CCH BUSINESS OWNER'S TOOLKIT™ &
CCH FINANCIAL PLANNING TOOLKIT™

TAX GUIDE 2007

A *CCH Toolkit*™ Publication

Paul N. Gada, J.D., LL.M., M.B.A.

CCH
a Wolters Kluwer business
Chicago

Published by CCH, a Wolters Kluwer business

Cover designed by Tim Kaage, Laurel Graphx, Inc.

Books may be purchased at quantity discounts for educational, business or sales promotion use. For more information please contact:

Consumer Media Group

CCH Tax and Accounting

2700 Lake Cook Road

Riverwoods, Illinois 60015

ISBN 0-8080-1473-0

Printed in the United States of America

FOREWORD

Welcome to another tax season and the latest edition of the *CCH Toolkit*™ *Tax Guide 2007.* As always, we are here to guide you through the agonizing process of filing your 2006 income tax returns.

Before you get too depressed thinking about the blank tax forms that await you, don't lose hope. There continue to be many juicy tax breaks to help you out again this year.

In 2006, taxpayers continue to receive the benefits of several major tax-cut packages enacted in 2001 through 2004. Although some popular tax law changes expired in 2006, many new tax laws were enacted in 2005 and 2006 to take their place.

For example, the Pension Protection Act of 2006 enacted earlier this year provides a long-overdue major overhaul to U.S. pension laws. The highlight of the new retirement savings provisions is the permanent extension of the many temporary retirement savings incentives enacted in 2001 that would have ended after December 31, 2010. The major provisions made permanent include:

- Permanent higher dollar amounts for IRA contributions
- Permanent higher dollar limits for various retirement plans and elective deferrals
- Permanent catch-up contributions for older workers
- Permanent faster vesting of employer matching contributions
- Permanent Roth 401(k)s
- Permanent enhanced rollover rules

If you haven't guessed this by now, our current tax laws are very complex and can easily become a taxpayer's worst nightmare (as if you needed a reminder of this unpleasant fact of life). Fortunately, our *Tax Guides* will provide the tax help you need to take advantage of the latest tax breaks being offered.

Because last minute developments may affect your 2006 filing season, you should regularly check our free Internet site, *CCH Business Owner's Toolkit*™, at http://www.toolkit.cch.com.

While surfing the net, you might also want to pay a visit to our financial planning site, *CCH Financial Planning Toolkit*™, at http://www.finance.cch.com. The site provides detailed and practical information on such topics as investing, insurance, retirement planning and estate planning. In addition, over 100 calculators and interactive planning tools are provided for your use.

Paul N. Gada

Senior Tax Analyst

CCH Business Owner's Toolkit™

December 1, 2006

THE CCH BUSINESS OWNER'S TOOLKIT™ TEAM

Drew Snider, Publisher, Consumer Media Group (*dsnider@cch.com*) has over 25 years experience with business-information services (SRDS), consumer magazines (*Golfweek*), and home-based software applications (Parsons Technology).

Joel Handelsman (*jhandels@cch.com*) has 25 years of experience writing about business, tax, and financial topics. He has been involved in multiple new product and business ventures in the publishing industry, and has held a variety of management positions. Joel holds degrees from Northwestern University's Medill School of Journalism and DePaul University College of Law.

Paul N. Gada (*pgada@cch.com*) has over 10 years of legal publishing experience, primarily in dealing with federal and state tax issues. He has helped create numerous editorial products, including newsletters, journals, books and electronic information systems. Paul is an attorney and holds degrees from the John Marshall Law School (LLM. - Tax and Employee Benefits), Southern Illinois University (JD), Northern Illinois University (MBA) and Loyola University of Chicago (BA).

Catherine Gordon (*cgordon@cch.com*) has over 15 years of experience in the tax, business, and financial publishing field and has worked as a tax consultant providing services to individuals as well as large and small companies. Catherine holds a juris doctorate degree from the State University of New York at Buffalo School of Law and a BA in sociology from the State University of New York at Stony Brook.

Alice H. Magos (*amagos@cch.com*) has over 35 years of experience running the operations of numerous small businesses. She is the author of the *CCH Business Owner's Toolkit*™ online advice column "Ask Alice." Alice is a popular instructor at small business seminars on accounting, financial planning, and using the Internet; is an accountant and a Certified Financial Planner; and holds degrees from Washington University in St. Louis and Northwestern University.

John L. Duoba (*jduoba@cch.com*) has almost 20 years of small business experience in book and magazine publishing, fulfilling various roles in editorial and production management. He has been involved in the publication of scores of titles, with multiple editions and issues raising the total well into the hundreds. John is a professional journalist and holds a degree from Northwestern University's Medill School of Journalism.

Table of Contents

Part I

Getting Started

Small business owners create the steam – and frequently design the tracks – on which the American economy runs.

Not only do small businesses create the vast majority of new jobs in this country, it's entrepreneurs like you who provide most of the innovation in products, services, delivery and marketing methods that continue to transform U.S. culture. The size and unrelenting persistence of our small business sector creates a vast virtual laboratory for testing out new ideas in the local, national, or even global marketplace.

A small business's size and the fact that there is usually only one layer of management make it the ideal business form to create and take advantage of newly emerging market niches and technological advances. In fact, it's been said that the best structure for an organization is one in which sales, marketing, operations and administration all sit in the same "business unit": the mind of an entrepreneur.

Being the owner of a small business in America means that you have to wear many hats, and that while you can delegate or outsource many tasks, the ultimate responsibility for all of them remains with you.

One of the most important of these tasks – and some say, one of the most onerous – is to stay on top of your numerous federal income tax obligations.

While many business owners delegate the preparation of tax returns to their accountant or professional preparer, the ultimate responsibility for a missed payment or filing deadline, an improperly claimed deduction, overlooked income, or incomplete records is yours alone.

Whether or not you plan to do your own taxes, you need to create (or at least oversee the creation of) the basic business records that will be used to complete the forms. And you need to know what kind of documentation to save throughout the year, not only to prepare your return, but also in case you're audited and you need to substantiate your responses to the questions on the forms. You can safely assume that a tax auditor won't look kindly on you if your only defense is "I didn't know I had to do that." The old legal saying that "ignorance of the law is no excuse" is perhaps most often applied in tax settings.

While the current U.S. tax code is almost unbelievably complicated – the law, regulations, and explanations run to over 42,000 pages in CCH's best-selling tax publication for professionals – it provides numerous opportunities for tax savings, if you know where to look.

Our goal in this book, and in all *CCH Toolkit*™ products, is to lay out the rules for you as clearly as possible. We know that your immediate concern is to get your taxes filed correctly and on time, so that you get any refund that's due and so you don't get socked with penalties and interest if you're selected for an audit.

We also want to tell you about the many ways you can save taxes by structuring your business operations to take the greatest possible advantage of the existing laws and regulations. While our main focus is on tax issues that impact your business as a sole proprietor, we'll also discuss taxes that apply to you and your family as individuals.

Tax laws change constantly – in fact, the last few years have seen a major overhaul of the IRS's structure; significant changes in taxpayer's rights; and changes in business tax credits and deductions, capital gains, Roth IRAs, the home office deduction, the child tax credit, education tax breaks, the $500,000 exclusion for gain on sale of a home, and the gradual elimination of the estate tax system beginning in 2002, to name just a few. It's important to keep up-to-date with all these changes in order to keep your tax bill to the minimum.

While we've taken great pains to bring you the latest information and tax forms available up to the date of publication, you can check for any late-breaking developments by going to our *CCH Business Owner's Toolkit*™ web site at http://www.toolkit.cch.com or our new *CCH Financial Planning Toolkit*™ web site at http://www.finance.cch.com.

How To Use This Book

We've designed this book to help you do two things:

(1) to get your tax return filed with as little pain and aggravation (and as large a refund) as possible, and

(2) for the long term, to make you aware of the opportunities for saving tax dollars in your business, and in your personal and family life.

For those of you who are familiar with filing your own returns, this book can be used as a handy reference as you gather your records and work through the forms. Find the topics that apply to you in the Table of Contents or the Index, and go directly to the appropriate section of the book. You'll find the examples, tips, and worksheets scattered throughout the text are a quick way to get a good understanding of the issues.

If you're a new business owner, or haven't tried doing your own taxes before, you may want to read through Part II, *Taxes and Your Business,* from start to finish. It will give you a good, easy-to-understand overview of how the system works. You'll also pick up scores of tax-saving ideas to help you organize your business activities, and to get the greatest possible after-tax return for your effort.

Take advantage of the book's special features to help you work more effectively:

- **Tax Forms:** At the back of the book, you'll find copies of the most commonly used tax forms and tax tables. Copy them, or tear them out and use them directly. You can also download copies of forms through the Internet by going to the IRS web site, http://www.irs.gov, or by calling the IRS at 1-800-TAX-FORM.

- **What's New This Year:** A thumbnail description of the most important changes for small business owners and individuals keeps you up to date.

- **Glossary:** Plain-language definitions of the more commonly used tax terms will help you decipher IRS instructions and other communications.

- **Tax Calendar:** To keep you on track with your due dates and filings, we provide a 2006 calendar of tax-related events.

FREE ONLINE TAX PREPARATION AND FILING WITH COMPLETETAX®

Understanding the tax rules and knowing what to report is half the battle – the other half is gathering all the records, receipts, and other pertinent financial data you've been generating throughout the year, and organizing it so you can actually complete the forms and send them to the IRS.

To that end, we're providing you with the opportunity to use CompleteTax, an Internet-based tax preparation service, to complete your federal and state tax returns and file them electronically, for free.

Getting started with CompleteTax is easy. Just follow these six steps:

1. Log onto the secure CompleteTax web site at http://www.completetax.com/taxguide2007.asp.

2. The CompleteTax program will guide you through an interview process customizing itself based upon your answers. Answering the questions and clicking "Continue" will take you through the interview, allow you to answer the questions and enter the information that relates to your tax situation.

3. When you reach the "End of Interview" page, click "Continue" to choose your filing options. You can choose to file your federal return, your state return or both by mail or electronically. You can also choose how to receive your refund or pay your balance due or you can use our optional Refund Anticipation Loan (for an additional fee).

4. After choosing your filing options and clicking "Continue," your return will be calculated, checked for errors and omissions and you will be given a summary of your return. You can return to any page and edit your information and then recheck your results as often as you like by clicking the "Review Return" link located at the bottom of any page.

5. As a purchaser of *CCH Toolkit™ Tax Guide 2007,* you are entitled to use CompleteTax to prepare one federal and one resident state tax return for free! For no additional cost, you can choose to file your federal and resident state return electronically. **Enter your promotional code (found on the inside back cover of this book) at Step 3, "Paying for your Tax Return." on the "Steps to File" page.** The "Steps to File" page is right after the summary. Note: If you wish to prepare additional returns, you can pay for them by credit card or you can have the fee deducted from your refund, if applicable.

6. After you have reviewed your return and checked it for errors, you can print a copy for your records, mail your return to the IRS and your state taxing authorities or you can E-file your federal and state return through CompleteTax for free.

Getting Started with CompleteTax®

CompleteTax is designed to focus only on the items that are relevant to your business and personal tax situation.

When you login to CompleteTax for the first time, you will need to enter your personal information, and then provide answers to a number of key questions on the "Interview Setup" page. Your answers to those questions will determine which of the tabs will appear at the top during the interview process.

The best way to move through the return is by selecting the "Continue" button at the bottom of each page. You may also move through the tabs in any sequence. As you open a new tab, the opening page for that tab will ask you a few basic questions. Your answers will determine which of the pages you will move to as you click the "Continue" button.

As you answer questions, additional questions may appear on subsequent pages. You will see these questions as you use the "Continue" button at the bottom of each page. Be sure to answer each "Yes" or "No" question to make sure that the correct additional questions appear. At the bottom of each page is a "Check if page is complete" box to indicate that you have answered all of the appropriate questions on that page. You should check this box on each page, even if no entries on that page apply to your return.

When you have checked all of the pages "complete" in a section, you will notice that a checkmark appears on the tab or sub-tab indicating that the section is complete.

When you have finished entering your relevant tax information, you can print your tax return for your records by clicking on the "Print or E-File" link at the bottom of any CompleteTax page. On the "Steps to File" page, click on the "View or Print" link (Step 4).

You can choose to file your return electronically or to mail the printed return to the IRS and state taxing authority.

Helpful Functions

Whenever you need further information about how to enter a particular item, click on any one of the "Help for this page", "Where do I enter" or "Customer Support" links on the right-hand side of your screen. Clicking on any of these links will bring up the "Resource Center" page.

In addition to the information on the links described above, you will find:

- Links to the IRS Pub 17
- Links to a glossary with definitions for tax terms
- Links to contact us via email or for a small fee via "Live Chat"
- Links to an online version of the *2007 Tax Guide*

What's New This Year

Like the weather, our tax laws are subject to frequent changes. Unfortunately, there continue to be many traps for the unwary and uninformed taxpayer.

Here are some highlights of changes in effect for 2006:

Personal exemption amount. This amount has increased to $3,300 per person for 2006.

Standard deductions. Standard deduction amounts have increased for 2006 as follows: singles and married filing separately, $5,150; heads of household, $7,550; married filing jointly, $10,300.

AMT exemption amount increased. The AMT exemption amount is increased in 2006 to $42,500 for singles, $62,550 if married filing jointly or a qualified widow(er), and $31,275 if married filing separately.

Reporting children's income. Starting with the 2006 filing season, children under 18 and their parents face new filing requirements. Also, the "kiddie tax" rules are now much less favorable to minor children with investment income and their families.

Standard mileage rate. The standard mileage rate for determining your deduction for the business use of a car has increased to 44.5 cents per mile in 2006. Those using their car for charitable purposes in 2006 can deduct 14 cents per mile. Cars used for deductible medical travel or moving can deduct 18 cents per mile in 2006.

Residential energy credits. Beginning in 2006 and through 2007, you may be able to take a residential energy credit for the costs of having qualified energy saving items installed in your main home. The credit is subject to a lifetime limitation of $500 and no more than $200 of the credit can be used towards the purchase of energy efficient windows.

There is also a new tax credit available to help individual taxpayers pay for residential alternative energy equipment. The credit is 30 percent of the cost of eligible solar water heaters, solar electricity equipment and fuel cell plants. The maximum credit is $2,000 per tax year for *each* category of solar equipment, and $500 for each half kilowatt of capacity of fuel cell plants installed per tax year.

Credit for federal telephone excise taxes paid. For 2006, individual taxpayers may request a telephone excise tax refund via their Form 1040. The standard refund amounts depend on the number of exemptions claimed and can be as high as $60 for four of more exemptions claimed.

Adoption tax credit. In 2006, the maximum credit allowed for an adoption of a special needs child or other adoption is $10,960. The credit begins to phase out for taxpayers with modified adjusted gross income over $164,410 and is completely phased out at $204,410.

IRA deduction. The maximum IRA deduction allowed per person continues to be $4,000 in 2006 and 2007. However, those who are at least 50 years old can now make an additional catch-up contribution of $1,000 to their IRA in each of those years.

Retirement plan elective deferral limits. An employee's maximum salary deferral to a 401(k) plan, a tax-sheltered 403(b) annuity, a salary reduction simplified employee pension (SEP) plan, or a government-sponsored 457 plan increases to $15,000 in 2006. Those 50 years or older can make additional catch-up contributions to their plans of $5,000 in 2006.

Elective deferrals to a SIMPLE plan increase to $10,000 in 2006. SIMPLE plan participants who are age 50 and over can make additional catch-up contributions of $2,500 in 2006.

Where to mail your return. The IRS has changed the mailing addresses (again) for filing an income tax return in several areas, so make sure that your return gets to its proper filing location.

Estate taxes. The amounts that can be excluded from an estate for estate tax purposes will increase to $2 million in 2006 through 2008.

Expired tax provisions. A number of tax benefits expired in 2006. For individual taxpayers, these include the deduction from gross income for educator expenses, the tuition and fees deduction, and the District of Columbia first time homebuyer credit. For business taxpayers, these include the R&D tax credit, the Work Opportunity Tax Credit, Welfare-to-Work incentives, and the Indian employment tax credit for wages and health insurance.

Changes Beyond 2006

It would easily take an entire book just to explain the many tax law changes enacted in 2001 through 2005 that will be phased in through 2010. The following, however, are some of the highlights you can look forward to in the years to come:

Personal exemption amount. This amount has increased to $3,400 per person in 2007.

Standard deductions. Standard deduction amounts have increased for 2007 as follows: singles and married filing separately, $5,350; heads of household, $7,850; married filing jointly, $10,700.

Standard mileage rate. The standard mileage rate for determining your deduction for the business use of a car has increased to 48.5 cents per mile in 2007. Those using their car for charitable purposes in 2007 can deduct 14 cents per mile. Cars used for deductible medical travel or moving can deduct 20 cents per mile in 2007.

Equipment expensing election. The $100,000 expensing limit (adjusted annually for inflation) and the $400,000 investment limitation are extended through 2009.

Adoption tax credit. In 2007, the maximum credit allowed for an adoption of a special needs child or other adoption is $11,390. The credit begins to phase out for taxpayers with modified adjusted gross income over $170,820 and is completely phased out at $210,820.

Retirement plan elective deferral limits. An employee's maximum salary deferral to a 401(k) plan, a tax-sheltered 403(b) annuity, a salary reduction simplified employee pension (SEP) plan, or a government-sponsored 457 plan will increase to $15,500 in 2007. Those 50 years or older can make additional catch-up contributions to their plans of $5,000 in 2007 and thereafter.

Elective deferrals to a SIMPLE plan increase to $10,500 in 2007 and thereafter. SIMPLE plan participants who are age 50 and over can make additional catch-up contributions of $2,500 in 2007 and later years.

Estate taxes. The amounts that can be excluded from an estate for estate tax purposes increase to $3.5 million in 2009. Estate taxes will be repealed for those dying in 2010, but may return unless Congress acts to make the repeal permanent.

2007 Tax Calendar

First Quarter

January 10

Employees who work for tips and received $20 or more in tips during December must report them to their employers. Form 4070, *Employee's Report of Tips to Employer,* can be used.

January 16

Make a payment of your estimated tax for the last quarter of 2006 if you did not pay enough income tax through withholding (see page 310). Use Form 1040-ES. You don't have to make this payment if you file your 2006 tax return (Form 1040) and pay any tax due by January 31, 2007.

Farmers and fisherman must pay estimated tax for 2006 using Form 1040-ES. You have until April 16 to file your 2006 income tax return on Form 1040. If you don't pay your estimated tax by this date, you must file your 2006 return and pay any tax due by March 1, 2007 to avoid an estimated tax penalty.

January 31

File your income tax return (Form 1040) for 2006 if you didn't pay your last installment of estimated tax by January 16. Filing your return and paying any tax due by January 31 prevents any penalty for late payment of the last installment.

All employers: Give copies B, C, and 2 of Form W-2 for 2006 to each employee, including household employees.

All businesses: Give annual information statements to recipients of payments you made during 2006, on the appropriate version of Form 1099 or other information return. Payments that must be included are:

- compensation for independent contractors
- dividends and other corporate distributions
- interest
- amounts paid in real estate transactions
- rent
- royalties
- amounts paid in broker and barter exchange transactions
- payments of Indian gaming profits to tribal members
- payments to attorneys
- profit-sharing distributions
- retirement plan distributions
- original issue discount
- prizes and awards
- medical and health care payments
- debt cancellation
- cash payments over $10,000

February 12

Employees who work for tips and received $20 or more in tips during January must report them to their employers. Form 4070, *Employee's Report of Tips to Employer,* can be used.

February 28

Businesses must file information returns (Form 1099) with the IRS for certain payments you made during 2006, as described under January 31. Use a separate Form 1096 to summarize and transmit the forms for each type of payment.

If you file Forms 1098, 1099 or W-2G electronically (not by magnetic media), your due date for filing them will be extended to April 2, 2007.

February 28

Employers must file copy A of all W-2 forms and one W-3 transmittal form with the Social Security Administration. If you file electronically, your due date is extended to April 2.

March 1

Farmers and fishermen must file their 2006 income tax return (Form 1040) to avoid an underpayment penalty if they owe estimated tax. However, they have until April 16 to file if they paid their 2006 estimated tax by January 16, 2007.

March 12

Employees who work for tips and received $20 or more in tips during February must report them to their employers. Form 4070, *Employee's Report of Tips to Employer,* can be used.

SECOND QUARTER

April 2

If you file Forms 1098, 1099, W-2 or W-2G electronically, this is the due date for filing them with the IRS. The due date for giving the payment recipient a copy of the form is still January 31.

April 10

Employees who work for tips and received $20 or more in tips during March must report them to their employers. Form 4070, *Employee's Report of Tips to Employer,* can be used.

April 16

File an income tax return for 2006 (Form 1040EZ, 1040A, or 1040) and pay any tax due. If you want an automatic six-month extension of time to file the return, file Form 4868, *Application for Automatic Extension of Time to File U.S. Individual Income Tax Return.* Then file your tax form by October 16.

If you paid cash wages of $1,500 or more in 2006 to a household worker, file Schedule H (Form 1040) with your income tax return and report any employment taxes. Report any federal unemployment FUTA tax on Schedule H if you paid total cash wages of $1,000 or more in any calendar quarter of 2005 or 2006 to household employees. Also report any income tax you withheld for your household employees.

Pay the first installment of estimated tax, using Form 1040-ES.

May 10

Employees who work for tips and received $20 or more in tips during April must report them to their employers. Form 4070, *Employee's Report of Tips to Employer,* can be used.

June 11

Employees who work for tips and received $20 or more in tips during May must report them to their employers. Form 4070, *Employee's Report of Tips to Employer,* can be used.

June 15

Make your second installment of quarterly estimated income tax on Form 1040-ES.

If you are a U.S. citizen or resident alien living, working, or on military duty outside the U.S. or Puerto Rico, file Form 1040 and pay any tax, interest, and penalties due.

THIRD QUARTER

July 10

Employees who work for tips and received $20 or more in tips during June must report them to their employers. Form 4070, *Employee's Report of Tips to Employer,* can be used.

August 10

Employees who work for tips and received $20 or more in tips during July must report them to their employers. Form 4070, *Employee's Report of Tips to Employer,* can be used.

September 10

Employees who work for tips and received $20 or more in tips during August must report them to their employers. Form 4070, *Employee's Report of Tips to Employer,* can be used.

September 17

Third payment of quarterly 2007 estimated tax is due, on Form 1040-ES.

Fourth Quarter

October 10

Employees who work for tips and received $20 or more in tips during September must report them to their employers. Form 4070, *Employee's Report of Tips to Employer,* can be used.

October 15

File a 2006 income tax return and pay any tax, interest and penalties due if you were given an automatic six-month extension.

November 13

Employees who work for tips and received $20 or more in tips during October must report them to their employers. Form 4070, *Employee's Report of Tips to Employer,* can be used.

December 10

Employees who work for tips and received $20 or more in tips during November must report them to their employers. Form 4070, *Employee's Report of Tips to Employer,* can be used.

Fiscal Year Taxpayers

If you are using a fiscal year as your tax accounting period, Form 1040 is due on the 15th day of the fourth month after the end of your tax year. Estimated tax payment are due on the 15th day of the 4th, 6th, and 9th months of your tax year and on the 15th day of the first month after the end of your tax year.

Chapter 1

The Basics of Tax Planning

Tax planning is a process of looking at various tax options in order to determine *when, whether,* and *how* to conduct business and personal transactions so that taxes are eliminated or reduced.

As an individual taxpayer, and as a business owner, you often will have several different options as to how you want to complete a certain taxable transaction. The courts strongly back your right to choose the course of action that will result in the lowest *legal* tax liability. In other words, *tax avoidance* is entirely proper.

Although tax avoidance planning is legal, *tax evasion* — the reduction of tax through deceit, subterfuge, or concealment — is not. Frequently, what sets tax evasion apart from tax avoidance is the IRS's finding that there was some fraudulent intent on the part of the business owner.

The following are four of the areas most commonly focused on by IRS examiners as pointing to possible fraud:

- a failure to report substantial amounts of income, such as a shareholder's failure to report dividends, or a store-owner's skimming cash from the register without including it in the daily business receipts

- a claim for fictitious or improper deductions on a return, such as a sales representative's substantially overstating travel expenses, or a taxpayer claiming a large deduction for charitable contributions when no verification exists

- accounting irregularities, such as a business's failure to keep adequate records, or a discrepancy between amounts reported on a corporation's return and amounts reported on its financial statements

- improper allocation of income to a related taxpayer who is in a lower tax bracket, such as where a corporation makes distributions to the controlling shareholder's children

A business owner may *not* reduce his or her income taxes by labeling a transaction as something that it's not. So, if payments by a corporation to its stockholders are in fact dividends, calling them "interest" or otherwise attempting to disguise the payments as interest will not entitle the corporation to an interest deduction.

Ultimately, it is the substance, not the form, of a transaction that determines its tax treatment.

How a tax plan works. There are countless tax planning strategies available to a small business owner. Some are aimed at the owner's individual tax situation, some at the business itself. But regardless of how simple or how complex a tax strategy is, it will be based on structuring the transaction to accomplish one or more of these often overlapping goals:

- reducing the amount of taxable income
- reducing your tax rate
- controlling the time when the tax must be paid
- reducing the amount of the tax itself by claiming tax credits
- controlling the effects of the alternative minimum tax

In order to plan effectively, you'll need to estimate your personal and business income for the next few years. This is necessary because many tax planning strategies will save tax dollars at one income level, but will create a larger tax bill at other income levels. You will want to avoid having the "right" tax plan made "wrong" by erroneous income projections. Once you know what your approximate income will be, you can take the next step: estimating your tax bracket.

The effort to come up with crystal-ball estimates may be difficult and by its nature will be inexact. On the other hand, you should already be projecting your sales revenues, income, and cash flow for general business planning purposes. The better your estimates, the better the odds that your tax planning efforts will succeed.

Reducing Taxable Income

The primary way to reduce the part of your income that is subject to tax is to take full advantage of all available tax deductions, both business and personal. In order to do this, you must become aware of what is deductible and what isn't, and the special rules that apply to certain types of deductions such as meals and entertainment, automobile expenses, and business travel (see Chapter 6).

In many cases, a business owner can deduct benefits that would otherwise be classified as nondeductible personal expenses. Don't overlook the possibility of purchasing health insurance, investing for your retirement, or providing perks like a company car through your business (see Chapter 6).

But do remember that claiming some kinds of deductions may have a tax impact in later years. An example of this is the recapture of certain depreciation deductions upon the sale of business property (see page 119).

Reducing Your Tax Rate

Although you can't *literally* reduce your federal income tax rate, you can take actions that will have a similar result. These include:

- Choosing the optimum form of business organization (such as sole proprietorship, partnership, or corporation). For example, the sole proprietorship or pass-through entities (partnerships, LLCs, S corporations) usually offer more tax benefits.
- Structuring a transaction so that some of the money that you receive is classified as capital gains. Long-term capital gains earned by noncorporate taxpayers are taxed at lower rates than ordinary taxable income.
- Shifting income from a high-tax-bracket taxpayer (such as yourself) to a lower-tax-bracket taxpayer (such as your child).

One fairly simple way to do this is by hiring your children. Another possibility is to make one or more of your children a part-owner of your business, so that net profits of the business are shared among a larger group. The tax law limits the usefulness of this strategy for shifting *unearned* income to children under age 14, but some tax-saving opportunities still exist.

When we say "tax bracket," we're referring to the highest federal tax rate that you pay on any of your taxable income. This is the rate that will apply to each additional dollar that you earn, until you earn so much that you graduate to the next bracket. You need to know your current tax bracket in order to make wise tax planning decisions, since many decisions will make sense for those in certain brackets, but not for those in others.

In 2006, there continue to be six tax brackets for individuals: 10 percent, 15 percent, 25 percent, 28 percent, 33 percent, and 35 percent. These rates reflect tax reductions enacted in 2001, with an accelerated phase-in period enacted in 2003.

The chart on the bottom of the page shows the income thresholds at which each tax bracket begins for 2006. The dollar amounts at which each bracket begins is different for each filing status (that is, whether you file as single, head of household, etc.) and are adjusted for inflation each year. Note that the dollar amount does not refer to your gross income, but rather, your taxable income — that is, income after you've subtracted any deductions and personal exemptions to which you're entitled.

Controlling the Due Date for Taxes

Although your former grade school teachers may not want to hear it, putting something off can sometimes be a good idea.

Putting it another way, "justice delayed" may be "justice denied," but taxes delayed can be taxes minimized!

The idea that we're trying to convey is that it's usually worthwhile to delay the due date for your tax liability, if you can do so legally.

This is true even if you figure that you'll be in the same tax bracket in all relevant years. What you gain is the use of your money for a longer period of time. The advantage may be as little as passbook earnings on the money, or as much as the growth resulting from a needed investment of money or equipment into your business.

Now, you generally don't have the option of actually delaying payment of the income tax you owe. While most taxpayers can get an automatic four-month extension of the time to file their return (e.g., until August 15), you still have to pay the taxes you owe by April 15 or face penalties and interest payments. It's possible to obtain an extension to pay tax if you can demonstrate to the IRS's satisfaction that you can't pay on time without undue hardship. However, this is not something that you'll want to do unless absolutely necessary, since even with this extension you will owe interest on the unpaid taxes, beginning on the original due date.

What we're really talking about is the fact that it's often possible to delay your taxes indirectly, by taking actions that delay the time when particular income items must be reported on your return.

For small business owners, a common way to do this is to postpone receipt of income until the next year, and accelerate payment of expenses into your current tax year. (This will be much easier to do if you are using the cash method of accounting – see page 41.) This will have the effect of delaying your tax liability to the next quarter, or even the next tax year.

2006 Tax Brackets

Tax Rate	Single	Married/Joint	Married/Separate	Head of Household
10%	$0.01	$0.01	$0.01	$0.01
15%	$7,550	$15,100	$7,550	$10,750
25%	$30,650	$61,300	$30,650	$41,050
28%	$74,200	$123,700	$61,850	$106,000
33%	$154,800	$188,450	$94,225	$171,650
35%	$336,550	$336,550	$168,275	$336,550

Year-End Tax Saving Strategies

- **Delay collections** — Delay year-end billings until late enough in the year that payments won't come in until the following year.
- **Delay dividends** — If you operate your business as a C corporation, arrange for any dividends to be paid after the end of the year.
- **Delay capital gains** — If you are planning to sell assets that have appreciated in value, delay the sale until next year if you can do so without reducing the price significantly.
- **Accelerate payments** — Where possible, prepay deductible business expenses, including rent, interest, taxes, insurance, etc.
- **Accelerate large purchases** — Close the purchase of depreciable personal property or real estate within the current year.
- **Accelerate operating expenses** — If possible, accelerate the purchase of supplies or services, or the making of repairs.
- **Accelerate depreciation** — Elect to expense the cost of new equipment if you are eligible to do so, instead of depreciating the equipment.

Another way to defer the day of reckoning is to plow as much money as you can into qualified, tax-free retirement plans. In most cases, the business will get a tax deduction for the amount contributed, but you won't have to pay income tax on the amounts until you start taking money out of the plan when you retire.

Meanwhile, any income earned on the investments made by the plan will build up, tax-free. As the owner, you have a great deal of control over the way the plan is set up, and there's sure to be a plan that fits your business goals and retirement objectives.

Postponing Income, Accelerating Deductions

As a general rule of thumb, you should *always* try to minimize your taxes in the present year, even if doing so means you may have to pay slightly more tax in the future.

After all, no one knows what the future holds. The tax laws are constantly changing, and there's a good chance that whatever you think you may owe in the future will be different by the time you get there. Furthermore, economic conditions or personal plans can change, and your business may look entirely different even one year down the road. In the worst-case scenario, you could die unexpectedly, and in some cases you can avoid tax altogether if you die before paying it.

In broad terms, you can minimize taxes in the current year by postponing the receipt of income so that more of it will be taxed next year, and by accelerating deductions into the current year.

A few more specific ideas for doing this are listed above. (Bear in mind, however, that any strategies aimed at changing the year in which items of income or deduction will be accounted for will be much easier to accomplish if you use the cash method of accounting.)

Using the Accrual Method

Although strategies aimed at changing the year in which income and deductions will be accounted for are usually more difficult to accomplish using the accrual method, this does not mean that they're impossible. You'll need to learn how to navigate through the accrual method accounting rules in a way to reach the tax result that you want:

- If you want to delay taxation of an item of income, make sure that all events fixing the liability for payment are *not* met by year's end.

For instance, if you're selling goods, delay shipment until next year.

- If you want to accelerate a deductible expense into the current year, make sure that all events fixing the liability and amount of payment, and the economic performance, have been completed by year's end. If you are purchasing goods, services, or the use of some property, make sure that you have a valid contract covering all necessary terms, and that the goods, services, or properties are delivered, performed or used by year's end. If you do this, you are "one up" on a business that uses the cash method of accounting: You have received the benefit and deduction for the expense item before you've actually had to pay for it.

Accelerating Income, Postponing Deductions

What if, after looking into your tax situation, you have decided that you should take steps to maximize the amount of income that will be taxed in your present tax year, because you'll probably be in a higher bracket next year? You can accomplish your goal by accelerating income, and postponing expenses into the following year. How do you go about doing this? In most cases, if you simply reverse our suggestions in the box on the previous page, you'll find that you can accomplish your goals. For example, instead of delaying your billings, send out all of your bills early and do everything you can to collect them before year's end.

Again, any strategies aimed at changing the year in which items of income and deduction will be accounted for will be much easier to accomplish if you use the cash method of accounting.

RESTRICTIONS ON TAX PLANNING

The fact that you chose to use one form of transaction rather than another in order to minimize tax will not invalidate a transaction for income tax purposes. The fact that one form is adopted rather than another in order to minimize tax will not necessarily deprive the owner of the tax benefits sought. However, even if the *form* of a transaction is valid, the IRS will look at the *substance* or true nature of the transaction in order to determine what the tax consequences should be.

Example

Jon Buford, the manager and principal stockholder of Oak Park Micro-Round Bearings, Inc. (a regular, as opposed to an S, corporation), lands a lucrative government contract. Because of this contract, corporate income jumps from $50,000 in 200X, to $500,000 in 200Y. Based on his view that landing the government contract proves that "he's worth a lot more" to the company, Jon raises his corporate salary ten-fold, to $450,000 in 200Y (up from $45,000 for 200X). His corporation takes a compensation-paid deduction of $450,000.

The IRS is likely to see things differently. If $100,000 is reasonable compensation for a manager in Jon's industry, then only that amount will qualify for the compensation deduction, and $350,000 will be treated as a disguised dividend (which does not qualify for the deduction).

Although the IRS says that the substance of a transaction, not its form, determines its tax consequences, a taxpayer who casts a taxable transaction in a particular form may have a difficult time changing his or her mind later, and then trying to convince the IRS that the substance of the transaction differs from its form for tax purposes.

So, the general rule is that the *IRS* may look behind the form of a transaction in order to determine its substance for tax purposes, but *taxpayers* are generally locked into the form of the transaction. The thinking here is that since a taxpayer can freely choose how to set up a transaction, it's only fair to require him or her to live with its tax consequences.

Step Transaction Doctrine

The IRS sometimes uses what is known as the "step transaction" doctrine to argue that the substance of a particular transaction is different from its form. When it relies on this doctrine, the IRS is generally saying that it will not break up a single transaction into two or more steps for income tax purposes.

So, the intermediate steps in an integrated transaction will not be assigned separate tax consequences.

Example

A transfer of property from Able to Baker, followed by Baker's transfer of the same property to Charlie, may, if the transfers are interdependent, be treated for tax purposes as a transfer from Able to Charlie.

Related Taxpayers

The IRS pays close attention to transactions that involve taxpayers who have close business and/or family relationships. In some cases, the tax laws have given the IRS special powers to deal with specific areas where related taxpayers in the past have used their relationships to unfairly cut their taxes.

Examples of this include the denial of interest-paid deductions to businesses that borrow money to purchase life insurance contracts benefiting their officers and employees, and the special accounting rules that apply to interest and expense payments between related parties.

Even beyond those areas in which the IRS has specific powers to deny tax benefits arising from transactions between related taxpayers, you can expect that its agents will closely scrutinize business dealings that you have with family members or other related parties.

Often, the IRS will combine its check of returns for a closely held corporation with a check of returns of the corporation's owners or principal officers, in order to discover any attempts to shift personal expenses to the corporation.

Warning

Among the items that IRS agents are likely to make special checks for are: vacation trips disguised as business trips, purchase of household furnishings or payment of household expenses (such as repairs and mortgage payments) charged off as corporate expenses, and excessive salaries paid to stockholders and relatives.

Chapter 2

Keeping Good Records

Everyone who pays taxes is required to keep accurate, permanent books and records so they can determine the various types of income, expenses, gains, losses, and other items that affect their income tax liability for the year.

Business-Related Records

For business owners, keeping good records takes on special significance, since it's only by keeping a watchful eye on your operations that you can determine whether your business is on the right track.

One of your most important management tools is financial analysis, based on your business records. Here are some of the reasons why you need a good financial recordkeeping system for your business:

Monitoring the success or failure of your business. It's hard to know how your business is doing without a clear financial picture. Am I making money? Are sales increasing? Are expenditures increasing faster than sales? Which expenses are too high based on my level of sales? Do some expenditures appear to be "out of control?"

Providing the information you need to make decisions. Evaluating the financial consequences should be a part of every business decision you make. Without accurate records and financial information, it may be hard for you to know the financial impact of a given course of action. Will it pay to hire another salesperson? How much will another production employee cost? Is this particular product line profitable?

Obtaining bank financing. Before approving a loan, a banker will usually want to see your financial statements: a balance sheet, income statement, and cash flow budget for the most current and prior years, as well as your projected statements showing the impact of the requested loan. A banker may even want to see some of your bookkeeping procedures and documents to verify whether you run your business in a sound, professional manner.

Obtaining other sources of capital. If you need capital and are thinking of taking in an outside investor or a partner, you will need to produce a lot of financial information. Even your suppliers and other creditors may ask to see certain financial records. Such information may be produced by an outside accountant, but it is based on your day-to-day recordkeeping.

Budgeting. All businesses should use a budget for planning purposes. A budget will help keep your business on track by forecasting your cash needs and helping you control expenditures. In addition, if you are seeking bank financing or other sources of capital, a banker or prospective investor will probably want to see your budget as evidence that your business is well planned and stable. You must have solid financial information to prepare a meaningful budget.

Submitting sales taxes. If you collect sales tax from your customers, good records will make it easy for you to compute the tax due and prepare the required reports.

Preparing your income tax return. With good records, preparing an accurate tax return will be easier and you're more likely to be able to do it on time. Poor records may result in your underpaying or overpaying your taxes and/or filing late (and paying penalties). Furthermore, you will have the records necessary to prove your income and deductions, should questions arise or should your return be selected for a tax audit.

Like many small business owners, you may find that it's too expensive to pay an accountant to do routine bookkeeping chores. Someone in your organization must take on the responsibility of keeping an accurate set of financial records. Fortunately, you may find this task easier than you thought, especially if you use your computer.

In most cases, with a little study and help from computer software, you should be able to manage your most basic financial records without the help of an accountant. This includes the daily recording of sales, recording of incoming cash if customers' payments come in after the sale is made, and maintenance of your disbursements. Depending on the size of your business and how it is set up, you may need to maintain other types of records such as accounts receivable and accounts payable ledgers.

Business Bank Accounts

Most small business owners rely primarily on their business checkbook as a recordkeeping device. It's extremely important that you keep a business bank account that is separate from your personal funds. When you make a deposit, you should note the source of the funds – which may be as simple as noting whether the deposit represented business receipts from a certain day or week, an infusion of personal funds, or a loan.

Once you've established your business checking account, you should pay all business expenses (and only business expenses) with a check from that account, or with a credit card. If you must pay an expense with cash, make doubly sure that you save the receipt.

Save Time

If you've graduated from using a manual checkbook to an electronic version, such as that found in Quicken or Microsoft Money, you can easily keep track of your expenses and reconcile your checkbook each month in just minutes. You'll also be able to print out a variety of reports on income and expenses, which is important in case you are ever audited by the IRS.

The exception to the "don't write checks payable to 'cash' " rule is that when you withdraw earnings from the business for your personal use, you may write a check payable to cash, to yourself, or to your personal bank account.

As your business grows, you may become ready to step up to a small business accounting software package. There are a number of good ones on the market, and we suggest that you poll your friends and associates about the packages they've tried and been happy with. If you work with an accountant, choose a software package that works with his or her system so that data can easily flow back and forth between you.

The IRS does not require you to keep any specific forms of records, so long as your records clearly show your income and expenses for the period. If you use a computerized system, you must be able to obtain printouts of your records that are easily read.

Supporting Documents

From the IRS's point of view, perhaps even more important than your overall business accounting system is your ability to produce the invoices, receipts, and other original documents that prove your items of income and expense.

To show your income, you should have original documents such as cash register tapes, bank deposit slips, receipts, invoices, credit card charge slips, and, if you're an independent contractor, Forms 1099-MISC.

If you carry inventory, you should have canceled checks, cash register tape receipts, credit card sales slips, and invoices.

To show your other business expenses, you should have canceled checks, cash register tapes, account statements, invoices, and credit card slips. Very small expenses paid in cash can be evidenced by a sales receipt.

Ideally, you should have two forms of records for each expense: a document showing you paid the expense, such as a cancelled check or credit card slip, and a document itemizing the expense, such as a sales receipt or invoice from the vendor.

Work Smart

If your financial institution does not provide you with cancelled checks, you can rely on an account statement that shows, for each check, the check number, amount, payee, and date the check amount was posted. Similarly, statements showing electronic funds transfers or credit card statements can also be used. However, these statements should not be your only record of your expenses: you should also have another form of proof for each expense, such as a receipt or an invoice.

Special Deduction Rules

In many cases, if you don't have records of a particular business expense but it's obvious that you must have incurred it, in an audit situation the IRS will estimate the amount of your expenses and allow you to deduct them. An example would be a retailer who has incomplete records of inventory purchases — the IRS will come up with a reasonable estimate of what the purchases should have been.

However, certain types of expenses, which the IRS has found to be particularly susceptible to cheating, are subject to special documentation rules. The following expenses must generally be proven by adequate records or other evidence; if you have no records, the deduction will be completely disallowed:

- expenses for travel away from home (including meals and lodging while traveling)
- meals and entertainment expenses
- business gifts
- cars and other means of transportation
- cellular phones, computers, and other property of a kind that is generally used for entertainment or recreation

For all these types of expenses, you must keep receipts for any expense that is at least $75, and for all lodging expenses whatever the amount. For transportation expenses, a receipt is not needed if it is not readily available.

You must also substantiate each individual expense as to: (1) amount, (2) time and place, and (3) business purpose. For entertainment and gift expenses, you must also note the business relationship of the person(s) being entertained or receiving a gift.

These things can be noted on the back of the receipt, or recorded in a formal expense log. For vehicle expenses, you'll also have to keep a mileage log.

Save Money

There is no requirement that you keep a contemporaneous log of your business deductions. However, the closer in time to the expenditure or use that you record the expense (and provide necessary documentary evidence), the more valuable it will be to prove the deduction. Also, if you get into the habit of systematically recording your expenses and all the necessary supporting facts and records, you may discover that you have many more perfectly legitimate deductions than you thought!

Keeping Automobile Records

If you want to deduct expenses for the use of a car for business or employment, for charitable work, or to get to medical appointments, you must keep mileage records of your driving for any of these tax-deductible purposes. In fact, the IRS specifically asks you on your tax return whether you have written evidence of your auto expenses and is likely to deny your deduction if you don't have them.

At a minimum, you should keep a notebook in the car and jot down your odometer reading at the beginning and end of the year. In between, you should jot down your starting and stopping odometer reading for each business trip you take and for any other deductible driving you do, as well as the reason for the trip. Most office supply stores carry notebooks designed for this purpose, in a size that's convenient for glove-box storage.

Save Money

If you have a good memory, you can choose to merely update your mileage records every week or two, but we don't recommend it: It's too easy to forget those short trips to the bank or office supply store. Over the course of the year, those forgotten trips can really add up! It's better to get into the habit of jotting down the facts at the start and end of every trip.

If you commute to a regular place of business, you'll also need to know the distance from your home to your workplace, as well as the number of commuting trips you made during the year, because the IRS specifically asks for this information.

At the end of the year, you'll need to compute the total number of miles you drove during the year and the total number of business miles. Then, you'll divide the number of business miles by the total number of miles driven. The answer you get represents your percentage of business use for the year. Save this number – you'll need it when you compute your deductible vehicle expenses!

Example

Mikio Nagano's initial odometer reading for the year was 23,456, and her ending reading was 33,500. So, her total mileage for the year was 10,044.

During the year, she recorded a total of 34 business trips, with a total mileage of 800 business miles.

So, her business usage of the vehicle was 800/10,044 = .0796, or about 8 percent.

You don't have to keep substantiating records for the business use of any vehicle that, by its very nature, is not likely to be used more than a very minimal amount for personal purposes. This includes various heavy trucks, buses, police and fire vehicles, cranes, forklifts, tractors, and similar vehicles.

For 2006, those using the standard mileage rate can deduct 44.5 cents per mile for every business mile they drove. In 2007, the rate will increase to 48.5 cents per mile. For both 2006 and 2007, those using their car for charitable purposes can deduct 14 cents per mile. Those using their car for deductible medical travel or moving expenses can deduct 18 cents per mile in 2006 and 20 cents per mile in 2006. Parking and tolls may be deducted in addition to these rates, so be sure to ask for a receipt at the toll booth.

Those opting to use the actual cost method for calculating their business-related auto expenses will also have to keep records for all car expenses during the year including gas and oil, cleaning and washing, repairs and maintenance, insurance, interest on a vehicle loan, tires and supplies, parking and garage rental, tolls, motor club membership, personal property taxes, depreciation if you own the vehicle, and lease payments if you lease the vehicle.

Capital Asset Records

For equipment, real estate, and other long-term assets that you use in your business or for investment purposes, you should have records that show when and how you acquired the asset, its purchase price, the cost of any improvements, any Section 179 deduction or tax deductions for depreciation, any deductions taken for casualty losses, when and how you disposed of the asset, the selling price, and any expenses of the sale. You can use the form on page 104 to summarize all this information in one place.

In addition, you should have supporting documents such as purchase and sales contracts or invoices, real estate closing statements, and canceled checks or credit card slips.

These recordkeeping rules generally apply to your personal residence as well. For more details, see page 207.

Other Personal Records

In addition to the records described above for automobile use (for charitable, moving, or medical expenses deductions) and for capital assets used as investments, you should retain basic records showing the source of all income you receive, including W-2 forms, 1099 and 1098 forms, and year-end comprehensive statements from financial institutions.

For any deductible item, you should retain documents proving the expense itself (a receipt, bill, or invoice) and proving that you paid it (a canceled check, credit card slip, or bank statement itemizing your checks).

If you are claiming employee business expenses, the recordkeeping rules for each type of expense are the same as those that apply to business owners, as discussed above.

If you receive or pay alimony, you should keep a copy of the separation agreement or divorce decree.

If you are claiming the child care credit, you must keep records of the name, address, and Social Security number or Employer Identification Number of all caregivers.

If you are claiming deductions for charitable contributions, you may need to get a receipt from the organization to which you made the donation, or an appraisal of the item. See page 268 for more details.

If you have gambling winnings, you should be keeping a diary of your winnings and losses that includes the date, type of activity, and location of the establishment, the names of other people who were present, and the amount you won or lost.

How Long Must Your Records Be Kept?

Your business records and your personal financial records must be retained for as long as they may be relevant for any tax purpose.

Generally, you will need to keep all records that support items on your tax return for at least four years, since the IRS may challenge your return for up to three years after its due date.

Records for capital assets, such as real estate, business equipment, and investments, should be maintained as long as you own the assets, since you will need them in order to determine your taxable gain or loss upon sale of the asset, and you may need them to support depreciation or casualty loss deductions along the way. If you rolled over gain in the asset, as was permitted under the old rollover replacement rule for personal residences, or because you traded some business or investment property in a tax-free exchange, you should keep records of the original asset until you dispose of the asset that took its place.

Also, be sure to keep copies of your income tax return itself. If you have ever made any nondeductible IRA contributions, you must retain the Forms 8606 from each year you made a contribution or received a distribution from any IRAs. But more generally, if your return is ever challenged for something serious such as fraud or not filing a tax return, the IRS can go back in time to examine your returns for as many years as it thinks necessary. The problem is that the IRS computer system might not have accessible copies of your returns from, say, 10 or 15 years ago. Therefore it is very important that you keep copies of your own tax records indefinitely, and preferably forever.

Tax Organizer Tip

Along with your tax returns, we suggest that you keep copies of any worksheets, itemized lists, supplementary records, or even scrap paper you used to organize your tax records. These can be very helpful if you ever need to figure out exactly how you arrived at a particular number on your tax return.

Part II

Taxes and Your Business

If you own a business, your business's tax situation has a tremendous effect on your personal or family tax situation.

At the simplest level, the tax you pay on your business income is unavailable for you to use, so obviously it's in your interest to reduce this tax burden as much as you legally can.

As an entrepreneur, you're likely to face many more volatile income fluctuations than you would as an employee of a large company, and you need to retain absolutely every penny you can to build up a cushion in case things get rough. Saving on taxes is one very important way to reduce your costs and keep more of what you earn.

On the other hand, owning a business also presents numerous opportunities for you to reduce your tax bill by having the business pay for things – for example, family health benefits, a retirement plan, and perhaps even some of the expenses of owning a home, a car, and a computer – that you would otherwise have to purchase on your own. In addition, if your spouse or other family members work in the business, you may be able to reduce your total tax bill by spreading the income and benefits among more people.

There are limits to how far you can go with these strategies, and numerous rules to follow and records to keep to make sure you stay within the parameters the IRS will permit. But if you become aware of the rules and the techniques that work in your favor, you can save a lot of money.

In Part II, we'll lay out the income tax rules that apply to your business clearly and concisely, to help you file your taxes as quickly and accurately as possible this year, and to tell you about planning strategies you can use to reduce your tax bill in the future.

Warning

As a small business owner, your primary concerns are usually expressed in terms of maximizing your revenue, minimizing your expenses, and ultimately, improving your bottom line. When it comes to taxes, however, the goal is usually the opposite: to defer income or receive it in tax-favored forms such as capital gains or employee benefits, to maximize *your expenses by making sure you claim every deduction you're entitled to, and to* minimize *your taxable net income.*

Because of these conflicting goals, which require very different approaches, business owners sometimes fall into the trap of making important business decisions based mainly on the tax consequences.

Don't let the tail wag the dog. Make sure that you consider all the consequences of a transaction or business practice – from a tax, financial, and strategic viewpoint – before finalizing your decision. What sounds good from a tax perspective does not always make sense in terms of your overall business objectives.

Our discussion of the income tax issues faced by your business is organized around seven key subjects.

Chapter 3: Forms of Business Organization provides an overview of how the way in which your business is organized influences your tax situation and the way in which you'll report your income. While this book focuses on the sole proprietorship, we explain how forms such as the partnership, limited liability company (LLC), C corporation, and S corporation operate from a tax perspective.

Chapter 4: Introducing the Schedule C discusses the threshold issues you need to consider, including whether you need to file as a business, how to identify your business, how to select your accounting method and year, and other preliminary matters.

Chapter 5: Business Income discusses the types of income that must be reported on your Schedule C, and for those who carry an inventory, how to compute your cost of goods sold.

Chapter 6: Deductible Business Expenses provides detailed explanations of the most commonly used business deductions, including car and truck expenses, travel expenses, meals and entertainment, employee compensation, health insurance, and retirement plans.

Chapter 7: Capital Assets and Depreciation shows how to handle your costs for real estate, equipment, and other long-term business assets. It also explains what to do when you sell, trade, or dispose of an asset used in your trade or business.

Chapter 8: Business Profit and Self-Employment Tax wraps up our explanation of how to compute your taxable net income, explains how to handle a business loss if you have one, and shows how to compute and pay your self-employment (SECA) tax.

Chapter 9: Business Tax Credits explains the federal tax credits that are available for hiring disadvantaged workers, improving access by the disabled, operating in an Empowerment Zone, and taking certain other actions the government is seeking to promote.

Tax Organizer Tip

Business-related income and expenses are entered on the "Employment" tab of CompleteTax. On the first page of the Employment tab, you'll see a list of questions. When you answer "Yes" to the question "Did you have any self-employment or business income?" a sub-tab for "Business" will be added. Click on that sub-tab to input your small business information. If you have more than one business, click on the "Add a New Business" button on the "Business" sub-tab to enter the information for each additional business.

As you continue to read through this book, we'll explain unfamiliar terms and tell you how to handle your various items of business income, expense, gain, loss, etc.

Chapter 3

Forms of Business Organization

One of the most important decisions that you made in connection with starting your business was the legal form in which you operate. And, as time passes and your business grows, you may decide to change the form to conform to your changing business goals.

You have a number of choices: a sole proprietorship, a partnership, a corporation (including an S corporation), or a limited liability company (LLC). As you can imagine, there are significant income tax consequences that flow from each of these choices. But as with every business decision you make, don't forget to weigh the tax issues against the non-tax issues.

In this case, you need to think about things like what type of business form will best help you to operate and grow the business, and what form, at your death, will make it easier for you to pass along the business to your heirs as a going concern if you desire.

While this book focuses primarily on tax issues for business owners operating as sole proprietors, it's worthwhile to spend a little time highlighting the differences between that form and the other possibilities. If you own interests in businesses that are organized as corporations, partnerships, or LLCs, we discuss how to report income from these forms of business on your individual tax return at page 173 (salary), page 227 (dividends), and page 239 (partnership, S corporation, and LLC distributions).

SOLE PROPRIETORSHIPS

A sole proprietorship is an unincorporated business with a single owner. It's the most commonly used form for new small businesses, and the easiest form to operate from a tax and recordkeeping perspective. If your business has only one owner, the IRS will presume that it's a sole proprietorship unless you incorporate under state law.

From the IRS's perspective, a sole proprietorship is not a taxable creature in itself. Instead, all of the business's assets and liabilities are treated as belonging directly to the business owner. The annual income and expenses generated by the business are reflected on Schedule C, *Profit or Loss From Business,* or Schedule C-EZ, *Net Profit From Business,* which is part of the business owner's individual tax return (Form 1040).

Beginning on page 33, we'll provide a detailed explanation of the information you need to fill out Schedule C.

For now, just the basics: Your gross revenue from sales and other business income is reported on the top of the Schedule C. Expenses of the business are subtracted from income to arrive at the net profit (or loss) figure at the bottom of the form.

The net profit or loss is carried over from the Schedule C and reported on page 1 of the owner's 1040. This means that there is no separate tax rate schedule that applies to a sole proprietorship — the business owner's individual tax rate will determine the amount of tax paid on the earnings of the business.

The main advantage of a sole proprietorship is simplicity. Because there is only one owner, the accounting rules are much easier to understand and to use. Also, a business owner may transfer money in or out of the business with no tax effects to keep track of.

Example

When you pay yourself as a sole proprietor, you simply withdraw money from your business checking account — you don't have to issue yourself a paycheck and make payroll tax deductions.

Similarly, if you decide to contribute some personal money to the business, you can simply add it to your checking account – you don't have to formally make (and keep track of) your capital contribution as you would with a partnership or a corporation, at least as far as the IRS is concerned.

Sole proprietors are generally required to pay self-employment taxes (see page 135) on all of the business's net profits computed on Schedule C. You must use Schedule SE of the annual income tax return to compute these taxes.

For each quarter, a sole proprietor generally needs to make an estimated tax payment that includes income tax and self-employment tax (see page 308). If you have employees, you may also need to make periodic payments of payroll taxes for them.

When the time comes to sell a business asset or even the business itself, the owner is treated as if he or she sold each individual item that was included in the sale, and gain or loss on each item must be computed separately. Intangible assets such as patents and copyrights are considered assets of the business, and separate gain or loss is computed on them (see page 118).

PARTNERSHIPS

A partnership is an unincorporated business with two or more owners. For businesses with more than one owner, the IRS will presume that your business should be taxed as a partnership unless you have incorporated under state law, or you elect to be taxed as a corporation by filing IRS Form 8832, *Entity Classification Election.*

A partnership is not a taxable entity under federal law — there is no separate partnership income tax, as there is a corporate income tax. Instead, income from the partnership is taxed to the individual partners, at their own individual tax rate.

However, the partnership is required to file a tax return (Form 1065) that reports its income and loss to the IRS, and also reports each partner's share of income and loss on Schedule K-1 of the 1065. For tax purposes, all of the income of the partnership must be reported as distributed to the partners, and they will be taxed on it through their individual returns. This is true whether or not the partners actually received their shares of the income, and even if the partnership agreement requires that the money be retained in the business as partnership capital.

Partnerships are generally the most flexible form of business for tax purposes, since the income and losses distributed to each of the partners can vary (e.g., one partner can receive 40 percent of any profits but 60 percent of any losses), as long as a business purpose other than tax avoidance can be shown for the split.

In the early years of most businesses, the company generates losses rather than profits, and the partnership form allows the partners to use these losses to offset other income they may have from investments or another job. One caveat: The partners may not deduct losses that exceed the amount of their investment in the business. But any losses that can't be deducted as a result of this rule can be deducted in subsequent years if the partner increases his or her investment.

Although the individual partners (not their partnership) are the ones paying the income tax for the business, most of the choices affecting how income is computed must be made by the partnership, rather than by the individual partners on their own returns. These choices include elections of general methods of accounting, methods of depreciation, and accounting for specific items such as organization and business startup expenses and installment sales. Partners are required to treat partnership items in the same way on their individual tax returns as they were treated on the partnership return.

There are a number of nontax factors that may influence your decision as to whether a partnership is the right form of business for you, and we recommend that you seek legal advice in setting up a partnership and writing up the partnership agreement.

LIMITED LIABILITY COMPANIES

The limited liability company (LLC) is a hybrid of a corporation and a limited partnership that is created under state law. For federal tax purposes, an LLC is treated as a partnership and it must file a Form 1065, *U.S. Partnership Return of Income.* (There is an exception to this rule for single-owner LLCs, which are treated identically to sole proprietorships and whose owners must simply file a Schedule C with their Form 1040.)

Under state laws, LLC owners are given the protection from liability that was previously afforded only to corporate stockholders. Although the LLC is a relatively new business form, all of the states have now enacted legislation providing for limited liability companies.

However, while LLCs are treated as partnerships for federal tax purposes, the same is not always true for state tax purposes. Your state department of revenue can tell you the rule in your state.

Comparison with S Corporations

While S corporations (see page 31) also provide limited liability for their owners and favorable pass-through tax treatment, LLCs do provide some special advantages to growing businesses. Like a partnership, an LLC has the ability to make disproportionate distributions to its owners (for example, an LLC member may have a 50 percent ownership interest in the LLC but be entitled to 60 percent of the annual income, if the operating agreement so provides). In contrast, S corporations must generally make all distributions pro-rata according to the number of shares held by each owner. An LLC can have an unlimited number of investors, but an S corporation is limited to 75 shareholders (100 shareholders for tax years beginning in 2005).

CORPORATIONS

Businesses that are engaged in operations that are considered "risky" or subject to frequent lawsuits are often encouraged by their legal advisors to incorporate. Using a corporate structure can also make it much easier to obtain investment capital and to pass the business down to the owner's children or other successors upon death or retirement.

From a tax perspective, there are two options for corporations under federal income tax law:

- C corporations are what we normally consider "regular" corporations and are subject to the corporate income tax.
- S corporations are corporations that have filed a special election with the IRS. They are not subject to corporate income tax but are treated as similar (but not identical) to partnerships for tax purposes.

There are a number of nontax factors that may influence your decision as to whether a corporation is the right form of business for you, and we recommend that you seek expert legal advice in setting up a corporation and writing up the articles of incorporation.

C Corporations

A C corporation (also known as a regular corporation) is taxed as a separate person or "entity" under the tax law. Income earned by the corporation is normally taxed at the corporate level, using the corporate income tax rates shown in the table on page 30.

After the corporate tax is paid on the business income, any distributions made to stockholders are taxed again at the individuals' rates, as dividends.

Because of these two levels of tax, a regular corporation may be a less desirable form of business than the other types of business entities (sole proprietorships, partnerships, limited liability companies, or S corporations).

Comparing Corporations to Other Forms

Because the taxation of income to sole proprietorships and partnerships is determined by the tax bracket that applies to each individual owner, a comparison of tax rates that apply to corporations and to individuals can give you some idea of which form of business would save taxes at a particular income level.

The chart that follows compares the marginal tax rates for tax years beginning in 2006 for corporations, married individuals filing jointly, and for singles. As the table shows, corporations generally have the same or a higher tax rate imposed on their income compared to those subject to individual tax rates. Also keep in mind that the rate comparison is only part of the tax picture to consider: distributions (money taken out) from a partnership are generally taxable only once on the partners' individual returns, while distributions made by a corporation to its shareholders after corporate tax is paid are taxed again as dividends on the shareholders' returns.

Salaries May Offset Tax

In comparing the tax advantages of operating a business as a partnership or sole proprietorship rather than as a corporation, it should be remembered that not all of the corporate profits will be subject to double taxation. The operators of the corporation may withdraw reasonable salaries, which are deductible by the corporation.

These salaries are therefore free from income tax at the corporate level (although the recipients will have to pay individual income tax, and both recipients and the business will have to pay FICA tax, on them). In some cases, the entire net profits of the business may be eaten up by salaries to the owners and other employees, so that no corporate income tax is due.

2006 Tax Rates

Taxable Income ($)	C Corporation	Married/Joint	Single
0 — 7,500	15%	10%	10%
7,501 — 15,100	15%	10%	15%
15,101 — 30,650	15%	15%	15%
30,651 — 50,000	15%	15%	25%
50,001 — 61,300	25%	15%	25%
61,301 — 74,200	25%	25%	25%
74,201 — 75,000	25%	25%	28%
75,001 — 100,000	34%	25%	28%
100,001 — 123,700	39%	25%	28%
123,701 — 154,800	39%	28%	28%
154,801 — 188,450	39%	28%	33%
188,451 — 335,000	39%	33%	33%
335,001 — 336,550	34%	33%	33%
336,551 — 10,000,000	34%	35%	35%
10,000,001 — 15,000,000	35%	35%	35%
15,000,001 — 18,333,333	38%	35%	35%
Over 18,333,333	35%	35%	35%

Note: Personal service corporations (those whose employees spend at least 95 percent of their time in the field of health, law, engineering, architecture, accounting, actuarial science, performing arts, or consulting) are taxed at a flat rate of 35 percent of net profits.

Warning

If your corporation is profitable but does not pay any dividends for an extended period of time, the IRS is likely to conclude that some of the salaries paid to owners are really disguised dividends. The IRS can disallow some or all of the salary deductions, resulting in a large tax bill plus interest and penalties. If you have a corporation, your best bet is to make sure all salaries are in line with industry standards, and to pay out at least some dividends each year.

S Corporations

An S corporation is a creature of the federal tax laws. For all other purposes, it's treated as a regular corporation.

This means that to form an S corporation you first have to incorporate under state law.

Then, you must file a special form electing to be taxed under a special provision of the tax law that preserves the corporation's limited liability under state law, but avoids taxation at the corporate level. As a result, the annual income or losses of the S corporation are passed through to shareholders in much the same way that a partnership passes through such items to partners.

One exception is that all S corporation profits, losses, and other items that pass through must be allocated according to each shareholder's proportionate shares of stock. For example, if you own 50 percent of the stock, you must receive 50 percent of the losses, profits, credits, etc. This is not the case with a partnership, where one partner can receive different percentages of different tax items if the partnership agreement so specifies.

While the technical requirements for S corporation status are restrictive, an S corporation is given significant flexibility in structuring its business operations. For example, by forming a partnership that includes S corporations, ineligible shareholders can participate as partners in the corporation's business without the risk of losing the S election. Also, business owners that "outgrow" their S corporation status are always free to choose an alternative entity structure that better meets their needs.

S Corporation Requirements

To obtain S corporation status under the federal income tax law, all of the following requirements must be met:

- The corporation must be a domestic corporation (a corporation organized under the laws of the United States, a state, or territory that is taxed as a corporation under local law).
- *All* shareholders must agree to the election.
- The corporation may not have more than one class of stock (voting and nonvoting shares are not considered to be two separate classes, however).
- The corporation may not have more than 100 shareholders.
- The corporation may not have any shareholder that is a nonresident alien or nonhuman entity (such as other corporations or partnerships), unless the shareholder is an estate or trust that is authorized to be an S corporation shareholder under the tax laws, or unless the shareholder is on the list of certain exempt organizations (such as qualified pension, profit-sharing, and stock bonus plans) that are be allowed to be shareholders.

Chapter 4

Introducing the Schedule C

For the rest of Part II, we'll concentrate on issues that apply to businesses organized as sole proprietorships.

If you are the sole owner of a business or operate as an independent contractor, you're going to become very well acquainted with the tax form used by all these businesses: the Schedule C, *Profit or Loss from Business,* or its shorter cousin, the Schedule C-EZ, *Net Profit From Business.*

Although the sole proprietorship is, by definition, a single-owner business, many family businesses are operated in this form even though both spouses consider themselves to be the owners.

If one spouse is the primary business operator, he or she can file as a sole proprietor even if the other spouse fills in as needed or consults on major decisions. If both spouses actively work in the business, you may consider one spouse to be the owner for IRS purposes, and the other may be considered an employee (or possibly even an independent contractor) which will save you the time and trouble of filing partnership tax forms.

You should be aware that under many state marital property laws, both spouses may be considered to be owners of the business assets in case of divorce, regardless of whose name is listed as the owner on the tax forms or the property records.

Work Smart

If both spouses work in the business and you want both to obtain wage credits toward Social Security disability and retirement benefits, you'll generally need to have paychecks issued, and payroll taxes withheld, for the spouse who is not listed as the sole proprietor.

DO YOU NEED TO FILE THIS FORM?

While we suspect that most of you already know the answer to that question, it pays to review the filing requirements just in case your business does not meet them for a particular year.

First of all, the income requirement: If you have $400 or more of business income over and above your expenses, you need to file a Schedule C and a Schedule

SE to pay self-employment tax, even if you would not otherwise have to file a tax return (see page 157).

Although you may know exactly what your business earnings are for normal accounting purposes, if you're close to the $400 threshold or actually had a loss for the year, you'll need to use IRS rules to compute net income for tax purposes in order to know the exact amount. For a complete description of what income you need to include as "business income," see Chapter 5.

Work Smart

Even if your business does have a loss for the year, consider filing a tax return anyway.

That way you can take advantage of the opportunity to carry losses back for two years and/or forward to future years, so you can deduct them in some other year(s) in which you do have a profit.

If your business is just starting out and you have a profit of less than $400, you may want to file a Schedule C to establish your business's existence and show that your business activity was undertaken for a profit motive. In this case, you would not have to file Schedule SE.

If you run more than one business as a sole proprietorship, you'll need to net them together to determine whether you've met the $400 threshold. For example, if one business has a profit of $2,000 and another has a loss of $1,700, your net profit from both businesses is only $300 and you won't need to pay any self-employment tax for the year. We recommend that you do file a Schedule SE anyway, just to demonstrate to the IRS that you computed your taxes correctly.

Do You Have a Profit-Seeking Trade or Business?

In general, in order to file a Schedule C and deduct all your business expenses, you must have been engaged in a "trade or business;" that is, an activity that is carried on for a livelihood or for profit.

A profit motive must be present (though you may in fact have experienced a loss for the year) and some type of economic activity must be conducted.

"Profit" for purposes of these business activity rules means real economic profit, not just tax savings. This profit motive is what separates a business from a hobby, which is an activity engaged in purely for self-satisfaction.

Hobby Loss Rules

What's so bad about hobbies? Well, if you are in business with the objective of making a profit, and it so happens that your deductions exceed your business income for the year, you can claim a loss up to the amount of your total income from all activities. Remaining losses can be carried over into other years.

Your ability to deduct these losses will be limited, however, if the IRS considers your "business" to be a hobby.

Hobby expenses incurred by individuals and even by partnerships and S corporations are generally deductible *only to the extent of the income produced by the hobby.* In other words, you can't use a hobby to generate a tax loss that can be used to shelter your other income. Some expenses, however, that would be deductible on your individual tax return regardless of whether they are incurred in connection with a hobby (such as real estate taxes, mortgage interest, and casualty losses) are deductible even if they exceed your hobby income. These expenses must be used to reduce the amount of the hobby income from which your other hobby expenses can be deducted.

Every bit of your hobby income is reported as "other income" on Line 21 of your Form 1040, *Individual Income Tax Return.* However, expenses associated with the hobby are only deductible if you itemize your deductions. What's more, they are considered "miscellaneous itemized deductions" and you can only deduct the portion of them that, along with any other miscellaneous deductions, exceeds 2 percent of your adjusted gross income.

Although the IRS is not limited in the kind of businesses that it can challenge as being hobbies, businesses that look like traditional hobbies (such as "gentlemen farming" and craft businesses run from the home) may well face a greater chance of IRS scrutiny than other types of businesses.

The absence of income, in itself, does not prevent an activity from being classified as a business activity. You can establish the profit motive of your business under the nine factors used by the IRS, as shown by the chart that follows. A "yes" answer supports a finding of a profit motive, although no one factor settles the matter.

You may also qualify for a presumption that you had a profit motive if your business shows a profit for three of the five years in question.

For a new business, this means that you don't have to show a profit for your first two years. (A narrow exception to this rule applies to horse breeding, training, and racing activities, where profitability must be shown in two out of seven consecutive years.)

If your business qualifies for this presumption, it means that the IRS (not you) has the burden of proving that your business is a hobby. If you don't qualify for the presumption, you may still show that you operated for profit under the nine factors listed below.

The IRS does provide a form (Form 5213, *Election To Postpone Determination as to Whether the Presumption Applies That an Activity Is Engaged in for Profit,* reproduced at the end of the book) on which you can officially elect to have the IRS wait until the first five years are up before examining the profitability of your business. If you use this form, it should be filed within three years of the due date of the return for your first year in business.

However, it's generally not necessary to file the form in order to take advantage of the presumption. If you don't file the form and you are audited by the IRS, you can file the form within 60 days of receiving the IRS notice, as long as your three-year period has not expired.

Nine Factors Used to Show a Profit Motive

1. **How the business is run** — Is the activity carried on in a businesslike manner? Does the owner keep complete, accurate business records and books? Has the owner changed business operations to increase profits?
2. **Expertise** — Does the owner have the necessary expertise to run the business? If not, does he or she seek (and follow) expert advice?
3. **Time and effort** — Does the owner spend the time and effort needed for the business's success? (Spending a lot of time on the activity will not, however, have much value to prove a profit motive if the type of activity has significant personal or recreational aspects.)
4. **Appreciation** — Is it likely that business assets will appreciate in value? (A profit objective can exist where an overall profit would result when the gain from the sale of the asset is added to the other income from the activity, even though a profit is not derived from current operations.)
5. **Success with other activities** — Has the owner engaged in similar (or dissimilar) activities in the past and converted them from unprofitable to profitable enterprises?
6. **History of income or loss** — Were the business losses that were incurred due to the business still being in a startup phase, or because of unforeseen circumstances?
7. **Amount of occasional profit** — Are the amount of occasional profits significant when compared to the size of the owner's investment in the activity, and the amount of losses suffered in other years? (An occasional small profit for an activity generating large losses, or in which the owner has a large investment, will not establish a for-profit objective.)
8. **Financial status of owner** — Is the business activity the only source of the owner's income?
9. **Personal pleasure or recreation** — Is the type of business one that is not usually considered to have elements of personal pleasure or recreation?

Work Smart

How you can go about showing that your activity is operated for profit will depend, in large part, on when you expect it to turn a profit.

Profit possible over short term — *By planning when to receive income and when to purchase items that generate deductions, try to maximize income (and minimize deductions) in at least three years (the "profit" years), and maximize deductions (and minimize income) in the remaining two years (the "loss" years). This may allow you to qualify for the presumption of profit motive discussed above.*

Profit possible only over long term — *If it appears that the business will not be profitable for some years, you won't be able to come within the presumption of profit motive. You'll have to rely on qualifying under the IRS's nine-point inquiry to establish profit motive.*

No possibility of profit — *Face it: What you have here is a hobby. You can try to argue that you qualify under the IRS's nine-point inquiry, but in all likelihood you'll fail. If you want to continue this activity, you may as well either resign yourself to the limitation on hobby losses, or figure out a way to conduct the activity in a way that generates profits.*

More Than One Business?

People who are endowed with an entrepreneurial spirit generally don't limit their efforts to one business activity. It's common for business owners to branch out into sideline activities that may or may not be related to their original activity, and that might be considered a separate business.

For example, a craft supply retailer might also offer classes in various types of arts and crafts. Or, a photography studio might offer photoprocessing of customers' ordinary snapshots, in addition to traditional professional photography. In each case, the question arises: Is this a single business, or two businesses that should be reported on two different Schedule Cs?

The tax laws and regulations are not very clear on this issue, probably because the facts and circumstances can vary so much from case to case. Generally speaking, if you have two or more separate business activities, you can't report them both on the same Schedule C. The instructions to Form 5213, *Election To Postpone Determination as to Whether the Presumption Applies That an Activity Is Engaged in for Profit,* state that in determining whether you are engaged in more than one activity, you must consider all of the following:

- the similarity of the activities
- the business purpose that is (or might be) served by carrying on the activities separately or together in a trade or business or investment setting
- the organizational and economic interrelationship of the activities

These factors are quite vague and subjective, even for the IRS. The general idea, however, is that if you provide similar products or services to similar clients, you have a single business. If you don't, you may have more than one business depending on how close the relationship is between the activities.

Other factors that should be considered include which spouse is the primary operator of the business (for instance, does one spouse run one activity while the other runs a second?) and the locations of the businesses (if you have two different but related businesses that occupy two separate sites, it's more likely that they should be considered two separate businesses).

If you receive income as a "statutory employee," a grouping that includes full-time life insurance agents, agent or commission drivers, commission traveling salespersons, and certain homeworkers, you must report this income on a Schedule C. If you also receive other income as a self-employed person, don't combine the two types of income – you must file a separate Schedule C for each type. See page 48 for more details.

One last factor to keep in mind is that the tax law provides for separate treatment of "passive activities" – basically, income or losses from a passive activity can only be offset by income or losses from other passive activities.

Real estate rentals are most often classified as passive activities which must be reported on Schedule E, *Supplemental Income and Loss,* not Schedule C. So, if your "sole proprietorship" involves some rental or leasing activities, you may need to treat the income and expense from these activities as separate passive activities (see page 216 regarding Schedule E).

Can You Use Form C-EZ?

The IRS does provide a simplified version of Schedule C, known as Schedule C-EZ, *Net Profit From Business*, that can be used by some small business owners, primarily those who work as independent contractors for one or more larger businesses. A copy of Schedule C is reproduced at the end of the book.

Whenever you have an option as to which tax form you can use, it's generally best to use the simplest form that's available to you. There is some evidence that the IRS is less likely to scrutinize tax returns that include the "EZ" versions of the forms.

So, you'll want to use Schedule C-EZ if you're eligible, which means that you:

- operated only one sole proprietorship business during the year
- did not have an inventory at any time during the year
- did not have any employees during the year
- had total business expenses that did not exceed $5,000
- do not deduct expenses for business use of your home
- use the cash method of accounting (see discussion page 41)
- did not have a net loss from your business
- do not have any prior-year unallowed passive activity losses for this business
- are not required to file a Form 4562, *Depreciation and Amortization,* for the year, which means that you did not place any depreciable property into service for the first time this year, and you're not claiming depreciation on any "listed property" such as a car, light truck, motorcycle, cell phone, computer or peripherals, or photographic, audio/video, or communications equipment (for more on depreciation, see page 99).

If you do not meet all of these requirements, you must file Schedule C this year instead of C-EZ.

IDENTIFYING YOUR BUSINESS

Whether you use Schedule C or C-EZ, the top of the form requires you to list your business name (if it's different from your own name), your principal business or profession, your principal business code, and your Employer Identification Number (EIN) if you are required to have one.

Employer I.D. Numbers

Sole proprietors need to have an EIN only if they have one or more employees, if they have a Keogh plan, or if they are required to file excise tax forms such as those for sales tax, alcohol or tobacco.

If you purchase a business for which an EIN is needed, use your own EIN or get a new one – don't use the EIN of the previous owner. If you operate more than one business as a sole proprietor, you should use the same EIN for each one; if you operate businesses in forms other than sole proprietorship, you'll need a separate EIN for each business entity.

To apply for an EIN, you can file a paper Form SS-4, *Application for Employer Identification Number,* with the appropriate IRS Service Center for your state. If you apply by mail, it generally takes about four weeks to receive the number. If you need to file your tax return before you receive the EIN, write "applied for" in the space where the EIN should go.

You can also get an EIN immediately over the phone by calling the number of the Tele-TIN in the chart on the next page; however, you'll still need to fill out a paper SS-4 form and mail or fax it to the Service Center within 24 hours. The IRS representative will give you the correct fax number. The advantage of using this system is that you will receive the EIN immediately and you can use it on your tax forms right away.

Business Codes

Whether you file a Schedule C or C-EZ, you'll need to enter a six-digit business code at the top of the form. We reproduce the complete list of codes on pages 38-40. It's very important that you use the correct business code. If your return is examined by the IRS, the agents may use this code as a screening device to determine whether your income and expenses are unusual for that type of business.

Where to Apply for an EIN	
If your principal business, office or agency, or legal residence in the case of an individual, is located in:	*Call the Tele-TIN or Fax-TIN number shown or file with the IRS Service Center at:*
Connecticut, Delaware, District of Columbia, Florida, Georgia, Maine, Maryland, Massachusetts, New Hampshire, New Jersey, New York, North Carolina, Ohio, Pennsylvania, Rhode Island, South Carolina, Vermont, Virginia, West Virginia	Attn: EIN Operations Holtsville, NY 11742-9003 Tele-TIN: TOLL FREE (800) 829-4933 Fax-TIN: (631) 447-8960
Illinois, Indiana, Kentucky, Michigan	Attn: EIN Operations Cincinnati, OH 45999 Tele-TIN: TOLL FREE (800) 829-4933 Fax-TIN: (859) 669-5760
Alabama, Alaska, Arizona, Arkansas, California, Colorado, Hawaii, Idaho, Iowa, Kansas, Louisiana, Minnesota, Mississippi, Missouri, Montana, Nebraska, Nevada, New Mexico, North Dakota, Oklahoma, Oregon, Puerto Rico, South Dakota, Tennessee, Texas, Utah, Washington, Wisconsin, Wyoming	Attn: EIN Operations Philadelphia, PA 19255 Tele-TIN: TOLL FREE (800) 829-4933 Fax-TIN: (215) 516-3990
If you have no legal residence, principal place of business, or principal office or agency in any state:	Attn: EIN Operations Philadelphia, PA 19255 Tele-TIN: NOT TOLL FREE (215) 516-6999 Fax-TIN: (215) 516-3990

If so, they may decide to dig further into your return (and ask you to produce a lot more records to prove your figures).

In the last several years, the IRS has been making an effort to educate its agents about typical operating procedures in different industries and even in specific types of businesses, so that the agents can more effectively ferret out underreported income and overstated deductions. If you report the wrong business code, the IRS may be judging you by the incorrect standard.

Example

If you operate a retail jewelry business, the IRS has a general idea of the percentage of your revenues that should be eaten up by your cost of goods sold. If you erroneously list your code as "453220" which applies to gift shops, your cost of goods sold may appear to be way out of line and your tax return may be flagged for an audit.

Principal Business or Professional Activity Codes

These codes for the Principal Business or Professional Activity classify sole proprietorships by the type of activity they are engaged in to facilitate the administration of the Internal Revenue Code. These six-digit codes are based on the North American Industry Classification System (NAICS).

Select the category that best describes your primary business activity (for example, Real Estate). Then select the activity that best identifies the principal source of your sales or receipts (for example, real estate agent). Now find the six-digit code assigned to this activity (for example, 531210, the code for offices of real estate agents and brokers) and **enter it on line B of Schedule C or C-EZ.**

Note. If your principal source of income is from farming activities, you should file **Schedule F,** Profit or Loss From Farming.

Accommodation, Food Services, & Drinking Places

Accommodation

- 721310 Rooming & boarding houses
- 721210 RV (recreational vehicle) parks & recreational camps
- 721100 Travel accommodation (including hotels, motels, & bed & breakfast inns)

Food Services & Drinking Places

- 722410 Drinking places (alcoholic beverages)
- 722110 Full-service restaurants
- 722210 Limited-service eating places
- 722300 Special food services (including food service contractors & caterers)

Administrative & Support and Waste Management & Remediation Services

Administrative & Support Services

- 561430 Business service centers (including private mail centers & copy shops)
- 561740 Carpet & upholstery cleaning services
- 561440 Collection agencies
- 561450 Credit bureaus
- 561410 Document preparation services
- 561300 Employment services
- 561710 Exterminating & pest control services
- 561210 Facilities support (management) services
- 561600 Investigation & security services
- 561720 Janitorial services
- 561730 Landscaping services
- 561110 Office administrative services
- 561420 Telephone call centers (including telephone answering services & telemarketing bureaus)
- 561500 Travel arrangement & reservation services
- 561490 Other business support services (including repossession services, court reporting, & stenotype services)
- 561790 Other services to buildings & dwellings
- 561900 Other support services (including packaging & labeling services, & convention & trade show organizers)

Waste Management & Remediation Services

- 562000 Waste management & remediation services

Agriculture, Forestry, Hunting, & Fishing

- 112900 Animal production (including breeding of cats and dogs)
- 114110 Fishing
- 113000 Forestry & logging (including forest nurseries & timber tracts)
- 114210 Hunting & trapping

Support Activities for Agriculture & Forestry

- 115210 Support activities for animal production (including farriers)
- 115110 Support activities for crop production (including cotton ginning, soil preparation, planting, & cultivating)
- 115310 Support activities for forestry

Arts, Entertainment, & Recreation

Amusement, Gambling, & Recreation Industries

- 713100 Amusement parks & arcades
- 713200 Gambling industries
- 713900 Other amusement & recreation services (including golf courses, skiing facilities, marinas, fitness centers, bowling centers, skating rinks, miniature golf courses)

Museums, Historical Sites, & Similar Institutions

- 712100 Museums, historical sites, & similar institutions

Principal Business or Professional Activity Codes *(continued)*

Performing Arts, Spectator Sports, & Related Industries

711410 Agents & managers for artists, athletes, entertainers, & other public figures
711510 Independent artists, writers, & performers
711100 Performing arts companies
711300 Promoters of performing arts, sports, & similar events
711210 Spectator sports (including professional sports clubs & racetrack operations)

Construction of Buildings

236200 Nonresidential building construction
236100 Residential building construction

Heavy and Civil Engineering Construction

237310 Highway, street, & bridge construction
237210 Land subdivision
237100 Utility system construction
237990 Other heavy & civil engineering construction

Specialty Trade Contractors

238310 Drywall & insulation contractors
238210 Electrical contractors
238350 Finish carpentry contractors
238330 Flooring contractors
238130 Framing carpentry contractors
238150 Glass & glazing contractors
238140 Masonry contractors
238320 Painting & wall covering contractors
238220 Plumbing, heating & air-conditioning contractors
238110 Poured concrete foundation & structure contractors
238160 Roofing contractors
238170 Siding contractors
238910 Site preparation contractors
238120 Structural steel & precast concrete construction contractors
238340 Tile & terrazzo contractors
238290 Other building equipment contractors
238390 Other building finishing contractors
238190 Other foundation, structure, & building exterior contractors
238990 All other specialty trade contractors

Educational Services

611000 Educational services (including schools, colleges, & universities)

Finance & Insurance

Credit Intermediation & Related Activities

522100 Depository credit intermediation (including commercial banking, savings institutions, & credit unions)
522200 Nondepository credit intermediation (including sales financing & consumer lending)
522300 Activities related to credit intermediation (including loan brokers)

Insurance Agents, Brokers, & Related Activities

524210 Insurance agencies & brokerages
524290 Other insurance related activities

Securities, Commodity Contracts, & Other Financial Investments & Related Activities

523140 Commodity contracts brokers
523130 Commodity contracts dealers
523110 Investment bankers & securities dealers
523210 Securities & commodity exchanges
523120 Securities brokers
523900 Other financial investment activities (including investment advice)

Health Care & Social Assistance

Ambulatory Health Care Services

621610 Home health care services
621510 Medical & diagnostic laboratories
621310 Offices of chiropractors
621210 Offices of dentists
621330 Offices of mental health practitioners (except physicians)
621320 Offices of optometrists
621340 Offices of physical, occupational & speech therapists, & audiologists
621111 Offices of physicians (except mental health specialists)
621112 Offices of physicians, mental health specialists
621391 Offices of podiatrists
621399 Offices of all other miscellaneous health practitioners
621400 Outpatient care centers
621900 Other ambulatory health care services (including ambulance services, blood, & organ banks)

Hospitals

622000 Hospitals

Nursing & Residential Care Facilities

623000 Nursing & residential care facilities

Social Assistance

624410 Child day care services
624200 Community food & housing, & emergency & other relief services
624100 Individual & family services
624310 Vocational rehabilitation services

Information

511000 Publishing industries (except Internet)

Broadcasting (except Internet) & Telecommunications

515000 Broadcasting (except Internet)
517000 Telecommunications

Internet Publishing & Broadcasting

516110 Internet publishing & broadcasting

Internet Service Providers, Web Search Portals, & Data Processing Services

518210 Data processing, hosting, & related services
518111 Internet service providers
518112 Web search portals
519100 Other information services (including news syndicates and libraries)

Motion Picture & Sound Recording

512100 Motion picture & video industries (except video rental)
512200 Sound recording industries

Manufacturing

315000 Apparel mfg.
312000 Beverage & tobacco product mfg.
334000 Computer & electronic product mfg.
335000 Electrical equipment, appliance, & component mfg.
332000 Fabricated metal product mfg.
337000 Furniture & related product mfg.
333000 Machinery mfg.
339110 Medical equipment & supplies mfg.
322000 Paper mfg.
324100 Petroleum & coal products mfg.
326000 Plastics & rubber products mfg.
331000 Primary metal mfg.
323100 Printing & related support activities
313000 Textile mills
314000 Textile product mills
336000 Transportation equipment mfg.
321000 Wood product mfg.
339900 Other miscellaneous mfg.

Chemical Manufacturing

325100 Basic chemical mfg.
325500 Paint, coating, & adhesive mfg.
325300 Pesticide, fertilizer, & other agricultural chemical mfg.
325410 Pharmaceutical & medicine mfg.
325200 Resin, synthetic rubber, & artificial & synthetic fibers & filaments mfg.
325600 Soap, cleaning compound, & toilet preparation mfg.
325900 Other chemical product & preparation mfg.

Food Manufacturing

311110 Animal food mfg.
311800 Bakeries & tortilla mfg.
311500 Dairy product mfg.
311400 Fruit & vegetable preserving & speciality food mfg.
311200 Grain & oilseed milling
311610 Animal slaughtering & processing
311710 Seafood product preparation & packaging
311300 Sugar & confectionery product mfg.
311900 Other food mfg. (including coffee, tea, flavorings, & seasonings)

Leather & Allied Product Manufacturing

316210 Footwear mfg. (including leather, rubber, & plastics)
316110 Leather & hide tanning & finishing
316990 Other leather & allied product mfg.

Nonmetallic Mineral Product Manufacturing

327300 Cement & concrete product mfg.
327100 Clay product & refractory mfg.
327210 Glass & glass product mfg.
327400 Lime & gypsum product mfg.
327900 Other nonmetallic mineral product mfg.

Mining

212110 Coal mining
212200 Metal ore mining
212300 Nonmetallic mineral mining & quarrying
211110 Oil & gas extraction
213110 Support activities for mining

Other Services

Personal & Laundry Services

812111 Barber shops
812112 Beauty salons
812220 Cemeteries & crematories
812310 Coin-operated laundries & drycleaners
812320 Drycleaning & laundry services (except coin-operated) (including laundry & drycleaning dropoff & pickup sites)
812210 Funeral homes & funeral services
812330 Linen & uniform supply
812113 Nail salons
812930 Parking lots & garages
812910 Pet care (except veterinary) services
812920 Photofinishing
812190 Other personal care services (including diet & weight reducing centers)
812990 All other personal services

Repair & Maintenance

811120 Automotive body, paint, interior, & glass repair
811110 Automotive mechanical & electrical repair & maintenance
811190 Other automotive repair & maintenance (including oil change & lubrication shops & car washes)
811310 Commercial & industrial machinery & equipment (except automotive & electronic) repair & maintenance
811210 Electronic & precision equipment repair & maintenance
811430 Footwear & leather goods repair

C-8

Principal Business or Professional Activity Codes *(continued)*

811410 Home & garden equipment & appliance repair & maintenance
811420 Reupholstery & furniture repair
811490 Other personal & household goods repair & maintenance

Professional, Scientific, & Technical Services

541100 Legal services
541211 Offices of certified public accountants
541214 Payroll services
541213 Tax preparation services
541219 Other accounting services

Architectural, Engineering, & Related Services

541310 Architectural services
541350 Building inspection services
541340 Drafting services
541330 Engineering services
541360 Geophysical surveying & mapping services
541320 Landscape architecture services
541370 Surveying & mapping (except geophysical) services
541380 Testing laboratories

Computer Systems Design & Related Services

541510 Computer systems design & related services

Specialized Design Services

541400 Specialized design services (including interior, industrial, graphic, & fashion design)

Other Professional, Scientific, & Technical Services

541800 Advertising & related services
541600 Management, scientific, & technical consulting services
541910 Market research & public opinion polling
541920 Photographic services
541700 Scientific research & development services
541930 Translation & interpretation services
541940 Veterinary services
541990 All other professional, scientific, & technical services

Real Estate & Rental & Leasing

Real Estate

531100 Lessors of real estate (including miniwarehouses & self-storage units)
531210 Offices of real estate agents & brokers
531320 Offices of real estate appraisers
531310 Real estate property managers
531390 Other activities related to real estate

Rental & Leasing Services

532100 Automotive equipment rental & leasing
532400 Commercial & industrial machinery & equipment rental & leasing
532210 Consumer electronics & appliances rental
532220 Formal wear & costume rental
532310 General rental centers
532230 Video tape & disc rental
532290 Other consumer goods rental

Religious, Grantmaking, Civic, Professional, & Similar Organizations

813000 Religious, grantmaking, civic, professional, & similar organizations

Retail Trade

Building Material & Garden Equipment & Supplies Dealers

444130 Hardware stores
444110 Home centers
444200 Lawn & garden equipment & supplies stores
444120 Paint & wallpaper stores
444190 Other building materials dealers

Clothing & Accessories Stores

448130 Children's & infants' clothing stores
448150 Clothing accessories stores
448140 Family clothing stores
448310 Jewelry stores
448320 Luggage & leather goods stores
448110 Men's clothing stores
448210 Shoe stores
448120 Women's clothing stores
448190 Other clothing stores

Electronic & Appliance Stores

443130 Camera & photographic supplies stores
443120 Computer & software stores
443111 Household appliance stores
443112 Radio, television, & other electronics stores

Food & Beverage Stores

445310 Beer, wine, & liquor stores
445220 Fish & seafood markets
445230 Fruit & vegetable markets
445100 Grocery stores (including supermarkets & convenience stores without gas)
445210 Meat markets
445290 Other specialty food stores

Furniture & Home Furnishing Stores

442110 Furniture stores
442200 Home furnishings stores

Gasoline Stations

447100 Gasoline stations (including convenience stores with gas)

General Merchandise Stores

452000 General merchandise stores

Health & Personal Care Stores

446120 Cosmetics, beauty supplies, & perfume stores
446130 Optical goods stores
446110 Pharmacies & drug stores
446190 Other health & personal care stores

Motor Vehicle & Parts Dealers

441300 Automotive parts, accessories, & tire stores
441222 Boat dealers
441221 Motorcycle dealers
441110 New car dealers
441210 Recreational vehicle dealers (including motor home & travel trailer dealers)
441120 Used car dealers
441229 All other motor vehicle dealers

Sporting Goods, Hobby, Book, & Music Stores

451211 Book stores
451120 Hobby, toy, & game stores
451140 Musical instrument & supplies stores
451212 News dealers & newsstands
451220 Prerecorded tape, compact disc, & record stores
451130 Sewing, needlework, & piece goods stores
451110 Sporting goods stores

Miscellaneous Store Retailers

453920 Art dealers
453110 Florists
453220 Gift, novelty, & souvenir stores
453930 Manufactured (mobile) home dealers
453210 Office supplies & stationery stores
453910 Pet & pet supplies stores
453310 Used merchandise stores
453990 All other miscellaneous store retailers (including tobacco, candle, & trophy shops)

Nonstore Retailers

454112 Electronic auctions
454111 Electronic shopping
454310 Fuel dealers
454113 Mail-order houses
454210 Vending machine operators
454390 Other direct selling establishments (including door-to-door retailing, frozen food plan providers, party plan merchandisers, & coffee-break service providers)

Transportation & Warehousing

481000 Air transportation
485510 Charter bus industry
484110 General freight trucking, local
484120 General freight trucking, long distance
485210 Interurban & rural bus transportation
486000 Pipeline transportation
482110 Rail transportation
487000 Scenic & sightseeing transportation
485410 School & employee bus transportation
484200 Specialized freight trucking (including household moving vans)
485300 Taxi & limousine service
485110 Urban transit systems
483000 Water transportation
485990 Other transit & ground passenger transportation
488000 Support activities for transportation (including motor vehicle towing)

Couriers & Messengers

492000 Couriers & messengers

Warehousing & Storage Facilities

493100 Warehousing & storage (except leases of miniwarehouses & self-storage units)

Utilities

221000 Utilities

Wholesale Trade

Merchant Wholesalers, Durable Goods

423600 Electrical & electronic goods
423200 Furniture & home furnishing
423700 Hardware, & plumbing & heating equipment & supplies
423940 Jewelry, watch, precious stone, & precious metals
423300 Lumber & other construction materials
423800 Machinery, equipment, & supplies
423500 Metal & mineral (except petroleum)
423100 Motor vehicle & motor vehicle parts & supplies
423400 Professional & commercial equipment & supplies
423930 Recyclable materials
423910 Sporting & recreational goods & supplies
423920 Toy & hobby goods & supplies
423990 Other miscellaneous durable goods

Merchant Wholesalers, Nondurable Goods

424300 Apparel, piece goods, & notions
424800 Beer, wine, & distilled alcoholic beverage
424920 Books, periodicals, & newspapers
424600 Chemical & allied products
424210 Drugs & druggists' sundries
424500 Farm product raw materials
424910 Farm supplies
424930 Flower, nursery stock, & florists' supplies
424400 Grocery & related products
424950 Paint, varnish, & supplies
424100 Paper & paper products
424700 Petroleum & petroleum products
424940 Tobacco & tobacco products
424990 Other miscellaneous nondurable goods

Wholesale Electronic Markets and Agents & Brokers

425110 Business to business electronic markets
425120 Wholesale trade agents & brokers

999999 Unclassified establishments (unable to classify)

C-9

If you find that your business does not fit neatly into one of the business code categories listed by the IRS, consider whether you might actually be operating more than one business, as discussed on page 36.

If you're still convinced that you're operating only one business, use the code that applies to the majority of your income and expenses. The IRS does provide a code 999999 for business owners that are unable to classify their operations, but we suggest that you use this only as a last resort.

Accounting Methods and Tax Years

As a small business owner, you frequently make business decisions that may have important tax implications, whether or not you realize it at the time.

However, there are some tax-related choices that tend to have a more general, long-term effect on how you determine your business income, and possibly even on how you run your business. Often, once made, these choices are more or less permanent — you may not be able to change without the IRS's permission, which may be difficult or time-consuming to get. While some of these decisions may seem rather technical, they can have a significant effect on your tax situation and you should have a basic understanding of the issues at stake.

The most commonly encountered decisions of this nature that you'll face are your choices of an accounting method and a tax year. For those of you who carry an inventory, another important decision relates to your inventory valuation method, discussed on page 52.

Accounting Methods

At the top of the Schedule C or C-EZ the IRS asks you to identify the accounting method you use by checking a box. There are two basic accounting methods available to most small businesses: cash and accrual. If you use a hybrid method (see page 43) or some special method for your industry, you must check the box marked "other" and give the name of the method.

The major difference between cash and accrual is that a cash method taxpayer recognizes income and expenses at the point in time that the money is actually received or paid. In contrast, an accrual method taxpayer generally reports income at the time the sale is made even if the customer does not pay at that time, and reports expenses as they become due rather than by the date that the checks go out.

Most taxpayers use the cash method of accounting for their personal life. It's very simple to use and requires little recordkeeping other than a checkbook register, bank statements and perhaps credit card statements.

You can continue to use the cash method for personal items even if you use the accrual method for your business. And if you have more than one business, you can use different methods for each business as long as you maintain a separate set of accounting books and records for each one.

Cash Method Accounting

The cash method is simple to use because it's usually obvious when you receive money from a customer or other payer, or when you pay an expense with cash, credit card or a check. When money comes in or goes out, it's recorded and recognized for tax purposes.

However, as you would expect, there are a few complicating factors to remember. For one thing, if you are paid in the form of property or services instead of money, or if you pay some of your own debts through some type of barter arrangement, you must recognize these payments at the fair market value of what you give or receive.

You can't delay recognition of income by not taking control of money that you're entitled to receive. Under the cash method, income is recognized when it is actually *or constructively* received. "Constructive receipt" occurs when money is made available to you without restriction, is posted to your account, or is received by your agent.

Example

If a customer pays you with a check on December 30, 2006, you have constructively received the money and must count it as income in 2006, even if you don't cash the check or deposit it into your bank account until sometime in January of 2007.

Similarly, if you receive interest on a money market account, you have constructive receipt of the money when it is credited to your account, not when it is withdrawn.

With most business expenses, the cash method allows you to deduct them in the year that you paid for them. However, some things are not entirely deductible in the year you pay for them; for example, the purchase price of capital assets must be depreciated or amortized over a number of years (see page 99). Generally, if you make advance payments for an expense that apply substantially beyond the end of the current year, the payments must be prorated and deducted proportionately over the period in which the payments apply.

Example

If you purchase a one-year business owner's insurance policy and coverage begins on July 1, 2006, you can only deduct six months' worth of premiums in 2006. The remainder would be deductible in 2007.

Some of the more common items that fall under this rule are amounts paid to obtain a loan, such as prepaid interest, points, and loan origination fees, which must ordinarily be deducted over the course of the loan.

Advance lease payments must be deducted in the year to which they apply, and amounts paid to acquire a lease from another lessee must be deducted evenly over the course of the entire lease.

Accrual Method Accounting

Under the accrual method, you record business income when a sale occurs, whether it be the delivery of a product or the rendering of a service on your part, regardless of when you get paid. You record an expense when you receive goods or services, even though you may not pay for them until later.

To be more precise, under the accrual method you recognize an item of income when all the events that establish your right to receive the income have happened, and when the amount of income you are to receive is known with reasonable accuracy. If you estimate an amount due to you with reasonable accuracy and record it as income, and the amount you eventually receive differs from your estimate, you should make an adjustment to your income in the year you actually receive the payment.

Example

You sold a big-screen television for $3,000 in December of 2006. You sent out a bill in January of 2007 and the customer paid you later that year. However, when he got the bill, your customer pointed out that your competitor, Store X, was selling the same model for $50 less, so you adjusted your price by $50 to avoid losing the sale.

Under the accrual method, you would recognize $3,000 of income in 2006, because that is when all events establishing your right to the income took place. You would reduce your 2007 income by $50 to reflect the lower actual payment you received.

The accrual method also says that you recognize an item of expense when you become liable for it, whether or not you pay for it in the same year. Becoming liable means that all events have occurred that establish your obligation, you can determine the dollar amount with reasonable accuracy, and "economic performance" has occurred. Economic performance means that the property or services have been provided or the property has been used.

Work Smart

The accrual method gives you a more accurate picture of your financial situation than the cash method. This is because you record income on the books when it is truly earned, and you record expenses when they are incurred. Income earned in one period is accurately matched against the expenses that correspond to that period, so you get a better picture of your net profits for each period.

Who must use accrual? Any type of business that has an inventory must use the accrual method, at least for sales and for purchases. Inventories are necessary in most marketing, manufacturing, retail, or wholesale businesses, or service businesses in which customers are charged for parts, materials, or components.

At the end of 2001, the IRS issued new rules allowing certain small service businesses that also sell related products and have average annual gross receipts under $10 million for the previous three year period to use the cash method of accounting for their income and expenses. The cash method, instead of the accrual method, can be used under the following four safe harbors:

- the principal business activity is not retailing, wholesaling, manufacturing, mining, publishing, or sound recording, determined by reference to the codes in the North American Industry Classification System published by the Department of Commerce (www.census.gov)
- the principal business activity is the provision of services, even if the taxpayer is providing property incident to the services
- the principal business activity is custom manufacturing
- regardless of the taxpayer's primary business activity, the taxpayer may use the cash method with respect to any separate and distinct trade or business that satisfies one of the first three safe harbors

There is an exception for artists, authors, and photographers who sell works that they have created by their own efforts. They are not required to assign their qualified creative expenses to the particular works they have created as "cost of goods sold," which generally means they don't need to keep track of inventory costs. "Qualified creative expenses" do not include expenses related to printing, photographic plates, film, videotape, etc., so if you are involved in mass reproduction or publishing of your own creative work, you'll have to use inventory accounting for that part of your business.

Hybrid methods. Since using two different accounting methods can be cumbersome, it's more practical for most businesses that carry inventory to simply use the accrual method for everything.

However, if you wish, you can use a hybrid method that uses accrual to the extent required by law, and uses cash for the remainder of your income and expenses. Consult your accountant for more details on how this would work.

Pros and cons of accrual. Even if your business does not have inventory, if you have a lot of complex transactions during the year you may find the accrual method more desirable, because expenses are deducted in the year in which the income to which they relate is reported. By using the accrual method, your net income tends to be leveled out, avoiding income "peaks" that are subject to higher tax rates.

For some business owners, the accrual method does not necessarily reduce taxes, and may create many unnecessary accounting headaches when compared with the cash method. On the other hand, most accountants feel that the accrual method is the only one that accurately reflects the true financial state of your business.

In selecting the most appropriate accounting method, there's one disadvantage of the accrual method that tax planners like to emphasize — it's considerably more difficult to minimize taxes by shifting items of income and expense from one year to another under the accrual method. The cash-method business owner may be able to collect fees, rents, interest, and other obligations in advance or put off payment until a later year. The cash-method owner can also usually control expenses to some extent by accelerating or deferring payment for items such as advertising, supplies, repairs, interest and taxes.

Controlling income and expenses is not nearly as easy for the accrual-method business owner. He or she can defer some income into the next tax year by shipping and invoicing as little as possible during the closing days of the year, but this may not be worth the cash-flow problem that it may cause. Or the owner can try to accelerate expenses by requesting the delivery and billing of supplies, etc., before the end of the year.

Other Accounting Methods

Certain kinds of businesses can use special accounting methods under the tax law. These include farmers, builders and contractors, and business owners receiving income under long-term contracts. If you're in one of these industries, your accountant can give you more information about your options.

Your Tax Year

Your tax year determines how your taxable income will be computed. All income received or accrued within a single year is reported on that year's tax return, along with all expenses paid or accrued, and the end of the year is the cut-off point for many tax-saving strategies.

In theory, your tax year, which is also known as your accounting period, may be either a calendar year or a fiscal year (a 12-month period that ends on the last day of any month other than December). Whether you knew it or not, you selected your tax year the very first time you filed a tax return as an individual, partnership, corporation, or trust. You must continue to use the same tax year that you used that first time, unless you get IRS permission to change.

Since a sole proprietorship does not exist apart from its owner (at least in the eyes of the IRS), a sole proprietorship must use the same tax year as the owner. The majority of sole proprietors use the calendar year as their tax year, since they must continue to use the same tax year that the owner used in his or her initial individual tax return (and since most of us began filing early in life, we automatically used the calendar year the first time).

Choosing a Fiscal Year

The tax year you use may determine the accuracy with which your business's income is matched with the expenses that generate the income, on your business's financial statements. So, in the case of a business that has seasonal cycles, ideally you would have the accounting period include the entire busy season. The accounting period generally should not begin in the middle of the season.

Example

A ski resort is open only during the months of December through March — the winter resort season. If the books are kept on the basis of a calendar year, the accounting period would split the season, and distortion of income would result.

So, what would appear as a profit as of December 31, the close of the calendar year, may turn out to be a loss, or vice versa, when the entire season from December through March is considered.

Moreover, the use of the calendar year would require the owners to take inventories and make other determinations in the middle of the season when they have the least amount of time available. The use of a fiscal year that included the entire season would allow them to avoid these difficulties.

If the nature of your business is such that the bulk of expenses and receipts for an operating cycle fall in different calendar years, it may be best to select an accounting period that includes both.

Example

Let's say that your business incurs most of its expenses in the fall and gets most of its income in the spring. In any one calendar year, expenses and receipts would have little relation to each other.

Receipts in 2006, for example, would not be offset by corresponding expenses, because these expenses would have been incurred in 2005. The 2006 receipts would be offset by 2006 expenses, although these expenses would relate to 2007 receipts. A fiscal year starting on July 1, August 1, or September 1 would more accurately reflect income for your natural business year.

If you want to switch from a calendar year to a fiscal year (or vice versa), you'll need permission from the IRS, and to get such permission you must demonstrate to the IRS's satisfaction that you have a valid business purpose other than tax avoidance. In most cases, a seasonal business would be able to show a valid business purpose for using a fiscal year. You can request approval by filing IRS Form 1128, *Application to Adopt, Change, or Retain a Tax Year.*

Warning

Except in unusual cases, once you have received permission to change your tax year, the IRS will not allow you to change it again within 10 years.

DID YOU MATERIALLY PARTICIPATE IN THE BUSINESS?

The top section of the Schedule C form asks you to answer yes or no to the question, "Did you materially participate in the operation of this business during 2006?"

Most business owners can safely check the box marked "yes," since owners typically expend much more time and effort on their operations than an employee might. Their participation in the business is not only material, it's absolutely crucial!

The IRS asks this question chiefly to screen out businesses that are really passive, investment activities for their owners instead of actively managed businesses. Passive activities are the classic vehicles for tax shelters, and they are now subject to strict rules regarding deduction of losses (see page 221).

Essentially, the IRS does not want you to try to disguise passive activity losses as regular business losses that are deductible against your ordinary income.

What's more, because passive activity losses can only be deducted against passive activity income, the IRS does not want you to call a profitable business a "passive activity" just so that you can deduct some passive losses against it.

Real estate rentals will always be considered a passive activity that should be reported on Schedule E, not Schedule C, regardless of whether the owner materially participates. An exception exists for real estate professionals who materially participate in the real estate rental activities. See the discussion of rental activities on page 216.

Beyond that important distinction, the IRS has devised a seven-step test for material participation. If you meet any of seven requirements, you have materially participated for the year, and you should check the "yes" box in answer to the question on Schedule C.

If you are married, your spouse's work in the business can be counted towards your own participation hours whether or not you file a joint tax return, and whether or not your spouse is a co-owner of the business. However, work done primarily as an investor in the business (such as reviewing or analyzing financial statements, or monitoring the finances or operations in a nonmanagerial capacity) does not count toward these tests.

If you do not meet any of these tests, you must check the "no" box, and you may have to complete Form 8582, *Passive Activity Loss Limitations.*

There is an exception for those who own working interests in oil or gas wells – they may check the "yes" box and complete Schedule C whether or not they meet any of the seven tests.

Seven Tests for Material Participation

1. You participated in the activity for more than 500 hours during the tax year.
2. You were substantially the only participant in the activity during the tax year.
3. You participated in the activity for more than 100 hours in the tax year, which was at least as much as any other participant, including employees and independent contractors.
4. The activity involves the conduct of a trade or business, you participated in the activity for more than 100 hours, none of the other six tests apply, and you participated in all such significant participation activities for more than 500 hours during the year.
5. You materially participated in the activity for any five of the preceding 10 tax years.
6. The activity is a personal service activity in which you materially participated for any three prior tax years. A personal service activity is one that involves performing services in the fields of health, law, engineering, architecture, accounting, actuarial science, performing arts, consulting, or any other trade or business in which capital is not a material income producing factor.
7. Based on all the facts and circumstances, you participated in the activity on a regular, continuous basis during the year, and you participated for more than 100 hours. Your participation in management will not count toward this test if anyone else was a paid manager or spent more hours than you in managing the business.

Chapter 5

Business Income

The starting point for computing your income tax is, of course, your gross business income. In this chapter we'll discuss some rules you need to know about what is and isn't reportable business income, and the distinctions between various types of income that must be reported in different places on your tax form.

INCOME REPORTED ON SCHEDULE C

The general rule is that any income you receive that's connected with your business is considered "business income" that should be reported on Schedule C. Income is considered "connected with your business" if it's clear that the payment would not have been made if you did *not* have the business.

The Schedule C provides you with two places to report your income. Line 1 is the place to report the gross income from sales of your product or service to customers. In most cases, this will be the bulk of the income you receive from actually operating your business.

Line 6 is where you report miscellaneous types of income that are not sales revenue. This is where questions arise and the answers can sometimes get complicated, since some types of income that you might consider to be business-related must be reported on other areas of your tax return.

Gross Income from Sales

Income you receive from sales to your customers is reported on Line 1 of Schedule C or C-EZ. You should only report income you received within your tax year, according to your established accounting method (see page 41).

If you work as an independent contractor and you have received one or more 1099-MISC forms from people or businesses you have done work for, the total amount you've received from all such sources is reported on Line 1.

For most people the income has been received in the form of cash, checks, or credit card charges, but if you receive income in the form of goods or services in some type of bartering transaction, you must report the fair market value of whatever you receive.

Example

You own a plumbing business and provide plumbing services for a friend of yours who owns a landscaping business. In return, your friend installs some new shrubs in front of your office. The IRS expects you to report the value of the shrubs and installation as income, although you can deduct any of your costs incurred in providing the plumbing services.

If the shrubs had been installed in front of your home instead of your office, their value would still be reported as business income. However, if you had received the shrubs in exchange for some personal, non-business service such as babysitting, they should be reported as miscellaneous personal income on Line 21 of your Form 1040.

If you receive a negotiable promissory note in payment for a sale and you use the cash method of accounting, the fair market value of the note is reported in gross income at the time you receive it. Accrual method taxpayers would generally recognize the discounted value of the note at the time of economic performance; e.g., when they had provided the services or goods to the customer.

Statutory Employees

Statutory employees occupy a sort of middle ground between independent contractors and regular employees. They can be defined as workers in certain occupations who would not be considered employees under the usual rules, but who have been declared employees under the federal tax laws so that their employers must withhold FICA taxes on their income.

If you are a classified as a statutory employee, you will also report your income on Schedule C, although your employer should give you a W-2 Form that reports this income and shows that payroll taxes were withheld on it.

Because FICA taxes have already been paid by your employer on this income, you don't have to file a Schedule SE and pay Self-Employment Contributions Act (SECA) tax on it. Just be sure to check the box on Line 1 on your Schedule C or C-EZ, so that the IRS doesn't go looking for a Schedule SE that's not there.

If you have both statutory employee income and other income from your own business, do not combine these two types of income on a single Schedule C. You must file two Schedule Cs, and only the income from your non-statutory-employee business will flow through to your Schedule SE.

People in occupations who may be considered statutory employees are:

- **Full-time life insurance salespersons** who work primarily for one insurance company.

- **Agent and commission drivers** who deliver specified products — individuals who (1) operate their own trucks or the trucks of the persons for whom they perform services, (2) serve customers designated by their principals and customers they solicit on their own initiative, (3) make wholesale or retail sales, and (4) are paid commissions on their sales or earn the difference between what they charge their customers and what they pay their principals for the products or services they sell. Such drivers are statutory employees if they distribute beverages (other than milk), meat, vegetables, fruit, or bakery products, or if they pick up and deliver laundry or dry cleaning.

- **Traveling or city salespersons** (other than agent or commission drivers) who work full time on the principal's behalf and remit orders from customers who are retailers, wholesalers, contractors, or operators of hotels, restaurants, or other businesses whose primary function is the furnishing of food or lodging. The orders must be for items that their customers will resell or will use as supplies in their business operations.

- **Homeworkers** who work on a contract or piecework basis, in their own homes or in the homes of others. For example, persons hired to type up correspondence and to do other word processing jobs on their home computers would be homeworkers.

Statutory employees are entitled to deduct their business expenses on Schedule C, and must pay income taxes on their net income since their employers are not required to withhold income taxes from their pay.

Miscellaneous Business Income

Income other than what you receive from your customers in the ordinary course of business is reported on Line 6 of Schedule C. If you're filing Form C-EZ, you will include this income in your total on Line 1.

Tax Organizer Tip

We suggest that you follow the IRS's lead and enter any income that will be reported on your Schedule C on the "Business" pages found on the "Employment" tab. As you click "Continue" on the "Business Income Information" page, you'll be able to enter your gross receipts or sales, and an itemized list of miscellaneous income amounts.

What kinds of income should be included here? Well, two common types of income that are *not* included are your gains or losses from sales of real or personal business property, which is reported on Form 4797, *Sales of Business Property* (see page 116), and any gains or losses from casualties or thefts, which are reported on Form 4684, *Casualties and Thefts.*

Another type of income that might be considered business income but that must be reported on a different tax form is rental income from real estate, including personal property leased with real estate. This income is reported on Schedule E, *Supplemental Income and Loss,* unless you are a dealer in real estate, a hotel or motel operator, or your business is focused on renting personal property (e.g., formalwear or power tools). See the discussion of Schedule E on page 216.

Investment Income

Income such as interest and dividends from bank accounts, stocks, and bonds are generally *not* considered business income for a sole proprietor, even if you think of them as reserve funds for business downturns. Instead, they are treated as personal items to be reported on Schedule B, *Interest and Ordinary Dividends,* which is part of your Form 1040. Any gains or losses on your investments are reported on Schedule D, *Capital Gains and Losses.*

One exception would be the situation where your business uses an interest-bearing account (for example, a money-market sweep account used in conjunction with your regular checking account). In that case, the interest paid should be reported on Line 6 of Schedule C or Line 1 of the C-EZ.

If you are in the business of lending money or if you are paid interest on notes receivable that you were given by your customers, you would report that interest income on your Schedule C or C-EZ. Dividends you received on business insurance policies should also be reported there.

Recaptured Depreciation

If you need to report recaptured depreciation because your business use of expensed business equipment or listed property (e.g., cars, computers, cellular phones and other property generally used for recreation) dropped to 50 percent or less, you would report that recaptured deprecation on Line 6 of Schedule C, after computing the amount on Form 4797. See the discussion of recaptured depreciation on page 119.

Royalties

Royalty income you receive on property you produce as part of your business (for instance, if you're a freelance writer and you receive royalties on a book you wrote) would be considered business income to be reported on Schedule C. But if you receive royalty payments on property you purchased or inherited, the payments should instead be reported on Schedule E, *Supplemental Income and Loss.*

Recovery of Items Previously Deducted

If in 2006 you recovered some item that you deducted in a prior year (such as a state tax refund or, for accrual method taxpayers, a recovery on a previously deducted bad debt), you should recognize the amount as income in 2006. You don't need to go back and amend the previous year's tax return.

However, if the original deduction did not reduce the amount of income tax you owed for that previous year (for instance, if your net income was too low to expose you to taxes), you don't have to include the amount. If this exception applies to you, you should attach a statement to your tax return explaining how you came to your conclusions. This is especially important in the case of tax refunds, since they are reported to the IRS by the taxing body.

Cancelled Debts

The general rule is that if a debt you owe is cancelled or forgiven, you must include the cancelled amount in your gross income. If the debt is connected to your business, it should be reported on Schedule C. The theory behind this is that in most cases you've already received some benefit in exchange for taking on the debt, so in effect, cancelling the debt is equivalent to the lender transferring some type of property to you free of charge.

However, there are a number of exceptions to this rule. One important question to ask is, if you had paid the cancelled amount, would the payment (not just the interest) have been deductible? If so, then the cancelled debt should not be reported as income.

Example

You are a cash-basis business owner and obtained some professional services on credit. Later on, when you were having some cash-flow problems, a portion of the debt was cancelled. You had not already deducted the price of the services, but would have been able to deduct the full price if you had paid it. In this case, you don't have to report the debt cancellation as income.

If you were using the accrual method, you would have recognized and deducted the full professional service expense at the time the services were rendered, so the debt cancellation would have to be treated as income.

Similarly, if you purchase some property for use in your business, and the seller reduces the price after the sale but before you pay for it, cash-method taxpayers don't need to report the reduction as income. Instead, it's simply a price adjustment similar to a discount, and you would record the new lower price as the cost of the property.

Another exception applies to debts that are cancelled in a bankruptcy or because you are insolvent. Generally, such debt forgiveness is not recognized as income to you, perhaps out of recognition that if you can't pay your debts, the government is unlikely to be able to collect any additional taxes from you!

There is also a special exception for forgiveness of qualified real estate business debts, but this gets into rather complicated territory. Consult your tax advisor if, for example, your lender allowed you to refinance some real estate for a lower principal amount, and you think you might qualify for relief under this provision.

Some Non-Income Items

Believe it or not, there are a number of items that the IRS does not require you to report as income or pay tax on:

- contributions to capital; for example, if you deposit personal funds in your business checking account to cover a temporary cash-flow problem
- proceeds from loans
- gifts
- cash discounts for prompt payment of bills (just report the net price after the discount as the amount of the expense; as an alternative, you can credit the amounts to a separate discount account, and include the credit balance in your business income at the end of the year)
- trade discounts you receive from suppliers
- consignments, which are not recognized as sales until the merchandise is actually sold by the person to whom you consigned the goods
- insurance reimbursements, up to the amount of your loss (but if you receive continuation-of-income benefits under a business insurance policy, these amounts must be treated as business income)
- improvements made by tenants to property they rent from you
- like-kind exchanges (see the discussion at page 103)

Damages

If you receive compensation because of a breach of contract or fiduciary duty, patent infringement, or antitrust injury, the amounts must be included in your gross business income. This rule applies to punitive damages as well. You may be entitled to a deduction against this income for legal fees and other expenses you had to pay in order to recover the amounts.

COMPUTING GROSS PROFIT

As we've discussed above on page 47, the Schedule C has two places to enter your business income. Miscellaneous business income goes on Line 6, while Line 1 is the place to enter your gross receipts from sales. In most cases, the income reported on Line 1 represents the bulk of your business income. But this is just a starting point. You must make a number of adjustments before arriving at your gross business income.

If, during the year, you booked some income but then accepted some returned merchandise or made an allowance to a customer for unsatisfactory products or services, you must enter the total of these amounts as "Returns and allowances" on Line 2, and subtract them from your gross sales receipts to arrive at your net receipts on Line 3. "Returns and allowances" can include things like rebates, cash refunds, or merchandise credits. Almost any kind of business can have returns and allowances, including professional service businesses.

If you have no inventory, you can stop here: Your net receipts will be the same as your gross profits, and you can proceed to determine your deductible business expenses (see Chapter 6).

If your business uses inventory, however, you'll need to go through a few more steps to complete the business income portion of your tax return. You need to compute your cost of goods sold, which means determining your change in inventory for the year.

Computing Your Cost of Goods Sold

It's a given that all manufacturers, retailers, and wholesalers must use inventories to accurately track their costs. Other types of businesses, such as those providing professional services or working in the trades, will need to use inventory accounting methods if they bill customers separately for materials and supplies. And under IRS rules most businesses that use inventory must use accrual accounting, at least for purchases and sales of inventory items.

Work Smart

Qualifying small business taxpayers whose average annual gross receipts for the prior three tax years are $1 million or less, or in certain cases over $1 million up to $10 million, may qualify for a less burdensome accounting method for their inventory costs. Under this method, inventory costs of raw materials purchased for use in producing finished goods and merchandise purchased for resale are deductible in the year the items are sold. To see if you qualify. consult page C-6, Part III of the instructions for Schedule C.

In general terms, the formula used to compute your cost of goods sold is the following:

	Inventory at beginning of year
+	**Purchases or additions during the year**
=	**Goods available for sale**
–	**Inventory at end of year**
=	**Cost of goods sold**

This equation is the basis for Part III on the flipside of the Schedule C. Inventory at the beginning of the year is reported on Line 35, purchases are reported on Line 36 (with a reminder to subtract the cost of items you withdrew for your own personal use), goods available for sale appears on Line 40, inventory at the end of the year is reported on Line 41, and the result is your cost of goods sold on Line 42.

If you are a reseller of goods, these would be the only five items you need. But if you are a manufacturer, things get a little more complicated.

As your additions and purchases during the year, a manufacturer would report the cost of raw materials or parts you purchased for manufacture into a finished product. You would also report the cost of labor on Line 37, including both direct labor costs for production workers, and indirect costs for other employees who perform a general factory function that is necessary for the manufacturing process. On Line 38 you would report the cost of materials and supplies used in the manufacturing process such as hardware, lubricants, abrasives, etc. And on Line 39 you would report the cost of overhead, which includes rent, utilities, insurance, depreciation, taxes, and maintenance for the production facility, as well as the cost of supervisory personnel.

In their accounting records, small manufacturers traditionally use three categories of inventory: raw materials, work in process, and finished goods awaiting sale. As raw materials are purchased, their costs (including delivery charges) are debited to the raw materials account. As materials are taken from storage and used in the manufacturing process, their costs are removed from (credited to) raw materials and added (debited) to the work in process account. The work in process account also collects the costs of direct and indirect labor and factory overhead. When the goods are finished, their costs are transferred (credited) out of work in process and added (debited) to the finished goods inventory. By taking beginning and ending counts of items in each of these three types of inventories, manufacturers can keep a handle on their costs.

Inventory Valuation Methods

Whether you are a retailer or a manufacturer, how do you determine the numbers to plug into the inventory equation?

As a starting point, you need to determine the number of items in your inventory (or each category you use) at the beginning and end of each year. You don't need to physically count your inventory at the end of the year, although that would be the most accurate way to do it. The IRS recognizes that requiring every business to do a complete inventory count on December 31 would be unworkable and would result in poor information, since workers would be rushed and not likely to make an accurate count.

As long as you take regular physical inventory counts at intervals during the year, you may extrapolate your beginning/ending amounts. The inventory at the end of year 1 becomes the beginning inventory for year 2; if there is a discrepancy, you should attach an explanation to your tax return.

But once you know the *number* of each kind of item in your inventory, how do you determine the *value* of the inventory at the beginning and at the end of the year, which will determine the value of inventory items sold during the year? There are two issues that need to be addressed before you can answer that question:

- Is the original cost, or the current market value, a better way to evaluate your inventory?
- How do you identify the particular inventory items that were sold?

Although there are many possible ways of valuing inventories, the IRS strongly prefers that small business retailers, wholesalers and manufacturers value inventories under either of these methods: (1) cost, or (2) cost or market, whichever is lower.

If you are using the cost method, the value of the inventory would be all the direct and indirect costs of acquiring it. For example, the cost of goods you purchased would be the invoice price, less appropriate discounts, plus transportation or other charges you incur in acquiring the goods. For goods that you produced, the cost would be the cost of labor, materials, and plant overhead used in production. Manufacturers must generally use the uniform capitalization ("unicap") rules to determine exactly which costs are to be included in the formula; if you are subject to these rules, you'll probably need an accountant's help to interpret and apply them. Resellers with average annual gross receipts of $10 million or less for the last three tax years are exempt from the unicap rules.

The second method—the lower of cost or market method—in effect permits you to reduce your gross income to reflect any reduction in the value of inventories. This method is based on the assumption that if the market price falls, the selling price falls correspondingly. If this is so, a business owner will report a lower income, and thus defer until the following year a part of the taxes that would otherwise have to be paid under the cost method. One big drawback to using this method is that you need to compute the value of your inventory both ways in order to determine which is lower.

Case Study — Inventory Valuation

In Year 1, John Newsome purchased merchandise for $50,000 and sold half of the goods for $60,000. On December 31, Year 1, his inventory was $25,000 (under the cost method) and $15,000 (under the lower of cost or market method). In Year 2, he sells the remaining goods for $50,000. If he had used the lower of cost or market method, his income would have been $10,000 less in Year 1 and $10,000 more in Year 2 than if he had used the cost method.

	Cost	Cost or Market
Year 1		
Sales	$60,000	$60,000
Cost of sales (purchases, less ending inventory)	- 25,000	- 35,000
Gross income	$35,000	$25,000
Year 2		
Sales	$50,000	$50,000
Cost of sales (beginning inventory)	- 25,000	- 15,000
Gross income	$25,000	$35,000

In this example, the selling price of the goods in Year 2 is $10,000 less than in Year 1, the same amount by which the market value of the goods sold in Year 1 fell below cost on December 31, Year 1. But suppose that the selling prices do not drop in relation to the market values. Then, the lower of cost or market method may produce a higher total tax over a two-year period than would the cost method because of an imbalance of income and the graduated tax rates. This could happen, for example, if a tax rate increase takes effect in Year 2.

If you are just starting your business and do not use the "Last In, First Out" (LIFO) cost method (see "Identification of Inventory Items," below), you may select either the cost or the lower of cost or market method of accounting.

Save Time

The IRS is less concerned about the nuances of the specific inventory procedures you use, than with your being consistent from year to year so that your inventory method accurately reflects your income.

You must use the same method to value your entire inventory, and you may not change to another method without the IRS's consent.

Identification of Inventory Items

Besides deciding how you will value your inventory — at cost, or at the lower of cost or market — you must also decide how you will identify which items were sold, and which are still in inventory. The most basic way of doing this is called the "specific identification method," which requires you to match each item sold with its cost (or market value).

The specific identification method is easy to understand, but may be totally impractical for your business. It may work well for companies that sell relatively few big-ticket items like cars or pianos. But if your business has a large, quick-moving inventory of smaller items, you soon would be doing little else than tracking inventory if you had to do it piece by piece.

Example

The "We're Widgets World Wide" ("4W") company, buys and sells thousands of widgets each year. Because 4W depends on several suppliers for widgets, and frequently must outbid other wholesalers for them, the price that 4W must pay usually varies daily. Listed below are just four of the thousands of widgets that came into 4W's inventory in 2006:

- *Widget 2301, bought 1/1/06, $49.00; sold 12/1/06*
- *Widget 3904, bought 6/1/06, $49.50; sold 9/1/06*
- *Widget 5039, bought 6/30/06, $50.45; sold 7/14/06*
- *Widget 7932, bought 7/1/06, $50.20; sold 12/15/06*

Although modern computer-based inventory control systems could allow you to track each widget, the IRS doesn't require this. Instead, you can usually choose one of two identification methods. These systems make broad *assumptions* about which inventory items were sold and which remain in inventory, without reference to the particular inventory items that were actually bought and sold. These two methods are known as the "first-in, first-out" (FIFO) and the "last-in, first out" (LIFO) methods.

The FIFO method assumes that sales are made from the items that have been longest in the inventory. This conforms to the usual business practice of trying to sell the older items first, before they become obsolete, spoiled, or out-of-fashion. This is also the method the IRS prefers.

In contrast, the LIFO method assumes that the most recently purchased items are the ones you sold, and the oldest items are still sitting in your warehouse or on your shelf.

One consequence of using FIFO is that if prices are generally going up over time, your gross income will be matched against the lowest-priced items in your inventory, resulting in higher net profits. In contrast, LIFO would match your gross income against the most expensive items in your inventory, resulting in lower net profits and, consequently, a lower tax bill. If your business and inventory are constantly growing over time, LIFO will generally be more preferable.

Example

Using the four widgets described in the example above, let's say you know that you sold two of these widgets this year, for a price of $60 each. Under FIFO, you'd be treated as having sold the first two widgets you purchased, so your net income would be $120.00 – ($49.00 + $49.50) = $21.50.

Under LIFO, you'd be treated as having sold the last two widgets you purchased, so your net income would be $120.00 – ($50.45 + $50.20) = $19.35.

The IRS does not favor LIFO, and if you want to use it, you must file IRS Form 970 and follow some very complex tax rules. There is also a "simplified" dollar-value LIFO method available to small businesses (those with average annual gross receipts of $5 million or less for the last three tax years). For more information, see your tax advisor.

Chapter 6

Deductible Business Expenses

Once you know what your gross profit is for the year, it's time to figure out how you can whittle that figure down by subtracting all your deductible business expenses. Digging up every legitimate deduction you have is usually your best bet for reducing your taxable income, and therefore your tax bill, as much as possible in the short run.

In the long run, there may be other ways to save even more tax dollars — such as by shifting income to other tax years and by taking advantage of tax credits — that can take a certain amount of advance planning. But for many small businesses the deduction rules are often the best place to look for tax savings.

Save Money

Getting a tax deduction may be nice, but before you pull out your wallet, make sure that the deductible expense is justified from a business operations perspective. Particularly if you are in the startup phase of your business, the money you have to spend is limited. You don't want to fall into the trap of justifying the purchase of a gold-plated white elephant by saying: "So what if I really don't need it, it's deductible!"

In this chapter we'll explain the basic rules about deductions, so that you'll be able claim all the deductions you've got coming this year and so that, in the future, you can become an expert at spotting deduction opportunities in time to take advantage of them.

To begin with, we'll go through some of the general rules that apply to all business deductions. After that we'll deal with more specific (and fruitful) areas like car expenses, travel and entertainment, and the home office deduction.

Tax Organizer Tip

Most business expenses that will be reported on your Schedule C should be entered in the "Business" pages, which are located within the "Employment" tab of CompleteTax.

One notable exception is contributions to retirement plans on your own behalf, which are entered on the "Retirement" tab.

Ordinary and Necessary Business Expenses

The first, most basic guideline to remember is that a deduction for an expense paid in connection with your business will be allowed only if the expense is "ordinary and necessary" for the operation of the business.

This doesn't mean that the IRS will attack all sorts of legitimately claimed business deductions, either on the ground that an expense would occur only occasionally (is it ordinary?), or that the expense would be helpful, but not vital to the business (is it necessary?).

In practice the IRS is rather flexible in this regard. It defines "ordinary" as common and accepted in a field of business, and defines "necessary" as helpful and appropriate to your business. "Ordinary" usually refers to expenses that are frequent and ongoing, such as amounts spent on gasoline or business meals, but can also apply to something that you pay only once, such an installation fee for utility service. And an expense does not have to be indispensable to be a necessary expense.

Example

The cost of holiday gifts and cards sent to customers is deductible as a necessary business expense if the items promote healthy customer relations.

However, the cost of a gun purchased for personal protection by an insurance agent, who is sometimes required to make business calls to private homes late in the evening, would not be deductible. While the expense of the handgun might be "ordinary," it is not "necessary" because it is not helpful or appropriate to the business of an insurance agent. It would be considered a nondeductible personal expense.

In addition to being "ordinary and necessary," it has been held that a business expense must also be "reasonable." Whether an expense is reasonable depends upon the facts and circumstances in the particular situation. In one case, for example, a chauffeured luxury car provided to an employee was not unreasonable given the nature of the employment and the congested area in which the car was driven. Entertainment and meal expenses are not deductible to the extent that they are lavish or extravagant, given the circumstances.

In applying the "ordinary and necessary" and "reasonable" deduction test, the IRS isn't looking to second-guess your business decisions. You can expect that almost any expense that's fairly common for your type of business will pass muster without serious question.

Rather, IRS agents use this test to make sure that the money was actually spent as you claim, and: (1) pertains to the business instead of personal or family needs, (2) is not also being deducted elsewhere on the return (such as in the cost of goods sold computation – see page 51), and (3) is a current, rather than a capital, expense.

Warning

There are a few types of expenses that might be seen as promoting the business, but are specifically made nondeductible. These include items such as lobbying expenses and political contributions, fines and penalties such as parking tickets, and illegal payments such as kickbacks.

For instance, a traveling salesman who receives a speeding ticket must pay it, or risk losing his driver's license and his ability to earn a living. It's arguable that the cost of the ticket is an ordinary and necessary business expense. Nevertheless, the law states that legal fines and penalties are never deductible, so the ticket must be paid out of the salesman's own pocket.

To be deductible, business expenses must be incurred in carrying on an *already existing* trade or business. Costs associated with starting up a business are considered a type of capital expenditure, and are not fully deductible as current expenses (see page 61).

Business vs. Personal Expenses

As a general principal, amounts that you spend for personal or family reasons are not deductible. In many instances this distinction may be difficult to make, especially if yours is a family business or you work out of your home. However, the IRS has been known to come down hard on those who don't keep their personal and business expenses separate, and who attempt to deduct personal living expenses against business income.

Example

A builder was not allowed a business deduction for expenses incurred as a result of his polo playing because he could not show a relationship between those expenses and a true business purpose.

The tax laws contain numerous very specific rules in areas where business expenses are difficult to disentangle from personal expenses. For example, commuting expenses are nondeductible, there are very specific rules on deducting business meals and entertainment, and certain types of property that are commonly used for recreation or amusement are subject to special depreciation rules and more stringent reporting. These rules are discussed in detail in later parts of this chapter.

If an expense is used partly for business and partly for personal purposes, you need to allocate the expense and deduct only the portion that pertains to business usage. The method of allocation depends on the nature of the expense. It can be done on the basis of time, space, usage or some other reasonable method.

Example

If you have an employee who cleans your office and also cleans your house, you can deduct the portion of the employee's wages and payroll taxes that compensate for the hours spent cleaning the office, but not the home. If you drive your car for both business and personal purposes, you must allocate your car expenses on the basis of the mileage driven for business purposes, as opposed to that for personal or commuting purposes.

As a rough rule of thumb, if you're in doubt about whether a particular expense qualifies as a business expense rather than a personal one, ask yourself whether you would still have to pay the expense if you had the same income but didn't work (perhaps all those direct-mail sweepstakes entries finally paid off). If so, there's a good chance that what you have is a personal expense, not a business expense.

To help you decide whether a particular expense is likely to be deductible, we've provided a list of the most common business deductions.

Following that is a list showing common items that usually *won't* be allowed as business deductions. In most cases, a deduction will be denied for these things either because they are nondeductible personal expenses, or because Congress specifically made them nondeductible. Where noted, some of these items may qualify for other tax benefits such as tax credits or recovery through depreciation.

Warning

Just because a particular item does not appear in the second list doesn't mean that it necessarily will be deductible. Any expense may be nondeductible if it does not meet the deduction rules outlined in this chapter. Whether a particular expense meets the deductibility requirements will depend on the facts and circumstances of your particular business.

Some Common Business Deductions

- advertising
- bad debts, for accrual method taxpayers
- bank fees on business accounts
- car and truck expenses
- commissions and fees
- depreciation
- dues for trade and business associations
- employee benefit programs
- meals and entertainment
- office expenses
- pension and profit-sharing plans
- publications
- rent or lease expense
- repairs and maintenance
- supplies and materials
- taxes and licenses

- gifts to customers, suppliers
- insurance (casualty and liability)
- legal and professional services
- travel expenses
- utilities
- wages for employees

Common Nondeductible Expenses

- bar or professional examination fees
- capital expenditures (not fully deductible in the year placed in service, but yearly deductions are allowed to recover cost of item over a specified time period)
- charitable contributions or gifts by a business that's not a C corporation (sole proprietors may deduct contributions on their individual tax returns, rather than on Schedule C).
- clothing, unless it's protective equipment or a uniform that would not be worn during non-working hours
- country or social club dues
- commuting expenses
- estate tax even if largely due to the ownership of a business interest
- expenses, including interest, paid to generate tax-exempt income
- federal income tax
- fines and penalties incurred for violations of law, such as child labor violations, federal income tax penalties, and traffic tickets
- gift tax; inheritance tax
- gifts to employees that are valued at more than $25
- gifts to individuals
- hobby losses
- interest on indebtedness incurred by a business taxpayer to purchase life insurance coverage in excess of $50,000 on the life of any its officers, employees, or other persons having a financial interest in the taxpayer's trade or business
- interest on indebtedness incurred to purchase single premium life insurance contracts, or any life insurance contract under a plan of financing the purchase by withdrawing some or all of the yearly build up in policy cash values
- job hunting expenses (new trade or business)
- life insurance premiums, if the business, or the business owner, is a direct or indirect beneficiary
- lobbying expenses (appearances before legislative bodies and expenses to influence voters)
- partnership organizational expenses, unless amortization election is made
- personal, living or family expenses — however, certain interest, taxes, bad debts, medical expenses, theft or casualty losses, or charitable contributions may be deductible in whole or in part as an itemized deduction on your individual tax return.
- political contributions, including tickets to political dinners
- tax penalty payments
- transfer taxes on business property

NONDEDUCTIBLE CAPITAL EXPENDITURES

One of the principles underlying the rules for tax deductions is that your income for the year should be offset only by those expenses that contributed to earning that income.

Example

If you add floor space to your facility or purchase a new delivery vehicle, you've acquired an asset that will benefit your business for a number of years. If you were allowed to deduct the full cost of such an asset in the year you acquired it, you'd effectively be understating your income during that first year and overstating your income during all the subsequent years that you use the asset in your business.

It may seem as though this shouldn't really be a problem, because everything would come out even in the end. However, what would have happened from the government's perspective is that you would have reduced your taxable income inappropriately in the year of acquisition and deferred the payment of some income taxes, which is not something the IRS usually likes to allow.

So, instead of letting you currently deduct your outlay for items of a more permanent nature (that is, items that will benefit your business beyond the current year), the tax rules provide that such expenditures generally must be capitalized.

What does it mean to "capitalize" an expense? Well, apart from the fact that it means the expense is not fully deductible this year, the act of capitalizing an expense is just an exercise in bookkeeping. The asset becomes a capital asset, against which you can take depreciation deductions each year. Depreciation is discussed at length in Chapter 7.

For now, let's just say that for tax purposes, you'll eventually recover the benefits of a capital expense through (1) annual depreciation deductions for the property and/or (2) a reduced amount of taxable gain or an increased amount of taxable loss when you sell or otherwise dispose of the property.

Although these two results are positive, they are usually not as good as a current deduction for the entire amount of the expense. Unfortunately, you normally won't have a choice as to how to treat a given expense. With certain exceptions, the tax rules specify whether an expense must be capitalized or deducted.

What, Exactly, Is a Capital Expenditure?

One type of capital expenditure occurs when you purchase or otherwise acquire any asset that will benefit your business for more than one year. Expenses that add to the value or useful life of an item of property also are considered capital expenditures.

In contrast, an expense that keeps an asset in an ordinarily efficient operating condition and that does not add to its value or substantially prolong its useful life is generally considered a deductible repair or maintenance expense.

Deciding whether a particular item should be classified as a capital expenditure or as a currently deductible expense is not always easy, particularly if it's debatable whether the expense represents a repair, or an improvement to a capital asset.

However, over time, the IRS and the courts have classified, on a case-by-case basis, some categories of items commonly considered to be capital expenditures. On the next page, we provide a listing of these items as a guide.

Warning

Remember that the same item that was a deductible expense to one taxpayer might be a capital expenditure to another.

That's mainly because the deduct-or-capitalize question does not just involve what was purchased, but also whether its benefits will be expected to last for more than one year. If two taxpayers use an identical item in different ways in their businesses, the item may represent a capital expenditure to one, but a currently deductible expense to the other.

Some Special Rules

In some cases, the tax laws depart from the general deduct-or-capitalize analysis by providing specific rules that govern how you may or must treat certain expenditures. For small business owners, the most commonly applied of these rules are:

- an equipment expensing election that allows you to deduct rather than to capitalize a specified amount of your costs in acquiring new business property (see page 103)
- elections to amortize business startup costs over a 60-month period, including costs associated with organizing a corporation or a partnership (see page 61)
- an election to capitalize rather than deduct taxes and other carrying charges (such as interest) on the property

Common Capital Expenditures

- abstracts of title costs
- appraisal costs paid in obtaining possession of premises
- author's publishing costs
- asbestos removal costs
- basement repair and waterproofing
- boiler patching and welding costs
- burglar alarm installation charges
- business facility improvement costs (for example, waterproofing; replacing a roof; planning, designing, and constructing an addition; remodeling costs)
- cable replacement costs upon sudden failure
- copyright development costs
- credit card membership fees
- drainage costs
- electric wiring costs (new wiring, replacement, and rearrangement)
- electrical system replacement costs
- Federal Communications Commission (FCC) license preparation fees
- fire escapes
- flood protection costs (such as costs of raising floors, or rearranging bins)
- insulation costs
- irrigation system costs
- merger negotiation costs
- office, cost of changing location and equipment
- package design costs
- performance bond premiums
- Security Exchange and Commission (SEC) statement preparation cost
- settlement costs for threatened lawsuit
- well (water) costs
- zoning change costs that increase the value of property beyond the tax year

BUSINESS STARTUP COSTS

Investigating the potential for a new business and getting it started can be an expensive proposition. However, under the general rules for business deductions, you couldn't deduct these expenses because only expenses for an *existing* trade or business can be deducted. By definition, you incur your startup expenses prior to the time that your business is born.

Fortunately, there is a way around this dilemma: If your startup expenditures actually result in an up-and-running business, you can elect to amortize the costs (that is, deduct them in equal installments over a set period of time) over a period of at least 60 months, beginning with the month in which your business opens.

This election enables you to eventually deduct both the cost of investigating the creation of the business and the costs of actually creating it. However, only those costs that would be deductible if they were incurred by an existing trade or business are eligible for the election.

What Costs Qualify?

Investigation expenses that can be deducted over the 60-month period include those relating to business conditions generally, and those relating to a specific business, such as market or product research to determine the feasibility of starting a certain type of business. The costs of checking out the various factors involved in site selection would also be an amortizable investigation expense.

Amortizable costs of creating a business include advertising, wages and salaries, professional and consultant fees, and costs of travel that is necessary before the business actually begins.

What Costs Don't Qualify?

Although they are frequently incurred before a new business goes into operation, the following costs don't qualify for 60-month amortization:

- Startup expenditures for interest, taxes, and research and experimental costs that are otherwise allowed as deductions do not qualify for amortization. These costs may be deducted when incurred.
- The costs of organizing a partnership or a corporation are not considered startup costs, but they may be eligible for separate amortization.
- The costs attributable to the acquisition of a specific property that is subject to depreciation or cost recovery do not qualify for amortization. Instead, the property should be depreciated under the appropriate rules.

Save Money

It's usually best to claim the 60-month amortization deduction as early as possible if there is any doubt about when the business began operating. If the IRS determines that your business began in a year before the election to amortize startup costs was made, the right to deduct these costs is lost.

What if You Change Your Mind?

If you ultimately decide *not* to go into business, what happens to your costs? The portion of costs you paid to generally investigate the possibilities of going into business at all, or to purchase a non-specific existing business, are considered personal costs and are not deductible. However, the total costs that you paid in your attempt to start or purchase a specific business would be considered a capital expense and you can claim it as a capital loss.

If you purchased any business assets along the way (for instance, some bagel-making machinery), you can claim a loss only if and when you sell or dispose of the property.

Claiming Amortization Expenses

Assuming your business was successfully launched and you want to amortize your startup costs, total up all the costs paid or incurred before your business opened and divide them by 60 months (or longer, if you desire). The result is the monthly deduction amount. Your amortization period will begin with the month in which your business opened.

Example

If you opened on October 31, 2006, you could deduct costs for October, November and December of 2006, which would be equal to 3/60ths of your total startup costs.

For the first year, your amortization deduction would be shown on Part VI of Form 4562, *Depreciation and Amortization,* and then carried over to your Schedule C as an "other" expense.

You'll need to attach a statement to your tax return itemizing the amortization costs, giving the date each cost was incurred, stating the month your business began operations, and specifying the number of months in your amortization period (not less than 60). The fact that you need to attach this statement precludes you from electronically filing your tax return this year.

In later years, if you are filing Form 4562 for some other reason (generally you must file this form in the first year you put a capital asset into service), you would continue to show your amortization costs on Part VI; if you don't need to file the 4562 in a particular year, simply list your amortization amount as an "other" expense on your Schedule C.

Tax Organizer Tip

When using CompleteTax, you can treat your total amount of amortizable startup expenditures as a business asset. On the "Business Income Information" page, answer "Yes" to the question "Do you have any depreciable assets related to this business?" and click on the "Continue" button to arrive at the "Business Property Depreciation Information" page. Choose "Other" as the type of asset, select "Amortization" from the drop-down list as your "Method of Depreciation," and enter the number of months over which to amortize the expense (generally 60). Your start up costs will be automatically amortized by the program.

SPECIAL DEDUCTION RULES

Having given you a broad overview of the rules for claiming business tax deductions, we're ready to get into the specific rules that apply to the most commonly encountered business deductions:

- expenses for cars, trucks, and other vehicles used in your business
- travel expenses for business trips
- meal and entertainment expenses when you entertain business guests
- business gifts you give to your clients and customers
- the home office deduction, for those with a home-based business
- wages and fringe benefits you provide to your employees
- health insurance for yourself
- retirement plan expenses

Most of these expenses are claimed on Part II of your Schedule C, which asks you to itemize your expenses in 20 categories (some with subcategories). For expenses that don't fit into any of the Part II categories, there is space on the back of the form (Part V) for you to describe and itemize any additional expenses.

Work Smart

If your gut feeling tells you that your dollar amount for any of the IRS expense categories is very large for a business of your type – perhaps large enough to raise an IRS agent's eyebrows – we recommend that you itemize the amounts on the back of the Schedule C. For example, if your travel expenses were unusually large this year, on Line 24a you might write "see itemization in Part V." Then, in Part V, you might break out the expenses into several categories such as "travel – sales calls; travel – conventions; travel – continuing education." This can sometimes save you from receiving an inquisitive letter from the IRS.

For a few categories of expenses, the IRS asks you to first fill out a specific form dealing with the expense, and then to transfer the net amount to your Schedule C. This is true of the home office deduction, and often true of your car expenses and depreciation expenses. There are also a few expenses that may be deducted directly on the front of your Form 1040, such as Keogh or SEP contributions for yourself, and one-half of the self-employment tax.

Also remember that if your business is a type that uses inventory, certain types of costs must be attributed to the inventory and are considered part of your cost of goods sold. As such, these costs will, in effect, be deducted when you sell the inventory to which they are attributed. There is an exception for authors, artists, and photographers who sell works created by their own efforts; these individuals can deduct their expenses without having to use inventory accounting. See page 51 for more information on costs of goods sold.

TAXES AND VEHICLES

Whether it's down payments, interest payments, gas, tires, or repairs, operating a car or truck can be expensive. If you're using a vehicle in business, it's important to get any tax breaks that you can for money spent on the vehicle. On the next few pages, we'll examine some of the common tax issues that relate to vehicles.

Obtaining a Business Vehicle

For every business owner, there comes a time when the old set of wheels will no longer suffice. Or, perhaps this was the year you needed a special purpose vehicle such as a delivery truck or van.

At some point, nearly every business owner will have to consider purchasing, leasing, or otherwise obtaining a vehicle. If you've purchased a car this year or are thinking about getting one in the near future, becoming familiar with the following tax issues may help you save money:

- There are several types of excise taxes that may be imposed on the vehicle that you purchase.
- Clean-fuel vehicles such as gas or electric-powered cars are eligible for special tax breaks.
- The expensing election may allow you to deduct up to $10,610 of the cost of a vehicle placed in service in 2004. For more on this, see page 113.

Save Money

Once you've made the decision that you need a vehicle for your business, our first recommendation is that you try to conserve your capital by converting a vehicle you already own to partial or full-time use in your business.

Cars and trucks generally depreciate in value very quickly and are poor investments in and of themselves. If you are the owner of a new business, whatever capital you have should be put into the things that will most directly generate revenue — and that usually won't include a new car.

Excise Taxes on New Cars

You need to be aware that purchasing certain vehicles may subject you to various excise taxes. The excise taxes may be related to the whole vehicle or only to certain vehicle components (e.g., tires).

These taxes may be hidden costs that could influence your decision in terms of choosing a vehicle. As such, it is well worth your time to discover if there are any applicable excise taxes before you commit to making a purchase.

Gas guzzler tax. This tax is imposed on new cars that fail to meet federal fuel economy standards. Although the tax is imposed on the manufacturer, it becomes part of the retail price. Before computing the depreciation deduction for a business car, you must reduce the basis of the car by the amount of any gas guzzler tax you paid. So, you can't recover this tax through depreciation. For more on how depreciation works, see page 99.

Tax Breaks for New Clean-Fuel Vehicles

There are two notable types of tax breaks available to purchasers of alternative-fuel vehicles.

Alternative motor vehicle credit. Starting in 2006, the Energy Tax Incentives Act of 2005 creates a series of new tax credits to encourage the development, manufacture and use of alternative fuel motor vehicles. The credits are collectively claimed under the title of the "Alternative Motor Vehicle Credit." This credit is equal to the sum of four separate credit components:

- the qualified fuel cell motor vehicle credit (available through December 31, 2014)
- the advanced lean burn technology motor vehicle credit (available December 31, 2010)
- the qualified hybrid motor vehicle credit

(available through December 31, 2010, for passenger automobiles or light trucks with a gross vehicle weight rating (GVWR) of no more than 8,500 pounds and through December 31, 2009, for qualified hybrid motor vehicles that are not passenger automobiles or light trucks and have a GVWR of more than 8,500 pounds)

- the qualified alternative fuel motor vehicle credit (available through December 31, 2010)

The amount of the credit may be as much as $3,400 for those who purchase the most fuel-efficient passenger automobiles and light trucks. Calculating the credit, however, can be extremely challenging because of the complexity involved.

Form 8910, *Alternative Motor Vehicle Credit*, is used to compute all components of the alternative motor vehicle credit, including the hybrid credit. If the vehicle is used for business purposes, the credit amount is also reported on Form 3800, *General Business Credit.* The credit amount for vehicles used for personal purposes is reported on line 55 of Form 1040.

Tax credit for electric vehicles. A 10 percent tax credit (based on your purchase price) is allowed for certain electric vehicles placed in service before January 1, 2007. The maximum credit may not exceed $3,000 in 2006. Unfortunately, the credit will be phased out entirely in 2007. The allowable credit is claimed on IRS Form 8834, *Qualified Electric Vehicle Credit.*

Using a Vehicle in Your Business

If you use your car, van, or some other type of vehicle exclusively for business purposes, you may generally deduct the full cost of operating the vehicle. But if, like most sole proprietors, you use a vehicle for business on a part-time basis, you will have to allocate your expenses based on your business and personal use.

The business portion of your costs will be deductible on Line 9 of Schedule C; the personal portion will be nondeductible except for any costs of using the vehicle for charitable purposes (see page 267), for medical purposes (see page 264), or for a tax-deductible move (see page 187). Also, if you or your spouse is employed by another business, a portion of the expenses for the car may be deductible as an employee business expense (see page 183).

But what, exactly, is "business use of a car?" Generally, the IRS divides all car usage into three categories: business, commuting, and personal. "Business use" generally means travel between two business destinations, one of which may be your regular place of business. Typical travel expenses that are deductible include expenses for:

- travel from one job to another
- travel from one customer or client to another
- travel from your office or business location in order to perform business tasks, such as to pick up supplies and inventory, to check your business post office box, or to make a bank deposit

In addition, if you have a regular place of business, the cost of traveling between your home and a temporary work site that is *not* the regular place of business is deductible, regardless of the distance traveled. A temporary work site is a place where you perform services on an irregular or short-term basis. The term "short-term" generally means a matter of days or weeks. Also, if you do *not* have a regular place of business and you travel outside of the metropolitan area in which you work to a temporary work site, you are allowed a deduction for your travel costs. Travel within the metropolitan area would be considered nondeductible commuting.

Commuting expenses. Vehicle expenses incurred in commuting between your home and your main or regular place of business are not deductible expenses. This is true even if you have an advertising display on your car, or you use the commute to listen to business books on tape or to phone your clients.

Save Money

Remember that costs of traveling between your home and a location that is not *your regular place of business are deductible. You can take advantage of this rule by making a business related-stop on the way to work and on the way home, thereby converting your nondeductible commute into deductible business travel!*

Travel from a Home Office

If you work out of your home and your home is your principal place of business (see page 79), you can generally deduct the cost of traveling from your home to any business destination.

Example

If you are a real estate agent and do most of your work at home, you can deduct the expenses that you incur in traveling between your home and the houses you're trying to sell.

Whether your home is your principal place of business is determined under the same standards that apply to home office deductions (see page 79).

Hauling Tools or Equipment

Commuting expenses may be partially deductible if you have to transport heavy or bulky tools, materials, or equipment to and from your workplace.

The catch is that you can only deduct the portion of the cost that is higher than the costs you'd normally face in commuting by that *same* mode of transportation *without* the work equipment. The fact that you would have used a less expensive mode of transportation were it not for the tools is immaterial.

Example

Robert Jensen takes the train from his home to his workplace each workday. His daily round-trip train ticket costs $10.00. Every few months he must bring drafting tools and display charts to his workplace for a presentation. When he transports these tools and materials he uses his car instead of taking the train. Driving to his workplace costs him $20.00 in gas, tolls, and parking fees. However, Jensen cannot deduct the extra $10.00 it costs him when he drives to his workplace, since he would have spent that amount driving regardless of what he was carrying with him.

If, however, Jensen's tools and materials were so bulky that he had to rent a trailer to carry them, he could deduct his costs for renting and parking the trailer.

Keeping Records of Business Use

If, like most business owners, you use your vehicle for both business and personal purposes, you must allocate your vehicle costs for business use separately from those associated with commuting or personal use. Even if you use a particular car or truck *only* for business purposes, you'll need to keep records to prove it unless the vehicle, by its nature, is not likely to be used more than a very minimal amount for personal purposes. Such vehicles would include various heavy trucks, buses, police and fire vehicles, cranes, forklifts, tractors, and similar vehicles. See the discussion of mileage records on page 21.

If you commute to a regular place of business, you'll also need to know the distance from your home to your workplace, as well as the number of commuting trips you made during the year, because the IRS specifically asks for this information.

At the end of the year, you'll need to add up the total number of miles you drove during the year and the total number of business miles. Then, you'll divide the number of business miles by the total number of miles driven. The answer you get represents your percentage of business use for the year. Save this number – you'll need it when you compute your deductible vehicle expenses!

Example

Joyce King's initial odometer reading for the year was 23,456, and her ending reading was 33,500. So, her total mileage for the year was 10,044.

During the year, she recorded a total of 34 business trips, with a total mileage of 800 business miles.

So, her business usage of the vehicle was 800/10,044 = .0796, or about 8 percent.

How to Compute Your Vehicle Expenses

If you use your vehicle for business driving, there are two methods that can be used to compute your vehicle expense deduction:

- the standard mileage rate, discussed below
- the actual cost method, discussed on page 67

The standard mileage rate is generally easier to use and doesn't require you to keep as many records; however, it's not available to everyone. It will generally be the preferred method if you do relatively little business driving.

The actual cost method may result in a larger deduction, particularly with a relatively expensive car; however, the burden of keeping records for every penny you spend on the car may cause more trouble than the deduction is worth.

Ideally, each year you (or your accountant) should compute your deduction under both methods and compare the results. Then, use the method that gives you the largest deduction in that particular year.

Warning

Remember that whichever method you choose, you may have a taxable gain when you sell or otherwise dispose of a vehicle used in business. *See page 116 for more on taxable gains and losses.*

The Standard Mileage Rate

If you use the standard mileage rate (SMR) method, you calculate the fixed and operating costs of your vehicle by multiplying the number of business miles traveled during the year by the business standard mileage rate. This rate is set by the IRS and adjusted annually. The rate is 44.5 cents per mile in 2006 and 48.5 cents per mile in 2007.

While very simple to use, the standard mileage rate is not available to everyone. Specifically, this rate may not be used to compute the deductible expenses for:

- vehicles used for hire, such as taxis
- two or more vehicles used simultaneously, as in fleet-type operations. This does not include situations where you own more than one vehicle (say, a car and a truck) but you don't use them at the same time; in that case, you can still use the SMR.

Save Time

As of 1998, the standard mileage rate can be used for cars that you lease, not just those that you own, provided that you continue to use this method for the entire lease term (or the remainder of the term, for leases that began before 1998).

For all practical purposes, if you want to use the SMR for a car that you own, you must use it in the very first year you place it in service for your business.

If you do that, in later years you can either use the actual cost method or the SMR, depending on which method yields the bigger deduction in any given year.

However, once you use the SMR, you must use the straight-line method of depreciation if you switch to the actual cost method for that car. Ordinarily straight-line gives you a smaller deduction than the quicker MACRS depreciation (see page 100 for a comparison of depreciation methods). The SMR and MACRS are basically incompatible, and if you've ever used MACRS for a car, you can never use the SMR method for that car.

What's included in the SMR? Using the SMR takes the place of deducting almost all the operating and fixed business costs of your vehicle, such as maintenance and repairs, tires, gas, oil, insurance, and license and registration fees.

However, you can still deduct parking fees and tolls that are directly related to business (i.e., not commuting), in addition to the standard mileage rate. For business owners, interest on loans for vehicles and taxes attributable to the operation of these vehicles are also deductible on top of the SMR.

Adjustments for depreciation. When you use the standard mileage rate method, a specific amount is included for depreciation. This means that you can't claim an additional deduction for depreciation when you use the standard mileage rate method.

It also means that if you use the SMR method, when you sell your car and need to determine whether you had any taxable gains, you must adjust the basis of your vehicle for each year the method was used.

You must multiply your business mileage for the year by a specified amount, as shown on the chart that follows, and then reduce your car's basis (and increase your potential taxable gains) by that amount.

Example

If a car was used for 7,000 business miles in 2006, the basis would be reduced by $1,190 (7,000 x $0.17).

Pre-1990 use of a vehicle in excess of 15,000 miles in one year is disregarded for the purpose of basis adjustment, even if the actual business mileage was higher.

Year method used	Amount of adjustment (cents per mile)
1989-91	11
1992-93	11.5
1994-99	12
2000	14
2001-02	15
2003-04	16
2005-06	17
2007	19

The Actual Cost Method

When you use the actual cost method of determining your vehicle deduction instead of the SMR, you must keep track of the actual amount of your costs during the year, including all the costs shown on the list below, to calculate your deductible vehicle expenses. The amount of your deduction depends, to a large extent, on how good you are at saving receipts and jotting down your costs throughout the year.

At the end of the year, you'll multiply your total expenses by your percentage of business use of the car. The business use percentage is calculated in the same way as described above, in the discussion of the standard mileage rate method:

business miles/total miles = business use percentage

Actual Cost Car Expenses

The cost of operating a vehicle includes these expenses:

- cleaning, inside and out; waxing
- depreciation, if you own the vehicle
- gas and oil
- insurance
- interest on a vehicle loan
- lease payments, if you lease the vehicle
- license fees, if substantially based on the value of the vehicle
- motor club membership
- parking and garage rental
- personal property taxes
- repairs and maintenance
- tires and supplies
- tolls

The cost of the vehicle itself is not a deductible expense, nor is the cost of a replacement, modification, or extensive repair that prolongs the useful life of the vehicle or increases its value. Instead, these costs are capitalized, which means they are added to your tax basis in the vehicle. These capitalized costs are recovered through depreciation deductions that are taken for a number of years after you place the vehicle in service.

You'll also need to calculate your depreciation amount for the car, as discussed in Chapter 7, *Capital Assets and Depreciation.* This amount is deducted as part of your depreciation expense on Line 13 of your Schedule C, not as part of the car and truck expenses reported on Line 9.

Deducting Vehicle Lease Payments

If you lease a vehicle for your business, you can generally deduct each lease payment as a rental expense. However, when business use of a leased vehicle is less than 100 percent, the rental deduction is scaled down in proportion to the personal use.

Example

If you drive a leased car, and 75 percent of the mileage driven was for business while 25 percent was for personal purposes and commuting, you can deduct only 75 percent of the lease payments.

The percentage of use for business is determined using your mileage records. The amount you deduct for a leased car is reported on Line 20a as rented or leased vehicles, machinery, and equipment; it is not added to the rest of your car and truck expenses on Line 9.

If a vehicle with a fair market value in excess of approximately $15,200 (for 2006) is leased, you must add back an additional amount (i.e., subtract it from your otherwise deductible amount) to offset a portion of the lease payments. This rule was enacted to prevent individuals from using leases to avoid the luxury car depreciation limits that apply to purchased vehicles. The amounts that must be added back are called "inclusion amounts" and are taken from a price-based table issued annually by the IRS.

Tables for 2006, 2005 and 2004 are reproduced on pages 69-71; if you leased your car before 2004, get IRS Publication 463, *Travel, Entertainment, Gift, and Car Expenses,* to find the tables for earlier years. Please note that there are separate tables for leased cars and leased trucks and vans. There is also a table to use if you happen to lease an electric automobile.

To use the table, find the value of your car on the first day of your lease term (or on the day you converted your personal car to business use) in the first column, and read across the line to the column that matches the year of your lease to find the dollar value to be included. Then prorate the dollar amount from the table for the number of days of the lease term included in your tax year, and multiply the prorated amount by your percentage of business use for the year (as calculated by using your mileage records).

Example

Let's say that on April 1, 2006, you leased a car with a fair market value of $31,700 for a four-year term. Assuming you are a calendar-year taxpayer and used the car only for business, your includible amount for 2006 is $82.12 (275/365 x $109). Your includible amounts for 2007, 2008, and 2009 are $238, $353, and $422, respectively. For 2010, your includible amount is $119.59 [90/365 x $485 (the dollar amount for the preceding year for the last year of the lease)].

IRS Tables Not Available at Press Time

See **http://www.toolkit.cch.com**

or

http://www.finance.cch.com

for the latest information

Inclusion Amounts for Trucks/Vans First Leased in 2005						
Fair Market Value		Tax Year During Lease				
Over	Not Over	1st	2nd	3rd	4th	5th and Later
$16,700	$17,000	3	6	8	10	11
17,000	17,500	4	10	14	17	20
17,500	18,000	7	15	21	26	30
18,000	18,500	9	20	29	35	40
18,500	19,000	11	25	37	43	51
19,000	19,500	14	30	44	52	61
19,500	20,000	16	35	51	62	71
20,000	20,500	18	40	59	71	81
20,500	21,000	20	45	67	79	92
21,000	21,500	23	50	74	88	103
21,500	22,000	25	55	81	98	113
22,000	23,000	28	63	92	111	129
23,000	24,000	33	73	107	129	149
24,000	25,000	38	83	122	147	169
25,000	26,000	42	93	137	165	190
26,000	27,000	47	103	152	183	210
27,000	28,000	51	113	167	201	231
28,000	29,000	56	123	182	218	253
29,000	30,000	60	133	197	237	272
30,000	31,000	65	143	212	254	294
31,000	32,000	70	153	227	272	314
32,000	33,000	74	163	242	290	335
33,000	34,000	79	173	257	308	355
34,000	35,000	83	184	271	326	376
35,000	36,000	88	193	287	344	397
36,000	37,000	93	203	302	361	418
37,000	38,000	97	214	316	380	438
38,000	39,000	102	223	332	397	459
39,000	40,000	106	234	346	415	480
40,000	41,000	111	244	361	433	500
41,000	42,000	115	254	376	451	521
42,000	43,000	120	264	391	469	542
43,000	44,000	125	274	406	487	562
44,000	45,000	129	284	421	505	583
45,000	46,000	134	294	436	523	603
46,000	47,000	138	304	451	541	624
47,000	48,000	143	314	466	558	645
48,000	49,000	148	324	481	576	666
49,000	50,000	152	334	496	594	687
50,000	51,000	157	344	511	612	707
51,000	52,000	161	355	525	630	728
52,000	53,000	166	364	541	648	748
53,000	54,000	170	375	555	666	769
54,000	55,000	175	385	570	684	789
55,000	56,000	180	394	586	701	811
56,000	57,000	184	405	600	720	830
57,000	58,000	189	415	615	737	852
58,000	59,000	193	425	630	755	873
59,000	60,000	198	435	645	773	893
60,000	62,000	205	450	667	800	924
62,000	64,000	214	470	697	836	966
64,000	66,000	223	490	727	872	1,007
66,000	68,000	232	510	757	908	1,048
68,000	70,000	241	531	786	944	1,089
70,000	72,000	251	550	817	979	1,131
72,000	74,000	260	571	846	1,015	1,172
74,000	76,000	269	591	876	1,051	1,213
76,000	78,000	278	611	906	1,087	1,254
78,000	80,000	287	631	936	1,123	1,296
80,000	85,000	303	666	989	1,185	1,368
85,000	90,000	326	717	1,063	1,274	1,472
90,000	95,000	349	767	1,137	1,365	1,575
95,000	100,000	372	817	1,212	1,454	1,678

Inclusion Amounts for Cars (Other Than Trucks, Vans and Electric Cars) First Leased in 2005						
Fair Market Value		Tax Year During Lease				
Over	Not Over	1st	2nd	3rd	4th	5th & Later
$15,200	$15,500	3	6	9	11	13
15,500	15,800	4	9	13	17	19
15,800	16,100	5	12	18	22	26
16,100	16,400	7	15	22	27	32
16,400	16,700	8	18	27	32	39
16,700	17,000	9	21	32	38	44
17,000	17,500	11	25	38	45	52
17,500	18,000	14	30	45	54	63
18,000	18,500	16	35	52	63	73
18,500	19,000	18	40	60	72	83
19,000	19,500	20	46	67	80	94
19,500	20,000	23	50	75	90	104
20,000	20,500	25	55	82	99	115
20,500	21,000	27	61	89	108	125
21,000	21,500	30	65	97	117	135
21,500	22,000	32	70	105	125	146
22,000	23,000	35	78	116	139	161
23,000	24,000	40	88	131	156	182
24,000	25,000	44	98	146	175	202
25,000	26,000	49	108	161	192	223
26,000	27,000	54	118	175	211	244
27,000	28,000	58	128	191	228	265
28,000	29,000	63	138	205	247	285
29,000	30,000	67	149	220	264	306
30,000	31,000	72	159	234	283	326
31,000	32,000	77	168	250	300	348
32,000	33,000	81	179	265	318	367
33,000	34,000	86	189	279	336	389
34,000	35,000	90	199	295	354	409
35,000	36,000	95	209	309	372	430
36,000	37,000	99	219	325	389	451
37,000	38,000	104	229	339	408	471
38,000	39,000	109	239	354	426	491
39,000	40,000	113	249	370	443	512
40,000	41,000	118	259	384	462	533
41,000	42,000	122	269	400	479	554
42,000	43,000	127	279	414	497	575
43,000	44,000	132	289	429	515	595
44,000	45,000	136	299	444	533	616
45,000	46,000	141	309	459	551	636
46,000	47,000	145	320	473	569	657
47,000	48,000	150	329	489	587	678
48,000	49,000	154	340	504	604	699
49,000	50,000	159	350	518	623	719
50,000	51,000	164	360	533	640	740
51,000	52,000	168	370	548	659	760
52,000	53,000	173	380	563	676	781
53,000	54,000	177	390	578	694	802
54,000	55,000	182	400	593	712	823
55,000	56,000	186	410	609	729	844
56,000	57,000	191	420	623	748	864
57,000	58,000	196	430	638	766	884
58,000	59,000	200	440	653	784	905
59,000	60,000	205	450	668	802	925
60,000	62,000	212	465	691	828	957
62,000	64,000	221	485	721	864	998
64,000	66,000	230	506	750	900	1,039
66,000	68,000	239	526	780	935	1,081
68,000	70,000	248	546	810	971	1,123
70,000	72,000	258	566	839	1,008	1,163
72,000	74,000	267	586	869	1,044	1,204
74,000	76,000	276	606	899	1,079	1,247
76,000	78,000	285	626	930	1,114	1,288

78,000	80,000	294	646	960	1,150	1,329
80,000	85,000	310	682	1,011	1,213	1,402
85,000	90,000	333	732	1,086	1,303	1,504
90,000	95,000	356	782	1,161	1,392	1,608
95,000	100,000	379	832	1,236	1,481	1,712

Inclusion Amounts for Trucks/Vans First Leased in 2004						
Fair Market Value		Tax Year During Lease				
Over	Not Over	1st	2nd	3rd	4th	5th and Later
$18,000	$18,500	7	15	21	26	30
18,500	19,000	9	18	28	33	38
19,000	19,500	11	22	34	40	47
19,500	20,000	13	26	39	48	55
20,000	20,500	14	31	45	54	63
20,500	21,000	16	35	51	61	72
21,000	21,500	18	38	58	68	80
21,500	22,000	20	42	63	76	88
22,000	23,000	23	48	72	87	100
23,000	24,000	26	57	83	101	117
24,000	25,000	30	64	96	115	133
25,000	26,000	34	72	108	129	149
26,000	27,000	37	81	119	143	166
27,000	28,000	41	88	132	157	183
28,000	29,000	44	97	143	172	198
29,000	30,000	48	104	155	187	215
30,000	31,000	52	112	167	201	231
31,000	32,000	55	121	178	215	248
32,000	33,000	59	128	191	229	264
33,000	34,000	63	136	203	243	281
34,000	35,000	66	145	214	257	298
35,000	36,000	70	152	227	271	314
36,000	37,000	74	160	238	286	330
37,000	38,000	77	169	249	301	346
38,000	39,000	81	176	262	314	364
39,000	40,000	84	185	273	329	379
40,000	41,000	88	192	286	343	396
41,000	42,000	92	200	298	357	412
42,000	43,000	95	209	309	371	429
43,000	44,000	99	216	322	385	445
44,000	45,000	103	224	333	400	462
45,000	46,000	106	233	345	413	479
46,000	47,000	110	240	357	428	495
47,000	48,000	114	248	369	442	511
48,000	49,000	117	257	380	457	527
49,000	50,000	121	264	393	471	544
50,000	51,000	125	272	404	486	560
51,000	52,000	128	280	417	499	577
52,000	53,000	132	288	428	514	593
53,000	54,000	135	297	440	527	610
54,000	55,000	139	304	452	542	626
55,000	56,000	143	312	464	556	643
56,000	57,000	146	321	475	571	659
57,000	58,000	150	328	488	585	675
58,000	59,000	154	336	499	600	691
59,000	60,000	157	345	511	613	708
60,000	62,000	163	356	529	635	733
62,000	64,000	170	372	553	663	766
64,000	66,000	177	389	576	692	798
66,000	68,000	185	404	600	720	832
68,000	70,000	192	420	624	749	864
70,000	72,000	199	436	648	777	897
72,000	74,000	206	453	671	805	931
74,000	76,000	214	468	695	834	963
76,000	78,000	221	484	719	863	996
78,000	80,000	228	501	742	891	1,029
80,000	85,000	241	528	785	940	1,087
85,000	90,000	259	568	844	1,012	1,168
90,000	95,000	277	609	902	1,084	1,250
95,000	100,000	296	648	962	1,155	1,333

Inclusion Amounts for Cars (Other Than Trucks, Vans and Electric Cars) First Leased in 2004						
Fair Market Value		Tax Year During Lease				
Over	Not Over	1st	2nd	3rd	4th	5th & Later
$17,500	18,000	11	23	33	42	48
18,000	18,500	13	26	40	49	56
18,500	19,000	14	31	46	55	65
19,000	19,500	16	35	51	63	73
19,500	20,000	18	39	57	70	81
20,000	20,500	20	43	63	77	89
20,500	21,000	22	47	69	84	97
21,000	21,500	23	51	75	91	106
21,500	22,000	25	55	81	98	114
22,000	23,000	28	61	90	109	126
23,000	24,000	32	69	102	123	142
24,000	25,000	35	77	114	137	159
25,000	26,000	39	85	126	151	176
26,000	27,000	43	93	137	166	192
27,000	28,000	46	101	149	180	209
28,000	29,000	50	109	161	194	225
29,000	30,000	54	116	174	208	242
30,000	31,000	57	125	185	223	257
31,000	32,000	61	133	197	237	274
32,000	33,000	64	141	209	251	291
33,000	34,000	68	149	221	265	307
34,000	35,000	72	157	232	280	323
35,000	36,000	75	165	244	294	340
36,000	37,000	79	173	256	308	357
37,000	38,000	83	181	268	322	373
38,000	39,000	86	189	280	337	389
39,000	40,000	90	197	292	351	405
40,000	41,000	94	204	304	365	423
41,000	42,000	97	213	316	379	438
42,000	43,000	101	221	327	394	455
43,000	44,000	105	228	340	408	471
44,000	45,000	108	237	351	422	488
45,000	46,000	112	245	363	436	504
46,000	47,000	115	253	375	451	520
47,000	48,000	119	261	387	464	538
48,000	49,000	123	269	398	479	554
49,000	50,000	126	277	411	493	570
50,000	51,000	130	285	422	508	586
51,000	52,000	134	292	435	522	603
52,000	53,000	137	301	446	536	619
53,000	54,000	141	309	458	550	636
54,000	55,000	145	316	471	564	652
55,000	56,000	148	325	482	578	669
56,000	57,000	152	333	493	593	685
57,000	58,000	155	341	506	607	701
58,000	59,000	159	349	517	622	718
59,000	60,000	163	357	529	636	734
60,000	62,000	168	369	547	657	759
62,000	64,000	176	384	571	686	792
64,000	66,000	183	401	594	714	825
66,000	68,000	190	417	618	743	857
68,000	70,000	197	433	642	771	890
70,000	72,000	205	448	666	800	923
72,000	74,000	212	465	689	828	956
74,000	76,000	219	481	713	856	990
76,000	78,000	227	496	738	884	1,022
78,000	80,000	234	513	760	914	1,055
80,000	85,000	247	540	803	963	1,112
85,000	90,000	265	580	862	1,035	1,194
90,000	95,000	283	621	921	1,105	1,277
95,000	100,000	301	661	980	1,177	1,359

Note that as of 1998, you can elect to use the standard mileage rate to compute your auto expenses for a leased car or truck, provided that you use this method for the entire period of the lease. If your lease began before 1998, you would need to use the SMR for the remainder of the lease term.

Claiming Your Business Vehicle Deductions

If you are self-employed, you will deduct your total vehicle expenses on Schedule C or C-EZ of IRS Form 1040.

Part IV of Schedule C or Part III of Schedule C-EZ may be completed if you are claiming the standard mileage rate and you are not required to file IRS Form 4562, *Depreciation and Amortization*, for any other reason.

If you are using the actual cost method and you are entitled to a depreciation deduction, Part V of Form 4562 must be completed, and the appropriate amount must then be transferred to Schedule C. And if you are required to complete Form 4562 for any other reason (i.e., you are claiming some other business depreciation deductions for the year), you must enter your auto expenses on Part V of the Form.

BUSINESS TRAVEL EXPENSES

Travel expenses are one of the most commonly encountered types of business tax deductions. However, this category is also one of the most confusing. When is the cost of a trip deductible as a business expense? How about conventions in other cities? What if you bring your family? It will be easier to plan your business trips, and to combine business with vacation when possible, if you become familiar with the IRS's ground rules.

Basically, to be deductible, your travel must meet two criteria:

- the travel expenses must be incurred in connection with an existing business
- the expenses must be incurred away from home

You can only deduct travel expenses if they are ordinary and necessary expenses that you incur in connection with the pursuit of an existing business. You can't deduct travel expenses to the extent that they are lavish or extravagant — the expenses must be reasonable considering the facts and circumstances. However, the IRS gives you a great deal of latitude here. Your expenses won't be denied simply because you decided to fly first class, or dine in four-star restaurants.

The expenses have to be incurred for an *existing* business — travel expenses you incur in connection with acquiring or starting a new business are not deductible. However, you can add these costs to your startup expenses and amortize them over 60 months – see page 61.

What about travel that has a combined business and personal aspect? Here's where it gets a bit more complicated. The IRS is on the lookout for taxpayers who might try to classify a nondeductible personal trip as a deductible business trip. So, if you travel to a destination and engage in both personal and business activities, you can deduct your traveling expenses to and from the destination only if the trip is *primarily* related to your business.

If the trip is primarily personal in nature you can't deduct any of your airfare, hotel, or other traveling expenses. This is true even if you engage in some business activities while you are there. (You can deduct particular expenses you incur while you're at your destination if they otherwise qualify as business deductions; for example, cab fare to an isolated business appointment.)

The primary purpose of a trip is determined by looking at the facts and circumstances of each case. An important factor is the amount of time you spent on personal activities during the trip as compared to the amount of time spent on activities directly relating to business. Travel expenses outside the U.S. may be further limited if part of your trip is for personal purposes – see the discussion of foreign travel below.

Away From Home

You may only deduct travel expenses incurred when you are "away from home." You are traveling away from home if you meet the following two conditions:

- Your trip is long enough or far away enough that you can't reasonably be expected to complete the round trip without obtaining sleep or rest. This doesn't mean that you need to stay overnight at the destination; for example, it may be that you had an all-day meeting and needed to catch a few hours sleep in a hotel before driving home.

- The travel is away from the general area or vicinity of your tax home.

Generally, your tax home is the entire general area or vicinity (e.g., a city and surrounding suburbs) of your principal place of business.

If you conduct your business in more than one place, you should consider the total time you ordinarily spend working in each place, the degree of your business activity in each place, and the relative amount of your income from each place to determine your "principal" place of business.

If you don't have a regular place of abode and no main place of business, you may be considered an itinerant: your tax home is wherever you work and you can never be "away-from-home." When you are temporarily (a year or less), as opposed to indefinitely, working away from your main place of business, your tax home doesn't change.

Defining Travel Expenses

Generally, deductible travel expenses are the ordinary and necessary expenses that you incur while you're away from home in pursuit of your trade or business. In order to claim travel expenses as deductions, you must keep adequate records and be able to prove the existence, amount, and business purpose of your expenses.

The chart below shows a list of expenses you may be able to deduct as travel expenses, depending on the facts and circumstances.

Meal Costs When Traveling

The cost of dining alone is a deductible expense only if your business trip is overnight or long enough to require that you stop for sleep or rest. (Of course, if you entertain business guests at home or away you may be able to deduct the cost, if you meet the usual deductibility rules for meals and entertainment as discussed on page 75).

In any case, you can deduct only 50 percent of the cost of the meals.

Deductible Travel Expenses

- 50 percent of the cost of meals when traveling (see discussion below)
- air, rail, and bus fares
- baggage charges
- cleaning and laundry expenses
- computer rental fees
- expenses of operating and maintaining a vehicle, including the cost of gas, oil, lubrication, washing, repairs, parts, tires, supplies, parking fees, and tolls
- expenses of operating and maintaining RVs or house trailers
- hotel expenses
- local transportation costs for taxi fares or other transportation between the airport or station and a hotel, from one customer to another, or from one place of business to another, and tips incidental to the foregoing expenses
- public stenographer or clerical fees
- telephone or fax expenses
- tips on eligible expenses
- transportation costs for sample and display materials and sample room costs

A special exception to the 50 percent rule for deducting meal costs applies to people who are away from home while working under Department of Transportation regulations. This group of workers includes air transportation employees, interstate truck and bus drivers, railroad employees, and merchant mariners. For these workers, meals will be 75 percent deductible in 2006 and 2007, and 80 percent deductible in 2008 and thereafter.

Standard Meal Allowance

Assuming that you are traveling away from home for the required length of time, you may elect to deduct half of a Standard Meal Allowance (SMA), rather than half of the actual cost of your meals, laundry, cleaning and tips.

The minimum standard meals and incidental expense allowance for the 2006 fiscal year (October 1, 2005, through September 30, 2006) is $39 a day for most areas in the U.S. Some locations in the U.S. are considered high-cost areas and qualify for higher rates of $44, $49, $54, $59 or $64 per day. The same rates apply for the 2007 fiscal year. These per diem rates are updated periodically to reflect regional inflation and are published at http://www.gsa.gov on the Internet and in IRS Publication 1542, *Per Diem Rates (for Travel Within the Continental United States).* Note that these sources also list a per diem rate that includes lodging as well as meals and incidentals, but this combined per diem generally can't be used by self-employed people.

For travel in areas outside the continental U.S., you must use federal per diem rates that are published monthly by the government. The foreign per diem rates can be purchased from the Government Printing Office and are also available on the Internet from the State Department at http://www.state.gov.

Save Time

The advantage to using the standard meal allowance is that you don't have to keep records of actual meal expenses, although you still have to keep records to prove the time, place, and business purpose of your travel.

A disadvantage is that the standard meal allowances are not very generous. Chances are that your actual expenses — and therefore your deductions — would be larger.

Spouses and Dependents

You may be wondering whether you can deduct the cost of bringing your spouse along on a business trip. The answer is generally no.

For the travel expenses of a spouse (or dependent or any other individual for that matter) to be deductible, the spouse (or other person) must also be an employee of the business. In addition, the spouse's travel must be for a bona fide business purpose and the expenses must be otherwise deductible by the spouse.

Conventions, Seminars, Meetings

You can deduct your travel expenses when you attend a convention if you can show that attending the convention benefits your business.

You can satisfy the business relationship test by showing that your business duties and responsibilities tie into the program or agenda of the convention. The agenda doesn't necessarily have to deal specifically with your duties or responsibilities—a tie-in is enough. You must, however, show some kind of income-producing purpose for attending the convention. In any case, you won't be able to deduct any nonbusiness expenses (sightseeing, for example) you incur while attending the convention.

The rules become even stricter when the convention is held outside North America or on a cruise ship. Basically, the IRS doesn't want people deducting their vacations. However, they recognize that at least some of these trips are for bona fide business purposes. Here's what you need to know:

Conventions held outside North America. In order to be able to deduct expenses for attending a convention outside the North American area, the convention must be directly related to your business and it must be as reasonable to hold the convention outside the North American area as in it. You must also satisfy the requirements for deducting business travel expenses outside the U.S.

Conventions held on cruise ships. The following requirements must be met before you can deduct expenses incurred for a convention or seminar held on a cruise ship:

- The convention must be directly related to the active conduct of your business.

- The cruise ship must be a vessel registered in the U.S.

- All of the cruise ship's ports of call must be located in the U.S. (or its possessions).

- You must attach to your income tax return a written statement signed by you that includes the total days of the trip (excluding the days you spent traveling to and from the ship's port), the number of hours each day that you devoted to scheduled business activities, and a program of the scheduled business activities of the meeting.

- You must attach to your income tax return a written statement signed by an officer of the organization or group sponsoring the convention that includes a schedule of the business activities of each day of the convention, and the number of hours you attended the scheduled business activities.

If you meet the requirements, you can deduct up to $2,000 annually of the expense of attending a seminar or convention on a cruise ship. In the case of a joint return, a maximum of $4,000 would be deductible if each spouse qualifying cruise ship conventions.

Foreign Travel

Simply stated, if you travel outside the U.S. purely for business purposes, all your travel expenses of getting to and from your business destination are deductible.

However, if you spend part of your time in a foreign country engaging in personal activities, you may have to allocate your travel expenses in proportion to the number of days you spent on nonbusiness activities during your trip, unless you meet one of the following conditions:

- You were outside the U.S. for a week or less, combining business and personal activities (a week is seven consecutive days, not counting the day you leave the U.S., but counting the day you return to the U.S.).

- You were outside the U.S. for more than a week, but you spent less than 25 percent of the total time you were in a foreign country on personal activities (counting both the day your trip began and the day it ended).

- You can establish that a personal vacation was not a major consideration for the trip.

If you meet one or more of these conditions, you're in luck! Your trip is considered entirely conducted for business and you can deduct all of your business-related travel expenses.

If you don't meet at least one of these conditions and you spent 25 percent or more of your time on personal activities, you'll have to allocate your travel expenses of getting to and from your destination between your business and personal activities to determine your deductible amount. You must allocate your expenses *even if* your trip was primarily for business reasons. Remember, if your trip was primarily for vacation purposes, the entire cost of the trip is a nondeductible personal expense. You would be able to deduct only the expenses that you incurred on the trip that were directly related to your business.

Claiming Your Travel Expenses

Sole proprietors claim their travel expenses, except for any meals or entertainment expenses, on Line 24a of their Schedule C. The full amount of meals and entertainment costs must be reported separately on Line 24b; the tax form asks you to compute 50 percent of this amount on the face of the form to make sure that you're only deducting half of the expenses.

Meal and Entertainment Expenses

As a small business owner, you may often find yourself in the position of having to entertain clients or customers. While this sort of thing is a necessary expense for many small business owners, the costs can really add up. You'll be glad to know that the IRS lets you take a deduction for 50 percent of qualifying entertainment expenses for yourself and your guests.

What requirements must your meal and entertainment expenses meet in order to be deductible? Generally, the answer is that you can deduct ordinary and necessary expenses to entertain a customer or client if:

- Your expenses are of a type that qualifies as meals or entertainment.

- Your expenses bear the necessary relationship to your business activities.
- You keep adequate records and can substantiate the expenses.

Defining Meals and Entertainment

What kind of expenses count as meal and entertainment expenses, for which a 50 percent deduction is allowed? Generally, expenses for any activity considered to provide entertainment, amusement, or recreation fall into this category.

For example, entertaining guests at nightclubs; at social, athletic, and sporting clubs; at theaters; at sporting events; or on hunting, fishing, vacation and similar types of trips is considered deductible entertainment. Meeting personal, living, or family needs of individuals (for example, providing meals, a hotel suite, or a car to business customers or their families) can be an entertainment expense as well.

Entertainment expenses include the cost of meals you provide to customers or clients, whether the meal alone is the entertainment or it's a part of other entertainment (for example, refreshments at a football game). A meal expense includes the cost of food, beverages, taxes, and tips.

You can also deduct 50 percent of business meals or entertainment expenses incurred while:

- entertaining business guests, whether it's at your place of business, a restaurant, or some other location
- attending a business convention, reception, meeting, or luncheon at a club
- traveling away from home on business, whether eating alone or with others on business.

It's important to note that the type of business you run can determine whether an activity is entertainment.

Example

If you're a freelance theater critic who is paid for your reviews, and you attend a theatrical performance in your professional capacity, this is not a 50 percent deductible entertainment expense; instead, it would be a 100 percent deductible business expense. Similarly, if a clothing designer puts on a fashion show to show his designs to a group of store buyers, it would not be considered entertainment. However, if you are an appliance distributor and you put on a fashion show for your retailers and their spouses, the show is considered entertainment and only 50 percent would be deductible.

The cost of entertainment tickets is generally deductible. However, you can only deduct the face value of the ticket *even if* you paid a higher price (for example, if you pay more than face value for a ticket from a scalper, ticket agency, or ticket broker).

You can, however, take the full cost you pay for a ticket into account, even if it's higher than face value, when the ticket is to a sporting event if the event's main purpose is to benefit a qualified charitable organization, the entire net proceeds go to the charity, and volunteers perform substantially all the event's work. Also, the 50 percent limitation on entertainment expenses doesn't apply to any expense covered by a package deal involving a ticket to a charitable sports event.

Entertaining Spouses

Can you deduct the cost of entertainment for your spouse or a customer or client's spouse? You can only deduct these costs if you had a clear business purpose, rather than a personal or social purpose, for providing the entertainment.

Example

You would be able to deduct otherwise permissible entertainment expenses of an out-of-town client's husband when it is impracticable to entertain the client for business purposes without him.

Business-Related Entertainment

Your expenses for meals and entertainment must be closely related to your business in order to be deductible. In the IRS's view, your expenses may qualify if they meet at least one of the following two tests:

- the directly-related test
- the associated-with test

You can't deduct meal and entertainment expenses to the extent that they are lavish or extravagant — the expenses must be reasonable considering the facts and circumstances.

Directly-Related Test

If the entertainment takes place in a clear business setting (for example, you provide a hospitality room at a convention) directly to promote your business, the expense satisfies the directly-related-to test. If you can't meet the clear business setting requirement, the expense must meet *all* of the following requirements:

- You must have more than a vague expectation of deriving some income or other specific business benefit (other than the goodwill of the person entertained) from the meal or entertainment. However, you don't need to show that income or some other business benefit actually resulted from each deducted expenditure.
- During the meal or entertainment, you actively engaged in business discussions.
- The main purpose of the combined business and entertainment was the active conduct of business.

What kind of expenses are generally *not* considered directly related? In situations when entertainment occurs where there are substantial distractions, such as meetings or discussions at night clubs, theaters, or sporting events; meetings or discussions at social gatherings, such as cocktail parties; and situations in which you meet with a group that includes persons other than business associates, for example cocktail lounges, country clubs, golf or athletic clubs, or at vacation resorts. For these types of meal and entertainment expenses, there's a presumption that the directly-related test is not met unless you clearly can show otherwise.

Associated-With Test

Meals and entertainment expenses may be deductible under this test if they meet the following two requirements:

- The expenses are associated with the active conduct of your business.
- The meal or entertainment directly precedes or follows a substantial and bona fide business discussion.

Entertainment that occurs on the same day as the business discussion automatically meets the "directly precedes or follows" requirement.

If the entertainment and the business discussion don't occur on the same day, the facts and circumstances of each case are considered. The relevant facts are the place, date, and duration of the business discussion, whether you and your business associate are from out of town (and the dates of arrival and departure), and the reasons the entertainment didn't take place on the same day as the business discussion.

Whether a business discussion (such as a meeting, negotiation, transaction, etc.) is substantial and bona fide depends on the facts and circumstances of each case. If the IRS challenged you on this, you would have to establish that you actively engaged in the business discussion (not the entertainment) for the purpose of obtaining income or some other type of specific business benefit. However, you *don't* have to show that more time was devoted to business than entertainment.

Claiming Meal and Entertainment Expenses

Your total meals and entertainment expenses would be reported on Line 24b of the Schedule C. This amount should include any meal expenses you incurred while traveling on business.

Line 24c requires you to multiply your total meals by 50 percent and to subtract it from the total, just to be sure that you're only deducting half of these costs. The remaining 50 percent is reported on Line 24d.

BUSINESS GIFT EXPENSES

As a small business owner, you may find yourself giving gifts to clients and customers in the course of your business, particularly around the holidays.

What you may not know is that you can deduct only part of the cost of certain gifts as a business expense.

For purposes of this discussion, a gift is any item that's excluded from gross income of the recipient under the gift tax laws. If an item is excluded from gross income under any other provision, then it's not considered to be a gift. For example, because scholarships are excluded from income under another tax law provision, they are not considered gifts. Similarly, a "gift" to an employee will be treated as taxable compensation for the employee, which is deductible for your business under the normal rules for employees' pay.

Dollar limitation. Basically, the IRS will let your business deduct only $25 or less for business gifts you give to any one person during your tax year.

This means that any number of your employees, co-owners or business partners may give a client business gifts. However, the deduction will be limited to $25 per recipient. Any amount of expense in excess of $25 is disallowed as a deduction.

Example

If you give a client a $50 plant as a gift, you can only take a $25 deduction.

In addition, if you and your spouse both give gifts, you're both going to be treated as one taxpayer, and together you can only deduct gifts of $25 per recipient. This is true even if you have separate businesses, are separately employed, or whether each of you has an independent connection with the gift recipient.

Direct and Indirect Gifts

The $25 limit for business gifts includes both direct and indirect gifts. Figuring out if you gave a direct gift is a pretty straightforward determination. If you gave fruitcakes to each of ABC Corporation's 10 employees, than you made a direct gift to each one of them.

Determining whether you made an indirect gift is trickier because the IRS isn't only going to look at who received the gift, but also at whom you actually intended to benefit by giving this gift.

Example

Let's say you give your client's live-in relative, Aunt Mabel, a single ticket for a basketball game. Now, at the time you gave her the ticket, you probably had a pretty good idea that she would ultimately give the ticket to your client who is an avid basketball fan. So, do you think the IRS will classify this as an indirect gift to your client? You can bet on it.

However, if you have bona fide business dealings with Aunt Mabel (let's say she is your supplier) then the gift is generally not considered an indirect gift. Still, the IRS will look at the gift to see whether your client, Aunt Mabel, (or any family member for that matter), was to have the eventual use or benefit of the gift. If your client is the intended beneficiary it may still be treated as an indirect gift.

Incidental Costs

The $25 limit for business gifts doesn't include incidental costs — for example, packaging, insurance, and mailing costs or the cost of engraving jewelry. Related costs are considered incidental only if they don't add some kind of substantial value to a gift.

Example

Let's say you send someone a fruit basket as a gift. If the basket has a substantial value as compared to the value of the fruit, the cost of the basket is not incidental and it must be included in the $25 limit. On the other hand, the cost of gift wrapping is incidental and doesn't have to be included in the $25 limit.

Exemptions From the Gift Limitations

If you give key chains or pens with your business name on them to customers and clients, are these considered gifts and subject to these rules? In a word, no. The following items are excepted from the $25 limit for business gifts and their cost is deductible without limitation:

- items that cost $4 or less, have your name clearly and permanently imprinted on them, and are one of a number of identical items you widely distribute

- signs, display racks, or other promotional material to be used on the business premises of the recipient

Entertainment Gifts

What happens if you give tickets to a play or sporting event to a customer or client? Is this a gift expense or an entertainment expense? The general rule is that any item that could be considered either a gift or an entertainment expense should be considered an entertainment expense.

However, under certain circumstances, you may have the choice of determining whether an item is either a gift or entertainment expense. For example, if you give a client tickets to go see a play or sporting event, you may treat the tickets as either a gift or an entertainment expense if you don't go with the client to the play or sporting event. If you do go with the client, you *must* treat the cost of the tickets as an entertainment expense – you don't have any choice.

Save Money

If you have the choice of treating an expense as a gift or entertainment, which should you choose? Taking into account the $25 limit for gifts and the 50 percent limitation on entertainment expenses, it's generally advantageous to treat an expense as entertainment when it is over $50. For example, let's say you gave a client ballet tickets that cost $140. If you deduct them as a gift expense, your deduction is limited to $25. If you deduct them as an entertainment expense, your deduction is one-half the cost or $70. Conversely, if you gave a client tickets to a movie premiere that cost $30, you would get a bigger deduction by claiming a gift expense ($25 as opposed to $15 for an entertainment expense).

What about food-related gifts? Should you treat their cost as a meal expense or a gift expense? If you give a customer or client packaged food or beverages that you intend them to use at a later date, treat the cost as a gift expense, not a meal expense.

Claiming Business Gift Expenses

Since Schedule C does not include a separate category for business gift expenses, you would need to list them as an "other" expenses in Part V of the Schedule C. You don't need to list each gift separately; it's fine to total them up and list them as a single line-item, "gifts."

BUSINESS-RELATED EDUCATION EXPENSES

Self-employed business owners can deduct the cost of seminars; training sessions; and vocational, technical, or academic classes that may or may not lead to a degree, if they are sufficiently related to the business activity. For more information, see the discussion of education expenses for employees on page 184.

THE HOME OFFICE DEDUCTION

If you use a part of your home for business — perhaps to perform paperwork; to store records, inventory, or samples; or even to meet customers — you may be able to claim a tax deduction for some of your expenses of maintaining the home.

You may have heard that the home office deduction is either one of the greatest money-savers available to American small business, or that it is a major red flag that will make you audit bait for the IRS. As a general rule, you should never shy away from taking a deduction you are legally entitled to. At the same time, we strongly recommend that you keep meticulous records of all your home office and other expenses so that you are able to back up any deductions you claim.

Tax Organizer Tip

As a reminder, your business home office expenses should be entered under the sub-tab for "Business" on the "Employment" tab of CompleteTax. Note: If you have an office in the home, you should enter the full amount of your home mortgage interest and real estate taxes on this tab instead of the "Deductions" tab. Do not duplicate entries on the "Deductions" tab.

Many Deductions, Not Just One

In reality, when we speak of the home office deduction, we're really talking about a series of smaller deductions. These deductions — which may include such items as part of your utility bills, mortgage interest, repairs, and depreciation — are totaled up to get an overall deduction amount which is reported on IRS Form 8829, *Expenses for Business Use of Your Home.* The common denominator among these deductions is that the IRS has devised a single test to determine whether you qualify for all of them.

Some deductions are available even if you don't qualify. A commonly held misconception is that you need to qualify for the home office deduction in order to claim *any* expenses associated with a home or a home-based business. This is simply not true.

For example, home mortgage interest and real estate taxes would be allowed as an itemized deduction on Schedule A of your Form 1040 in any case, even if you can't take a home office deduction. Office supplies, postage, and the cost of bringing a second telephone line into your home for business use may also be deductible. Moreover, you may be able to write off the cost of computers and office furniture you buy to use at home, even if you're not allowed to deduct the cost of the office itself (see Chapter 7 regarding depreciation).

Having said that, we're ready to discuss the details of the home office deduction and to help you calculate your deduction amount.

Qualifying for a Home Office Deduction

The requirements of the home office deduction are fairly strict. Generally, to qualify, your home office must be used exclusively and regularly for business *and* either:

1. be your "principal place of business" *or* be normally used to personally meet with clients or customers

2. be a separate structure that is not attached to your house or residence, in which case it merely has to be used in your trade or business

Exclusive and Regular Business Use

Everyone who wishes to claim the home office deduction must use a portion of the home exclusively and regularly for business.

You don't necessarily have to use the space as an office; it could be a showroom, lab, or storage area. However, you must use it *regularly*, not just occasionally. Ordinarily, "exclusive use" means that the business part of the home may not be used for any personal, family, or investment activities, or for any other business activities that don't meet the home office requirements.

There is an exception to the "exclusive use" requirement if your home is the only fixed location of a retail or wholesale business. In that case, you can deduct expenses that pertain to the use of part of your home for the storage of inventory or product samples.

Example

Patrick Daily's home is the sole, fixed place of his business selling personal computers at retail. He regularly uses half of his basement for inventory storage, although he also uses that part of the basement for personal purposes when his inventory is low.

The expenses allocated to the storage space are deductible even though he does not use that part of the basement exclusively for business.

There is also an exception to this exclusive use requirement for those who operate a child care business in their home. The portion of the home that is used regularly for day care qualifies as a "home office," even if it is also used for personal and family living space. However, day care operators face an additional time restriction: They may only deduct expenses for the actual time the day care center was open (see page 83).

Other Requirements

As we mentioned above, in addition to the exclusive and regular use tests, you must meet *one* of the following requirements:

- The part of the home must be your principal place of business, *or* you must use it as a place to personally meet clients or customers in the normal course of your business (telephone calls don't count).

- If it is a separate structure that is not attached to your house or residence, it merely has to be used in your trade or business.

The "principal place of business" definition is significantly easier to meet than it once was. A home office will qualify as the principal place of business if: (a) the office is used by the taxpayer to conduct administrative or management activities of a trade or business, and (b) there is no other fixed location where the taxpayer conducts substantial administrative or management activities of the trade or business.

This means that the fact that you may conduct management activities in a non-fixed location, such as a car or hotel room, will not cause you to lose the deduction. Similarly, the fact that you conduct some management activities in another fixed location of the business will not cause you to lose the deduction, as long as those activities are not "substantial."

Example

Joe Ditto operates his photocopier service and repair business out of his home. His only office is a room in his house used solely for business purposes.

Although Joe never meets with customers in his home office, he spends about 12 hours per week working there, scheduling service calls and writing up orders and other reports. He spends an average of 30 hours per week on service calls at his customers' businesses at various locations in the metropolitan area. Joe keeps the few tools and supplies necessary to his business in the trunk of his car.

Joe's home qualifies for the home office deduction. Even though the essence of his business requires him to service and repair photocopiers at the customers' places of business, and he spends less time in his home office than he does at the customers' offices, his home office is considered his principal place of business because it is the only fixed location from which he conducts administrative and management functions.

The same result would apply to a restaurant owner who serves his customers in a retail setting, but conducts management activities such as ordering food and supplies, scheduling employees' working time, and doing bookkeeping and payroll chores out of his home.

He will qualify for the home office deduction, as long as this is the only place he conducts substantial management activities; the fact that some of his employees may conduct management activities at the retail location does not matter.

Are You Eligible as an Employee?

If you or your spouse is an employee, including an employee/shareholder of a small corporation, there is another requirement that you must meet in addition to those discussed above. You must be using your home for the convenience of your employer in order to qualify for the home office deduction. If your employer provides you with office space, you probably can't take the home office deduction because your home would not be considered your principal place of business.

The IRS specifically prohibits you from taking the home office deduction if you rent all or part of your home to your employer and then use the rented portion to work in as an employee.

Computing Your Home Office Deduction Amount

Once you've determined that you qualify for the home office deduction, you can determine the actual dollar amount that you can deduct.

This amount depends on a surprisingly large number of factors. But don't be alarmed – we'll walk you through them.

First, you need to know what you spent for each component of the home office deduction:

- rent if you don't own the home
- mortgage interest and real estate taxes if you do own the home
- depreciation if you own
- insurance, utilities and services, repairs, and decorating, whether you own or rent
- casualty losses whether you own or rent

Of course, for all these expenses, you can only deduct the portion that pertains to your home office, not the full amount that applies to the entire residence. There are two factors to consider in determining the "home office portion":

- space: the size of the area that was used
- time: the portion of the year that the home office was used, if not the entire year

Finally, some business owners will find that their home office deduction is limited by their business income. The tax law states that the home office deduction, plus all your other deductible business expenses, cannot exceed your business income for the year. In other words, the home office deduction cannot be used as a tax shelter to offset other income you (or your spouse) may have.

Business Portion of the Home

An important part of the qualification requirements for a home office is that a portion of your residence be used regularly and exclusively for business purposes, whether it be as an office, a conference room, a lab area, storage room, or some other type of business usage.

But, if you do have an area that you use regularly and exclusively for business, you can deduct a portion of certain expenses relating to your home. For most types of home office expenses, the amount you may deduct depends primarily on the percentage of the space in the residence that is used for business.

There are two common ways to determine this, and you can use whichever method results in the larger deduction.

The first method looks at the number of rooms used for business, divided by the total number of rooms in your house. The second method looks at the square footage of the space used for business, divided by the total square footage of the house.

Example

If you have an eight-room house and use one room as an office, the business use portion will be 1/8 or 12.5 percent of the home. Alternately, if your home office was 168 square feet and your home was a total of 2000 square feet, your business use percentage will be 168/2000 or 8.4 percent.

Most of your home expenses (such as rent or real estate taxes and mortgage interest) must be multiplied by the larger of these two fractions to determine the portion that's deductible as a home office expense.

Day care providers. Home day care operators get a special tax break: They can count all the space they regularly use for their day care business as the "business portion of the home" even though the same space is used for personal or family purposes. For example, they may include the bathroom, the kitchen where day care meals are prepared, and the family bedrooms where naps are taken. However, unlike most home business operators, they must prorate these expenses for the hours in which the day care is offered, as discussed below.

Partial-Year Home Offices

Most people do not start up a new business precisely on January 1. Most likely, you opened your business at some point between January 1 and December 31, and your first year in the home office was not a complete one. Similarly, people who close down their business don't always do it precisely on the last day of their tax year.

As a result, for the first year in which you began using your home office, or the year in which you closed your business, you'll have to prorate your home office expenses based on the percentage of the time your home office was actually used.

Example

If you began using your home office on July 1 of this year and continued to use it through the end of the year, you can use only your expenses for the last half of the year in computing your home office deduction.

Special rules for depreciation. For the first year you begin using your home office, the IRS provides a table showing the fraction of your depreciable basis you can deduct, based on the month in which you started using the office. See Table A-7a on page 129.

For the last year, you'll need to determine the amount of depreciation you'd normally deduct for the year, under the usual rules. Then multiply this amount by a fraction: The numerator will be the number of months that you used the office, and the denominator will be 12. Count the month in which you stopped using the property as half a month. For example, if you stopped using your office in October, the fraction will be 9.5/12.

Day care operators. As mentioned above, home day care operators can count as "business-use space" whatever portion of the home is regularly used for day care purposes, even if the same space is also used for personal living space. However, they must prorate their home office expenses based on their hours of operation.

Example

A home day care operator's expenses for mortgage interest, real estate taxes, depreciation, utilities, and property insurance amounts to $10,000. She estimates that 80 percent of her home is used regularly for day care activities. The day care center is open 12 hours per day, five days per week, which amounts to 60 hours out of a possible 168.

She must multiply her home office expenses of $10,000 by .80 to arrive at $8,000, which is her business use percentage of these expenses. Then she must multiply this amount by 60/168 to arrive at her allowable deduction of $2,857.

Rent, Interest, and Taxes

For those who rent their home, the major advantage of the home office deduction is that a portion of your rental payments will be deductible. Renters who don't qualify for the home office deduction ordinarily can't deduct any of their rental payments, so working out of your home can result in significant tax savings.

Homeowners. For homeowners, your deduction is not based on the fair rental value of your home. Instead, you may deduct a portion of your real estate taxes and your qualified mortgage interest (but not principal) payments on the home. You can also claim a depreciation deduction to recover some of the home's purchase price.

"Real estate taxes" include the amount of taxes actually paid to the taxing authority on your behalf during the year, which may be different from the amount that your mortgage holder requires you to pay into an escrow account. Real estate taxes do not include amounts paid to any homeowner's association or condominium association. They also don't include assessments for local benefits like streets, sidewalks, or water and sewer systems – instead, these amounts may be depreciated (see the discussion of home office depreciation, below).

"Qualified mortgage interest" may include interest on a second mortgage or a home equity loan. However, there are dollar limits that apply. Only interest on mortgages up to $1,000,000 ($500,000 if married filing separately) used to buy, build, or improve your property, and interest on home equity loans up to $100,000 ($50,000 if married filing separately), is considered "qualified." If you think either of these limits might apply to you, consult your tax advisor or get IRS Publication 936, *Home Mortgage Interest Deduction,* for more detailed information on computing your deduction.

For both renters and homeowners, the deductible portion of the rental, tax, or interest payments depends on the percentage of the home's space that is used for business (see page 82 for the rules on computing the business percentage of your home). If you start or stop using the office during the year, the percentage of time that the office is used will also be a factor.

Save Money

Of course, as a homeowner, you can claim all your real estate taxes and qualified mortgage interest as itemized deductions, regardless of whether you use your home for business purposes. Claiming these expenses as part of the home office deduction basically means shifting them to a different tax form (Form 8829).

One major advantage to this shift is that by claiming these amounts as a business deduction, you reduce the net business income on which you must pay self-employment taxes.

For higher income taxpayers, there can be another advantage, because most itemized tax deductions are phased out for those with high levels of income while business expenses, including the home office deduction, are not.

Claiming the home office deduction also means that some of your real estate taxes and mortgage interest will be used to reduce your adjusted gross income (AGI), which in turn can improve your eligibility for numerous tax benefits including IRAs (see page 251), miscellaneous itemized deductions (see page 274), and the deduction for medical expenses that exceed 7.5 percent of AGI.

Depreciation on a Home Office

If you qualify for the home office deduction and you own your home, you can't directly deduct the price you paid for the home, the principal payments you make on the mortgage, or the fair rental value of the home.

Instead, you can recover the cost of the business percentage of the home through depreciation deductions.

Before you can calculate the dollar amount of your depreciation, however, you will need to know the tax basis of your home. To determine your home's tax basis, you start with the lower of:

- the home's fair market value at the time you begin using the home office, or
- the cost of the home (not including the cost of the land underneath it), plus the value of any permanent improvements you made before using the home office, and minus any casualty losses you deducted before using it.

In most cases you'll be using the second of the two items listed above, but if you suspect that your home has slid down in value since you bought it, you should have an appraisal done when you start using the home office in order to fix the fair market value at that point in time.

The cost of the home generally includes not only the price you paid to the seller, but also various closing costs and settlement fees such as abstract fees, installation of utility services, legal fees, recording fees, surveys, transfer taxes, title insurance, and any amounts you agree to pay on behalf of the seller such as back taxes or interest, sales commissions, or charges for improvements or repairs. Some fees and costs you may not include are insurance premiums, rent for occupancy before closing, and charges connected with getting a loan such as mortgage insurance, credit reports, appraisal fees, loan assumption fees, and points.

You must reasonably allocate the total costs of the property between the land and the buildings on it to compute your tax basis for depreciation. If your sales contract did not explicitly allocate the price, you should allocate the costs on the basis of the fair market values of the land and buildings at the time of purchase. Your realtor or insurance agent may be able to help you make a reasonable estimate of fair market value.

Your tax basis must be multiplied by the business percentage of your home (see page 82), to arrive at the amount you can depreciate.

Once you know the tax basis of the depreciable portion of the home, you multiply it by a percentage determined by the IRS, based on the month and year you bought the home. Table A-7a showing these percentages is included on page 129. Generally speaking, for home offices that you began using for business on or after May 13, 1993, the depreciation period will be 39 years and in every year but the first and the last, the applicable percentage will be .02564. For the first and last years, the fraction will depend on the month in which business use began or ended.

If you began using your home office before May 13, 1993, continue using the depreciation method that you originally started out with.

Capital improvements. If, after you begin using your home for business, you make a significant, permanent improvement to the property (as opposed to a repair) you will need to depreciate this capital expenditure as well. For example, if you put on a new roof or buy a new furnace for your home, you would depreciate the business percentage of the cost of the improvement over 39 years, beginning with the month and year of installation. See page 60 for a list of items that are generally considered capital improvements, not repairs.

Warning

It's important to recognize that when you eventually sell your home, you'll be required to pay tax on the amount of capital gain (if any) that's equal to the amount of depreciation you claimed over the years on your home, including depreciation from a home office. The maximum tax rate on this "recaptured" depreciation is 25 percent.

Insurance, Utilities, Services, Repairs, and Decorating

If you qualify for the home office deduction, you may claim a portion of certain types of expenses that are associated with your home but are not deductible by the average homeowner. These expenses include insurance, utilities, repairs, security system expenses, maid service, garbage disposal, and decorating expenses.

With all of these expenses, the general rule is that if a given expense pertains only to the home office, the entire expense will be deductible as a "direct" home office expense. If the expense applies to the entire house, it's an "indirect" home office expense and only a proportionate part of it will be deductible. And if the expense applies only to the non-business portion of the house, none of the expense will be deductible. Also, if you did not operate the business for the entire year, you may only deduct expenses that pertain to the portion of the year in which the office was used.

Insurance. You may deduct the business percentage of your homeowner's or renter's insurance as part of the home office deduction.

Do not include the costs of any business insurance you carry or special home office policy riders in this figure. Those costs apply specifically to the business portion of your home, and are fully deductible as ordinary business expenses, not as part of the home office deduction. This distinction can become important if your home office deduction is limited by the amount of your business income (see page 86).

Utilities and services. As a general rule, you can deduct the business percentage of your utility payments for heat and electricity, and for services that pertain to the entire house such as trash collection, security services, and maid or cleaning services.

Warning

IRS regulations indicate that lawn service is generally not *deductible as part of the home office deduction, even when the home office is used as a meeting place with clients (who presumably view the lawn as they enter the residence).*

If you pay for a utility or service that's not used in your business at all, you can't deduct any portion of the expense. For instance, if you buy propane fuel that is used only in your kitchen and your business does not involve cooking, no part of the propane bill is deductible.

If you believe that your business accounts for significantly more (or less) of a particular utility, you should increase (or decrease) your business percentage of that utility bill accordingly. This is not an exact science, and the IRS will accept a reasonable estimate.

Example

Leona Grossberg is a cosmetics company representative who qualifies for the home office deduction. She has an electric bill of $400 for lighting, cooking, laundry and television. Only the lighting is used for business. She figures that $250 of the bill is for lighting alone. Because she uses 10 percent of the house for business, $25 may be deductible as a business expense.

Telephones. Telephone bills are considered direct business expenses, and are not part of the home office deduction. Therefore, you may be able to deduct a portion of your home or cellular phone bill even if you don't qualify under the home office rules.

In any event, you can't claim any deduction for the basic telephone service on the first telephone line in your home, or on your cellular phone. These are considered to be personal expenses that you would incur even if you did not own a business. However, you *can* deduct any separately stated charges for local or long distance business calls. You can also deduct the cost of bringing a second phone line into your home, if you use the line exclusively for business.

Repairs and decorating expenses. Expenses that exclusively benefit your business (for example, repairing the drywall and repainting a former bedroom that is now your office) are considered "direct" home office expenses and are fully deductible. Expenses that benefit the entire home (for example, patching the roof so it doesn't leak, or recarpeting the entire house) are considered "indirect" home office expenses that are proportionately deductible. And expenses that benefit only the personal portion of the home (for example, installing a whirlpool tub in the master bedroom suite) are not deductible at all.

It's sometimes difficult to distinguish between a repair, which is deductible (fully or partially) in the year it was done, and an improvement, which must be depreciated over the course of property's useful life. The IRS says that an improvement is something that materially adds to the value of your home, considerably prolongs its useful life, or adapts it to new uses. A repair, on the other hand, is something that keeps your home in ordinary efficient operating condition but does not add to the value of your home or prolong its life. If repairs are done as part of extensive remodeling or restoration, the entire job is considered an improvement.

Example

Generally speaking, patching walls and floors, painting, repairing roofs and gutters, fixing a furnace or air conditioner, and mending leaks would be considered repairs. Installing new flooring, roofs and gutters, furnaces, or air conditioners would be considered capital improvements.

Home Office Casualty Losses

If your home office is damaged or destroyed by a burglary or a disaster such as a hurricane, flood, fire, accident, riot, or vandalism, you may be able to deduct some of your losses as part of the home office deduction. For a detailed discussion of casualty loss deductions, see page 269.

If the loss occurs only to the home office, treat it as a "direct" expense that is fully deductible. If it applies to the entire home (such as storm damage to your roof), you can deduct a proportionate part of it as a business expense (based on your business use percentage), and the remainder as a personal expense. If the loss occurred only to the personal part of the home, you may not deduct any of it as a business expense, although you may be able to deduct it as a personal expense.

Business vs. personal loss. The rules for deducting casualty losses are more favorable for business property than for personal property.

For one thing, losses on personal property are generally subject to two thresholds: a $100 per occurrence threshold (the first $100 is not deductible at all) and a 10 percent of adjusted gross income (AGI) limit. In other words, after the first $100 is subtracted, you can only deduct the portion of the remaining loss that exceeds 10 percent of your AGI. Neither of these limits applies to casualty losses on business property.

Secondly, business casualty losses are measured using slightly different rules. For both kinds of losses, if the property is only damaged, you must take the *lower* of the decrease in the property's fair market value (FMV) as a result of the loss or the property's adjusted basis before the casualty loss. From this you subtract any insurance reimbursement, to arrive at the amount of loss. If personal property is completely destroyed, use the lower of the property's FMV or adjusted basis before the loss. But if business property is completely destroyed, use the adjusted basis before the loss minus any salvage value; the property's FMV is not considered.

In order to claim a casualty loss on your home office, you must compute the loss both ways. First, compute the amount of loss that you'd be allowed to deduct if the office was *not* used for business, using the $100 and 10 percent-of-AGI thresholds described above.

Then, compute the amount of loss on the home office as a business expense. The easiest way to compute these two amounts is to use IRS Form 4684, *Casualties and Thefts,* as a worksheet. Complete Section A as if the loss were on personal property, and then complete Section B as if the property were business.

While the amount that would be deductible as a personal loss (as shown on Section A) is always deductible as an itemized deduction, the difference between the personal loss and the business loss will only be deductible this year if your business income is sufficient to cover all your business expenses. If not, you can carry over the excess and deduct it next year.

Adjustments to basis. Your deductible casualty losses must be used to reduce your tax basis in the business portion of the home. For the year of the loss and for subsequent years, you will need to use this new basis in calculating your depreciation deductions. For more information, see IRS Publication 946, *How To Depreciate Property.*

Business Income Limitation

With most of your ordinary business expenses, if you have more expenses than you have income, your business can show a net operating loss that may be deductible against any other regular income you have (such as interest, dividends, or income from another job or business). This may even be true if the loss is a "paper loss" resulting from depreciation.

However, it is not true of the home office deduction.

Your home office deduction is limited by the amount of your net business income. If your net income is too low, you won't be able to deduct the entire amount of your home office deduction this year (although you may carry it over and deduct it in a later year when your net business income is higher).

The IRS has developed a rather lengthy computation that must be used in applying this limit, which is incorporated into Form 8829.

Basically, you must start with your gross business income from all sources (sales, interest on bank accounts, etc.), less all of your business expenses that are not part of the home office deduction. This is your tentative profit as shown on Line 29 of your Schedule C, and is the maximum amount you can claim as a home office deduction this year.

Then, subtract the portion of your home office deduction expenses that you could otherwise use as itemized deductions: home mortgage interest, real estate taxes, and casualty losses computed as if the home office was your personal residence. (If the answer is zero or a negative number, you may be better off not claiming the home office deduction, and instead claiming these amounts as regular itemized deductions. This is especially true if you think your tax bracket next year won't be higher than your bracket this year.)

Assuming the answer to the previous step was a positive number, subtract the portion of your home office deduction expenses that would not otherwise be deductible as itemized deductions: insurance, repairs and maintenance services, utilities, and rent if you don't own the home.

Finally, you may subtract the extra business portion of any casualty losses, depreciation on your home, and any carried-over home office expenses from previous years. If the end result is zero or a positive number, you can deduct all your home office expenses. If the end result is a negative number, you may carry over the nondeductible portion to be subtracted on next year's tax return.

Home Office Deduction Forms

As with most other business expenses, the way in which you claim your home office deduction depends on your employment status:

If you are self-employed. Self-employed people must fill out a special form to claim the home office

Case Study

Sylvia Pappas is employed as an outside salesperson, and she meets all the requirements for deducting expenses for a home office. In 2006, her computation of expenses for the business use of her home is as follows:

Gross income from business:	$6,000
less: direct business expenses (business phone, car expenses)	-2,000
Balance:	4,000
less: deductible mortgage interest and taxes	-3,000
Home office deduction limitation	1,000
less: other expenses for business use of home	-2,400
Balance (carried over to the next year)	-1,400

deduction. You must complete Form 8829, *Expenses for Business Use of Your Home,* and then transfer the total to your Schedule C. Unfortunately, Schedule C-EZ, which is a much simpler form, can't be used if you're claiming the home office deduction. The business portion of your home mortgage interest and real estate taxes is claimed on Form 8829 and cannot be claimed again as an itemized deduction on Schedule A of your return.

If you are an employee. Employees are not required to complete Form 8829. Your unreimbursed home office deductions are usually claimed on Form 2106, along with your other unreimbursed employee business expenses.

Then, the total of such expenses is included in your miscellaneous deductions on Schedule A of your individual income tax return. As such, they are subject to the 2 percent floor; in other words, you can deduct only the portion of all miscellaneous expenses that is more than 2 percent of your adjusted gross income.

In some cases, you might be able to avoid filing Form 2106. If your only reason for filing the form would be to claim the home office deduction, and your employer did not reimburse you for any home office expenses, you don't have to file the 2106. Instead, you can claim the deduction directly on the bottom of your Schedule A.

DEDUCTIBLE WAGES FOR EMPLOYEES

If you have employees, you can claim a tax deduction for the salary, wages, commissions, bonuses, and other compensation you pay them. In fact, it's likely that your deductions for employee compensation will be one of your largest deductible expenses.

To be deductible, the compensation must be ordinary and necessary, reasonable in amount, based on services rendered, and actually paid or incurred in the year for which the deduction is claimed (as shown by your payroll records).

The timing of your deduction will depend on whether you use the cash or accrual method of accounting. If you use the cash method, you must deduct your expense for each salary, wage, or benefit payment in the year it's paid to the employee. If you use the accrual method, you must generally deduct the expense when you establish your obligation to make the payment and when the services are performed, even if the actual paycheck is distributed later.

If the compensation is paid in some form other than cash, the deductible amount is generally equal to the fair market value of the property transferred. For example, if you give your employees gold-plated cell phones at Christmas, the cost you paid for the gifts would be deductible.

What is "reasonable" compensation to employees depends on the facts and circumstances at the time the compensation is paid. Ordinarily, the IRS will not challenge the amount of the compensation as unreasonable unless the employee has some control over the employer (e.g., is a large stockholder) or has some personal relationship with the owners.

Warning

This discussion of employees' wages does not include payments to independent contractors. The gross amount you pay an independent contractor is deductible. If, in the course of business, you pay $600 or more to an independent contractor, or you pay $600 or more in rents, services including parts and materials, or attorney fees, you must report the payment on IRS Form 1099-MISC. Give a copy to the contractor by January 31, and send a copy to the IRS by March 1. These rules generally don't apply to payments made to corporations. Form 1099-MISC is a machine-readable form, and you must use the official IRS version (call 1-800-TAX-FORM for a copy) or a pre-approved computer-generated form (software is available in most larger office supply stores).

Awards and Bonuses

You can deduct the cost of any bonuses you pay to your employees, as long as the bonus represents pay for services rather than a gift, and it's reasonable in view of the employee's services and performance.

If you're a cash method taxpayer, you must have paid the bonus before December 31, 2006 in order to deduct it in 2006.

If you're using the accrual method, you can deduct it in 2006 as long as you established the amount and the employee's right to the bonus before the end of the year – you can pay the amount in 2007 if you prefer.

Warning

There is an exception to this rule for related taxpayers: If your bonus-achieving employee is your spouse, child, brother or sister, parent or grandparent, you may only deduct the payment in the year in which the employee reports the payment as income. This means that if the recipient is using the cash method (as most individuals do), you may only deduct the bonus in the year you pay it, after all.

Awards. Employee achievement awards made under a written plan that does not discriminate in favor of highly compensated employees, and which average $400 or less during the year, are deductible as "qualified" plan awards. Other awards are considered "nonqualified" and no more than $400 in nonqualified awards can be deducted for any one employee. No more than $1,600 in total awards, both qualified and nonqualified, can be deducted for any one employee per year.

Loans or Advances

If you make a loan to an employee which you don't expect to be repaid, you can deduct the amount as compensation. If you do expect the loan to be repaid, it would not be deductible unless and until the employee defaults.

If an employee has outstanding loans over $10,000 and you are not charging interest, or you are charging interest at a rate below the applicable federal rate, you may have to report "imputed interest" income at the federal rate, and also report this imputed interest as additional compensation to the employee. You can find out the current applicable federal interest rate by calling the IRS at 1-800-TAX-1040. Consult your tax advisor for more information if you think this rule applies to you.

Vacation Pay and Unpaid Salaries

If you use the cash method, it's simple: You only deduct what you actually paid to your employees during your tax year, whether you're talking about vacation pay or that last December paycheck.

If you're on the accrual method, you may be able to deduct vacation pay or unpaid salaries before the payment is actually made, so long as the employee's right to the payment is fixed and unconditional, and the employee has done the work on which the payment is based. For example, if the employee's pay period ended on December 31 and your paychecks are issued a week later, you could deduct the amount for that last pay period of the year. Accrued vacation pay must be paid within 2½ months to come under this rule.

There is an exception to the rule for employees who are related to you – see the discussion above under "Awards and Bonuses."

Meals and Lodging

If you pay your employees in the form of food or housing, you can deduct your costs of providing these items. You would deduct them as direct costs of your business, not as employees' wages.

Example

If you rent a house for your temporary workers, you can deduct the cost of the rental payments as "rental expenses" on Line 20b of your Schedule C, not as "wages" on Line 26.

Meals provided to employees for the convenience of the employer are 100 percent deductible by the employer, but are not taxable to the employees. To be considered "for the convenience of the employer," they must be taken on the business premises. Also, if an employer provides meals to its employees on the premises, and more than one-half of the employees are receiving the meals "for the convenience of the employer," the meals will not be taxable to any of the employees and the employer can deduct the entire cost of all the meals.

The question of exactly what "convenience of the employer" means remains an unsettled question in the law. Generally, if your employees must remain on the premises in order to be available to work if needed, or if the lunch breaks are too short to allow employees to go out to eat, the meals would be considered to be for the employer's convenience.

If the meals do not meet this test, the costs of the meals would be only 50 percent deductible unless you include the value of the meals in the employee's taxable wages.

Work Smart

You can deduct the full cost, not just 50 percent, of providing an occasional social or recreational event for your employees, such as a company picnic or holiday party.

Payment of Employees' Expenses

Frequently it happens that employees pay some of your company's expenses out of their own pocket, and then ask you for reimbursement. This is often the case with car, travel, or meal expenses. How do you treat these expenses for tax purposes?

The answer is that reimbursements made under an "accountable plan" are deductible for your business, and are also excluded from the employee's gross income for payroll tax purposes. You would deduct these expenses in the Schedule C categories to which they pertain; for example, reimbursed employee travel expenses would be added to your own travel expenses on Line 24a; reimbursed meals would be reported on Line 24b etc.

However, if the reimbursements are not made under an accountable plan, you must include the reimbursements in the employee's taxable wages on IRS Form W-2. In that case, the employee must generally claim a miscellaneous itemized deduction for the allowable business expenses if he or she wants to get any tax benefits from them. You will be able to deduct the reimbursements as compensation to the employee, on Line 26 of Schedule C, "wages."

The catch is that you are required to withhold income taxes and employment taxes on reimbursements made, or considered made, under a nonaccountable plan because the reimbursements are included in the employee's taxable wages. You'll also have to pay your portion of the payroll taxes on these amounts.

Clearly, reimbursing under an accountable plan is better for both you and your employees, from a dollars-and-cents perspective. So, what is an accountable plan? A reimbursement arrangement that meets the following three requirements is considered an accountable plan:

- The reimbursements must be for your deductible business expenses that are paid or incurred by an employee in the course of performing services for you.

- The employee must be required to substantiate the amount, time, use, and business purpose of the reimbursed expenses to you. In order to do this, the employee should submit an account book, diary, log, statement of expense, trip sheet, or similar record, supporting each of these elements, that is recorded at or near the time of the expenditure. The records should include any supporting documentary evidence, such as receipts. An employee who receives a mileage allowance is considered to have substantiated the amount of the expenses if the employee substantiates the time, place (or use), and business purpose of the travel.

- The employee must be required to return to you any excess of reimbursements over substantiated expenses within a reasonable period of time.

How long is a "reasonable period?" The IRS will generally accept your plan if the employee is required to provide substantiation within 60 days or return unsubstantiated amounts within 120 days after an expense is paid or incurred. Again, you can use a mileage allowance — *even one that exceeds the 2006 standard mileage rate of 44.5 cents per mile* — and if it is reasonably calculated not to exceed the employee's actual or anticipated expenses, it will be treated as meeting this return requirement even if the employee does not have to return the excess of the allowance over the standard mileage rate.

Save Money

While having an accountable plan is not required, the fact that you won't have to pay FICA on these amounts could make it a real moneysaver in the long run, depending on how many employees you have and the extent to which reimbursement plays a part in your business.

Salaries of Owners

Sole proprietorships may deduct wages paid to employees, but the owner of the business is not considered an employee and the owner's salary or draw is not deductible. All the net profits of the business are taxable income to the owner, and self-employment tax applies to the entire amount (see page 135).

Claiming Deductions for Wages and Benefits

Generally, the value of wages and salaries you pay to your employees is reported on Line 26 of Schedule C. Payments for employee benefit plans are reported separately. Retirement plan contributions are reported on Line 19, and your contributions for all other employee benefit plans are reported on Line 14.

However, if you are a manufacturer, the wages and benefits of production workers, indirect factory workers, and supervisors must be included in your cost of good sold, as discussed on page 51.

Finally, your payments of payroll taxes such as FICA, FUTA, and state unemployment taxes are reported on Schedule C, Line 23, "taxes and licenses."

Warning

You should be aware that if you have employees, you will have some additional tax obligations because of them. You'll need to withhold and/or pay federal, state, and perhaps local income taxes; Social Security and Medicare taxes; federal and state unemployment taxes; and, in some states, disability insurance taxes. All of these payroll taxes must be paid over to the various government agencies, along with employment tax returns; for small employers this is generally done on a quarterly basis. You'll also need to give each employee a W-2 form at the end of the year, detailing their pay and the amounts deducted.

Payroll tax reporting is beyond the scope of this book. For more information, some good references are the CCH Business Owner's Toolkit at www.toolkit.cch.com and the IRS's free Publication 15, Employer's Tax Guide.

EMPLOYEE BENEFIT PLANS

Employee benefits can be considered a special type of fringe benefits – benefits that provide things for employees that, if they purchased them for themselves, would normally be considered personal or family expenses.

You can generally deduct the *cost* of providing benefits such as accident and health plans, group-term life insurance, adoption assistance, dependent care assistance, educational assistance, and welfare benefit funds. These costs would be deductible on the "employee benefits" line (Line 14) of Schedule C.

Note that the issue here is different from the issue of whether the benefit is taxable to the employee for purposes of computing payroll taxes. For payroll tax purposes, some types of benefits are not taxable to the employee for purposes of FICA or income tax withholding, and they are not taxable to you as the employer for FICA or FUTA tax purposes. Common examples of this are health insurance, qualified retirement plan contributions, and group-term life insurance up to $50,000. However, the cost of providing these benefits is deductible by the employer.

Fringe benefits that are not specifically excluded from employees' income under the tax laws must be included in the employee's taxable income, at their value. This is also true when the benefits are of a type that would be excludible if they met all the federal requirements, but for some reason your plan does not meet the requirements. For instance, some types of benefit plans are not permitted to discriminate in favor of highly compensated employees such as the business owners. If the plans do discriminate, the value of the benefits will generally be taxable compensation to the highly compensated employees who receive them. However, the cost of the benefit is still deductible to your business.

Life Insurance

The cost of group-term life insurance coverage up to $50,000 per employee is deductible on the "employee benefits" line of your Schedule C, unless you are directly or indirectly a beneficiary of the policy. Life insurance on yourself as the business owner is not deductible on your Schedule C.

Health Insurance

Group health benefits that you provide to employees and their dependents are generally deductible. Beginning in 2003, the cost of your own benefits under the plan is also 100 percent deductible.

Unless you operate in Hawaii, there are no federal or state laws that require you to have a health plan. However, if you do have a health plan, your plan must meet certain federal requirements or be subject to punitive excise taxes.

To avoid these excise taxes, your plan must include certain accessibility and portability features, most notably those that impose strict limits on the extent to which preexisting health conditions of employees or their dependents can be used to limit coverage. You must provide COBRA benefits to employees who lose coverage under the plan – that is, you must continue to allow them to purchase coverage at their own expense for up to 18 or 36 months, depending on the reason for the loss of coverage. COBRA coverage is not required, however, if you have fewer than 20 employees.

Work Smart

If you haven't spoken to your insurance representative recently, we suggest you contact him or her to be sure your plan provides the required coverage.

Health Insurance for the Owner

Since 2003, health insurance premiums are completely deductible for sole proprietors, partners, LLC members, and S corporation shareholders owning more than 2 percent of the shares. Previously, only a portion of a self-employed individual's health insurance premiums could be deducted.

Health insurance premiums for yourself and your dependents are deductible on the first page of your Form 1040 (Line 29), rather than on the Schedule C.

As a result, the cost of the premiums serve to reduce your adjusted gross income (AGI), which in turn can increase your ability to take advantage of certain tax breaks like Roth IRAs and tax breaks for education. Since the premiums are not considered an itemized medical deduction, they are not limited by the 7.5 percent of AGI floor, as are most medical deductions.

Medical Savings Accounts (MSAs)

Under an IRS pilot program that has been extended through the end of 2005, employees of small businesses and self-employed individuals can set up Archer Medical Savings Accounts (MSAs) to pay health care expenses, provided the accounts are used in connection with high-deductible health insurance. After 2005, no new MSAs may be established, but contributions to existing Archer MSAs may continue (nonactive employees of participating employers would also be eligible for an Archer MSA contribution).

MSAs are similar to IRAs in the sense that each employee (including the small business owner) can make tax-free contributions to an account. But instead of withdrawing the funds at retirement as you would with an IRA, you withdraw them to pay for certain types of medical care. In effect, you're being allowed to pay some of your medical costs with pre-tax dollars, which is a lot cheaper than paying for it with post-tax dollars.

Any unused money in the account is allowed to accumulate from year to year, to be used in later years when medical expenses are higher or to be saved until retirement.

Here's how MSAs work. A business may offer its employees, or a self-employed person may purchase, a high-deductible health insurance plan (often referred to as a "catastrophic health plan"). For 2006, the deductible must be a minimum of $1,800 for individual coverage and $3,650 for family coverage, and can be as high as $2,700 for an individual and $5,450 for a family (these amounts are indexed for inflation periodically). The employer and employee may then make tax-free contributions to an MSA. Total annual contributions are limited to 65 percent of the deductible for individuals and 75 percent of the deductible for families.

Contributions. Contributions to the account by an individual are deductible from gross income, and contributions made by an individual's employer are excluded from income (unless they are made through a cafeteria plan). Contributions may be made for a tax year at any time until the due date of the return for that year (not including extensions). Employer contributions must be reported on the employee's W-2. Earnings of the fund are not included in taxable income for the current year.

Withdrawals. Funds may then be withdrawn from the MSA, tax-free, to pay for minor medical expenses — routine checkups, dental exams, eyeglasses, drugs, even minor surgery. Any funds that are left in the MSA at the end of the year remain in the account, and can be used in succeeding years, or saved until retirement. Thus, unlike flexible spending accounts, there is no "use it or lose it" requirement.

If you have few medical expenses over a period of years, the account may grow to a tidy sum. If funds are withdrawn for nonmedical purposes, a 15 percent penalty will be assessed (plus the funds will be taxed as ordinary income). However, after age 65 or if you become disabled, you may use your MSA monies for any purpose, just like an IRA, and pay only the tax on withdrawn funds.

Reporting MSA contributions. The health insurance feature of the MSA would be treated like any other health insurance: Benefits you pay for your employees are reported as employee benefits on Line 14 of the Schedule C, and your own benefits would be included on Line 29 of your Form 1040.

If you make contributions to your employee's MSA accounts (i.e., other than what they voluntarily have deducted from their paychecks), you must do so at a uniform rate or dollar amount. If so, you can deduct the contributions as employee benefits on Line 14 of the Schedule C.

Contributions you make to your own MSA are reported on a special IRS Form 8853, *Archer MSAs and Long-Term Care Insurance Contracts,* and the deductible amount is transferred to Line 29 of your Form 1040.

Long-Term Care Insurance

Long-term health care contracts are relatively new arrangements designed to provide coverage if you become chronically ill or disabled after reaching a specified age, such as 50. Long-term care policies greatly expand the time period over which benefits will be paid out, when compared to standard accident and health policies. Another advantage is that, unlike Medicare coverage, long-term care contracts will cover the cost of custodial care, as well as skilled nursing care. These two advantages often make long-term care contracts a preferred way of pre-funding nursing home care for the elderly.

If certain specified requirements are met, long-term care insurance contracts issued after December 31, 1996 will generally receive the same income tax treatment as accident and health policies.

That means that amounts received under a long-term care insurance contract are nontaxable, although the exclusion is capped at $250 per day on *per diem* contracts in 2006 and $260 per day in 2007 (this amount is adjusted annually for inflation). It also means that company-paid premiums for long-term care are not taxable for the employee. If you purchase the policy as an individual rather than through your company, the premiums count as deductible medical expenses.

Employer-provided long-term care premiums are deductible by the employer as employee benefits. For the business owner, they are treated as health insurance premiums, which means that, from 2003, they are also 100 percent deductible.

Retirement Plans for the Self-Employed

Before 1963, sole proprietors and partnerships were allowed to have qualified pension and profit-sharing plans for their employees, but the owners of these businesses could not get the tax benefits of the plans. The only way to get the maximum retirement plan tax benefits for the owner was to incorporate.

The Self-Employed Individuals Tax Retirement Act of 1962 (also called HR-10 or the Keogh Act) and its later amendments made it possible for owner-employees of unincorporated businesses and other self-employed persons to be covered under qualified retirement plans. Over the years, this tax-favored treatment for retirement plans was extended to individuals not covered by other private qualified retirement plans, and made available through Individual Retirement Accounts (IRAs) and Simplified Employee Pension (SEP) plans.

As a self-employed business owner, your major pension options are:

- Keogh plans
- Simplified Employee Pensions (SEPs)
- SIMPLE plans
- Individual Retirement Accounts (IRAs) (discussed on page 251)

Keogh Plans

Generally, a Keogh plan is a defined benefit or a defined contribution retirement plan set up by a self-employed person or partnership. The plan must meet the same eligibility and coverage requirements, contribution limits, vesting requirements, rules for integration with Social Security, and other plan requirements, as any qualified retirement plan covering corporate employees.

If you have employees, they must be allowed to participate in the Keogh plan. Also, an individual who has another job during the day, but decides to supplement his or her income by turning a weekend avocation into a business, is eligible to open a Keogh plan based on the net earnings derived from the part-time self-employment.

Warning

It's important to remember that to take a deduction for contributions to a Keogh plan on behalf of yourself, you must have some net earnings – you cannot use Keogh plan contributions to create a business loss.

Qualified plans. These plans are those that meet the requirements of the Employee Retirement Income Security Act of 1974 (ERISA) and the federal tax laws, and qualify for four significant tax benefits.

1. The income generated by the plan assets is not subject to income tax, because the income is earned and managed within the framework of a tax-exempt trust.
2. An employer is entitled to a current tax deduction for contributions to the plan.
3. The plan participants (the employees or their beneficiaries) do not have to pay income tax on the amounts contributed on their behalf until the year the funds are distributed to them by the employer.
4. Under the right circumstances, beneficiaries of qualified plan distributions are afforded special tax treatment.

Nonqualified plans. These plans are those not meeting the ERISA guidelines and the requirement of the federal tax laws. They do not get all of the preferential tax treatment of qualified plans, but employers may still deduct contributions to these plans, generally at the time that employees become vested in the benefits. Nonqualified plans are usually designed to provide deferred compensation exclusively for one or more executives.

Requirements for Qualified Plans

To satisfy the general requirements, a qualified plan must be permanent, meaning it cannot have a planned expiration date. Although the employer may reserve the right to change or terminate the plan or to discontinue operations, abandoning the plan for any reason other than business necessity within a few years is evidence that the plan was not a bona fide program from its inception.

The plan must be a definite written program that is communicated to all employees. All plan assets must be held in trust by one or more trustees. The plan must be for the exclusive benefit of the employees and their beneficiaries. Assets can't revert to the employer, except for forfeitures (for example, if an employee leaves before vesting in benefits). Funding can be provided from employer or employee contributions, or both.

Participation/coverage rules. To meet the minimum standards, at least a certain percentage of the non-highly-compensated employees must be covered by the plan and a certain number of those covered employees must actually be in the plan. The plan cannot discriminate in favor of employees who are officers, shareholders, or highly compensated, by making larger contributions on their behalf or providing them with better benefits. The plan may condition eligibility on age and service, but generally cannot postpone participation beyond the date the employee attains the age of 21 and the date on which the employee completes one year of service.

Vesting rules. The process of acquiring a nonforfeitable right to the money being set aside for you is called vesting, and means that you have to stick around in order to earn full benefits. There are two permitted vesting methods: five-year cliff vesting in which the participant becomes fully vested after five years of service (with zero vesting in the first four years) and seven-year gradual vesting in which the participant becomes increasingly vested (usually 20 percent per year) after three years of service. Although the employer can have vesting rules more lenient than these, the rules cannot be more restrictive. An employee must become fully vested no later than the normal retirement age specified in the plan. The plan must also provide rules on how breaks in service affect vesting rights.

Beginning in 2002, an accelerated vesting schedule applies to employer matching contributions to a defined contribution plan. An employer may choose either a three-year cliff vesting schedule, which provides 100 percent vesting after three years of employee service, or a two- to six-year graded vesting schedule, with 20 percent being vested after two years of service and each year thereafter.

When an employee leaves your business, you may "cash out" the employee's pension benefits if the vested portion of the benefits is equal to or less than $5,000. Starting in 2002, when the cash out amount is over $1,000, the distribution must automatically be rolled over directly to an IRA account designated by the employer unless the employee elects to have the distribution go elsewhere (i.e. another IRA, another qualified plan, or directly in the employee's pocket). This rule is intended to limit the temptation for employees to squander retirement savings when a cash out distribution occurs.

Required communications. Each year the employer must furnish a document called a Summary Plan Description, written in plain English understandable to the average plan participant, detailing the amount of pension benefits, requirements for receiving those payments, and any conditions that might prevent someone from receiving them.

Integration with Social Security. Many companies integrate their pension schemes with Social Security. This integration reduces your employer-provided pension benefit by a percentage of the amount of your Social Security benefit. The employer argues that since it must pay over 7 percent in Social Security taxes and also fund the pension program, without integration it is supporting two pension systems. However, although a certain degree of integration is allowed by law, an employee must be guaranteed at least 50 percent of the pension he or she earned when Social Security is merged with the pension.

Example

If your employer-provided pension benefit is $2,000 per month and your Social Security benefit is $1,200 per month, the amount you will actually receive from your employer must be at least $1,400 [$2,000-(50 percent x $1,200) = $1,400]. Your total monthly income may be as low as $2,600 [$1,200 Social Security + $1,400 pension], not the $3,200 you might have anticipated.

Retirement plans (including Keogh plans) are also divisible into the following broad categories: defined benefit plans, defined contribution plans and hybrid plans.

Defined Benefit Plans

A defined benefit plan is one set up to provide a predetermined retirement benefit to employees or their beneficiaries, either as a certain dollar amount each month, or a percentage of compensation.

Employer contributions to a defined benefit plan are very complex to determine and require the work of an actuary. The assets of the plan are held in a pool, rather than individual accounts for each employee, and as a result, the employees have no voice in investment decisions. Once the plan is established, the employer must continue to fund it, even if the company has no profits in a given year. Since the employer makes a specific promise to pay a certain sum in the future, it is the employer who assumes the risk of fluctuations in the value of the investment pool.

There are three basic types of defined benefit plans:

- **Flat benefit plan** — All participants receive a flat dollar amount as long as a predetermined minimum years requirement has been met.

Example

A plan might pay 20 percent of average compensation for the last five years, or $500 per month, to each retiree with at least 10 years of service.

- **Unit benefit plan** — The benefit is either a percentage of compensation or a fixed dollar amount multiplied by the number of qualifying years of service.

Example

A plan might provide a benefit of 2 percent of the average compensation of the employee's five highest consecutive years, or a $20 monthly retirement benefit, for each year of service.

- **Variable benefit plan** — Benefits are based on allocating units, rather than dollars, to the contributions to the plan. At retirement, the value of the units allocated to the retiring employee would be the proportionate value of all units in the fund.

The maximum annual contribution you can make in 2006 to a defined benefit plan is one that would be projected to yield a benefit equal to the lesser of $175,000 ($180,000 in 2007) or 100 percent of the participant's average compensation for the three highest consecutive years.

Very few defined benefit plans provide for the benefits to be adjusted each year to reflect the effects of inflation (called the Cost of Living Adjustment, or COLA), so over the years of your retirement, the value or purchasing power of your benefits may shrink considerably.

The Pension Benefit Guarantee Corporation (PBGC). With a defined benefit plan the employer is legally required to make sure there is enough money in the plan to pay the guaranteed benefits. If the company fails to meet its obligation, the federal government steps in. Defined benefit plans are the only type of pension insured by the PBGC. The insurance works similarly to the federal deposit insurance that backs up your bank accounts. If your plan is covered and the sponsoring company goes bust, PBGC will take over benefit payments up to a maximum amount. The insurance protection helps make your pension more secure, but it is not a full guarantee that you will get what you expected.

Defined Contribution Plans

Defined contribution plans, which are less expensive and more flexible than defined benefit plans, are actually a broad range of programs including profit-sharing plans, money-purchase plans, 401(k) plans, and others. Either you alone, or you and your employee, make contributions into the plan, usually based on a percentage of the employee's annual earnings.

Each participant has an individual, separate account. There is no way to determine in advance what the final payout at retirement will be. Each employee's benefits depend on how much was contributed in his or her name and how well the pension fund investments performed. So, the risk of fluctuations in investment return is shifted to the employees.

The government sets a limit on how much can be contributed in your name each year no matter how many different plans you participate in. The total amount that can be contributed in one employee's name in 2006 is the lesser of $44,000 ($45,000 in 2007) or 100 percent of compensation.

Contributions are allocated to separate accounts for each participant based on a definite, predetermined formula. Contributions by self-employed persons are treated like those made on behalf of employees, except the tax deductions may be limited. Forfeitures can be reallocated to remaining participants.

Profit-sharing plans. Profit-sharing plans are now the most popular type of plan, especially for small businesses. They offer the greatest flexibility in contributions and are simple to administer. Initially developed to encourage hard work and loyalty, the plans encourage companies to set aside money in the employees' names when the company shows a profit. In 2006, the employer has the discretion to contribute up to the lesser of $44,000 ($45,000 in 2007) or 25 percent of compensation for each plan participant. For yourself, however, the applicable percentage limit is only 20 percent. The employer may decide *not* to contribute in any given year, if it so desires.

Money-purchase plans. In a money-purchase plan, the employer is obligated to contribute each year even if the company didn't make a profit. The contributions are determined by a specific percentage of each employee's compensation and must be made annually. In 2006, the employer may contribute up to the lesser of $44,000 ($45,000 in 2007) or 100 percent of each employee's compensation. You, as the business owner, may contribute and take a tax deduction in 2006 for the lesser of $44,000 ($45,000 in 2007) or 20 percent of your net earnings.

401(k) plans. Many qualified defined contribution plans permit participating employees to make contributions to a plan, so they can save for retirement on a before-tax basis. The employees authorize their employer to reduce their salary and contribute the salary reduction on their behalf to a qualified retirement plan.

In addition to the employees' elective deferrals, an employer can make supplemental contributions on behalf of employees. These employer contributions can be subject to a vesting schedule, but the employees' own contributions must be nonforfeitable.

The employee's elective deferral to all 401(k) plans is limited to $15,000 for 2006 ($15,500 for 2007), and the employer contribution is also subject to separate, complex limitations. Generally, withdrawals from 401(k) plans are not permitted before age $59^1/_2$ unless the employee retires, dies, becomes disabled, changes jobs, or suffers a financial hardship as defined by Internal Revenue Service regulations. 401(k) plans are often offered in combination with other plans, such as profit-sharing plans.

Save Money

While 401(k) plans are popular with large corporate employers, they are not the most popular plans for small business owners since they severely limit the amount of money a business owner can sock away on his own behalf. If you're going to the trouble and expense of setting up a pension plan, a money-purchase plan would generally offer you more flexibility and the opportunity to defer tax on a much larger nest egg.

Setting up a Keogh plan

To qualify for tax deductions, the Keogh plan must be in writing and must be communicated to the employees. Most Keogh plans follow a standard form (a master or prototype plan) approved by the Internal Revenue Service, and provided by the bank or financial services company that administers the plan. If you prefer, you can set up an individually designed plan to meet specific needs, but you will usually need the help of a professional in doing so. You can set up a trust or custodial account to invest the funds, or buy a contract from an insurance company.

Reporting Keogh Contributions

Contributions made for employees to a Keogh are reported on Line 19 of Schedule C, "Pension and profit-sharing plans." Contributions made on your own behalf would be reported on Line 28 of your Form 1040.

There are also reporting requirements with regard to the Keogh plan itself. Generally, an annual report on IRS Form 5500 must be filed with the IRS by the last day of the 7th month after the close of the plan year. Single-participant plans can use form 5500-EZ. See the instructions for these forms (available from the IRS by calling 1-800-TAX-FORM, or at their website http://www.irs.gov) or see your professional tax advisor.

Tax Organizer Tip

Contributions you make for employees should be entered as a business expense on the "Business" pages of the "Employment" tab. Answer "Yes" to the question, "Did you have any operating expenses?" When you select "Continue" you will be taken to a page where you can enter this expense. Contributions made on your own behalf should be entered on the "Retirement" tab of CompleteTax.

Simplified Employee Pensions (SEPs)

A simplified employee pension (SEP) is a written arrangement that allows an employer to make contributions toward his or her own and employees' retirement without becoming involved in more complex retirement plans. Contributions are made to special IRAs (SEP-IRA) set up for each individual qualifying employee.

An employer can use IRS Form 5305-SEP to satisfy the written arrangement requirement for a SEP. A SEP can be established at any time during the year, or up to the original due date of the tax return for the year (April 15th for most people). Contributions to the SEP for a given year must be made by the due date of the income tax return, including any extensions, for that tax year.

If you have a SEP plan in place, you don't have to make any contributions to the plan in any given year. But, if you do make contributions for a year, the contributions must be based on a written allocation formula (for example, "2 percent of each employee's pay") and must not discriminate in favor of highly compensated employees.

For 2006, the SEP rules permit an employer to contribute, and deduct, an annual maximum of 25 percent of the employee's compensation or $44,000 ($45,000 in 2007), whichever is less, to each participating employee's account. For the business owner, however, the contribution limit is lower. The business owner's maximum contribution is the net earnings of the business, minus the deduction for one-half the self-employment tax, multiplied by a percentage that is somewhat lower than the percentage used to compute the employees' contribution. For example, if your employees were receiving the maximum contribution of 25 percent of pay, you would have to use 20 percent. If your employees receive 15 percent, your percentage would be 13.0435. You can compute your percentage for other rates by taking the employees' rate, expressed as a decimal, and dividing it by that rate plus one.

Example

If the employees' rate was 10.5 percent, you could compute the owner's rate by dividing 0.105 by 1.105 to arrive at .0950, or 9½ percent.

Prior to 1997, an employer could establish a Salary Reduction Arrangement SEP (SARSEP) under which employees could elect to make contributions out of their own pay, up to a certain dollar limit per year, per employee. This choice is called an elective deferral. Although new SARSEPs can no longer be set up, you may continue to make contributions to a SARSEP that was established before 1997. For 2006, the dollar limit for each employee's elective deferrals is $15,000 ($15,500 in 2007).

SIMPLE Plans

Employers with 100 or fewer employees who received at least $5,000 in compensation during the preceding year can adopt a relatively new type of simplified retirement plan, the Savings Incentive Match Plan for Employees (SIMPLE plan). If you want to establish a SIMPLE, it must be the only retirement plan you have — if you've already established another plan, you'd have to terminate it or convert it to a SIMPLE.

The plan allows employees to make elective contributions of up to $10,000 in 2006 ($10,500 in 2007), and requires employers to make matching contributions on a dollar-for-dollar basis, up to 3 percent of each employee's pay. Alternately, you can decide to make "nonelective" contributions of 2 percent of each participating employee's pay regardless of whether they make any elective contributions. When figuring matching contributions, no more than $220,000 of an employee's 2006 compensation can be taken into account ($225,000 in 2007).

Assets in the account are not taxed until they are distributed to an employee, and employers may generally deduct contributions to employees' accounts. In addition, the SIMPLE plan is not subject to the nondiscrimination rules or other complex requirements applicable to qualified plans, mainly because the contributions to each employee's account must follow exactly the same formula.

SIMPLE plans may be structured as an IRA or as a 401(k) plan. All contributions to an employee's SIMPLE account must be nonforfeitable. If a SIMPLE plan is adopted, it must be open to every employee who is reasonably expected to receive at least $5,000 in compensation during the current year and received at least $5,000 in compensation from the employer during any two preceding years. Self-employed individuals are also eligible to establish a SIMPLE plan.

Distributions from a SIMPLE account are generally taxed like distributions from an IRA. Participants may roll over distributions from one SIMPLE account to another free of tax. In addition, a participant may roll over a distribution from a SIMPLE account to an IRA without penalty if the individual has participated in the SIMPLE plan for at least two years. Participants who take early withdrawals from a SIMPLE account before age $59^{1}/_{2}$ are generally subject to the 10 percent early withdrawal penalty. However, employees who withdraw contributions during the two-year period beginning on the date that they first began participating in the SIMPLE plan will be assessed a 25 percent penalty tax.

Deducting SIMPLE Contributions

Contributions for employees to a SIMPLE plan would be reported on Line 19 of your Schedule C, as a "pension and profit sharing plan." Contributions for yourself are reported on Line 28 of your Form 1040. There are also reporting requirements associated with setting up and maintaining the plan itself; see IRS Publication 560, *Retirement Plans for Small Business,* for more details.

Catch-Up Contributions

Those who are age 50 and older and participate in a retirement plan may elect to save even more each year to their employer's plan by making "catch-up contributions." Qualified participants in a 401(k) or SEP plan may save an additional $5,000 in 2006 and 2007. Participants in a SIMPLE plan who meet the age threshold can save an extra $2,500 in 2006 and 2007.

Chapter 7

Capital Assets and Depreciation

Almost every business must invest in some major equipment, vehicles, machinery, or furniture in order to operate. Some businesses will require assets such as land, a building, patents, or franchise rights. Major assets that will be used in your business for more than a year are known as "capital assets" and are subject to special treatment under the tax laws. Most importantly, you generally can't deduct the entire cost of acquiring such an asset in the year you acquire it.

Why not? Because one of the goals of accounting is to accurately measure a business's gross income, expenses, and net income (earnings) during a given period of time, usually a year. If a business were allowed to reduce one year's gross income by an expense deduction for the total cost of an item that will be used for several years, the result would be an understatement of earnings in the year the asset was purchased, and an overstatement of earnings during the following years.

It follows that, for "capital assets" (assets that have a useful life of more than one year), the cost must be written off (that is, depreciated or amortized) over more than one year.

Theoretically, the cost of an asset should be deducted over the number of years that the asset will be used, according to the actual drop in value that the asset will suffer each year. At the end of each year, you could subtract all depreciation claimed to date from the cost of the asset, to arrive at the asset's "book value," which would be equal to its market value. At the end of the asset's useful life for the business, any undepreciated portion would represent the salvage value for which the asset could be sold or scrapped.

Since the actual drop in value of each business asset would be difficult and time-consuming to compute (if indeed it could be computed at all), accountants use a variety of conventions to approximate and standardize the depreciation process.

For example, the straight-line method assumes that the asset depreciates by an equal percentage of its original value for each year that it's used. In contrast, the declining balance method assumes that the asset depreciates more in the earlier years. The following table compares the depreciation amounts that would be available under these two methods, for an asset that cost $1,000, and is expected to be used for five years and then sold for $100 in scrap.

	Straight-Line Method		Declining-Balance Method	
Year	*Annual Depreciation*	*Year-End Book Value*	*Annual Depreciation*	*Year-End Book Value*
1	$900 x 20% = **$180**	$1,000 - $180 = **$820**	$1,000 x 40% = **$400**	$1,000 - $400 = **$600**
2	$900 x 20% = **$180**	$820 - $180 = **$640**	$600 x 40% = **$240**	$600 - $240 = **$360**
3	$900 x 20% = **$180**	$640 - $180 = **$460**	$360 x 40% = **$144**	$360 - $144 = **$216**
4	$900 x 20% = **$180**	$460 - $180 = **$280**	$216 x 40% = **$86.40**	$216 - $86.40 = **$129.60**
5	$900 x 20% = **$180**	$280 - $180 = **$100**	$129.60 x 40% = **$51.84**	$129.60 - $51.84 = **$77.76**

As you can see, the straight-line method results in the same deduction amount every year, while the declining-balance method results in larger deductions in the first years and much smaller deductions in the last two years. One implication of this system is that if the equipment is expected to be sold for a higher value at some point in the middle of its life, the declining balance method can result in a greater taxable gain that year because the book value of the asset will be relatively lower.

You Must Follow the Rules

Most people realize that if they claim more depreciation than they're entitled to, they may suffer penalties in a tax audit. What you may not know is that if you *don't* claim all the depreciation deductions that you're entitled to, you will still be treated as having claimed them when it comes time to compute your taxable gain or loss upon sale or disposal of the asset.

In some cases, the IRS gives you a choice between two or more different methods, but you must choose one of them — you can't create your own system.

Example

You can't choose to depreciate your computer over three years, when the IRS mandates a five-year period, even though you may know your particular computer will be obsolete and replaced within three years.

If you make a mistake and claim the wrong depreciation amount, you can generally file an amended tax return (Form 1040X) for the year at issue, and correct your deduction. However, if you make the same mistake for two or more consecutive tax years and the mistake is not a simple math error (for example, you realize that you've been using the wrong table), you've effectively chosen an accounting method, and you cannot correct the mistake by filing an amended return. Instead, you must file IRS Form 3115 requesting permission to change accounting methods.

Tax Organizer Tip

To add tax basis and depreciation information, use the "Business" sub-tab on the "Employment" tab in CompleteTax. For assets used in your trade or business, answer "Yes" to the question, "Did you have any depreciable assets related to this business?" As you continue forward, you will open a page that allows you to enter your information. For assets used in your home office, answer "Yes" to the question, "Did you use part of your home exclusively for business?" As you continue forward, you will add information for your home that will include a page for your home office depreciation information.

Which Assets Can Be Depreciated?

In general, property that you own can be depreciated if it meets all of the following requirements:

- It is used in a trade or business (which is the focus of our discussion here), or held for the production of income as investment property.
- It has a finite period of usefulness in your

business that can be estimated with some confidence, and that is longer than one year.

- It wears out, decays, gets used up, becomes obsolete, or loses value from natural causes.

Examples of depreciable assets are cars, computers, office furniture, machines, buildings, and significant additions or improvements to these kinds of property.

See page 59 regarding the distinction between improvements, which must be depreciated, and repairs, which can be fully deducted when made.

Which Assets Are Not Depreciable?

Land is probably the most commonly encountered property that is *not* depreciable. As a rule you can only "recover" the cost of land when you eventually sell it, at which point you'll subtract the cost from the sales price to determine your taxable gain. So, when you purchase a business building and the land on which the building is situated, the cost of the land must be subtracted from the total cost of the property. Only then can you determine the depreciation expense for the building itself.

The costs of clearing, grading, planting, landscaping, or demolishing buildings on land are not depreciable, but are added to the tax basis of the land, so they can reduce your taxable gains on the property when it comes time to sell.

Depreciation is not allowed on personal assets, such as a residence used by you and your family, or an automobile or boat used for pleasure purposes only. If an asset is used partly for personal purposes and partly for business, only the portion of the asset used for business purposes is depreciable.

Other items that are not depreciable are inventory and property you lease or rent from others. However, if you pay for some permanent improvements on property that you lease (for example, you remodel your leased office or store), you can depreciate the cost of the improvements.

Amortizable Assets

Some business assets are not depreciable, but the costs can be recovered through amortization; that is, they can be deducted in a series of equal amounts over a specified period of time. An example of this is the cost of starting your business, which can be deducted over a period of 60 months after the business begins to operate (see page 61).

Intangible assets purchased after August 10, 1993, including agreements not to compete, franchise rights, business licenses, and patents, copyrights, trademarks, trade names, business goodwill, and going concern value that are acquired as part of the acquisition of a substantial portion of a business, must be amortized over the course of 15 years. Most intangible assets acquired before that date cannot be amortized at all; others, such as patents and copyrights, agreements not to compete, designs and patterns, franchises, and customer or subscriber lists, must be depreciated using the straight-line method over their useful life.

Off-the-shelf computer software purchased after August 10, 1993 must be amortized over 36 months from the date of purchase (However, beginning in 2003 through 2007, off-the-shelf computer software may be expensed in the first year of service—see page 105). Customized software purchased after that date must be amortized over a 15-year period.

For software purchased before August 11, 1993, if it was purchased as part of a computer, the software should have been treated as part of the computer and depreciated as a single asset; if you purchased the software separately you could depreciate it using the straight-line method over five years (or a shorter period if you could prove that its usefulness was less than five years).

As a general rule, any intangible assets created by your business (rather than purchased from someone else) cannot be depreciated or amortized.

Depreciable Value of an Asset

The starting point to determine how much depreciation you can claim on a business asset is a value for the asset known as its "tax basis." Usually, the tax basis is equal to the asset's purchase price, minus any discounts and plus any sales taxes, delivery charges, installation fees, or other acquisition costs.

Example

If you bought a piece of machinery priced at $1,000, you paid 8 percent in sales tax, and it cost $200 to deliver the item, the tax basis would be $1,280 and that's the amount that you could write off as depreciation over the life of the asset.

For real estate, you can also include costs of legal and accounting fees, revenue stamps, recording fees, title abstracts/insurance, surveys, and real estate taxes assumed for the seller. Some special rules apply where you trade in business equipment; see page 103.

If you acquire property by gift, the tax basis for depreciation will be the same as the donor's basis at the time of the gift.

If you convert personal property to business use, the basis will be the *lower* of (a) the fair market value at the time of the conversion, or (b) the cost plus any additions or improvements, and minus any deducted casualty losses, up to the time of the conversion.

Partly Depreciable Assets

Things aren't always so simple. What if, for a single purchase price, you purchase an asset that is only partly depreciable? What you need to do is to allocate the price between the depreciable part and the nondepreciable part.

Example

Raymond Anthony buys some real estate for use in his auto repair business for $100,000. On the lot is a building that was formerly used as a gas station. Considering the size and location of the property, and the size and repair of the building, a fair allocation of the price paid for the property might be $70,000 for the building and $30,000 for the land.

In this example, the $70,000 paid for the building could be recovered through depreciation, while the $30,000 paid for the land could not, because land is not depreciable. But wouldn't it be better to allocate as much as possible to the building (say, $90,000), so Ray's depreciation deductions would be greater and his tax bill would be lower?

Absolutely, but you can expect the IRS to attack your allocation if it doesn't reflect economic reality.

If an IRS auditor raises objections, you may need to bring in a real estate appraisal to support the allocation you use. In some states, real estate tax bills will show a separate assessment for the buildings and the land on a piece of property, which can be useful evidence in an IRS audit. Ideally, the allocation should have been made as part of the sales contract in which you originally acquired the property, and you should be prepared to prove that the allocation was a part of good faith negotiations between yourself and the seller.

If you acquire a number of assets at the same time (for example, you acquire a number of business assets in the course of buying a business), you need to allocate the purchase price among the various assets you purchased. The IRS provides special rules for doing this — consult your tax advisor for more details.

Mixed-Use Property

You also need to make an allocation if you have a single asset that is used partly for business and partly for personal purposes; for example, if you have a home office, or a car that you use sometimes for work and sometimes for family driving.

You will need to allocate the cost of the asset according to the percentage of usage that is strictly for business. For example, if 20 percent of the square footage of your home is used as an office, you may be able to depreciate 20 percent of the cost of the home (see page 84); if 60 percent of the mileage you drive in your car is for business purposes, you may be able to depreciate 60 percent of the cost of the car (see page 113).

For other business assets, the allocation would ordinarily be based on the amount of time you used the asset for business, compared to the amount of time you used it for personal or family purposes.

Example

Although you don't qualify for the home office deduction, you have a computer at home on which you keep a backup copy of your accounting records, and which you use for other business purposes in the evenings. You also use the computer to keep track of your investments, surf the Internet, send and receive social E-mail, etc. Your computer time log (see page 113) shows that you've spent approximately 10 hours per week on the computer for business reasons, and approximately 5 hours per week for other purposes. Therefore, you can depreciate 2/3 of the cost of the computer.

Adjustments to the Basis

If, like most taxpayers, you use the standard depreciation charts to compute your depreciation expense each year, your tax basis for the asset at the time you begin depreciating it will generally remain the same. You will multiply your original basis by a fraction that may change each year. For an example of how this works, see page 110.

In addition to the *original* basis of the asset, you may also need to know your *adjusted* basis if you sell, trade or dispose of the asset, or suffer a casualty loss.

Once you've claimed some depreciation on a piece of business property, the depreciation would be deducted from the cost to arrive at the adjusted basis. It's important that you (or your accountant) keep capital asset records that include the amount of accumulated depreciation you've claimed for each asset over the years, so you can easily compute the adjusted basis when the need arises. You can use the depreciation worksheet on page 104 to keep track of your tax basis over time. These records should be retained as long as you own the asset.

Other events that can require an adjustment to the basis are casualty losses for which you've claimed a tax deduction, or additions or improvements to the property. You'll need to keep a record of these items, too, and save them until you eventually dispose of the property.

When you file your tax return, additions or improvements are treated like separate, depreciable assets that have the same depreciation period as the underlying property. However, when the underlying property is sold, any undepreciated value of the additions or improvements must be added to the asset's tax basis to compute your taxable gains. For more on sales of capital assets, see page 116.

Casualty loss deductions (see page 269) *are* subtracted from your adjusted tax basis in the property as of the year the loss occurred. Once you have a deductible casualty loss, you must use the new, adjusted basis of the property, instead of the original basis, for depreciation purposes. What's more, you can no longer use the tables to compute your depreciation expense. Instead, you'll have to use the actual formulas on which the tables are based. Consult your tax advisor or the IRS's free Publication 946, *How to Depreciate Property,* for details on how this is done.

Effect of Trade-In on Basis

If you trade in some business equipment that was used 100 percent for business for new business equipment of the same asset category, the transaction will not be a taxable event because it will be treated as a "like-kind exchange," as discussed on page 116.

However, the tax basis of the new equipment will be equivalent to the adjusted basis of the old equipment, plus any additional cash you paid for the new equipment. This tax basis represents the maximum amount you can claim as depreciation for the item for tax purposes.

If you trade in a *vehicle* that was used partly for business for another vehicle that will be used in your business, you must use the following computation to determine the tax basis of the replacement vehicle. (For cars acquired before June 19, 1984, consult your tax advisor for the proper method to use.)

The basis for figuring depreciation for the replacement vehicle is:

1. the adjusted basis of the old vehicle, plus
2. any extra amount paid for the replacement vehicle, minus
3. the excess, if any, of the total amount of depreciation that would have been allowable during the years before the trade if 100 percent of the use of the vehicle had been business and investment use, divided by the total amounts actually allowable as depreciation during those years.

To see how this would work, check out the case study that follows.

WRITING OFF ASSETS IN THE FIRST YEAR

As we've been saying, you normally can't take a current business deduction for the entire cost of a capital asset in the year you purchase it, because the asset's usefulness to your business will extend beyond the year of purchase. However, there is an important exception to this rule for small businesses.

Depreciation Worksheet (Keep for your records.)

Description of Property	Date Placed in Service	Cost or Other Basis	Business/ Investment Use %	Section 179 Deduction and Special Allowance	Depreciation Prior Years	Basis for Depreciation	Method/ Convention	Recovery Period	Rate or Table %	Depreciation Deduction

A special tax provision allows you the option of claiming a deduction in the first year for the entire cost of qualifying business assets, up to $108,000 in 2006 and $112,000 in 2007. If you fully qualify for this deduction, known as the expensing election or Section 179 deduction, you can get what amounts to a significant, up-front reduction in the out-of-pocket cost of a needed piece of business equipment.

Example

For 2006, if you are a sole proprietor in the 25 percent tax bracket, the net after-tax cost of buying a $50,000 piece of machinery is reduced to $37,500.

If you want to make use of this election, you must do so on your original tax return for the period, on Form 4562, or on an amended tax return filed before the due date for your original return (including any extensions). If you don't claim it, you cannot change your mind later by filing an amended tax return after the due date.

What Qualifies for the Election?

To qualify for this expensing election, the property that you purchase must be tangible personal property: that is, property other than real estate that can be seen or touched, such as a typewriter, chair, or desk. This includes property that is not a building or a structural component of a building, but is an integral part of manufacturing, production, or extraction, or of furnishing transportation, communications, electricity, gas, water, or sewage disposal services; or a research or storage facility used in connection with any of these processes. It can also be a single-purpose livestock or horticultural structure, or a petroleum products storage facility that is not a building.

New for this year, off-the-shelf computer software placed in service in tax years beginning after 2002 and before 2010 qualifies for the expensing election. This refers to software that is readily available for purchase by the general public, is subject to a nonexclusive license, and has not been substantially modified. Qualifying software does not include any database or similar item unless it is in the public domain and is incidental to the operation of otherwise qualifying computer software.

An air conditioning or heating unit doesn't qualify, nor does intangible property such as a patent, contract right, stock or bond, etc. To qualify, the property must be something that you actively use in your business, for which a depreciation deduction would be allowed. The property must have been purchased specifically for your business, whether it is new or used — property that you previously owned but recently converted to business use does not qualify. Also, property you acquired by gift or inheritance does not qualify, nor does property you acquired from related persons such as your spouse, child, parent, some other ancestor or descendent, or another business with common ownership.

The property must be used more than 50 percent for business. If you want to expense property that will be used partly for personal or family reasons (e.g., a home computer that you use for business only 75 percent of the time), you can expense only the portion of the property's tax basis that corresponds to its percentage of business use.

Warning

If, in any year after the year you claimed the expensing election, you either sell the property or stop using it more than 50 percent in your business, you may have to recapture or "give back" part of the tax benefits that you previously claimed. The recaptured amount is equal to the difference between the amount you expensed, and the amount you would have been able to depreciate under the normal rules. *See page 108 for instructions on how to do this.*

So, if you think you'll only be using the equipment for a year or two, it may be better to forego the expensing election and avoid the recapture problem.

Annual Deduction Limit

The maximum amount that can be expensed each year is subject to a ceiling amount of $100,000 in 2003 through 2009. This dollar amount will be adjusted for inflation after 2003 (e.g., $108,000 for 2006; $112,000 in 2007).

If the cost of all qualified property placed in service by a business during the year is more than $430,000 in 2006 ($450,000 in 2007), the ceiling for that business is reduced by the amount over $430,000. This limit is intended to keep the expensing election targeted toward small businesses.

Example

In 2006, Bobscarts, Inc., a company that manufactures electric golf carts, purchases for $438,000 *a machine to be used in its business. Bobscarts would be able to expense $100,000 of the cost of the machine ($108,000 - [$438,000 - $430,000]).*

Empowerment zone businesses. If substantially all of the property's use is in a trade or business located in an empowerment zone, the annual deduction limit is increased an additional $35,000 (e.g., to $143,000 in 2006). Some special requirements will apply, so consult your tax advisor or IRS Publication 946, *How To Depreciate Property,* if you think this higher limit might apply to you.

Gulf Opportunity Zone. For qualified Gulf Opportunity Zone property (i.e., property in areas impacted by Hurricanes Katrina, Rita, and Wilma) acquired on or after August 28, 2005, and placed in service before January 1, 2008, the first-year write-off is increased by an additional $100,000. The investment limitation is increased by an additional $600,000. A taxpayer may also claim a 50-percent additional depreciation allowance on qualified Gulf Opportunity Zone property acquired on or after August 28, 2005, and placed in service before January 1, 2008 (January 1, 2009 in the case of residential rental and nonresidential real property).

Equipment Over the Limit

If you purchased equipment that exceeds the $108,000 limit, you can depreciate the excess amount under the usual rules.

Example

Say that you purchased a full suite of office furniture and equipment for $110,000 in 2006, and this was your only capital expense for the year. You could expense $108,000 of the cost in 2006, which would leave a remaining balance of $2,000. You could then depreciate the $2,000 over seven years, yielding a 2006 depreciation deduction of $285.71.

Your total write-off for the furniture in 2006 would be $108,000 + $285.71 = $108,285.71.

If your equipment purchases for the year exceed the expensing dollar limit, you can decide to split your expensing election among new assets any way you choose.

Save Money

Generally speaking, where you have a choice, it's best to expense those assets with the longest depreciation periods (e.g., seven-year property), so you can claim a quicker write-off for them. If the asset has a shorter depreciation period (e.g., three-year property), expensing it in the first year is not going to make as much of a difference. See page 110 for more on the depreciation periods that apply to various assets.

Special Rules for Cars

For many small business owners, the only time they would even approach the $108,000 limit would be the year they purchase a new car. But as fate would have it, there is a special rule that prevents you from deducting the full price of the car. Generally, for cars, the amount that may be expensed the first year under the special write-off election is limited to $2,960 for vehicles placed in service in 2006 (this amount increases periodically because of inflation). For more details on depreciating your car, see page 112.

Timing Your Purchases

As long as you start using your newly purchased business equipment before the end of the tax year, you get the entire expensing deduction for that year, whether you started using the equipment in January or on December 31st. The amount that can be expensed depends upon the date the qualifying property is placed in service, not when it's purchased or paid for.

Save Money

If, toward the end of your tax year, you're thinking about purchasing equipment that you can expense, you may do well to complete the purchase and start using the property before the end of the year if you can benefit from deducting the property's cost on your current year's tax return.

However, if you expect your taxable income to be much higher in the following year, you may want to hold off on the new equipment until the beginning of the next tax year.

Business Income Limitation

The total cost of property that may be expensed for any tax year cannot be higher than the total amount of taxable income that you get from the active conduct of any trade or business, including any salary or wages from other jobs you (or your spouse) may have.

So, if your business is facing a loss, you might not get

the full benefit of the expensing provision. Costs that can't be deducted because of this limit can be carried forward to future years, so the fact that this income limitation rule knocks out a portion of your expensing deduction does not mean that it is permanently lost.

Work Smart

The way in which taxable income is computed under the expensing rules may especially benefit a small business owner who operates the business in either an unincorporated form (a sole proprietorship or partnership) or as an S corporation. This is because in determining the taxable income limit of such taxpayers, all wages and income are included — even those from another job or a separate business activity. Married business owners filing joint returns can also count their spouses' wages and business income.

Sharing the Election

Allocation rules determine how the benefits of the expensing deduction are to be split up between spouses, certain related corporations, partnerships and their partners, and S corporations and their shareholders. These rules are designed to make sure that a purchase of business equipment in a particular year cannot be used by related parties to gain more than the total allowed for expense deductions.

- **Married taxpayers filing separate returns** — For purposes of the expensing amount ceiling, they are treated as one taxpayer. Unless they elect otherwise, 50 percent of the cost of the property is allocated to each spouse.

- **Related corporations** — If you operate your business as a corporation that controls other corporations, the corporations will be limited to one total deduction amount for business property purchased.

- **Partnerships and S corporations** — The deduction limit applies separately to the partnership or S corporation itself and to each partner or S corporation shareholder.

Example

In 2006, Sam Smith and Linda Lane form a partnership to operate a bakery. The partnership buys new ovens and a refrigerator for a total cost of $108,000. In addition, Lane also enters into a separate business venture, a flower shop, by herself, for which she buys $5,000 worth of equipment.

Assuming the partnership has taxable income that exceeds $108,000, it can elect to expense up to $108,000 of the cost of the oven and refrigerator. If it does so, each partner's share of the expensing deduction is $54,000. In addition, Lane can elect to expense the entire $5,000 cost of her equipment, assuming her taxable income derived from the flower shop exceeds $5,000.

Recapturing the Expensed Amount

Remember that to claim the expensing election for a piece of property, you must use the property more than 50 percent for business purposes. If your business usage drops below 50 percent during some year before the ordinary depreciation period for this property ends (see the chart on page 110), you will have to "give back" or recapture some of the amount you expensed.

To figure the recaptured amount, compare the amount you expensed, and the total amount you would have been entitled to deduct so far under the quickest depreciation method allowed for that type of property (see page 109). If the amount you expensed was greater, the difference between the two amounts must be reported as ordinary income.

The recapture is reported on IRS Form 4797, *Sales of Business Property,* in Part IV at the end of the second page. If the property was listed property, use Column (b) of Lines 33 through 35. If not, use Column (a). See the case study below for an illustration of how this works.

When Does Depreciation Begin?

Your depreciation or expensing election deductions for a piece of property begin in the tax year in which you place it in service.

That means that just buying a piece of depreciable property is not enough: In order to claim a depreciation deduction for the property in 2006, you must have put it to some productive use in your business before the end of the year.

If you are using the expensing election, the timing doesn't matter much; as long as you began using the property before the end of the year, you get the entire deduction.

But if you have property that's not eligible for the $108,000 expensing election described above (for example, your home office or other business real estate, or the portion of business equipment that exceeds $108,000), the date on which you placed the property in service and the total amount of property placed in service during the year are the two factors that determine how much of a full year's deduction you will get for the first year. If you sell or dispose of the property within the year you got it, you can't claim a depreciation deduction at all.

Mid-Month Convention

Nonresidential real estate, a classification that includes home offices, is treated as being placed in service in the middle of the month in which you actually placed it in service. You will get a deduction for half of that month, plus the rest of the months for the remainder of the year. This principle (known as the mid-month convention) is factored into the depreciation tables used for this type of property (see Table A-7a, page 129).

Half-Year Convention

For most depreciable property other than real estate, no matter what month of the year you begin using the property, you treat it as if you began using it in the middle of the year. So, you will generally get one-half of the first year's depreciation, regardless of when you placed the property in service. Again, this principle (known as the half-year convention) is factored into the depreciation tables used for most depreciable property (see Table A-1, page 126).

Mid-Quarter Convention

However, there's an important exception to the half-year convention described above. Think of it this way: If Uncle Sam were going to give you a half year's tax break for a purchase made *any time in the year*, what would keep you from routinely purchasing all your business assets and starting to use them in the final days of December?

Presumably, that would allow you to get a deduction for a half-year's worth of depreciation, while avoiding any actual cash outlay until late in the year. Good deal? You bet! Unfortunately, the IRS is well aware of this strategy, and has imposed some special rules to prevent you from using it.

Case Study

In 2004, John Able purchased a new computer to use for in his startup boat chartering business, and expensed 75 percent of the $3,000 cost in the year of purchase. He used the computer 75 percent for business in 2004 and 2005. In July of 2006, John decided to buy a new business computer and retired the old one to his family room, to be used for business purposes only 10 percent of the time. Since John's computer was "listed property" (see page 112), his allowable depreciation must be computed using the straight-line method, over a five-year recovery period. John's recapture amount would be computed as follows:

Section 179 expensing election:	$3,000 x .75 =		**$2,250**
Allowable depreciation:			
2004:	$3,000 x .75 x .10 =	$225	
2005:	$3,000 x .75 x .20 =	$450	
2006:	$3,000 x .10 x .20 =	$ 60	**$ 735**
2006 recapture amount:			**$1,515**

John would report the amounts in bold in Column (b), Lines 33-35, of his IRS Form 4797, *Sales of Business Property.*

These rules, called the mid-quarter convention rules, apply if you place more than 40 percent of your total new property for the year into service in the last quarter. If you do, you will have to use these rules for all assets placed in service during the year. Under the mid-quarter rules, assets are considered to be placed in service at the midpoint of the quarter in which they were actually placed in service. So, for the first year, depending on which quarter in which you placed the asset in service, you would get the following portions of a full year's depreciation:

First quarter:	**87.5%**
Second quarter:	**62.5%**
Third quarter:	**37.5%**
Fourth quarter:	**12.5%**

Don't worry about having to use these percentages – they are factored into the depreciation charts used for mid-quarter property, on pages 126-128.

If you want to avoid the mid-quarter rule, you can't be too aggressive about placing a lot of property in service late in the year. However, there may be times when using the mid-quarter convention can work to your advantage. If you place a large, expensive asset in service in the first quarter, you may be able to claim more depreciation by placing slightly more than 40 percent of new assets in service in the last quarter.

Example

If you placed five-year assets with a total value of $10,000 in service at various points during the year, but no more than $4,000 in assets were placed in service in the fourth quarter, you'd ordinarily be able to claim a total of $10,000 x .20 = $2,000 in the first year.

If, however, $5,999 in assets were placed in service in the first quarter and $4,001 in the fourth quarter, your depreciation deduction (using Table A-2 on page 126 and Table A-5 on page 128) would be ($5,999 x .35) + ($4,001 x .05), which equals $2,099.65 + $200.05 for a total deduction of $2,300 in the first year.

DEPRECIATION METHODS

The depreciation method that you use for any particular asset is fixed at the time you first place that asset into service. Whatever rules or tables are in effect for that year must be followed as long as you own the property. Since Congress has changed the depreciation rules many times over the years, you may have to use a number of different depreciation methods if you've owned business property for a long time.

Class of Property	Items Included
3-year property	Tractor units, racehorses over two years old, and horses over 12 years old when placed in service.
5-year property	Automobiles, taxis, buses, trucks, computers and peripheral equipment, office machinery (faxes, copiers, calculators etc.), and any property used in research and experimentation. Also includes breeding and dairy cattle.
7-year property	Office furniture and fixtures, and any property that has not been designated as belonging to another class.
10-year property	Vessels, barges, tugs, similar water transportation equipment, single-purpose agricultural or horticultural structures, and trees or vines bearing fruit or nuts.
15-year property	Depreciable improvements to land such as shrubbery, fences, roads, and bridges.
20-year property	Farm buildings that are not agricultural or horticultural structures.
27.5-year property	Residential rental property.
39-year property	Nonresidential real estate, including home offices. However, a new law temporarily assigns a 15 year MACRs recovery period to qualified restaurant and leasehold improvement property placed in service after October 22, 2004, and before January 1, 2006. (Note: the value of land may not be depreciated.)

For most business property placed in service after 1986, if you don't claim the equipment expensing deduction for the full cost of the item, the IRS requires you to depreciate the asset using a method called "MACRS," which stands for Modified Accelerated Cost Recovery System. This method categorizes all business assets into classes and specifies the time period over which you can write off assets in each class. The most commonly used items are classified as shown in the chart above. Some assets are not eligible for MACRS depreciation, including intangible assets such as patents, trademarks, and business goodwill. Generally these must be written off in equal amounts over a 15-year period, beginning in the month of acquisition (see page 116). Off-the-shelf computer software must be amortized over 36 months.

Once you know the classification and the tax basis of the asset you need to depreciate (see page 101), you can use a special table provided by the IRS to determine the percentage of the item's tax basis that can be deducted each year. MACRS provides for a slightly larger write-off in the earlier years of the cost recovery period. We include the most commonly used depreciation tables beginning on page 126.

Case Study

As an example, the following chart shows the depreciation amounts under MACRS for office furniture purchased in 2006 for $10,000, and used 100 percent for business. The amounts in the third column are taken from the MACRS half-year convention table, which is the one most commonly used.

Sample Depreciation Table

Year	Basis x	Percent =	Deduction
2006	$10,000	14.29%	$1,429
2007	10,000	24.49%	2,449
2008	10,000	17.49%	1,749
2009	10,000	12.49%	1,249
2010	10,000	8.93%	893
2011	10,000	8.92%	892
2012	10,000	8.93%	893
2013	10,000	4.46%	446

Notice that the asset's tax basis does not change over the years—only the percentage used as a multiplier changes each year.

If you do not use the asset 100 percent for business, then each year you must multiply the asset's total tax basis by the business percentage for that year, and then multiply the result by the fraction found in the table.

If, in 2007, you use the office furniture from the previous example only 50 percent for your business, you would multiply the $10,000 tax basis by .50, and then multiply the result by .2449 to get your final depreciation figure.

Groups of Assets

If you place more than one asset of the same type into service during the year, and the assets are in the same class, with the same recovery period, and use the same depreciation method, you can elect to group the assets into a "general asset account." For example, if you purchase five computers to use in your business in 2007, you can create a general asset account for them.

This basically means that you will treat them as a single asset for depreciation purposes. You can only do this for assets that are used 100 percent for business in the first year you place them into service.

Warning

Although the general asset account can simplify your recordkeeping, it can also cause problems if you sell one, but not all, of the assets in the group before the end of the recovery period. In that case you might have to recognize the full amount of the sales price as ordinary income (not the sales price minus the tax basis of the item, as in the usual case). You would continue to depreciate the entire group of assets for the remainder of the class life, including the computer you've already sold.

Be sure to check with your tax advisor if you think you want to use a general asset account for large, relatively expensive assets.

Variations on MACRS

The MACRS charts we've provided on pages 126-129 are the most commonly used and generally the most favorable to taxpayers, because they provide for the largest possible deductions in the earliest years. However, you do have the option of using slower depreciation methods.

While normal MACRS uses a 200 percent declining balance method for 3-, 5-, 7- and 10- year property, there is also a 150 percent declining balance method that is available as an option for most business owners, and that *must* be used for all farm property, and for all nonfarm property in the 15- and 20-year property classes. Charts for this method begin on page 129. Most often the 150 percent declining balance method is used for the same recovery periods as normal MACRS, but you do have the option of using the longer ADS recovery periods as described below.

Normal MACRS uses a straight-line method for real estate, which is property in the 27.5- or 39-year class. However, you can also choose to use straight-line depreciation for any other property, if you wish.

Warning

Generally, if you exercise your option to use any of the variations of MACRS you must use it for all assets of the same class that you placed in service during the year. Once you make the election you cannot change it.

Alternative Depreciation System

There is also an alternative MACRS system known as ADS, under which depreciation is deducted over generally longer periods than under regular MACRS, using the straight-line method. The chart beginning on page 133 compares the depreciation periods for various classes of property under the ADS system and MACRS.

The ADS straight-line method must be used in certain situations when normal MACRS is not available; for example, if you've used the Standard Mileage Rate method of deducting vehicle expenses and want to switch to the actual cost method in a later year (see page 66). ADS must also be used if your business use of "listed property" drops to 50 percent or less for a year (see page 113).

For property purchased before 1999, the ADS system *must* be used to compute your alternative minimum tax (AMT) liability, if you're unlucky enough to have to worry about the AMT (see page 310). Taxpayers who have paid or are likely to pay AMT will need to maintain depreciation records under both the alternative system and the regular MACRS. The depreciation tables that must be used for AMT purposes are reproduced beginning on page 130.

Save Time

For depreciable real estate *placed into service in 1999 or later, you will be able to use the same depreciation allowable under MACRS even if you are subject to the AMT, so you no longer have to maintain two sets of records.*

For non-real estate property *purchased in 1999 or later, you may use the MACRS recovery* periods *for AMT purposes but must use a slower recovery* method*; namely, either the straight-line or the 150 percent declining balance method, rather than the 200 percent declining balance method.*

You can elect to use the slower ADS depreciation even if you are not required to use it by law; for example, if you want your earnings to appear larger on your income statement, you might opt to use ADS for any new property you purchase because it will result in lower depreciation deductions.

However, if you begin depreciating a particular asset using ADS, you must continue using it for the life of the asset — you can never switch back to the ordinary MACRS system. Also, if you elect this method for one item in an asset class, you must use it for all assets of that class that you placed into service that year, unless the asset is real estate.

Pre-1987 Property

If you began operating your business before 1987, you might be using some assets that were put into service before that year. If so, you'll have to continue to use a set of depreciation methods known as "ACRS," which stands for Accelerated Cost Recovery System.

ACRS used shorter recovery periods for most assets than those currently in use under MACRS. Personal property was classified as 3-year (cars, trucks, racehorses, tractors); 5-year (computers, copiers, equipment, furniture, petroleum storage facilities, single-purpose horticultural and agricultural buildings); or 10-year (theme-park structures, public utility property, manufactured homes and railroad tank cars). The normal ACRS recovery periods for property of these types purchased before 1987 would already have expired, unless a longer period was elected.

Under ACRS, real estate is depreciable over 15 years if placed into service after 1980 but before March 16, 1984; over 18 years if placed into service on or after March 16, 1984 but before May 9, 1985; and over 19 years if placed into service on or after May 9, 1985 through the end of 1986.

To find the depreciation deduction for any of these properties, get a copy of IRS Publication 534, *Depreciating Property Placed in Service Before 1987,* which you can obtain for no charge by calling 1-800-TAX-FORM, or download it from the IRS website at http://www.irs.ustreas.gov.

Even Older Methods

For property placed into service before 1981, you could generally use any reasonable method for depreciating property based on its tax basis, useful life, and salvage value. If you still hold such property and it is not yet fully depreciated, you must continue to use the same method you've established in previous years, or get IRS permission to change your accounting method by filing IRS Form 3115. There is an exception to this rule if you want to change to a straight-line method; in that case, you generally don't need advance permission, although you must attach a statement to your tax return that explains what you're doing. See IRS Publication 534, *Depreciating Property Placed in Service Before 1987,* for more details.

CARS AND OTHER LISTED PROPERTY

Certain types of business property are called "listed property" and are subject to even more depreciation rules and regulations.

Listed property includes:

- cars and other vehicles (but not those over 14,000 pounds, or those that are unlikely to be used for personal purposes because of their design such as construction vehicles, moving vans, tractors etc.)
- cellular phones
- equipment that's normally used for entertainment or recreation such as photographic, audio, communication, and video recording equipment

- computers and peripherals *unless* they are used at a regular business establishment, including an office that qualifies for the home office deduction, and are owned or leased by the business operator
- significant additions or improvements to listed property

Generally, your business use of listed property must exceed 50 percent in order for you to take the special expensing election or to depreciate the property under MACRS. Otherwise, you must use straight-line depreciation under the ADS method, using the appropriate ADS class lives for the items. Depreciation charts for this method are included at page 130, and the class life chart is at page 133.

Warning

Commuting to work is not considered "business use" of the car, even if you do work while driving such as calling customers or dictating letters.

If your employees use your car, you can count as "business use" any mileage they drive for business purposes, plus other mileage if the value of the car's use is treated as compensation to the employees. See page 64 for more on which trips are considered "business use."

If your business use drops below 51 percent in any year after the first year you use the property in your business, but before the property's depreciation period expires, you may have to pay back some of the excess depreciation you claimed.

Specifically, you'll have to treat the difference between the ADS depreciation and the depreciation you actually claimed (including any amount you expensed in the first year) as ordinary income in the first year you no longer use the asset more than 50 percent for business. For an example of how this would work, see the Case Study on page 108.

And, as you might guess, you'll have to keep records showing that your business usage was at least 51 percent of total usage of the property. This means that you should keep a log showing each time the property was used, for how long, and for what purpose.

For cars, your mileage records (see page 21) will generally suffice. For computers, cameras, audio/video equipment etc., you should keep a log noting the date, length of time, and purpose for each use of the item. Personal or family use can simply be designated "personal" but business use should show enough detail to enable you to prove the relationship to your work, if necessary in an audit.

Depreciation Limits for Passenger Cars

While the expensing limit for general business property is $108,000 in 2006 the limit for passenger cars is much lower: $2,960 is the maximum amount of depreciation of any type that can be written off in the first year ($3,260 for trucks and vans placed in service in 2006). This limit does periodically increase to reflect inflation.

The maximum amounts that may be deducted under the MACRS depreciation method (ACRS for cars placed in service before 1987), and/or under the Section 179 expensing election for the first year, are known as the "luxury car limitations," although in reality they apply to cars valued at a moderate cost. They are provided by the IRS in the form of a chart, reproduced on the next page.

Note that the maximum annual amounts shown in the chart assume that the vehicle was used 100 percent for business. The amounts must be proportionately reduced if your business use of the vehicle was less than 100 percent.

Year Placed in Service	Passenger Car Depreciation Allowable in—			
	Year 1	*Year 2*	*Year 3*	*Year 4 and later years*
1991	2,660	4,300	2,550	1,575
1992	2,760	4,400	2,650	1,575
1993	2,860	4,600	2,750	1,675
1994	2,960	4,700	2,850	1,675
1995 and 1996	3,060	4,900	2,950	1,775
1997	3,160	5,000	3,050	1,775
1998	3,160	5,000	2,950	1,775
1999	3,060	5,000	2,950	1,775
2000 through 2003	3,060	4,900	2,950	1,775
2004	2,960	4,800	2,850	1,675
2005	2,960	4,700	2,850	1,675
2006	2,960	4,800	2,850	1,775

Example

In 2006, you purchased a new car. Sixty percent of the mileage you drove during the year was for business purposes. So, your maximum depreciation deduction for the first year would be $2,960 x .60 = $1,776.

This table represents the *maximum* depreciation you can claim. For the first year, if you used the car more than 50 percent for business, you may claim a proportionate part of the full amount, regardless of the actual cost of the car.

Beginning in 2003, separate maximum depreciation caps apply to trucks and vans. The following amounts are for trucks and vans placed in service in 2006: $3,260 in year one; $5,200 in year two; $3,150 in year three; and $1,875 for each year thereafter.

For later years, you must compute your depreciation on the car using the usual methods, but can't deduct more than the amount shown in the chart. As long as you continue to use the car more than 50 percent for business, you would multiply the business percentage of the car's cost by the percentage shown in the MACRS table for five-year property. The dollar amounts in the chart above, reduced proportionately for any non-business use of the car, acts as a ceiling on the amount of depreciation you can actually claim.

If you use the car 50 percent or less for business, you must use the straight-line ADS method for five-year property for that year, and for every subsequent year.

If you started out depreciating the car under MACRS, but then your business use dropped to 50 percent or less which required you to switch to the straight-line ADS method, you will have to "give back" some of the depreciation you claimed. Specifically, you'll have to report as income the amount (if any) by which the total MACRS depreciation you claimed is greater than the total straight-line depreciation you would have been entitled to claim.

Save Money

If you use a van, truck, or sport-utility vehicle (SUV) that weighs over 6,000 pounds in your business, it is not *subject to the annual depreciation dollar caps nor the annual lease income inclusion rules. In addition, the luxury car excise tax does not apply to these types of vehicles.*

The American Jobs Creation Act of 2004, however, limits the cost of an SUV that may be expensed in the first year under the expensing election (see page 103) from $108,000 to $25,000, even if the SUV is exempt from the depreciation limitations. The reduced election amount applies to SUVs placed in service after October 22, 2004. The rules, otherwise, remain the same.

If you own a relatively lower-priced car, you can expect to recover the entire basis of the business portion of the car over the six tax years for which the

MACRS depreciation deductions are generally claimed.

However, when part of the normal MACRS deduction is disallowed because of the luxury car limitations, you'll recover only a portion of the car's basis during the normal recovery period. In that case, you may continue to depreciate the car for as long as it takes to recover the remaining basis *of the business portion* of the car.

When Does Depreciation End?

Whatever method you use, you must stop claiming depreciation when the total amount of depreciation you've claimed over the years is equal to your original cost or other basis for the asset, or when you stop using the asset in your business.

Warning

One of the more common mistakes business owners make is to continue depreciating property beyond the end of its recovery period. This is not permitted, except in the case of "luxury cars" where the dollar limits prevented you from claiming the full depreciation amounts within six years after the car's purchase.

If the asset is sold, scrapped, or otherwise disposed of, you can claim a depreciation deduction for the year of disposal, based on the depreciation convention you used. For example, if you were using the usual MACRS method, which includes a half-year convention, you're treated as owning the asset for half of the final year and can claim a half-year's depreciation; if you were using the mid-month or mid-quarter convention, you're treated as owning the asset until mid-way through the month or quarter in which you stopped using it.

Claiming Your Depreciation Deductions

In most cases, your depreciation deductions will be entered on Form 4562, *Depreciation and Amortization,* and then the total amount will be carried over to Line 13 of your Schedule C.

You must file a Form 4562 for the first year you claim depreciation or amortization on any particular piece of property, for any year you claim a Section 179 expensing election (including an amount carried over from a previous year), and for every year you claim depreciation on a car or other vehicle or on any other type of listed property (see page 112). You don't have to file this form if you are simply claiming continued depreciation on property that is not considered listed property, or if you are claiming auto expenses based on the Standard Mileage Rate.

Do not combine depreciation expenses for more than one business or investment activity on the same Form 4562. If you operate more than one business, or if you conduct some other type of activity for which you can deduct depreciation (e.g., you own some rental real estate that will be reported on Schedule E), you'll need to consider each activity's expenses separately in determining whether you need to file a Form 4562 for that business. It's very common to include several 4562s in the same tax return. Just be sure that, at the top of the form, you write the name of the business or activity to which that copy of the form relates, along with its Employer Identification Number if you have one.

If you (and your spouse, if filing jointly) are filing more than one Form 4562, you should use one of the forms as a "master" and complete Part I on that form only. This section of the form computes your Section 179 expensing election and applies the $108,000 limit, and since the limit applies "per taxpayer" rather than "per business activity," you need to total up all your elected amounts in one place.

If you use the worksheet on page 104 to keep track of your depreciable assets, you'll have all the information you need to complete your 4562.

Part V of the form relates to cars and other listed property and should generally be completed first. The total section 179 expensing election claimed for this type of property, if any, is entered on Line 29 and carried over to the front of the form (Line 7). The total amount of regular depreciation on listed property is entered on Line 28 and is carried over to the front of the form (Line 21).

Once you've taken care of Part V, you can go back and complete Part I, which helps you to compute your Section 179 expensing election for any new property placed in service during the year, or any carryover of an elected amount from previous years.

Then, complete Part II for any new property other than cars and listed property placed in service during the year. If you have more than one piece of property in an asset class (for instance, you purchased several pieces of office furniture which are considered seven-year property), your entry for column (c) in Part II will be the total basis for all items in the class, and your entry for column (g) will be the total depreciation deductions for all items in the class.

Part III asks you to total up your depreciation deductions for "old" property—that is, any property not first placed in service in 2006. The total for property placed in service in 1987 or later is entered on Line 17.

The grand total of your depreciation deductions are calculated on Line 22, and then carried over to the appropriate Schedule C (or other form).

Amortization deductions are treated separately, on Part VI of the Form 4562 (Lines 42-44). Once entered here, they are not added to the rest of your depreciation deductions. Instead, they are carried over as "other expenses" to your Schedule C, and must be listed separately on the back of that form. See page 61 for more on computing your amortization expenses, in the context of business startup expenses.

Disposing of Capital Assets

When you sell, scrap, retire, or otherwise remove a capital asset from your business, you'll have to report the change to the IRS and pay tax on any gain from the sale.

The good news is that long-term capital gains are taxed at a lower rate than other income, and if you have a loss on property used in a trade or business, you can deduct it.

Save Money

In some cases, if you trade business property for other business property of the same asset class, you do not need to recognize a taxable gain or loss.

Instead, you'll be treated as making a nontaxable like-kind exchange, in which the tax basis of the old property becomes the tax basis of the new property. The most common situation in which this rule arises is when you trade in an old vehicle for a new one (see page 103).

Consult your tax advisor for more details if you think you may want to arrange another type of like-kind exchange, since there are some very complicated rules to follow.

When you dispose of a capital asset, your gain (or loss) is computed by subtracting your adjusted tax basis for the property from your net proceeds on the sale.

Your proceeds from the sale include the cash you receive in the sale, the fair market value of any property or services you receive, and the value of any of your existing mortgage, loans, and other debts that are assumed by the buyer. From these proceeds you may subtract any costs you had in effecting the sale such as brokers' commissions, advertising expenses, appraisal fees, legal fees, surveys, abstract and recording fees, title insurance, and transfer or stamp taxes.

Your adjusted tax basis is generally your original cost for the property, plus the cost of any improvements or additions, and minus any depreciation you've claimed or casualty losses you've deducted over the years.

If you (or your accountants) have carefully maintained capital asset records for all your assets on forms like the one on page 104, it will be relatively quick and easy for you to compute any taxable gains or losses.

Tax Rate on Capital Gains

Business property that is held for one year or less is considered to be held on a short-term basis. If you sell, scrap, retire, or otherwise dispose of a short-term capital asset, any related gains will be taxed at your ordinary income tax rate.

Gain or loss is long-term if the asset's holding period is more than a year. Although short-term capital gain is taxed at ordinary income tax rates, long-term capital gains of noncorporate taxpayers are generally taxed at lower rates.

For tax years ending on or after May 6, 2003, up to four different rates could apply to long-term capital gains: 28 percent for collectible gain and gain on qualified small business stock, 25 percent for unrecaptured gain from the sale of certain depreciable realty, 15 percent for other gain, or five percent for other gain for taxpayers in the 10 percent or 15 percent income tax rate brackets. For tax years beginning after 2007, the five percent rate is reduced to zero.

These reduced rates will expire for tax years beginning after December 31, 2010. Unless the tax laws are changed, the capital gains rates that existed for tax years ending before May 6, 2003 will once again apply.

Calculating Net Capital Gains

Okay, so you understand the basic principle that sales price – cost of selling – adjusted tax basis = taxable gain (or loss). But what happens if you sell more than one capital asset during the year? What if you take a loss on one sale, but a gain on another? How do you determine the amount of your gains or losses, and will they be short- or long-term?

The general principle is that you must net your short-term gains against your short-term losses, to get a total short-term gain or loss. Then, you net your long-term gains against your long-term losses, to get a total long-term gain or loss. Finally, you net your total short-term gain or loss against your total long-term gain or loss.

If the ultimate result is a long-term gain, it will be subject to the maximum capital gains tax rate of 20 percent. If the result is a short-term gain, it will be subject to tax at your regular income tax rate.

If the result is a loss, whether short-term or long-term, up to $3,000 of it will be deductible from your ordinary net income (or up to $1,500 for married people filing separately). If your losses exceed this amount, you can carry them over and deduct them in subsequent years until they are used up.

Allocating Gains of Part-Business Property

For depreciable property that is used for both business and personal purposes, both the tax basis and sale proceeds of the property must be allocated between the two types of usage.

Essentially, the property will be treated as if it were two separate pieces of property. This applies to both real estate (e.g., your home office), and to property like cars, computers, office furniture, and equipment.

As a general rule, the taxable gain or loss on the business portion's disposition will be reported on Form 4797, *Sales of Business Property*.

In contrast, gain or loss on the personal portion will generally be reported on Schedule D of your individual income tax return. Note that any losses on the personal portion of your home or equipment are *not* deductible, although gains on this portion are taxable.

In the case of a home office, a special provision in the law says that up to $250,000 in capital gains (or $500,000 on a joint return) will be excluded upon sale of the home, if the home has been used as a principal place of residence for two out of the last five years before the sale. If you have been using part of your house as a home office for more than three years out of the last five years, you cannot meet the "two out of five years" residence rules for that portion of the home, since you have been using the office as a place of business, not your residence. Therefore, you would need to treat the property as two separate assets, and only the gain on the home would be excludable.

If you have used your home office for no more than three years out of the last five, you do not need to treat the home office as a separate business asset. However, you would still need to recapture any depreciation claimed on the home for periods after May 6, 1997 (see page 120). Except for the recaptured depreciation, the gain on the entire home would be excludible.

Selling a Business

If you sell your sole proprietorship business, each of the assets sold with the business is treated separately.

So, you would need to determine the adjusted basis of each and every asset in the sale (you can lump some of the smaller items together, however, in categories such as office machines, furniture, production equipment, etc.). The problem becomes one of allocation: if you negotiate a total price for the business, you and the buyer must agree as to what portion of the purchase price applies to each individual asset, and to intangible assets such as goodwill. The allocation will determine the amount of capital or ordinary income tax you must pay on the sale.

Allocation of the price can be a big bone of contention. The buyer wants as much money as possible to be allocated to items that are currently deductible, such as a consulting agreement, or to assets that can be depreciated quickly under IRS rules. This will improve the business's cash flow by reducing its tax bill in the critical first years.

The seller, on the other hand, wants as much money as possible allocated to assets on which the gain is treated as capital gain, rather than to assets on which gain must be treated as ordinary income. The reason is that the tax rate on long-term capital gains is limited to 15 percent (from May 6, 2003, for property held for more than 12 months), while the tax rate on short-term gains or ordinary income can be as high as 35 percent. Most small business owners who are successful in selling their companies are in high tax brackets, so the rate differential is very important.

Any gains on property held for one year or less, inventory, or accounts receivable are treated as ordinary income. Amounts paid under noncompete agreements are ordinary income to you and amortizable over 15 years by the buyer, *unless* the IRS successfully argues they are really part of the purchase price. And amounts paid under consulting agreements are ordinary income to you and currently deductible to the buyer.

Case Study

You've been using a room in your house as a home office for the last four years. Your original basis in the home was $120,000, and you sold it in 2006 for $300,000. Your costs of selling were $21,000. The total area of the home is 2,400 square feet and your office is 120 square feet, or 5 percent of the total.

You must treat the sale as the sale of two pieces of property: your home, which is 95 percent of the total property, and your office, which is 5 percent of the total:

	Home	**Office**
Selling price	$285,000	$15,000
Less: selling expenses	-19,950	-1,050
Amount realized:	265,050	13,950
Cost basis:	114,000	6,000
Less: depreciation	-0	-622
Adjusted basis	114,000	5,378
Gain (amount realized minus adjusted basis)	$151,050	$ 8,572

The sale of the office portion would be reported on Form 4797, *Sales of Business Property.* Because the gain on the "home" portion of the property is less than $250,000, it does not have to be reported; if it had been over that amount (or over $500,000 on a joint return), it would be reported on Schedule D.

IRS allocation rules. As you can imagine, the IRS has come up with some rules for making allocations of the purchase price. Generally speaking, they require that each tangible asset be valued at its fair market value (FMV), in the following order: (1) cash; (2) CDs, government securities, readily marketable securities and foreign currency; (3) all other assets except intangible assets; (4) intangible assets such as patents, trademarks, trade names, copyrights, a trained workforce, the value of business records, covenants not to compete, customer relationships, supplier relationships, licenses or permits; and (5) goodwill.

The total FMV of all assets in a class are added up and subtracted from the total purchase price before moving on to the next class. Thus, intangible assets such as goodwill get the "residual value," if there is any. However, remember that FMV is in the mind of the appraiser. You still have some wiggle room in allocating your price among the various assets, provided that your allocation is reasonable and the buyer agrees to it. Your odds are even better if your allocation is supported by a third-party appraisal.

According to IRS rules, the buyer and seller must use the same price allocation, so the allocation will have to be negotiated and put in writing as part of the sales contract. The allocation must be reported to the IRS on Form 8594, *Asset Acquisition Statement Under Section 1060,* which must be attached to the tax returns of both parties for the year in which the sale occurred. The allocation will be binding on both parties unless the IRS determines that it is not appropriate.

Recapture of Depreciation Deductions

If you realize a capital gain on the sale or other disposition of property used in your trade or business, you probably won't get the benefit of the special capital gains tax rate on the entire amount of your gain.

Why not? Because Congress wants to first take back, or "recapture," some of the benefits of the depreciation deductions you've been claiming for all the years you owned the property.

The tax rules for recapture differ, depending on whether the property is real estate or personal property. For business real estate, there is a special, more generous rule for home offices.

Recapture Rules for Personal Property

If you have a capital gain on any depreciable personal property other than real estate, you must report all or part of the gain as ordinary income to reflect the amount of depreciation, and any first-year expensing deductions that were claimed on the asset. The amount that must be reported as ordinary income ("recaptured") is not eligible for the special long-term capital gains rates described above, and is equal to the lesser of:

- the total of depreciation and expensing deductions allowable on the asset, and
- the total gain realized

If the total gain realized is more than the amount that must be recaptured, the excess will be taxed at the long-term capital gain rate, provided that the asset has been held for more than one year. If the total of the depreciation deductions is greater than the gain realized, the entire amount of the gain is reported as ordinary income.

Case Study

On April 30, 2006, Albert Edwards sold a car for $5,000. The original cost of the car in 2000 was $12,000. The car had been driven 75,000 miles, 60,000 of which were attributable to business usage. Edwards used the standard mileage rate to claim car deductions, so his depreciation equals the depreciation component of the SMR for each year, multiplied by the business miles driven that year. Assume the depreciation treated as allowable for those years was $6,300. Edwards sold no other business property during the year. Edwards has a business gain of $700, computed as follows:

	Total	***Business (80%)***	***Personal (20%)***
Cost of car	$12,000	$9,600	$2,400
Less: depreciation	-6,300	-6,300	--0--
	----------	---------	-----------
Adjusted basis of car	5,700	3,300	2,400
Less: sale proceeds	-5,000	- 4,000	-1,000
	-----------	----------	-----------
Gain (loss)	($700)	$700	($1,400)

The full amount of the business gain of $700 is treated as ordinary income because it is less than the amount of depreciation that was taken on the car. Remember, the personal loss is not deductible!

Recapture of Real Estate Depreciation

Gain on the sale of real estate is treated as ordinary income to the extent of additional depreciation allowed or allowable on the property. For property held over a year, the additional depreciation is the actual depreciation adjustments that are more than the depreciation using the straight-line method.

Depreciation recapture for real estate is computed on Form 4797, *Sales of Business Property*.

Planning for Depreciation Recaptures

If you choose to depreciate a property quickly, the property's adjusted basis will be reduced more quickly than if you had depreciated the property more slowly, and if you sell in the first few years you will have more taxable gain upon sale of the asset.

Moreover, as a general rule, *the faster you depreciate property, the more likely it is that you will have a recapture liability when you sell the property, and the more likely that this liability would be larger than if you have chosen slower depreciation.*

All things being equal, it's probably best to be hit with a recapture in a year in which your business has an operating loss (which can be used to offset the recapture amount), rather than in profit years, when the recapture will increase your taxable income, and possibly even move you into a higher tax bracket.

Warning

Don't let the tail wag the dog. Strategies aimed at the timing or minimization of depreciation recaptures may be worthwhile, but don't fall in the trap of over-focusing on tax issues. First, consider the operational aspects when deciding whether and when you should sell an asset. Tax considerations should run a distant second when making these kinds of decisions.

Foreclosures and Involuntary Conversions of Property

If your property is foreclosed upon, repossessed, or destroyed due to theft, condemnation, or other casualty, you should report the event as a sale of the property.

A foreclosure or repossession is generally treated in the same way as a sale. Your gain or loss for tax purposes is the difference between your adjusted basis in the property, and the amount (if any) you receive. Cancellation of debt is treated as an amount that you received for this purpose.

If your property is lost or destroyed by theft, vandalism, condemnation, or a natural disaster such as a fire, tornado, flood, landslide etc., you may have a taxable gain if you receive some insurance payment, condemnation award, or damages in a lawsuit. If the amount you receive is less than the amount of your loss, you may have a deductible loss provided that the property was used in a trade or business or was investment property.

However, even if there is a taxable gain, you generally can postpone payment of tax on the gain if you reinvest the proceeds in similar property costing at least as much as the amount you received. Your tax basis in the new property would be the same as your tax basis in the old, destroyed property, and you would not be taxed on the cumulative gains until you sell the replacement property. The replacement property would generally have to be purchased within two years of receiving any payments that exceed your tax basis in the old property, or within three years if the property was used in a trade or business, or for investment. A special four-year replacement period applies to homes (and their contents) damaged by Presidentially declared disasters.

The Katrina Emergency Tax Relief Act of 2005 extends the replacement period for both business and personal residence property to five years. The longer time period applies to property damaged on or after August 25, 2005, as a result of Hurricane Katrina. In addition, the replacement property must be located in the Katrina disaster area to qualify for the extended replacement period. For a discussion of how to report casualty losses (and gains), see page 269.

Installment Sales

The installment method can be used to defer some tax on capital gains, as long as you receive at least one payment for a piece of property after the year of the sale. It can't be used if the sale results in a loss.

The bad news is that payments for many (or even most) of the assets of your business are not eligible for installment sale treatment.

Assets Eligible for Installment Treatment

Generally, anything on which gains must be treated as ordinary income will not be eligible for installment sale treatment. That includes payments for your inventory, for accounts receivable, and for property that's been used for one year or less. It also includes payments for any personal property or real estate to the extent of any depreciation that must be recaptured, based on deductions you've claimed over the years (see page 119). For all these items, you must pay tax on any gains in the year of the sale, even if you haven't yet received payments for the items.

Looking at it another way, in most cases only gain on assets that have appreciated in value beyond their original purchase price will be eligible for installment sale treatment. In most cases, that means real estate. For older businesses, gain on intangible assets such as goodwill will also be eligible for installment sale treatment, because under the law prior to 1993 goodwill could not be depreciated or amortized (hence, there's no depreciation to be recaptured).

Using the Installment Method

To use the installment method, you must allocate the total purchase price you received among all the assets you've sold in the transaction.

Then, for each asset to which the installment method applies, you must compute your "gross profit percentage." This is basically your gross profit (your selling price minus: the tax basis of the property, selling expenses, and any depreciation recapture) divided by the selling price of the asset. Then, each time you receive a payment from the purchaser, the principal portion of the payment (i.e., everything but the interest) is multiplied by the gross profit percentage to determine the amount that must be reported as taxable gain for the year.

Case Study

Let's say that on January 1, 2006, you sold some commercial real estate. The total price was $600,000, of which $500,000 was allocated to the building and $100,000 was for the land underneath. Selling expenses were $37,500. You originally purchased the property 10 years ago for $300,000 ($250,000 for the building and $50,000 for the land). Over the years you've claimed $61,168 in depreciation using the straight-line method. For simplicity, we'll assume you're a cheapskate and made no capital improvements to the building during the time you owned it.

The buyers made a $200,000 down payment and will pay the rest off at 10 percent interest on a 20-year amortization schedule, except that at five years the unpaid principal will be due in a balloon payment.

First, separate the transaction into two portions: the building, and the land:

	Building	**Land**
Cost basis:	$250,000	$ 50,000
Less: depreciation	-61,168	-0
	188,832	50,000
Plus: expenses of sale	+31,250	+ 6,250
Adjusted basis:	$ 220,082	$56,250

Now let's consider the "building only" portion of the transaction. Your net gains on the sale of the building alone will be the sales price minus the adjusted basis computed above, or $500,000 - $220,082 = $279,918. Since this amount is greater than the $61,168 in depreciation, all of the depreciation you claimed over the years would be "recaptured" and taxed in the year of the sale.

The remainder of your profit on the building, or $218,750 (since $279,918 - $61,168 = $218,750) would be divided by the selling price of $500,000 to arrive at your gross profit percentage for the building: $218,750/$500,000 = .4375, or 43.75 percent.

For the land, no depreciation was deductible, so there is no recapture. Your profit on the land is the price less the adjusted basis, or $100,000 - $56,250 = $43,750. Your gross profit percentage of the land would be $43,750/100,000 = .4375, or 43.75 percent.

For every payment you receive, including the down payment and the balloon, separate the principal from any interest (all interest is taxed as ordinary income).

Of the principal, 1/6 will represent a payment for the land, and 5/6 will represent a payment for the building. Of the payment for the land, 43.75 percent will be taxed as capital gains, and the remainder is a return of your capital, which is not taxed. Of the payment for the building, 43.75 percent of each payment will be taxed as capital gains, and the rest represents either the recaptured depreciation, which was taxed in the year of the sale, or the return of your capital which is not taxed.

Installment sales are reported on IRS Form 6252, *Installment Sale Income.* A separate form should be filed for each asset you sell using this method. You must file this form in the year the sale occurs, and in every later year in which you receive a payment.

If the buyer assumes any of your debt as part of the installment deal, the assumption is treated as a payment to you for purposes of the installment sale rules. If the buyer places some of the purchase price in an escrow account, it's not considered a payment until the funds are released to you, as long as there are some substantial restrictions on your ability to get the money.

If your deal includes an enrapt provision under which you may be entitled to additional payments based on future performance of the business, special rules apply. Please see your tax advisor for details.

Reporting Sales of Assets

If you sell or dispose of property used in a trade or business, it must be reported on IRS Form 4797, *Sales of Business Property.* This form is divided into several sections, which are used for different types of property.

Part II, "Ordinary Gains and Losses," is used for property held for one year or less, and for property not eligible for the long-term gain rate such as accounts receivable and inventory sold as part of a sale of your business.

Part III, "Gain from Disposition of Property Under Sections 1245, 1250, 1252, 1254, and 1255," is used for reporting the sale of depreciable personal property (known as 1245 property) and depreciable real estate (known as 1250 property). The other forms of property are less commonly used, but a translation is: 1252 property is farmland held more than one year but less than 10 years; 1254 property is oil, gas, or geothermal property place in service before 1987, and 1255 property is property for which you received certain types of government conservation program payments.

Part III is where your depreciation recapture (if any) will be figured. The net result of this section will be carried over to Part II on the front of the form.

Part I is used to report the sale of property not included in Part III, such as land, and gains from installment sales (originally reported on Form 6252 and carried over to Line 4 of Part I) and like-kind exchanges (originally reported on Form 8824).

Finally, Part IV is used to report an event that may not look like a sale, but is treated as a taxable event by the IRS: the recapture of some of your depreciation deductions when your business use of "listed property" drops below 51 percent (see page 112) and the recapture of some of your Section 179 expensing election when your business use drops below 50 percent for property you've previously expensed.

Purchasing vs. Leasing

Depreciation generally may be claimed by the *owner* of a capital asset. If you lease your equipment instead of purchasing it, you can't depreciate the equipment. However, you will generally be able to deduct the lease payments you make, at the time that you make them, which can result in a larger tax benefit than you'd get if you bought the equipment outright.

If you lease property that is used for both business and personal purposes, you must prorate the lease payments and deduct only the portion of the lease that corresponds to your business use percentage. See page 102 for more details on how to calculate business usage for various types of property.

Inclusion Amounts for Listed Property

If, instead of purchasing it, you lease your car, computer system, audio/visual equipment, or other listed property as defined on page 112, you may have to include an additional amount known as the "inclusion amount" in your gross income. This extra amount is intended to place you on the same financial footing as someone who has purchased similar equipment and can only deduct the depreciation, which is typically less than your lease payments would be.

If you lease a car, you must calculate an inclusion amount for every year you deduct lease payments; see page 68 for instructions on how this is done.

If you lease some other type of listed property, you only need to calculate an inclusion amount if your business usage of the property drops to 50 percent or less for a year. The inclusion amount is added to your income only for that year.

This could easily happen, for instance, if you have not claimed the home office deduction, but have been leasing a computer predominantly for business at home, and then you find that your family is using the computer more than you!

Inclusion Amount Worksheet for Leased Listed Property Used 50% or Less for Business

1. Fair market value of the asset	________	
2. Business/investment use for the first year that business use is 50% or less	________	
3. Multiply line 1 by line 2	________	
4. Rate from Table A-19 (below)	________	
5. Multiply line 3 by line 4		________
6. Fair market value of the asset	________	
7. Average business/investment use for all years property was leased before the first year that investment use fell to 50% or less	________	
8. Multiply line 6 by line 7	________	
9. Rate from Table A-20 (below)	________	
10. Multiply line 8 by line 9		________
11. Add lines 5 and line 10. This is your inclusion amount		________

RATES TO FIGURE INCLUSION AMOUNTS FOR LEASED LISTED PROPERTY

Table A-19. **Amount A Percentages**

Recovery Period of Property Under ADS	First Tax Year During Lease in Which Business Use is 50% or Less											
	1	2	3	4	5	6	7	8	9	10	11	12 & Later
Less than 7 years	2.1%	−7.2%	−19.8%	−20.1%	−12.4%	−12.4%	−12.4%	−12.4%	−12.4%	−12.4%	−12.4%	−12.4%
7 to 10 years	3.9%	−3.8%	−17.7%	−25.1%	−27.8%	−27.2%	−27.1%	−27.6%	−23.7%	−14.7%	−14.7%	−14.7%
More than 10 years	6.6%	−1.6%	−16.9%	−25.6%	−29.9%	−31.1%	−32.8%	−35.1%	−33.3%	−26.7%	−19.7%	−12.2%

Table A-20. **Amount B Percentages**

Recovery Period of Property Under ADS	First Tax Year During Lease in Which Business Use is 50% or Less											
	1	2	3	4	5	6	7	8	9	10	11	12 & Later
Less than 7 years	0.0%	10.0%	22.0%	21.2%	12.7%	12.7%	12.7%	12.7%	12.7%	12.7%	12.7%	12.7%
7 to 10 years	0.0%	9.3%	23.8%	31.3%	33.8%	32.7%	31.6%	30.5%	25.0%	15.0%	15.0%	15.0%
More than 10 years	0.0%	10.1%	26.3%	35.4%	39.6%	40.2%	40.8%	41.4%	37.5%	29.2%	20.8%	12.5%

To calculate your inclusion amount for items other than cars, you need to know the fair market value of the item on the first day of the lease term. Alternately, if the capitalized cost of the item is specified in the lease, you must treat that amount as the "fair market value."

Then, you can use the worksheet above to determine your inclusion amount. The final result from the worksheet must be included as "other income" on Line 6 of your Schedule C.

As we've said, inclusion amounts for listed property other than cars are included in gross income only in the first year that business use drops to 50 percent or less.

There is an exception to this rule if the lease term began within the last nine months of your tax year and extends into the next year, and you did not use the property more than 50 percent for business in the first year of the lease. In that case, you would calculate your average business use percentage for the first and second calendar years (Worksheet Line 2) and the percentage amount for the first year (Worksheet Line 4). The inclusion amount would be added to your income for the second year, not the first.

True Leases vs. Financial Leases

In certain situations, the IRS may deny your deduction of lease payments if it audits your return and concludes that your lease is not in reality a true lease, but a financial lease, which can be treated as an installment or conditional sale. To understand why the IRS would even care whether you characterize your acquisition as a lease or a purchase, consider the following example:

Example

Jiffy Company is interested in a piece of equipment that sells for $25,000. However, instead of purchasing the equipment, Jiffy negotiates to lease the equipment for three years at an annual rent of $8,500. The lease grants Jiffy the option to purchase the equipment at the end of the lease for $2,400. The fair rental value of the equipment is only $3,000. Why would Jiffy and the leasing company do this?

From Jiffy's perspective, leasing the equipment allows it to effectively recover the equipment's cost over three years via its deductions of the rental payments. If it had purchased the equipment, it likely would have recovered the cost over five years via depreciation deductions. And the IRS really frowns upon the improper acceleration of deductions.

From the lessor's perspective, leasing the equipment allows it to spread its recognition of income over the three-year lease period. The improper deferral of income is another thing the IRS dislikes. Furthermore, the lessor would be able to claim depreciation deductions with respect to the equipment while it is being leased and thereby reduce its current income even more.

If the IRS does recharacterize your lease as a sale, your rental payments will not be deductible. Instead, you'll be entitled to depreciation deductions as the owner of the property for tax purposes. Moreover, a portion of your rental payments, which the IRS effectively recharacterizes as being installment payments on a purchase price, will likely be considered interest that you can currently deduct.

The leasing transaction in the example above is one that the IRS would likely recharacterize. What types of factors attract the IRS's attention? Here are some examples:

- A portion of your rental payments establishes equity in the leased property.
- You acquire title to the property after paying a specified amount of rent.
- Your rental payments are made over a relatively short period of time and are inordinately large in comparison to the amount required to purchase the property.
- Your rental payments substantially exceed the fair rental value of the property.
- You can acquire the property under a purchase option for a price that is nominal in relation to the property's value at the time you can exercise the option or that is nominal in comparison to your total payments under the lease.
- A portion of your rental payments is specifically designated as being interest or is readily recognizable as being the equivalent of interest.

If any of these factors describe an equipment lease you're preparing to enter, you should proceed with caution to avoid interest and penalties if the IRS recharacterizes the transaction. If you have any doubt as to how the IRS may view the lease, have your accountant or lawyer review the agreement.

Table A-1. **3-, 5-, 7-, 10-, 15-, and 20-Year Property Half-Year Convention**

Year	Depreciation rate for recovery period					
	3-year	5-year	7-year	10-year	15-year	20-year
1	33.33%	20.00%	14.29%	10.00%	5.00%	3.750%
2	44.45	32.00	24.49	18.00	9.50	7.219
3	14.81	19.20	17.49	14.40	8.55	6.677
4	7.41	11.52	12.49	11.52	7.70	6.177
5		11.52	8.93	9.22	6.93	5.713
6		5.76	8.92	7.37	6.23	5.285
7			8.93	6.55	5.90	4.888
8			4.46	6.55	5.90	4.522
9				6.56	5.91	4.462
10				6.55	5.90	4.461
11				3.28	5.91	4.462
12					5.90	4.461
13					5.91	4.462
14					5.90	4.461
15					5.91	4.462
16					2.95	4.461
17						4.462
18						4.461
19						4.462
20						4.461
21						2.231

Table A-2. **3-, 5-, 7-, 10-, 15-, and 20-Year Property Mid-Quarter Convention Placed in Service in First Quarter**

Year	Depreciation rate for recovery period					
	3-year	5-year	7-year	10-year	15-year	20-year
1	58.33%	35.00%	25.00%	17.50%	8.75%	6.563%
2	27.78	26.00	21.43	16.50	9.13	7.000
3	12.35	15.60	15.31	13.20	8.21	6.482
4	1.54	11.01	10.93	10.56	7.39	5.996
5		11.01	8.75	8.45	6.65	5.546
6		1.38	8.74	6.76	5.99	5.130
7			8.75	6.55	5.90	4.746
8			1.09	6.55	5.91	4.459
9				6.56	5.90	4.459
10				6.55	5.91	4.459
11				0.82	5.90	4.459
12					5.91	4.460
13					5.90	4.459
14					5.91	4.460
15					5.90	4.459
16					0.74	4.460
17						4.459
18						4.460
19						4.459
20						4.460
21						0.557

Table A-3. **3-, 5-, 7-, 10-, 15-, and 20-Year Property Mid-Quarter Convention Placed in Service in Second Quarter**

Year	Depreciation rate for recovery period					
	3-year	5-year	7-year	10-year	15-year	20-year
1	41.67%	25.00%	17.85%	12.50%	6.25%	4.688%
2	38.89	30.00	23.47	17.50	9.38	7.148
3	14.14	18.00	16.76	14.00	8.44	6.612
4	5.30	11.37	11.97	11.20	7.59	6.116
5		11.37	8.87	8.96	6.83	5.658
6		4.26	8.87	7.17	6.15	5.233
7			8.87	6.55	5.91	4.841
8			3.33	6.55	5.90	4.478
9				6.56	5.91	4.463
10				6.55	5.90	4.463
11				2.46	5.91	4.463
12					5.90	4.463
13					5.91	4.463
14					5.90	4.463
15					5.91	4.462
16					2.21	4.463
17						4.462
18						4.463
19						4.462
20						4.463
21						1.673

Table A-4. **3-, 5-, 7-, 10-, 15-, and 20-Year Property Mid-Quarter Convention Placed in Service in Third Quarter**

Year	Depreciation rate for recovery period					
	3-year	5-year	7-year	10-year	15-year	20-year
1	25.00%	15.00%	10.71%	7.50%	3.75%	2.813%
2	50.00	34.00	25.51	18.50	9.63	7.289
3	16.67	20.40	18.22	14.80	8.66	6.742
4	8.33	12.24	13.02	11.84	7.80	6.237
5		11.30	9.30	9.47	7.02	5.769
6		7.06	8.85	7.58	6.31	5.336
7			8.86	6.55	5.90	4.936
8			5.53	6.55	5.90	4.566
9				6.56	5.91	4.460
10				6.55	5.90	4.460
11				4.10	5.91	4.460
12					5.90	4.460
13					5.91	4.461
14					5.90	4.460
15					5.91	4.461
16					3.69	4.460
17						4.461
18						4.460
19						4.461
20						4.460
21						2.788

Table A-5. **3-, 5-, 7-, 10-, 15-, and 20-Year Property**
Mid-Quarter Convention
Placed in Service in Fourth Quarter

Year	Depreciation rate for recovery period					
	3-year	5-year	7-year	10-year	15-year	20-year
1	8.33%	5.00%	3.57%	2.50%	1.25%	0.938%
2	61.11	38.00	27.55	19.50	9.88	7.430
3	20.37	22.80	19.68	15.60	8.89	6.872
4	10.19	13.68	14.06	12.48	8.00	6.357
5		10.94	10.04	9.98	7.20	5.880
6		9.58	8.73	7.99	6.48	5.439
7			8.73	6.55	5.90	5.031
8			7.64	6.55	5.90	4.654
9				6.56	5.90	4.458
10				6.55	5.91	4.458
11				5.74	5.90	4.458
12					5.91	4.458
13					5.90	4.458
14					5.91	4.458
15					5.90	4.458
16					5.17	4.458
17						4.458
18						4.459
19						4.458
20						4.459
21						3.901

Table A-6. **Residential Rental Property**
Mid-Month Convention
Straight Line—27.5 Years

Year	Month property placed in service											
	1	2	3	4	5	6	7	8	9	10	11	12
1	3.485%	3.182%	2.879%	2.576%	2.273%	1.970%	1.667%	1.364%	1.061%	0.758%	0.455%	0.152%
2–9	3.636	3.636	3.636	3.636	3.636	3.636	3.636	3.636	3.636	3.636	3.636	3.636
10	3.637	3.637	3.637	3.637	3.637	3.637	3.636	3.636	3.636	3.636	3.636	3.636
11	3.636	3.636	3.636	3.636	3.636	3.636	3.637	3.637	3.637	3.637	3.637	3.637
12	3.637	3.637	3.637	3.637	3.637	3.637	3.636	3.636	3.636	3.636	3.636	3.636
13	3.636	3.636	3.636	3.636	3.636	3.636	3.637	3.637	3.637	3.637	3.637	3.637
14	3.637	3.637	3.637	3.637	3.637	3.637	3.636	3.636	3.636	3.636	3.636	3.636
15	3.636	3.636	3.636	3.636	3.636	3.636	3.637	3.637	3.637	3.637	3.637	3.637
16	3.637	3.637	3.637	3.637	3.637	3.637	3.636	3.636	3.636	3.636	3.636	3.636
17	3.636	3.636	3.636	3.636	3.636	3.636	3.637	3.637	3.637	3.637	3.637	3.637
18	3.637	3.637	3.637	3.637	3.637	3.637	3.636	3.636	3.636	3.636	3.636	3.636
19	3.636	3.636	3.636	3.636	3.636	3.636	3.637	3.637	3.637	3.637	3.637	3.637
20	3.637	3.637	3.637	3.637	3.637	3.637	3.636	3.636	3.636	3.636	3.636	3.636
21	3.636	3.636	3.636	3.636	3.636	3.636	3.637	3.637	3.637	3.637	3.637	3.637
22	3.637	3.637	3.637	3.637	3.637	3.637	3.636	3.636	3.636	3.636	3.636	3.636
23	3.636	3.636	3.636	3.636	3.636	3.636	3.637	3.637	3.637	3.637	3.637	3.637
24	3.637	3.637	3.637	3.637	3.637	3.637	3.636	3.636	3.636	3.636	3.636	3.636
25	3.636	3.636	3.636	3.636	3.636	3.636	3.637	3.637	3.637	3.637	3.637	3.637
26	3.637	3.637	3.637	3.637	3.637	3.637	3.636	3.636	3.636	3.636	3.636	3.636
27	3.636	3.636	3.636	3.636	3.636	3.636	3.637	3.637	3.637	3.637	3.637	3.637
28	1.97	2.273	2.576	2.879	3.182	3.485	3.636	3.636	3.636	3.636	3.636	3.636
29							0.152	0.455	0.758	1.061	1.364	1.667

Table A-7. **Nonresidential Real Property**
Mid-Month Convention
Straight Line—31.5 Years

Year	Month property placed in service											
	1	2	3	4	5	6	7	8	9	10	11	12
1	3.042%	2.778%	2.513%	2.249%	1.984%	1.720%	1.455%	1.190%	0.926%	0.661%	0.397%	0.132%
2–7	3.175	3.175	3.175	3.175	3.175	3.175	3.175	3.175	3.175	3.175	3.175	3.175
8	3.175	3.174	3.175	3.174	3.175	3.174	3.175	3.175	3.175	3.175	3.175	3.175
9	3.174	3.175	3.174	3.175	3.174	3.175	3.174	3.175	3.174	3.175	3.174	3.175
10	3.175	3.174	3.175	3.174	3.175	3.174	3.175	3.174	3.175	3.174	3.175	3.174
11	3.174	3.175	3.174	3.175	3.174	3.175	3.174	3.175	3.174	3.175	3.174	3.175
12	3.175	3.174	3.175	3.174	3.175	3.174	3.175	3.174	3.175	3.174	3.175	3.174
13	3.174	3.175	3.174	3.175	3.174	3.175	3.174	3.175	3.174	3.175	3.174	3.175
14	3.175	3.174	3.175	3.174	3.175	3.174	3.175	3.174	3.175	3.174	3.175	3.174
15	3.174	3.175	3.174	3.175	3.174	3.175	3.174	3.175	3.174	3.175	3.174	3.175
16	3.175	3.174	3.175	3.174	3.175	3.174	3.175	3.174	3.175	3.174	3.175	3.174
17	3.174	3.175	3.174	3.175	3.174	3.175	3.174	3.175	3.174	3.175	3.174	3.175
18	3.175	3.174	3.175	3.174	3.175	3.174	3.175	3.174	3.175	3.174	3.175	3.174
19	3.174	3.175	3.174	3.175	3.174	3.175	3.174	3.175	3.174	3.175	3.174	3.175
20	3.175	3.174	3.175	3.174	3.175	3.174	3.175	3.174	3.175	3.174	3.175	3.174
21	3.174	3.175	3.174	3.175	3.174	3.175	3.174	3.175	3.174	3.175	3.174	3.175
22	3.175	3.174	3.175	3.174	3.175	3.174	3.175	3.174	3.175	3.174	3.175	3.174
23	3.174	3.175	3.174	3.175	3.174	3.175	3.174	3.175	3.174	3.175	3.174	3.175
24	3.175	3.174	3.175	3.174	3.175	3.174	3.175	3.174	3.175	3.174	3.175	3.174
25	3.174	3.175	3.174	3.175	3.174	3.175	3.174	3.175	3.174	3.175	3.174	3.175
26	3.175	3.174	3.175	3.174	3.175	3.174	3.175	3.174	3.175	3.174	3.175	3.174
27	3.174	3.175	3.174	3.175	3.174	3.175	3.174	3.175	3.174	3.175	3.174	3.175
28	3.175	3.174	3.175	3.174	3.175	3.174	3.175	3.174	3.175	3.174	3.175	3.174
29	3.174	3.175	3.174	3.175	3.174	3.175	3.174	3.175	3.174	3.175	3.174	3.175
30	3.175	3.174	3.175	3.174	3.175	3.174	3.175	3.174	3.175	3.174	3.175	3.174
31	3.174	3.175	3.174	3.175	3.174	3.175	3.174	3.175	3.174	3.175	3.174	3.175
32	1.720	1.984	2.249	2.513	2.778	3.042	3.175	3.174	3.175	3.174	3.175	3.174
33							0.132	0.397	0.661	0.926	1.190	1.455

Table A-7a. **Nonresidential Real Property**
Mid-Month Convention
Straight Line—39 Years

Year	Month property placed in service											
	1	2	3	4	5	6	7	8	9	10	11	12
1	2.461%	2.247%	2.033%	1.819%	1.605%	1.391%	1.177%	0.963%	0.749%	0.535%	0.321%	0.107%
2–39	2.564	2.564	2.564	2.564	2.564	2.564	2.564	2.564	2.564	2.564	2.564	2.564
40	0.107	0.321	0.535	0.749	0.963	1.177	1.391	1.605	1.819	2.033	2.247	2.461

Table A-13. **Straight Line**
Mid-Month Convention

Year	Month property placed in service											
	1	2	3	4	5	6	7	8	9	10	11	12
1	2.396%	2.188%	1.979%	1.771%	1.563%	1.354%	1.146%	0.938%	0.729%	0.521%	0.313%	0.104%
2–40	2.500	2.500	2.500	2.500	2.500	2.500	2.500	2.500	2.500	2.500	2.500	2.500
41	0.104	0.312	0.521	0.729	0.937	1.146	1.354	1.562	1.771	1.979	2.187	2.396

Table A-8. **Straight Line Method**
Half-Year Convention

Year	Recovery periods in years							
	4	5	6	9	10	15	18	20
1	12.5%	10.0%	8.33%	5.56%	5.0%	3.33%	2.78%	2.5%
2	25.0	20.0	16.67	11.11	10.0	6.67	5.56	5.0
3	25.0	20.0	16.67	11.11	10.0	6.67	5.56	5.0
4	25.0	20.0	16.67	11.11	10.0	6.67	5.55	5.0
5	12.5	20.0	16.66	11.11	10.0	6.67	5.56	5.0
6		10.0	16.67	11.11	10.0	6.67	5.55	5.0
7			8.33	11.11	10.0	6.67	5.56	5.0
8				11.11	10.0	6.66	5.55	5.0
9				11.11	10.0	6.67	5.56	5.0
10				5.56	10.0	6.66	5.55	5.0
11					5.0	6.67	5.56	5.0
12						6.66	5.55	5.0
13						6.67	5.56	5.0
14						6.66	5.55	5.0
15						6.67	5.56	5.0
16						3.33	5.55	5.0
17							5.56	5.0
18							5.55	5.0
19							2.78	5.0
20								5.0
21								2.5

Table A-9. **Straight Line Method**
Mid-Quarter Convention
Placed in Service in First Quarter

Year	Recovery periods in years							
	4	5	6	9	10	15	18	20
1	21.88%	17.5%	14.58%	9.72%	8.75%	5.83%	4.86%	4.375%
2	25.00	20.0	16.67	11.11	10.00	6.67	5.56	5.000
3	25.00	20.0	16.67	11.11	10.00	6.67	5.56	5.000
4	25.00	20.0	16.67	11.11	10.00	6.67	5.56	5.000
5	3.12	20.0	16.66	11.11	10.00	6.67	5.55	5.000
6		2.5	16.67	11.11	10.00	6.67	5.56	5.000
7			2.08	11.11	10.00	6.67	5.55	5.000
8				11.12	10.00	6.66	5.56	5.000
9				11.11	10.00	6.67	5.55	5.000
10				1.39	10.00	6.66	5.56	5.000
11					1.25	6.67	5.55	5.000
12						6.66	5.56	5.000
13						6.67	5.55	5.000
14						6.66	5.56	5.000
15						6.67	5.55	5.000
16						0.83	5.56	5.000
17							5.55	5.000
18							5.56	5.000
19							0.69	5.000
20								5.000
21								0.625

Table A-10. **Straight Line Method**
Mid-Quarter Convention
Placed in Service in Second Quarter

Year	Recovery periods in years							
	4	5	6	9	10	15	18	20
1	15.63%	12.5%	10.42%	6.94%	6.25%	4.17%	3.47%	3.125%
2	25.00	20.0	16.67	11.11	10.00	6.67	5.56	5.000
3	25.00	20.0	16.67	11.11	10.00	6.67	5.56	5.000
4	25.00	20.0	16.66	11.11	10.00	6.67	5.56	5.000
5	9.37	20.0	16.67	11.11	10.00	6.67	5.55	5.000
6		7.5	16.66	11.11	10.00	6.67	5.56	5.000
7			6.25	11.11	10.00	6.66	5.55	5.000
8				11.12	10.00	6.67	5.56	5.000
9				11.11	10.00	6.66	5.55	5.000
10				4.17	10.00	6.67	5.56	5.000
11					3.75	6.66	5.55	5.000
12						6.67	5.56	5.000
13						6.66	5.55	5.000
14						6.67	5.56	5.000
15						6.66	5.55	5.000
16						2.50	5.56	5.000
17							5.55	5.000
18							5.56	5.000
19							2.08	5.000
20								5.000
21								1.875

Table A-11. **Straight Line Method**
Mid-Quarter Convention
Placed in Service in Third Quarter

Year	Recovery periods in years							
	4	5	6	9	10	15	18	20
1	9.38%	7.5%	6.25%	4.17%	3.75%	2.50%	2.08%	1.875%
2	25.00	20.0	16.67	11.11	10.00	6.67	5.56	5.000
3	25.00	20.0	16.67	11.11	10.00	6.67	5.56	5.000
4	25.00	20.0	16.66	11.11	10.00	6.67	5.56	5.000
5	15.62	20.0	16.67	11.11	10.00	6.67	5.55	5.000
6		12.5	16.66	11.11	10.00	6.67	5.56	5.000
7			10.42	11.11	10.00	6.66	5.55	5.000
8				11.11	10.00	6.67	5.56	5.000
9				11.11	10.00	6.66	5.55	5.000
10				6.95	10.00	6.67	5.56	5.000
11					6.25	6.66	5.55	5.000
12						6.67	5.56	5.000
13						6.66	5.55	5.000
14						6.67	5.56	5.000
15						6.66	5.55	5.000
16						4.17	5.56	5.000
17							5.55	5.000
18							5.56	5.000
19							3.47	5.000
20								5.000
21								3.125

Table A-12. **Straight Line Method**
Mid-Quarter Convention
Placed in Service in Fourth Quarter

Year	Recovery periods in years							
	4	5	6	9	10	15	18	20
1	3.13%	2.5%	2.08%	1.39%	1.25%	0.83%	0.69%	0.625%
2	25.00	20.0	16.67	11.11	10.00	6.67	5.56	5.000
3	25.00	20.0	16.67	11.11	10.00	6.67	5.56	5.000
4	25.00	20.0	16.67	11.11	10.00	6.67	5.56	5.000
5	21.87	20.0	16.66	11.11	10.00	6.67	5.55	5.000
6		17.5	16.67	11.11	10.00	6.67	5.56	5.000
7			14.58	11.11	10.00	6.67	5.55	5.000
8				11.11	10.00	6.66	5.56	5.000
9				11.11	10.00	6.67	5.55	5.000
10				9.73	10.00	6.66	5.56	5.000
11					8.75	6.67	5.55	5.000
12						6.66	5.56	5.000
13						6.67	5.55	5.000
14						6.66	5.56	5.000
15						6.67	5.55	5.000
16						5.83	5.56	5.000
17							5.55	5.000
18							5.56	5.000
19							4.86	5.000
20								5.000
21								4.375

Table A-14. **150% Declining Balance Method**
Half-Year Convention

Year	Recovery periods in years						
	3	5	7	10	15	20	25
1	25.0%	15.00%	10.71%	7.50%	5.00%	3.750%	3.000%
2	37.5	25.50	19.13	13.88	9.50	7.219	5.820
3	25.0	17.85	15.03	11.79	8.55	6.677	5.471
4	12.5	16.66	12.25	10.02	7.70	6.177	5.143
5		16.66	12.25	8.74	6.93	5.713	4.834
6		8.33	12.25	8.74	6.23	5.285	4.544
7			12.25	8.74	5.90	4.888	4.271
8			6.13	8.74	5.90	4.522	4.015
9				8.74	5.91	4.462	3.774
10				8.74	5.90	4.461	3.584
11				4.37	5.91	4.462	3.583
12					5.90	4.461	3.584
13					5.91	4.462	3.583
14					5.90	4.461	3.584
15					5.91	4.462	3.583
16					2.95	4.461	3.584
17						4.462	3.583
18						4.461	3.584
19						4.462	3.583
20						4.461	3.584
21						2.231	3.583
22							3.584
23							3.583
24							3.584
25							3.583
26							1.792

Table A-15. **150% Declining Balance Method Mid-Quarter Convention Property Placed in Service in First Quarter**

Year	Recovery periods in years						
	3	5	7	10	15	20	25
1	43.75%	26.25%	18.75%	13.13%	8.75%	6.563%	5.250%
2	28.13	22.13	17.41	13.03	9.13	7.008	5.685
3	25.00	16.52	13.68	11.08	8.21	6.482	5.344
4	3.12	16.52	12.16	9.41	7.39	5.996	5.023
5		16.52	12.16	8.71	6.65	5.546	4.722
6		2.06	12.16	8.71	5.99	5.130	4.439
7			12.16	8.71	5.90	4.746	4.172
8			1.52	8.71	5.91	4.459	3.922
9				8.71	5.90	4.459	3.687
10				8.71	5.91	4.459	3.582
11				1.09	5.90	4.459	3.582
12					5.91	4.460	3.582
13					5.90	4.459	3.582
14					5.91	4.460	3.582
15					5.90	4.459	3.582
16					0.74	4.460	3.582
17						4.459	3.582
18						4.460	3.582
19						4.459	3.581
20						4.460	3.582
21						0.557	3.581
22							3.582
23							3.581
24							3.582
25							3.581
26							0.448

Table A-16. **150% Declining Balance Method Mid-Quarter Convention Property Placed in Service in Second Quarter**

Year	Recovery periods in years						
	3	5	7	10	15	20	25
1	31.25%	18.75%	13.39%	9.38%	6.25%	4.688%	3.750%
2	34.38	24.38	18.56	13.59	9.38	7.148	5.775
3	25.00	17.06	14.58	11.55	8.44	6.612	5.429
4	9.37	16.76	12.22	9.82	7.59	6.116	5.103
5		16.76	12.22	8.73	6.83	5.658	4.797
6		6.29	12.22	8.73	6.15	5.233	4.509
7			12.23	8.73	5.91	4.841	4.238
8			4.58	8.73	5.90	4.478	3.984
9				8.73	5.91	4.463	3.745
10				8.73	5.90	4.463	3.583
11				3.28	5.91	4.463	3.583
12					5.90	4.463	3.583
13					5.91	4.463	3.583
14					5.90	4.463	3.583
15					5.91	4.462	3.583
16					2.21	4.463	3.583
17						4.462	3.583
18						4.463	3.583
19						4.462	3.583
20						4.463	3.583
21						1.673	3.583
22							3.583
23							3.583
24							3.582
25							3.583
26							1.343

Table A-17. **150% Declining Balance Method Mid-Quarter Convention Property Placed in Service in Third Quarter**

Year	Recovery periods in years						
	3	5	7	10	15	20	25
1	18.75%	11.25%	8.04%	5.63%	3.75%	2.813%	2.250%
2	40.63	26.63	19.71	14.16	9.63	7.289	5.865
3	25.00	18.64	15.48	12.03	8.66	6.742	5.513
4	15.62	16.56	12.27	10.23	7.80	6.237	5.182
5		16.57	12.28	8.75	7.02	5.769	4.871
6		10.35	12.27	8.75	6.31	5.336	4.579
7			12.28	8.75	5.90	4.936	4.304
8			7.67	8.74	5.90	4.566	4.046
9				8.75	5.91	4.460	3.803
10				8.74	5.90	4.460	3.584
11				5.47	5.91	4.460	3.584
12					5.90	4.460	3.584
13					5.91	4.461	3.584
14					5.90	4.460	3.584
15					5.91	4.461	3.584
16					3.69	4.460	3.584
17						4.461	3.584
18						4.460	3.584
19						4.461	3.584
20						4.460	3.584
21						2.788	3.585
22							3.584
23							3.585
24							3.584
25							3.585
26							2.240

Table A-18. **150% Declining Balance Method Mid-Quarter Convention Property Placed in Service in Fourth Quarter**

Year	Recovery periods in years						
	3	5	7	10	15	20	25
1	6.25%	3.75%	2.88%	1.88%	1.25%	0.938%	0.750%
2	46.88	28.88	22.41	14.72	9.88	7.430	5.955
3	25.00	20.21	17.24	12.51	8.89	6.872	5.598
4	21.87	16.40	13.26	10.63	8.00	6.357	5.262
5		16.41	13.10	9.04	7.20	5.880	4.946
6		14.35	13.10	8.72	6.48	5.439	4.649
7			13.10	8.72	5.90	5.031	4.370
8			4.91	8.72	5.90	4.654	4.108
9				8.72	5.90	4.458	3.862
10				8.71	5.91	4.458	3.630
11				7.63	5.90	4.458	3.582
12					5.91	4.458	3.582
13					5.90	4.458	3.582
14					5.91	4.458	3.582
15					5.90	4.458	3.582
16					5.17	4.458	3.583
17						4.458	3.582
18						4.459	3.583
19						4.458	3.582
20						4.459	3.583
21						3.901	3.582
22							3.583
23							3.582
24							3.583
25							3.582
26							3.135

Table B-1. **Table of Class Lives and Recovery Periods**

Asset class	Description of assets included	Recovery Periods (in years) Class Life (in years)	GDS (MACRS)	ADS
	SPECIFIC DEPRECIABLE ASSETS USED IN ALL BUSINESS ACTIVITIES, EXCEPT AS NOTED:			
00.11	**Office Furniture, Fixtures, and Equipment:** Includes furniture and fixtures that are not a structural component of a building. Includes such assets as desks, files, safes, and communications equipment. Does not include communications equipment that is included in other classes.	10	7	10
00.12	**Information Systems:** Includes computers and their peripheral equipment used in administering normal business transactions and the maintenance of business records, their retrieval and analysis. Information systems are defined as: 1) Computers: A computer is a programmable electronically activated device capable of accepting information, applying prescribed processes to the information, and supplying the results of these processes with or without human intervention. It usually consists of a central processing unit containing extensive storage, logic, arithmetic, and control capabilities. Excluded from this category are adding machines, electronic desk calculators, etc., and other equipment described in class 00.13. 2) Peripheral equipment consists of the auxiliary machines which are designed to be placed under control of the central processing unit. Nonlimiting examples are: Card readers, card punches, magnetic tape feeds, high speed printers, optical character readers, tape cassettes, mass storage units, paper tape equipment, keypunches, data entry devices, teleprinters, terminals, tape drives, disc drives, disc files, disc packs, visual image projector tubes, card sorters, plotters, and collators. Peripheral equipment may be used on-line or off-line. Does not incude equipment that is an integral part of other capital equipment that is included in other classes of economic activity, i.e., computers used primarily for process or production control, switching, channeling, and automating distributive trades and services such as point of sale (POS) computer systems. Also, does not include equipment of a kind used primarily for amusement or entertainment of the user.	6	5	5
00.13	**Data Handling Equipment; except Computers:** Includes only typewriters, calculators, adding and accounting machines, copiers, and duplicating equipment.	6	5	6
00.21	**Airplanes (airframes and engines), except those used in commercial or contract carrying of passengers or freight, and all helicopters (airframes and engines)**	6	5	6
00.22	**Automobiles, Taxis**	3	5	5
00.23	**Buses**	9	5	9
00.241	**Light General Purpose Trucks:** Includes trucks for use over the road (actual weight less than 13,000 pounds)	4	5	5
00.242	**Heavy General Purpose Trucks:** Includes heavy general purpose trucks, concrete ready mix-trucks, and ore trucks, for use over the road (actual unloaded weight 13,000 pounds or more)	6	5	6
00.25	**Railroad Cars and Locomotives, except those owned by railroad transportation companies**	15	7	15
00.26	**Tractor Units for Use Over-The-Road**	4	3	4
00.27	**Trailers and Trailer-Mounted Containers**	6	5	6
00.28	**Vessels, Barges, Tugs, and Similar Water Transportation Equipment, except those used in marine construction**	18	10	18
00.3	**Land Imporvements:** Includes improvements directly to or added to land, whether such improvements are section 1245 property or section 1250 property, provided such improvements are depreciable. Examples of such assets might include sidewalks, roads, canals, waterways, drainage facilities, sewers (not including municipal sewers in Class 51), wharves and docks, bridges, fences, landscaping shrubbery, or radio and television transmitting towers. Does not include land improvements that are explicitly included in any other class, and buildings and structural components as defined in section 1.48-1(e) of the regulations. Excludes public utility initial clearing and grading land improvements as specified in Rev. Rul. 72-403, 1972-2 C.B. 102.	20	15	20

Table B-2. **Table of Class Lives and Recovery Periods**

Asset class	Description of assets included	Recovery Periods (in years)		
		Class Life (in years)	**GDS (MACRS)**	**ADS**
	DEPRECIABLE ASSETS USED IN THE FOLLOWING ACTIVITIES:			
01.1	**Agriculture:** Includes machinery and equipment, grain bins, and fences but no other land improvements, that are used in the production of crops or plants, vines, and trees; livestock; the operation of farm dairies, nurseries, greenhouses, sod farms, mushroom cellars, cranberry bogs, apiaries, and fur farms; the performance of agriculture, animal husbandry, and horticultural services.	10	7	10
01.11	**Cotton Ginning Assets**	12	7	12
01.21	**Cattle, Breeding or Dairy**	7	5	7
01.221	**Any breeding or work horse that is 12 years old or less at the time it is placed in service****	10	7	10
01.222	**Any breeding or work horse that is more than 12 years old at the time it is placed in service****	10	3	10
01.223	**Any race horse that is more than 2 years old at the time it is placed in service****	*	3	12
01.224	**Any horse that is more than 12 years old at the time it is placed in service and that is neither a race horse nor a horse described in class 01.222****	*	3	12
01.225	**Any horse not described in classes 01.221, 01.222, 01.223, or 01.224**	*	7	12
01.23	**Hogs, Breeding**	3	3	3
01.24	**Sheep and Goats, Breeding**	5	5	5
01.3	**Farm buildings except structures included in Class 01.4**	25	20	25
01.4	**Single purpose agricultural or horticultural structures (within the meaning of section 168(i)(13) of the Code)**	15	10***	15
10.0	**Mining:** Includes assets used in the mining and quarrying of metallic and nonmetallic minerals (including sand, gravel, stone, and clay) and the milling, beneficiation and other primary preparation of such materials.	10	7	10
13.0	**Offshore Drilling:** Includes assets used in offshore drilling for oil and gas such as floating, self-propelled and other drilling vessels, barges, platforms, and drilling equipment and support vessels such as tenders, barges, towboats and crewboats. Excludes oil and gas production assets.	7.5	5	7.5
13.1	**Drilling of Oil and Gas Wells:** Includes assets used in the drilling of onshore oil and gas wells and the provision of geophysical and other exploration services; and the provision of such oil and gas field services as chemical treatment, plugging and abandoning of wells and cementing or perforating well casings. Does not include assets used in the performance of any of these activities and services by integrated petroleum and natural gas producers for their own account.	6	5	6
15.0	**Construction:** Includes assets used in construction by general building, special trade, heavy and marine construction contractors, operative and investment builders, real estate subdividers and developers, and others except railroads.	6	5	6
57.0	**Distributive Trades and Services:** Includes assets used in wholesale and retail trade, and personal and professional services. Includes section 1245 assets used in marketing petroleum and petroleum products.	9	5	9****
57.1	**Distributive Trades and Services—Billboard, Service Station Buildings and Petroleum Marketing Land Improvements:** Includes section 1250 assets, including service station buildings and depreciable land improvements, whether section 1245 property or section 1250 property, used in the marketing of petroleum and petroleum products, but not including any of these facilities related to petroleum and natural gas trunk pipelines. Includes car wash buildings and related land improvements. Includes billboards, whether such assets are section 1245 property or section 1250 property. Excludes all other land improvements, buildings and structural components as defined in section 1.48-1(e) of the regulations. See *Gas station convenience stores* in chapter 3.	20	15	20
79.0	**Recreation:** Includes assets used in the provision of entertainment services on payment of a fee or admission charge, as in the operation of bowling alleys, billiard and pool establishments, theaters, concert halls, and miniature golf courses. Does not include amusement and theme parks and assets which consist primarily of specialized land improvements or structures, such as golf courses, sports stadia, race tracks, ski slopes, and buildings which house the assets used in entertainment services.	10	7	10
	Certain Property for Which Recovery Periods Assigned A. Personal Property With No Class Life Section 1245 Real Property With No Class Life		 7 7	 12 40

* Property described in asset classes 01.223, 01.224, and 01.225 are assigned recovery periods but have no class lives.

** A horse is more than 2 (or 12) years old after the day that is 24 (or 144) months after its actual birthdate.

*** 7 if property was placed in service before 1989.

**** Any high technology medical equipment as defined in section 168(i)(2)(C) which is described in asset guideline class 57.0 is assigned a 5-year recovery period for the alternate MACRS method.

Chapter 8

Business Profit and Self-Employment Tax

Once you have added up all your gross business income, and you've dug up all your deductible business expenses for the year, you can calculate your net business income by subtracting your expenses from your income. Hopefully, you still have some income left over after expenses are deducted, and this amount is your profit for tax purposes.

This calculation is made on Line 31 of your Schedule C or on Line 3 of your C-EZ. If you have more than one Schedule C, the results from each one are computed separately.

The results from any and all Schedule Cs you have are totaled up and carried over to your individual income tax return (Form 1040, Line 12), where they will become part of your adjusted gross income (AGI). If you are filing jointly with your spouse, the net income from any Schedule Cs filed by your spouse is also included.

Owning a business is full of surprises, both good and bad. In some years you may find that your expenses exceed your gross business income, which means that you have a loss for the year. This can be deducted against any other income you or your spouse may have, or carried over to other years in which you have more income, provided you meet certain requirements, as discussed on page 139 below.

Your net business income is important for another reason: it is the amount on which you must pay self-employment taxes. So, your net business profit or loss is also carried over to Line 2 of Schedule SE, which is used to compute your self-employment (SECA) tax.

SELF-EMPLOYMENT TAX

Brand-new business owners are sometimes surprised to find out that in addition to their federal income taxes, they must also pay a significant percentage of their income as SECA taxes.

The Self-Employment Contributions Act (SECA) tax is basically the business owner's version of the FICA tax that employees pay. Like FICA, it is made up of your "contributions" to both the Social Security and Medicare programs. However, the tax rate for the self-employed under SECA is twice the rate that employees must pay on their paychecks as FICA tax, to reflect the fact that employees pay one-half of the FICA tax and employers pay the other half.

What Income Counts?

For starters, you don't have to worry about paying the SECA tax at all if your total business income, from all Schedule Cs combined, is less than $400. But if your total income is $400 or more, you must file a Schedule SE (Form 1040) and pay SECA tax on your entire profits, including the first $400.

If you are filing jointly and your spouse also files one or more Schedule Cs, each spouse must count his or her own income separately.

Example

You own two small businesses and file two Schedule Cs. Business A had net income of $80,000 and Business B had a net loss of $5,000. Your spouse also operated a business as a sole proprietor, and had net income of $20,000. On Line 12 of your Form 1040, you would report all Schedule C income earned by both you and your spouse: $80,000 + $20,000 - $5,000 = $95,000.

However, for SECA tax purposes, your total net business income would be $80,000 - $5,000 = $75,000. Your spouse's total net income for SECA purposes would be $20,000. You must each file one Schedule SE and attach both of them to your joint Form 1040.

Since it's the net income from your *business* that is the basis of SECA tax, certain types of income are not included: interest and dividends, sales of business property or other assets, and rental income from real estate or personal property. There's an exception to this rule if generating that income is your core business; for instance, if you are a real estate developer in the business of renting or selling property, you operate a bank, or you are in the rent-to-own business. Do not count any income from your hobbies, as defined on page 34.

Farmers

Farmers who file Schedule F with their Form 1040 must include as self-employment income their net income from farming, as shown on Line 36 of their Schedule F.

Partners

Partners must also include their distributions from the partnership, as well as any guaranteed payments they receive for their services, as net self-employment income. These amounts should be shown on the Schedule K-1 information return that a partner receives from the partnership at the end of the year. For all general partners, this is true whether you are an active or inactive member of the partnership. For limited partners, you need only to include any guaranteed payments, such as salary or professional fees received during the year.

There is an exception to this rule if the partnership is an investment club, and the club limits its activities to investing in CDs and securities, and collecting income on the investments.

If you are a retired partner, you do not need to include your retirement income received from the partnership in net earnings from self-employment if all of the following are true:

- You are receiving periodic payments for life.
- Your share of the partnership capital has been fully repaid. The partnership owes you nothing but the retirement payments.
- You performed no services for the partnership this year.

Corporate Payments

If you are an S corporation shareholder, unlike a partner, your distributions from the organization generally do not count as self-employment income and are not subject to SECA tax. However, if you are a shareholder and also an officer of the company who performs substantial services, you are considered an employee. Some reasonable amount of compensation for your services must be considered salary or wages, on which regular payroll taxes, including Social Security, Medicare, and income tax withholding, must be paid.

Corporate directors of either C or S corporations who receive fees are not considered employees. Instead, their fees are considered self-employment income. However, if you are a corporate officer or other employee, your income is subject to regular payroll taxes (including FICA) and you aren't considered self-employed for purposes of SECA tax.

Religious Exemptions

There are some special exemptions from self-employment income that may apply if you are a member of certain religions, or you work for a religious group.

If you are a member of a religious order who has taken a vow of poverty, you are exempt from self-employment tax as long as you are working for the church or a church agency. But if you are working for yourself, you must pay SECA tax.

If you have not taken a vow of poverty, but you are a minister, member of a religious order, or a Christian Science practitioner, you can get an exemption from SECA tax if you file IRS Form 4361, *Application for Exemption from Self-Employment Tax for Use by Ministers, Members of Religious Orders, and Christian Science Practitioners.* To get a copy, call the IRS at 1-800-TAX-FORM.

If you are a member of a recognized sect that has been in existence since December 31, 1950 and that is opposed to insurance, you may be exempt from Social Security and Medicare tax (and thus, SECA tax) if you are conscientiously opposed to pension plans or life, disability, or medical insurance and you waive all Social Security benefits. To get the exemption, you must file IRS Form 4029, *Application for Exemption from Social Security and Medicare Taxes and Waiver of Benefits*, which you can obtain by calling 1-800-TAX-FORM.

If none of the above apply to you and you are an employee of a church or church-controlled organization that has itself elected exemption from Social Security and Medicare taxes, you will have to pay SECA tax if you are paid $108.28 or more in a year by the church or organization.

Aliens

Aliens who are residents of the United States are generally subject to the same rules as U.S. citizens, including SECA tax rules. Residents of the Virgin Islands, Puerto Rico, Guam, or American Samoa are also subject to SECA tax. Self-employment activities of U.S. citizens in these regions plus the Northern Mariana Islands are subject to SECA tax.

Nonresident aliens will be subject to SECA tax on income earned in the U.S. unless they are citizens of a country that has a social security agreement or treaty in effect with the U.S. If an agreement is in effect, the terms of the agreement will dictate the rules. Currently there are agreements with Australia, Austria, Belgium, Canada, Finland, France, Germany, Greece, Ireland, Italy, Luxembourg, the Netherlands, Norway, Portugal, South Korea, Spain, Sweden, Switzerland, and the United Kingdom. For more information, contact a country's social security agency, or the Social Security Administration, Office of International Programs, P.O. Box 17741, Baltimore, MD 21235-7741.

Other Miscellaneous Income

If you are the executor or administrator of a deceased person's estate, your fees are exempt from SECA tax and are simply reported as miscellaneous income on Line 21 of your Form 1040. An exception to this rule applies if you are a professional fiduciary, or the estate includes an active trade or business that you participate in and your fees are related to operating the business, or your administrative duties are so extensive over a long period of time that they should be considered a trade or business. In any of these cases, you'd need to file a Schedule C to report the income and, in turn, a Schedule SE to report self-employment income.

Since statutory employees already have FICA tax withheld from their payments, they do not have to pay SECA tax. See page 48 for more on statutory employees.

Fees received as a notary public are not subject to SECA tax.

The $94,200 Ceiling

In computing your SECA tax, the Medicare portion of the tax is imposed on 2.9 percent of all your net business income, with no upper limit.

The Social Security portion of the tax is 12.4 percent, but it only applies to the first $94,200 you earn in 2006 ($97,500 in 2007). This dollar amount increases every year to reflect increases in the average American wage.

For purpose of determining whether you meet the $94,200 ceiling, only your own earnings – and not those of your spouse – are counted.

If you have earnings from a regular job, or perhaps more than one job, your employer will automatically be withholding FICA tax on your wages. Your wages, salary, bonus, tips, etc. earned on the job will count towards the $94,200 amount, and at most your SECA tax will apply to the difference.

Overpayments of FICA Tax

If you had more than one job during the year, and the total of all your income from those jobs added up to more than $94,200, it's likely that too much Social Security tax has been withheld from your paychecks.

Take a look at the amount in Box 4 on all of your W-2 Forms. If you add them up and the sum is more than $5,840.40 ($94,200 x 6.2 percent), you've paid too much tax. The overpayment (what you've paid, minus $5,840.40) can be claimed as a subtraction from your tax bill on Line 67 of Form 1040. You cannot use Forms 1040EZ or 1040A to claim this overpayment.

Computing Your SECA Tax

Your SECA tax is computed by filling out either the long or the short version of Schedule SE.

Most people can use the short version of the form. Those who cannot include those whose total wages, tips, salary and earnings from self-employment were more than $94,200 in 2006; religious workers who owe self-employment taxes (see discussion above); or farmers or low-income people using one of the optional methods discussed below (which generally require you to pay higher SECA taxes).

Unless you are using one of the optional methods, to compute your SECA tax you will transfer your net self-employment income to Lines 1 and 2 of the short SE form or the long SE.

Then, you will multiply your total net self-employment income by 92.35 percent (.9235) to get your taxable net earnings from self-employment. This fraction has the effect of giving you a deduction from your income for one-half of the SECA taxes you'd otherwise have to pay, to reflect the fact that employees don't have to pay FICA tax on the portion of FICA that their employers pay them.

Then, multiply the result by 15.3 percent to arrive at your SECA tax, unless your combined wages, tips, salary, bonus and your net earnings from self-employment are greater than $94,200. If they are, you will be using the long form of Schedule SE, which will allow you to make sure you're paying Social Security only on the first $94,200 you make.

Finally, you will enter the amount of your SECA tax on Line 5 of the short SE or Line 12 of the long SE, and then transfer it to Line 58 of your Form 1040 and add it to the income tax you owe.

Don't forget the very last step, which is to give yourself an income tax deduction for one-half of your SECA tax (computed on Line 6 of the short SE and Line 13 of the long one). This amount is transferred to Line 27 of your Form 1040. It has the effect of allowing you to avoid paying income tax on one-half of your SECA tax amount, just as employees do not have to pay income tax on the amount of FICA tax that their employers pay for them.

Optional Methods

As we mentioned above, there are two optional methods of computing your SECA tax.

To understand why these optional methods exist, you have to realize that Social Security disability and retirement benefits are conditioned on your having worked a certain amount during your lifetime; generally you need to have worked for at least 40 calendar quarters (or 10 years) in which you were covered by Social Security and earned a minimum amount. For 2006, you must earn $970 ($1,000 in 2007) to get a quarter of coverage; if you earn $3,880 or more ($4,000 in 2007) you will be credited with four quarters.

When the Social Security system was enacted, people who were relatively close to retirement, or who had been out of the workforce or had worked for many years at very low-paying jobs, were in danger of not qualifying for retirement benefits. This is less of a problem today, when most workers earn many more quarters than the minimum needed to qualify; however, there are still a few people who might be in danger of falling outside the Social Security system if they did not have a special way to qualify. In particular, some farmers whose income fluctuates a great deal from year to year and who often suffer an annual financial loss may need some help in gaining more quarters of coverage.

Hence, the optional methods of computing net earnings from self-employment, which operate by allowing you to pay SECA tax as if your net earnings were higher than they actually were.

Can I Use the Optional Methods?

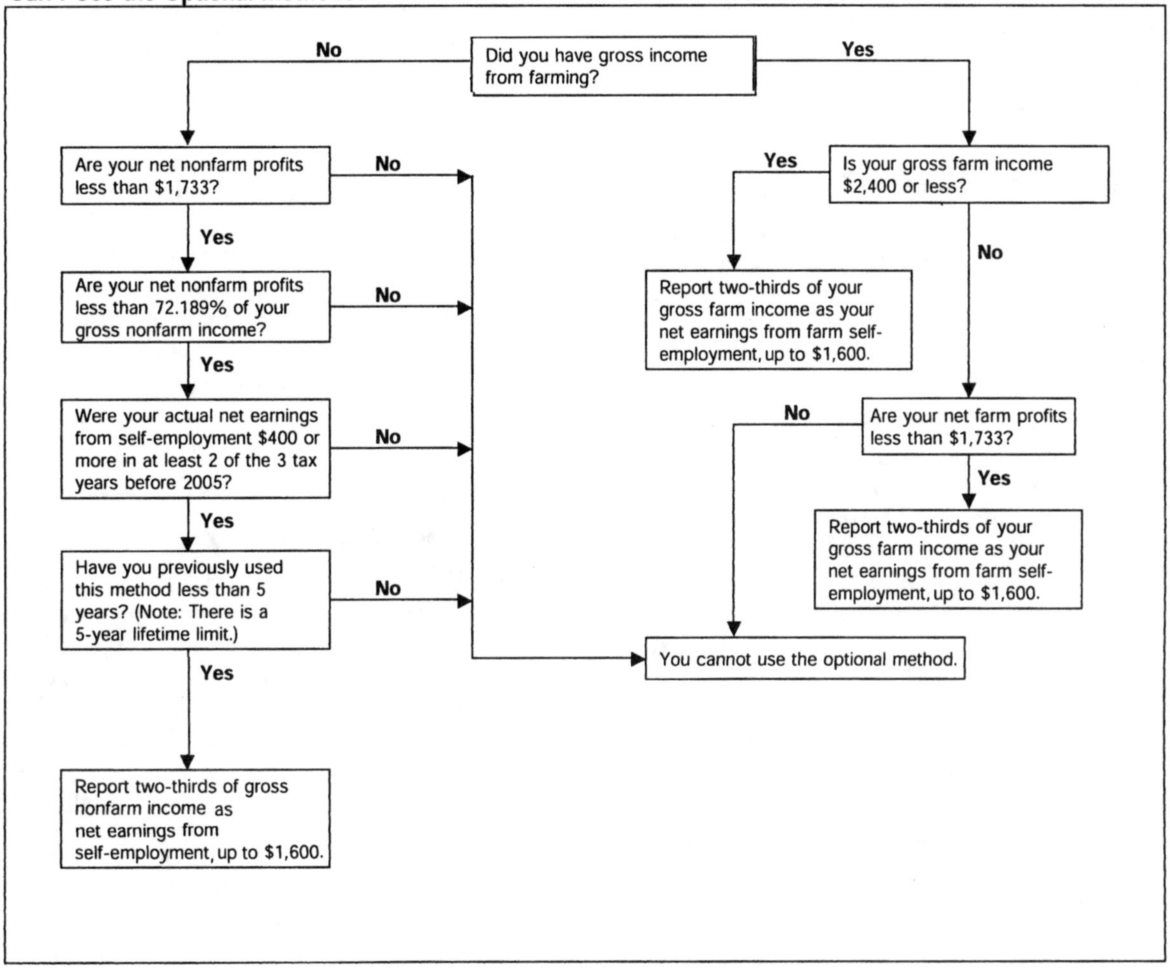

There is a special optional method for farmers, and a slightly less lenient method for low-income non-farmers. Either of these methods can also help you if you are entitled to the Earned Income Credit (EIC) and increasing your net self-employment income will help you to obtain a higher EIC amount.

The flow chart above will tell you whether or not you qualify to use one of these methods. If you are eligible, Part II of the long version of Schedule SE will walk you through the computations.

NET OPERATING LOSSES

If you're like most small business owners, you won't see a profit in your first year of operation. And as your business grows, you may face one or more years in which your business's expenses exceed its income. In other words, the business may have a loss for the year.

Although it may be small comfort, if you have a loss, you'll normally be able to deduct it from your total income from other business ventures or from any salary, wages, or other earnings. If the business loss exceeds your total income for the year, any unused portion of the loss, which is known in the tax laws as a net operating loss (NOL), can be used to offset income and reduce taxes in another year.

The net operating loss deduction is an exception to the general income tax rule that your taxable income is determined on the basis of your current year's events. This deduction allows you to offset one year's losses against another year's income. A net loss from the operation of a trade or business, casualty losses, and losses resulting from employee business expenses are included in this computation, but losses from a trade or business are the most common occurrence.

Calculating an NOL can be tricky and we suggest that, if you have one, you consult a professional to help ensure you do it correctly, or get the IRS's free Publication 536, *Net Operating Losses.* The following discussion is intended to give you a basic understanding of how NOLs work

Do You Have an NOL?

If you complete your 2006 tax return and you have a negative number on Line 41 of your Form 1040, you may have an NOL that may potentially be carried over to other years. If so, 2006 will be called your "NOL year."

The next step is to determine whether or not you have a deductible NOL. Schedule A of Form 1045, *Application for Tentative Refund,* should be used to compute the amount of your NOL. This can become complicated, because a number of things that are ordinarily deductible on your tax return cannot be deducted for purposes of determining whether you actually have an NOL: personal exemptions for yourself, spouse, and dependents; net capital losses, which are subject to different carryover rules; nonbusiness losses; NOL deductions from other years; and nonbusiness deductions such as alimony, medical deductions, charitable deductions, real estate tax on your residence, deductible IRA contributions, or the standard deduction if you don't itemize.

Net operating losses generally may be carried back for two years (or for three years, in the case of a casualty loss) before the year of the loss (called the NOL year). The loss is used to offset the taxable income of those previous years, for the earliest year first. Any unused portion of the loss may be carried forward for up to 20 years after the NOL year. If the entire loss isn't used up within the permitted period, no further net operating loss carryover is permitted.

To "carry a loss back" that occurred in 2006, you may file a Form 1045 within one year of the end of the NOL year, or you can file an amended tax return on Form 1040X for the year in question no later than three years after the due date of the return for the applicable tax year (not recommended).

Example

If your NOL year was 2006 and you filed your tax return on April 16, 2007, you can file Form 1045 any time on or after April 16 of 2007 but before January 1, 2008, to claim a refund for 2004.

Whichever form you use to claim the carryback, you must use Schedule A of Form 1045 to compute the amount of the NOL.

A taxpayer can elect to forgo the carryback period, instead choosing to deduct the net operating loss only over the next 20 years in the future. If so, you must attach a statement to your tax return for the NOL year, or to an amended return for that year filed within six months of its due date excluding extensions. The statement must assert that you are electing to forgo the carryback period under Section 172(b)(3) of the Internal Revenue Code.

Save Money

Because carrying back a net operating loss to a prior tax year can result in a quick tax refund, it will usually be unwise to pass up the carryback period, unless you're quite sure that your business will be in a higher tax bracket in the future.

When you carry back an NOL, you must refigure your tax for the carryback year by recomputing your adjusted gross income (AGI) for that year. Then you must recompute any items that were limited by your AGI amount, such as the special allowance for passive activities, taxable Social Security benefits, IRA deductions, and excludable savings bond interest.

Next, refigure your taxable income if needed to reflect the change in your itemized deductions for medical expenses, casualty losses, miscellaneous itemized deductions, and the overall limit on itemized deductions and phaseout of personal exemptions for higher-income taxpayers. You will also have to refigure your AMT, if it applied to you. However, do not refigure your self-employment tax for the carryback year.

If you don't use up your entire NOL in the first carryback year, you may have a carryover, and you'll need to use Schedule B of Form 1045 to compute the amount.

If you carry forward an NOL, things are a little simpler. You would list your NOL figure as a negative amount on the "other income" line of Form 1040, and attach a statement showing how you computed the NOL.

Chapter 9

Business Tax Credits

Besides taking care to claim every single tax deduction that you qualify for, you can minimize your income tax bill by claiming any and all the business tax credits available to you. When they're available, tax credits are generally a better deal than tax deductions would be, because credits are subtracted directly from your tax bill. On the other hand, deductions are subtracted from the *income* on which your tax bill is based.

So, a dollar's worth of tax credit reduces your tax bill by a whole dollar, but a dollar's worth of deductions lowers your tax bill by only 35 cents if you're in a 35-percent bracket, by 33 cents if you're in a 33-percent bracket, etc. If you have a choice between claiming a credit or a deduction for a certain expense, you're generally better off claiming the credit.

As wonderful as tax credits can be, with the IRS (as you've probably figured out by now) there's almost always a catch. In this case, the catch is that business tax credits are only available for certain very specific situations. Many of them apply only to certain industries (like restaurants and bars, or energy producers). And credits come with a set of very complicated rules, which you (or, more likely, your tax pro) must follow in order to claim them.

Most federal tax credits currently available to business owners are very narrowly targeted to encourage you to take certain actions that lawmakers have deemed desirable; generally, to benefit disadvantaged or low-income individuals or the environment. There are also a few credits designed to prevent double taxation, and a few designed to encourage certain investments that are considered socially beneficial.

The forms and procedures used to calculate and claim business tax credits are quite complicated. In fact, we recommend that you leave the technical details to your tax adviser. However, we do provide an outline of the basic rules, including the dollar limits, carryback and carryforward rules, and recapture rules, so you can decide whether to pursue arranging your business affairs to take advantage of a credit.

As you go through this section, please be aware that Congress failed to renew many tax credits that have been around for many years. These credits include the R&D tax credit, the Work Opportunity Tax Credit, Welfare-to-Work incentives, and the Indian employment tax credit for wages and health insurance. They continue to be included here, though, because there is still a good chance that they will be extended for 2006.

CREDITS FOR CERTAIN TAXES

You might not believe it, but sometimes the IRS does have a heart. It occasionally gives certain people a break for taxes that might be considered unfair. There are four business tax credits that give a "rebate" for certain kinds of taxes.

Credit for FICA Tax on Tips

Under current law, employees who get $20 or more in tips in a single month must report their tips to their employers. If you have tipped employees, you have to pay Social Security and Medicare (FICA) taxes to the tune of 7.65 percent on tips that are reported to you, even though you don't have any control over the amounts. The purpose of the rule is to make sure that tipped employees are adequately covered by Social Security pension, disability, and survivors' benefits. However, the rule was believed to place a particularly heavy burden on the restaurant industry.

So, if your business is one that provides food or beverages for customers to consume on or off the premises, and if your waiters, waitresses, or delivery personnel are customarily tipped by your patrons, you're entitled to a tax credit for any FICA taxes you pay on the tips.

The upshot of all this? Your workers receive Social Security credits towards their future benefits on account of the tips, but you don't have to pay for these benefits. Note that there's an exception to the general credit rule: If you pay your employees below the minimum wage, with the expectation that tips will bring them up to the minimum, you can't claim the credit for FICA on the portion of the tips that is used to bring them up to the minimum wage.

No double-dipping is allowed. If you are eligible for and decide to claim this credit, you can't deduct the FICA taxes on which the credit is claimed as a business expense. However, because tax credits are generally worth more than deductions, this is not usually a problem.

The FICA tax credit is claimed on Form 8846, *Credit for Employer Social Security and Medicare Taxes Paid on Certain Employee Tips,* and is part of the general business credit.

The total of all your general business credits can't reduce your current year's tax bill below the larger of (a) your tentative minimum tax or (b) 25 percent of the part of your regular tax bill that exceeds $25,000.

Gasoline Tax Credit

You can claim a credit for any federal excise taxes you pay on gasoline and special fuels (like undyed diesel, heating oil, liquefied petroleum gas, and compressed natural gas), when you use the fuel for certain purposes: for farming; for nonhighway purposes of your trade or business; for intercity, local, or school buses; or for export or foreign trade. You can't claim this credit for any personal (nonbusiness) use, so forget about claiming it for your snowmobile or pleasure boat! The credit is claimed on Form 4136, *Credit for Federal Tax Paid on Fuels.* It is *refundable*, meaning that the IRS will pay it to you even if you have no tax liability for the year.

Foreign Tax Credit

You can claim a credit for foreign income taxes, or taxes imposed by possessions of the U.S., that you paid or accrued during the tax year. For example, you might have become liable for foreign taxes on profits from overseas operations or investments. You can elect to deduct these taxes instead of taking the credit, if you prefer, although claiming the credit will generally save you more money. The credit is claimed on Form 1116, *Foreign Tax Credit.*

Prior Years' AMT Credit

If you paid alternative minimum tax (see page 305) in a prior year, you may be eligible for a credit for a portion of it against your regular tax liability for the current year, and for subsequent years as well. The credit is claimed on Form 8801, *Credit for Prior Year Minimum Tax—Individuals, Estates, and Trusts.*

Save Time

If you have paid AMT in prior years and think you might be eligible for this credit, see your tax adviser. The AMT rules are a morass of confusion, and interpretation of them is best left to professionals.

CREDITS BENEFITING DISADVANTAGED GROUPS

The tax laws have historically been used to encourage certain activities that the government deems desirable, but that people might not otherwise undertake on their own because the economic rewards are perceived as insufficient. This group of tax credits is a good example of that type of policy.

Welfare-to-Work Credit

A tax credit is provided to employers who hire qualified long-term family assistance (AFDC or its successor program) recipients. The credit is equal to 35 percent of up to $10,000 of wages in the first year and up to 50 percent of up to $10,000 in the second year of employment, for a two-year maximum credit of $8,500 per employee. The credit is available for employees hired from January 1, 1998 and before January 1, 2006, and is claimed on Form 8861, *Welfare-to-Work Credit.*

Work Smart

Note that if you claim the welfare-to-work credit for an employee, you can't also claim the work opportunity credit for that employee. The welfare-to-work credit is more generous, so it will usually be more beneficial to claim it, rather than the work opportunity credit, where the employee would qualify for both.

Work Opportunity Credit

This credit was designed to provide an incentive to hire persons from certain disadvantaged groups that have a particularly high unemployment rate (including urban youths, government assistance recipients, ex-convicts, veterans, and vocational rehabilitation referrals). It was created in 1996 to replace the expired targeted jobs credit. The credit is claimed on Form 5884, *Work Opportunity Credit.*

The Work Opportunity Tax Credit (WOTC) is available for a limited time—it applies to the wages of employees who began work after October 1, 1996, and before January 1, 2006.

For targeted employees hired in 2005, employers may generally claim a credit equal to 40 percent of the first $6,000 of qualified wages paid during an employee's first year of employment, provided the employee performs at least 400 hours of service. If an employee works less than 400 hours, but at least 120 hours, the credit is reduced to 25 percent. No credit is available for employees who work fewer than 120 hours.

The credit applies to the wages of the following groups:

- families receiving cash welfare benefits for at least nine months
- veterans who are members of families receiving assistance or food stamps
- high-risk youth aged 18 through 24 on their hiring date who live in an empowerment zone or enterprise community
- vocational rehabilitation referrals certified to have a physical or mental disability
- qualified summer youth employees aged 16 or 17 on the hiring date who live in an empowerment zone or enterprise community, perform services during a 90-day period between May 1 and September 15, and who have not previously worked for the employer
- ex-felons hired not more than one year after the later of their conviction or release from prison, who are members of low-income families
- individuals aged 18 to 24 who are in families that have been receiving food stamps for six months
- Supplemental Security Income (SSI) recipients

Under special provisions, an employer's credit for hiring an eligible summer youth employee is only 40 percent of the first $3,000 of wages earned during the 90-day period. If the summer youth employee continues working for the employer after the 90-day period, the employer can get an additional credit until the employee earns $6,000 for the year if the employee qualifies as a member of another targeted group (e.g. part of a family receiving food stamps for six months).

The Katrina Emergency Tax Relief Act of 2005 expands the work opportunity tax credit to include a new target group for the WOTC, "Hurricane Katrina employees." A Hurricane Katrina employee is an individual whose principal place of residence was in the core disaster area on August 28, 2005. If a business employed a particular worker on August 28, however, it is ineligible for a WOTC for that worker.

Employers must take the credit for an individual hired to work in a core disaster area by August 27, 2007; employers can take the credit for a displaced individual hired by December 31, 2005, regardless of where the employee works. The expiration date of the WOTC is waived for these employees.

Employee Retention Credit

The Katrina Emergency Tax Relief Act of 2005 also offers a new tax credit to encourage small employers to keep employees on their payrolls. Like the WOTC, the Employee Retention Credit is 40 percent of the first $6,000 in wages paid to each eligible employee after August 28, 2005, and before January 1, 2006, by employers located in a core disaster area (i.e., presidentially declared disaster area), for the period the business is rendered inoperable as a result of damage caused by Hurricane Katrina. This credit is only available to small employers, defined as a business that employed an average of no more than 200 employees during the tax year.

Disabled Access Credit

Under the Americans with Disabilities Act of 1990 (ADA), businesses that are open to the public ("public accommodations," in legal language) must help or accommodate persons with disabilities seeking to use their services. They must also remove physical barriers to the disabled, if removal is "readily achievable."

Example

The regulations say moving tables in a restaurant is "readily achievable," but widening a doorway is not.

What's more, any renovations or new construction must include provisions for access by the disabled, in accordance with certain very technical specifications.

Small businesses that are faced with making changes to obey the ADA have been given a "carrot," in the form of a tax credit, to encourage them to comply with the law. For any year, you may claim a credit for 50 percent of your eligible access expenditures that exceed $250 but don't exceed $10,250. So, you can't claim more than $5,000 in any one year.

The "eligible access expenditures" include not only expenses for removal of physical barriers (in renovations, but not new construction), but also expenses for deaf interpreters; readers for the blind; equipment or devices to make services available to the deaf, blind, or other disabled persons; or similar expenses.

Save Money

If you anticipate that your disabled accommodation expenses will exceed $10,250, try to spread them over more than one year in order to take maximum advantage of the tax credit.

This tax credit is available only to small businesses—that is, those having: (1) gross receipts of $1 million or less, or (2) having no more than 30 full-time employees.

The disabled access credit is claimed on Form 8826, *Disabled Access Credit,* and is part of the general business credit discussed on page 148.

Empowerment Zone Employment Credit

If your business is located in a federal "empowerment zone," and you hire workers who also live and work within the zone, you can get a tax credit for 20 percent of the first $15,000 of wages paid to each of your workers (i.e., $3,000 maximum credit per employee each year). The workers can be full-time or part-time, so long as substantially all of their work is done within the zone and as part of your trade or business. You can't count wages paid to employees who worked for less than 90 days (unless the worker became disabled or was fired for misconduct); employees who are closely related to you; employees who own 5 percent or more of the business; or employees at golf courses, country clubs, massage parlors, hot tub facilities, suntan facilities, racetrack or gambling facilities, or liquor stores.

Where are these zones? The initial zones created involve certain designated parts of Atlanta, Baltimore, Chicago, Detroit, New York, and Philadelphia; portions of Clinton, Jackson, and Wayne Counties in Kentucky; portions of Bolivar, Sunflower, Leflore, Washington, Humphreys, and Holmes Counties in Mississippi; and portions of Starr, Cameron, Hidalgo, and Willacy Counties in Texas. The phase out of the credit for these areas that was to begin in 2002 has been eliminated.

In 1999, 20 more empowerment zones were designated, located in Boston; Bridgeton/Vineland, New Jersey; Cincinnati, Columbia/Sumter, South Carolina; Columbus, Ohio; El Paso, Texas; Gary/East Chicago, Indiana; Huntington, West Virginia; Ironton, Ohio; Knoxville, Tennessee; Miami, Florida; Minneapolis, Minnesota; New Haven, Connecticut; Norfolk/Portsmouth, Virginia; Santa Ana, California; St. Louis, Missouri /East St. Louis, Illinois; Cordele, Georgia; Fargo, North Dakota; Oglala Sioux Reservation in Pine Ridge, South Dakota; Riverside County, California; and Ulline, Illinois. These empowerment zones were not eligible for a wage tax credit until 2002. To help compensate for this, eligible employers may expense (rather than depreciate) $35,000 of additional qualified zone property in 2002.

Beginning in 1998, portions of Washington, D.C. have been designated as enterprise zones that are eligible for the empowerment zone wage tax credit. This law is scheduled to expire on December 31, 2003. In contrast, the lives of all the other enterprise zones have been extended through December 31, 2009.

In 2002, the following eight new zones were designated: Pulaski County, Arkansas; Fresno, California; Jacksonville, Florida; Syracuse, and Yonkers, New York; Oklahoma City; and San Antonio, Texas. Business in the new zones will share the same tax incentives as other existing zones (i.e., a 20 percent wage credit, $35,000 of additional expensing of property and enhanced tax-exempt financing benefits). The tax incentives would begin in 2002 and end December 31, 2009.

If you live in one of these designated cities or areas, contact your city or county government to find out the exact boundaries of the empowerment zones.

The empowerment zone employment tax credit is claimed on Form 8848, *Empowerment Zone Employment Credit,* and is part of the general business credit (see page 148).

Indian Employment Credit

If your business is located on an Indian reservation, and you have employees who live on or near the reservation, you may be eligible for a special tax credit. You can claim a credit for 20 percent of your wages or health insurance costs for the year (up to $20,000 per employee) that exceed the total of comparable costs you had in 1993. However, the employee must be an enrolled member, or the spouse of an enrolled member, of an Indian tribe.

Until it expires at the end of 2005, the credit is claimed on Form 8845, *Indian Employment Credit.*

Community Development Corporation Credit

The government wants to encourage you to make gifts or long-term loans to community development corporations (CDCs) that provide employment and business opportunities to low-income individuals. So, you can claim a tax credit for 5 percent of the amount you contribute, for each of 10 tax years beginning with the year you make the contribution. Eventually, you'll get tax credits for 50 percent of the contribution.

If the contribution is a gift, you can also take a charitable contribution deduction for the full amount, in the year you make it. If the contribution is a loan, the loan term must be at least 10 years. The CDC must be one of 20 organizations selected by the Secretary of HUD.

The CDC contribution credit is claimed on Form 8847, *Credit for Contributions to Selected Community Development Corporations.*

New Markets Credit

This tax credit for qualified equity investments made after December 31, 2000, to acquire stock in a community development entity (CDE). The credit includes any capital or equity investment in, or loan to, any qualified active low-income community business or qualified community development entity.

A CDE is any domestic corporation or partnership whose primary mission is serving or providing investment capital for low-income communities or low-income persons, that maintains accountability to residents of low-income communities through representation on governing or advisory boards of the CDE, and is certified by the Treasury Department as an eligible CDE. Examples of CDEs include community development banks, venture funds, and new investment companies.

The credit is worth over 30 percent of the amount invested (in present value terms). An investor is allowed a five percent credit for the year in which the equity interest is purchased from the CDE and for the first two anniversary dates after the purchase from the CDE. The investor is also entitled to a six percent credit on each anniversary date thereafter for the following four years. The credit is recaptured if the entity fails to continue to be a CDE or the interest is redeemed within seven years. The maximum annual amount of qualifying equity investments is capped at $3.5 billion for 2006 and 2007.

An additional amount equal to $300,000,000 for 2005 and 2006, and $400,000,000 for 2007, is available for qualified CDEs to make qualified low-income community investments within the hurricane-ravaged Gulf Opportunity Zone. To qualify for this allocation, a qualified CDE must have as a significant mission the recovery and redevelopment of the Gulf Opportunity Zone.

The credit is claimed on Form 8874, *New Markets Credit.*

Low-Income Housing Credit

A tax credit is available for low-income housing that's constructed, rehabilitated, or acquired after 1986. The credit amounts to 70 percent of the qualified basis of non-federally subsidized units, or 30 percent of the qualified basis of units financed with tax-exempt bonds or other federal subsidies, but it must be claimed over a period of 10 years. The property must continue to meet the "low-income" requirements for at least 15 years. If you purchase qualified property on which the credit is being claimed, before the 10-year period is up, you may be able to "step into the shoes" of the seller and claim the remainder of the credit.

The credit is claimed on Form 8586, *Low-Income Housing Credit.*

Warning

If you're interested in investing in low-income housing to take advantage of the tax credit, you will definitely need the assistance of an attorney who is well-versed in this very complicated subject.

Credits Benefiting the Environment

Currently, the largest group of tax credits are those designed to encourage energy conservation or other actions to help the environment. However, most of these credits are very narrowly targeted, so the number of people eligible for them is actually quite small.

Credit for Qualified Electric Vehicles

A 10-percent tax credit (based on your purchase price) is allowed for certain electric vehicles placed in service after June 30, 1993, and before January 1, 2007. The maximum credit may not exceed $3,000 in 2006. Unfortunately, the credit will be eliminated entirely in 2007. While it lasts, the allowable credit is claimed on Form 8834, *Qualified Electric Vehicle Credit.*

Energy Credit

An energy credit is allowed for 10 percent of the cost of the following types of property placed in service during the year: (1) equipment that uses solar energy to generate electricity, heat or cool a structure, provide hot water, or provide solar process heat; or (2) equipment used to produce, distribute, or use geothermal energy stored in rocks, water, or steam. The property must be depreciable (i.e., tangible personal property used in your business).

Starting in 2006, the business investment credit for solar energy property and hybrid solar lighting systems is increased to 30 percent under the Energy Tax Incentives Act of 2005. In addition, the definition of energy property is expanded to include qualified fuel cell property and stationary microturbine property. The energy credit for qualified fuel cell property is also 30 percent. For stationary microturbine property and other energy property, the credit remains at 10 percent.

The energy credit is part of the investment tax credit, and can be recaptured (paid back to the IRS) if the qualifying property is sold or disposed of before the end of its recovery period. It is claimed on Form 3468, *Investment Credit.*

Alcohol Fuels Credit

Producers of alcohol fuels or mixtures such as gasohol or ethanol can receive a tax credit for any sales or use of such fuels. The alcohol fuels credit is part of the general business credit. It's claimed on Form 6478, *Credit for Alcohol Used as Fuel.*

Enhanced Oil Recovery Credit

If you begin or significantly expand a domestic oil recovery project that uses certain tertiary recovery methods — such as the injection of liquids, gasses, or other matter — to increase crude oil production, you can take a credit for 15 percent of your qualified enhanced oil recovery costs for the tax year. The enhanced oil recovery credit is part of the general business credit. It's claimed on Form 8830, *Enhanced Oil Recovery Credit.*

Renewable Resources Electricity Production Credit

This credit is based on electricity that was produced from wind or closed-loop biomass (organic material grown exclusively for electricity production) and sold to third parties, from facilities placed in service after 1992 and before January 1, 2008, or wind energy facilities placed in service after 1993 and before January 1, 2008.

The credit for calendar year 2006 is 1.9 cents per kilowatt-hour of such electricity sold. The credit is claimed on Form 8835, *Renewable Electricity Production Credit.*

CREDITS FOR CERTAIN INVESTMENTS

A small number of tax credits remain for investments that are not necessarily targeted towards the disadvantaged or the environment. In some cases, investments that take advantage of one of these credits can become, in effect, a tax shelter for cash-rich small businesses. In other cases, certain investments to improve the employee benefits offered by your business are rewarded with a tax credit, in addition to the increased ability to attract and retain your employees. Consult your tax adviser for more details.

R&E Credit

The research and experimentation (R&E) credit encourages businesses to increase the amounts they spend on scientific research. The credit applies to qualified research expenses paid or incurred before January 1, 2006.

The credit generally equals 20 percent of the amount by which your research expenses for the year are higher than your "base amount," which is a figure based on the percentage of gross receipts you spent on research for 1984 through 1988. New companies' base amounts are set by a formula in the law.

To qualify for the credit, the research must be done for an existing business, and must be technological in nature (not research in the social sciences, arts, or humanities). It must relate to a new or improved function, performance, reliability, or quality. Qualified expenses includes in-house research, 65 percent of research costs of a person other than an employee of the taxpayer, and 75 percent of the costs paid to a qualified scientific research consortium.

The R&E credit is claimed on Form 6765, *Credit for Increasing Research Activities.*

Orphan Drug Credit

The orphan drug credit is designed to encourage development of drugs for diseases and conditions that are so rare that drug development would otherwise be economically unfeasible.

The credit is equal to 50 percent of the qualified clinical testing expenses for the year. The orphan drug credit operates in much the same fashion as the R & D credit, except that there is no requirement that expenses exceed a base amount. Where the same expenses would qualify for both the orphan drug credit and the R & D credit, you must choose between them — the same expenses can't be claimed as a credit twice. The orphan drug credit is claimed on Form 8820, *Orphan Drug Credit.*

Rehabilitation Credit

This tax credit is designed to encourage the rehabilitation of older real estate or certified historic buildings. It allows you to take a tax credit for the expenses you have for renovating, restoring, or rehabilitating (but not enlarging or adding new construction to) certain structures. The percentage of expenses you can take as a credit is 10 percent for buildings originally placed in service before 1936, and 20 percent for buildings listed in the National Register of Historic Places. The credit is further limited to the tax paid on $25,000 and is phased out for taxpayers with adjusted gross incomes between $200,000 and $250,000. If a project involves both rehabilitation and enlargement, only the costs of rehabilitation are eligible for the credit.

If you claim this credit, you must reduce the depreciable tax basis of the property by the amount of the credit.

The rehabilitation credit is part of the investment tax credit, and can be recaptured (paid back to the IRS) if the qualifying property is sold or disposed of within five years of the time it's placed in service. The credit is claimed on Form 3468, *Investment Credit.*

Retirement Plan Startup Credit

In order to stimulate greater retirement saving, small employers who establish new retirement plans are now entitled to a tax credit for doing so. The credit is only available to employers with 100 employees or less who have not maintained a qualified retirement plan during the three-year period immediately before the first effective year of the new plan. This credit is set to expire for tax years beginning after 2010.

The credit amounts to 50 percent of the costs incurred in creating or maintaining a new qualified plan, up to a maximum of $500 in each of the first three years the plan is effective. Essentially, this means that you have to spend at least $1,000 per year to get the full credit. Any set-up and administration costs not offset by the tax credit (i.e. those above $1,000 in the first three years and those incurred after the first three years) are deductible as ordinary and necessary business expenses.

Employer-Provided Child Care Credit

For tax years beginning before 2011, small, as well as middle-sized, businesses will be eligible for a tax credit of 25 percent of the qualified child care expenses they provide and 10 percent of the cost of qualified child care resource and referral services they offer. The employer-provided credit is capped at $150,000 per tax year.

Expenses eligible for the credit include payments under a contract with a qualified child care facility to provide child care services to the business's employees. Qualified childcare expenses also include the amounts paid or incurred by the employer to acquire, construct, establish, and operate a qualified child care facility for employees. The facility itself must meet any state and local government laws and regulations, like licensing requirements, that may apply for its location.

Claiming Federal Income Tax Credits

Once you've decided that one or more of the available tax credits apply to you, how do you go about claiming it? The easy answer is, you don't— you leave it up to your tax pro, because the rules for most credits are too complicated for the average small business owner to handle.

However, we're including the basic concepts here, so that you can ask intelligent questions of your accountant or lawyer, and see that he or she is earning the fees that you pay. You can also use this information as a starting point if you are a stouthearted do-it-yourselfer.

There are a number of steps you must take in the process of computing and claiming your tax credits:

First, compute your regular tax liability. You need to know what your income is for the year, subtract all your allowable deductions, and compute your tax liability on that basis (as if you had no credits). If you're a sole proprietor, part of the process will be completing Schedule C, *Profit or Loss From Business,* so you can determine your net income for your business.

Second, compute your alternative minimum tax (AMT) liability, if any. Generally, credits cannot be claimed to the extent that they would reduce your tax bill below your tentative minimum tax. See page 305 for a discussion of how AMT works.

Third, compute your nonrefundable credits and subtract them in the prescribed order. The order is important because each credit is limited to the amount of the tax minus the credits previously taken. Claim credits in the following order:

1. personal nonrefundable credits, such as the credit for child and dependent care, the credit for the elderly and disabled, the adoption credit, the child credit, and the credit for interest on certain home mortgages

2. the foreign tax credit

3. the alternative fuels credit

4. the credit for qualified electric vehicles

5. the general business credit, which is made up of the following parts: the investment credit, the work opportunity credit, the welfare-to-work credit, the alcohol fuels credit, the research credit, the low-income housing credit, the enhanced oil recovery credit, the disabled access credit, the renewable energy production credit, the empowerment zone employment credit (which is part of the general business credit but is not claimed on Form 3800), the Indian employment credit, the employer FICA credit on tips, the orphan drug credit, and the community development corporations credit. The investment credit, in turn, is made up of the rehabilitation credit, the energy credit, and the reforestation credit.

Fourth, compute any carryback or carryover amounts, as discussed below.

Finally, compute and subtract your refundable credits from your remaining tax liability, if any. Refundable credits include the earned income credit, credit for any income taxes withheld on your paycheck, and the credit for gasoline and special fuels taxes. If subtracting these credits leaves you with a tax liability below zero, the IRS will send you a check for the difference.

Dollar Limits on Credits

In most cases, the limit on the credits you can claim for the year is computed as follows: take your regular tax liability, subtract your tentative minimum tax liability, and the result is the dollar limit on credits you can claim for the year. The credits are subtracted in a prescribed order, and some, including the general business credit, have additional limits that must be observed.

Tax Forms To Use

Most of the credits must be computed on their own special IRS forms. In addition, if you are claiming more than one of the components of the general business credits, if you have a carryback or carryover, or a credit from a passive activity, you will also need Form 3800, *General Business Credit,* to compute any limitations on the combined credit components.

The General Business Tax Credit

In order to provide some uniform rules about dollar limitations, carrybacks and carryforwards, and other technical details, many of the federal income tax credits available to businesses that were discussed above are lumped together and treated as components of the "general business credit."

The order in which the components are claimed is important. If you plan to claim more than one of these credits for the year, you must claim them in the prescribed order, using Form 3800, *General Business Credit* — that way, if you exceed your credit dollar limit for the year, the credits further down the list will be the ones that are carried back or carried over to other years.

Dollar Limits on General Business Credits

Your total general business credit for the year can't exceed your net income tax, minus the greater of (1) your tentative minimum tax, or (2) 25 percent of your net regular tax liability that is more than $25,000 ($12,500 for marrieds filing separately). Your net income tax is your net regular tax liability plus your alternative minimum tax.

Carrybacks and Carryforwards

If the dollar limitations on the general business credit prevent you from claiming all of it in the year that it was earned (the "credit year"), for credits arising in 1998 and later, you can carry unused amounts back for one year, and forward for 20 years. The foreign tax credit may be carried back to the past two years and forward for five years, if it is necessary to use it up. To claim a carryback, you must generally file an amended return (Form 1040X, *Amended U.S. Individual Income Tax Return)* for the tax year to which you're carrying the credit. You can also apply for a quick refund of taxes for a prior year by filing Form 1045, *Application for Tentative Refund.*

The Investment Tax Credit

The investment tax credit is a credit against your federal income tax. Currently, it's made up of three components: the rehabilitation credit, the energy credit, and the reforestation credit. The investment tax credit is itself one of the components of the general business credit and is subject to the limitations, carryback and carryforward rules, etc. that apply to all the other components of that "umbrella" credit. The investment credit is claimed on Form 3468, *Investment Credit.*

Basis Adjustment

When you claim an investment tax credit for a business asset, you must generally reduce the depreciable tax basis of the property. The basis reduction would be equal to 100 percent of the rehabilitation credit you claimed, and 50 percent of the reforestation and energy credits.

Part III

Personal Tax Issues

The first half of this book dealt with the many questions and issues that can arise on the business portion of your tax return. In many cases, keeping your business taxes low is the best way to keep your overall tax bill as low as possible.

However, even if your business occupies the majority of your time and efforts, and presents the most thorny issues at tax time, don't neglect the personal and family side of your tax return.

For a sole proprietor, the income tax forms you need to file for your business (Schedules C and SE of Form 1040, and perhaps other forms depending on your business activity) are only one part of your individual income tax return that you must file.

Personal and family tax issues must be sorted out and addressed in the course of preparing your return. Depending on the age, size, income level and activities of your family, the personal side of your tax return may be as complicated as the business side.

What's more, there are numerous opportunities to save money on taxes on the personal side. Buying or refinancing a home, contributing to a regular or Roth IRA, investing in higher education, or riding the Wall Street rollercoaster all present you with potential tax breaks. If you become familiar with the rules and keep up with the annual changes, you will be able to take advantage of all the breaks available to you.

Our discussion of non-business tax issues is organized into the following topical areas:

Chapter 10: Filing Status and Exemptions explores the basic questions of who must file a tax return, who qualifies as a dependent, and what are your options as to filing jointly or separately if married, or as single or head of household if not married.

Chapter 11: Employment Income and Related Deductions discusses the tax treatment of income reported to employees on W-2 forms, as well as income received by farmers, and various types of miscellaneous income such as unemployment benefits, disability benefits, and gambling winnings. This chapter also discusses tax breaks that may be claimed by employees and the self-employed, including moving expenses, the tax credit for child and dependent care, and miscellaneous deductions for employee business expenses.

Chapter 12: Real Estate covers the tax benefits of owning a home, such as the itemized deductions for home mortgage interest and real estate taxes. It also addresses the issues that must be faced by investors in real estate, or those who rent out their home or a vacation home for some part of the year. Finally, this chapter discusses recordkeeping for homeowners and the tax consequences of selling a home or other real estate.

Chapter 13: Investments discusses the tax treatment of interest and dividend income; capital gains on investment sales; and income from other entities such as estates and trusts, partnerships, LLCs and S corporations, and REMICS. Also discussed are itemized deductions related to investments, and special rules for handling the investment income of a minor child.

Chapter 14: Retirement explains how to report periodic payments from pension and annuity plans, as well as lump-sum distributions and Social Security benefits. It also covers all the rules related to IRAs – both Roth and traditional – whether you are making contributions or taking distributions.

Chapter 15: Standard and Itemized Deductions covers the standard deduction as well as itemized deductions not discussed elsewhere in the book: medical and dental expenses, state and local taxes, interest, charitable contributions, casualty and theft losses, and miscellaneous itemized deductions. It also explains the limit on itemized deductions that applies to high-income taxpayers.

Chapter 16: Tax Credits and Miscellaneous Issues for Families deals with some of the latest new tax breaks for individuals: the $1,000-per-child tax credit, tax benefits for adoption, and tax breaks for education. It also covers the credit for the elderly and the disabled, and the earned income credit for low-income families. The tax aspects of alimony and child support are also discussed.

Chapter 17: Calculating Your Tax explains how to pull everything together and calculate the amount of federal income tax you owe, so you can determine the amount of your refund (or the amount you'll have to send in to the government). It also discusses two other types of taxes you may have to pay: payroll taxes on household employees, and the alternative minimum tax.

Chapter 18: Dealing with the IRS covers the mechanical issues of when and where to file your tax return, how to get an extension, and how to figure your quarterly estimated tax bill, and offers some tips on dealing with IRS audits.

Chapter 10

Filing Status and Exemptions

Thanks to legislation enacted in 2003, tax rate reductions that were to take effect in 2006 are accelerated to 2003. Also for the next several years, those filing a joint return will find some relief from the "marriage penalty," with their tax brackets and standard deductions being more on par with single filers.

For 2003 through 2010, the tax rates are set at 10, 15, 25, 28, 33, and 35 percent. Each succeeding rate applies to a tier of your income. For example, a certain amount of your initial income is taxed at 10 percent, than a certain amount of income above that is taxed at the 15 percent rate, and so on.

Although the six rates are the same for everyone, the dollar levels at which the different tax rates kick in depend on your "filing status"—that is, whether you file your tax return as a single individual, as a head of household, or as married filing jointly or separately. For almost any given income level, the IRS tax tables provide four different amounts of tax that will apply, depending on filing status.

Your filing status is the first item you need to complete on your tax return, after your name, address, and Social Security number. This is appropriate, because your filing status is the starting point for determining whether you need to file a tax return at all, and, if you must file a return, the tax rates that will apply to your income.

Your status also has a wide-ranging effect in determining how numerous other tax rules will apply to you including the standard deduction, IRA contribution limits, credits for children or for education expenses, taxation of Social Security benefits, credits for the elderly or disabled, the adoption credit, the earned income credit and the phaseouts of exemptions and deductions for high-income taxpayers.

Once you've determined your filing status, you need to know how many personal exemptions you can claim, since the law allows you a tax exemption of $3,300 for each member of your family in 2006.

The rules are fairly straightforward for most people. You can claim one exemption for yourself, one for your spouse if married and filing jointly, and one for each minor child living with you. But what about your older children, parents, extended family members you support, or children from a previous marriage? The surprisingly complex rules are explained on page 163.

Tax Organizer Tip

When entering information into CompleteTax, choose your filing status on the "Taxpayer" page on the "Personal" tab. If you indicate that your filing status is married, a sub-tab will appear for your spouse's information. If you answer "Yes" to the question, "Will you be claiming any of the following: children or other dependents; Child Care Credit for someone other than a dependent; Earned Income Credit with a qualifying person other than a dependent; or qualifying person for Head of Household filing status?" a sub-tab will appear for your dependents' information.

CHOOSING YOUR FILING STATUS

To claim your filing status on IRS Form 1040A or Form 1040, you simply check the box in front of the status that applies to you. If you choose "married filing separate returns," you'll need to enter the name of your spouse on Line 3, and also include your spouse's Social Security number at the top of the form directly below your own. This is required so that the IRS can match up your two forms in case of an audit. If you choose "head of household" status, you must enter on Line 4 the name of your qualifying person if it is a child who's not your dependent (see page 163).

Taxpayers who are able to file Form 1040EZ can only use "single" or "married filing jointly." If they are married, they must write both spouses' names and Social Security numbers on the return, which automatically places them in the "joint filers" category; otherwise they will be considered single.

While actually claiming your filing status on your tax return couldn't be simpler, knowing which status to claim is not always so easy. The primary factor in determining your status is whether you are married or not. If you are married, you and your spouse must decide whether to file jointly or separately (see page 155). In some cases, recently widowed persons can be treated as married, and some married people who are not living with their spouses can be treated as single.

Generally, if you are not currently married, you can be classified as a "head of household" if you meet the requirements for supporting at least one other person, or as "single" if you don't. Head of households face a significantly lower tax rate than singles for the same level of income, but must file IRS Form 1040A or 1040 to claim this status.

Are You Married?

The rule for determining marital status is a simple one. If you are married on the last day of the tax year (December 31, for most people), you are considered to be married for the whole year. Conversely, if you are divorced during the year and don't remarry before December 31, you will be considered unmarried for the entire year.

Save Money

If you are planning a winter wedding and your income level is much higher or lower than that of your future spouse, marriage can actually lower your tax bill, and a December wedding would be preferable to a January wedding. If you are married by December 31, you'll be treated as if you were married for the whole preceding year.

However, if you and your intended have relatively similar income levels, marriage is more likely to increase your tax bill. In that case, waiting until January to get married will allow you one extra year of more favorable single status.

In a divorce situation, the parties are considered to be married until a final decree of divorce or legal separation is issued. The validity of the divorce is determined under the law of the state of domicile (legal residence). Taxpayers who live apart and have obtained an interim decree of divorce or separation, but have not yet been granted a final decree, are treated as married for tax purposes.

What about common-law marriages? Generally speaking, if your state recognizes such marriages and you meet all the state law requirements, the IRS will recognize your marriage as well.

Spouses Living Apart

A special rule allows a married person who is living apart (but not necessarily legally separated) from the spouse, and who is caring for a dependent child, to be treated as single and eligible to use the head of household filing status. In the absence of this rule, these individuals would probably have to file as "married filing separately," a much less advantageous status.

In order to take advantage of this special rule, all of the following conditions must be met:

- You must file a separate tax return.
- You must pay more than half of the cost of maintaining your household for the year.
- Your spouse must not have been a member of your household during the last six months of the tax year.
- Your household must, for more than six months of the year, have been the principal home of at least one of your dependent children. See page 163 for the definition of "dependent." "Child" includes your legally adopted children and foster children; however, if the child is a foster child, he or she must reside in your household for the entire year.

Recently Widowed Persons

An exception to the "December 31 rule" for determining whether a person is considered to be married applies to those whose spouses have died in the past year.

Generally, you can file a joint return with your spouse for the year in which your spouse dies, and you'll be treated as married for the entire year. You can also claim the whole personal exemption for the deceased spouse. However, in order to file jointly, you must have the consent of the personal representative (executor or administrator) of the deceased spouse's estate, if you are not the representative.

This rule does not hold if you remarry within the year. In that case, you can file jointly with your new spouse, but not with the old one. The return of the deceased spouse would have to be filed as "married filing separately" for the final year.

Qualifying widows or widowers. Some surviving spouses can continue to use the "married filing jointly" tax rates for up to two years *after* the year in which their spouse died. To take advantage of this option, all of the following must be true:

- You have not remarried.
- Your home was the principal residence of a dependent child or stepchild for the entire year, and you must have provided more than half of the cost of maintaining the home.
- You must have been eligible to file a joint return with your deceased spouse in the year he or she died.

Surviving spouses who meet these tests and are able to continue using the joint return rates are called "qualifying widows or widowers" and must check off the box for that filing status on Line 5 of Form 1040. They must also write the year in which their spouse died in the blank provided for that purpose on Line 5, so that the IRS can be sure they aren't using this status for more than two years after the year the death occurred.

As a result, they have the advantage of continuing to use the joint return tax amounts in the tax table, although they may not claim a personal exemption for the deceased spouse for any year after the year in which the spouse died.

Most Married People File Jointly

If you're married, you and your spouse must decide whether to file jointly or separately.

In the vast majority of cases, filing jointly will result in a lower total family tax bill. The tax rates for joint filers have the effect of "leveling out" the income, exemptions, and deductions of each spouse, so that each spouse is essentially treated as having half of the total net income. For slightly more than half of married couples, this results in a "marriage bonus," so that the couple pays less in tax than they would if they each made the same income and were single. This is usually the case where one spouse's earnings are much higher than the other's.

For couples where each spouse makes roughly the same income, however, there is often a "marriage penalty" in which the second wage earner's income pushes the couple into a higher tax bracket than either spouse would face if they were single. This situation can sometimes, but unfortunately not often, be helped if the couple files separately rather than jointly.

However, the IRS does not smile on couples who file separately, perhaps because it has to incur the extra charges of processing two tax returns rather than only one.

In order to strongly encourage married couples to file jointly, Congress has provided that for people who are treated as "married," certain tax benefits are available *only* if a joint return is filed, as shown in the chart that follows (but note that certain legally separated couples or spouses living apart from each other are not treated as "married" for this purpose – see page 154). When you consider the effects of not being able to claim any of these benefits, it's usually clear that filing separately would result in a larger tax bill.

Thanks to legislation enacted in 2001, 2003 and 2004, those suffering under the marriage penalty will see some relief as various deductions, limits, and phaseout points continue to be gradually adjusted through 2008. In 2006, for example, the standard deduction for most joint filers has increased to $13,000, which is twice that of single filers. Also, the 15 percent tax bracket for joint filers has been expanded to twice the income range as that of single filers through 2007.

Joint Returns May Be Prohibited

In a few limited situations, married taxpayers have no choice and must file separately:

- if the spouses have different tax years, and this difference is not due to the death of either spouse (if filing separately is not beneficial, either spouse may be able to obtain IRS consent to change to a "matching" tax year by filing Form 1128, *Application to Adopt, Change, or Retain a Tax Year*; after consent is obtained, you can file jointly)

- if either spouse is, at any time during the year, a nonresident alien and the couple chooses not to treat the nonresident alien spouse as a U.S. resident subject to tax on worldwide income (see page 158 for more on this situation)

- if a spouse has died during the year, and the personal representative of the estate elects to file a separate return

Tax Breaks Not Available to Married People Filing Separately

- the dependent care credit (see page 191)
- the earned income credit (see page 291)
- the HOPE scholarship credit (see page 288)
- the lifetime learning credit (see page 289)
- the deduction for interest on education loans (see page 290)
- the adoption credit (see page 284)
- the exclusion for interest income on Series EE U.S. Savings Bonds used for higher education expenses (see page 226)
- the $4,000 ($5,000 if age 50 or older at the end of 2006) deduction for IRA contributions for a nonworking or low-income spouse (see page 251)

In addition, married couples who lived together at any time during the year must file jointly in order to claim any of the following:

- the more lenient phaseout rules (i.e., phaseout between $150,000 and $160,000 in AGI) for the IRA deduction when an individual does not participate in an employer-sponsored plan, but their spouse is covered by an employer's pension plan (see page 254)
- the credit for the elderly or the disabled (see page 286)
- the $25,000 rental loss allowance under the passive loss rules (see page 221)

Beyond these listed items, you should be aware that if a couple files separately and one spouse itemizes his or her deductions, the other spouse must follow suit - the standard deduction may not be used. Also, if either spouse is receiving Social Security benefits, the amount of benefits on which income tax must be paid is higher for spouses filing separately.

When Is a Separate Return Better?

If spouses file separately, each must report only his or her own income, exemptions, and deductions on his or her tax return. However, in community property states, the general rule is that each spouse must report one-half of the combined community income.

To be absolutely certain whether joint or separate returns are better, you should compute your tax liability both ways and compare the results. It's especially important to run the numbers where one or both spouses may be liable for the alternative minimum tax (see page 305).

Itemized Deductions

If both spouses have similar income levels but one spouse has a much higher amount in deductible expenses, it may be advantageous to file separately.

For example, medical expenses are deductible only to the extent that they exceed 7.5 percent of the taxpayer's adjusted gross income (AGI). If one spouse had the majority of the family medical expenses, the 7.5 percent threshold may be easy to overcome if only that spouse's income is counted. A similar situation exists for miscellaneous itemized deductions, including employee business expenses (2 percent of AGI threshold) and nonbusiness casualty losses (10 percent of AGI threshold).

However, keep in mind that if one spouse itemizes deductions, the other will have to itemize as well, even if the second spouse winds up with few or no allowable deductions. If you're a high-income earner, it may also be important to consider how separate filing alters the impact of the limitation on itemized deductions faced by high-income taxpayers (see page 275).

Dependents

If you have dependents and file separately, you must divide their exemptions between yourself and your spouse, but no single exemption can be split.

Save Money

If you have numerous dependents and one spouse claims them all, you might come out ahead, particularly if the other spouse's income is so high that his or her personal exemptions would be phased out. Just make sure that the spouse who claims the exemptions can meet all the tests for claiming each dependent as described on page 163; generally this would require that the spouse claiming the exemptions earned enough money to provide more than one-half of the dependents' support.

Limiting Your Liability for the Return

It's important to note that if you file a joint tax return with your spouse, both of you are legally responsible for the accuracy of information shown on the tax return, as well as for the entire amount of tax that is owed.

Spouses who are separated often file separate returns simply because they do not have access to complete financial information about the other party.

In other situations, where one spouse actually suspects that the other spouse is not being completely truthful, he or she should consider filing a separate return to avoid possible civil or criminal penalties.

It is possible, but difficult, to obtain "innocent spouse relief" and avoid having to pay taxes, interest and penalties on amounts that were actually owed by the other spouse. You must establish that you did not know, and had no reason to know, that your joint return failed to report some income or claimed some erroneous deductions, credits, or other tax breaks. If so, you can be relieved of liability for tax on that item.

To obtain innocent spouse relief, you have to apply for it using IRS Form 8857, *Request for Innocent Spouse Relief*, which can be obtained by calling 1-800-TAX-FORM. You must file this form within two years after the IRS begins collection activities.

Work Smart

The law permits a taxpayer who is divorced, legally separated or living apart from a spouse for at least one year to limit his/her liability in instances where a former spouse may have made erroneous statements on a previous joint tax return.

To make the election, the ex-spouse must file IRS Form 8857, and establish the unpaid taxes that should be allocated to the other spouse. The election can't be made if the IRS demonstrates that the spouse seeking the election had actual knowledge of the matter relating to the unpaid taxes when the return was signed. This is a more lenient standard than the innocent spouse relief rule, but it is available only to spouses who have split up.

The divorced husband or wife has two years after the IRS begins collection activities to make this election of separate liability, which will excuse the innocent spouse from paying any additional taxes owed or interest and penalties on the item(s) in question.

Nonresident Alien Spouses

If a U.S. citizen or resident alien is married to a nonresident alien, a joint return may not be filed unless both spouses file an election with the IRS to treat the nonresident alien as a resident alien.

While it may appear that a nonresident alien who has no income from U.S. sources need not be concerned with filing status, since he or she is not subject to taxation by the U.S. government, the filing of a joint return may at least reduce his or her spouse's U.S. tax bill on income subject to U.S. taxation. If the nonresident alien has U.S. source income, an election for a joint return may be doubly beneficial, since he or she may be taxed on the U.S. income anyway.

Contrast Between Tax Treatments

Nonresident aliens who are not treated as resident aliens generally are taxed only on their income from U.S. sources. Investment income from U.S. sources is taxed at a flat 30 percent rate. Regular U.S. income tax rates for a married person filing separately are imposed on income from a job in the U.S. This income may be offset by deductions.

In contrast, when a nonresident alien is treated as a resident alien, he or she is subject to U.S. taxation on worldwide income (i.e., income from foreign sources as well as U.S. sources). However, as with any other U.S. citizen or resident alien, the alien is eligible for a foreign tax credit or an itemized deduction for taxes paid to a foreign government on income earned in those countries. The alien may also exclude up to $80,000 of foreign earned income from U.S. taxation (in 2005) and may be eligible to exclude or deduct some of the cost of foreign housing.

How to Make the Election

You can make the election to treat a nonresident alien spouse as a resident alien by attaching a statement to that effect, signed by both you and your spouse, to the joint return for the first tax year of the election. The election is effective for all later tax years unless it is revoked by the spouses or the IRS, one spouse dies, or the spouses are legally separated. It will also be suspended as of any year in which neither spouse is a U.S. citizen or a resident alien.

Are You a Head of Household?

Next to the joint return rates, the best tax rate schedule applies to single taxpayers who qualify for head of household (HOH) status.

However, some complicated rules determine whether you are eligible to file as an HOH. Whether you are divorced or have never been married is not important; what is important is that you maintain a home for one or more of your children or dependent relatives.

Beginning with the 2005 tax year, a taxpayer qualifies for head of household status if he/she is unmarried at the end of the tax year, is not a surviving spouse, pays at least half of the costs to maintain a home, and shares that home with:

- at least one qualifying child;
- a dependant for whom the taxpayer is entitled to claim a personal exemption (e.g., $3,300 per person in 2006); or
- his/her mother or father, provided that the taxpayer is entitled to claim a personal exemption for the mother or father

A qualifying child is an individual who:

- is a child (including an adopted or foster child) , brother, sister, stepbrother, stepsister, or descendant of any such relative of the taxpayer;
- has the same principal place of abode as the taxpayer for more than half the tax year;

- is 18 years old or younger at the close of the calendar year in which the taxpayer's tax year begins or is a student that is 23 years old or younger (this rule does not apply if the individual is permanently and totally disabled); and

- has not provided for over one-half his/her own support for the calendar year in which the taxpayer's tax year begins.

If you are not married, and you can't qualify as a head-of-household, you are treated as single for federal income tax purposes.

Maintaining a Household

In order to be considered to be "maintaining a household," you must provide more than one-half the cost of keeping up a home. Costs of maintaining a household include rent or mortgage interest, real estate taxes, insurance on the home, repairs, utilities, and food eaten in the home. They do not include the costs of clothing, education, medical treatment, vacations, transportation, life insurance, or the value of services.

Save Money

The test described above for "maintaining a household" is less demanding than the test for supporting a dependent, discussed on page 166. As a result, you may be entitled to file as an HOH even though you can't claim any dependency exemptions.

One common situation where this rule comes into play is where a couple is divorced, and the lower-paid spouse retains custody of the children. The couple may agree to give the dependency exemptions to the noncustodial parent (because that parent can gain more tax benefits from the exemptions), but the custodial parent would still retain the tax benefits of filing as an HOH.

Residing in the Same Household

You must live in the same household as your "qualifying person" *unless* the person is your father or mother. In that case, you can be an HOH if you pay for at least half the cost of maintaining your father or mother's main home for the entire year, even if your parent(s) lives apart from you in a house or apartment, or in a nursing home or other care facility for the elderly.

If the "qualifying person" is anyone other than your mother or father, the person must live in your household for more than half of your tax year. However, temporary absences for vacations, illnesses, military service, or time spent in college are permissible for either you or the qualifying person, provided that you reasonably anticipate that the absentee will return and you continue to maintain a household during the absence.

Also, if the qualifying person is born or dies during the tax year so that he or she is alive for less than six months in the year, you can still file as an HOH if the qualifying person lived with you for the whole period in which he or she was alive during the year.

WHO MUST FILE A RETURN?

If you're reading this book, you probably don't have any doubt about whether you need to file a tax return. Most small business owners need to file, because anyone with net self-employment income of $400 or more must file a tax return to report and pay their self-employment tax.

However, you may have questions about whether your child, parent, or some other person for whom you're responsible needs to file a return.

The basic rule is that if you are a citizen or resident of the United States, or a resident of Puerto Rico, you must file a tax return if you have gross income at or above a certain dollar amount. The dollar amount depends on your filing status, and on your age if you are 65 or older at the end of the year. The same rules apply to U.S. citizens living outside the United States.

If you are a nonresident alien, different rules may apply which are not covered in this book. See IRS Publication 519, *U.S. Tax Guide for Aliens*.

Filing Thresholds for 2006

If your gross income meets or exceeds the following levels and you are under age 65, you must file a tax return:

Single	**$ 8,450**
Head of Household	**$ 10,850**
Married Filing Jointly	**$ 16,900**
Married Filing Separately	**$ 3,300**
Qualifying Widow or Widower	**$ 13,600**

If you are 65 or older by the end of 2006, you can add $1,250 to the amounts shown above for single or head of household. If one of the spouses filing jointly is 65 or older, add an extra $1,000. If both spouses are 65 or older, on a joint return, you can add $2,000 to the amount shown, so the threshold would be $18,900.

Filing for Dependents

Children or other people who can be claimed as dependents on someone else's tax return (see discussion below) generally must file a tax return if they have more than $850 of unearned income (interest, dividends, capital gains), or earned income over $5,150, or their total income was more than the larger of $850 or their earned income (up to $4,850) plus $300.

If the dependent is age 65 or over or blind, he or she generally must file a return if their unearned income was more than $2,100 for singles or $1,850 for marrieds. If the dependent was *both* 65 or over *and* blind, you can add to these amounts an extra $1,250 for singles or $1,000 for marrieds.

When tallying up a dependent's income, "unearned income" includes interest, dividends, capital gains, unemployment compensation, taxable Social Security benefits, pensions, annuities, and trust distributions. "Earned income" includes wages, salaries, tips, and net income from a business; it also includes taxable scholarship and fellowship grants.

If the child or other dependent is too young or otherwise incapable of filing a tax return, his or her parent, guardian, or other legally responsible person must file the tax return for the dependent. In that case the responsible adult filing the return would sign the return for the dependent, and add their own name; for example, "John Jones, Jr., by John Jones, parent of minor child."

If the child is under age 18 and his or her only income is interest and dividends, the parent has the option to include the child's income on the parent's return by filing IRS Form 8814, *Parent's Election to Report Child's Interest and Dividends*, along with the parent's return.

Save Money

Combining a child's income with that of the parents would save the child from having to file his or her own tax return; however, it frequently results in a slightly larger tax bill since the child's income will increase the parents' AGI and possibly reduce the deductible portion of the parents' itemized medical expenses, miscellaneous deductions, casualty losses, and IRA deductions. There are many other tax breaks that are phased out at higher levels of AGI and that can potentially be lost or reduced if a child's income is combined with the parents' income, so in most cases the family will be better off if the child files a separate return.

Others Who Must File a Tax Return

Even if you don't have sufficient income to meet the filing thresholds for your filing status, you must file a tax return in order to get an IRS refund for any overpaid estimated taxes or amounts withheld from your paycheck.

You must also file a tax return if any of the following apply to you:

- You received an advance earned income credit from your employer (this would be shown in Box 9 of your W-2 Form).
- You had net earnings from self-employment of at least $400, as shown on Schedule C or C-EZ.
- You had wages of at least $108.28 from a church or church organization that is exempt from Social Security (see page 137).
- You owe any special taxes, such as: uncollected FICA tax on tips, uncollected FICA tax on group-term life insurance over $50,000, alternative minimum tax (AMT – see page 305), tax on a pension plan or IRA, tax on a medical savings account (MSA), recapture tax on a home purchased with a federally subsidized mortgage, recapture of the qualified electric vehicle credit, or recapture of investment credit or low-income housing credit (see page 145).

Which Tax Form Should You Use?

For business owners, the answer to this is cut and dried: If you file a Schedule C or C-EZ, or if you must report a taxable sale of business property, you must file the "long form" (Form 1040) for your federal income tax.

Since some of you may have dependents who must file tax returns, or may be overseeing tax preparation for other people who do not own a business, we'll go over the rules for the shorter income tax forms as well. The general idea is that you should always use the simplest tax form that applies to you.

If you cannot use the 1040EZ or the 1040A under the rules discussed below, you must use the regular 1040 form.

Rules for Form 1040EZ

The simplest, one-page tax form has become more and more complicated in recent years, and as a result it can be used by more and more taxpayers.

You can use the 1040EZ if all of the following are true:

- Your filing status is single, or married filing jointly.
- You (and your spouse, if filing jointly) were both under 65 and not blind.
- You are not claiming any dependents (but you may use this form if you are claimed as a dependent on someone else's tax form)
- Your taxable income is less than $100,000.
- Your income is only from wages, salaries, tips, unemployment compensation, Alaska Permanent Fund dividends, taxable scholarship and fellowship grants, and taxable interest of $1,500 or less.
- You're not claiming a student loan interest deduction or an education credit
- You did not receive any advance earned income credit payments.
- You are not claiming an education credit, the retirement savings contributions credit or the health insurance credit for eligible recipients.
- You do not owe any household employment taxes on wages you paid to a household employee (see page 306).

Rules for Form 1040A

Form 1040A is the "medium form." It's not quite as long as Form 1040, but can be used if you don't qualify for the 1040EZ and meet all of the following requirements:

- Your taxable income is less than $100,000.
- Your only income is from wages, salaries, tips, IRA distributions, pensions and annuities, taxable Social Security or railroad retirement benefits, taxable scholarships or fellowships, interest, dividends (including Alaska Permanent Fund dividends) and unemployment compensation.
- Your only adjustments to income are the deduction for contributions to an IRA or the student loan interest deduction; you don't have an adjustment for a medical savings account, moving expenses, penalty on early withdrawal of savings, or alimony.
- You are claiming the standard deduction rather than itemized deductions.
- Your only taxes are the income tax as shown in the Tax Table, the alternative minimum tax (AMT), and/or the advance earned income credit (EIC).
- Your only tax credits are the child tax credit, the credit for child and dependent care expenses, the credit for the elderly and the disabled, the EIC, the retirement savings contribution credit, education credits, and/or the adoption credit.
- You don't have an AMT adjustment on stock acquired from the exercise of an incentive stock option.

Rules for Using Form 1040

You must file your income taxes using Form 1040 if *any* of the following are true.

1. You had $400 or more in self-employment income.
2. Your taxable income is $100,000 or more.
3. You choose to itemize your deductions.
4. You received capital gain distributions (e.g., from a mutual fund) or nontaxable dividends.
5. You had taxable gain from the sale of your home or other property, barter income, alimony income, taxable refunds of state or local income taxes, or self-employment income (including farm income).
6. You sold or exchanged capital assets or business property.
7. You had any of the following adjustments to gross income: payments to a medical savings account; moving expenses; payments for self-employed health insurance; one-half of the self-employment tax; payments to a Keogh, SEP or SIMPLE retirement plan; penalty for early withdrawal of savings; alimony paid; certain required repayments of supplemental unemployment benefits; jury duty pay turned over to your employer; qualified performing artists' expenses; or other allowable adjustments to income.
8. Your Form W-2 shows uncollected FICA tax on tips or group-term life insurance over $50,000 in Box 12.
9. You received $20 or more in tips in any one month and did not report all of them to your employer.
10. You received or paid accrued interest on securities transferred between interest payment dates.
11. You receive a distribution from a foreign trust, or you had a bank, securities, or other financial account in a foreign country at any time during the year.
12. You have to recapture an investment tax credit, a low-income housing credit, a qualified electric vehicle credit, or an Indian employment credit you claimed in a previous year.
13. You have to recapture tax on the disposition of a home purchased with a federally subsidized mortgage.
14. You have to pay tax on excess golden parachute payments.
15. You claim any of the following tax credits: mortgage interest credit, foreign tax credit, any general business credit (see page 148), credit for prior years' AMT, credit for fuel from a nonconventional source, credit for federal tax on fuels, qualified electric vehicle credit, or the regulated investment company credit
16. You file any of the following forms: Form 2555, *Foreign Earned Income;* Form 2555-EZ, *Foreign Earned Income Exclusion;* Form 4563, *Exclusion of Income for Bona Fide Residents of American Samoa;* Form 4970, *Tax on Accumulation Distribution of Trusts;* Form 4972, *Tax on Lump-Sum Distributions;* Form 5329, *Additional Taxes Attributable to Qualified Retirement Plans (Including IRAs), Annuities, Modified Endowment Contracts, and MSAs;* Form 8271, *Investor Reporting of Tax Shelter Registration Number;* Form 8814, *Parents' Election to Report Child's Interest and Dividends;* Form 8853, *Medical Savings Accounts and Long-Term Care Insurance Contracts.*

Exemptions and the Dependency Test

In computing how much of your income is actually subject to federal income tax, you're automatically entitled to subtract two amounts: a personal exemption and a standard deduction. The sum of these amounts is not taxed, period. Of course, you can choose to itemize your deductions rather than claiming the standard deduction, if itemizing would result in a lower tax bill. Deductions are discussed in Chapter 15; the remainder of this chapter explains personal exemptions and how to determine whether a particular person is your dependent or not.

The rule is that one (and only one) personal exemption is available for every individual – adult or child. The amount of the exemption is $3,300 for 2006 and is indexed for inflation every year.

So, on a joint return, you could automatically claim one exemption for yourself and one for your spouse, for a total of $6,600. You can claim an exemption for your spouse even if he or she died during the year, provided you have not remarried. However, if you obtain a final decree of divorce, you can't claim your spouse's exemption.

If you are married filing separately, you can claim your spouse's exemption on your own return only if your spouse had absolutely no gross income for the year and was not the dependent of any other individual.

Besides the personal and spousal exemptions, you should also claim an exemption for each of your dependents. The catch is that if you can claim a dependency exemption for an individual, that person may not claim a personal exemption on his or her tax return.

Warning

There is nothing optional about this rule. If you are eligible to claim, say, an exemption for your child who is away at college, you cannot choose to let the child claim his or her own exemption even if you want to. This is true even if you are going to lose some or all of your personal exemptions because your income is too high *(see page 167).*

One possible way around this rule is to make a hefty gift to the child in one year, and then refrain from paying more than half of the child's support in later years. The child could use the gift money to support himself or herself and could then claim the personal exemption on his or her own return.

Claiming Your Dependents' Exemptions

To claim an exemption for a dependent, you must use IRS Form 1040A or the long Form 1040. You must write each dependent's first and last name and Social Security number on Line 6c of either form, and also write in the dependent's closest relationship to you (or your spouse, if filing jointly).

Then, you must total up your dependents in three categories: children who live with you, children who don't live with you because of divorce or separation, and other dependents. The total number of exemptions (including one for yourself and, if applicable, your spouse) is entered on Line 6d of either form.

Social Security Number Required

You must list a Social Security number on your tax return for each dependent, even if the dependent was born late in 2006. Otherwise, your dependency deduction may be denied.

If you don't have a number for one of your dependents and don't expect to get it before April 15th, file an extension request on IRS Form 4868, *Application for Automatic Extension of Time to File U.S. Individual Income Tax Return,* so that you have an extra four months in which to obtain a number. In the meantime, you or your dependent should get a number from the Social Security Administration by filing Form SS-5, *Application for a Social Security Card,* as soon as possible. Contact your local SSA office for more information.

If you are adopting a child who has been placed with you by an authorized agency, you may be able to claim an exemption for the child. If you don't know the child's Social Security number you can get an adoption taxpayer identification number from the IRS by filing Form W-7A, *Application for Taxpayer Identification Number for Pending U.S. Adoptions.* You can call the IRS at 1-800-TAX-FORM to get a copy of this form.

Similarly, if your dependent is a resident or nonresident alien, you will need to get a special identification number from the IRS by filing Form W-7, *Application for IRS Individual Taxpayer Identification Number.*

Tests for Dependency

Deciding whether a given household member is your dependent is usually obvious. In most cases, the person is a minor child living with one or both parents, and there is no doubt that the child is being supported by his or her parent(s).

However, in cases where a child who has substantial income is a member of the household, where an extended family lives under one roof, or where a family supports someone who is living elsewhere, there may be questions as to whether a certain individual qualifies for a dependency exemption. The IRS has come up with a five-part test to determine whether a person is really your dependent.

Briefly, if the individual meets all of the following tests, he or she is your dependent and is not permitted to claim an individual exemption on his or her own tax return:

- the member-of-household or relationship test
- the citizenship test
- the joint return test
- the gross income test
- the support test

Each of these tests is described in more detail below. If your child meets all five of the tests, you can claim a full exemption for the child even if he or she was born on the last day of the year.

If your child or other dependent died during the year but would otherwise have met all five tests, you can still claim the exemption for the dependent. Also, a child who qualifies as a dependent immediately prior to being kidnapped by a nonrelative (as determined by law enforcement authorities) continues to be considered a dependent for all tax years during the period of the kidnapping until the first tax year after the year in which the child is determined to be deceased (or, if earlier, the year in which the child would have turned 18).

The Member-of-Household or Relationship Test

Basically this test is met if the individual is closely related to you *or* was a member of your household for the entire year.

Relationship Test

A person automatically meets this test if he or she is one of the following:

- your child, grandchild, or great-grandchild (legally adopted children are treated as children; before legal adoption, a child is treated as your child if he or she was placed with you by an authorized agency and is a member of your household)
- your stepchild (but not a step-grandchild)
- your brother, sister, stepbrother, stepsister, half-brother, or half-sister
- your parent, grandparent, or other direct ancestor (but not a foster parent)
- your stepfather or stepmother (but not a step-grandparent)
- your aunt, uncle, niece, or nephew by blood; that is, the brother or sister of your father or mother, or the child of your brother or sister
- your father-in-law, mother-in-law, son-in-law, daughter-in-law, brother-in-law, or sister-in-law

The person must bear the listed relationship to you or, on a joint return, to your spouse. You don't need to show that the person is related to the particular spouse who actually provided the financial support unless you are married filing separately.

Example

Peter Lake is the primary support for the uncle of his wife, Vera, although the uncle lives in his own apartment. If the Lakes file a joint return, they may claim the uncle as a dependent. However, if they file separately, neither spouse can claim the exemption because Peter does not bear the required relationship to the uncle or live with him for the whole year, and Vera does not provide more than one-half of the uncle's support.

You may have noticed that your spouse is not on the list of close relationships, above. That's because the spousal exemption is not treated as a dependency exemption, and the five tests do not apply to your spouse. On a joint return, you can automatically claim the exemption for your spouse, simply because you're married. If you file separately, you can claim the exemption for your spouse only if the spouse had no gross income at all and was not the dependent of any other taxpayer. However, in that situation you'd ordinarily have a much lower tax bill if you filed jointly.

Member of Household Test

If the individual is not a close relative under the IRS's definition, he or she can still meet the first test by living with you for the entire year as a member of your household.

Temporary absences from the home will not cause you to fail this test, whether it's you or the dependent who's absent. Temporary absences may be due to illness, education, business, vacation, military service, or temporary placement in a nursing home. If a person died or was born during the year, but was a member of the household for the entire time he or she was alive during the year, the test was met.

Foster children (or adults) can be treated as dependents if they live with you for the entire year, *unless* you receive payments as a foster parent from a state government, a political subdivision, or a tax-exempt child-placement agency. If you receive any such payments, you can't claim a dependency exemption for the child.

Save Money

If you receive some payments as a foster parent, you can claim a charitable deduction for the excess expenses, if your actual expenses for the child are higher than the amount of payments you receive.

Exception for employees. Your maid, babysitter, *au pair,* or any other employee is not considered your dependent even if the employee lived in your household for the entire year.

Citizenship Test

This test for dependency status is met if the person is a U.S. citizen or resident alien, or is a resident of Canada or Mexico for at least part of the calendar year in which your tax year begins.

Children are usually considered to be citizens or residents of their parents' country. In most cases, children born of an American parent are considered to be U.S. citizens for dependency purposes, even if the other parent is a nonresident alien and the child does not live in the U.S., Mexico, or Canada.

Foreign exchange students placed in American homes for a temporary period are not considered U.S. residents, so they don't qualify for a dependency exemption.

Joint Return Test

This test refers to the tax return (if any) filed by the dependent, not your own tax return. In most cases, you can't claim a dependency exemption for any married person who files a joint return with his or her spouse.

There is an exception to this rule if both of the following are true:

- Neither the dependent nor his or her spouse is required to file a tax return, but they file one merely to get a refund.
- Neither the dependent nor his or her spouse would owe any tax if they filed separately rather than jointly.

Gross Income Test

This is another either/or test. The dependent must either (a) be your child who is age 18 or younger, or age 23 or younger and a student, *or* (b) have gross income that is less than the amount of the dependency exemption for the year, which means less than $3,300 for 2006.

Some Definitions

The definition of "child" includes a stepchild, legally adopted child, or a child placed with you by an authorized agency for legal adoption. A foster child who was a member of your household for the entire year is also considered your child.

The child must meet the age requirement for the entire year. If the child was not a student, you don't meet the test for the year in which the child turns 19, even if the child was 18 for most of the year. For that year, the child must have income that is lower than the exemption amount or you'd lose the exemption.

The definition of "student" means a full-time student for some portion of at least five months in the calendar year. Therefore, you can usually count your child as a dependent for the year in which he or she graduates from school.

The school can be an elementary school; middle school; junior or senior high school; a college or university; or a technical, trade, or mechanical school. However, it can't be a correspondence school, night school, or an on-the-job training course (certain on-farm training courses are permitted, though). People who work in co-op programs that are part of the school's prescribed course of study are considered full-time students. Also, students who attend some classes at night as part of a full-time program are considered full-time students.

Income Under $3,300

At the end of 2006, if the person is not your child under age 19 or a full-time student under age 24, the amount of income he or she received in 2006 must have been under $3,300.

You must count all the taxable income the person received during the year, whether in the form of money, property, or services. "Income" includes all unemployment compensation and the taxable portion of any pension income, but does not include gifts, support from you, or tax-exempt Social Security payments.

Also not included are scholarship funds used for tuition, fees, books, or equipment needed for school, or income received by a totally and permanently disabled person for working in a sheltered workshop.

Support Test

The final part of the dependency test requires that you provide more than half of the person's total support during the calendar year.

Save Time

In practice, most parents of minor children are assumed to provide at least half of the support. They don't need to do the formal calculations described below unless the dependent received a significant amount of income during the year and spent it on "support items" as described below.

Technically speaking, to apply the support test you must first calculate the total amount spent for the individual's support during the year, and then calculate how much of that support was provided by you (or your spouse, if filing jointly). If you provided more than half, the individual meets this test to be your dependent.

Total Support for the Year

The first step is to determine how much was actually spent on the individual's support during the year.

"Total support" includes amounts spent to provide food, clothing, lodging, education, medical and dental care, health insurance, recreation, transportation, and similar necessities. Other items can be included, depending on the situation. For example, if you pay someone to provide child care or disabled dependent care, you can include the payments as support even if you claim a tax credit for them.

Items not included as support are federal, state and local taxes; life insurance premiums; funeral expenses; savings and investments; and scholarships received by your child if the child is a full-time student.

Each item you provided is valued at its actual cost. In the case of lodging, the cost is determined as a portion of the fair rental value of the home provided to the dependent. The fair rental value usually includes utilities and furnishings.

Where the precise cost of the support items provided to the dependent can't be determined (e.g., the value of groceries consumed by the person is unknown), you must compute the cost of the item for the entire household in the year, and assign a proportionate share to each member of the household.

Where Did the Support Come From?

Once you know the total value of support received by the individual, you must compute how much of it was provided by yourself (and your spouse, if filing jointly) and then compare the amounts. If you provided one-half or more of the total support, the individual is your dependent under this test.

In some cases, the individual may be receiving income from outside sources such as Social Security, a welfare program, an educational institution, or other individuals. None of this income is treated as support provided by you.

If you are an employer of the individual (for example, if you hire your child to perform office work), the wages you pay are not treated as support provided by you. Also, if the individual takes out a loan and uses the proceeds for educational or other expenses, the loan proceeds count toward total support but not toward support provided by you.

However, the fact that the individual is receiving outside income does not automatically mean that it is being used to support that individual. Amounts that the person saves or invests, or spends on non-support items like life insurance, are not treated as support. This is true even if you encourage the person to save his or own money (and perhaps to open an IRA) and you make up for the amount saved by providing a comparable amount of support.

You can use the worksheet provided on the next page to see whether a particular dependent qualifies under the support test.

Case Study

Troy Smith owns a home in which he lives with his wife, two children, and his mother, Blanche. Blanche is a U.S. citizen and receives annual pension benefits of $3,000, of which $1,800 is taxable gross income. She spends her entire pension on clothing, recreation, and other support items.

Troy's total food expenses for the household were $5,000. He also paid his mother's medical expenses, amounting to $4,000. The fair rental value of the room furnished to Blanche, based on the cost of comparable rooming facilities, was $2,400 per year.

Blanche's total support is computed as follows:

Fair rental value of lodging:	$ 2,400
Direct expenses paid by Blanche:	3,000
Medical expenses paid by Troy:	4,000
Blanche's share of food expenses:	1,000
Total support:	$10,400

Because Troy furnished support worth $7,400, he paid more than one-half of Blanche's support and can claim her as a dependent.

If we change the facts slightly to provide Blanche with nontaxable Social Security benefits of $8,000 in addition to her $3,000 pension, she would remain Troy's dependent as long as she spent less than Troy did ($7,400) on her own support. The remainder of her pension and benefits could be saved or invested, perhaps with the idea that upon her death the savings would go to Troy's children.

Worksheet for Determining Support

Income of the Person You Supported	
1) Did the person you supported receive any income, such as wages, interest, dividends, pensions, rents, social security, or welfare? (If yes, complete lines 2, 3, 4, and 5. If no, go to line 6.)	☐ Yes ☐ No
2) Total income received	$
3) Amount of income used for support	$
4) Amount of income used for other purposes	$
5) Amount of income saved	$
(The total of lines 3, 4, and 5 should equal line 2)	
Expenses for Entire Household (where the person you supported lived)	
6) Lodging (Complete item a or b)	
a) Rent paid	$
b) If not rented, show fair rental value of home. If the person you supported owned the home, include this amount in line 20.	$
7) Food	$
8) Utilities (heat, light, water, etc. not included in line 6a or 6b)	$
9) Repairs (not included in line 6a or 6b)	$
10) Other. Do not include expenses of maintaining home, such as mortgage interest, real estate taxes, and insurance.	$
11) Total household expenses (Add lines 6 through 10)	$
12) Total number of persons who lived in household	
Expenses for the Person You Supported	
13) Each person's part of household expenses (line 11 divided by line 12)	$
14) Clothing	$
15) Education	$
16) Medical, dental	$
17) Travel, recreation	$
18) Other (specify)	$
19) Total cost of support for the year (Add lines 13 through 18)	$
Did You Provide More Than Half?	
20) Amount the person provided for own support (line 3, plus line 6b if the person you supported owned the home)	$
21) Amount others provided for the person's support. Include amounts provided by state, local, and other welfare societies or agencies. Do not include any amounts included on line 2.	$
22) Amount you provided for the person's support (line 19 minus lines 20 and 21)	$
23) 50% of line 19	$

Is line 22 more than line 23?
Yes. You meet the support test for the person. If the other exemption tests are met, you may claim an exemption for the person.
No. You do not meet the support test for the person. You cannot claim an exemption for the person unless you can do so under a multiple support agreement.

Support Test for Children of Divorced or Separated Parents

Special rules apply for determining who can claim the dependency exemption for a child in cases where the parents are divorced, legally separated, or have lived apart for the last six months of the calendar year, and are not filing a joint tax return.

For these rules to apply, the support provided by the parents is combined, and the sum must be greater than one-half of the child's total support. The parent who has custody of the child for the greater part of the year is generally treated as the parent who has provided more than one-half of the child's support.

The question of who has custody of the child is normally determined under the divorce decree, separation agreement, or custody agreement. If there is no such agreement, physical custody of the child is the controlling factor.

The parent who does not have custody of the child for the greater portion of the year can take the dependency exemption if either:

- The custodial parent waives the exemption by signing IRS Form 8332, *Release of Claim to Exemption for Child of Divorced or Separated Parents,* or a similar statement.

- A decree or agreement signed before 1985 provides that the noncustodial parent gets the exemption, and that parent provided at least $600 for the child's support during the year.

Multiple Support Agreements

A situation that frequently arises, particularly with elderly persons, is that a number of people are contributing to an individual's support but no one is paying more than one-half of the support.

The IRS has devised a special rule to cover situations where two or more individuals would have been eligible to claim the dependency exemption if not for the support test, and together these individuals provide more than half of the support.

They can agree among themselves that one of them who provides more than 10 percent of the support will get the exemption. Each of the others must sign an IRS Form 2120, *Multiple Support Declaration,* or another written statement agreeing not to claim the exemption for that year. These forms or statements must be filed along with the income tax return of the person who's claiming the exemption.

In making the decision as to who will get the most tax savings from the exemption, it's important to consider the marginal tax rates of the eligible contributors as well as the effect of the phaseout of personal exemptions discussed below.

Example

Amy, Betty, Carl, and Donald together provide 80 percent of the total support for their mother, Evelyn in the following amounts:

Amy	*35 percent*
Betty	*20 percent*
Carl	*20 percent*
Donald	*5 percent*
	80 percent

Evelyn receives nontaxable Social Security benefits to cover the remaining 20 percent of her expenses.

Because Amy, Betty, and Carl all provide more than 10 percent of Evelyn's support, they may choose which one of them should get the exemption, provided that the other two sign statements to that effect. Donald does not need to sign a statement since his contributions were not greater than 10 percent.

Phaseout of Exemptions for High-Income Families

Taxpayers in the higher brackets will find that, even if they are entitled to one or more exemptions for dependents, they may not get the full benefit of the exemptions on their tax return. In fact, your dependency exemptions may be phased out entirely if your income is high enough.

The threshold amounts of adjusted gross income (AGI) at which you must begin to reduce your personal exemptions are adjusted each year for inflation. The amounts shown in the chart below apply for 2006.

Filing Status	Phaseout Begins At:	Phaseout Complete Above:
Married filing separately	$112,875	$174,125
Single	150,500	273,000
Head of household	188,150	310,650
Married filing jointly	225,750	348,250

If your income exceeds the amount at which the phaseout begins for your filing status, you have to determine the amount of the excess income, and divide it by $2,500 ($1,250 if married filing separately). Take this result and round it up to the nearest whole number. Then multiply this whole number by two percent. Your answer is the percentage by which you must reduce your otherwise allowable exemptions.

Reverse Planning for Exemptions

While those in lower income brackets will want to arrange their affairs to allow as many people as possible to qualify as dependents, it can sometimes pay to "reverse plan" for those in higher income brackets. If you stand to partially or completely lose your exemptions, but you have dependents that have significant taxable income of their own from wages or investments, you might consider allowing some of your dependents to "lose" their dependent status in the future so they will be able to claim their own personal exemptions.

An added benefit of this strategy stems from the fact that individuals who may be claimed as dependents on your tax return are allowed a lower standard deduction on their own tax return. As long as they are considered dependents in 2006, they may claim only the greater of $850 or the amount of their earned income as a standard deduction. If dependent status is lost, they will be eligible for the full $5,150 standard deduction for singles in 2006.

In the case of a child who is age 14 or older, you might also consider transferring some additional income-producing assets to the child to ensure that the child will be able to use the full amount of the exemption and the higher standard deduction.

Case Study

Lincoln and Shabona Park are married and have one child, Grant. The Parks file a joint return and have a joint adjusted gross income of $240,250. They claim three exemptions. The reduction of the Parks' exemptions for 2006 will be calculated as follows:

Adjusted gross income	$240,250
Less: threshold for joint filers	- 225,750
Amount exceeding threshold	$ 14,500

The $14,500 figure is divided by $2,500 to reach the result of 5.8. Rounding up 5.8 to the nearest whole number gives us 6. 6 x 2 percent = 12 percent, which is the percentage of their exemptions that the Parks will lose.

Because the Parks would have an unreduced exemption amount of 3 x $3,300 = $9,900 for 2006, and 12 percent x $9,900 = $1,188, the Parks may claim exemptions of only $8,712 ($9,900 - $1,188).

Example

Mary and Carl Black file jointly, have one child, and have a taxable AGI of $250,000 for 2006. Their daughter, Carrie, is a college student who earns $6,000 in summer employment and also has $5,000 in investment income. It may be beneficial to have Carrie pay more than one-half of her own support so that she may claim a personal exemption on her tax return.

Filing Returns for the Deceased

If your spouse or another family member passes away during the year, a tax return may have to be filed for him or her.

The rule is that if the deceased person met any of the filing thresholds for the year so that he or she would have been required to file a tax return if alive, then a final return for the year of death must be filed.

Example

A 2006 tax return must be filed for a single person over age 65 if he or she had already received taxable income over $9,700 for the year, or more than $400 in self-employment income.

What income is included, in determining whether the thresholds are met and in filing the tax return itself? On the final income tax return, you report only income that the decedent received (for cash-basis taxpayers) or accrued (for accrual basis taxpayers) up to the date of death. Any income received or accrued after that date is ordinarily reportable on the estate's income tax return. If the account is transferred immediately to another beneficiary (such as to the joint owner on a bank account), the beneficiary must report any income earned after the date of death.

If the decedent receives any year-end 1099 forms from banks, savings and loans, brokerages, mutual fund companies, or other financial institutions reporting interest or dividends earned both before and after death, the institutions must be contacted so they can correct their records and issue corrected 1099 forms. Special care should be taken to make sure that the new 1099 forms correctly allocate the amounts between the final individual return and the estate or beneficiary's income tax return.

If the decedent had a capital loss in the period before death, it can be netted against capital gains as discussed on page 237. Any remaining loss up to $3,000 can be deducted on the final return; if the loss exceeded $3,000, the remainder cannot be deducted by the estate or carried over to any succeeding tax years.

Due Dates and Filing Requirements

The due date for the final tax return is the same due date the deceased person would have faced if alive, which is generally April 15th of the year after the year of death, although extensions may be available under the usual rules.

The person responsible for filing the final return is the individual's executor, administrator, or personal representative, if one has been appointed.

An "executor" is the person named in the deceased's will to gather the deceased assets, pay debts and taxes, and distribute any remaining assets according to the directions in the will. An "administrator" has similar duties but is appointed by the probate court if no executor was named, or the named executor is unable to serve. The term "personal representative" is used to refer to both executors and administrators. Often, but not always, a surviving spouse is chosen as the personal representative.

If no personal representative has been formally appointed by the time the tax return is due, the surviving spouse (if there is one) is responsible for filing the last tax return. If there is no surviving spouse, the person who is in charge of the deceased's property must file the final return, and would write the words "Deceased," the decedent's name, and the date of death across the top margin of the tax return.

Filing Status on the Final Return

If the decedent was married at the time of death and the surviving spouse does not remarry before the end of the year, the decedent's final return can be in the form of a joint return with the surviving spouse. The income reported is that of the decedent for the portion of the year he or she was alive, and that of the spouse for the entire calendar year. A full personal exemption can be claimed for the decedent even if his or her income was less than the minimum filing amount.

Filling a joint return usually results in significantly lower overall taxes, but this election must be agreed to by both the surviving spouse and the personal representative (if there is one who is not the surviving spouse). Otherwise, both the survivor and the decedent will have to file as "married filing separately."

If a personal representative was not appointed before the date the tax return is due, but is later appointed, he or she can file an amended return to change the deceased's filing status. If the status will be changed from "separate" to "joint," the surviving spouse must agree to the change. If the status will be changed from "joint" to "separate," the personal representative must file a separate return for the deceased within one year from the due date of the return; in that case, the original joint return would become the separate return of the surviving spouse.

The personal representative or other person filing the final return must sign it, and state his or her capacity (e.g., "Sharon Smith, executor for the estate of Sally Ann Smith"). If the final return is a joint return with the surviving spouse, the spouse must also sign it.

Claiming the Decedent's Refund

The surviving spouse can claim a refund on a final joint return, and no special forms are necessary.

However, if the deceased's return is filed separately, the person filing the return must generally attach IRS Form 1310, *Statement of Person Claiming Refund Due a Deceased Taxpayer,* with the return. A court-appointed personal representative can avoid filing this form if he or she attaches a copy of the court certificate showing the appointment.

Chapter 11

Employment Income and Related Deductions

Many business owners have working spouses who are pulling down a salary, and who will need to report income and associated deductions from a W-2 on their joint return.

What's more, many business owners themselves start out as moonlighters while holding down a day job for a larger company. Even after a small business is established, it's not uncommon (or a bad idea) for the owner to have another job on the side, to provide supplemental income when business is slow.

If any of these scenarios apply to you, you'll need to be aware of the rules for reporting income from a job on your tax return.

Some of you may also have farm income that must be reported on Schedule F, or other types of miscellaneous income. In this chapter we'll provide you with a list of various types of income that are or are not taxable, and tell you how to handle the taxable ones on your income tax return.

The second part of this chapter will discuss employee business expenses, such as expenses for cars, travel, entertainment, and job-related education. We'll also cover the rules for two types of tax breaks that can apply to both those who are self-employed, and those who are employed by others: deductible job-related moving expenses, and child or dependent care credits, for those who can claim them.

Tax Organizer Tip

Most of the income and deduction items we'll be discussing in this chapter should be entered on the "Employment" tab of CompleteTax. Some types of miscellaneous income (such as gambling income and alimony) are entered on the "Miscellaneous" tab.

EMPLOYMENT INCOME

For the most part, employees have it very easy when it comes to reporting their taxable earnings.

They simply look at the W-2 forms they've received from their employers, take the number in Box 1 of the W-2, and report it on Line 1 of Form 1040EZ, or Line 7 of Form 1040A or Form 1040.

If they had more than one job during the year, or they are filing jointly with a spouse, they must add up all the numbers in Box 1 from all the W-2s that they (and their spouse) received, and report the total on Line 7.

There are numerous types of employee benefits that are exempt from federal income tax. For example, health and accident insurance, qualified retirement plan contributions, certain types of education assistance, reimbursements for business expenses, qualified transportation benefits, and group-term life insurance up to $50,000 can all be excluded if certain conditions are met. However, it will be up to your employer to determine whether or not you've received nontaxable benefits, to determine the appropriate value of the benefits, and to adjust your taxable earnings amount accordingly so that only the taxable amount is reported in Box 1.

Your employer must give you a W-2 Form by January 31, 2007, to report all taxable salary, tips, wages and other compensation earned in 2006. A copy of each W-2 you (or your spouse, if filing jointly) receive must be attached to your tax form.

If the employer makes a mistake in these calculations, you must inform the employer and ask for a corrected Form W-2. Employers send a copy of all W-2s directly to the government, and if your reported income does not match what the employer has reported, you may get a letter from the IRS asking for more tax money, plus interest, and penalties.

If you don't receive a W-2 at all, you should contact the employer to find out why not, and ask that one be sent to you. If this doesn't work and by February 15 you still haven't received a W-2, call the IRS at 1-800-TAX-1040 to ask them to help you fill out a copy of Form 4852, *Substitute for Form W-2*.

Employees' Fringe Benefits

Certain types of fringe benefits that you may receive from your employer have been singled out for special treatment by the IRS.

If you received these benefits during the year, your employer must determine the amount that it expects to be deductible on your tax return, and does not include that amount in your taxable wages as reported in Box 1 of your W-2 Form. However, you will have to report the amount separately, somewhere else on your tax return.

The benefits to which this applies are:

- **Dependent care benefits:** If your employer reports these in Box 10 of your W-2, you must file IRS Form 2441, *Child and Dependent Care Expenses,* to determine whether you can exclude the full amount from your taxable income. See page 198.
- **Adoption benefits:** If your employer reports these in Box 12, code T, you must file IRS Form 8839, *Qualified Adoption Expenses,* to determine whether you can exclude the full amount from your taxable income. See page 284.
- **Employer's contributions to an Archer Medical Savings Account (MSA):** If your employer reports these in Box 12, code R, you must file IRS Form 8853, *Archer MSAs and Long-Term Care Insurance Contracts,* to determine whether you can exclude the full amount from your taxable income.
- **Advance Earned Income Credit payments:** If your employer reports these in Box 9, you must report them on Line 61 of your Form 1040, or Line 36 of Form 1040A. You will also have to complete Schedule EIC.

If any of these benefits apply to you, you will have to complete the applicable form to determine whether some of the benefit amount might have to be added back in to your taxable income on Line 7 of Form 1040 or 1040A.

There are a number of other items that may have to be included in your total on Line 7, which are discussed in more detail below.

Excess Salary Deferrals

If an employee makes an elective deferral to a 401(k) plan, the entire amount (including any excess over the annual deferral limit) is reported in Box 12 of your W-2 with code D. Any voluntary after-tax contributions may be reported in Box 14, although this is optional. (If your plan was a tax-sheltered annuity plan or an eligible plan of a state or local government or non-profit organization, a higher limit may apply. Contact your employer if you have questions about your plan, or see IRS Publication 575 for details.)

Corrective Distributions

If too much of your salary was withheld or contributed to a retirement plan (other than an IRA) and your employer corrected the amounts, the corrections should have been reported to you on Form 1099-R, and you must include the amounts that were repaid to you on Line 7 of Form 1040 or 1040A.

Disability Pensions

If you received a disability pension reported on Form 1099-R and you have not reached the minimum retirement age set by your employer, report the amount on Line 7. Otherwise, pensions are reported on Lines 16a and 16b of Form 1040, or Lines 12a and 12b of Form 1040A.

Back Pay Awards

If you received a settlement or a judgment for back pay, it should be reported to you on a W-2 Form and included in the total on Line 7 of Form 1040 or 1040A. The taxable amount can include damages, unpaid life insurance premiums, or unpaid health insurance.

Severance Pay

Severance pay is taxable compensation and should be reported on Line 7 of Form 1040 or 1040A. Also include any amounts you receive to compensate for cancellation of an employment contract.

Tips

If you or your spouse received tips from customers in 2006, any tips that exceeded $20 in a single month should have been reported to your employer over the course of the year. These tips should be reported to you in Box 1 of your W-2 Form.

If, in addition to your reported tips, your employer allocated tips to you (as shown in Box 8 of your W-2) you generally must add these amounts to your Form 1040 Line 7 salary and wages. Allocation is done for employees of larger restaurants, bars, or similar businesses when an employee's reported tips did not equal at least 8 percent of the employer's gross sales that were attributable to you. When you add your allocated tips to your Line 7 wages, remember that FICA tax has not been paid on these tips. Therefore, you will also have to file IRS Form 4137, *Social Security and Medicare Tax on Unreported Tip Income,* to compute and pay the FICA tax, and you will have to file IRS Form 1040 (not 1040A or 1040EZ).

You do not have to add your allocated tips in Box 8 to your reported tips in Box 1 (and pay the extra FICA tax on Form 4137) if you kept a daily record of tips in 2006. In that case, you can use your actual amount of tips, as shown in your tip diary or records.

Work Smart

Technically, all employees who receive tips are supposed to keep a daily tip record – otherwise, how can they accurately report their tips to their employers each month? In actuality, the IRS recognizes that this recordkeeping duty is not always carried out. This is the reason that larger employers have to make a tip allocation.

As an employee, you can save yourself from having to pay unexpectedly large amounts of taxes on April 15th if you carefully keep track of your tips during the year. All it takes is a notebook showing your name, the employer's name, and, for each workday, the date, amount of cash tips, amount of credit card tips, and amount of any non-cash tips. You can also use IRS Form 4070A, Employee's Daily Record of Tips, *found in IRS Publication 1244,* Employee's Daily Record of Tips and Report to Employer. *If you split your tips with other workers you must also write down the names of the other employees and the amounts you paid to them.*

Clergy and Religious

Clergy members must include in their income offerings and fees they receive for performing religious ceremonies such as weddings, baptisms, funerals, etc. But if the offering is made to the religious organization, it is not taxable to you. If you're a clergy member or retired clergy (but not a teacher or administrator of a church school or college), you do not pay tax on the rental value of a home or a housing allowance that's paid as part of your salary, and designated a housing allowance by the church or organization that employs you. If you own the home, you may deduct real estate taxes and mortgage interest (see page 201) even if you pay these expenses with your housing allowance.

Members of religious orders who have taken a vow of poverty and who turn their wages or salary over to the order are not taxed on these earnings, provided that they perform the services as duties required by the order, for the church or another agency of the church or an associated institution. If they work outside the church, they must pay tax on the income.

Miscellaneous Forms of Income

The general rule is that, if you are a U.S. citizen, you must report all income from any source and any country – your total worldwide income – unless it is explicitly exempt under U.S. law. This includes income received in the form of money, property, or services. The following pages explain how to report some commonly encountered forms of income.

Alaska Permanent Fund Dividend Income

If you receive this type of income, you should receive a statement from the State of Alaska showing the total amount. Report it on Line 21 of Form 1040, on Line 13 of the 1040A, or Line 3 of the 1040EZ.

Alimony

For the treatment of alimony paid, as well as alimony received, see page 282.

Cancelled Debts

If you had a debt that was cancelled by the person to whom you owe money, the debt may be treated as taxable income. It will not be taxable if the cancellation was intended as a gift, or as a bequest. It will also not be taxable if the debt was cancelled in a bankruptcy case or when you are insolvent.

Certain student loans that are cancelled because the student worked for a certain period of time in a certain profession (such as teaching) are not treated as income. To qualify, the loan generally must have been made by an educational institution, a tax-exempt organization, or a government agency or instrumentality.

See also the discussion of cancelled business debts on page 49.

Corporate Director Fees

Report these on Line 7 of Form 1040 or 1040A, or Line 1 of Form 1040EZ. Generally, you should receive a W-2 Form showing these payments in Box 1.

Court Awards, Damages, and Legal Settlements

These amounts are either taxable or nontaxable, depending on the nature of the injury that they are designed to compensate you for.

Compensatory damages for personal physical injury or physical sickness are not taxable. However, the following types of damages would be taxable as ordinary income:

- Interest on any type of award
- Compensation for lost wages or lost profits
- Punitive damages
- Amounts received to settle pension rights, if you did not contribute to the plan
- Compensation for patent or copyright infringement
- Compensation for breach of contract
- Compensation for interference with business operations
- Back pay and damages for emotional distress in a Civil Rights Act claim.

Credit Card Insurance Payments

If you receive payments under an insurance plan that makes your credit card payments if you cannot pay because of unemployment, illness, or injury, you must report as "other income" on Line 21 of Form 1040 the amount of benefits you receive during the year that exceeds the amount of premiums you paid during the year.

Disability Pay

If you receive payments because of disability under a plan paid for by your employer, the benefits will be taxable; if you paid for the plan yourself, they are not taxable. "Paying for the plan yourself" includes paying through payroll deductions that were made from your after-tax income. If you paid for the plan through pre-tax payroll contributions, as in a cafeteria-plan arrangement, the benefits you receive are taxable.

Certain types of military and government disability pensions are not taxable. VA disability payments are not taxable, including awards made retroactively after retirement for length of service, and the equivalent of VA benefits that would have been paid if you receive a lump-sum disability severance award. Disability payments for combat-related injuries, or injuries sustained in a terrorist attack while serving as a U.S. government official, are tax-exempt. Also persons who were eligible to receive a disability payment before September 25, 1975 may generally exclude their disability payments.

If the benefits are taxable, they are reported on Line 7 of Form 1040 or 1040A until you reach minimum retirement age. Beginning on the day after you reach minimum retirement age under your employer's plan, the benefits are treated as pension benefits and reported on Lines 16a and 16b of Form 1040, or on Lines 12a and 12b of Form 1040A.

Dividends

See the discussion in Chapter 13.

Election Official Fees

If you are paid for performing services as an election officer or worker, you should receive a W-2 Form reporting this income. Include it in the total reported on Line 7 of Form 1040 or Form 1040A, or on Line 1 of Form 1040EZ.

Estate and Trust Income

See the discussion of investment income in Chapter 13.

Executors and Trustees

If you are not in the business of being a professional fiduciary, fees you receive in these capacities are treated as "other income" to be reported on Line 21 of Form 1040. If being a fiduciary is part of your trade or business, or your duties are so extensive as to constitute a trade or business for a substantial period of time, you will have to report the fees you receive on Schedule C or C-EZ. See Chapter 13.

Gains and Losses

See the discussion of investment gains and losses in Chapter 13.

Gambling Winnings

If you have winnings from a lottery, raffle, or some other gambling activity, it must be reported on Line 21 of Form 1040. If any taxes were withheld from your winnings, you should receive a Form W-2G that shows the total paid to you in Box 1, and the amount of income taxes withheld in Box 2. Be sure to include the amount in Box 2 in the amount of taxes paid on Line 64 of your 1040.

Hobby Income

Income you receive from an activity that is not considered a for-profit business (see page 34) is reported as "other income" on Line 21 of Form 1040. Expenses you incurred in generating this income are deductible as miscellaneous itemized deductions on Schedule A.

Illegal Income

Bribes, kickbacks, push money, stolen or embezzled funds, and other illegal income must be reported on Line 21 of Form 1040, or on Schedule C or C-EZ. While obviously this is rarely done, failure to report opens the door to imposition of tax fines and penalties, as well as criminal penalties, on illegal activities.

Interest

See the discussion in Chapter 13.

Jury Duty Pay

All jury duty pay you receive must be reported as "other income" on Line 21 of Form 1040. If the pay is turned over to your employer, you should treat the amount you repay to your employer as an adjustment to income on Line 34. Write "Jury Pay" and the amount that was repaid on the dotted line next to Line 34.

Pension Benefits

For a discussion of the treatment of retirement and Social Security payments, see Chapter 14.

Prizes and Awards

If you win a prize in a contest, drawing, or raffle, you must report it on Line 21 of Form 1040. If the prize takes the form of a car, merchandise, a gift certificate, or free services, the fair market value of the item is the value that you must report.

There is a very narrow exception for prizes in recognition of past accomplishments (such as a Nobel, Pulitzer, literary prize, citizen-of-the-year award, etc.). You don't have to include the award as income if you were selected without any action on your part to enter the contest, you don't have to perform future services, and you transfer the award directly to a tax-exempt charitable organization or government unit.

Refunds or Recoveries of Previously Deducted Items

If you recover or receive back an amount that you had already deducted on a prior year's return, you generally must report the recovered amount as income in the year you receive it. This rule saves you the trouble of having to file an amended tax return for the prior year.

State or local income tax refunds are the most commonly encountered items of this type. Therefore, they have been assigned their own line (Line 10) on Form 1040. If you itemized your deductions in the year to which the refund applies, you must report the refund as income on Line 10. If you did not itemize, you don't have to report the refund since you didn't gain any tax benefit from it. Federal tax refunds are not reported because you cannot claim an itemized deduction for your federal taxes.

This rule – the rule that you must report the refund or recovery only if you got some tax benefit from it in a previous year – applies generally to all types of refunds and recoveries, except that recoveries other than state and local tax refunds, credits and offsets are reported on Line 21 of Form 1040.

You only have to report recoveries of items to the extent that they helped your itemized deductions to exceed the standard deduction for the year in question.

Example

In 2005, your filing status was single, which would have qualified you for a standard deduction of $5,000. Instead, you claimed itemized deductions of $5,400.

In 2006, you received a $1,000 refund of state income tax. Since your itemized deductions minus your standard deduction was only $400, you must report $400 of the recovery as income for 2006. The remaining $600 of the recovery is not taxable.

If your deduction for the item was less than the amount you recovered, you only have to report a taxable recovery for the amount that you had actually deducted.

Example

In 2005, your employee business expenses were $1,000, but since your adjusted gross income was $40,000, you faced the 2 percent of adjusted gross income limitation on miscellaneous deductions (including employee business expenses). So, you had to subtract $40,000 x .02 = $800 from the expense amount, to arrive at an allowable deduction of $200.

In early 2006, your employer reimbursed you for $300 of your business expenses. Your taxable recovery is limited to the amount you deducted, or $200.

Taxpayers who itemized their deductions for the year to which the recovery applies, but had their deductions limited because they were high-income taxpayers (see page 275), must go through some special calculations to determine how much of the recovery they must report. Basically, this involves determining how much of a deduction they would have been able to claim for the item if it were reported accurately, as compared to the amount they actually were able to claim for the item, taking the limitation into account.

Example

In 2005, $9,000 in state income taxes were withheld from your paycheck, but you could only *deduct $3,600 of these taxes because your itemized deductions were reduced by 3 percent of the amount by which your income exceeded $145,950. In 2006, you received a state tax refund of $2,000. If you had correctly reported your state taxes for 2005 as $7,000, your itemized deduction for taxes would have been $1,800. Therefore, the difference between what you actually claimed, and what you should have claimed, is your reportable recovery amount ($3,600 - $1,800 = $1,800).*

Rents and Royalties

See the discussion in Chapter 13.

Scholarships

Scholarship or fellowship grants are excludable from income if you are a degree candidate, and the amounts received are for tuition, fees, books, supplies, or equipment required for courses. Room and board do not qualify. If you receive payments for services, they must be included in your taxable income even if such services are required of all candidates for the degree.

Veterans' Administration payments are not taxable. Qualified tuition reduction for undergraduates, or tuition waivers or reductions for graduate students engaged in teaching or research activities, are not taxable.

If you received taxable money under a grant, you must report it on Line 7 of your 1040 form, whether or not it was reported on a W-2 form.

Social Security Benefits

See the discussion in Chapter 14.

State Tuition Programs

Distributions from a qualified state tuition program are tax-free up to the amount that was contributed to the program; amounts over the contributions are taxable.

Unemployment Compensation

All unemployment compensation you may receive is taxable. If you received any during the year, you should receive a Form 1099-G showing the amount. that was paid to you. Report it on Line 19 of Form 1040, Line 13 of Form 1040A, or Line 3 of Form 1040EZ.

If you receive supplemental unemployment benefits from a fund that was created by your employer, these benefits are taxable for income tax purposes and are reported on Line 7 of Form 1040 or 1040A.

If you received payments from a union, they are reported on Line 21 (the "Other Income" line) of Form 1040. And if you received payments from a private unemployment fund to which you contributed, only the portion that exceeds your total contributions are taxable, and reported on Line 21.

Nontaxable Income

The following items are generally not reported as taxable income.

- Accelerated death benefits under a life insurance contract that are paid to a terminally or chronically ill person by the insurance company or a viatical settlement company
- Accident and health insurance benefits
- Black lung benefits
- Cash rebates (for example, you receive $500 after purchasing a new car)
- Casualty insurance and other reimbursements for theft or casualty loss (see page 271)
- Child support payments

- Damages for physical injury or sickness
- Energy conservation subsidies provided by public utilities for purchase or installation of energy-saving devices in dwellings
- Federal Employees' Compensation Act payments
- Foster-care payments, unless you are paid for care of more than five people age 19 or older, or you receive difficulty-of-care payments for more than five people age 19 or older, or more than 10 people under 19
- Gifts, bequests, and inheritances
- Government cost-of-living allowances for civilian employees stationed outside the continental U.S. or in Alaska
- Life or accident insurance proceeds, unless the policy was turned over to you for a price. However, if you cash in a policy, you must include in taxable income any amount that exceeds the total premiums you paid less any rebates, refunds, dividends, or unrepaid loans.
- Living expenses paid by insurance, because of a casualty loss to your home, to the extent the payments compensate for extra expenses you would not have had if the casualty had not occurred
- Long-term care insurance benefits from qualified plans, up to $250 per day or $91,250 per year in 2006 ($260 per day or $94,900 per year in 2007).
- Medical savings account withdrawals, if used to pay for qualified medical expenses for you, yourself, or your dependents (withdrawals to pay for health insurance premiums are qualified expenses only if you are unemployed, buying COBRA continuation coverage, or buying long-term care coverage)
- Military allowances
- Supplemental Security Income (SSI) payments
- Veterans' benefits
- Welfare benefits, including disaster relief grants, mortgage assistance programs, and payments to reduce cost of winter energy
- Workers' compensation

Farm Income

Farmers must report their income from farming in a variety of different ways.

If you are in the trade or business of farming, you must complete and file Schedule F, *Profit or Loss from Farming,* along with your IRS Form 1040. This form is very similar to Schedule C and most of your expense deductions, tax credits, and gains and losses are computed using the same rules discussed in Part II for small business owners. For example, for the treatment of car or truck expenses, see page 63 relating to small business car or truck expenses. For the treatment of sales of assets, see page 116 relating to sales of business assets.

Note that sales of livestock held for breeding, dairy, draft, or sport purposes are treated as sales of business assets reported on Form 4797, *Sales of Business Property,* while sales of livestock raised or purchased for resale are reported on Schedule F.

Schedule F, Line E, asks whether you "materially participated" in the farming business. The standard for "material participation" for this question relates to the passive activity rules and is basically the same as the standard for materially participating in a small business; see page 44 for more details.

As a farmer, you can be treated as materially participating under two additional situations: (1) if you are a retired or disabled farmer, and you materially participated for five of the eight years preceding your retirement or disability, or (2) if you are a surviving spouse of a farmer, you actively manage the farm, and the property used for farming meets the special use valuation of a farm property under the estate tax rules.

Net farm income as computed on Schedule F is carried over to Line 18 of Form 1040, and self-employment tax is computed on the Schedule F net income using Schedule SE. See the discussion of self-employment taxes on page 135.

Beginning in 1998, a special rule permits farmers to average their income over three years. This will allow you to pay less in taxes in an unusually good year. If you elect to average farm income, you must complete Schedule J and file it with your Form 1040. You'll figure the current year's tax by following these steps:

1. Subtract the elected part of your current year's taxable farm income (elected farm income) from your total taxable income.

2. Figure the tax on the amount in Step 1 using the current year's tax tables or tax rate schedules.

3. For each of the previous three years, make the following computation:

   (a) Add one-third of the current year's elected farm income to your taxable income for that year.

   (b) Figure the tax on the amount in (a) using the tax tables or rate schedules for that year.

   (c) Subtract that year's actual tax from the tax in (b).

4. Add the amounts in step 3(c) to the amount in Step 2. The result is the tax for the current year.

Rent Based on Crop or Livestock Sharing

If you are involved in a crop or livestock sharing arrangement with a tenant who does most of the work of operating the farm and you don't meet the special active participation test described below, you should report your income and expenses on Form 4835, *Farm Rental Income and Expenses,* instead of Schedule F. In that case, your net income from Form 4835 is carried over to Schedule E, *Supplemental Income and Loss.* It is treated like rental income and will not be subject to self-employment tax.

In order to use this form (and avoid self-employment tax on the income), you must *not* have materially participated in the activity. You *did* materially participate if you meet one of the following four tests:

1) You do any three of the following four things: pay or stand good for at least half the direct costs of producing the crop; furnish at least half the tools, equipment, and livestock used in producing the crop; consult with your tenant; inspect production activities periodically.

2) You regularly and frequently make, or take an important part in making, important management decisions.

3) You work 100 hours or more spread over five weeks or more in activities connected with crop production.

4) You do things which, considered in their total effect, show that you are materially and significantly involved in the production of the farm commodities.

Rent Based on Flat Charge

Finally, if you rent cropland, farm buildings, etc. for a flat charge (rather than a percentage of the value of the yield produced by the tenant), report the activity directly on Schedule E, *Supplemental Income and Loss.* Again, net income from this type of activity will not be subject to self-employment tax.

More Farming Information

Farmers are subject to some special, generally more lenient accounting rules and some very specific rules about income recognition. We recommend that you get a copy of the IRS's free Publication 225, *Farmer's Tax Guide,* for help in completing Schedule F or Form 4835. For more on Schedule E, see Chapter 12.

EMPLOYEE BUSINESS EXPENSES

If you've read Part II of this book, you know that business owners must report their sales and other income on Schedule C, and then are entitled to deduct all their legitimate business expenses before arriving at the net income that will be subject to tax.

If you are an employee, your income from your job is reported to you on a W-2 form, and the expectation is that your employer is providing you with the location, materials, tools and equipment, and other things you need to do your work. However, it's not always the case that employers pay for *all* of an employee's business expenses.

So, the IRS does give employees the opportunity to claim some tax deductions if you spend money on your job; e.g., on business meals and entertainment, local transportation, gifts, travel, education, supplies, tools, uniforms and other customary business expenses, so long as the expenses are considered reasonable and meet certain requirements.

The way in which your business expenses are written off for tax purposes depends on whether your employer reimburses you for your expenses and, if so, what type of reimbursement plan the employer uses.

Generally speaking, you'll get the full benefit of all your allowable deductions if they are reimbursed by your employer under what is known as an "accountable plan." This is a plan under which you have to report and document your expenses for your employer, and you have to return any expense allowance amounts over and above the expenses you have proven. Your employer then subtracts the reimbursements from your taxable income when filling out your annual W-2 form, so you pay no tax on the amount of the reimbursements.

Unreimbursed Expenses

If you have expenses that are not reimbursed by your employer, or if your employer does not use an accountable plan, you'll generally have to claim the nonreimbursed expenses on Form 2106, *Employee Business Expenses.* In some cases you may be able to use Form 2106-EZ, *Unreimbursed Employee Business Expenses.* Then the total amount of your expenses from either of these forms is transferred to Line 20 of Form 1040 Schedule A, *Itemized Deductions.*

Warning

We might as well warn you upfront that Schedule A requires that your employee business expenses be classified as "miscellaneous deductions" that must be reduced by 2 percent of your adjusted gross income (AGI) before they can be deducted. In other words, you'll automatically lose the benefit of some of your expenses, up to the amount of 2 percent of AGI.

And, if you can't itemize your deductions because all of your deductible expenses don't add up to more than the standard deduction for your filing status *(see page 259)**, you will lose the tax benefits of your employee business expenses entirely.*

Therefore, it becomes very important to keep track of your expenses so that your allowable deductions will be as large as possible. Sometimes a few extra dollars of expenses will make the difference when you're deciding whether it's worthwhile to itemize in a particular year.

This is the basic story, but as you might guess, there are a few wrinkles to be aware of. On the next few pages, we'll first go over the most common types of employee business expenses, and then explain exactly how to claim them on your tax return.

What Expenses are Deductible for Employees?

For the most part, employees can deduct all "ordinary and necessary" business expenses, using the same definition that is used by a business owner. An "ordinary" expense is one that is common and accepted in your line of work. A "necessary" expense is one that is appropriate or helpful for the work you do, even if it's not absolutely indispensable to your business.

For employees, expenses may be considered "unnecessary" if you could have been reimbursed for them, but you neglected to ask the employer for reimbursement.

As a general principle, amounts that you spend for personal or family reasons are not deductible. While it's sometimes difficult to tell the difference, the IRS has specific rules in a number of areas (such as car expenses, travel, meals and entertainment, and education) to help you determine what portion of an expense is truly business-related. If you pay for property or have some other expense for both business and personal purposes, you must allocate the expense between the two types of usage. The allocation must be made on a reasonable and consistent basis, depending on the nature of the expense.

Example

If a car is used partly for business and partly for personal purposes, the allocation is based on the number of miles driven during the year for business, compared to the miles driven for personal use. If you use a room in your home as a home office, the allocation is based on the number of square feet in the office as compared with the square footage of the entire home.

See page 57 for more information on how to make this type of allocation.

Certain expenses, while they may be ordinary and necessary, must be treated as capital expenditures.

Generally speaking, the cost of equipment or business real estate that will be used for more than one year must be treated as a capital expenditure and depreciated. Employees may claim a depreciation deduction for equipment they need in their job (such as a cellular phone or a laptop computer) and would use a separate Form 4562, *Depreciation and Amortization,* to compute the proper amount. The result from Form 4562 would be carried over to Line 4 of the Form 2106 or 2106-EZ. For a detailed explanation of capital assets, depreciation, and how to treat the sale of a business asset, see Chapter 7.

Finally, certain types of expenses are not deductible even if they meet the "ordinary and necessary" tests, and are not personal or capital expenses. This category includes illegal payments (e.g., bribes or kickbacks) and payments of fines or penalties (such as parking or traffic tickets).

Cars, Meals and Entertainment, Travel, Home Offices, and Gifts

The most commonly deducted employee business expense is undoubtedly the cost of a car. The IRS has a large number of very specific rules about deductible costs of operating a vehicle. The rules for employees are basically the same as the rules for self-employed people, as described beginning on page 63.

One departure from the ordinary rules that employees should be aware of is that an employee using the actual expense method cannot deduct any part of the interest payments on a car loan (while a self-employed person can).

In order to claim the deduction for car expenses, you'll have to keep records that satisfy the IRS. The best way to be sure you'll get to claim all your deductions is to keep a written record of your business mileage whenever you drive, and also keep a record of all car expenses as you pay them. It's a good idea to save all your receipts for expenses as well. See the discussion of recordkeeping in Chapter 2.

If your employer pays you a mileage allowance, you can simplify your recordkeeping a bit. Generally, if the mileage allowance is no higher than the government's standard mileage rate (44.5 cents per mile in 2006 and 48.5 cents per mile in 2007) you will only be required to prove to the employer the time, number of miles, and business purpose of your car trips, and this will be enough to satisfy the IRS. If, however, your employer pays you more than the standard mileage rate (SMR), the SMR amount will be shown in Box 12 of your W-2 Form with Code L, and the excess will be reported as taxable income to you in Box 1 of the W-2 Form.

For employees, car expenses can be reported on Form 2106-EZ if you own your car and use the standard mileage rate for 2006, and if you are not required to file Form 2106 for any other reason. Otherwise, you must use Form 2106 to report car expenses.

Meals, entertainment, travel, gifts, and home offices. Most other types of employee business expenses follow the same rules that apply to small business owners. For the rules regarding meals and entertainment, see page 75; for rules on deductible travel expenses, see page 72; for rules on business gifts, see page 77; and for rules on home offices, see page 79. Note that for an employee to claim a home office expense, he or she must be using the office for the convenience of the employer (not just his or her own convenience), in addition to meeting all the other requirements for the home office deduction.

Employees' Education Expenses

Educational expenses for employees can yield tax benefits under two different law provisions, each of which has its own detailed requirements.

In addition, there are several types of tax credits that apply to educational benefits for all individuals, not just employees. For a discussion of the Hope Scholarship Credit and the Lifetime Learning Credit, see page 288; for a discussion of the exclusion of education loan interest, see page 290.

In this section, we'll concentrate on two types of educational benefits: employer-provided educational assistance, and qualifying work-related education.

Employer-provided assistance. Up to $5,250 per year can be provided to an employee as reimbursement for educational expenses as part of an employee benefit plan. Tuition, fees, books, supplies, and tools are considered reimbursable "educational expenses."

The tax law does not require the education to be related to the job, or part of a degree program, although some employers may impose these requirements under their particular plan. Also, covered educational expenses may include graduate level course work, even courses leading to a professional degree.

Work Smart

Note that the benefits must be provided under a written plan that does not discriminate in favor of officers, shareholders, or highly compensated employees, and no more than five percent of the benefits provided during a year can be paid to the business owner's family. Therefore, small business owners can't use this type of plan to finance their own or their family's education.

If you receive benefits under this type of plan, they are completely tax-free, and they will not be reported as income on your W-2 form. You don't have to take any further action to claim your exemption.

Work-related education. If you don't receive employer-provided assistance under the type of plan described above, or if the assistance you receive is more than $5,250 per year, there is another law provision under which you may receive a tax break for education.

Under the qualifying, work-related education rules, education of any type (whether or not it leads to a degree, and whether it is technical, vocational, undergraduate, graduate, or professional) will be deductible if it meets either of these requirements:

1. The education must be required by your employer or the law to keep your present salary, status, or job (and serve a business purpose of your employer).

2. The education must maintain or improve skills needed in your present work, including refresher courses, seminars, and academic courses.

However, even if the education meets these requirements, it is not qualifying education if either:

1. It is needed to meet the minimum educational requirement for your present trade or business as in effect when you first got the job.

2. It is part of a program of study that can qualify you for a new trade or business, even if you have no plans to enter that trade or business. Bar review or CPA review courses or exams don't qualify.

The education must relate to your present work, not just to work you may take up in the future or work that you held in the past. However, if you stop work for a year or less (for example, to go to school full-time) and then resume your work, this temporary absence will not render the education nonqualifying.

If all of these rules are met, you can deduct your educational expenses. Furthermore, if the employer reimburses you for these expenses, it can be treated as a nontaxable working-condition fringe, and the reimbursements should not be reported as taxable income on your W-2 form. Nondiscrimination rules do not apply to this type of working-condition fringe benefit, so small business owners can take advantage of this deduction as well.

Types of expenses that qualify. Under the qualifying work-related education expense rules, you can deduct a much broader range of expenses: the costs of tuition, fees, books, supplies, transportation and travel costs, and other expenses such as the cost of research, typing and copying when writing a paper as part of an educational program.

Generally, you can deduct the standard mileage rate of 44.5 cents per mile in 2006 (48.5 cents in 2007) for the mileage you drive one way from work to school; alternately, you can deduct the cost of bus, subway, train, cab, or even airfare to get to school. If you are regularly employed and go to school on a temporary basis (generally, irregularly or for a matter of days or weeks), you can also deduct the cost of going from school to home. However, if you go from home directly to school you can deduct the round-trip costs only if you are going from home to school on a temporary basis.

If you drive, you can choose to use the actual cost method to compute your vehicle costs (see page 67); however, this generally involves a great deal of recordkeeping for very little payback. Regardless of whether you use the standard mileage rate or the actual cost method, you can always deduct the cost of parking and tolls.

If you must travel and stay overnight to get to school or to a particular seminar, training course, trade or business association meeting, etc., you can deduct the cost of travel, lodging, and 50 percent of the cost of meals for yourself under the usual rules related to travel (see page 72). However, you cannot deduct the cost of travel that is in itself a form of education – there must be some type of specific class, seminar, convention, etc., involved.

Claiming work-related education expenses. For employees, if you are deducting transportation, travel, or meals in connection with qualified education, these should be added to your other expenses of the same type and deducted on IRS Form 2106 or 2106-EZ.

Example

You traveled 10 miles from work to school and 12 miles from school back home, and made this trip once a week for a six-week period. Since this was a "temporary" situation you can deduct the cost of driving 22 miles, for each of the six classes, or a total of 132 miles. This mileage would be added to any other business mileage you drove during the year and reported on Line 13 of Form 2106, or Line 8a on Form 2106-EZ.

Other education costs of employees (the costs of tuition, fees, books, supplies, etc.) would normally be reported on Line 4 of either Form 2106 or 2106-EZ.

If you are self-employed, education costs would be reported on Schedule C, with most costs being reported on Line 27 as "other expenses" but the costs for your car or truck, meals, and travel being added to Lines 9, 24b, and 24a respectively. If you file Schedule C-EZ, deduct these expenses on Line 2.

More Employee Business Expenses

Along with the expenses we've already mentioned, you can deduct almost any other ordinary and necessary business expense you have as an employee. Some of the more common ones are discussed below.

Computers. You can claim a first-year expensing election for a home computer (see page 103) if you use it more than 50 percent for business; otherwise, or for later years, you may depreciate the business percentage of the cost. See Chapter 7 for the rules related to long-term business assets.

Dues. You can deduct membership fees and dues to professional societies, the chamber of commerce, boards of trade, business leagues, civic or public service organizations, real estate boards, or trade associations if membership helps you in your job; however, you can't deduct any portion of the dues that is used for lobbying or political activities. Your organization should tell you the percentage of your dues, if any, that are used for this purpose. Dues to airline clubs, social clubs, or country clubs are not deductible.

Office furniture used at home. Even if you can't claim the home office deduction, you can expense or depreciate the cost of a desk, chair, file cabinets, lighting, etc. you use when you work at home, provided you meet the usual requirements (see Chapter 7).

Subscriptions. You can deduct the cost of professional, trade, or business publications and newspapers.

Telephones. The installation and monthly charges for the first telephone line you bring into your home is not deductible. But if you have a second line for business, or you can determine the cost of specific long-distance or local charges for business calls, you can deduct those amounts even if you don't qualify for the home office deduction.

Work clothes and uniforms. These are deductible only if you must wear certain items as a condition of your employment and they are not suitable for normal wear; for example, firefighters, delivery people, waiters, health care workers, and others required to wear specific uniforms may claim the deduction, but not those who are merely required to conform to a dress code, or to dress in a certain style or color. If your clothing qualifies, so does the cost of upkeep and cleaning. You can also deduct the cost of protective clothing or items like hard-hats, safety glasses, work gloves, steel-toed boots, etc.

Other deductions. Here are a few more potentially deductible items that are often overlooked:

- Breakage fees
- Business cards
- Business liability or malpractice insurance, for wrongful acts committed on the job
- Damages for breach of employment contract that you pay to your former employer
- Legal fees (for example, to negotiate an employment contract)
- Medical exams required by the employer
- Occupational taxes and license fees
- Office supplies and postage
- Passport fee for a business trip
- Tools and other supplies used in your work
- Union dues

Claiming Employee Business Expenses

If you receive an advance to pay for your employee business expenses, or reimbursements for expenses you have already incurred, the way you report your expense depends on how your employer reimburses you.

The key distinction to be made is whether the employer's plan is "accountable" or "nonaccountable." Your employer should be able to tell you which type it is using.

Accountable plans. If the plan is accountable, and you are reimbursed for the exact amount of the expense, you are among the lucky ones. Your reimbursements are simply excluded from your income – that is, they are not reported as income on your W-2 form, and you don't have to pay income tax, Social Security tax, or Medicare tax on them. You don't have to file a Form 2106 to claim your expenses as deductions because they are already subtracted from your pay.

Under accountable plans, you report your expenses to the employer, and provide it with all the receipts, credit card slips, and other documentation you would normally need for the IRS. This takes the place of retaining all these records in case the IRS asks for them.

Nonaccountable plans. However, if the plan is not considered accountable, or if your employer does not reimburse you for all of your allowable expenses, you'll have to claim the deductions on your tax return.

Your employer will include any reimbursements it makes in your taxable income (in Box 1 on your W-2), and will withhold income tax, Social Security tax, and Medicare tax on them. Any reimbursements that are *not* reported in Box 1 must be subtracted from your deductible expenses on Form 2106, *Employee Business Expenses.*

If you are not reimbursed for your employee business

expenses (other than taxable amounts included in Box 1), you can generally report your expenses on Form 2106-EZ, *Unreimbursed Employee Business Expenses,* provided that if you are claiming vehicle expenses, you are using the standard mileage rate (SMR) to compute your expenses.

If you use the actual expense method of claiming car expenses, or if you were reimbursed for expenses, you will have to use the longer Form 2106, *Employee Business Expenses.*

Save Time

If you are not claiming any car, parking and tolls, local transportation charges, travel, or meal and entertainment expenses, and you didn't receive any reimbursements that weren't reported as taxable income, you don't have to use either version of the 2106. Instead, you can simply claim these expenses as miscellaneous deductions on Line 20 of Schedule A.

However, you may want to file a Form 2106 anyway, particularly if you are claiming a large amount of expenses, just to provide the IRS with some additional information and, hopefully, prevent them from writing you a letter that questions your deduction.

Some special rules. Qualified performing artists, and disabled employees with impairment-related work expenses, are subject to some special, more lenient ways to claim their employee business expenses.

A qualified performing artist can deduct employee business expenses as an adjustment to gross income (on Line 24 of Form 1040). As a result, such artists don't need to itemize expenses to get the benefits of their deductions. They would still need to complete Form 2106 to compute their expenses, and then write the total amount on Line 24 on the 1040.

Qualified performing artists are those who perform services for at least two employers during the tax year, receive at least $200 from two different employers, have related performing-arts business expenses over 10 percent of their gross income, and have adjusted gross income of not more than $16,000 before deducting those expenses. If married, the artist must file jointly unless living apart from the spouse at all times during the tax year, and joint adjusted gross income may not be more than $16,000 before deducting the expenses.

Employees with physical or mental disabilities, who have impairment-related work expenses, can deduct those expenses without regard to the usual 2 percent of adjusted gross income threshold for miscellaneous deductions. They would complete Form 2106 or 2106-EZ, and enter impairment-related expenses directly onto Line 27 of Schedule A, *Itemized Deductions.*

DEDUCTIBLE MOVING EXPENSES

Moving to a new location to take a new job or start a new business is something that hopefully doesn't happen every year. However, if you did move last year, your moving costs may have eaten up a significant portion of your income.

The tax laws permit some limited tax breaks for job-related moves, if you meet all the requirements. If your employer pays for some or all of the costs, you won't be taxed on the reimbursements. And if you pay for the costs yourself, you can deduct them "above the line"; that is, you don't have to itemize your deductions in order to get the benefit of your moving expenses. Moreover, your moving expense deduction will serve to reduce your adjusted gross income (AGI), which may help you qualify for other tax breaks that are phased out at higher AGI levels.

Which Moves Qualify?

Before you can start to add up the amounts you spent on your move, you have to determine whether your move met the IRS's requirements for a deductible move.

There are three parts to the test that you must meet:

1. Was the move closely related to the start of work?
2. Did the move meet the distance test?
3. Did your work in the new location meet the time test?

Closely Related to Start of Work

For any moving expenses to be deductible, your move must have been closely related to the start of work in your new location, in both time and in space.

Being closely related in time means that the expenses occurred within one year before, or one year after, you go to work or start a business in the new location.

You may qualify for an exemption from this rule if you have a good reason for incurring the expense of moving outside the one-year period.

Example

You were transferred to a new job on the West Coast and began working there, but the rest of your family did not move from the Midwest until 18 months later so that your son could finish high school. The costs of moving your family would be deductible even though they were incurred more than one year after your new job began.

Being closely related in place generally means that the distance from the new job to the new home is not more than the distance from the new job to the old home.

Again, there may be an exception to this rule if you can show that either your employer requires you to live at the new home as a condition of employment, or you will actually spend less time or money commuting to the new job from your new home.

For purposes of measuring distances, the "new job" is considered to be located at your principal place of work, which is the place where you spend most of your working time. If there is no one location where you spend most of your time, consider your principal place of work to be the main office, station, check-in point, or place where you receive instructions. If you have more than one job, you'll have to decide which is your main job, based on the time spent at each job, the amount of work you do at each place, and the amount of money you earn at each place.

Also, your "home" for these purposes means your main home, not a summer home, second home, or a home kept up by other family members.

Distance Test

There is another test related to distance that must be met if you want to deduct moving expenses.

The distance between your old home and your new job must be at least 50 miles farther than the distance from the old home to the old job. In other words, your new job would have increased your commuting distance by at least 50 miles, if you hadn't moved.

Example

Sally travels 60 miles one way to get to work. She takes a new job that would require her to travel 65 miles and, since she feels the extra time makes her commute just too long, she bites the bullet and buys a new home only two miles from the new job. Sally cannot deduct her moving expenses, because the new job would only have increased her commute by five miles.

For those who are seeking their first full-time job or have been out of the workforce for a significant period of time, the new place of work must be at least 50 miles from your old home.

Time Test

The third and final test for a deductible move is that, if you're an employee, in the first year after you start work in the new location you must work full time for at least 39 weeks.

If you are self-employed (as a sole proprietor or partner), you must work full time for at least 39 weeks in the first year, and you must also work full time for at least 78 weeks in the first two years.

The weeks need not be consecutive, and they don't have to be with the same employer or in the same business activity if you are self-employed. "Full-time work" means whatever is considered full time in your occupation and region. Also, vacation time or time off because of illness, strikes, layoffs, natural disasters, or similar causes counts as time worked. If you are using the self-employed rule, you can count time spent as an employee as well as time working for your own company towards the 78-week requirement.

This rule can be waived only if your work is cut short due to death or disability, or if you obtained full-time work but you were transferred by the employer or were laid off for a reason other than misconduct.

If you are filing a joint return, the move is deductible if either spouse meets the 39-week test, or the 78-week test if self-employed. However, time worked by one spouse can't be added to time worked by the other spouse.

Example

K.C. Jones decides to move from Boston to Dallas because he believes there are better job prospects there. He moves himself and his family to Dallas at his personal expense, where he finds a job with an oil company. After working full-time for 30 weeks, his job ends. He then moves to Santa Fe and gets a job there, which he holds for more than 39 weeks.

Meanwhile his wife, Tracy, found a job in Dallas at the same time as her husband and worked there for nine weeks after he left for Santa Fe. Since Tracy met the 39-week requirement for work in Dallas, the entire family's move from Boston to Dallas is deductible if the couple files a joint return. Since K.C. met the 39-week requirement in Santa Fe, the family's moving expenses from Dallas to Santa Fe will also be deductible.

Obviously, the one-year period after you begin work in a new location might not coincide with your tax year, which is a calendar year for most individuals. The IRS very graciously allows you to deduct your moving expenses on this year's tax return even if you have not yet met the 39-week or 78-week requirements, as long as you reasonably expect to meet them within the allotted time.

If it later turns out that you can't meet the test, and you don't qualify for any of the exceptions, you have a choice: either amend your tax return for the year you claimed the moving expenses using IRS Form 1040X, or add back the expenses as miscellaneous income to your tax return for the year in which you fail the test.

Example

You moved in December of 2005 to transfer to a new location and take a different job with your employer of 20 years, and because it seemed likely that your job would continue indefinitely, you deducted your moving expenses on your 2005 tax return.

However, in May of 2006, your employer offers you a buy-out for early retirement, and you decide to accept the offer and retire to the beach. Because you did not work for 39 weeks at the new location, your moving expenses were rendered nondeductible. You could file an amended return for 2005 to rescind the deduction; however, since your income (and your tax rate) is lower in 2006 due to your retirement, you decide instead to report the moving expenses as miscellaneous income (on Line 21 of your Form 1040) in 2006.

Some Special Rules

There are special, more lenient rules on moves for the military, and for those who move back to the U.S. to retire or because their spouse has died.

First, the rules for members of the U.S. Armed Forces: You can deduct moving expenses and do not have to meet the time or distance tests described above if you are moving because of a permanent change of station. If a member of the armed services is imprisoned, deserts, or dies, a permanent change of station for the spouse or dependents includes a move to the place of enlistment; the member's, spouse's or dependent's home of record; or a nearer point in the United States. Finally, if the military moves a member and his or her family to or from separate locations, the moves are treated as a single move to the new main job location and all moves will be deductible.

Retirees whose former main job location and main home were outside the U.S. can deduct their moving expenses to the U.S. or one of its possessions without having to meet the time test described above, provided they are permanently retiring.

Spouses or dependents of people who die overseas can deduct expenses for a move that begins within six months of the death. The deceased person must have had a main job location outside the U.S., and the survivor(s) must have been living there also.

Which Moving Expenses are Deductible?

In general, there are only two categories of expenses that can be deducted as moving expenses:

1. the cost of moving household goods and personal effects, including temporary storage costs

2. the cost of a one-way trip for all household members to the new home, including lodging expenses (but not meals)

"Household members" includes all who reside in both the old and the new location, but does not include domestic help or tenants unless they're your dependents (see the rules for dependents, page 163).

The trip must be taken by conventional, reasonable means considering the circumstances of the move. If you make side trips along the way, the side trips are not deductible expenses.

If you travel by train, air, bus, etc., the cost will generally be the cost of the tickets, plus taxis or other ground transportation if applicable. If you travel by car, you have the choice of deducting 18 cents per mile in 2006 (20 cents per mile in 2007), or your actual expenses for gasoline, oil, repairs, etc. In either case, you can also deduct parking fees and tolls. It's not necessary that all family members travel together or by the same method.

The cost of the trip includes the cost of lodging along the way, including lodging in the vicinity of your old home within one day of the time you could no longer stay in the old home because your furniture was moved, and expenses for the day you arrive in the new location.

The cost of moving household goods and personal effects includes the possessions of all members of the household as defined above, including pets and cars. It includes costs of packing, crating, and insuring them. It also includes the cost of storing them for up to 30 consecutive days between the time they are removed from your old home and the time they are delivered to your new home. If goods are being moved from another location besides your old residence, you can't deduct more than the cost of moving them from your old residence.

Example

John Grey is moving from Chicago to Los Angeles. John also wants to move furniture and other personal effects stored at his parents' home in New York. He can deduct the cost of moving goods from both Chicago and New York, but for the New York items, he can only deduct an amount equivalent to what it would have cost to move them from Chicago.

A Special Rule for Foreign Moves

For a move by a U.S. citizen or resident alien to a new place of work outside the U.S. or its possessions, the moving expense deduction also includes the reasonable expenses of moving household goods and personal effects to and from storage, and the cost of storing such items for part or all of the period during which the taxpayer worked at the new, foreign location as his or her principal place of work.

However, if the individual also qualifies for the foreign earned income exclusion (see page 158), unreimbursed moving expenses may be disallowed to the extent that they are allocated to or chargeable against the excluded earned income.

Nondeductible Moving Expenses

The following are now considered nondeductible expenses, although you may remember that some of them were deductible as moving expenses under prior law. If your employer reimburses you for any of these expenses, the reimbursements are taxable (and your employer should add them to your taxable income, as shown in Box 1 of your W-2 Form).

- any part of the purchase price of your new home
- car license plates, stickers, or other registration
- drivers' licenses
- expenses of breaking or getting a lease
- expenses of buying or selling a home
- home improvements to help sell your home
- loss on the sale of your home

- losses from disposing of club memberships
- meal expenses
- mortgage prepayment penalties
- pre-move househunting trips
- real estate taxes
- refitting carpets and draperies
- security deposits
- storage charges other than those incurred in a 30-day period between when your goods were moved, and when they arrived at the new home
- temporary living expenses

Claiming Moving Expenses

Moving expenses are reported on IRS Form 3903, *Moving Expenses,* which is one of the simpler and more self-explanatory tax forms that you will run across. Moves to a location outside the U.S. are also reported on Form 3903. If you move to more than one location during the year, you'll need to fill out two forms.

Either of these forms will ask you to add up your total moving expenses in the two categories of deductible expenses described above. Then, you will subtract any reimbursements you receive from your employer that were not included in Box 1 of your W-2 form along with your other taxable wages. The amount of these reimbursements, if any, should have been shown in Box 12 of your W-2 form and marked with Code P.

If your employer's payments were higher than your deductible expenses, you must report the excess as income from wages, salaries, or tips on Line 7 of your 1040 Form.

If your expenses were higher than any reimbursements you received, the difference will be your deductible moving expenses, which are carried over to Line 26 of your 1040 Form. You cannot claim moving expenses on either Form 1040EZ or 1040A.

Timing the Deduction

If you, like most people, are a cash-method taxpayer, you can deduct your moving expenses either when you owe them, or when you pay them. If you moved near the end of the year, you may be able to deduct some expenses in two different calendar years.

If you are reimbursed for moving expenses by your employer, you may be able to deduct the expenses in the year you receive reimbursement, even if that's not the same year that you paid the expenses. You can do this if either of the following is true:

1. You actually paid the expenses in the year preceding the reimbursement.
2. You actually paid the expenses in the year after you received the reimbursement, and you paid them on or before the due date of the tax return for the reimbursement year.

The Credit for Child and Dependent Care

Congress and the IRS both recognize that in many situations you have to spend money to make money. This is especially true of working parents, many of whom would find it impossible to look for a job, let alone actually work at it, without paying someone to look after their children. Those who are responsible for looking after an aged parent or a disabled relative often find themselves in the same position.

To lighten some of the extra burden that falls upon working parents and those caring for disabled dependents, Congress has provided three basic types of tax benefits for employees or the self-employed:

- the credit for child or dependent care
- the exclusion for employer-provided care
- the earned income credit (EIC)

This section will focus on the first two of these tax benefits. The EIC is discussed on page 291.

There is also a $1,000-per-child credit for 2003 through 2010, but it is available to all parents and does not depend on whether or not one or both parents work outside the home. For a discussion of this credit, see page 283.

You Must Choose Your Benefit

To some extent, the child and dependent care credit, and the exclusion for employer-provided dependent care assistance, are mutually exclusive. If you use one, you might be totally or partially precluded from using the other.

Thus, if your employer offers any assistance for dependent care, you'll have to decide which strategy saves you more money: taking advantage of your employer's assistance program or claiming the tax credit. In certain limited circumstances you might be able to combine methods.

Save Money

The decision as to which tax break is best for you depends on factors including the kind of assistance your employer offers, your marginal tax bracket (see page 15 if you don't know your bracket), whether you have one qualified dependent or more, and the amount of qualified expenses you had this year.

As a rule of thumb, if you have an adjusted gross income of more than approximately $25,000, you'll save more money by taking full advantage of any assistance offered by your employer, even if that means giving up the tax credit.

In other situations, the answer is not so simple and you may have to figure out your tax bill both ways before you can tell which strategy is best for you.

How the Tax Credit Works

If your employer does not offer any type of dependent care assistance, this tax credit may be your only chance to recover some tax benefits for your child or other dependent care expenses. It's available in varying degrees to anyone who has children under the age of 13, who supports a disabled relative, or who has a disabled spouse.

If your employer does provide dependent care assistance, the tax credit may still be a better deal, particularly if you are in the 15 percent marginal tax bracket. If you meet all the qualifications described on the following pages, you can reduce your tax bill by up to $1,050 if you have one qualifying dependent, or by up to $2,100 if you have two or more.

If your employer provides only a small amount of dependent care assistance (under $3,000 for one child or under $6,000 for more than one), but you have expenses that exceed what your employer paid, you may be able to take advantage of your employer's plan and claim the tax credit for your excess expenses. See page 198.

How Much Is the Credit Worth?

Basically, the credit works like this: you get a tax credit of between 20 and 35 percent of your qualifying child care expenses, but you can only count expenses of up to $3,000 for one dependent, or up to $6,000 for two or more dependents.

Whether you can claim 20 percent, 35 percent, or somewhere in between depends on your adjusted gross income (that is, your net taxable income before subtracting your exemptions or deductions).

The following table shows the applicable percentages. These figures are not adjusted for inflation.

Adjusted Gross Income		Percentage of Expenses	Maximum Credits	
Over	*But Not Over*		*One Person*	*More Than One*
$0	$15,000	35%	$1,050	$2,100
$15,000	$17,000	34%	$1,020	$2,040
$17,000	$19,000	33%	$990	$1,980
$19,000	$21,000	32%	$960	$1,920
$21,000	$23,000	31%	$930	$1,860
$23,000	$25,000	30%	$900	$1,800
$25,000	$27,000	29%	$870	$1,740
$27,000	$29,000	28%	$840	$1,680
$29,000	$31,000	27%	$810	$1,620
$31,000	$33,000	26%	$780	$1,560
$33,000	$35,000	25%	$750	$1,500
$35,000	$37,000	24%	$720	$1,440
$37,000	$39,000	23%	$690	$1,380
$39,000	$41,000	22%	$660	$1,320
$41,000	$43,000	21%	$630	$1,260
$43,000	no limit	20%	$600	$1,200

Eligibility for the Credit

As you might expect, there a number of requirements you must meet before you can claim any portion of the tax credit. The requirements are summed up in the checklist that follows, and described in more detail below.

Eligibility Requirements To Claim the Child or Dependent Care Credit

- You must have incurred expenses for the care of at least one qualifying person.
- The expenses must have been incurred to allow you to work or to look for work.
- You (and your spouse, if married) must keep up a home in which you live with the qualifying person (exceptions exist for divorced or separated parents).
- You (and your spouse, if married) must have earned some income during the year, unless you or your spouse were disabled or a full-time student.
- The care provider must be someone that you can't claim as a dependent.
- You must identify the care provider by name and Social Security number (or employer I.D. number).
- If married, you must file a joint return unless you meet the "abandoned spouse" exception.
- To claim the expenses you must file IRS Form 2441, *Child and Dependent Care Expenses,* along with your Form 1040, or file Schedule 2 along with your Form 1040A. You can't claim the expenses by filing Form 1040EZ.

Qualifying Person

There are three basic categories of people who may be qualifying persons for purposes of this credit:

- Any child under the age of 13 for whom you can claim a dependency exemption. For more details about dependency exemptions, see page 163.
- Any dependent, regardless of age, who is disabled. For purposes of this rule only, "dependent" means any disabled dependent who received more than half of his or her total support from you, even if the dependent received more than $3,300 in gross income for the year.
- Your disabled spouse, regardless of age, amount of support, or place of abode.

"Disabled" means having a physical or mental condition that makes the person incapable of dressing, feeding, or cleaning himself or herself. Also, if a person requires constant attention to prevent injury to self or others, the person is considered disabled.

If a person meets the requirements for only part of the year, you can count only the expenses you had during the period he or she was qualified.

Example

Lois and Kent Clark enrolled their dependent son, Jimmy, in an after-school program because neither of them arrives home from work before 5:30 in the evening. Jimmy turned 13 on March 15, 2006. When figuring their 2006 tax credit for child care, Lois and Kent can count the cost of the program only through March 14.

Child of separated or divorced parents. Ordinarily, the custodial parent, or the parent who has actual custody of the child for more than half of the year, is the parent who can claim the child as a "qualifying person." This is true even if the other parent is entitled to the child's dependency exemption under the divorce decree. This rule applies if you are legally divorced or separated, or if you've lived apart from your spouse for all of the last six months of the year.

Social Security number required. You will need to report the Social Security number of your qualifying persons (up to two) on Form 2441 or on Schedule 2 of Form 1040A.

Keeping Up a Home

In order to meet this test, you (and your spouse, if married) must pay at least half of the expenses of maintaining your household for the year, and the qualifying individual must live there with you.

The costs of maintaining a household include:

- Rent
- Mortgage interest
- Property taxes
- Utility charges
- Home repairs
- Food eaten at home
- Homeowner's or renter's insurance

Costs of maintaining a household do not include:

- Clothing
- Vacations, recreation
- Education
- Life insurance
- Transportation
- Mortgage principal
- Medical treatments
- Permanent improvements or replacement of property

Living in the home. Individuals are considered to be living in the home if it continues to be their main home, even if they are temporarily away because of illness, school, business, vacations, military service or a custody agreement. So, either you or your qualifying person can be temporarily absent without failing this requirement.

Earned Income Test

Another requirement for claiming the tax credit is that you (and your spouse, if you're married) must have some earned income during the year. You can only claim child care expenses up to the amount of the lower of your income or your spouse's earned income.

"Earned income" includes your net earnings from self-employment, wages, salaries, tips, other employee compensation, strike benefits, and any disability pay that is taxable as wages.

It does not include pensions, annuities, Social Security benefits, worker's compensation, interest, dividends, unemployment compensation, or scholarship or fellowship grants (except amounts paid for teaching, research, or other services).

Exception for disabled spouses or student-spouses. So long as one spouse is working, the other spouse may be a nonworking disabled person or a full-time student without losing the credit.

If this situation applies to you, the nonworking spouse will be treated as having earned $250 a month for one qualifying person, or $500 for more than one qualifying person, for every month in which the spouse was physically or mentally incapable of self-care or was a full-time student at an elementary school; junior or senior high school; college university; or technical, trade, or professional school. This does not include night school or correspondence school. Therefore, if the nonworking spouse was a student or disabled for the entire year, you will be able to claim the maximum amount of expenses.

"Full-time student" means a person maintaining a schedule that is considered full-time by the institution attended, but the schedule must extend over some part of at least five months of the year.

This $250- or $500-per-month rule applies to only one spouse per month. If both you and your spouse are unemployed because each is either disabled or a full-time student (or for any other reason), you cannot claim dependent care expenses for the month because of the work-related expenses test discussed below.

Work-Related Expenses

The tax credit for child and dependent care expenses was intended only to help those who incur these expenses in order to enable them to earn income. So, you can only claim expenses that are work-related; that is, they must be necessary to allow you to work or to look for work.

Example

You can't claim expenses for a babysitter while you run errands or do volunteer work.

If you are married, the expenses must be required to allow both you and your spouse to work or to look for work, unless one of you meets the criteria above for being disabled or a full-time student.

"Work" includes any gainful full-time or part-time work, self-employment, and even work performed in your own home, but does not include volunteer work.

If you are actively looking for work, you can claim expenses for the period of your job search, but only up to the amount of your actual earned income for the year (or your spouse's income, if lower).

Kinds of Expenses To Count

A wide variety of child or dependent care expenses are counted. The care can be provided in your own home, another's home, or at a daycare center. However, if the care is provided outside your home, the qualifying person must be either your dependent under age 13, or any other qualifying person who regularly spends at least eight hours each day in your household. In other words, boarding school does not qualify.

If you use a dependent care center (that is, a place that provides care for more than six persons and charges a fee), the center must comply with all applicable state and local regulations.

Expenses of caring for the qualifying person do not include amounts spent for food, clothing, and entertainment unless the costs can't be separated out of the other costs you pay for the individual's care.

Education. You can count the total cost of sending your child to school if the child is not yet in first grade, and the amount you pay for schooling is incidental to the cost of care.

If your child is in the first grade or higher, or the cost of care can be separated from the cost of school, you can only count the cost of care.

Examples

Carla Webb sends her three-year-old child to a nursery school that provides lunch and educational activities as a part of its preschool program. She can count the total cost of the school in figuring her credit.

However, Wilbur Mudd sends his five-year-old child to kindergarten in the morning. In the afternoon, the child *attends an after-school daycare program in the same school. Mudd's total tuition cost is $3,000, of which $1,800 is for the after-school program. Only the after-school program qualifies in figuring Mudd's credit.*

Camp. You can deduct the full cost of sending your child to day camp, provided the money was spent to ensure the child's well-being during your absence from the home while at work. However, the cost of sending your child to overnight camp is not deductible at all.

Household services. If you pay someone to perform household services, you can count the fees or wages as long as the services are at least partly for the well-being and protection of a qualifying person.

In this context, household services are the ordinary and usual services done in and around your home that are necessary to run your home. They can include the services of a nanny, babysitter, nurse's aid, housekeeper, maid, or cook, but not a driver, bartender, or gardener.

If one individual performs some services that don't qualify (e.g., your cook doubles as a driver), you can't count the part of the payment that applies to the non-household services. However, you don't have to allocate the payments if only a small part applied to nonqualified purposes.

Example

Basil Holmes pays a housekeeper to care for his children, aged nine and 15, so that he can work. The housekeeper spends most of the time doing normal household work, but also spends 30 minutes each day driving the children to and from school.

Holmes can treat the entire expense of the housekeeper as work-related, because the time spent driving is minimal. He doesn't need to apportion the housekeeper's wages between the two children, because the household services are at least partly for the care of the nine-year-old, who is a qualifying person. However, he can only count the first $3,000 that he pays the housekeeper for the year, because he has only one qualifying person (the 15-year-old is too old to qualify).

Meals and lodging that you provide to a household worker count as child or dependent care expenses.

If the person performing services in your home is your employee, you may have to pay federal and state employment taxes (Social Security, Medicare, and unemployment taxes – see page 306). If the services qualify for the dependent care credit, any taxes you pay on the services are also qualified expenses.

Prepaid or postpaid expenses. If you prepaid for some 2007 child care expenses in 2006, you can claim them only in the year that the dependent care is actually received. In that case, you'll fill out your Form 2441 (for Form 1040) or Schedule 2 (for Form 1040A) for 2007 as if the prepaid expenses were paid in the same year that the care was received.

However, if you received some care in 2006 but won't pay for it until 2007, you can claim the care only in the year you paid for it. You will have to file Forms 2441 and 1040 (not Form 1040A and Schedule 2) in order to get any credit for this care.

Dependent care assistance provided by your employer. Any child or dependent care expenses that were paid for or reimbursed by your employer can't be counted for purposes of the tax credit for dependent care.

Moreover, if you received any such assistance from your employer, you will have to subtract the amount of assistance from your applicable credit expense limit (the limit is $3,000 for one qualifying person and $6,000 for more than one). If the answer is a positive number, that answer is the maximum amount of expenses you can claim when computing your tax credit for dependent care. For more on employer-provided assistance, see page 198.

Payments to Dependents or Household Members

Payments that you make to a person for whom you or your spouse can claim a dependency exemption, or to your child who is under the age of 19 at the end of the year even if not your dependent, can't be counted for purposes of the dependent care credit.

You can count work-related expenses that you pay to persons who live in your home, even if they are related to you, as long as they are not your dependents. This includes payments to live-in babysitters or housekeepers.

Identification of Care Provider

You must provide the IRS with the name, address, and Social Security number (for individuals) or the Employer Identification Number (for organizations) of the person or organization that provided the care. The information must be included on Part I of Form 2441 or Schedule 2.

I.D. numbers are not required if the care provider is a tax-exempt organization, such as a church or nonprofit school. In that case, simply write "tax-exempt" in the space provided for an I.D. number.

If the care provider refuses to give you all the information you need, you should report whatever information you have on the tax form you use to claim the credit. On the bottom of the second page of the form, you should write a note saying that you asked the care provider for the information but he or she didn't give it to you.

Joint Return

If you're married at the end of the tax year, you must file a joint return in order to claim this credit. The only exception to the joint return rule is that you can be considered unmarried if you are legally separated, or if all of the following are true:

- You file a separate return.
- Your home is the home of a qualifying person for more than half the year.
- You pay more than half the cost of keeping up your home for the year.
- Your spouse does not live in your home for the last six months of the year.

If all of these apply to you, you can claim the credit on your separate tax return.

Medical Expense Deductions

Some expenses, like the costs of at-home nursing care for a disabled dependent, would ordinarily be deductible as medical expenses. If they enable the taxpayer to be gainfully employed, they can also qualify as employment-related dependent care.

However, you can't use the same expenses for both the medical deduction and the dependent care credit. You'll have to decide which tax benefit will help you more.

Generally speaking, if you have a choice, it's better to maximize your child or dependent care credit up to the applicable dollar limitations ($3,000 for one qualifying person, or $6,000 for two or more). If your expenses exceed this limitation, any excess that qualifies as a medical deduction should be treated as such.

Remember that only medical expenses that exceed 7.5 percent of your adjusted gross income are deductible, and high-income taxpayers may lose some of their deductions above 7.5 percent (see page 275). If you do have sufficient medical expenses to exceed the 7.5 percent threshold, and your tax bracket is 28 percent or higher, you may be better off claiming the expenses as a medical deduction.

Example

During 2006, John and Mary Davis paid $10,000 of work-related expenses for the care of their physically handicapped daughter. The work-related expenses were for services performed in the Davis' home and qualified as medical expenses. The Davis' adjusted gross income for 2006 was $60,000.

If they take the maximum of $3,000 of these expenses into account for purposes of the dependent care credit, they can claim a 20 percent credit of $600, and treat the balance, or $7,000, as medical expenses. Because the Davises had no other medical expenses, they can deduct $2,500 ($7,000 minus 7.5 percent of $60,000, or $4,500) as a medical expense. Since they are in the 25 percent bracket, the $2,500 deduction saves them $625 in taxes. Total tax savings: $600 + $625 = $1,225.

However, if they claim the full $10,000 as a medical expense, subtracting the 7.5 percent of AGI amount ($4,500) leaves a deduction of $5,500. In the 25 percent bracket, this deduction would save $1,375 in taxes. The Davises are better off forgoing the child and dependent care credit, and instead claiming the full medical expense deduction for their daughter's expenses.

Claiming the Credit

To claim the credit for child and dependent care expenses, you need to fill out Parts I and II of IRS

Form 2441, *Child and Dependent Care Expenses,* if you're filing IRS Form 1040. If you are filing the 1040A, you may use Schedule 2, Parts I and II.

Either of these forms requires you to provide identification information for both the care provider(s) and the qualifying children or disabled persons. The forms help you to compute your credit by comparing your allowable expenses with your wages and other earnings (and those of your spouse, if married). Your credit amount as shown on Line 11 of the 2441 is carried to Line 48 of your Form 1040, where it will be directly subtracted from the taxes you owe. If you use Schedule 2, the credit amount as shown on Line 11 is carried to Line 29 of Form 1040A.

If you are using Form 2441 to claim a credit for expenses you incurred in 2005 but did not pay until 2006, you can increase the amount of credit you can claim, but you will have to attach a statement to your tax return explaining how you computed the credit, as well as the name, I.D. number, and address of the care provider for the 2005 expenses. Get IRS Publication 503, *Child and Dependent Care Expenses,* for more details. You can obtain any IRS Publication for free by calling 1-800-TAX-FORM; most popular publications are also posted on the IRS website at www.irs.gov.

DEPENDENT CARE PROVIDED BY YOUR EMPLOYER

In order to retain valued employees and improve the corporate image, and at the same time gain tax benefits for themselves, many companies offer some type of financial help to employees who must pay for child or dependent care in order to work.

These benefits can take a number of forms. In some cases, the employer has set up on-site daycare centers, to which employees can send their young children. In other cases, employers subsidize the costs of child care by reimbursing employees for certain expenses.

However, the majority of companies that provide dependent care assistance do so by allowing employees to contribute part of their pretax wages to individual accounts under a "Flexible Spending Arrangement." The money is then used to reimburse the employee for child or dependent care expenses.

All these types of assistance can be provided to the employee as tax-free fringe benefits, provided certain rules are met.

Employers may also offer a number of other dependent-related services, such as referrals to area day care centers, seminars or informational meetings, or employee assistance programs that provide counseling for personal problems that affect an employee's work. In most cases, these benefits are considered tax-free fringe benefits for employees because they fall into the category of *"de minimis"* benefits. Their value is relatively small and difficult to measure, so the IRS essentially ignores them when it comes to imposing taxes.

Dependent Care as a Fringe Benefit

Your employer can provide you with a substantial amount of dependent care assistance as a nontaxable fringe benefit. However, it must meet certain criteria.

From the employee's standpoint, the most important requirement is probably the fact that the amount of tax-free assistance is limited to $5,000 a year per family, or to the total amount of the lower-paid spouse's salary, whichever is lower. If one spouse is totally disabled or a student, that spouse is treated as earning $200 per month for one dependent, or $400 per month for two.

Unlike the child and dependent care credit, employer-provided dependent care can be claimed by a married couple filing separately. In that case the maximum dollar limit is $2,500 per spouse. Only the spouse whose employer provides assistance can claim the exclusion; if both spouses' employers provide assistance, they can each claim $2,500.

Warning

To qualify for tax benefits, the dependent care assistance must be offered by the employer under a written plan that does not discriminate in favor of the most highly paid workers. The tax laws say that no more than 25 percent of the amounts paid by the employer for dependent care assistance during the year may be provided for shareholders or owners (or their spouses or dependents), who own more than 5 percent of the stock or of the capital or profits interest in the employer on any day in the year. This means that dependent care programs generally can't be used by very small, family-owned businesses.

Rules for tax credit apply. The kinds of dependents and expenses that may be covered by an employer's dependent care plan are the same as those that would qualify for the tax credit for child and dependent care. So, the rules relating to keeping up a home for at least one qualifying individual, the earned income test, the work-related expenses test, and the other rules discussed on pages 193-197 all apply to the employer-provided assistance.

Salary Reduction Arrangements

Employers can give you tax-free dependent care assistance in a number of ways. Dependent care assistance is usually delivered by means of a Flexible Spending Arrangement, or FSA plan. Under such plans, employees request that an annual amount of up to $5,000 be withheld in equal installments from their paychecks and set aside in a special account by the employer. The employees benefit because the salary reductions are made before any federal income, Social Security, or Medicare taxes are paid – in effect, the employee is able to pay for child care with pretax dollars.

Save Money

Where both spouses work for employers that provide FSAs, and one spouse has a salary that is higher than the Social Security ceiling ($94,200 for 2006), the other spouse should be the one to sign up for the FSA to maximize family tax savings. This is because FSA amounts are not taxed for income, Social Security, and Medicare taxes. Your "discount" for using the FSA will be greater if you would otherwise have been subject to Social Security taxes on the amount.

During the year, each employee using an FSA submits bills for daycare, babysitting, and other qualified expenses to the plan, and is reimbursed up to the amount set aside in his or her individual account. Requests for reimbursement are monitored to make sure that the expenses are work-related, apply to a qualified individual, and meet the other requirements.

One drawback to the arrangement is that you must decide how much you want to contribute to your FSA once a year, usually in November or December for the coming year. Once requested, the amount may not be changed during the calendar year unless you experience a "major life event" such as a birth, death, marriage, or divorce.

If you don't have enough qualifying expenses during the year to use up your FSA contributions, you forfeit the remainder of your account back to your employer.

Comparison with the Tax Credit

Child care expenses for which you're paid or reimbursed under an employer's plan cannot be used again in determining whether you're eligible for the tax credit for child and dependent care, discussed beginning on page 191. Obviously, if your employer doesn't offer any assistance, the tax credit is your only choice.

One difference between the two types of tax breaks is especially important for those with only one child or qualifying individual. Under the tax credit, you are only allowed to count the first $3,000 you spend for care of that individual ($6,000 for more than one individual). However, under the employer assistance plan, you may count up to $5,000, whether it's spent on one person or several.

The second factor to consider is your tax bracket. If you're in the 25 percent bracket, your federal tax "discount" for using the employer's plan will probably equal 32.65 percent of your allowable expenses (25 percent federal income tax + 7.65 percent FICA tax), unless your salary is over the Social Security ceiling. Even if it is, you'll still have a 26.45 percent discount (25 percent income tax + 1.45 percent Medicare tax). However, families with taxable income higher than $43,000 who use the tax credit will get a credit of only 20 percent of their allowable expenses.

A third factor to consider is the alternative minimum tax (AMT). Ordinarily, if you are subject to the AMT, your tax credit may be limited or potentially extinguished.

However, employer-paid dependent care assistance is subtracted from your adjusted gross income before the AMT is calculated, so it will not be affected by the AMT calculation (and in fact can help you to avoid the AMT by keeping your AGI lower).

Reduced Retirement Benefits

One more factor to consider when deciding whether to take advantage of your employer's plan or to go for the tax credit is the Social Security angle.

Because you don't pay social security tax on the amounts that are withheld from your paycheck to fund your dependent care reimbursement account, these amounts aren't counted as part of your salary when you eventually retire and collect Social Security benefits. So, you might qualify for a slightly lower benefit at retirement because of the dependent care benefits you're getting now.

In most cases, this benefit reduction would be slight, particularly if you have a long working career but receive dependent care benefits for only a few of those years. Moreover, it's generally better to save tax dollars now, rather than to pay more tax now in the hope of getting a larger retirement benefit 20 or 40 years down the road. It's quite likely that the rules for computing Social Security benefits will have changed by then, anyway.

Claiming Employer-Provided Assistance

If your employer provided you with any dependent care assistance in 2006, it should have been reported in Box 10 of your W-2 Form. If more than $5,000 was provided, the extra amount is taxable and should have been included in Box 1 of the W-2.

To report this amount, you need to complete Parts I and III of Form 2441, *Child and Dependent Care Expenses,* if you are filing Form 1040. If you are filing Form 1040A, you can use Schedule 2 of that form and, again, complete Parts I and III.

Note that either of these forms will ask you whether you forfeited any benefits this year; that is, whether you had more deducted from your paycheck than you were able to claim reimbursement for. If you have a forfeiture, you don't have to pay taxes on this amount. However, if the amount you had withheld from your paycheck was more than your total wages (or those of your spouse, if married, which is the more likely scenario) you can only deduct the dependent care assistance up to the amount of the wages earned. Anything above that amount would be taxable and must be included in your taxable income amount on Line 7 of your Form 1040 or 1040A.

Chapter 12

Real Estate

For many people, a home is not only a shelter for their family, but also the only real tax shelter available.

The opportunity to reduce your income taxes by deducting your mortgage interest payments, the points you may have paid when taking out your loan, and your real estate taxes is one of the most important reasons for owning a home.

In order to claim these tax breaks, you'll need to itemize your deductions. It's important to note that if you're itemizing in order to claim home mortgage and real estate taxes, you'll also be able to claim any itemized deductions for state and local income taxes, charitable contributions, casualty losses, employee business expenses and other miscellaneous deductions that exceed 2 percent of your adjusted gross income (AGI), and medical expenses that exceed 7.5 percent of your AGI. These deductions can save you many tax dollars—and most people who don't own a home can't take advantage of them.

On the next few pages we'll outline the major rules you need to know in order to maximize your home-related tax deductions. This chapter will also discuss how to handle the purchase or sale of your principal residence. Generally the first $250,000 in gains on the sale of your home will be tax-free (and the first $500,000 will be tax-free, if you are married filing jointly), provided that you meet certain requirements. Losses on sales of your personal residence are generally not deductible, unless you used part of the property for business purposes or rented it out.

Finally, for those of you who own investment real estate, we'll discuss the rules related to reporting rental income and deductions, and handling the purchase or sale of rental property, including second homes.

Tax Organizer Tip

Most of the income and deductible expenses discussed in this chapter should all be entered on the "Real Estate" tab of CompleteTax. One notable exception is the home mortgage interest deduction and real estate taxes on your residence. These items should be entered on the "Deductions" tab.

THE HOME MORTGAGE INTEREST DEDUCTION

In most cases, you can deduct all of the interest you pay on any loan that is secured by your home, whether the loan is called a mortgage, a second (or third, fourth, fifth, etc.) mortgage, a home equity loan, a line of credit, or a home improvement loan. Your lender will mail you an end-of-year statement that breaks down your house payment into components, and tells you exactly how much interest you paid. You can't deduct the portion of the payment that goes towards repaying the principal amount of the loan.

A loan "secured by your home" means that, under the loan agreement, the lender has the right to take the house ("foreclose") if you don't make the payments. This generally means that if you or your spouse take a loan from a 401(k) plan at work to make a down payment on a house, you can't deduct interest on the 401(k) loan because it is not secured by a mortgage on the house.

Generally, as long as the loan is secured by the home, if doesn't matter what you actually spend the money on. For example, you can take out a home equity loan and use the money to buy a car, take a vacation, consolidate credit card debts, or anything else you choose. However, the dollar limits discussed below can differ, depending on how the loan proceeds are spent.

Limits on Deductibility

Beginning in the late 1980s, Congress placed certain limits on the types and amounts of loans that qualify for the mortgage interest deduction.

If you took out a mortgage on or before October 13, 1987, all of the interest is fully deductible, regardless of the amount of the loan. This is called "grandfathered debt."

If you had such a mortgage and you refinanced it after that date, the new mortgage is treated as grandfathered debt to the extent of the principal balance remaining on the pre-October 13, 1987 loan. Any mortgage amount over that limit may be eligible for treatment under category (A) or (B) discussed below.

If you had established a home equity line-of-credit as of October 13, 1987 and you borrowed amounts against it after that date, then those amounts are treated under category (A) or (B), below, depending on how the proceeds were used. Amounts borrowed before that date are fully deductible grandfathered debt.

Post-1987 Loans

Loans that were taken out after October 13, 1987, will qualify for the mortgage interest deduction if they meet the criteria in either (A) or (B):

(A) Interest paid on mortgages used to buy, build, or substantially improve your first or second home is deductible (referred to as home acquisition debt), to the extent that the total of all these mortgages, plus any grandfathered debt, does not exceed either the lower of:

1. the total cost to buy or build the home, plus the cost of any improvements

2. $1 million (for married taxpayers filing separately, this second limit is $500,000 each)

(B) Interest paid on mortgages used for any other purpose (commonly known as home equity debt) is deductible only to the extent that such mortgages totaled $100,000 or less throughout the year and totaled no more than the fair market value of your home, reduced by any grandfathered or home acquisition debt. The limit is $50,000 each for married taxpayers filing separately. You can't deduct the interest, however, if you used the money to generate tax-exempt interest (e.g., if you bought tax-free municipal bonds).

It is important to keep in mind that if the total amount of all loans secured by a home is more than the fair market value (FMV) of the home, you can't deduct interest on the portion of debt that exceeds the FMV. In recent years, some lenders in some areas of the country have been willing to extend loans that exceed 100 percent of the home's value; the interest on the excess portion of the debt is not deductible.

If you are married filing separately, who gets to deduct the interest? Generally, a taxpayer can deduct interest he or she pays on a mortgage if the taxpayer is the legal or equitable owner of the property. In the marital setting, ownership rights and their tax treatment when filing separately can get complicated. If a home is owned jointly, each spouse can deduct half the interest payments. If two houses are involved and the spouses are filing separately, each spouse can treat one houses as their qualified residence for interest deduction purposes unless both spouses agree in writing to a different arrangement.

Mixed-Use Mortgages

If you took out a mortgage after October 13, 1987 and use the money both to buy, build, or substantially improve the home and for other purposes, then it is considered a mixed-use mortgage. The loan amount must be divided between categories (A) and (B) above, to determine whether the deductibility limits have been reached.

Example

Alice Gamos took out a $100,000 mortgage to buy her home in 1986. In March of 1994, when the home had a fair market value (FMV) of $220,000 and she owed $95,000 on the mortgage, she took out a second mortgage of $80,000. She used $60,000 of the loan proceeds for home improvements and the remaining $20,000 for other personal purposes.

All of the interest is deductible. The interest on the first mortgage is deductible simply because it was taken out before October 13, 1987.

Of the second mortgage, the $60,000 used to improve the home falls into category (A), above. The $60,000 must be added to the balance on the existing loan to be sure that the $1 million limit is not exceeded; in this case, $60,000 + $95,000 = $155,000, well short of $1 million. The remaining $20,000 is subject to the limits on home equity loans in category (B); because it is less than $100,000 and does not exceed the home's FMV reduced by grandfathered and home acquisition debt (i.e., $220,000-$95,000-$60,000=$65,000), it is fully deductible.

Which Homes Qualify?

You can deduct mortgage interest on both your main home and one other qualified residence each year, but all the mortgages on both homes must be combined for purposes of the dollar limits discussed above.

If more than one person owns the home (for instance, you purchased a vacation home jointly with your brother), each of you can deduct your proportionate part of the interest.

A "home" for tax purposes can be a house, condominium, cooperative, mobile home, motor home, timeshare condominium, or boat. At a minimum, the "home" must contain sleeping space, a toilet, and cooking facilities.

If the home is a condominium, you can deduct interest paid on a mortgage you take out to purchase your individual unit. If there is a blanket mortgage over the entire property, you can deduct interest on the portion of the blanket mortgage that applies to your unit. Similarly, if you own a co-op, you can deduct interest paid on a mortgage to purchase shares in the building that pertain to your individual unit; you can also deduct interest paid or incurred by the corporation on loans taken out to acquire, construct, alter, rehabilitate, or maintain the co-op buildings or land.

Your main home is generally the place where you spend the most time.

Save Money

If you have a second home that you don't rent out to others, it can be treated as your "other qualified residence," even if you don't set foot in it all year. If you have several vacation homes, you can claim the interest deduction for a different home each tax year.

If you rent out your vacation home to others for any part of the year, it is a qualified residence only if you use if for personal purposes for more than 14 days or more than 10 percent of the rental days in the tax year, whichever is longer. If you don't use it long enough, it is considered "rental property" and a different set of rules apply. These rules are covered beginning on page 215.

Timeshares

In the case of a timeshare arrangement, you count your use and rental of the home only during the time you have a right to use it.

Example

If you have the right to use a timeshare condo for one week each year, you could claim the mortgage interest deduction for a loan on the condo if you either use the week or leave the condo vacant for the week. If you rented it for even one day during the week, you'd lose the deduction for the year since it would be impossible for you to meet the greater-of-14-days-or-10-percent rule.

Home Being Built

You can treat a home that is under construction as a qualified home for a period of up to 24 months, but only if it becomes your qualified main or secondary home at the time it is ready for occupancy. The 24-month period can start any time on or after the day construction actually begins.

Save Money

If you delay making a mortgage payment and, consequently, have to pay an extra "late fee" to the lender, the late fee is deductible as home mortgage interest, as long as it was not for a specific service performed by the lender.

Prepaying Your Mortgage Interest

If you, like most individuals, are a cash-method taxpayer, you ordinarily deduct interest in the year that you pay it. However, if you prepay your mortgage interest, you can't fully deduct the prepaid amount in the year you pay it. Instead, you must deduct the interest in the year to which it applies (but see the exception for "points," below).

An apparent exception to this rule applies if you make your first payment of the next tax year during the last month of the preceding year (for example, you make your January 1st mortgage payment sometime in December). Mortgage interest is due after the month to which it applies; therefore, your January 1st payment is for interest you owe for the month of December and can be deducted in the earlier year.

Work Smart

Be aware that if you use this strategy to reduce your taxes, the mortgage interest statement you receive from your lender may not reflect that last pre-January 1st payment. If not, you should deduct the correct amount on your tax return and attach a short statement explaining why the lender's statement is incorrect.

Interest Paid at Settlement

At the settlement or closing on a new home loan, it's common for the buyer to be charged a small amount of "prepaid interest." This generally represents mortgage interest on your loan amount from the day of settlement to the end of the current month, so it's less than an ordinary monthly mortgage payment. Such prepaid interest is deductible home mortgage interest, and since it applies to the portion of the month immediately following the closing date, for calendar year taxpayers it would be deductible for the same tax year in which the closing date falls.

You cannot count as "interest" the fees your lender charges you to make the loan, such as an application fee, appraisal fee, credit check fees, fees for private mortgage insurance (PMI), etc. These amounts are not deductible, nor are they added to the cost of your home for purposes of calculating gains or losses when you sell.

Points

As mentioned above, as a general rule you can't deduct prepaid interest ahead of the year to which it relates. The most common form of prepaid interest is "points."

A point is a charge paid by the borrower to the lender upon taking out the loan. One point equals one percent of the amount borrowed; thus, on a $100,000 loan, three points equals $3,000, but on a $250,000 loan, three points equals $7,500.

Under the general rule, you could deduct points as mortgage interest but you'd have to spread your deduction for points out over the entire life of the loan, even though you actually paid the amount if the first year.

Fortunately, there is an exception that allows many borrowers to deduct their points in the year paid.

Points on Home Mortgage or Improvement Loans

You may deduct points in the year you pay them if all of the following are true:

1. The loan is used to buy, build or improve your principal home, and the loan is secured by the home. Thus, second mortgages or home equity loans qualify if the proceeds are used for home improvement – but not otherwise.

2. The payment of points is an established business practice in your area.

3. The points paid don't exceed the number of points generally charged in the area. If lenders in your area generally charge three points and you pay four, you can deduct the first three in the first year. The fourth point must be deducted over the entire term of the loan.

4. The points aren't paid in place of amounts that are usually separate charges, such as appraisal, inspection, title, or attorney fees

5. The points are computed as a percentage of the principal amount of the mortgage and are clearly shown on the settlement statement (such as the Uniform Settlement Statement, Form HUD-1) as points charged for the mortgage.

6. If the loan is used to buy your main home, you must have provided funds at the time of closing that are at least equal to the points charged, outside of the money obtained from the lender. For this purposes, the funds you provided don't have to be applied specifically as payment of points; they can be applied to your down payment, earnest money, or other funds actually paid over at closing.

7. You must use the cash method of accounting, which is the way most people keep track of their income and expenses (i.e., reporting them for the year they come up).

The deduction for points applies only to buyers, and not to sellers, of homes. If the seller pays some points to enable the buyer to get a loan, the buyer may deduct the points. The seller treats the amount paid as a selling cost that helps to reduce his or her taxable profits on the sale.

Second Homes

The rules above apply only to your main home. If you pay points on a loan secured by a second home, those points can only be deducted over the entire term of the loan.

Refinancing

Points paid in refinancing a mortgage on your main home are generally not deductible in the year paid. They must be prorated and deducted over the entire loan period.

However, if the proceeds of your refinancing are used both to pay off the old mortgage and to pay for home improvements, the portion of the points that pertain to the home improvements can be deducted in the first year. The remaining portion must be prorated over the loan's entire term.

Mortgage Paid Off Early

If your mortgage is paid off early (perhaps because you sell the home, refinance to get a lower interest rate, or make enough extra principal payments to retire the loan), at that time you can deduct any portion of points on the old loan that have not yet been deducted.

Example

Sharon Flint refinanced her mortgage in 2002 to get a lower interest rate. At that time, she paid $3,000 in points that were required to be spread over the 15-year term of her new loan. Through 2005, she had deducted $800 of the points. In 2006, Sharon paid off her mortgage in full. She can then deduct the remaining $2,200 of points in 2006.

Mortgage Credit Certificates (MCCs)

If you reside in one of the few states or localities that have chosen to issue MCCs and you obtain a certificate, then you can claim a tax credit (rather than a deduction) based on the amount of interest you paid. Generally, credits are more valuable than deductions because they reduce your taxes dollar-for-dollar, while deductions reduce your taxes by only a percentage of the amount in question (i.e., if you're in the 25 percent tax bracket, a deduction reduces your taxes by 25 percent of the dollar amount of your mortgage interest).

Even within the localities that issue MCCs, these certificates are generally available only to first-time homebuyers whose income is below the median income for the area where they live. If you are eligible for the credit, it must be claimed on IRS Form 8396 *Mortgage Interest Credit,* which must be filed with your Form 1040.

Claiming the Home Mortgage Interest Deduction

If you paid mortgage interest to a financial institution, by January 31 you should be sent a Form 1098 reporting the amount of interest and points you paid during the previous year.

The amount shown in Box 1 of the 1098 is the amount of interest you paid, and the amount shown in Box 2 is the amount of points paid. These amounts are added together (and if you have a mortgage on a second home, add the amounts on the 1098 from that mortgage also), and entered on Line 10 of Schedule A *Itemized Deductions.*

If the amounts shown on Form 1098 don't agree with what you actually paid (for example, the bank did not add in the interest from that extra payment you made at the end of December), enter the correct amount but attach a short statement to the return explaining the discrepancy.

If you paid interest that was not reported on a 1098, it should be entered on Line 11 of the Schedule A. In most cases this will be interest you paid to an individual, such as a seller who took back a mortgage, or your rich Uncle Harry who lent you the money for part of the down payment. You'll need to enter the person's name, Social Security number, and address on the dotted lines next to Line 11.

On Line 12, report any points that were not reported on Form 1098 (for example, if you paid off a loan you had already refinanced at least once).

Lines 10, 11, and 12 are added up, together with any amount on Line 13 for investment interest (see page 242), and the total is entered on Line 14 of the Schedule A. Certain high-income taxpayers may have all of their itemized deductions limited – see page 275 for more details.

THE DEDUCTION FOR REAL ESTATE TAXES

Next to the home mortgage interest deduction, the most important tax break for homeowners is probably the deduction for state and local taxes, including real estate taxes.

Your real estate taxes are fully deductible, whether they are imposed by the state, county, city, township, or some other local government body.

You can deduct taxes on all your real estate – your deduction is not limited to only two principal residences, as it is with the home mortgage interest deduction. Real estate taxes you paid on all real estate you own for personal or family purposes is deductible on Line 6 of Schedule A, *Itemized Deductions.* However, if you own commercial or residential rental real estate, the taxes would be deducted on your Schedule E, *Supplemental Income and Loss* (see page 218) or on Form 4835 for farms (see page 181), not Schedule A. See also page 215 for information about real estate that is rented out some of the time, and used for personal purposes at other times.

Deductible "taxes" do not include charges for services performed, such as a unit fee for water consumed or a periodic fee for trash removed. Taxes also don't include assessments for local benefits that tend to increase the value of your property, such as for the construction of streets, sidewalks, or sewers. Any such charges must be added to the tax basis of your property – they'll eventually reduce the amount of taxable profit on your property when you sell.

However, there is a distinction to be made between *improvements* and *repairs.* Assessments for repairs, such as repair of a broken sidewalk, or for maintenance, such as mowing, are deductible if the charges are broken out separately on your tax bill.

The general rule is that the person who owns the real estate and, therefore, owes the taxes is the person who can deduct them, provided that he or she actually paid the amounts. Co-owners should divide the tax bill and the deduction according to the percentage of their ownership interest. If you pay taxes for someone else (for example, your aged parent) on property that they own, you cannot deduct them.

However, if you are divorced and your separation agreement or divorce decree requires you to pay real estate taxes on property owned jointly by you and your ex-spouse, the amount you pay on the ex-spouse's portion may be deductible as alimony (see page 282).

Condos and Co-Ops

You can't deduct homeowners' association assessments, including condominium association assessments, if they are for maintaining common areas and/or for the recreation, health, safety, and welfare of residents.

However, condo owners can deduct real estate taxes assessed against the unit. In some jurisdictions, the unit owner receives a single assessment covering both the unit and the percentage interest that the owner has in the common elements of the condo building or community. In other jurisdictions, the unit owner receives an assessment against his or her unit, and the condominium association receives an assessment covering all the common elements. The association collects a share of its tax bill from each unit owner. Each owner can deduct the share of this bill that he or she pays.

Co-op owners. Under a cooperative housing arrangement, the owner in a co-op building does not own title to the building or to any real estate. Rather, he or she owns shares of stock in a corporation; the corporation, in turn, owns title to the land and building. The shareholder receives a proprietary lease entitling him or her to occupy a unit within the building. Nevertheless, the tenant-shareholder can deduct amounts paid to the co-op corporation, to the extent that they represent his or her proportionate share of real estate taxes paid or incurred by the corporation.

When Taxes Are Deductible

You can deduct real estate taxes that are imposed on you and that you paid either at the settlement or closing of a sale, or to a taxing authority during the year.

If your monthly house payment includes an amount placed in the care of the lender ("escrow") to be saved up and used to pay real estate taxes when due, you can deduct only the amount that the lender actually pays to the taxing body even though this may be more or less than the amount you have contributed to escrow during the year. You cannot deduct the portion of your escrow payment that goes to pay homeowner's insurance, unless you have a qualifying home office (see page 79 for complete details on the home office deduction).

Taxes Paid at Settlement

At the closing, it's customary for the seller and the buyer to allocate the real estate taxes for the current year between themselves. If taxes for the year have already been paid, the buyer may have to pay a portion of that amount to the seller; on the other hand, if the taxes for the year are not yet due, the seller will generally give the buyer a credit for the portion that the seller is estimated to owe. Occasionally, one party will agree to pay all taxes for the year.

For federal tax purposes, the actual arrangements made between the buyer and the seller don't matter. Instead, taxes for the year of sale must be divided between the parties on the basis of the number of days each party owned the property during the year. The seller can deduct the taxes up to the date of sale; the buyer can deduct taxes beginning with the date of sale through the rest of the year.

Generally, the seller can claim this deduction in the year of sale; the buyer may claim the deduction only when the tax bill is actually paid – which sometimes means the following year.

Example

Gus Pappageorge's property tax year is the same as the calendar year, but the property taxes are not due until the following October 31 (e.g., 2006 taxes are payable by October 31, 2007).

On March 2, 2006, Gus sells his home to Joel Page. The 2006 real estate taxes on the home are $4,500. Gus is treated as having paid $740 of the tax (he owned the home for 60 days out of 365; $4,500 x 60/365 = $739.73). He can deduct this amount in 2006.

Joel is treated as having paid the remainder of the tax or $3,760. He must deduct this amount in 2007 because the taxes will not be paid until then.

Buying a Home

If you bought a home in 2006, you've undoubtedly been busy with a glut of activities including shopping for a house and a mortgage, negotiating the purchase price, moving, and setting up your household in a new location.

You can add to this list of duties one fairly simple, but important task: collecting and retaining the records that show the basis of your home.

Why Track Your Basis?

While some brokers and advisers will tell you that keeping track of your basis is now unnecessary, since the first $250,000 in gain on sale of your home won't be taxed (see page 212) and probably won't even need to be computed, you're on much safer ground if you retain these records.

Knowing the basis of your home is important for several reasons besides computing your gain when you eventually sell the home.

For example, if you suffer a casualty loss to the home, your deductible losses may be limited by the amount of your tax basis in the home. If you don't have accurate records of that, you may lose some of your tax benefits at a time when you need them most.

If you ever decide to rent out some or all of your home (for example, if you decide to move when the housing market is very slow and you need to find a tenant to cover your mortgage payments with some income for an extended period of time), you'll need to know your tax basis in order to determine your depreciation deductions. Similarly, if you ever decide to use part of your home for business (see page 79), depreciation is usually computed on the business portion of the home's tax basis.

If you purchased your first home many, many years ago and since then you've moved several times, deferring gain each time by purchasing a more expensive home under the old rollover replacement rule, you may have deferred tens or hundreds of thousands of dollars already, and the basis of your current home may be very low. If so, you may hit the $250,000 in capital gains mark very quickly.

Finally, if it turns out that you stay in your home for a long time, you should realize that the $250,000 exclusion of taxable gain on the sale of the home is not indexed for inflation. The value of the exclusion is bound to be eroded as time passes.

Example

If we look at the exclusion in today's dollars, at a modest 3 percent inflation rate, the value of $250,000 in ten years will be only $186,023. In 20 years it will be worth $138,418, and in 30 years it will be worth only $102,996 in 2005 dollars.

Long-time homeowners may well find that they end up paying some capital gains tax on their home, but they may pay more than necessary if they haven't kept track of their basis over the years.

And all of this assumes that Congress won't change the law to either increase or, more likely, decrease the amount of the exclusion or change the rules for claiming it!

Computing Your Initial Basis

The starting point for your home's tax basis is the sales price and the charges you paid upon purchasing or building the home (if you did not purchase the home but acquired it by gift, inheritance, transfer in a divorce, etc., see the discussion on page 210). The key document that you'll need for tax purposes is the HUD statement or other settlement document that shows all the settlement costs paid by yourself and the seller.

Of course, for legal purposes, you'll also want to keep the signed sales contract that shows the legal description of the property, the sales price, and the terms of your sale in a safe place like your safe deposit box at the bank. But the settlement statement will generally provide the information you need for tax purposes.

Work Smart

You should keep these documents for at least as long as you own the home, but preferably for the rest of your life since it may turn out that your executor or heirs need this information.

To compute your basis for a home that you purchased, start with the sales price you paid, which is generally composed of your down payment (including any earnest money) plus the principal amount of any mortgage or other debt you took out or assumed.

If you built the home, the starting point would be your basis in the land the home is built on, plus the costs of building the house including labor and materials, contractor's fee, architect fee, building permit charges, and legal fees directly connected with building the home. If you worked on the home yourself, you can count the value of materials and supplies you used, but not the value of your labor.

Settlement or Closing Costs

In addition to the direct costs of the house, you can add to your basis certain costs that you paid at the settlement or closing.

First of all, remember that prepaid interest or points are deductible in the year of the purchase, under the rules outlined above. Real estate taxes for the day of the purchase and afterwards are also deductible by you, whether you paid them or the seller actually paid them. Real estate taxes up to and including the day before the sale are deductible by the seller. If either party actually paid taxes for any period when they did not own the home, the amount of taxes they paid is not deductible, but is added to their tax basis in the property.

Other settlement costs that can be added to your basis are listed below, along with some costs that may not be added to your basis. The general rule of thumb is that you can deduct most fees directly associated with acquiring the home, as opposed to costs associated with living in it, but you can deduct only those fees that you would have had if you had paid cash for the home. In other words, costs specifically incurred to take out a mortgage are not deductible.

Items Added to Purchaser's Tax Basis

The following items are commonly paid at settlement and can be added to your tax basis:

- attorney's fees
- abstract fees
- charges for installing utility services
- transfer and stamp taxes
- surveys
- owner's title insurance
- unreimbursed amounts that the seller owes but that you pay for back taxes or interest, recording fees for the deed or the mortgage, charges for improvements or repairs done before the sale, and selling commissions

Items Not Added to Purchaser's Tax Basis

The following items are *not* added to your basis and are not deductible:

- fire or liability insurance premiums
- charges for using utilities
- rent for occupying the home before closing
- any other fees or charges connected with occupying the home
- charges connected with getting or refinancing a mortgage loan, such as: FHA mortgage insurance premiums or VA funding fees, private mortgage insurance (PMI) premiums, loan assumption fees, cost of a credit report, cost of a preapproval or prequalification letter, fee for an appraisal required by the lender, and application fees, document fees, and any other miscellaneous fees imposed by the lender

Home Acquired by Gift, Inheritance or Other Transfer

If you received the home (or the part you did not already own) as part of a settlement in a divorce, you generally have no gain or loss at the time of the transfer. Thereafter you will essentially "stand in the shoes" of your former spouse and take whatever basis he or she had in the property, as to the part you received in the settlement. If the home was originally purchased by you and your former spouse together, the basis of the home will generally be figured based on its cost, as discussed above.

If you received your home by bequest or inheritance, your initial basis is the fair market value of the home on the date of the former owner's death, or the alternate valuation date if the estate is using that date for estate tax purposes. If an estate tax return was filed, use the amount shown for the home on the tax return. If the estate was too small to require the filing of an estate tax return, you may need to get an appraisal showing the home's value as of the date of death. Special rules apply where in community property states, where the death of one spouse causes the home to pass to the other spouse. Consult your attorney or tax professional for more details.

If you received the home as a gift, your initial tax basis will generally be the same as that of the person who gave it to you. You can add to this basis the part of any federal gift tax paid by the donor that is attributable to the increase in the home's value. See IRS Publication 551, *Basis of Assets,* or your tax adviser for more details.

Home That Was Purchased Under Rollover Replacement Rule

Under the tax laws that were in effect before May 7, 1997, you could avoid capital gains tax on the sale of your home if, within two years before or after the sale, you purchased and lived in another main home that cost more than the sales price of the old home.

If you took advantage of this rule in previous years, the gain on the sale of your earlier homes was deferred, not wiped out. The amount of gain you would otherwise have recognized (and paid tax on) was deducted from the cost of your replacement home, so the basis of your current home is likely to be somewhat lower than your cost.

If this is your story, you'll need to look back into your tax records for the IRS Form 2119, *Sale of Your Home,* that was filed in the year you sold your most recent earlier home. That form (which became obsolete for sales after 1997) required you to compute the adjusted basis of the replacement home, which is what you must use as the initial basis.

Adjustments to Your Home's Basis

Over the years that you own your home, your initial tax basis may need to be adjusted to reflect several kinds of events.

The most common reason for an addition to your basis is that you made a permanent improvement, such as a room addition, kitchen remodeling, installation of air conditioning or heating, new sidewalks or landscaping, etc. "Improvements" are generally defined as things that add to the value of the home, prolong its useful life, or adapt it to new uses. In contrast, "repairs" are things that keep your home in good working condition and maintain, but do not add to, its value. However, if jobs that would normally be considered repairs are done as part of a larger improvement project, all of the expenses can be treated as an improvement and added to your basis.

As you complete and pay for improvements, you should retain receipts and cancelled checks for the payments you make. You may find it helpful to use a form like the one that follows to keep track of your improvements over the years.

Save Money

Although the list of improvements included in the form concentrates on big-ticket items, remember that an improvement need not be large in order to be deductible. For example, drapery rods, window shades, bathroom towel racks, updated lighting fixtures, and even new handles on your kitchen cabinets can all be considered "improvements." If you keep careful track of these items over the years, they can really add up.

Capital Improvements Worksheet (keep for your records)

These are improvements made to your home that add to its value, prolong its useful life, or adapt it to new uses. Examples are listed below.

Caution: *Do not include improvements that are no longer part of your main home. For example, if you put wall-to-wall carpeting in your home and later replaced it with new wall-to-wall carpeting, do not include the cost of the first carpeting as a capital improvement.*

(a) Type of Improvement	(b) Year	(c) Amount
Additions		
Bedroom		
Bathroom		
Deck		
Garage		
Porch		
Patio		
Storage shed		
Fireplace		
Other		
Lawn & Grounds		
Landscaping		
Driveway		
Walkway		
Fence		
Retaining wall		
Sprinkler system		
Swimming pool		
Exterior lighting		
Other		
Communications		
Satellite dish		
Intercom		
Security system		
Other		
Miscellaneous		
Storm windows and doors		
Roof		
Central vacuum		
Other		

(a) Type of Improvement	(b) Year	(c) Amount
Heating & Air Conditioning		
Heating system		
Central air conditioning		
Furnace		
Duct work		
Central humidifier		
Filtration system		
Other		
Electrical		
Light fixtures		
Wiring upgrades		
Other		
Plumbing		
Water heater		
Soft water system		
Filtration system		
Other		
Insulation		
Attic		
Walls		
Floors		
Pipes and duct work		
Other		
Interior Improvements		
Built-in appliances		
Kitchen modernization		
Bathroom modernization		
Flooring		
Wall-to-wall carpeting		
Other		

Total capital improvements. Add the amounts in column **(c).** Enter the total here and on line 6 of the **Adjusted Basis of Home Sold Worksheet** on page 4. . . . . $ ________

Besides additions or improvements, you may need to record an increase in your home's tax basis if you pay a special assessment to your taxing body for a local improvement such as a sidewalk, paving an alley, etc. You should also increase your basis by the amounts you spend to restore damage to your home caused by a casualty, vandalism, etc.

Decreases to your basis will need to be made for the following amounts:

- casualty losses, whether they are covered and reimbursed by insurance, or not covered by insurance and deductible (see page 269)
- payments you receive for granting an easement or right-of-way
- depreciation, if you used your home for business or rental purposes (see page 219)
- residential energy credit claimed for the cost of energy-related improvements that you added to the basis of your home (the credit was available from 1977 through 1987)
- energy conservation subsidy that was excluded from your gross income because it was received from a public utility after 1992

to buy or install any energy conservation measure

- adoption credit you claimed for improvements that you added to the basis of your home, and nontaxable adoption assistance received from your employer that you used for improvements that you added to the basis of your home (see page 285)

Selling Your Home

Because of changes to the tax laws that went into effect in May of 1997, most homeowners will be exempt from paying tax on gains from the sale of their main home.

More specifically, you may be able to exclude up to $250,000 in gains when you sell your home, provided that you have both owned and used your home as a principal residence for at least two of the five years immediately preceding the sale (five years minimum ownership for sales and exchanges after October 22, 2004 if the residence was acquired in a like-kind exchange).

Married couples can exclude up to $500,000 in gains if they file a joint return, provided that both spouses meet the two-year use test, at least one spouse can meet the two-year ownership test, and neither spouse has excluded gain from the sale of another home in the last two years (counting sales since May 6, 1997).

As a reminder, losses on the sale of your personal residence are not deductible. There is an exception to this rule if part of your home was rented out or used for a home office (see page 79), or your home was converted to a rental property before you sold it. In any case, only losses on the business portion of the home would be deductible. See page 116 for more on sales of rental or commercial real estate.

Period of Ownership and Use

To take advantage of the exclusion for sales and exchanges, you must have *owned* and *used the home as a principal residence* for at least two of the five preceding years. The two years for each test need not have occurred at the same time.

Example

In 1999, Sharon Rose was living in a rented apartment. The apartment was converted into a condominium, and in 2001 Sharon purchased her apartment. In 2004, Sharon became ill and on April 14 of that year, she moved to her daughter's home. She never moved back to the condo and on July 10, 2006, she sold it.

Sharon can exclude up to $250,000 in gain on the sale of her condo because she met both tests, at different times. Her five year-period began on July 10, 2001 and ended on July 10, 2006. Within that period she lived in the condo from July 10, 2001 until April 14, 2004, which is more than two years. Also within that period she owned the home from sometime in 2001 until July 10, 2006, which is also more than two years.

In tallying up the time periods, you can count short periods of absence for vacation, seasonal absences, or any other temporary absence (generally, anything under one year) as time that you spent using the home.

Also, there are some grandfathering provisions in the law, which say that if you previously owned a home and rolled over the capital gains from that home into your current home under the old rollover-replacement rule, you can count the time you owned and/or lived in that previous home towards your two-year period. To take advantage of this exception, you can't have sold another home within two years of your sale, or since May 7, 1997 (whichever period is shorter). This is true even if your previous home was condemned or destroyed.

Finally, if you can't meet the two-year rules because you became physically or mentally incapable of self-care, you qualify for the exemption if you owned and lived in the home for at least one year.

In a new twist to these rules, the American Jobs Creation Act of 2004 requires that a principal residence be owned for at least five years prior to a tax-free sale or exchange if the residence was acquired in a like-kind exchange. This change applies to sales or exchanges occurring after October 22, 2004. However, the two-year ownership rule still applies for other types of acquisitions (e.g., purchasing a residence). Also, in any case, the two-year period of use as a principal residence remains unchanged.

Reduced Exclusion

You might qualify for a partial exclusion even if you don't meet the two-year rules, if the reason that you can't meet them is because you suffered a "change in place of employment, health, or unforeseen circumstances." Exactly what type of "change" is serious enough to warrant this tax break has not yet been defined in the regulations or any official pronouncements by the IRS. If you think this exception might apply to you, for the time being, we advise you to think about what a "reasonable" person would think was justification for moving. For example, taking a job in another city; moving to a warmer, drier part of the country due to severe asthma; or selling your home because of a drop in income would probably warrant a partial exclusion.

You can compute a partial exclusion by using the worksheet below. At this time, it is unclear whether the reduced exclusion will apply when a home acquired in a like-kind exchange does not meet the five-year ownership period due to one of the special circumstances.

If You Are Married

If you and your spouse file a joint return for the year, you can exclude up to $250,000 in gain if either spouse meets the ownership and use test, and up to $500,000 if both spouses meet the use test and at least one spouse meets the ownership test.

If each spouse sells a different home, each spouse can deduct up to $250,000 in gain provided that each meets the ownership and use test with regard to their own home.

Work Smart

This rule can come into play if, for example, an older couple gets married and each spouse brings a home into the marriage. If they want to sell the old homes and purchase a new one together, they can sell either home before or after the marriage without losing the full exclusion; furthermore, it's not necessary to buy a home that costs more than either (or both) of the homes to qualify for a tax break, as under prior law.

Reduced Exclusion for Gain on Sale of a Principal Residence

Complete Column B only if you are married and filing a joint return.

	You	Your Spouse
(1) Maximum amount	$250,000	$250,000
(2a) Number of days you used the property as a main home during the 5-year period ending on the date of sale	________	________
(2b) Number of days you owned the property during the 5-year period (if one spouse owned it longer than the other, enter the longer period in both columns)	________	________
(2c) Enter the smaller of Line 2a or 2b.	________	________
(3) Are you or your spouse excluding gain from the sale of another home after May 6, 1997? If no, skip Line 3 and enter the number of days from Line 2c on Line 4. If yes, if the other home was sold before this one, enter the number of days between the date of sale of the other home and the date of the sale of this home. Otherwise, skip Line 3 and enter the number of days from Line 2c on Line 4.	________	________
(4) Enter the smaller of Line 2c or Line 3.	________	________
(5) Divide the amount on Line 4 by 730 days.	________	________
(6) Multiply the amount on Line 1 by the decimal on Line 5.	________	________
(7) Add the amounts in columns a and b of Line 6. This is your reduced maximum exclusion.	________	________

If one spouse dies before a sale is accomplished, the other spouse can use the decedent's time of ownership and use in order to qualify for the exemption.

Divorce

If a home is transferred from one spouse to the other as part of a divorce settlement, the recipient is treated as having owned the home during any time the donor owned it.

Also, in cases where the home is not sold for a while after the divorce (for example, the couple agrees to maintain joint ownership, so one spouse can live there with the children until they finish high school), you are considered to have used the property as your main home during any period when you owned it, and your spouse or former spouse is allowed to use it under a divorce or separation instrument.

Calculating Gains on Sale

To determine the amount of your gains, and whether the $250,000 or $500,000 exemption is large enough to save you from paying any tax on the sale of your home, compute your gains as shown in this example:

Example

Kelly Vargas, a single person, sold her main home on September 15, 2006. She had owned and lived in it as her main home for seven years. She computed her gain as follows:

Selling price of home	*$195,000*
Minus: selling expenses	*- 15,000*
Amount realized on sale	*$180,000*
Minus: adjusted basis of home	*- 50,000*
Gain on sale	*$130,000*

Since Kelly's gain is less than $250,000, she will not be taxed on the sale.

Selling expenses that Kelly can subtract from the selling price of her home include the broker's commission, title insurance or abstract fees, legal fees, recording fees, advertising, escrow fees, geological surveys, and interest reimbursed on money borrowed for an option to purchase.

Reporting Gains on Sales

Historically, the IRS had required all homeowners to complete and file IRS Form 2119, *Sale of Your Home,* in the year that they sell a home. Form 2119 is no longer required for 1998 and thereafter. Those who owe some tax on the sale of a principal residence will report the sale as short-term or long-term gain on Schedule D, *Capital Gains and Losses.*

If you owned the home for up to one year, any non-exempt gain would be considered short-term gain taxable at ordinary rates. If you owned the home for more than one year, it would be taxed at the long-term rate.

Home Offices

If you have used part of your home as a home office, you haven't been using that part of your home as a principal residence at the same time. Fortunately, you don't need to allocate the basis of the property and the amount realized between the business portion of the home and the residential portion. However, gain must be recognized to the extent of claimed depreciation.

The rule is different when a separate part of the property was used for business purposes or rental income. For example, this situation would occur if the individual owned an apartment building and lived in one unit and rented out the other units. Generally, if the separate part of the property is used for business or rental purposes in the year of sale, the individual must treat the sale of the property as the sale of two properties (i.e., a residence and business or rental property). The sale of the business or rental portion of the property is reported on Form 4797, *Sales of Business Property.*

Example

Bob Bruhaha sold his main home in 2006 at a $30,000 gain. He meets the ownership and use tests to exclude the gain from his income. However, he used part of the home as a business office in 2005 and claimed $500 depreciation.

Because the business office was part of his home (not separate from it), he does not have to allocate the basis and amount realized between the business part of the property and the part used as a home. In addition, he does not have to report any part of the gain on Form 4797.

Bob reports his gain, exclusion, and taxable gain of $500 on Schedule D (Form 1040).

Case Study

Tom Stonehouse, a 72-year-old taxpayer, owns a four-unit apartment building that he had purchased five years ago. He occupies one unit as his personal residence and rents out three units. Desiring to move to a warmer climate, Tom decides to sell the building and move in with his nephew. Tom's records show the following:

Cost of building	$80,000
Capital improvements	+ 8,000
	$88,000
Less: Depreciation on rental units	- 10,100
Adjusted basis	$77,900

Tom sells the building on May 1, 2006, for $220,000 and incurs selling expenses of $10,000. Since only one-fourth of the building was used as his personal residence, Tom would compute his gain as follows:

	Apartment Residence (1/4)	Rental Building (3/4)
(1) Selling price	$55,000	$165,000
(2) Selling expenses	-2,500	-7,500
(3) Amount realized (adjusted sales price)	$52,500	$157,500
(4) Basis (including improvements)	$22,000	$ 66,000
(5) Depreciation		-10,100
(6) Adjusted basis	$22,000	$ 55,900
(7) Realized gain [(3) minus (6)]	$30,500	$101,600
(8) Gain subject to exclusion	$30,500	
(9) Gain subject to tax		$101,600

Of the gains subject to tax on line (9), $10,100 would be taxed at a 25 percent rate since it represents deprecation that must be recaptured, and the remainder would be taxed at a maximum rate of 15 percent.

VACATION HOME RENTALS

A second home in the country, a condo in the city, or a houseboat on the lake can all be a pleasant place to spend your vacation. They can also be made to partially pay for their own costs, if you can rent them out to others for at least a few days or weeks each year.

The IRS basically uses a two-week *de minimus* rule. If you rent out a vacation home for two weeks or less during the year, you don't have to report any rental income you receive, but you can't deduct any rental expenses you have (except for the normal home mortgage interest and real estate tax deductions you'd have anyway). Essentially the IRS will ignore this small amount of rental activity.

If you have property that is rented out for more than 14 days during the year, and you or your family, or any co-owner or his or her family, use it for personal purposes for *even one day* of the year, you have to divide all the expenses of the property into two buckets: "personal" and "rental."

The rental expenses will generally be deductible on Schedule E, *Supplemental Income and Loss,* and the personal expenses will not be deductible except for mortgage interest, real estate taxes, and casualty losses that you could ordinarily claim on Schedule A.

On Schedule E you can deduct the entire amount of expenses that apply only to renting, such as advertising, commissions, credit checks, etc. For all expenses that apply to the entire home, such as mortgage interest, real estate taxes, insurance, utilities, and repairs and maintenance on the furnace, roof, electric system, etc., you must generally divide the expenses on the basis of days spent for personal use, compared to days that the property was rented at a fair market rate; the total need not add up to 365 days.

When counting days of "personal use," you must include any days that you donated the use of your property to a charitable organization (for example, if you allowed a charity to auction off a week in your lakefront house). Also count as "personal" any days that you traded with someone else for the use of a different property, or any days for which you charged less than fair market rent. However, don't count as "personal" the days you stayed in the home because you were having repairs or maintenance done, even if your family stayed with you.

Example

You have a cabin in the mountains that you generally rent out during a three-month ski season; this year, the rental agent was only able to rent the property for 60 days out of the 90 days it was available. You donated a week of this unrented period to a local charity. Also, you spent a week at the cabin cleaning and making repairs before the rental period began.

You would count as "personal use" the 7 days you donated to charity, and you would count as "rental use" the 60 days you actually rented the property. Therefore, 7/67 of your expenses would be treated as "personal" and deductible, if at all, on Schedule A. 60/67 of your expenses would be treated as "rental" and deductible on Schedule E, subject to the limits discussed below. The 7 days spent cleaning and making repairs do not count as either personal or rental use.

Dwelling unit used as a home. An even more severe restriction applies if you (or your family, or any co-owners or their families) use the property for personal purposes for more than the greater of 14 days, or 10 percent of the days it is rented out to others.

In that case, not only do you have to apportion your expenses between the "rental" and the "personal" portion, but also if your rental expenses exceed your rental income for this mixed-use property, you can only deduct your expenses up to the amount of your income. Any remaining expenses can be carried over and deducted in the next year, however.

You don't have to apply this additional limit if you converted rental property to a personal residence during the year.

You also don't have to apply it if you converted a personal residence to a rental during the year and you rented or tried to rent it out for at least 12 months, or if you would have rented it for at least 12 months except that you sold or exchanged the property before the 12 months were up.

You can use the following worksheet to compute the additional limit on rental deductions for a mixed-use property.

RENTAL REAL ESTATE INCOME AND EXPENSES

If you rented out residential or commercial real estate during the year, you will normally report your income and expenses from this activity on Part I of Schedule E, *Supplemental Income and Loss.*

Worksheet for Figuring the Limit on Rental Deductions for a Dwelling Unit Used as a Home

Use this worksheet only if you answer "yes" to all of the following questions.
- Did you use the dwelling unit as a home this year?
- Did you rent the dwelling unit 15 days or more this year?
- Are the total of your rental expenses and depreciation more than your rental income?

1. Enter rents received . . . . ______

2a. Enter the rental portion of deductible home mortgage interest (see instructions) . . . . ______
b. Enter the rental portion of real estate taxes . . . . ______
c. Enter the rental portion of deductible casualty and theft losses (see instructions) . . . . ______
d. Enter direct rental expenses (see instructions) . . . . ______
e. **Fully deductible rental expenses.** Add lines 2a–2d . . . . ______

3. Subtract line 2e from line 1. If zero or less, enter zero . . . . ______

4a. Enter the rental portion of expenses directly related to operating or maintaining the dwelling unit (such as repairs, insurance, and utilities) . . . . ______
b. Enter the rental portion of excess mortgage interest (see instructions) . . . . ______
c. Add lines 4a and 4b . . . . ______
d. **Allowable operating expenses.** Enter the smaller of line 3 or line 4c . . . . ______

5. Subtract line 4d from line 3. If zero or less, enter zero . . . . ______

6a. Enter the rental portion of excess casualty and theft losses (see instructions) . . . . ______
b. Enter the rental portion of depreciation of the dwelling unit . . . . . . ______
c. Add lines 6a and 6b . . . . ______
d. **Allowable excess casualty and theft losses and depreciation.** Enter the smaller of line 5 or line 6c . . . . ______

7a. **Operating expenses to be carried over to next year.** Subtract line 4d from line 4c . . . . ______
b. **Excess casualty and theft losses and depreciation to be carried over to next year.** Subtract line 6d from line 6c . . . . ______

Enter the amounts on **lines 2e, 4d, and 6d** on the appropriate lines of Schedule E (Form 1040), Part I.

Worksheet Instructions

Follow these instructions for the worksheet above. If you were unable to deduct all your expenses last year, because of the rental income limit, add these unused amounts to your expenses for this year.

Line 2a. Figure the mortgage interest on the dwelling unit that you could deduct on Schedule A (Form 1040) if you had not rented the unit. **Do not** include interest on a loan that did not benefit the dwelling unit. For example, **do not** include interest on a home equity loan used to buy, build, or improve the dwelling unit, or to refinance such a loan. Enter the rental portion of this interest on line 2a of the worksheet.

Line 2c. Figure the casualty and theft losses related to the dwelling unit that you could deduct on Schedule A (Form 1040) if you had not rented the dwelling unit. To do this, complete Section A of Form 4684, treating the losses as personal losses. On line 17 of Form 4684, enter 10% of your adjusted gross income figured **without** your rental income and expenses from the dwelling unit. Enter the rental portion of the result from line 18 of Form 4684 on line 2c of this worksheet.

Note. Do **not** file this Form 4684 or use it to figure your personal losses on Schedule A. Instead, figure the personal portion on a separate Form 4684.

Line 2d. Enter the total of your rental expenses that are directly related only to the rental activity. These include interest on loans used for rental activities other than to buy, build, or improve the dwelling unit. Also include rental agency fees, advertising, office supplies, and depreciation on office equipment used in your rental activity.

Line 4b. On line 2a, you entered the rental portion of the mortgage interest you could deduct on Schedule A if you had not rented out the dwelling unit. Enter on line 4b of this worksheet the rental portion of the mortgage interest you could not deduct on Schedule A because it is **more than** the limit on home mortgage interest. **Do not** include interest on a loan that did not benefit the dwelling unit (as explained in the line 2a instructions).

Line 6a. To find the rental portion of excess casualty and theft losses, use the Form 4684 you prepared for line 2c of this worksheet.

A. Enter the amount from line 10 of Form 4684 . . . . . ______
B. Enter the rental portion of **A** . ______
C. Enter the amount from line 2c of this worksheet . . . . ______
D. Subtract **C** from **B.** Enter the result here and on line 6a of this worksheet . . . . . . ______

Allocating the limited deduction. If you cannot deduct all of the amount on line 4c or 6c this year, you can allocate the allowable deduction in any way you wish among the expenses included on line 4c or 6c. Enter the amount you allocate to each expense on the appropriate line of Schedule E, Part I.

Schedule E has space for up to three different real estate or royalty properties. Line 1 asks you to identify the type of property (such as "apartment building," "store," etc.) and the street address. You should also show your percentage of ownership in the property, if you (and your spouse, if filing jointly) own less than 100 percent. If you own, say, half of the property with another owner, you would report half of the income and half of the expenses on your tax return, regardless of which of you actually received the check for the income or paid the expenses out of pocket.

For each property, you are asked to answer "yes" or "no" to the question of whether you or your family used it for more than the greater of 14 days or 10 percent of the total days rented. See the discussion on page 215 explaining how to make the count.

Income and expenses for each property are reported separately in columns A, B, and C, and the totals from all properties combined are entered in the "totals" column. If you have more than three properties, use as many copies of Schedule E as you need. Just be sure to fill out the "totals" column on only one of the copies, which will become the "master."

Schedule E is not used to report farm rental income if the rent is paid in the form of a percentage of the crops or livestock produced on the farm. In that case, you must use Form 4835, *Farm Rental Income and Expenses,* instead (see page 180). But if the farm rent is paid in terms of a flat fee, use Schedule E.

Also, if you provide a large number of services to tenants in a residential property, you may have to treat your activity as being more akin to running a hotel (reported on Schedule C) than investing in real estate. The IRS says that providing maid service to tenants can transform your activity into a business, not a Schedule E rental. However, providing occasional cleaning or concierge services would probably not be sufficient to change the nature of your activity.

Rental Real Estate Income

Rent you recognize during the year for each property under your accounting method is entered in the appropriate column on Line 3 of Schedule E. For most taxpayers, this means all rent received during the calendar year, whether it's received directly or indirectly (for example, if your tenant makes repairs for you in exchange for a rent credit, or pays some tax, utility, or repair bills you owe under the terms of the lease).

If you receive a security deposit, it doesn't count as rent unless and until you determine that you're entitled to keep some of the deposit because your tenant violated the lease or damaged your property in some way. Also, if your tenant buys out the remainder of the lease term with a cash payment, the payment counts as rent. However, if you receive some rent in advance of when it's due, you must count it as income regardless of your accounting method.

If you are leasing the property with an option to buy, the payments you receive are considered rent. If and when the tenant exercises the option to buy, payments received after the date of the sale would be considered part of the selling price.

Rental Property Expenses

Expenses paid on your rental property are reported on Lines 5 through 18 on Part I of Schedule E. The rules for most of these expenses are the same as those discussed in Chapter 6 for small businesses, or in the first part of Chapter 12 for real estate taxes and mortgage interest.

The major categories of expenses that you can deduct are listed on the front of Schedule E. On the next page we discuss a few of the more important types of deductible expenses, and a few types of expenses that are often forgotten.

Interest Expenses

There is no upper dollar limit on the amount of mortgage interest you can deduct on rental property, as there is with home mortgage interest.

Furthermore, you can deduct almost any type of interest you pay when you borrow money to further your rental activity, such as interest on a revolving charge account or even credit card late fees.

Example

You purchase new kitchen appliances for a home that you rent out to others, and charge the amounts on your department store credit card. You can deduct the interest charges until you pay off the appliances.

The loan need not be secured by the property, but you must be liable for repayment, and the proceeds of the loan must be used for the rental activities. If you don't use the money immediately to pay for a particular expense (such as to buy or improve the property) you must keep records showing where the loan money went.

Save Time

Ideally, you should keep a separate bank account for each major type of activity you have. Don't commingle funds from your small business with funds from your rental activities. Having separate checking accounts, and separate deposit and check records, will also help you to limit the scope of an IRS audit if one of your activities (but not the others) draws the focussed attention of the IRS.

Unlike other types of investment interest, interest on loans pertaining to rental real estate activities in which you actively participate (see page 221) is not limited by the amount of income you receive from the activity.

However, you can't deduct prepaid interest, and there is no exception for points paid to obtain a mortgage on a rental property as there is with home mortgage loans. Consequently, points you pay to obtain a mortgage for commercial or residential property must be spread over the life of the loan, and deducted in equal amounts over the entire period.

Fees and charges you pay to obtain a mortgage on rental real estate, such as application fees, appraisals, abstract fees, recording fees, cannot be deducted as interest but can be amortized (deducted evenly) over the life of the mortgage.

Repairs vs. Improvements

The discussion that begins on page 59 regarding how to distinguish between repairs, which can be deducted in the year they are paid for, and improvements, which must be depreciated over a time period that matches the class life of the asset, applies to rental real estate as well.

Depreciation

Generally speaking, all assets that will be used for more than one year (and are not trivial in cost, such as paper clips or extension cords) are treated as capital assets.

For property used in your rental activity, you *cannot* make the election to expense up to $100,000 (indexed for inflation) in 2003 through 2009 in new equipment in the year you purchase it, under Section 179 of the tax law.

Instead, you'll have to depreciate your rental property, any capital improvements you make to it, and any tools or equipment you need to carry out this activity, such as power mowers or tools, vacuum cleaners, and even your computer, cellular phone, and answering machine.

Aside from the lack of availability of the Section 179 expensing election, all the rules for depreciation discussed in Chapter 6 apply equally to rental real estate. If the real estate is used for residential purposes, such as an apartment building, rental house, mobile home, houseboat, etc., the buildings and any capital improvements on it must be depreciated over 27.5 years. If the property is used for other commercial purposes, it must be depreciated over 39 years. Land itself is never depreciable; only the buildings and improvements on the land can be written off.

If you purchased property for personal use and then changed it to rental use, your depreciable basis will generally be the lesser of its adjusted basis, or its fair market value at the time of the conversion.

Depreciation is claimed on Form 4562, *Depreciation and Amortization.* Don't mix depreciation on rental property with any depreciation claimed on business assets; instead, file a separate Form 4562 for each activity you engage in.

Other Rental Expenses

The chart that follows shows some of the types of expenses you may be able to deduct.

Save Money

Unfortunately, you cannot deduct the cost of your own labor if, for example, you paint a rental apartment or install a lock yourself instead of hiring a painter or a locksmith. However, if you hire a non-owner (such as your child or, possibly, your spouse), you can deduct the payments.

Other Rental Deductions

The following is a list of other frequently overlooked rental deductions.

- 50% of meals and entertainment expenses while traveling, or when entertaining business guests
- cleaning supplies
- credit check fees for tenants
- finance charges on a credit card used for business
- janitorial or cleaning service

- legal fees related to drawing up leases, resolving disputes with tenants or repair contractors, tax advice, etc; however, legal fees incurred in connection with buying or selling the property are added to the property's tax basis
- landscaping maintenance
- local licenses, taxes, inspection fees etc.
- car and truck expenses or local transportation expenses, to inspect the property, collect rents, interview prospective tenants, or to call on contractors, suppliers, vendors, your insurance agent etc; if you claim these expenses, be sure to report them on Form 4562, *Depreciation and Amortization*
- miscellaneous repairs and maintenance
- rental fees for power tools, painting equipment, etc.
- safe deposit box rental, if you keep your deed, mortgage, or insurance policy there
- stamps, if you pay bills by mail
- stationery
- tax return preparation, if you pay someone to complete your Schedule E, associated depreciation tax forms, etc.
- telephone calls, although you can't deduct any part of the first telephone line into your residence

Gains and Losses from Rental Activities

Like any business-related activity, to calculate your taxable profits from rental activities, you subtract your deductible expenses from your gross income, and if the answer is a positive number, you have a taxable profit or gain. This will be initially reported on Line 22 of Schedule E.

In the case of real estate rental activities, it frequently happens that the answer isn't positive, it's negative, and you have a loss for the year. In some cases it's only a "paper loss" because you deducted depreciation expenses that don't represent out-of-pocket expenses, but in other cases it is a real loss. Investors in real estate are frequently willing to accept small losses in the short term, if they believe that their property will appreciate sufficiently over the years to result in a big gain over the long term.

However, the IRS is ever vigilant against the possibility that you are merely trying to create a tax shelter for other types of income. Therefore, there are some special rules that may prevent you from deducting some (or all) of your real estate losses.

At-Risk Limitations

Line 22 says that if the result is a loss, you may have to fill out IRS Form 6198, *At-Risk Limitations*. The at-risk limitations apply to relatively few small-business owners, and they don't apply to losses from holding real estate placed in service before 1987 (except mineral property).

In a nutshell, if they apply, the at-risk rules limit your deductible losses to the amount that you have at risk and could actually lose from the activity.

A taxpayer is "at risk" to the extent of cash and the adjusted basis of property contributed to the business activity, as well as to the extent of loans on which he or she is personally liable or has provided collateral. Having insurance will not render you "not at risk" or cause you to have to fill out this form. A real estate lessor is "not at risk" to the extent that he or she is protected by non-recourse financing not secured by real estate, guarantees by others, stop-loss agreements or similar arrangements.

If any of these items apply to you and you are not at risk for some amounts in your rental activities, you may have to complete Form 6198. You can obtain a copy of this form and its instructions from the IRS by calling 1-800-TAX-FORM, or by downloading it from the IRS website at www.irs.gov.

Passive Activity Losses

Line 23 of Schedule E cautions you that for some people, real estate losses are limited regardless of the at-risk rules.

In contrast to the at-risk limitations, the passive activity loss rules apply to a larger group of taxpayers. They generally prevent taxpayers with adjusted gross income (AGI) above $100,000 ($50,000 if married filing separately) from deducting some or all losses from real estate rentals, other than the rental of your home that was also used for personal purposes.

There is an exception to these rules for real estate professionals, defined as those who spend more than 750 hours per year and more than half their working time in developing, managing, and/or selling real estate.

If you're not a real estate professional, here's the basic rule: Taxpayers with modified AGI of $100,000 or less can deduct up to $25,000 in net losses from rental real estate activities in which they "actively participate." If you are married, you must file a joint return to take advantage of this deduction unless you lived apart from your spouse for the entire year; in that case, you can deduct up to $12,500 in losses on a separate tax return.

"Active participation" means that you have significant participation in making management decisions or arranging for others to provide services. These management decisions might include approving new tenants, deciding on rental rates and terms, and approving capital or repair expenditures. However, you're not considered to have "actively participated" if you own less than 10 percent of the property.

"Modified AGI" means your AGI as shown on Form 1040, Line 37, without taking into account any passive activity losses, taxable Social Security benefits, deductible IRA contributions, the deduction for one-half the self-employment tax, and the exclusion for amounts received under an employer's adoption assistance program. Also, if you filed Form 8815, *Exclusion of Interest from Series EE and I U.S. Savings Bonds Issued After 1989,* you must add back the savings bond interest excluded on Line 14 of that form.

If your modified AGI is more than $100,000, if you don't materially participate, if you have more than $25,000 in real estate losses, or if you are carrying over any losses that were not allowed in previous years, your losses may be limited. Generally, the rule is that you can deduct passive losses to the extent that you have passive income from other activities, and all rental real estate activities are treated as passive. For information on which trade or business activities are treated as passive, see page 44.

If you have more passive losses from real estate than you have passive income, your deduction of $25,000 will shrink as your AGI rises. You'll lose $1 of the deduction for every $2 that your AGI rises above $100,000; if your modified AGI is $150,000 or more, you can't deduct any excess passive losses this year.

If your losses are limited under any of these rules, you must complete Form 8582, *Passive Activity Loss Limitations.* The allowed loss, if any, shown on the bottom of Form 8582 is transferred to Line 23 of Schedule E.

Losses that cannot be deducted in the current year are carried over to later years until they can be offset by passive income, until you can use the special $25,000 deduction, or until you sell your entire interest in the property to an unrelated third party.

SALE OF RENTAL REAL ESTATE

If you sell or dispose of any rental real estate during the year, the sale will be reported on Form 4797, *Sales of Business Property.* For detailed information, see the discussion of disposing of capital assets beginning on page 116.

Chapter 13

Investments

For a large number of taxpayers, reporting interest and dividends on investments is very simple. Just collect all the 1099-INT and 1099-DIV forms you've received at the beginning of 2006, enter the amounts in Schedule B of Form 1040 or Schedule 1 of Form 1040A, add up the totals, transfer them to the front page of your main tax form, and you're done.

However, if you bought or sold any investments during the year, or if you had any of the many types of investments that followed special rules, including mutual funds, tax-free municipal bonds or bond funds, U.S. Savings Bonds, OID interest, nominee interest, amortizable bond premiums, accrued interest, foreign investments, or income from partnerships, S corporations, trusts, or estates, your situation will be a little more complicated.

You may also have some investment-related deductions for interest, investment advice, financial publications or software, or custodial fees. We'll help you deal with those as well.

If you have a child with investment income, you may have the option to report that income on your own return, or to file a separate tax return for the child. This issue is discussed beginning on page 240.

Tax Organizer Tip

Most investment-related data should be entered on the "Investments" tab of CompleteTax. However, information about royalty income and expenses, and investment real estate, should be entered on the "Real Estate" tab.

INTEREST INCOME

Interest from bank accounts or accounts at other financial institutions, certificates of deposits, and bonds should be reported to you by the payer on Form 1099-INT. These forms should be sent out by the end of January.

Save Time

If you receive an incorrect 1099 form, you should contact the financial institution involved and ask them to issue a corrected one. Copies of all 1099s are sent to the IRS and are matched with your tax return. Mix-ups are especially prone to occur if your bank completed a merger this year and, for example, your bank accounts were reported to the IRS under a different bank's name than the one you used on your tax return, or if you had multiple accounts at a single bank and they were not all reported on the same 1099.

As a general rule, if you are required to file Schedule B or Schedule 1, every total shown in Box 1 of every 1099 that you receive should appear on your tax form somewhere, so that the IRS knows you are reporting it. If your institution reported multiple accounts on the same form, you should report them the same way. If they sent you separate 1099 forms for different accounts, report them separately.

If you received $1,500 or less in interest from all sources and none of the special situations described below apply to you, you don't have to file a separate schedule reporting interest, although you can if you wish.

If you do receive more than $1,500 in taxable interest, you must complete Parts I and III of Schedule B (for Form 1040) or Part I of Schedule 1 (for 1040A).

Save Money

If any federal income tax was withheld on your interest income, it will be reported in Box 4 of Form 1099-INT. Be sure to include this as "federal income tax withheld" on Line 64 on the back of your 1040, or Line 38 on the 1040A. You can generally avoid backup withholding (which is set at 28 percent in 2006) if you provide your financial institution with an accurate Social Security number for the owner of the account.

What Is "Interest"?

Generally, the payer of the amount you receive will distinguish between interest and dividends, and will send you the appropriate form reporting the correct dollar amount you received during the year.

Some items that you might consider to be "interest" are treated as dividends by the IRS (for example, income from money market funds) and some things you might think of as "dividends" are treated as interest (for example, dividends from tax-free municipal bond funds).

Other items that are commonly called "dividends" but that are treated as interest and reported in Part I of Schedule B are income from accounts in cooperative banks, credit unions, domestic building and loan associations, domestic savings and loans, federal savings and loans, and mutual savings banks.

U.S. Government Obligations

Interest on all federal government bonds is generally taxable for federal income tax purposes, but it is tax-free for state and local income tax purposes.

Generally, interest on treasury notes and bills is paid either at maturity (for instruments with a maturity of one year or less) or at six-month intervals. You must report it in the year you receive it.

There is a special rule for Series E or EE U.S. Savings Bonds. While interest on these bonds accrue each year, if you're a cash-basis taxpayer, you don't have to pay tax on the interest until you cash in the bond, and most people choose to go this route. However, you do have the option of reporting and paying tax on this interest each year, if you want to avoid a big tax bill in the final year or if you think you'll be in a higher tax bracket at that time.

If you've been accruing interest on savings bonds without reporting it, you can switch to the annual reporting method without seeking IRS permission, but you'll have to switch for all bonds you own, and you'll have to report and pay tax on all interest owed on all bonds to date. You can also switch back to the "postpone recognition of interest" method later, but you'll have to write to the IRS for permission in that case.

Save Money

If your minor child was given U.S. Savings Bonds at birth or soon thereafter, and you haven't been reporting annual interest, you might think about switching to the "annual reporting" method in the year your child turns 18. For that year and all later years, the child's interest income will no longer be taxed at the parent's (usually higher) tax rate. Since savings bonds generally mature in 30 years, your child will probably be in a lower tax bracket at age 18 than he or she will be at age 30 or 31 when the bond is cashed, and under the annual reporting method, a minimum of about half the interest will be taxed at the lower age-18 rate.

Also, see page 226 for information about the special tax break for savings bonds redeemed to pay for higher education expenses.

Tax-Exempt Interest

While you don't have to pay ordinary income tax on it, the IRS wants to know how much tax-exempt interest you are receiving, and in some cases it can be used to limit your qualification for certain other tax breaks. Therefore, tax-exempt interest from state and local municipal bonds, including mutual funds that invest in these bonds, must be listed on the dotted lines provided for detailed information under Line 1 on the Schedule B, but it is not included in the "Amount" column on the right side of the page.

Tax-exempt interest is not required to be reported to you on Form 1099-INT or Form 1099-DIV, but your financial institution will generally send you a notice or year-end statement that includes the annual amount.

Work Smart

To clearly differentiate your tax-exempt interest, some tax practitioners recommend splitting the "dotted line" area into two columns labeled "tax-exempt" and "taxable," to make it very clear how much of which types of interest you've received. Or, you may want to add a separate page to your return that clearly details these amounts.

The total amount of tax-exempt interest you receive during the year must also be carried over to the front of your tax return, on Line 8b of both Form 1040 and 1040A.

Penalty on Early Withdrawal of Savings

If you paid a penalty for the early withdrawal of funds from a time savings account or certificate of deposit, you can deduct it, even if it exceeds the interest income you earned on the account during the year.

You must first report the gross amount of interest that would have been paid or credited to your account during the year without the penalty, on Line 1 of Schedule B. Then, you deduct the penalty amount on Line 30 of Form 1040 (you can't claim this deduction on Form 1040A or –EZ).

You don't have to compute the amount of the deduction, because it will be shown in Box 2 of your Form 1099-INT.

Special Situations

If any of the following items apply to you, you'll have to complete Part I of Schedule B or Schedule 1, even if you received $1,500 or less in total interest: you received interest from a seller financed mortgage, nominee interest, accrued interest, original issue discount (OID), or amortizable bond premiums; or you are claiming the exclusion for Series EE U.S. Savings Bonds used for higher education expenses.

Seller-Financed Mortgages

If you are holding a mortgage on property that the buyer is using as a personal residence, you must list the amount of interest received from the buyer as your first interest item on the lines provided for details under Line 1 of Schedule 1 or B. Also include the buyer's name, Social Security number and address. If you don't, you can get socked with a $50 fine.

Nominee Interest

If two or more people are listed as owners on a bank account or another type of investment account, the associated 1099-INT form will generally be sent to the person whose Social Security number is listed first on the account. The bank will report to the IRS that all income on the account was paid to that person. However, tax on the income should actually be split among all owners of the account, according to their proportionate ownership interest (which is determined under state law, but generally reflects the proportions that each person originally contributed to the account).

If you received a 1099-INT form that includes interest that is actually owed to someone else (for example, another joint owner of the account who is not your spouse), you can avoid tax on the full amount if you give the actual owner an 1099-INT form by the end of January, and file a copy of this form with the IRS along with IRS Form 1096, *Annual Summary and Transmittal of U.S. Information Returns,* by the end of February.

In that case, you would report on Line 1 of Schedule B the full amount shown on the 1099-INT you received; after you list all your taxable interest items, subtract the amount of interest you reported to the other owners and label it "nominee distribution." Then show the result (total interest minus nominee distribution) on Line 2.

Original Issue Discount on Bonds

Original issue discount (OID) is a feature of bonds that are purchased for less than their face value. The discount, or the difference between the amount you paid for the bond and its "face value" (face value is the amount you get at maturity) is generally taxed as it is earned each year, even though you won't actually receive it until the bond matures. A zero-coupon bond is an example of a bond with OID. You don't have to report OID from U.S. Savings Bonds, or from bonds with a maturity of one year or less.

Generally, if you are deemed to receive OID you'll receive an information return (Form 1099-OID) from the issuer of the bond, or from the brokerage or other institution holding your bonds.

Save Money

Remember that your tax basis in the bond is increased by the amount of OID you report over all the years that you own it, thus reducing the amount of capital gains tax that will be due when you sell the bond.

Income from a bank certificate of deposit, or a similar type of instrument at another institution, that has a maturity longer than one year can also be considered a form of OID, but it's generally reported to you on Form 1099-INT.

Accrued Interest

If you purchased a bond between interest dates and paid some accrued interest to the seller, this interest is taxable to the seller. If you find that it has been reported to you on a 1099-INT Form, you should, as your last item reported in the Line 1 area of Schedule B, take a subtotal of all reported interest, and then subtract the amount of accrued interest that was paid and is rightfully taxable to others. Be sure to label the amount you subtract "accrued interest." The remainder of the interest will be reported on Line 2.

Amortizable Bond Premiums

If you paid a premium to buy a bond (that is, you paid more than the bond's face value, most likely because the bond's stated interest rate is higher than the current interest rate at the time you bought it), you can make the election to deduct a portion of the premium each year while you hold the bond.

If you make this election, you must make it for every bond you own and for every bond you purchase in the future, until you revoke the election. You'll probably need the assistance of your accountant or financial advisor in determining the amount of amortization to deduct. If the bond was acquired after 1987, you can deduct this amount from the rest of your interest income on Line 1 of Schedule B. Take a subtotal of your interest income, subtract the amortizable bond premium (label it "ABP") and report the remaining interest on Line 2.

If the bond is a tax-exempt issue, you *must* amortize any premium you paid in your own records, but you can't deduct the amortization. Instead, it will reduce your tax basis in the bond and will potentially increase your capital gains when you sell the bond.

Savings Bonds Used for Higher Education

If you redeemed Series E or EE U.S. Savings Bonds in 2006 to pay higher education expenses you had this year, you may be able to avoid paying tax on the bond interest. The operative word here is "may." There are a lot of restrictions and requirements on this tax break, and many people find that it doesn't actually help them.

The first requirement is that the bonds must have been issued in 1990 or later, to a person who was at least 24 years old before the bond's issue date.

Save Time

The "24 or older at the time the bond was issued" rule eliminates all those bonds your children may have received when they were born or at birthdays, graduations, or other milestone events. In effect, it usually means that the parents must be the owners of bonds used to pay for their children's education.

Also, to qualify for the tax break, your income (not your child's, even if he or she is the one in college) must be below certain limits. For singles or heads of households in 2006, the tax break begins to be phased out at $63,100 of AGI and is completely phased out at $78,100 (phased out between $65,600 and $80,600 in 2007). For marrieds filing jointly, the phaseout begins at $94,700 in 2006 and is complete at $124,700 (phased out between $98,400 and $128,400 in 2007). Marrieds filing separately can't claim the exclusion at all.

If you can meet these requirements, a bond that was issued in your name or your spouse's name qualifies if you paid higher education expenses for yourself, your spouse, or your dependent children. Qualified education expenses include only tuition and fees – not room and board. However, as of 1998 you can include any contribution you make to a qualified state prepaid tuition program as an educational expense.

The qualified educational expenses must be reduced by any nontaxable scholarships, veterans' education assistance, benefits under a qualified state tuition program, or nontaxable employer-paid education benefits. Also, you cannot use the same expenses to qualify for the savings bond exclusion and either the Hope credit or the Lifetime Learning credit (see page 289).

Then, compare your qualified education expenses with the total amount of proceeds from any savings bonds you redeemed – "proceeds" includes principal as well as interest. If the total proceeds are less than your total qualified expenses, you can exclude all the interest on the bonds.

If the total proceeds were more than the total expenses, you can only exclude some of the interest. To find out how much, divide your qualified expenses by the total bond proceeds to get a percentage, and multiply that percentage by the interest you received on the bonds. That's the amount of interest you can exclude, unless you're subject to the AGI limits.

If your AGI is within the phaseout range, take your AGI, subtract the bottom rung of the phaseout range (see above), and divide the result by $15,000 if single, or $30,000 if married. The resulting percentage is multiplied by your excludible interest (as calculated in the preceding paragraph), and the result is the amount of the exclusion you lose because your AGI was too high.

The exemption must be computed on IRS Form 8815, *Exclusion of Interest From Series EE and I U.S. Savings Bonds Issued After 1989,* which must be attached to your Form 1040 or 1040A.

Work Smart

If you claim this exclusion, make sure that you retain records such as tuition bills, cancelled checks, or credit card statements showing the amount of your qualified higher education expenses. You'll also need to keep a record of the bonds you redeemed including the serial number, issue date, face value, and redemption proceeds. You can use optional IRS Form 8818 to keep this record (call 1-800-TAX-FORM or go to the IRS's website at www.irs.gov to get a copy).

DIVIDENDS

If you received dividends from a corporation in which you owned stock, they will generally be reported to you on a copy of IRS Form 1099-DIV. The ordinary dividends you received are shown in Box 1 on the form. However, you must report all dividends you receive even if you don't receive the 1099-DIV, for example, if you took some distributions from your small C corporation business that should be treated as dividends, not salary.

You'll also receive a Form 1099-DIV from mutual funds or real estate investment trusts (REITs) that pay dividends during the year. If the total amount of all ordinary dividends you received for 2006 from all sources is $1,500 or less, you don't have to itemize your dividends on Schedule B of Form 1040 or Schedule 1 of Form 1040A. If they totaled more than $1,500, you must complete Part II of the Schedule B or Schedule 1.

An exception to the $1,500 dollar rule applies if you received some dividends as a nominee (that is, some dividends were reported as income to you on a 1099-DIV form, but they really belonged to another taxpayer who is not your spouse, perhaps because you were joint owners of the account). In that case, you must complete Part II even if total dividends were less than $1,500; show your total dividends received, and then subtract the amounts you reported to the nominees on another 1099-DIV. The net result will be the total taxable dividends.

If you did receive dividends as a nominee, you'll have to send a 1099-DIV to the actual owner(s) of the dividends by January 31, plus a copy to the IRS along with Form 1096 by February 28. If you need to file these forms, you must use official forms printed with special, machine-readable ink – you can't use paper forms that you downloaded from the Internet and printed from your home computer.

Call the IRS at 1-800-TAX-FORM and ask them to send you copies of the official forms.

What are "Dividends"?

Some items that you might think of as interest are treated by the IRS as dividends, and vice versa. For example, distributions by money market mutual funds are considered "dividends," but ordinary distributions by tax-free municipal bond mutual funds are treated as "interest." See the discussion on page 224.

As of 1998, "ordinary dividends" you received from mutual funds reported in Box 1 of the 1099-DIV *do not* include the amount of any long-term capital gains distributions (i.e., net gains from sales of securities by the fund, which are passed through to the shareholders). Instead, your total long-term capital gain distributions are included in Box 2a, with more specific types of capital gain shown in Box 2b, 2c, 2d, and 2e. You then report these amounts directly on Schedule D, *Capital Gains and Losses*, Line 13, or to one of the worksheets indicated in the instructions to Schedule D. This allows you to more easily compute your tax at the special, lower long-term capital gains rate on Schedule D.

You must report and pay tax on the gross amount of all the ordinary dividends you were entitled to receive, even if you never actually received them because you reinvested them through a common-stock dividend reinvestment plan (DRIP) or a mutual fund reinvestment plan. If you paid any commissions or fees for reinvesting, you may be able to deduct them as investment expenses– see page 243.

Save Money

If you do reinvest dividends, make sure that you keep track of them by saving the annual statements on which they are reported. If you keep good records, when you sell the investment, you'll be able to add the reinvested amounts to your basis in the investment, and pay less in capital gains tax. If you lose your records, in some cases the issuer of the stock or mutual fund will be able to tell you what your reinvestments were, but they might not be able to locate records that go back as far as you need.

If you sold stock after a dividend was declared, but before it was paid, you are still treated as having received the dividend, and you must pay tax on it.

Nontaxable Distributions

Some of the amounts reported to you on Form 1099-DIV will not be taxable, because they are really a return of your original investment, or a return of capital. If you received this type of distribution, it will generally be reported in Box 3. Once you have received all capital you paid in to the investment, any further amounts will be taxable income.

While return of capital amounts will not appear on your tax return, you should keep a record of them, since they must be used to reduce your basis in the stock when you sell.

Stock dividends and distributions. If a corporation of which you're a shareholder pays dividends in the form of shares of stock, or spins off a subsidiary and gives all shareholders of record some shares in the newly created company, the distribution is not taxable until you sell the shares at some point down the road.

An exception to this rule applies if you receive stock or stock options or rights when you or any other shareholder had the choice between receiving such rights or cash, or when different shareholders receive different types of stock or stock options. In that case, the stock or options would be taxable at their fair market value. For more information on this subject, see the IRS's free Publication 550, *Investment Income and Expenses*.

Liquidating distributions. If the corporation is being liquidated, you may receive payments shown in Boxes 8 or 9 of Form 1099-DIV. These are nontaxable distributions to the extent that they repay your basis in the investment. If you receive more than your basis, the excess will be considered capital gains. If you ultimately receive less than your basis, you may have a deductible capital loss. See the discussion of gains and losses beginning on page 229.

Dividends on an insurance policy. Occasionally, certain forms of insurance companies send "dividends" to their policy holders, generally in years when the company has taken in more premium payments than it needs for operating expenses, reserves, and benefit payouts. These dividends are treated as a rebate of premiums you paid and are not taxable as dividends on Schedule B.

Foreign Investment Accounts and Trusts

While we're on the subject of Schedule B, if you were required to complete Part I or II of Schedule B because you had more than $1,500 in interest payments or ordinary dividend distributions in 2006, you must also complete Part III. Also, every taxpayer who had a foreign account or was a beneficiary, grantor, or transferor to a foreign trust must complete Part III.

Part III asks you to answer "yes" or "no" to two questions. The first question is, did you, at any time during the tax year, have an interest in or signature or other authority over a bank account, securities account, or other financial account in a foreign country? However, do not check the "yes" box if the combined value of the accounts was $10,000 or less during the year; if the accounts were with a U.S. military banking facility; or if you are an officer or employee of a commercial bank supervised by a U.S. agency, or of a domestic corporation listed on a national exchange or with assets of more than $1 million and with at least 500 shareholders, and you had no personal interest in the account.

Otherwise, check the "yes" box if you own more than half of the stock in a company that owns one or more foreign bank accounts, or you directly own or have an interest in such an account. This does not include foreign securities held in a U.S. securities account.

If you checked the "yes" box, you must write the name of the country or countries on Line 7b, and also file Form TD F 90-22.1, *Report of Foreign Bank and Financial Accounts,* with the Treasury Department by June 30, 2007. This is not a tax form, so don't attach it to your tax return. You can still get a copy of this form by calling 1-800-TAX-FORM, or you can download it from the IRS's website at www.irs.gov.

The second question is, did you receive a distribution from, or were you the grantor of or transferor to, a foreign trust? You may have to file IRS Form 3520, *Annual Return to Report Transactions with Foreign Trusts and Receipt of Certain Foreign Gifts.* This form can get complicated, so we suggest that you check with your tax advisor if you think it may apply to you.

Foreign Tax Credit

If you paid taxes to a foreign country, either directly or through a conduit such as a mutual fund, you may be entitled to a tax credit. Generally you have the option of claiming foreign taxes as an itemized deduction on Schedule A, or claiming the foreign tax credit on Form 1116, *Foreign Tax Credit.*

Save Time

Claiming the credit will nearly always save you more money, but this form is relatively lengthy and complicated to fill out, so it might not be worthwhile unless you've paid large amounts in foreign taxes. For more information, get IRS Publication 514, Foreign Tax Credit for Individuals.

STOCK, BOND, AND OTHER CAPITAL ASSET SALES

If you sold any stocks, bonds, options, or other securities; a home or other real estate; art, antiques, rugs, jewelry, precious metals, other collectibles, or property used in a trade or business or used to generate income; or if you had any capital gains distributions from mutual funds or REITs; you will have to complete and file Schedule D, *Capital Gains and Losses,* and file it with your Form 1040. You won't be able to use either the 1040A or the 1040EZ form.

Some of these items are first reported on another tax form, and then the results computed on that form are transferred to the appropriate line of Schedule D.

Example

Sales of property used in a trade or business, including business real estate, must first be reported on IRS Form 4797. See Chapter 7 for a discussion of the rules that apply to these kinds of assets. Form 8824 is used to report like-kind exchanges (see page 103), and Form 6252 is used to report installment sales (see page 121). All of these forms will separate your long-term gains and losses from your short-term gains and losses, and they will generally require you to transfer the amounts to Part I (short-term) and Part II (long-term) of the Schedule D. Short-term gain or loss from Form 4797, however, is transferred directly to Line 14 of Form 1040.

For special rules related to the sale of your home, see page 212.

Capital Gains Tax Rate

The advantage of capital gains, as opposed to ordinary income, is that the basic maximum tax rate on capital gains for property held for more than one year is currently 15 percent or lower. In contrast, the top four ordinary income tax rates are all higher than this, with the top rate at 35 percent in 2006.

Work Smart

Capital gains rates are, like anything else, always subject to change. This is especially true in recent years where there have been a number of tax law changes made.

For tax years ending on or after May 6, 2003, and through the end of 2010, up to four different rates could apply to long-term capital gains: 28 percent for collectible gain and gain on qualified small business stock, 25 percent for unrecaptured gain from the sale of certain depreciable realty, 15 percent for other gain, or five percent for other gain for taxpayers in the 10 percent or 15 percent income tax rate brackets. For tax years beginning after 2007, the five percent rate is reduced to zero.

There are some situations where other rates will apply to gains on certain types of property. The long-term capital gains rate on business or investment real estate (called "section 1250 property" on the tax forms) will be 25 percent up to the amount of depreciation on the property while you owned it. However, there are no losses counted in the 25 percent rate group and any loss from this group must be taken into account in computing net gain or loss in the 15 percent rate group. Also, the long-term capital gains rate on collectibles such as art, rugs, jewelry, precious metals or gemstones, stamps or coins, fine wines, or antiques is 28 percent.

For small business owners, capital gains have another advantage worth mentioning. Unlike the money you earn in your business, capital gains are not subject to the 15.3 percent self-employment tax. However, if a major activity of your business is buying or selling property that would be capital gains property in the hands of the average taxpayer–for example, you're a dealer in coins or stamps, or you're a real estate developer–you will have to treat your gains on sales as ordinary business income, reported on Schedule C rather than Schedule D. In that case, you would be subject to self-employment tax on these gains.

Computing Capital Gains

Generally, the proceeds of any stock, bond, or other securities you sold during 2006 will be reported to you on IRS Form 1099-B by the brokerage or financial institution that carried out the sale for you. The form will state the proceeds from the sale in Box 2 (except for certain futures contracts, reported in Boxes 6 – 9).

The institution may choose to report the gross proceeds, or the net proceeds (gross proceeds minus any commissions, option premiums, state or local transfer taxes, brokers' fees, etc.), in Box 2. Next to the amount reported, the appropriate box for the method used should be checked. If the broker reported net proceeds, you can simply enter the amount shown for each item in column (d) of Part I or II, Schedule D; otherwise, you'll have to check the broker's statements or other notices or documents you've received to determine the amount of commissions and other transaction costs you can deduct.

In the most general terms, your net proceeds, minus your tax basis for the item, will be the amount of capital gains you must report.

For each item you sold, you'll be asked to give a short description of the item (such as "100 shares of IBM common stock"), the date purchased, the date sold, the sales price, the cost or other basis, and the gain or loss you realized. If you run out of space on Schedule D, you can use Schedule D-1, *Continuation Sheet for Schedule D,* or you can create your own continuation sheet by repeating all the column headings on another piece of paper.

Which Asset Sales Are Reported?

Sales of inventory or other items held as stock-in-trade in your business are not considered capital assets. Sales of this type of property are reported on Schedule C or C-EZ (see page 47). Similarly, sales of accounts receivable or notes you received in the ordinary course of business are reported on Schedule C, as are any sales of copyrighted literary or musical compositions or artwork you created.

If you have a gain on property held for personal use such as a home, car, furnishings, clothing, etc. it will be taxable on Schedule D (but see page 212 regarding the exemption for gains on personal residences); if you have a loss, you can't deduct it. If you do have a loss on non-real estate property held for personal use, you don't have to report the sale at all.

Virtually any property that you hold as an investment will generate a taxable gain, or a deductible loss, that should be reported on Schedule D, or on one of the more specialized forms that feed into Schedule D:

- Form 4797, for sales of property used in a trade or business (see Chapter 7)
- Form 4684, for involuntary conversions due to casualties or theft (see page 269)
- Form 8824, if you made one or more like-kind exchanges (see page 103)
- Form 6781, if you had gains or losses from Section 1256 contracts and straddles (these are generally regulated futures contracts, foreign currency contracts, and certain options contracts, or hedging positions; for more information, see IRS Publication 550, *Investment Income and Expenses)*
- Form 6252, if you received payments for the asset over more than one year (but installment sale treatment is not permitted for stocks, bonds, and other securities sold by cash-basis taxpayers); see page 121

What Counts as a "Sale"?

Generally, if you receive money or other property in exchange for your asset, a sale has occurred and Uncle Sam will want a cut.

A redemption of stock, or a redemption or retirement of a bond, is considered a sale, and should be reported even if you have no gains or losses on the transaction (for instance, if you held a bond until maturity and received an amount exactly equal to your tax basis).

You can have a taxable gain caused by a casualty loss, although this can generally be avoided by purchasing replacement property for the items that were damaged or destroyed – see page 269 for more details.

Also, if stock, stock options or rights, or bonds that you owned became worthless, you may have a deductible loss. The "sale" is treated as occurring on the last day of the year in which the item became worthless, which means that your holding period (for determining whether the loss was short- or long-term) ends on December 31. If this applies to you, on the line where you report the sale, write "worthless" in Columns (c) and (d) of Part I or II, Schedule D, which is the space provided for the date and amount of the sale).

Save Money

If you learned this year that securities you own became worthless in some earlier year, you can file an amended tax return on Form 1040X for the year in which the investment became worthless, and deduct the loss. You must claim the deduction within seven years of the due date of your return for loss year, or within two years of the date you paid taxes for that year, whichever is later.

Bad debts. Occasionally, a taxpayer may be able to take a deduction for a bad debt not related to their trade or business. However, in order to deduct a nonbusiness bad debt, you must already have some basis in the debt – that is, you must have loaned out your cash, or you must already have included some expected money in your income. If you're a cash-basis taxpayer, you can't deduct a bad debt if someone merely reneges on a promise to pay you some income such as wages, rent, fees, interest, or dividends, unless you had already included the amount in taxable income (although you might be able to deduct the expense you had in earning this income). You should also have some documentation that the debt exists, such as a signed promissory note or loan agreement.

If you do have a deductible bad debt, you would record it as a short-term capital loss on Line 1, Part I of Schedule D. Enter the name of the debtor, and write "statement attached." Be sure to attach a statement to your tax return that shows the name of the debtor, and any business or family relationship you have with him or her; a description of the debt, the date it became due, and the amount; the efforts you made to collect it; and why you decided it was completely worthless (e.g., the debtor went bankrupt or legal action to collect would probably not result in any payment).

You can only deduct a nonbusiness bad debt in the year it became totally worthless; however, if you discover that a debt had become worthless in an earlier year, you can file an amended tax return within seven years of the due date for that year's taxes. Use Form 1040X.

Nontaxable transactions. There are a few types of transactions that are not considered taxable events. For one thing, if you redeem shares of a money market mutual fund, it's not a taxable event because the value of each share is fixed at $1. Your redemption price for each share will be exactly the same as your tax basis in each share, so no gain or loss is recognized.

Any transfer of property from one spouse to another, either while married, or incident to a divorce or separation agreement, is not taxable. Generally, the spouse receiving the property must continue using the same tax basis as the property had in the hands of the donor spouse (which means that the recipient will eventually get stuck with the capital gains tax bill when the property is sold).

Exchanging one life insurance policy for another or for an endowment or annuity contract, exchanging an endowment contract for an annuity contract or for another endowment contract that provides for regular payments beginning no later than the date on the original contract, or exchanging one annuity contract for another is not a taxable event, as long as the insured person or annuitant is the same under both the old contract and the new one.

Certain types of stock trades are not taxable events:

- exchanges of stock for other stock in the same corporation, as long as the exchange is common stock for common, or preferred stock for preferred, whether the trade is between two stockholders or between the corporation itself and a stockholder

- exchanges of stock for other stock in the same or a different corporation that occur because of a merger, acquisition, recapitalization, or some other form of reorganization, provided certain rules are followed

- conversion of a convertible bond into stock shares, or convertible preferred into common shares, according to the terms of the security

- transfers of property to a corporation in exchange for stock in the corporation, if you (or your group of investors) own at least 80 percent of the corporation after the transfer (for small businesses, this generally means that incorporating your business is not a taxable event)

Aside from these listed exceptions, you can't treat a trade of one type of stock, bond, note, beneficial interest, or partnership interest for another as a nontaxable like-kind exchange.

However, if you exchange other types of business or investment property (such as a store for an apartment building, a car for a truck, etc.), you may be able to avoid tax on the exchange if certain rules are met. In most cases we'd advise you to see a professional tax advisor to make sure that your transaction qualifies under the "like-kind exchange" rules and that you retain proper records, including the tax basis of the new property you receive, for the transaction.

What Is the Basis?

The starting point for determining the tax basis of an asset you purchased is its cost, plus any commissions or other transaction fees you pay on the sale.

If you didn't purchase the asset, determining the basis can be more complicated.

If you received property from your spouse, you'll take the same basis that your spouse had before the transfer.

If you received property in a nontaxable exchange, your basis will generally be the same as that of the asset(s) you gave up, plus any cash you added into the bargain.

If you received property as a bequest or inheritance, your basis will be the fair market value of the property on the date of death, or on the alternative valuation date if the decedent's executor chooses to use that date for estate tax purposes. Special valuation rules may apply to a farm or a closely-held business, but generally, the value shown on the estate tax return is the value that you must use. If there was no estate tax return, you may need to have the property appraised.

Save Time

For securities traded on a national exchange, you won't need an appraisal, and values are usually readily available for any date you need – consult your attorney or accountant for information.

If you received property in exchange for services, the fair market value of the property was taxable to you at the time you received it, and that FMV is the property's basis. If your right to receive the property was restricted or not fully vested, your basis will generally be the FMV at the time you no longer have a substantial risk of forfeiting it, unless you elected to pay tax on the property at an earlier point in time. For more information, see IRS Publication 525, *Taxable and Nontaxable Income.*

If you received property as a gift, your basis will generally be the same basis that the donor had at the time the gift was made. There is an exception to this rule if the fair market value of the property was lower than the donor's basis at the time the gift was made, and if you sell the property at a loss. In that case, you must use the FMV at the time of the gift.

Example

The rule described above can sometimes lead to a strange result.

Let's say your uncle made you a gift of some investment property having an adjusted basis of $10,000 at the time of the gift. The FMV at the time of the gift was $9,000. You later sell the property for $9,500. Your basis for figuring gain would be the donor's basis, or $10,000, but considering your sales price of $9,500, you would not have a gain. However, your basis for figuring loss would be the FMV or $9,000, but considering your sales price of $9,500 you would not have a loss.

In this case, you don't have a taxable gain or a loss. When reporting the sale on Schedule D, list the item's basis as being the same amount as the sales proceeds.

Adjustments to Basis

Stocks, bonds, and collectibles are not subject to depreciation deductions, unlike real estate investments and assets used in your trade or business. However, you may need to make some other types of adjustments to the tax basis of this kind of asset while you hold it.

If you deducted the amortization of bond premiums (see page 226), the deductions will reduce your basis in the bond. Conversely, if you were required to report original issue discount (OID) as income (see page 226) you should increase the basis of the bond to reflect the amounts you included as income.

If you received corporate dividends in the form of stock, the additional shares (or fractions of shares) were not taxable when you received them, but as a result of the distribution, you will have to recompute your basis in the shares you own. A similar computation is necessary if stock that you own splits. Basically, to compute the new basis of your shares, you take your existing basis in the investment, and divide it among the shares you now own as a result of the distribution or split.

Example

Flo Plummer originally bought 100 shares for a net $50 per share after commissions, so her original basis for the investment is $5,000. After several years the shares split 3-for-2, and she now has 150 shares. Her total basis has remained the same – $5,000 – but since it is now spread over more shares, her basis in each share is $33.33.

Reinvested shares. If you participate in a dividend reinvestment plan of a corporation or a mutual fund, don't forget to add the amount of all your reinvested dividends over the years to the basis of your investment. Otherwise, you'll be taxed twice on the dividends: once when you receive them as income, and once when you sell them as capital gains.

What Is the Holding Period?

As we've mentioned above, long-term gains (on property held more than one year) are taxed at a special lower rate, generally at no more than 15 percent; gains on property held for one year or less is taxed at your ordinary income tax rate, which may be as high as 35 percent in 2006. Short-term gains are reported in Part I of Schedule D, and long-term gains are reported in Part II.

Save Money

When counting the days that you held the property, the holding period begins on the day after *you bought the property, or the day after the trade date for stocks and other securities sold in an established market. This can be a trap for the unwary – try to avoid selling investments exactly one year after you bought them, or you'll end up with short-term, not long-term, gain.*

If you acquired property in a nontaxable trade, your holding period for the property will begin on the day following the date you acquired the original property that you gave up in the trade.

If you received property by gift and your basis is determined by your donor's basis (see page 232), your holding period begins when the donor acquired the property. If you must use the FMV at the time of the gift as your basis, your holding period begins when you received the gift.

If you received the property by bequest or inheritance, your holding period is always considered "long term" and you will get the benefit of the lower tax rate on capital gains even if you sell the property the day after you receive it.

Warning

If you are selling inherited property within one year of receiving it, report it as a sale of long-term property in Part II of Schedule D, and write "INHERITED" in Column (b) instead of the date you received the property. Otherwise, the IRS may question your long-term treatment.

If you sell stock that you acquired as part of a spin-off or stock dividend, your holding period begins on the same date as the original investment.

Multiple Stock Purchases on Different Days

If you've made more than one purchase of shares of the same company's stock or the same mutual fund, perhaps because you were participating in a dividend reinvestment plan, or because you were dollar-cost averaging by making regular periodic investments over an extended period of time, determining the basis and the holding period of the shares you sold can be more complicated.

If you sold the entire investment and you stopped reinvesting dividends more than a year before the sale, it's fairly simple. The entire gain will be considered long-term, to be reported in Part II of Schedule D. Just total up the costs of all the purchases you made over the years (less any transaction costs) and that will be your tax basis, to be entered in Column (e). In Column (b), write "various" instead of all the dates you actually purchased shares.

If you continued to reinvest income or make purchases up to the date of sale, you can follow the same procedure described above, except that any dividends reinvested or purchases made within the last year will be reported in Part I of Schedule D for short-term gains. Total up these dividends or purchases and use that amount as the cost basis for the short-term portion of the gains. Then multiply the number of shares (including fractional shares) purchased with those dividends by the price per share on the date of sale, and use that amount as the sales proceeds (Column (d)) to arrive at your short-term gains.

If you sold only part of your investment, and you purchased shares at various times during the year(s), you may have a choice as to which shares you can treat as the ones you sold. If, before the sale, you inform your broker or financial institution as to which specific shares you want to sell, you can treat those specifically identified shares as the ones that were sold. This gives you the opportunity to plan (some would say manipulate) the timing and amount of your gains.

Example

If, at various times over the course of several years, you purchased 100 shares of AT&T at $35, 200 shares at $42, and 100 shares at $55, and you now want to sell 200 shares, you can tell your broker to sell the most recently purchased shares. In that case, your tax basis would be 100 x $42 plus 100 x $55 = $9,700. However, if the most recent purchase was less than one year ago, you would probably prefer to tell the broker to sell the 200 shares purchased at $42, to take advantage of the lower tax rate.

If you don't specifically identify the shares of stock that you sold, the IRS requires you to assume that the shares you sold were the first ones you purchased. Since over time, stock prices tend to rise, this first-in, first-out (FIFO) method tends to result in higher gains reporting. It's not surprising that the IRS prefers it. On the upside, it will usually result in your reporting long-term gains if at all possible, rather than short-term gains.

If you own shares in a mutual fund and want to sell some, but not all, of them, it will be very difficult, if not impossible, to ask the fund in advance to sell specific shares. You can use FIFO to determine your basis and holding period for the shares you sell.

However, you can also use something called "average cost basis," which is an average of the prices you paid for all shares you own at the time of the sale. Many mutual fund companies will automatically calculate average cost at the time of the sale, and if they do, this is an easy way to report your sale. If it's not automatically calculated, however, it can be very difficult to compute.

Once you choose a method for selecting the shares you sold in a partial sale (e.g., FIFO, specific identification, or average cost), you must stick with it for that particular investment. For more information, see IRS Publication 564, *Mutual Fund Distributions.*

Capital Gains Distributions

If you own shares in a mutual fund or real estate investment trust (REIT) that pays out capital gains to shareholders every year or so, these amounts are also reported on Schedule D. The mutual fund company will report the total long-term gains on sales of securities during the year, and report them in Box 2a of Form 1099-DIV. Any short-term gains are included in the amount of ordinary dividends, and they are simply taxed as dividends.

Report your total capital gain distributions on Line 13 of Schedule D. You do not have to file a Schedule D if all of the following apply: the only amounts you have to report are from Box 2a of Forms 1099-DIV; none of your Forms 1099-DIV have an amount listed in Boxes 2b, 2c, 2d, or 2e; and you are not filing Form 4952 or the amount on line 4e of that form is zero. Instead, you can enter your capital gain distributions on Line 13 and check the box on that line. However, in that case you must figure your tax using the worksheet on page 38 of the 2006 1040 Instructions to get the benefit of the special 15 or 5 percent tax rate on capital gains.

Undistributed Capital Gains

Some mutual funds and REITs keep their long-term gains and pay tax on them, rather than distributing them to shareholders. If you've invested in one of these, you'll receive an IRS Form 2439, *Notice to Shareholder of Undistributed Long-Term Capital Gains.* Attach Copy B to your Form 1040.

Your undistributed capital gains will appear in Box 1a of the Form 2439, and it will be reported on Line 11 of Schedule D. You can claim a tax credit for the amount of tax paid by the fund or REIT on Line 70 of your Form 1040. Just check Box "a" indicating that the payment was shown on Form 2439.

Save Money

You should also keep a copy of Form 2439 in your records, so that when you sell the investment, you can increase its tax basis by the difference between the gain you reported over the years, and the tax credit you claimed. If you do, it will reduce the amount of capital gains you report for the sale.

Special Situations

There are several types of transactions or situations that call into play a number of more technical rules. In some cases, the special rules will operate to disallow the tax break for capital gains. If any of the situations discussed below (sales to related parties, wash sales, short sales, commodity sales, straddles, or gains on qualified small business stock) apply to you, you may need the assistance of a tax professional to sort out the facts and make sure that you pay the least possible amount of tax.

Sales to Related Parties

If you sell capital assets to a close family member, or to a business entity that you own or control, you might not get all the benefits of the capital gains tax rates, and you might not be able to deduct all of your losses.

Gain on sale of depreciable property. If you sell property to a corporation or partnership of which you directly or indirectly have more than 50 percent of the control, and the property is depreciable in the hands of the party who receives it, the gain will be taxed at ordinary rates, rather than the special lower capital gains tax rate.

Losses on sales or trades of property. If you sell or trade property at a loss, other than in the complete liquidation of a corporation, you can't deduct the loss if the transaction is directly or indirectly between you and the following types of related parties:

- members of your family, including your spouse, siblings or half-siblings, ancestors, or descendants
- a partnership or corporation in which you control more than 50 percent of the interests
- a tax-exempt or charitable organization controlled by you or a member of your family

Losses on sales between certain closely related trusts or business entities controlled by the same owners are also disallowed. If you sell multiple pieces of property, and some are at a gain while others are at a loss, the gains will generally be taxable while the losses cannot be used to offset the gains. What's more, when the related person or entity sells the item, he or she (or it) won't be allowed to deduct, as a capital loss, the amount of losses that were disallowed to the original seller.

Like-kind exchanges. If you trade business or investment property to a related party, ordinarily no gain or loss is recognized (under the usual rules – see page 103). However, if the related party sells the property he or she received within two years, both parties will be taxable on any gains they deferred through the exchange. This two-year rule does not apply if the sale occurred because of the death of either related person, an involuntary conversion (due to casualty loss, condemnation, etc.), or if the parties can establish that the main purpose of the exchange and later sale were not mainly designed to avoid taxes.

Wash Sales

If you sold any stock, bonds, or stock options at a loss and then purchased substantially identical securities within 30 days before or after the sale, the loss on the sale will not be deductible. Essentially, it will be ignored because your sale was a "wash." However, you can add the disallowed loss to the basis of your new investment, so that you are not in a worse position than you were before the sale. Moreover, you can add your holding period for the old stock to that of the new stock, for purposes of determining the holding period when you eventually sell the new investment.

Short Sales, Commodity Sales, and Straddles

A short sale occurs when you sell property that you don't actually have, or don't wish to part with at the present time. The sale occurs in two steps. First you make the sale, and then at some later date, you close the sale by either buying the promised property and delivering it to the buyer, or giving up some property you already own.

Generally, a short sale is taxable at the time the property is delivered (the second step, above). The amount of time you actually held the property delivered to the buyer determines whether it's a long-term or short-term gain or loss.

A straddle is any set of offsetting positions on personal property (generally, stock or other securities). For example, a straddle can consist of a call option and a put option written at the same time on the same number of shares. Generally, you can deduct a loss on one position only to the extent that it exceeds unrecognized gains you have in offsetting positions.

The wash sale rules take on special significance in the context of short sales. Moreover, numerous other technical rules apply to short sales, straddles, and to sales of options and commodities. If you are involved in any of these types of investments, we suggest you talk to your tax advisor or get the IRS's free Publication 550, *Investment Income and Expenses,* for more information.

Qualified Small-Business Stock

A special tax break is designed to help qualifying small businesses raise capital by allowing long-term noncorporate investors in original issue stock to cut the tax on their profit. If a five-year holding period is met, qualifying investors can exclude 50 percent of their gains. The nonexcluded portion is taxed at the maximum rate of 28 percent, for an effective tax rate of 14 percent (50 percent x 28 percent). However, through 2010, one-half of the excluded gain (7 percent of the 50 percent exclusion gain for dispositions beginning May 6, 2003) is a preference item for AMT purposes (see page 305).

In order to qualify for this special break, taxpayers must jump through a large number of hoops.

Qualifying for the Small-Business Stock Exclusion

The 50 percent capital gains exclusion applies only to gain on eligible stock (1) originally issued by a qualifying corporation after August 10, 1993, and (2) held for more than five years. The highlights of this break follow:

- The stock must be acquired in an exchange for money or other property (other than stock), or as compensation for services provided to the corporation (other than acting as the stock's underwriter).

- The small business must be a regular C corporation; it must have $50 million or less in aggregate capital as of the date of stock issuance; and at least 80 percent by value of corporate assets must be used in the active conduct of one or more trades or businesses.

- The corporation cannot be involved in the performance of personal services (such as health or law) or in the finance, banking, leasing, real estate, farming, mineral extraction, or hospitality industries. A number of other types of businesses, such as mutual funds and REITs, are also disqualified.

- The exclusion for each eligible corporation applies only to the extent that the gain does not exceed the greater of (1) 10 times the taxpayer's adjusted basis in the stock disposed of during the tax year (post-issuance additions to basis are disregarded), or (2) $10 million ($5 million for marrieds filing separately), reduced by gain excluded in earlier years from sales of stock in the corporation.

- Although a post-issuance purchaser of otherwise qualified stock doesn't get the exclusion, the tax break is preserved for those who receive such stock as a gift or due to the death of the original purchaser. The transferor's holding period also carries over to the transferee. Similar rules apply to qualified stock distributed by a partnership to its partners.

- Individuals can roll over, tax-free, gain realized on the sale or exchange of qualified small business stock provided that the proceeds are used to purchase other qualified small business stock within 60 days of the sale.

Netting Short-Term and Long-Term Gains and Losses

We're into the final stretch of the Schedule D, the part where you actually compute your gains and losses.

In Part I of Schedule D, you'll net your short-term gains and losses from sales of investment assets, as well as any from bad debts, casualty losses, installment sales, and like-kind exchanges, and also from partnerships, S corporations, or estates and trusts as reported on Schedule K-1 (see page 239). You'll also net any carryovers of short-term losses from previous years. By "netting" we mean that your total short-term losses are subtracted from your total short-term gains, and the result will be a net gain or loss.

Then, in Part II of Schedule D, you go through the same process with your long-term gains and losses. In Part II you are required to report separately (in Column (g)) any long-term gains or losses from art, jewelry, antiques, precious metals, etc., which are termed "collectibles," and up to 50 percent of the eligible gain on qualified small business stock (see page 236), which are taxed at a 28 percent rate. The result will be a net long-term gain or loss.

Then, you net your short-term gain or loss against your long-term gain or loss.

Gains. If the result is a gain, it must be reported on Line 13 of the 1040 Form. Then, go on to complete the rest of your 1040 Form. After you complete the rest of your income, adjustments, and deductions, and you're ready to figure out the actual amount of tax you owe, you must come back to Part III of the Schedule D to compute your taxes using the special lower rates for various types of capital gains.

Part III of Schedule D looks much more daunting that it actually is. You must follow the directions for each line, to the letter, but if you do that you'll effectively separate out any gains on collectibles and eligible small business stock, or on unrecaptured real estate depreciation, and tax them at 28 percent and 25 percent, respectively. The computations will also help you find out whether you're in the 10 or 15 percent tax bracket and, if so, tax your long-term capital gains at only 5 percent.

A note on Line 19 asks for your unrecaptured section 1250 gain, if any. This refers to depreciation you claimed on business or investment real estate over the years. If you invested in any REITs or mutual funds that invest directly in real estate, the amounts you need will be shown in Box 2c of Form 1099-DIV. If you sold any business or commercial real estate last year, you'll need to see the directions for Schedule D in order to complete this item. If you didn't receive a copy with your IRS tax package and instructions, you can get a copy by calling 1-800-TAX-FORM.

Losses. If you subtract your losses from your gains and the net result is a loss, you can claim a capital loss on your tax return. Transfer the loss amount to Line 13 of your Form 1040, and enclose it in parentheses to indicate that it should be subtracted from your other income items.

If your capital loss for 2006 is more than $3,000 (more than $1,500 for marrieds filing separately), you may not be able to deduct the entire loss. In most cases any amount above $3,000 will have to be carried over to later years, and deducted at the rate of $3,000 per year until the entire loss is used up. When you carry over a loss, it retains its character as short-term or long-term.

Save Money

When you complete your carryover loss computations, be sure to keep a copy in your records so that you remember to deduct the carryover loss next year, and so that you have proof of the amounts in case you are audited.

INCOME FROM ESTATES AND TRUSTS

If you were a beneficiary of an estate or trust in 2006, the estate or trust will have to file its own income tax return on Form 1041. Then, each beneficiary's share of income, deductions, credits and other tax items is reported to him or her on a Schedule K-1. One copy of each K-1 is filed with the estate or trust's income tax return, and each beneficiary receives a copy of his or her own K-1.

If you receive a K-1 from an estate or trust, don't file it with your tax return. Instead, each item that is separately stated on the K-1 is transferred to the appropriate section of your own Form 1040. For example, Line 1 on the K-1, "Interest income," should be transferred to Line 1, Part I, of your own Schedule B.

For the average trust, most items on the K-1 consist of interest, dividends, and capital gains and will be transferred to your Schedules B and/or D. However, if the trust operates a business or some rental real estate, income from these activities will be reported on Part III of your Schedule E, *Supplemental Income and Loss.*

The K-1 form contains line-by-line instructions as to exactly where on your tax form each item must be reported. If you disagree with the treatment or amount of any item, you'll need to take it up with the trustee or other fiduciary who prepared the K-1s, and ask them to change their treatment on the copy filed with the IRS. If you can't reach an agreement, you can file IRS Form 8082, *Notice of Inconsistent Treatment or Administrative Adjustment Request,* to explain the discrepancy.

Note that the amounts reported to you on the K-1 may be different from the amounts you actually received. If the trust instrument requires that the beneficiaries be paid all current income, each beneficiary will be taxed on his or her own share, whether or not he or she has actually received it (for example, if there is a time lag and the fiduciary did not pay the income over until the tax returns were filed).

INCOME FROM PARTNERSHIPS, LLCS, AND S CORPORATIONS

A partnership is not a taxable business entity, but while it generally pays no tax on its income, it must file a tax return with the government on Form 1065, U.S. Partnership Return of Income. As part of the Form 1065, it will include a Schedule K-1 for each partner showing his or her share of all partnership tax items. The partner then must report these items on the appropriate line of his or her tax return, generally in Part II of Schedule E

Limited liability companies (LLCs) with multiple owners are treated as if they were partnerships under federal tax law, so they will also file for 1065 and give each LLC member a copy of his or her Schedule K-1.

Warning

While the partnership will report your share of any partnership losses on your K-1, you might not be able to deduct them all. Your deductions are generally limited to your tax basis: the amount you have invested in the partnership, plus your share of any partnership liabilities, net income or gains, and minus previous distributions to you. The partnership isn't responsible for keeping track of your tax basis as time passes; you are. However, the K-1s you receive over the years will generally provide a good foundation for your records.

S corporations may have to pay some tax in certain circumstances. For the most part, however, they follow the partnership pattern of passing through most items of income, deductions, credits, etc. to the shareholders through a K-1 form. The shareholders report these items on their own Form 1040, generally in Part II of Schedule E.

Passive activities. If you own a partnership, LLC or S corporation interest that is classified as a passive activity (see page 44) and you have losses for the year, you will have to complete Form 8582, *Passive Activity Loss Limitations,* to compute your allowable passive losses. Generally passive losses are allowed only to the extent that you have passive income for the year. Any amounts that are disallowed are generally deductible in full in the year you dispose of the activity. For more information, see IRS Publication 925, *Passive Activity and At-Risk Rules,* which can be obtained for free by calling 1-800-TAX-FORM or by accessing the IRS website at www.irs.gov.

Royalty Income

"Royalties" can generally be described as payments you receive for the use of your property, that are based in some way on the number of units sold.

The two types of royalties most commonly encountered are royalties for the use of copyrights, trademarks, and patents, and royalties from the extraction of oil, gas, or minerals from your property. However, other types of royalties are possible, such as those paid for the use of a name, the sale of products using certain proprietary processes, etc. In any case, income and deductions related to your royalties are generally reported on Schedule E, *Supplemental Income and Loss.*

However, if you are in business as a self-employed artist, author, photographer or inventor, and the royalties relate to a self-created copyright, trademark, or patent, you would report the payments as part of your business income on Schedule C.

Similarly, if you hold an operating oil, gas, or mineral interest in land, you would report your gross income and expenses on Schedule C or C-EZ. Numerous special rules apply to the ownership and taxation of mineral property, and they're beyond the scope of this book. If you own any investments of this nature, we recommend that you consult a qualified tax professional for details.

Income from REMICs

A real estate mortgage investment conduit (REMIC) is basically an entity formed to hold a number of mortgages secured by property, and to pay out the income to investors.

If you hold a "regular" interest in a REMIC, your investment income is treated as interest, and it will be reported to you on Form 1099-INT and Form 1099-OID. You'll have to report any OID, or market discount that applies, under the rules for bonds discussed on page 226. The issuer should send you a notice with enough information to allow you to calculate the amounts to include in income. A "regular" interest is one that unconditionally entitles the holder to a specific principal amount. Any interest payments must be based on a specified interest rate (or formula for a variable rate) or a specified percentage of the interest on the mortgages.

Any interest in a REMIC that is not a "regular" interest is a "residual" one. If you own a residual interest, you should receive a Schedule Q from the issuer at the end of the year. Information from the Schedule Q is transferred to Part IV of your Schedule E, *Supplemental Income and Loss,* according to the instructions on Schedule Q. Don't file the Schedule Q itself with your tax return.

INVESTMENT INCOME OF YOUR MINOR CHILD

Beginning in 2006, the "kiddie tax" rules are much less favorable to minor children with investment income and their families. Unless the parent(s) of a child under the age of 18 (previously 14 prior to 2006) make a special election to include the child's income on a parent's return, the child's unearned income is taxed to the child at his or her parents' top marginal rate. The child is not allowed a personal exemption if he or she can be claimed as a dependent on his or her parents' return.

However, the child can use up to $850 for 2006 of his or her standard deduction to offset unearned income. Thus, only unearned income in excess of $1,700 for 2006 is taxed at the parents' top marginal rate. These amounts are indexed annually for inflation.

In computing the parents' top marginal rate, all unearned income of children under age under age 18 in 2006 in excess of $1,700 is added to the parents' otherwise taxable income. The result is that, in some circumstances, the unearned income of a child under age 18 may be taxed at the 35 percent rate, while the parents' top rate would otherwise (based on their actual income) be lower.

Reporting Your Child's Income on Your Tax Return

A parent may elect to include a child's income in the parent's income if the following are true:

- the child's income consists entirely of interest and dividends
- the child's income does not exceed $8,500 for 2006
- no estimated tax payments have been made in the name of the child
- the child is not subject to backup withholding

The election must be made by the due date (including extensions) of the regular tax return.

If the election is made, the parent must pay added tax of up to $85 for 2006. The $85 or whatever lesser amount the parent is called upon to pay is only what the child would have had to pay on income that is in excess of $850 and less than $8,500 for 2006.

The new kiddie tax rules do have some advantages, though. One situation in which the election might produce significant tax savings is where the parent is, for example, in the 35 percent tax bracket and cannot deduct investment interest because he or she does not have enough investment income. The election should enable the parent to treat the child's income as the parent's own investment income so that the parent would be able to make use of the interest deduction. Charitable contribution deductions also may be increased.

Another benefit would be relief from having to file the complicated "kiddie tax" form (Form 8615, *Tax for Children Under Age 14 With Investment Income of More Than $1,600*), especially where more than one child is involved. However, the election involves filing Form 8814, *Parents' Election to Report Child's Interest and Dividends*, with the parents' annual tax return.

On the negative side, including the child's income could result in a reduction in the parents' deduction for medical expenses, IRA contributions and casualty losses. Also, the income may increase family state income taxes that otherwise would not be payable absent the election.

Save Money

These new tax rules can be an unexpected burden for many families saving for college. However, the following gift-giving strategies can help reduce or even eliminate the kiddie tax and cut the overall family tax bill:

- *Buy Series EE bonds for the child and have the child elect to defer tax on the interest as it accrues.*
- *Invest the child's money in securities with low yields but strong appreciation potential. If the securities are retained until age 18 or later, appreciation during the child's younger years escapes the kiddie tax.*
- *Invest in raw land with appreciation potential.*

From the tax viewpoint, the land should be held until the child reaches age 18 or later.

- *Buy cash-value life insurance. Inside build-up from the policy will accumulate tax-free.*
- *If the child is a beneficiary of a trust, coordinate trust income with income from outside of the trust. Although this is a less attractive option, one can still accumulate trust income up to the amount taxed to the trust at the 15 percent rate ($2,050 for tax years beginning in 2006).*
- *Place UGMA and Uniform Transfers to Minors Act (UTMA) funds in tax-exempt bonds until the child reaches age 18. Tax-exempt zero coupon bonds may be a particularly good way to avoid the kiddie tax and build a college fund. Another approach is to buy stripped municipal bonds.*
- *Buy market discount bonds for the child, keeping the current yield below $1,700 (for 2006) so that the kiddie tax will not apply. When the bond is redeemed (or sold) after the child reaches age 18, the built-in discount will be taxed at the child's rates.*
- *Set up a gift-giving program that keeps the child's unearned income below the $1,700 threshold until he or she reaches age 18. For example, a cash gift to a 10-year-old child of $9,000, earning interest at eight percent, could grow over $3,000 by the time the child reaches age 18, and each year's interest will not exceed $1,300. Thereafter, the parent can set aside larger amounts for the child and continue to achieve effective family income-splitting.*
- *Employ the child in the family business or in the performance of chores supporting the payment of earned income. The income can be sheltered by the standard deduction. Even a young child can perform compensable services.*

INVESTMENT-RELATED EXPENSES

If you have investment-related income, it's likely that you'll have at least a few investment-related expenses as well. Unfortunately, many taxpayers aren't able to deduct these expenses because most of them are classified as miscellaneous itemized deductions, which are only deductible to the extent that they exceed 2 percent of your adjusted gross income.

However, if you have interest expenses related to your investments, it may be a different story. Read on to see how to deduct your interest and other expenses related to investments.

Investment Interest Deduction

The tax laws make a big distinction between interest on loans you take out for personal purposes, and loans you take out for your business, or to produce income through investments.

Interest on loans used for personal purposes is not deductible unless it's qualified home mortgage interest or, in some cases, interest on student loans.

However, you can deduct interest on loans taken out to purchase business assets or inventory, for working capital, or for some other business-related reason. Interest on business-related loans would be deductible on your Schedule C (see page 49).

If you take out a mortgage or other loans related to your ownership of investment real estate, the interest would be deductible on Schedule E (see page 218).

You may also be able to deduct interest on margin loans from your broker, or other loans you took out in order to purchase investments. These loans are the focus of our discussion in this section.

Where Did the Money Go?

It doesn't matter what, if anything, you use for collateral in order to get the loan. What the IRS is looking at is *how you spent the money*. If you spent the money on property that produces dividends, interest, annuities, royalties, or gains or losses, and it is not a trade or business or a passive activity, it will be considered "investment interest." However, you can't deduct interest on loans taken out to purchase tax-exempt investments, such as municipal bonds; on loans taken out to purchase single-premium life insurance, annuity, or endowment contracts; or on loans to purchase certain types of straddles.

Since the IRS is interested in where the money went, you need to be sure that you have a paper trail, including deposit slips, cancelled checks, or account statements (and preferably all three) so that you can prove you actually spent the money on investment property. If you took out a loan and deposited the proceeds in your bank account (for example, while you investigated a number of investment opportunities), any interest you pay is considered "investment interest" unless and until you spend the money on personal items.

We mentioned that interest related to passive activities is not considered "investment" interest. This may seem strange, considering that most people think of passive activities as precisely that – investments, rather than actively conducted businesses. However, the IRS draws another distinction between (a) passive activities, losses (and deductions) for which can only be offset by income from other passive activities, and (b) portfolio or investment assets. For that reason, you may deduct passive activity interest from passive activity income, and investment interest from investment income – the lines may never cross. For more on the definition of what is or isn't a passive activity, see page 44.

Limits on Deductible Interest

The general rule is that you may deduct interest on investment-related loans, up to the amount of your investment income for the year. If you paid more interest than the income you received, you can carry over the disallowed portion of the income to later years, when you can offset it by other investment income.

Your allowable deduction for investment interest is calculated on IRS Form 4952, *Investment Interest Expense Deduction.* You must complete this form and attach it to your return unless all of the following are true:

- Your only investment income was from interest or dividends; that is, you had no annuity or royalty income, no rental income from nondepreciable property, no equity-financed lending activities, and no interests in partnerships or LLCs licensing intangible property. In counting investment income, you must include investment income reported to you by any partnerships or S corporations on a K-1, by an estate or trust, or your child's investment income that you elected to report on your own return.
- You have no other deductible expenses connected with the production of interest or dividends.
- Your investment interest is less than or equal to your total investment income.
- You have no carryover interest deductions from previous years.

If even one of the previous statements is not true, you must complete Form 4952. Luckily, this form is relatively simple. It will ask you to add up your investment income, subtract any deductible investment expenses, and then subtract interest payments up to the remaining investment income.

In adding up your investment income, we mentioned above that you can include investment income of a child, if you opted to report that child's income on your own return. There's another option to consider, which is that you can, if you want, include some or all of your capital gains for the year, including any capital gains distributions from mutual funds. However, if you do, your deductions will offset those gains and you will lose the benefit of the lower tax rate for capital gains.

Save Money

If you're expecting to have significantly more investment income in later years, you may be better off not *including the capital gains so that you get the benefit of the lower capital gains tax rate this year. Instead, carry over the interest deduction to next year, so it offsets more of your ordinary income at higher tax rates.*

In subtracting your deductible investment expenses on this form, you only need to subtract the expenses you will actually be able to deduct; that is, expenses that exceed 2 percent of your adjusted gross income (AGI). If your itemized deductions are limited because your AGI is very high (see page 275), include only investment expenses that are left, after the limit is applied.

The total amount of allowable investment income is transferred from Form 4952 to Line 13 of Schedule A, *Itemized Deductions.*

Investment Expenses

You can deduct, as a miscellaneous itemized deduction, investment expenses you incurred to produce, manage, or collect income, dividends, gains, losses, etc. that are taxable to you.

The catch is that, like all miscellaneous deductions, the portion that is equal to 2 percent of your AGI will not be deductible. For most taxpayers, it means that these expenses are "lost." Still, it pays to look over your records and see how much you can dig up. You may surprise yourself.

What do investment expenses include? Things like subscriptions to investment on-line services; publications or newsletters; ongoing accounting or attorney fees related to the investment; investment advice; money management fees; dividend or automatic reinvestment plan fees; clerical help; the indemnity bond premium you'd pay to replace lost or missing securities; safe deposit box rent; custody fees for sponsored investment plans; trustee fees for revocable trusts; investment expenses passed through to you from an S corporation, partnership, or REMIC; and even office rent.

Some items are not deductible, but must be added to the tax basis of the investment, to reduce your capital gains when you sell: broker's commissions, state or local transfer taxes, and any fees to set up the investment.

Some items are not deductible at all: transportation to stockholder meetings, expenses of attending investment-related seminars and conventions, and expenses related to tax-exempt investments. If you have some expenses (for example, financial advisory fees) that relate to both taxable and tax-exempt income, you have to prorate the expenses and deduct only the part pertaining to taxable expenses.

Claiming Your Deduction

Your investment expenses are among the miscellaneous deductions that must be listed on Line 22 of Schedule A, *Itemized Deductions*. If you don't have room to list the categories of expenses you paid on the dotted lines following Line 22, you can attach additional sheets of paper to your return.

Chapter 14

Retirement

Because of the ups, downs, and other unpredictable changes that are part of life in a small business, sole proprietors need to plan carefully to meet their retirement needs. Having a good retirement plan allows you to build up a solid investment fund outside your business and gain significant tax benefits along the way – and as an added benefit, qualified retirement plans offer some protection from creditors should some unexpected event threaten your business and personal assets.

While we've already discussed how to deduct your contributions to a business-related retirement plan in Chapter 6, you or your spouse may be receiving payments from retirement plans from former employers, or you may have purchased a commercial annuity that provides you with income. This chapter will explain the treatment of both periodic or annuity-type pension payments, and lump-sum distributions.

If you're receiving Social Security benefits, you'll need to be able to calculate the portion (if any) that is taxable. We'll provide a simple worksheet that explains how.

And finally, this chapter discusses individual retirement accounts, a type of plan that's gotten a lot of attention because of the addition of Roth IRAs to the menu in 1998, and the enhanced availability of regular deductible IRAs.

Tax Organizer Tip

Both distributions from retirement plans including IRAs and annuities, and contributions to such plans, should be entered on the "Retirement" tab of CompleteTax.

DISTRIBUTIONS FROM A PENSION PLAN OR ANNUITY

First, a few definitions and explanations. Distributions from retirement and annuity plans can be made in several ways, depending on the terms of the plan. The typical types of distribution choices are:

- **Annuities.** Usually paid under a contract, this alternative makes regular distributions, generally in equal monthly amounts based on the life expectancy of the beneficiary.

- **Installments.** This alternative can offer a variety of payout periods and equal or unequal payments.

- **Lump sum.** This form of payout distributes the entire vested balance in one payment. It can be made in cash, in securities, or both.

Common types of annuities are:

- **Fixed period.** Distributions are made at regular intervals and have a predetermined amount and period of duration.

- **Single life.** Distributions are made at regular intervals, but payouts end at the beneficiary's date of death.

- **Joint and survivor.** The first annuitant receives a predetermined amount at regular intervals for life. After his or her death, the survivor receives a predetermined amount at regular intervals for life, which can be the same as, or different from, the original amount

- **Variable.** Distributions may fluctuate as a function of profits or economic indices, but the payout period is either fixed in duration or set only for the recipient's life. Employer-provided plans generally do not permit variable distributions, but some annuities purchased through insurance companies may.

Annuities and Pension Plan Installment Payments

Generally, amounts distributed by a qualified retirement plan or annuity are taxable to the recipient as ordinary income in the year they are received. The big exception to this rule is that if the taxpayer made any nondeductible or after-tax contributions to the plan, a portion of each payment will be tax-free, to reflect the amount of his or her contributions.

If you received pension or annuity payments during the year, you should receive an information return, Form 1099-R, from the plan sponsor. This form shows the gross amount of the payments in Box 1, the taxable amount in Box 2a, and the amount of federal income tax withheld (if any) in Box 4. If any tax was withheld, you'll have to attach a copy of the 1099-R to your tax return.

The taxable amount in Box 2a is generally the amount of income you must report on Line 16b of your 1040 or Line 12b of the 1040A, although in some cases you will need to modify these amounts. If your pension was fully taxable, leave Line 16a or 12a blank; these lines are used only if some portion of the payment represents a return of your original after-tax investment in the plan.

The plan sponsor, insurance company, or other payer will withhold federal income tax from your pension or annuity payments unless you specify in writing that you choose not to have tax withheld. If you don't want tax to be withheld on these payments (or if you need to change the withholding amount), notify the payer. You will generally be asked to fill out a form (IRS Form W-4P, or a substitute) showing your correct address and Social Security number. If there is no withholding on your pension, you may need to make quarterly estimated federal tax payments — see page 310.

Partially Nontaxable Payments

Some employment-based retirement plans are "noncontributory" — the employer pays for the entire plan on behalf of the employees. Others, such as 401(k) plans, permit employees to make voluntary, pre-tax contributions from their paychecks. Payments from either of these types of plans are fully taxable when the employee eventually receives the benefits.

However, if you, as an employee, made some *nondeductible, after-tax* contributions to the pension over the years, or if you purchased a commercial annuity with after-tax funds, you can recover the amount of your contributions tax-free over the period you are to receive the payments. A portion of each payment you receive will be nontaxable. Generally, the amount of the after-tax contributions that you received during the year will be shown in Box 5 of the 1099-R, but if your pension began before 1993, the payer is not required to compute this amount.

How is the nontaxable portion of the payment computed? It depends on the date the pension or annuity payments began. Congress has changed the rules several times over the years, so there are a number of different methods that may be applied to your situation.

If the payments began after November 18, 1996, and they are from a qualified retirement plan payable over your life, or your life and that of your beneficiary, you are required to use the "Simplified Method." You can use the worksheet below to figure your taxable annuity amount. After you have recovered your entire cost in the plan, the entire benefit will be fully taxable.

If the payments began after July 1, 1986 but before November 19, 1996, you may use the Simplified Method if the payments are from a qualified plan; you also have the option of using the General Rule Method. You may be able to switch from one method to the other within three years of your first pension year, by filing an amended return on Form 1040X using your new method for the first pension year and for each subsequent year.

If you received the payments from something other than a qualified retirement plan, such as a commercially purchased annuity or a nonqualified plan, you must use the General Rule Method. This method computes your investment in the contract as a percentage of your expected return, based on your life expectancy under IRS tables. With the General Rule Method, as with the Simplified Method, you can exclude the portion of the payments that represent your investment in the plan up to the point where you have recovered your entire cost for the plan; after that point, the entire payment is taxable. For detailed information on how the General Rule works, and worksheets and actuarial tables you can use to compute your taxable benefit amount, get IRS Publication 939, *General Rule for Pensions and Annuities.*

If the payments began before 1987, you can continue to take your monthly exclusion for as long as you receive the payments, even if you ultimately receive more tax-free benefits than the total amount of your contribution.

Simplified Method Worksheet—Lines 16a and 16b

Keep for Your Records

Before you begin: √ If you are the beneficiary of a deceased employee or former employee who died **before** August 21, 1996, include any death benefit exclusion that you are entitled to (up to $5,000) in the amount entered on line 2 below.

Note. If you had more than one partially taxable pension or annuity, figure the taxable part of each separately. Enter the total of the taxable parts on Form 1040, line 16b. Enter the total pension or annuity payments received in 2006 on Form 1040, line 16a.

1. Enter the total pension or annuity payments received in 2006. Also, enter this amount on Form 1040, line 16a . . . . . 1. ______

2. Enter your cost in the plan at the annuity starting date . . . . . 2. ______

Note. If you completed this worksheet last year, skip line 3 and enter the amount from line 4 of last year's worksheet on line 4 below (even if the amount of your pension or annuity has changed). Otherwise, go to line 3.

3. Enter the appropriate number from **Table 1** below. **But** if your annuity starting date was **after** 1997 **and** the payments are for your life and that of your beneficiary, enter the appropriate number from **Table 2** below . . . . . 3. ______

4. Divide line 2 by the number on line 3 . . . . . 4. ______

5. Multiply line 4 by the number of months for which this year's payments were made. If your annuity starting date was **before** 1987, skip lines 6 and 7 and enter this amount on line 8. Otherwise, go to line 6 . . . . . 5. ______

6. Enter the amount, if any, recovered tax free in years after 1986 . . . . . 6. ______

7. Subtract line 6 from line 2 . . . . . 7. ______

8. Enter the **smaller** of line 5 or line 7 . . . . . 8. ______

9. **Taxable amount.** Subtract line 8 from line 1. Enter the result, but not less than zero. Also, enter this amount on Form 1040, line 16b. If your Form 1099-R shows a larger amount, use the amount on this line instead of the amount from Form 1099-R 9. ______

10. Was your annuity starting date before 1987?

☐ **Yes.** STOP Leave line 10 blank.

☐ **No.** Add lines 6 and 8. This is the **amount you have recovered tax free** through 2006. You will need this number when you fill out this worksheet next year . . . . . 10. ______

Table 1 for Line 3 Above

IF the age at annuity starting date (see page 27) was . . .	**AND your annuity starting date was—** **before** November 19, 1996, enter on line 3 . . .	**after** November 18, 1996, enter on line 3 . . .
55 or under	300	360
56–60	260	310
61–65	240	260
66–70	170	210
71 or older	120	160

Table 2 for Line 3 Above

IF the combined ages at annuity starting date (see page 27) were . . .	**THEN enter on line 3 . . .**
110 or under	410
111–120	360
121–130	310
131–140	260
141 or older	210

Lump-Sum Distributions

If you received a lump-sum distribution from a qualified retirement plan, or from an annuity or endowment policy you bought from an insurance company, you may have several choices to make that can have a major effect on the tax on your benefits.

First of all, you won't be taxed on any portion of the payment that represents your cost of the plan — that is, any premiums you paid or after-tax contributions you made.

Generally, you have the option of receiving your payment in cash, or rolling it over into an IRA or another qualified plan (such as a new employer's 401(k) plan, or one established by your own business). The amount that represents your investment in the contract is not eligible for a rollover, however. The plan sponsor will report only the taxable amount in Box 2a of Form 1099-R, and that is the amount you can roll over to an IRA.

If you don't roll the payment into an IRA but receive it in cash, the taxable portion of it will be taxed as ordinary income in the year it is received, unless you are one of the few people who still qualify for any of the special tax treatments described below (capital gains treatment, or 5- or 10- year averaging). What's more, you may have to pay an extra 10 percent penalty if the distribution was made "prematurely." In any case, 20 percent of your payment will be withheld for income taxes.

If you roll the amount over into an IRA, you can generally avoid current taxation on the lump-sum, and the amount invested in the IRA will build up tax-free. However, you will be taxed at ordinary rates on all withdrawals as you take money out of the IRA, unless you elect to convert the IRA to a Roth IRA (see page 255).

Rollovers to an IRA

You can avoid current tax on some or all of your lump-sum distribution by rolling it over into an IRA account.

Work Smart

If you go this route, you'll also have the option of rolling the payment into your own small business's plan or another employer's plan at some point down the road, provided you keep the payment in a new IRA account (sometimes called a "conduit IRA") that's separate from any other IRAs you may have established.

You'll need to make the rollover within 60 days of receiving the lump sum, and you cannot revoke this decision once you make it.

If you make a direct, trustee-to-trustee rollover from your retirement plan to the IRA sponsor, there will be no income tax withholding on your lump-sum payment.

However, if you accept the lump sum in cash with the intention of rolling it over within 60 days, the retirement plan sponsor must withhold 20 percent of the payment for income taxes. In order to avoid all taxes on your lump sum, you will need to roll over 100 percent of the amount, which means that you will have to find some other source (perhaps even a loan) to temporarily replace the 20 percent that was sent to the IRS. Then, when you get your tax refund for the year, you can replenish the other source or repay the loan.

If you do roll over a lump sum you received in 2005, you will receive a 1099-R Form from the plan sponsor that shows the amount paid to you in Box 1. Report the total amount on Line 15a of Form 1040, or 11a of Form 1040A. Report any amount that was *not* rolled over on Line 15b or Line 11b (if you rolled over the entire amount, enter a zero on Line 15b or 11b). You will also need to write the word "rollover" in the margin of your tax return, next to Line 15 or 11.

If you don't roll over the entire amount and you are under age 59½, you may have to pay a 10 percent "premature distribution" tax on the amounts you took in cash – see the discussion on page 251 below.

Lump Sums Taxed as Ordinary Income

Generally, if you receive a lump sum from a retirement plan, any portion that is not rolled over into an IRA or another qualified retirement plan will be taxed as ordinary income. This can have the effect of pushing you into a much higher tax bracket than you'd usually face.

If you were born before 1936 and received a lump sum distribution from a qualified retirement plan, you may be eligible to elect optional methods of figuring the tax on the distribution which will end up saving you money. The part from active participation in the plan before 1974 may qualify as capital gain subject to a 20 percent capital gains tax rate. The election is claimed by filling out Part II of IRS Form 4972, *Tax on Lump Sum Distributions.* Any amount earned after 1973 or not reported as capital gain is treated as ordinary income.

In addition, a ten-year averaging option is available to figure the tax on the ordinary income part. The averaging treatment usually has the effect of taxing your payment in a lower tax bracket than you'd otherwise face.

If you choose the 10-year option, you'll basically figure your tax on 10 percent of the amount using a special chart based on the 1986 tax rates for a single person, as shown below. Then multiply this amount by 10 to find your total tax on the lump sum.

If you think you want to use any of the special tax methods, Part III of Form 4972 will walk you through the computations, and help you choose the method that will result in the lowest total tax bill.

10-Year Averaging Rate Table

Amount Subject to Averaging:

Over	*But Not Over*	*The Tax Is*	*Of the Amount Over*
$ 0	$1,190	11%	0
1,190	2,270	$ 130.90 + 12%	1,190
2,270	4,530	260.50 + 14%	2,270
4,530	6,690	576.90 + 15%	4,530
6,690	9,170	900.90 + 16%	6,690
9,170	11,440	1,297.70 + 18%	9,170
11,440	13,710	1,706.30 + 20%	11,440
13,710	17,160	2,160.30 + 23%	13,710
17,160	22,880	2,953.80 + 26%	17,160
22,880	28,600	4,441.00 + 30%	22,880
28,600	34,320	6,157.00 + 34%	28,600
34,320	42,300	8,101.80 + 38%	34,320
42,300	57,190	11,134.20 + 42%	42,300
57,190	85,790	17,388.00 + 48%	57,190
85,790	......	31,116.00 + 50%	85,790

Ten Percent Penalty

If you receive a lump-sum distribution under conditions that the IRS considers "premature," you may be subject to a 10 percent excise tax penalty, in addition to the ordinary income tax on the amount. You can generally avoid this tax by rolling over the entire amount into an IRA and leaving it there; just remember that nearly identical penalties apply for premature distributions from IRAs.

As a general rule, a 10 percent penalty applies for taking a lump-sum distribution before age 59½. A higher penalty (25 percent) applies for taking a distribution from a SIMPLE plan within the first two years of participation. Your 1099-R should show a distribution code of "S" in Box 7 if this 25 percent rate applies.

The 10 percent penalty does not apply to qualified plans or IRAs if the distributions are:

- made to a beneficiary or the estate of the plan participant on or after the participant's death
- made because you are totally and permanently disabled
- not more than your deductible medical expenses (those over 7½ percent of your AGI), whether or not you itemized deductions in 2006
- made as part of a series of substantially equal periodic payments, at least annually, over your life (or life expectancy) or the joint lives (or expectancies) of you and your beneficiary; if from a qualified employee plan, benefits must start after separation from service

Work Smart

If you want to take advantage of this last exception, talk to your financial planner about setting up a series of equal payments. There are a number of ways to calculate the payments that are acceptable to the IRS, and your choice among them should depend on things like the size of your lump sum and whether you need more or less cash from the plan each year.

However, once you set up a method, you must stick with it. If you deviate from your chosen method before the end of five years or your attainment of age 59½ (whichever takes longer), for any reason other than death or disability, you'll generally have to pay a recapture tax, plus interest, on all distributions received thus far.

For more on premature distributions from IRAs and some special exceptions that can apply, see page 256.

The 10 percent penalty does not apply to qualified plans if the distributions are:

- made to you after you separated from service if the separation occurred during or after the calendar year in which you reached age 55
- paid to alternate payees (such as a divorced spouse) under a qualified domestic relations order (QDRO)
- dividend distributions from an employer's securities held in an employees' trust or annuity plan
- made to correct excess deferrals, excess contributions, or excess aggregate contributions

The 10 percent penalty does not apply to payments from deferred annuity contracts *not* purchased by qualified employer plans (i.e., deferred annuities you purchased from a commercial provider) if the payments are:

- allocable to investment in a deferred annuity contract before August 14, 1982
- from an annuity contract under a qualified personal injury settlement
- made under an immediate annuity contract
- made under a deferred annuity contract purchased by your employer at the termination of a qualified retirement plan or qualified annuity that is held by your employer until you separate from service

Reporting the Excise Tax

If you owe only the extra 10 percent tax on premature distributions, and distribution code 1 is shown in Box 7 of your 1099-R, you can simply enter 10 percent of your taxable distribution on Line 60 of Form 1040. Write "no" on the dotted line next to Line 60 to show that you don't have to file Form 5329.

Otherwise, you must complete IRS Form 5329, *Additional Taxes Attributable to IRAs, Other Qualified Retirement Plans Annuities, Modified Endowment Contracts, and MSAs* and attach it to your tax return. This form is also required if you meet an exception to the tax, but your 1099-R form does not show distribution code 2, 3, or 4 in Box 7, or the code is incorrect.

TAXATION OF SOCIAL SECURITY BENEFITS

Depending on your total annual income, a portion of your Social Security benefits, or those of your spouse if filing jointly, may be subject to income tax.

If the total of your taxable pensions, wages, interest, dividends, and other taxable income, plus any tax-exempt interest income, plus half of your Social Security benefits are more than a base amount, some of your benefits will be taxable. The base amount is $0 for marrieds filing separately who lived with their spouses at any time during the year; $25,000 for singles, heads of households, and marrieds filing separately who didn't live with their spouses; and $32,000 for those who are married filing jointly. These dollar amounts are not indexed for inflation.

The amount of your Social Security benefits that you must include in taxable income depends on the total of your income plus half of your benefits. The higher the total, the more benefits that must be included in taxable income. You may have to pay income tax on anywhere from 50 percent to 85 percent of your Social Security benefits.

You can use the chart that follows to compute the amount of your Social Security benefits that are subject to tax.

INDIVIDUAL RETIREMENT ACCOUNTS (IRAS)

Individual Retirement Accounts (IRAs) function as personal, tax-qualified retirement savings plans. Anyone who works in 2006 or 2007, whether as an employee or self-employed person, can set aside up to $4,000 for the year in an IRA ($5,000 if age 50 or older in 2006 and 2007), and the earnings on these investments grow, tax-deferred, until the eventual date of distribution. Moreover, certain individuals are permitted to deduct all or part of their contributions to the IRA. As an alternative option, you may be able to set up a "Roth IRA," contributions to which are not deductible, but from which withdrawals at retirement won't be taxed.

IRAs are set up as trusts or custodial accounts for the exclusive benefit of an individual and his or her beneficiaries. You can set up an IRA simply by choosing a bank, mutual fund, brokerage house or other financial institution to act as trustee or custodian. The institution will give you the necessary forms to complete. A lesser-known alternative is to purchase an individual retirement annuity contract from a life insurance company. An individual cannot be his own trustee.

Contributing to Your IRA

The most that you can contribute to your retirement IRA in 2006 and 2007 is the smaller of $4,000, or an amount equal to your compensation includible in income for the year. Also, those who are at least age 50 in any of these years can make an additional "catch-up" contribution for the year, increasing their allowable contribution limits $5,000 in 2006 and 2007.

The same general contribution limits apply if you have more than one IRA or more than one type of IRA. The contribution must be from "compensation," which means wages, salaries, commissions, net self-employment income, and other sources of earned income. It does not include deferred compensation, retirement payments, or portfolio income such as interest or dividends. When both a husband and wife have compensation, the limit applies separately to each, so that as much as $8,000 can be contributed.

If one spouse does not work or has very little income, a married couple filing jointly may still contribute up to $4,000 for each spouse's account, as long as the couple's joint earned income exceeds their joint IRA contributions. Separate accounts must be used for each spouse.

Save Money

Starting in 2007 and through 2009, the Pension Protection Act of 2006 allows eligible individuals who are affected by an employer's bankruptcy can elect to make additional contributions to an IRA of up to $3,000. To be eligible to make additional contributions to an IRA, the following conditions must be met:

- *an individual must have been a participant in an employer's 401(k) plan under which the employer matched at least 50 percent of the employee's contributions with the employer's stock*
- *the employer must have been a debtor in bankruptcy in a preceding tax year*
- *the employer or any other person must have been subject to an indictment or conviction in a preceding tax year resulting from business transactions related to the bankruptcy case*
- *the individual must have been a participant in the employer's 401(k) plan on the date six months before the bankruptcy case was filed*

Taxpayers who elect to make additional contributions to an IRA under this provision cannot make catch-up contributions to an IRA that may otherwise be allowed for taxpayers aged 50 and older.

Form 1040—Lines 20a and 20b

Social Security Benefits Worksheet—Lines 20a and 20b *Keep for Your Records*

Before you begin:
- √ Complete Form 1040, lines 21, 23 through 32, and 34 if they apply to you.
- √ Figure any write-in adjustments to be entered on the dotted line next to line 36 (see the instructions for line 36 on page 34).
- √ If you are married filing separately and you lived apart from your spouse for all of 2006, enter "D" to the right of the word "benefits" on line 20a.
- √ Be sure you have read the **Exception** on page 27 to see if you can use this worksheet instead of a publication to find out if any of your benefits are taxable.

1. Enter the total amount from **box 5** of **all** your **Forms SSA-1099** and **Forms RRB-1099.** Also, enter this amount on Form 1040, line 20a . . . . . . **1.** ________
2. Enter one-half of line 1 . . . . . . **2.** ________
3. Enter the total of the amounts from Form 1040, lines 7, 8a, 9a, 10 through 14, 15b, 16b, 17 through 19, and 21 . . . . . . **3.** ________
4. Enter the amount, if any, from Form 1040, line 8b . . . . . . **4.** ________
5. Add lines 2, 3, and 4 . . . . . . **5.** ________
6. Enter the total of the amounts from Form 1040, lines 23 through 32, line 34, and any write-in adjustments you entered on the dotted line next to line 36 . . . . . . **6.** ________
7. Is the amount on line 6 less than the amount on line 5?
   - ☐ **No.** STOP None of your social security benefits are taxable. Enter -0- on Form 1040, line 20b.
   - ☐ **Yes.** Subtract line 6 from line 5 . . . . . . **7.** ________
8. If you are:
   - Married filing jointly, enter $32,000
   - Single, head of household, qualifying widow(er), or married filing separately and you **lived apart** from your spouse for all of 2006, enter $25,000
   - Married filing separately and you lived with your spouse at any time in 2006, skip lines 8 through 15; multiply line 7 by 85% (.85) and enter the result on line 16. Then go to line 17

   . . . . . . **8.** ________
9. Is the amount on line 8 less than the amount on line 7?
   - ☐ **No.** STOP None of your social security benefits are taxable. Enter -0- on Form 1040, line 20b. If you are married filing separately and you **lived apart** from your spouse for all of 2006, be sure you entered "D" to the right of the word "benefits" on line 20a.
   - ☐ **Yes.** Subtract line 8 from line 7 . . . . . . **9.** ________
10. Enter: $12,000 if married filing jointly; $9,000 if single, head of household, qualifying widow(er), or married filing separately and you **lived apart** from your spouse for all of 2006 . . . **10.** ________
11. Subtract line 10 from line 9. If zero or less, enter -0- . . . . . . **11.** ________
12. Enter the **smaller** of line 9 or line 10 . . . . . . **12.** ________
13. Enter one-half of line 12 . . . . . . **13.** ________
14. Enter the **smaller** of line 2 or line 13 . . . . . . **14.** ________
15. Multiply line 11 by 85% (.85). If line 11 is zero, enter -0- . . . . . . **15.** ________
16. Add lines 14 and 15 . . . . . . **16.** ________
17. Multiply line 1 by 85% (.85) . . . . . . **17.** ________
18. **Taxable social security benefits.** Enter the **smaller** of line 16 or line 17. Also enter this amount on Form 1040, line 20b . . . . . . **18.** ________

TIP *If any of your benefits are taxable for 2006* ***and*** *they include a lump-sum benefit payment that was for an earlier year, you may be able to reduce the taxable amount. See Pub. 915 for details.*

Need more information or forms? See page 7. **- 28 -**

An IRA can be established, and/or a contribution made, after year-end. It must be made no later than the due date for filing the income tax return for that year, not including extensions. This generally means that you have until April 15th of the following year to make the contribution, and to deduct it on your tax return if you qualify for the deduction.

You don't have to contribute the full $4,000 every year. You may skip a year or even several years. You may resume making contributions in a later year, but you cannot "catch up" for years no contribution was made.

If you contribute more than the allowable amount, a 6 percent excise tax penalty will be assessed. This penalty is due for the year of the excess contribution and for each year thereafter until corrected. However, you can generally avoid this tax by removing any excess contributions by the end of the tax year for which they were made.

No contributions may be made to an inherited IRA, in a form other than cash, or during or after the year in which the individual reaches age $70^1/_2$. For Roth IRAs, however, there is no upper age limit on when contributions can be made.

Form 1040A—Lines 14a and 14b

Social Security Benefits Worksheet—Lines 14a and 14b *Keep for Your Records*

Before you begin:

√ Complete Form 1040A, lines 16, 17, and 19, if they apply to you.

√ If you are married filing separately and you **lived apart** from your spouse for all of 2006, enter "D" to the right of the word "benefits" on line 14a.

√ Be sure you have read the **Exception** on page 28 to see if you can use this worksheet instead of a publication to find out if any of your benefits are taxable.

1. Enter the total amount from **box 5** of **all** your **Forms SSA-1099** and **Forms RRB-1099**. Also, enter this amount on Form 1040A, line 14a . . . . . 1. ______

2. Enter one-half of line 1 . . . . . 2. ______

3. Enter the total of the amounts from Form 1040A, lines 7, 8a, 9a, 10, 11b, 12b, and 13 . . . . . 3. ______

4. Enter the amount, if any, from Form 1040A, line 8b . . . . . 4. ______

5. Add lines 2, 3, and 4 . . . . . 5. ______

6. Enter the total of the amounts from Form 1040A, lines 16, 17, and 19 . . . . . 6. ______

7. Is the amount on line 6 less than the amount on line 5?

☐ **No.** STOP None of your social security benefits are taxable. Enter -0- on Form 1040A, line 14b.

☐ **Yes.** Subtract line 6 from line 5 . . . . . 7. ______

8. If you are:
- Married filing jointly, enter $32,000.
- Single, head of household, qualifying widow(er), or married filing separately and you **lived apart** from your spouse for all of 2006, enter $25,000.
- Married filing separately and you lived with your spouse at any time in 2006, skip lines 8 through 15; multiply line 7 by 85% (.85) and enter the result on line 16. Then go to line 17.

. . . . . 8. ______

9. Is the amount on line 8 less than the amount on line 7?

☐ **No.** STOP None of your social security benefits are taxable. Enter -0- on Form 1040A, line 14b. If you are married filing separately and you **lived apart** from your spouse for all of 2006, be sure you entered "D" to the right of the word "benefits" on line 14a.

☐ **Yes.** Subtract line 8 from line 7 . . . . . 9. ______

10. Enter: $12,000 if married filing jointly; $9,000 if single, head of household, qualifying widow(er), or married filing separately and you **lived apart** from your spouse for all of 2006 . . . . . 10. ______

11. Subtract line 10 from line 9. If zero or less, enter -0- . . . . . 11. ______

12. Enter the **smaller** of line 9 or line 10 . . . . . 12. ______

13. Enter one-half of line 12 . . . . . 13. ______

14. Enter the **smaller** of line 2 or line 13 . . . . . 14. ______

15. Multiply line 11 by 85% (.85). If line 11 is zero, enter -0- . . . . . 15. ______

16. Add lines 14 and 15 . . . . . 16. ______

17. Multiply line 1 by 85% (.85) . . . . . 17. ______

18. **Taxable social security benefits.** Enter the **smaller** of line 16 or line 17. Also enter this amount on Form 1040A, line 14b. . . . . . 18. ______

TIP *If any of your benefits are taxable for 2006* ***and*** *they include a lump-sum benefit payment that was for an earlier year, you may be able to reduce the taxable amount. See Pub. 915 for details.*

- 29 - ***Need more information or forms? See page 7.***

2006 Maximum IRA Deduction if Covered by a Retirement Plan		
If you file a single return and AGI is no higher than:	If you file a joint return and AGI is no higher than:	Maximum deduction is lesser of 100% of compensation or
$50,000	$75,000	$4,000
$51,000	$76,000	$3,600
$52,000	$77,000	$3,200
$53,000	$78,000	$2,800
$54,000	$79,000	$2,400
$55,000	$80,000	$2,000
$56,000	$81,000	$1,600
$57,000	$82,000	$1,200
$58,000	$83,000	$ 800
$59,000	$84,000	$ 400
$60,000	$85,000	$ 0

Deductible IRA Contributions

Everyone is eligible to establish and maintain an IRA, but whether your contributions into the IRA this year will be deductible depends on your (or, if married, you and your spouse's) income level and whether or not you are covered by another pension plan at work.

If neither you nor your spouse is covered under another retirement plan, you may both take full advantage of the tax deduction for the amount contributed, regardless of your income level.

If the individual making the contribution is covered under another retirement plan, the amount of the contribution eligible for deduction is determined by the filing status and adjusted gross income (AGI) of the couple, as shown on Line 37 of their Form 1040. Note that the test here is AGI–not earned income. That means that interest, dividends, capital gains, etc. are included in the total; what's more, AGI for this purpose is computed without considering the exclusion of Series EE bond interest shown on Form 8815, or the exclusion of employer-paid adoption expenses shown on Form 8839.

The table above shows the limits that apply for 2006. These dollar amounts will increase in the future. For joint returns, the phaseout threshold will increase by $5,000 per year in 2007. Ultimately, in 2007 the phaseout range for joint returns will be $80,000 to $100,000, and the range for singles will be $50,000 to $60,000.

AGI limits when only one spouse is covered. If the individual making the contribution is not covered by another retirement plan at work, but his or her spouse is covered by such a plan, the non-covered individual may make deductible contributions to an IRA. The AGI phase-out range for such contributions is $150,000 to $160,000, as shown on the following chart.

If your contribution to an IRA is deductible, you don't need to file any special form to claim it, nor do you need to itemize deductions on Schedule A. Simply write the amount of your contribution (and your spouse's contribution, if married filing jointly) on Line 32 of Form 1040, or Line 17 of Form 1040A.

Roth IRAs

As of 1998, some taxpayers can set up an IRA that is backloaded, meaning that the contributions are not deductible, but the withdrawals from the account, including all the buildup in value over the years, are tax-free as long as certain conditions are met; namely, that the withdrawals are made five years or more after the account was opened, and after you attain age 59$^1/_2$ or have become disabled.

In 2006, joint filers with income under $150,000 can make full contributions of $4,000 ($5,000 if age 50 or older) apiece to Roth IRAs; for those with income between $150,000 and $160,000, the contribution amount is phased down, until it is phased out completely at $160,000. For singles, the phase-out range is between $95,000 and $110,000, and for marrieds filing separately, the range is between $0 and $10,000.

For tax years beginning in 2007, the income limits for Roth IRA contributions will be indexed for inflation and rounded to the nearest multiple of $1,000. In 2007, for example, the contribution limit to Roth IRAs is $156,000 for taxpayers filing a joint return, $99,000 for all other taxpayers (except married taxpayers filing separately), and $0 for married taxpayers filing separately. However, the inflation indexing does not affect the phase-out ranges under present law. The phase-out range remains $15,000 for single taxpayers and $10,000 for married taxpayers.

Since contributions to Roth IRAs are not deductible, they are not reported on Form 1040 or 1040A.

Maximum Contribution When One Spouse is Covered by a Retirement Plan	
If you file a joint return and AGI is no higher than:	Maximum deduction is lesser of 100% of compensation or
$150,000	$3,000
$151,000	$2,700
$152,000	$2,400
$153,000	$2,100
$154,000	$1,800
$155,000	$1,500
$156,000	$1,200
$157,000	$ 900
$158,000	$ 600
$159,000	$ 300
$160,000	$ 0

You may be able to convert a "regular" IRA to a Roth IRA, if your adjusted gross income is under $100,000 (single or joint). The catch is that you must pay current income tax on the entire converted amount. If the conversion took place in 1998, the IRS allowed you to spread the tax over four years. The converted amount must remain in the account for five years; if it is withdrawn prematurely a 10 percent penalty will apply and any tax due on the conversion that has not already been paid (for instance, if it was to have been spread forward for four years) will become due in the year of the withdrawal.

If you make a conversion from a traditional IRA to a Roth, you must report the conversion on IRS Form 8606, *Nondeductible IRAs*. If you converted in 1998 and elected to spread the amount over four years, report this year's taxable amount on Form 1040, line 15b.

Nondeductible IRA Contributions

To the extent that you can't meet the requirements for deductible IRAs or Roth IRAs, you may still make a *nondeductible* contribution to an IRA.

However, your total annual contributions to any type of retirement IRA may not exceed $4,000 in 2006 ($5,000 if age 50 or older).

Just be sure that whatever you do, you don't mix deductible and nondeductible contributions in the same account. The earnings on nondeductible contributions will still accumulate on a tax-deferred basis, and when you make withdrawals from your account, you'll be able to receive your original contributions (but not the additional buildup in value over the years) tax-free.

To report nondeductible contributions, you must file Form 8606, *Nondeductible IRAs,* with your tax return.

Warning

If you do decide to make nondeductible IRA contributions, you should be aware that when you make withdrawals from the account after retirement, every withdrawal will be treated as if it included both taxable and nontaxable amounts. The computations of what percentage of each payment is nontaxable can become quite complicated, and you may need the assistance of an accountant or tax advisor to figure them out.

IRA Transfers and Rollovers

The shifting of funds from one IRA trustee/custodian directly to another trustee/custodian is called a transfer. It is not considered a rollover because nothing was paid over to you. You can have as many transfers as you like each year; transfers are tax-free, and there are no waiting periods between transfers. They don't have to be reported on your tax return.

A rollover, in contrast, is a tax-free distribution to you of assets from one IRA or retirement plan that you then contribute to a different IRA or retirement plan. Under certain circumstances, you may either roll over assets withdrawn from one IRA into another, or roll over a distribution from a qualified retirement plan into an IRA. Beginning in 2002, rollovers are also generally permitted from IRAs to a qualified retirement plan. If the distribution from a qualified plan is made directly to you, the payer must withhold 20 percent of it for taxes. You can avoid the withholding by having the payer transfer the funds directly to the trustee/custodian of your IRA.

To avoid tax, a rollover must be made within 60 days of receipt of the distribution. You cannot deduct the rollover contribution, but you must report it on your tax return, as follows: Enter the total amount of the distribution on Line 15a of Form 1040 or Line 11a of Form 1040A; then enter the taxable amount, if any (i.e., any amount that was not rolled over) on Line 15b or Line 11b. If you are rolling over a distribution from an employer's plan to an IRA, the distribution and the taxable portion (if any) are reported on Lines 16a and 16b of Form 1040, or Lines 12a and 12b of Form 1040A.

Rollovers not completed within 60 days can have horrible tax consequences. First of all, they are treated as taxable distributions. On top of the regular income tax on the entire amount, you may also have to pay a 10 percent excise tax penalty if the distribution was considered "premature". If you place the amount into another IRA account, you must treat it as a brand-new IRA contribution for the tax year in which it is made, and another 15 percent excise tax penalty will apply to any portion of the amount that exceeds $4,000 ($5,000 for those age 50 and above in 2006). These defective rollovers must be reported on Form 5329, *Additional Taxes Attributable to IRAs, Qualified Retirement Plans, Annuities, Modified Endowment Contracts, and MSAs.*

Victims of Hurricane Katrina who take a distribution from an IRA (or other eligible retirement plan) on or after August 25, 2005, and before January 1, 2007, may get tax-free rollover treatment if they repay the distributions within three years. Distributions are limited to $100,000 per taxpayer. The three-year period begins on the day after the date on which the distribution is received. Taxpayers who cannot avoid income tax on their penalty-free withdrawals are allowed to spread that income evenly over three years (unless they elect out of this special treatment).

A rollover from one IRA to another enables you to change your investment strategy and enhance your rate of return. It can also be used to obtain a short "bridge loan" from yourself, since you'll have the use of the funds for any purpose you want, for up to 60 days. This type of rollover may be made only once a year, but the once-a-year rule applies separately to each IRA you own. If property other than cash is received, that same property must be rolled over. Except for an IRA received by a surviving spouse, an inherited IRA cannot be rolled over into, or receive a rollover from, another IRA.

Beginning in 2007, the Pension Protection Act of 2006 allows distributions from an eligible retirement plan of a deceased participant/owner to be rolled over by a nonspouse beneficiary. If a direct trustee-to-trustee transfer is made to an IRA that has been established to receive the distribution on behalf of a beneficiary who is not the participant/owner's surviving spouse, the following treatment applies:

- the transfer is treated as an eligible rollover distribution
- the transferee IRA is treated as an inherited account
- the required minimum distribution rules applicable where the participant/owner dies before the entire interest is distributed apply to the transferee IRA; the special rules for surviving spouse beneficiaries do not apply

Withdrawals/Distributions from an IRA

In general, all withdrawals from a regular, deductible IRA account are fully taxable and reported on Line 15b of Form 1040, or Line 11b of Line 1040A. However, if you made any nondeductible contributions to IRAs over the years, a portion of your withdrawal will be treated as a withdrawal of the nontaxable cost basis of your IRAs, and no tax or penalties will apply to this portion.

Premature Withdrawals

Speaking of penalties, there are a number of rules limiting the withdrawal and use of your IRA assets. Violation of the rules generally results in taxation of the withdrawn amount as ordinary income *plus* a penalty equal to 10 percent of the withdrawal. The rules apply equally to SEP-IRAs and IRAs established under SIMPLE plans, except that the penalty for a withdrawal from a SIMPLE plan within the first two years of participation is 25 percent. Also, there are more lenient rules for Roth IRAs, discussed below.

Generally, you violate the rules if you withdraw assets from your regular IRA before you reach the age of 59$^1/_2$. However, there are a number of exceptions to these rules for cases that might be considered hardship withdrawals. If you can use any of these exceptions, you won't have to pay the penalty, but you will still be taxed at ordinary rates on the amount of the withdrawal. Also, you must complete IRS Form 5329, *Additional Taxes Attributable to IRAs, Other Qualified Retirement Plans (Including IRAs), Annuities, Modified Endowment Contracts, and MSAs,* and give the reason that the distribution is escaping from the penalty.

First, if you become disabled before you reach age 59½, you don't have to pay the additional 10 percent tax if you can furnish proof of your disability, as determined by your physician.

Second, you can receive distributions from your IRA that are a series of substantially equal distributions over your life (or life expectancy) or the lives of you and your beneficiary (or your joint life expectancies). You must use an IRS-approved calculation method, you must take at least one distribution annually, and you must continue the payment method until you reach age 59½ or for five years, whichever is longer. If you want to take advantage of this exception, consult your tax advisor or get IRS Publication 590, *Individual Retirement Arrangements,* for further information.

Third, there is an exception that allows you to take penalty-free distributions from an IRA if the amounts are used to pay medical expenses in excess of 7.5 percent of adjusted gross income, or if the distributions are used to pay health insurance premiums for yourself, your spouse, or dependents if you lost your job, you received unemployment compensation for 12 consecutive weeks, you made the withdrawals during the year you were unemployed or the following year, and you made the withdrawals no later than 60 days after you were reemployed. Self-employed persons can use this exception if they would have met all the requirements except for the fact that they could not receive unemployment benefits because they had been self-employed.

Fourth, as of 1998, you can take a penalty-free withdrawal of up to $10,000 from any type of IRA to purchase a first home for yourself, your spouse, your child or spouse's child, your grandchild or spouse's grandchild, your parent or other ancestor, or your spouse's parent or other ancestor. A "first home" actually means the person's first home within the last two years. Additionally, taxpayers who withdrew funds from an IRA after February 28, 2005, and before August 29, 2005, for a first-time home purchase but who could not complete that purchase because of Hurricane Katrina may put the funds back in their IRAs without penalty, if done by February 28, 2006.

Fifth, as of 1998, you can take a penalty-free withdrawal from an IRA that is not a Roth IRA to pay certain higher education expenses for yourself, your spouse, your children, or your grandchildren. Qualified higher-education expenses include tuition, fees, books, supplies, or equipment; if the individual is at least a half-time student, room and board are also qualified expenses.

Sixth, victims of Hurricane Katrina may withdraw up to $100,000 from an IRA (as well as a 401(k) or similar savings plan) without penalty for distributions made on or after August 25, 2005, and before January 1, 2007. Qualifying victims must have had their principal home in the Katrina disaster area on August 28, 2005, and must have sustained an economic loss. The $100,000 limit is applied for each taxpayer and not to each retirement account.

Seventh, under the Pension Protection Act of 2006, a qualified reservist distribution after August 17, 2006 from an IRA or attributable to elective deferrals under a 401(k) plan, 403(b) annuity, or certain similar arrangements are not subject to the 10 percent early withdrawal tax if a qualified reservist was ordered or called to active duty for a period in excess of 179 days.

Finally, if you make a contribution to an IRA (perhaps mistakenly), you take no deduction for it, and you withdraw your contribution before the due date (including extensions) of your income tax return for that year, the withdrawal is not a taxable distribution. However, any interest or income on the amounts (which must also be withdrawn) are treated as taxable income in the year the contribution was made. The income must be reported on Form 5329.

Withdrawals from a Roth IRA

The great thing about Roth IRAs is that qualified distributions from them are not subject to tax. The catch, however, is that you cannot make any withdrawals in the first five tax years your Roth IRA is open and, once you do make a withdrawal, it has to be under one of the following circumstances: you have attained age $59^1/_2$; you became disabled; the distribution was used to pay for qualified first-time homebuyer expenses; or the withdrawal was made to a beneficiary after your death. As long as you follow these rules, there should be no problem.

If the rules aren't followed, any nonqualified distributions from a Roth IRA may be taxable. For ordering purposes, withdrawals are first treated as coming from regular contributions (which are not taxed since you made the contributions on an after-tax basis); then from traditional IRA conversion contributions on a first-in first-out basis (treated as taxable to the extent they are included in income); and finally from earnings on contributions (considered taxable income). The 10 percent penalty for early withdrawals does not apply to qualified distributions from Roth IRAs, but may apply to nonqualified distributions unless they fall under one of the general exceptions to premature withdrawals for regular IRAs.

Taxable withdrawals from a Roth IRA are reported on IRS Form 8606, *Nondeductible IRAs.*

Withdrawals from Partially Nontaxable IRAs

If you've ever made nondeductible contributions to any of your IRAs, then whenever you take a distribution from a non-Roth IRA, part of the distribution will be treated as coming from the nontaxable part. You must compute the taxable and nontaxable portions of the withdrawals by completing IRS Form 8606, *Nondeductible IRAs,* and attaching it to your tax return. This can be a complicated process, so make sure that you follow the instructions to the form very closely.

Mandatory Withdrawals

You must begin taking distributions from an IRA (including a SIMPLE IRA) no later than April 1st of the year following the year in which you reach age 70½, or the year in which you retire, whichever is later. For any year after your 70½ year, you must take the minimum distribution by December 31st of that year. There's an exception to this rule for Roth IRAs, which carry no mandatory distribution requirements.

The amount of your mandatory distributions must be calculated under a formula prescribed by the IRS; if you take less than the required distribution, you may have to pay a 50 percent excise tax on the amount not withdrawn as required. You can always take more than the required amount (assuming you're over age 59½) but the extra withdrawals don't count towards your minimums for future years.

Uniform Distribution Period Table for Determining Required Lifetime Minimum Distributions

Age of Individual	*Number of Payout/ Distribution Years*	*Age of Individual*	*Number of Payout/ Distribution Years*
70	27.4	93	9.6
71	26.5	94	9.1
72	25.6	95	8.6
73	24.7	96	8.1
74	23.8	97	7.6
75	22.9	98	7.1
76	22.0	99	6.7
77	21.2	100	6.3
78	20.3	101	5.9
79	19.5	102	5.5
80	18.7	103	5.2
81	17.9	104	4.9
82	17.1	105	4.5
83	16.3	106	4.2
84	15.5	107	3.9
85	14.8	108	3.7
86	14.1	109	3.4
87	13.4	110	3.1
88	12.7	111	2.9
89	12.0	112	2.6
90	11.4	113	2.4
91	10.8	114	2.1
92	10.2	115 and older	1.9

Under new rules that officially went into effect in 2003, one simple and uniform table allows most participants to determine the required minimum distributions. The new table provides a uniform distribution for all participants who are the same age. The table assumes that each participant has a beneficiary who is exactly 10 years younger. Thus, a retiree determines the required annual distribution by:

- locating his or her current age on the table to obtain the distribution period, and
- dividing that number into the account balance as of the end of the previous year.

By using the uniform distribution period table on this page, most participants will be able to determine their required minimum distribution for each year based on just their current age and the account balance as of the end of the prior year.

The minimum distribution rules refer to the dollar amounts you must withdraw. You must calculate the minimum withdrawals *separately* for each account that you have (mainly because the IRS lets you have different beneficiaries on different accounts). You can actually make all the withdrawals from a single account, or spread the required withdrawals across all of your accounts in any manner you choose.

Warning

Computing minimum IRA distributions can be a rather daunting task, especially if you've established numerous IRAs over the years. Many financial institutions are willing to help you compute the minimums if you consolidate your accounts with them. Otherwise, you might consider hiring a financial planner or accountant to help you set up a withdrawal schedule, since the 50 percent penalty for making a mistake in this area is quite severe.

Special rules, too numerous to relate here, apply if your spouse is more than 10 years younger than you, your beneficiary is not your spouse and is more than 10 years younger than you, if you change beneficiaries, if your beneficiary dies or if you receive an inherited IRA account. For more detailed information, see IRS Publication 590, *Individual Retirement Arrangements (IRAs).*

Beginning in 2003, IRA trustees are required to provide account holders with a statement of their year-end account balances by January 31. In addition, the trustee is also required to state the amount of the required distribution and the date by which such amounts must be distributed. This is great news for IRA holders because it will relieve them of the burden of making mandatory distribution calculations and staying in compliance.

Chapter 15

Standard and Itemized Deductions

Throughout this book, we've discussed a wide range of deductible expenses, in the context of the type of income to which they pertain.

For example, Part II of this book dealt extensively with tax deductions relating to your small business. Chapter 11 covered deductible employee business expenses and moving expenses, and Chapter 12 covered deductions related to rental real estate, and to the home mortgage interest and real estate tax deductions for your home. Chapter 13 discussed deductions related to investment income.

In this chapter, we're going to wrap up our discussion of tax deductions, by first exploring the choice between using the standard deduction and itemizing your deductions on Schedule A of Form 1040.

Second, we'll discuss in more detail the few types of itemized deductions that we haven't covered elsewhere: the deductions for medical expenses, charitable contributions, casualty deductions, taxes other than real estate, and other miscellaneous deductions.

Finally, we'll explain how those of you in the higher income ranges may be required to cut back your itemized deductions, and suggest some ways to minimize the damage for those of you who are affected by the phaseout.

THE STANDARD DEDUCTION

Almost any taxpayer who does not wish to itemize deductions in any particular year can choose to use the standard deduction. For 2006, the standard deduction amounts for most individuals will be:

Single	**$5,150**
Head of Household	**$7,550**
Married Filing Jointly	**$10,300**
Married Filing Separately	**$5,150**

Those who can be claimed as a dependent on someone else's return must generally use a standard deduction of the greater of $850, or the dependent's earned income plus $300. However, the dependent's standard deduction may not be greater than the normal deduction for someone with the same filing status; for example, a single dependent with a lot of earned income can't claim a standard deduction higher than $5,150.

Those who are 65 years old or older at the end of the year, or who are blind, or who file jointly with a spouse who has one or both of these attributes, get a somewhat higher standard deduction. For those who are single or heads of households, being over 65 or blind merits an extra $1,250 added to the normal deduction amount; being both over 65 and blind merits an extra $2,500. For those who are married, each of these conditions for either spouse merits an extra $1,000 whether you file separately or jointly.

Example

Sarah and Jay Jackson are both over age 65 at the end of 2006, and Sarah is blind. They are filing a joint tax return. Their standard deduction for 2006 is computed as follows: $10,300 + $1,000 + $1,000 + $1,000 = $13,300.

Anna Thompson is Sarah's elderly mother, whom Sarah and Jay claim as a dependent. Anna has no earned income. Her standard deduction is $850 + $1,250 = $2,100.

Who Can't Use the Standard Deduction?

There are a very few people who aren't eligible to use the standard deduction. Most importantly, if you are married and filing separately from your spouse, and one of you itemizes deductions, the other must itemize as well or use a standard deduction of zero. This is the IRS's way of making sure you don't abuse the situation by having one spouse claim all the itemized deductions for the couple, while the other spouse claims a full standard deduction.

Others who can't use the standard deduction are nonresident aliens, or those who were both nonresident and resident aliens during the year, unless they are married to U.S. citizens or residents and elect to be taxed as residents for the year; and those who are filing a tax return for a short tax year because they are changing to a fiscal year.

Claiming the Standard Deduction

To claim the standard deduction, enter the appropriate amount on Line 40 of your Form 1040, Line 24 of Form 1040A, or Line 5 of Form 1040EZ.

If you (or your spouse, if filing jointly) are over age 65 and/or blind, you must use Form 1040A or 1040, and you'll also have to check boxes showing your status on Line 39a (Form 1040) or Line 23a (Form 1040A).

ITEMIZED DEDUCTIONS

If your deductible personal and family expenses, as defined by the IRS, add up to more than the standard deduction for your filing status, *and* you have the records to prove them, you should itemize your deductions instead of claming the standard deduction. To do that, you'll have to file Form 1040, and complete Schedule A and attach it to your tax return.

Save Time

As a general rule, most taxpayers who own their own homes will come out ahead by itemizing; those who don't are unlikely to be able to itemize unless they have extraordinary amounts of medical expenses, charitable gifts, or casualty losses during the year.

Schedule A divides your itemized deductions into six major categories: medical and dental expenses, state and local taxes, interest, gifts to charity, casualty and theft losses, and miscellaneous deductions. We'll discuss each of these categories in the next few pages.

Tax Organizer Tip

When using CompleteTax to pull together your personal tax-related information, most of the items that are discussed in this chapter should be entered on the "Deductions" tab. This includes home mortgage interest.

Investment real estate interest should be reported on the "Real Estate" tab; other investment interest should be reported on the "Investment" tab; business-related interest should be reported on the "Business" pages of the "Employment" tab; and qualified student-loan interest should be reported on the "Education Expenses" page of the "Miscellaneous" tab.

MEDICAL AND DENTAL EXPENSES

You can deduct the amount of medical and dental expenses you had during the year that were not reimbursed by insurance. You can also deduct the amount of health insurance premiums you paid out of pocket – that is, not including amounts paid by your employer, or paid with pre-tax dollars through withholding from your paycheck.

However, your medical and dental expense deduction is extremely limited in that only the portion that exceeds 7.5 percent of your adjusted gross income (as shown on Line 37 of your Form 1040) is deductible. For that reason, generally only those with severe chronic or catastrophic medical problems or those who must pay for their own health insurance will benefit from this deduction.

Save Money

For self-employed people in 2003 and beyond, 100 percent of health insurance premiums for themselves, their spouse, and dependents are deductible directly on the front of Form 1040 (Line 29), rather than on Schedule A. You're eligible to claim this deduction for any months that you were not covered or eligible to be covered under an employer's plan for yourself or your spouse. This is great news since self-employed people could only directly deduct a portion of their premiums in prior years (e.g., 70 percent in 2002).

Whose Medical Expenses Are Deductible?

You can deduct your own medical expenses, those of your spouse, and those of anyone you can claim as a dependent (see page 163 for rules on dependency status). For a married couple filing jointly, this makes it simple – you can add up both spouses' expenses, those of all your children, and those of any other dependents you are supporting in the hopes of reaching the 7.5 percent AGI limit.

However, if you're married filing separately, this means that you can deduct only those expenses that you actually pay for yourself or your spouse, and those that you actually pay for anyone claimed as a dependent on your separate return. Once again, you can see why filing separately is often unattractive for most married couples.

For divorced or separated parents, the IRS is slightly more lenient. As long as either parent can claim the child as a dependent, both parents can deduct any medical expenses they personally paid for the child.

If you are adopting a child, you can deduct expenses that you paid for the child before the adoption was finalized, so long as the child qualified as your dependent at the time the expenses were incurred or paid. If you pay back an adoption agency or anyone else (such as a birth mother) for medical expenses after the adoption goes through, you can deduct the expenses, except for those incurred before the adoption negotiations began. See also the discussion of the adoption tax credit on page 284.

Deductible Medical and Dental Expenses

- abortions, if legal
- acupuncture treatments
- alcoholism treatments, both inpatient treatments (including meals and lodging), and transportation costs to attend Alcoholics Anonymous meetings if you attend under medical advice
- ambulance payments
- artificial limbs
- birth control pills, injections, devices
- Braille books and magazines, to the extent that they cost more than an ordinary book or magazine
- capital expenses for equipment installed in your home, to the extent that they don't increase the value of your home, provided that the main purpose is medical care for yourself, your spouse or a dependent, or to accommodate the residence to such a person's disabled condition. The following are not treated as increasing the value of your home: adding entrance or exit ramps; widening doorways or hallways; installing railings, support bars, or other modifications to bathrooms; lowering or modifying kitchen cabinets or equipment; moving or modifying electrical outlets or fixtures; installing lifts other than elevators; modifying stairways; installing handrails or grab bars; modifying hardware; or grading ground or making other modifications outside doorways. However, elevators and air conditioning systems generally do increase the value of your home to some extent, and would not be fully deductible. Any operation and upkeep expenses (such as electric bills) for such capital improvements would be deductible, even if the original improvement was only partly deductible.
- car modifications to accommodate a disability, and the amount by which a specially modified car costs more than an ordinary car, but not operating expenses for the car
- chiropractors
- Christian Science practitioners
- contact lenses, including the cost of equipment and supplies to clean and maintain them
- crutches, walkers, canes, etc.
- dental treatment including x-rays, fillings, braces, extractions
- dentures, bridges, and implants
- drug addiction treatments at an inpatient facility, including room and board
- drugs if medically prescribed, and insulin, but not over-the-counter drugs
- eyeglasses and eye exams
- guide dogs or other animals to help the blind, hearing impaired, or people with other physical disabilities; including food, vet. bills, and other care expenses
- HMO premiums, deductibles, and copayments

- hearing aids
- home care, to the extent the services are of a type generally performed by a nurse; most personal or household services don't qualify unless they qualify as long-term care (see below)
- hospital services, including room and board for inpatients
- insurance premiums for policies that cover hospitalization, surgical fees, X-rays, prescription drugs, replacement of lost contact lenses, and HMOs, PPOs, etc. Long-term care policies are also deductible within limits (see below). Insurance premiums are not deductible if they are exempt from tax because they are paid under an employer-sponsored plan. However, you can deduct any deductibles, copayments, and noncovered charges under your insurance plan.
- laboratory tests and fees
- lead-based paint removal to prevent a child who has or has had lead poisoning from eating the paint (You can deduct the cost of removing or covering the paint with wallboard or paneling, but not the cost of repainting.)
- legal fees that are necessary to gain access to mental health treatment or other medical treatment, but not for the management of a guardianship estate or financial affairs
- lifetime care – advance payments for care under an agreement with a retirement home, or for treatment of dependents with disabilities
- lodging, up to $50 per night per person, while away from home to obtain medical care from a doctor or licensed medical facility, provided there's no element of vacation or lavish accommodations (You can deduct lodging for the person receiving the care and a companion.)
- long-term care contracts, if they are guaranteed renewable; have no cash surrender value; provide that refunds other than in case of death or policy cancellation may be used only to reduce premiums or increase benefits; and cover medical, therapeutic, maintenance, and personal care required by a chronically ill person under a plan of care prescribed by a licensed health care practitioner. A chronically ill person must be unable to perform at least two activities of daily living without substantial assistance, or require substantial supervision to prevent injury due to cognitive impairment. Payments from such contracts are not taxed, up to $250 per day in 2006 ($250 in 2007). Any unreimbursed expenses are deductible. Also, premiums paid in 2006 for such insurance are deductible up to the following annual amounts: age 40 or less -- $280; age 41 to 50 -- $530; age 51 to 60 -- $1,060; age 61 to 70 -- $2,830; and age 71 and above -- $3,530.
- medical information plans that keep your medical history available
- medical savings account contributions are deductible on Form 8853, *Medical Savings Accounts and Long-Term Care Insurance Contracts,* and not as an itemized medical deduction, see page 92 (Any amounts reimbursed by your medical savings account cannot be claimed as an itemized deduction.)
- medical services of physicians, surgeons, specialists, or other medical practitioners such as osteopaths and podiatrists
- Medicare Part B premiums deducted from Social Security checks, and Part A premiums for those who are not eligible for Social Security but voluntarily enroll in Medicare (Medicare payroll taxes are not deductible.)
- mentally retarded home costs, or those for similar disabilities
- nursing home costs, if the main reason for being there is to get medical care

- nursing services connected with caring for the patient's condition, as well as bathing and grooming, but not household help unless the expenses qualify as long-term care expenses (If the nursing services qualify, you can also deduct the cost of food and lodging for the nurse, as well as payroll taxes.)
- organ, bone marrow, etc. donation expenses, whether or not the donation is successfully completed
- oxygen and oxygen equipment
- psychiatric care, psychoanalysis, and psychologist counseling, but not marriage counseling
- schools, education, and tutoring costs for the blind, disabled, and learning disabled, including room and board
- sterilization
- stop smoking programs and prescribed drugs to alleviate nicotine withdrawal
- surgery that is legal and not purely cosmetic, even if it is elective
- telephone equipment for the hearing-impaired
- television modifications or special equipment for the hearing impaired
- therapy treatments, such as physical, occupational, or speech therapy
- transportation to obtain medical care, for a parent who must go with a child who needs care, or for a nurse traveling with a patient. Transportation expenses for cars can be computed as the actual cost of gas and oil, or at the rate of 18 cents per mile in 2006 (20 cents per mile in 2007); to this amount you can add parking fees and tolls. You can also deduct bus or cab fare, train or plane tickets, etc.
- weight loss programs for treatment of a specific disease
- wigs purchased for cancer patients to improve mental health, if on the advice of a physician
- wheelchairs
- x-rays, MRIs, etc.

Expenses That Are Not Deductible Medical Expenses

- cosmetic surgery including hair transplants, electrolysis, and liposuction, unless necessary to correct a congenital abnormality, an injury, or a disfiguring disease
- cost of diet food
- dancing lessons, swimming lessons, etc., even if they are recommended by a doctor
- Medicare tax payments
- funeral, burial or cremation costs
- health club dues or treatments, unless related to a specific medical condition (not general health and well-being)
- illegal operations, treatments, and drugs

- insurance premiums for life, disability, or accident insurance; policies that pay a stated amount each week if you are hospitalized; or the portion of your car insurance that covers medical expenses
- maternity clothes
- meals, unless part of inpatient care
- nonprescription medications
- trips to enhance general health even if taken on advice of a doctor
- vitamins, herbs, etc. to enhance general health
- weight loss programs to improve appearance or promote general health

STATE AND LOCAL TAXES

Generally, you don't have to pay federal tax on the amount of state and local taxes you pay. There are a few exceptions to this rule (most notably, sales tax) and a rather strict definition of what, exactly, is a "tax" instead of a license, but generally the principle holds true.

We've already discussed real estate taxes, which are deducted on Schedule C for business property, on Schedule E for rent-producing property, and on Line 6 of Schedule A for personal residence property (see page 206).

Income Taxes

The other big-ticket item among deductible taxes are state and local income taxes, in areas that have them. You can deduct all state and local income taxes that have been withheld from your paycheck during 2006 as shown on Form W-2, from your pension on Form 1099-R, from investment income on Forms 1099-INT or 1099-DIV, or from other payments on Form 1099-MISC.

Deduct tax payments in the year that you make them. If it later turns out that you get a refund, don't subtract the refund from your otherwise deductible taxes – include it as income on Line 10 of Form 1040, but only if you itemized deductions in the year to which the refund pertained.

On the other hand, if your withheld state and local income taxes were not enough to cover your tax bill for last year and you had to send in a check along with your tax return last April 15, don't forget to include the amount as taxes paid in 2006 on Line 5 of Schedule A.

State Disability Fund Taxes

If you, as an employee, had amounts withheld from your paycheck to pay taxes to one of the following state benefit funds, you can deduct the amounts: California, New Jersey, or New York Nonoccupational Disability Benefit Fund; Rhode Island Temporary Disability Benefit Fund; and Washington State Supplemental Workmen's Compensation Fund.

Foreign Income Taxes

Generally, you have the choice between deducting foreign taxes on Schedule A, or claiming a tax credit for them on Form 1116. Usually, the credit will do you the most good. See the discussion on page 229.

Personal Property Taxes

In some states, taxes are imposed on the value of certain personal property that you own such as cars, trucks, or investments. You can deduct such taxes on Line 7 of Schedule A, but only to the extent that they are based on the value of the item.

Example

Your state charges an annual motor vehicle registration tax based on 1 percent of the car's value plus 50 cents per hundred pounds. You paid $167 based on the car's value ($15,000) and its weight. You can deduct only the $150 that reflects 1 percent of the car's value.

Other Taxes

Several types of taxes might be deductible on other parts of your tax return:

- Any taxes paid as part of your business operations are deductible on Schedule C.
- Self-employment tax you paid on net earnings is deductible up to 50 percent of the amount paid, on Line 27 of Form 1040 (see page 135).
- Payroll taxes on nannies, babysitters, etc. may be deductible as part of the dependent care credit (see page 306).
- If you received income in respect of a decedent, you can deduct the portion of the decedent's federal estate tax that applied to this income as a miscellaneous deduction (Line 27 of Schedule A) that is not subject to the 2 percent of AGI floor (Line 25 of Schedule A). The decedent's executor should tell you the relevant amounts, if they apply to you.
- Any deductible taxes not included on lines 5, 6, or 7 of Schedule A can be go on line 8 of Schedule A. This is also where you would include taxes paid to a foreign country or U.S. possession, unless you claim the foreign tax credit on line 47 of Form 1040.

You can't deduct penalties, fines, or license fees paid for personal purposes such as driver's licenses, dog tags, marriage licenses, etc.

INTEREST

Two major categories of interest payments are deductible on Schedule A: qualified home mortgage interest, which is discussed on page 201, and investment interest, which is discussed on page 242.

Some other types of interest are deductible in other places on your tax return. Business-related interest payments are deducted on Schedule C (see Chapter 6), interest on rent-producing property is deductible on Schedule E (see page 218), and, as of 1998, qualified student loan interest is deductible on Line 33 of your Form 1040 (see page 290).

GIFTS TO CHARITIES

Making a gift of cash or property can be a good way to save some money on your tax bill, as well as to do some good for a cause you believe in.

You can generally deduct contributions to or for the use of qualified charities that you made during 2006, and in some cases you can deduct your out-of-pocket expenses incurred while donating your time to the charity. For small business owners, gifts made by your business should be deducted on Schedule A, not Schedule C.

Qualifying Organizations

Not all organizations that solicit your funds qualify as charities, to which gifts are deductible. Generally, only the groups listed below can qualify:

1. corporations, trusts, funds, foundations, or community chests organized and operated for charitable, religious, scientific, literary, or educational purposes or for the prevention of cruelty to children or animals, or that foster national or international sports competitions. This includes churches, synagogues, temples, mosques and other religious institutions; nonprofit schools and hospitals; groups like the Salvation Army, Red Cross, Goodwill Industries, Girl Scouts; medical research organizations; and nonprofit museums and cultural institutions
2. veterans' organizations
3. domestic fraternal societies, orders, and associations operating under the lodge system, only if used for charitable purposes
4. certain nonprofit cemetery companies or corporations, unless used for the care of a particular lot or crypt
5. the United States, a state, possession, or any political subdivision of a state, possession, or an Indian tribal government

Gifts that Don't Qualify for the Charitable Deduction

- gifts to civic leagues, social and sports clubs, labor unions, and Chambers of Commerce
- gifts to groups run for personal profit
- gifts to groups whose purpose is to lobby for law changes
- gifts to homeowners' associations
- direct donations to needy individuals or families
- gifts to political groups or candidates for public office
- cost of raffle, bingo, or lottery tickets
- dues, fees, or bills paid to fraternal organizations, country clubs, or similar groups
- tuition
- gifts made after August 15, 2006, of a clothing or household item (e.g., furniture, furnishings, electronics, appliances, linens, and other similar items) by an individual, partnership or corporation if the item has minimal monetary value and is not in good used condition or better

In most cases the charity must be a U.S. organization, but if you have Canadian income you may be able to deduct contributions to Canadian charities, and if you have income from sources in Mexico you may be able to deduct contributions to Mexican charities.

If you're in doubt about whether a particular organization qualifies for tax-deductible contributions, ask them directly, or check IRS Publication 78, which lists most qualified organizations. You can also call the IRS at 1-800-TAX-1040 to find out.

Which Contributions Are Deductible?

You can deduct outright gifts of money or property that you make to a qualified charity, or that you place in a trust for the use of the charity.

However, if you receive some benefit from the gift, you generally can only deduct the portion of the gift that exceeds the value of the benefit you receive.

Example

Jim and Shirley Jackson paid $1,000 for a table at a dinner to benefit a children's aid organization. They and eight friends attended the dinner, which would have ordinarily cost $30 per person. The Jacksons can deduct $1,000 less the $300 value of the dinners, or $700.

If you purchase items at a charitable sale or auction, you can only deduct the portion of the price you paid that exceeds the value of the item.

You can generally deduct the entire membership fee or dues you pay to a qualified organization, provided that you receive only nominal benefits in exchange, such as discounts on goods and services, free parking, and free or discounted admission to the group's events, or if you receive only token items such as mugs, T-shirts, calendars, etc.

If you make a payment over $75 that is partially in exchange for some goods or services, the organization must give you a written statement that tells you the amount you can deduct.

Donated Services

Although you can't deduct the value of your time, you can deduct the out-of-pocket expenses you incur in donating your time and efforts to a charity. The expenses must be unreimbursed, and directly connected with the services.

If you use your car in the service of the charity, you can deduct your actual cost of gas and oil, or you can deduct 14 cents per mile in 2005. However, you'll have to keep written records of the mileage you drive, the name of the charity and the purpose for which you drove, and the records should be made at or near the time you actually did the driving.

The Katrina Emergency Tax Relief Act of 2005 increases the statutory standard mileage reimbursement rate for charity work related to Hurricane Katrina from 14 cents per mile to 70 percent of the standard business mileage rate for the period beginning on August 25, 2005, and ending on December 31, 2006, rounded up to the next highest cent. The standard business mileage rate is 44.5 cents per mile in 2006. Therefore, the special mileage rate for charity work related to Hurricane Katrina is 32 cents-per-mile in 2006.

You can deduct travel expenses, including meals and lodging, if you travel away from home to perform services for a charity, or if you are a chosen representative of a qualified organization at a convention. However, you can't deduct travel expenses if you attend a convention only as a member, rather than a chosen representative. In any case, you can't deduct the costs of bringing your spouse or dependents along, and you can't deduct costs of sightseeing, parties, etc.

Foster parents can deduct any expenses for caring for their foster children that exceed the nontaxable payments they received (if any). If you host a foreign exchange student under an agreement with a qualified organization, you can deduct up to $50 for each month or half-month that the student lives with you.

The Katrina Emergency Tax Relief Act of 2005 rewards generous homeowners and renters who give shelter to Hurricane Katrina evacuees with a special tax deduction for tax years beginning in 2005 or 2006. Individuals who use their principal residence to provide housing free of charge to evacuees (referred to as Hurricane Katrina displaced individuals) for at least 60 consecutive days may claim a special $500 deduction from taxable income for each evacuee residing in the taxpayer's home. The deduction is capped at $2,000 total and may be claimed once for all tax years (which effectively limits it to providing shelter for four evacuees). The shelter must be in the taxpayer's principal residence. The evacuee's principal place of residence must have been in the Hurricane Katrina disaster area as of August 28, 2005.

Contribution Valuation and Recordkeeping

If you give cash or checks, the value of the gift is easy to determine. If the value is less than $250, you must keep a cancelled check or credit card slip, a receipt, or some other reliable written record or evidence.

If the cash gift was $250 or more, your own records won't be enough. You must get a written acknowledgement of the gift from the organization which states the amount of the gift, and the amount of goods or services you received in return (if any). For gifts made in 2006, you must get this acknowledgment before you file your tax return for 2006 or the due date of the return, including extensions, whichever is later.

If you made more than one small donation (under $250) to the same group, but the total for the year was more than $250, don't worry about getting a statement from the organization. Each gift is counted separately, unless you wrote two checks on the same day to the same organization.

If you made gifts through payroll deductions (such as to the United Way), you don't need an acknowledgement letter unless any single deduction exceeded $250. In that case, save a copy of your pay stub and also a pledge card stating that the organization does not provide goods or services in exchange for payroll contributions.

Starting with the 2007 tax year, donors of charitable contributions of cash, checks or other monetary gifts must retain certain records of the gift, regardless of the amount. Specifically, the donor must maintain either:

- a bank record
- a receipt, letter, or other written communication from the donee indicating the name of the donee organization, the date the contribution was made, and the amount of the contribution

If these records are not kept for each donation made, then no deduction is allowed for the charitable contribution.

Noncash Gifts

If you donate property to a charity, the value of the donation is sometimes difficult to determine. Generally the value of the gift is the fair market value of the property at the time of the donation, but there are some exceptions to this rule.

If you're donating used clothing, furniture, household goods, toys, books, etc., the value of the gift is the same as you would pay in a thrift or consignment shop. You should keep an itemized list of the goods you donate and, if possible, get the charity's representative to stamp or sign it; at a minimum, they should give you a receipt for the goods you donate showing the name of the charity and date.

Similarly, if you're donating a car, boat, etc., you should determine the current fair market value, and get a receipt describing the item from the charity. For donations made in 2005 and beyond, the American Jobs Creation Act of 2004 significantly increased the substantiation requirements for charitable contributions of most vehicles. Not only is donating a vehicle for tax purposes harder, it is also less rewarding for both the donor and the charity. To learn more about the pitfalls in this area, please review IRS Publication 4302, *A Charity's Guide to Car Donations*, and IRS Publication 4303, *A Donor's Guide to Car Donations.*

If you donate items from your inventory (for example, you're a restaurant owner and you donate the food for a charitable event) you can deduct the cost of the items to you, not their value.

If you donate property that has increased in value, the amount that you can deduct depends on whether, if you had sold the property, you would have realized ordinary gains or capital gains. For ordinary gains property (most property you held for a year or less, works of art you created, or inventory) you can deduct only the lower of fair market value at the time of the gift, or your basis in the property (which is generally your cost).

However, if the property would have resulted in capital gains if you had sold it, you can use the fair market value at the time of the gift. This includes stocks and bonds held for more than one year, real estate, and depreciable business property held for more than one year.

Documenting noncash gifts. For noncash contributions under $250, you need to get a receipt from the charity showing its name, the date, and a reasonably detailed description of the property. You also need to keep records showing the property's fair market value, and its cost if it has appreciated in value.

For noncash contributions of $250 to $500, you must get a written acknowledgement of your contribution from the charity, stating how much (if anything) you received in return for your gift.

If you made total noncash gifts over $500 for the year, you must complete and attach to your tax return IRS Form 8283, *Noncash Charitable Contributions.* If any single gift or group of similar gifts was valued at over $5,000, you must also get an appraisal of the item from a qualified appraiser. The cost of the appraisal itself is not a charitable contribution, but can be deducted as a miscellaneous deduction on Line 22 of Schedule A.

The American Jobs Creation Act of 2004 increased the reporting requirements for noncash charitable contributions made after June 3, 2004. For more details, please consult IRS Publication 526, *Charitable Contributions*, after it is revised to reflect the recent legislative changes.

CASUALTY AND THEFT LOSSES

If you've suffered the results of a theft, accident, fire, flood, or some other casualty during the year, you may be able to deduct some of your unreimbursed losses.

Save Money

In particular, it's important to know that if you're in an area that was declared a federal disaster area by the President, the tax deduction for your casualty losses can be claimed retroactively, by treating them as if they occurred in the previous year and filing an amended tax return for that year. This allows you to receive a quick tax refund – money that you can use right away.

Casualty losses are treated somewhat differently depending on whether the loss occurred to property used in your trade or business, property used to generate investment income, or property used for personal or family purposes. However, regardless of the type of property, the loss must first be reported on IRS Form 4684, *Casualties and Thefts.* For that reason we're going to discuss all types of casualties, both business and personal, on the following pages.

What Is a Casualty?

A casualty is a sudden, unexpected, or unusual loss or damage to some property you own. Examples of events that typically cause casualty losses are earthquakes, hurricanes, tornadoes, floods, storms, volcanic eruptions, shipwrecks, cave-ins, sonic booms, fires, car accidents, airplane crashes, riots, vandalism, burglaries, larcenies, or embezzlement. Examples of events that are not considered deductible casualties are progressive deterioration caused by age, wind and weather, wood rot, termites or other insect infestation, or drought.

Work Smart

There are situations where insect infestation can be considered a casualty for tax purposes, if the destruction was very sudden and severe. Also, drought can be considered a casualty if the property was used for a trade or business or in some other transaction entered into for profit, such as an investment in farmland.

Simply misplacing or losing property does not qualify as a tax-deductible casualty, even though your insurance company may consider it a reimbursable loss. However, if you lose property in conjunction with another accident, it may qualify. For instance, if you were involved in a car accident that scattered your property into the surrounding area and some of your jewelry was never found, you can deduct the loss of the jewelry.

Work Smart

Losses of business inventory can be treated as either a casualty loss or as part of your cost of goods sold.

Treating this kind of loss as part of your cost of goods sold will generally mean that you'll have less net income from your business, which, depending on your income level, may save you some Self-Employment Contributions Act (SECA) tax.

Measuring the Loss

First of all, only losses to your property are deductible. You can't deduct the loss of earnings if your business is damaged in a fire, nor can you deduct the loss of time you spent cleaning up after the fire (although you could deduct the cost of hiring a clean-up crew for your business, but not for a fire in your home). For personal losses, you can't deduct the extra living expenses you may have such as renting a car after your personal automobile was damaged in an accident.

How do you measure the amount of damage to your property? The IRS uses a rather conservative yardstick. You must use either the property's adjusted tax basis immediately before the loss, or the property's decline in fair market value due to the casualty, *whichever is lower.* IRS Form 4684 requires you to compare these two figures and will only allow you to deduct the smaller amount. This means that if your property has increased in value since you purchased it, you're out of luck, and you can only deduct the property's cost. However, if your property has decreased in value, your loss is limited to the lower current value.

Your adjusted tax basis for property generally is equal to the costs of acquiring it, plus the cost of any improvements, less any depreciation deductions or previous casualty losses. See Chapter 7 for more details on calculating your tax basis.

Example

You purchased a table at an auction for $100. Later you discovered that the table was actually an antique and its fair market value was $1,000. If the table was destroyed in a fire, your loss would be limited to the $100 you paid for it.

If the property was totally destroyed in a casualty, rather than just damaged, the value of the loss depends on what the property was used for. If it was used for personal purposes, the rule stated above still holds. But if it was used in a business or to produce income, you simply use the property's adjusted tax basis after the loss, minus any salvage value – the fair market value does not come into play at all.

If a single casualty or theft involves more than one piece of property, you must calculate the value of the loss separately for each item. There's an exception to this rule if the loss was to your home or other personal-use real estate. In that case, you can treat the entire property as a single item (including all buildings, improvements, trees and landscaping). But generally, each item will be listed in a separate column on the appropriate section of your IRS Form 4684.

Proving the Loss

In order to claim a deduction for your casualty loss, you must be prepared to prove it. Specifically, if your tax return is audited, you should be prepared to show all of the following:

- that you owned the property
- the amount of your basis in the property
- the pre-disaster value of the asset
- the reduction in value caused by the disaster
- the lack or insufficiency of reimbursement to cover the costs

To claim the deduction, generally, you must be the owner of the property. Therefore you can't claim a loss for the destruction of property owned by, say, your dependent parent. If more than one person owns the property, the loss must be allocated among the owners in proportion to their ownership interests. However, if the risk of loss was shifted to you by a contract, you can claim a deduction even if you didn't own the property.

Example

If the rental agreement for your office space says that you must pay for any damages to the building resulting from a casualty, then you are entitled to claim a loss deduction for the damages.

Proving the basis of business property is generally not a problem, since you should have adequate records of the property's original cost or other basis, plus any additions or subtractions to the basis, for tax and accounting purposes.

For personal property, proving the basis may be more difficult. For larger items such as your home, you should have retained the sales contract or closing documents in your safe-deposit box, but for furniture, cars, clothing, household items etc., it's quite impractical to save every sales slip. Perhaps luckily, since these items typically depreciate in value over time, their loss would generally be measured by the fair market value at the time of the casualty, not their cost basis to you.

Appraisals and Other Evidence

A professional appraisal is often the best evidence you can obtain of the value of property before and after a casualty. Ideally, the appraiser would be someone who was at least passingly familiar with your property before and after the theft, who has adequate knowledge of sales of comparable property in the area, who is familiar with conditions in the area, and who uses conventionally accepted appraisal methods.

Save Money

The cost of obtaining an appraisal is not itself part of your casualty loss, but it can be deducted as a miscellaneous itemized deduction (see page 274).

While professional appraisals are nice to have, they are not always required, especially for inexpensive items. An insurance adjuster's appraisal may do just as well. If you sell the property after the casualty, the sales price will be evidence of its fair market value (FMV).

For cars, you can often rely on "blue books" or similar sources that provide retail values for cars by age, make, model, condition, mileage, etc.

For property that has been damaged, you can use the cost of cleaning it up or repairing it to bring it back to its condition before the casualty as a measure of the difference in fair market value before and after the casualty, so long as the repairs do not actually increase the property's value above its pre-casualty value. Finally, if you have photographs (before and/or after), videotapes, an insurance inventory, any receipts or other documentation, they may all be useful in establishing the property's value.

Work Smart

You may find the IRS's free Publication 584, Nonbusiness Disaster, Casualty, and Theft Loss Workbook, *helpful if your home and personal belongings have been largely destroyed by a disaster. It goes through the house room by room and prompts your memory with lists of items commonly found in a typical home, which can also be useful in filing your insurance claim. You can get a copy by calling 1-800-TAX-FORM.*

Loss Reimbursements

If your property loss was covered by insurance, you must submit a timely claim for reimbursement with the insurance company in order to deduct any casualty losses for property damage. The exception to this rule is that if your policy requires you to pay a deductible amount, this amount counts as a loss even if you don't file a claim.

Once you've determined the amount of your loss, you must subtract the value of the insurance reimbursements you received, to arrive at your deductible casualty loss. If the reimbursements are greater than your losses as calculated under IRS rules, you may actually have a gain as a result of the casualty.

Example

If you are reimbursed on the basis of your home's appreciated value, but for tax purposes you can only claim the original cost of the home as a loss, you may experience a gain upon receiving the insurance money. You can generally avoid paying tax on the gain if you purchase qualified replacement property within two years – see page 272 below.

Insurance payments are the most common form of reimbursement for casualty losses, but you will also have to count any condemnation awards, disaster relief grants, or cancellation of disaster relief loans.

However, if you receive money to help you recover from a disaster that is not specifically earmarked for repair or replacement of damaged property, it is not considered a reimbursement for tax loss purposes.

If your insurance company pays you for living expenses because you have to move out of your damaged home, these payments are not subtracted from your casualty loss. However, you may have to declare some of the payments as taxable income, if they exceed the actual amount of the extra expenses you had.

Example

You had a fire in your apartment and had to move out for a month and stay in a hotel. Your rent is normally $500 per month, but the hotel cost $1,200. Your insurance company paid $1,000 for living expenses.

You don't have to subtract any of the payment from your allowable casualty loss. The amount by which your hotel bill exceeds your rent ($1,200 - $500 = $700) is tax-free. However the remaining $300 would have to be declared as extra income on Line 21 of Form 1040, unless you can show that your food, transportation, and other costs were $300 higher for the month because of the damage to your home.

If, at the time your tax return is due, you haven't yet received the final word from your insurance company on what your reimbursement will be, you must take a stab at an approximation, and subtract that amount. If it later turns out that you receive less than you expected, you can deduct the difference as a casualty loss on the tax return for the later year in which the insurance claim is finalized.

If it turns out that you receive more than you expected, you will have to include the excess amount in income in the year you receive it. However, if any part of your original deduction did not reduce your tax bill, you don't have to include that part of the reimbursement in your income.

Example

In December of 2006, you suffered a personal loss of $5,000 and expected to receive $3,000 from your insurance company. However, due to the application of the $100-plus-10 percent rule (discussed below), you were unable to deduct any of your loss in 2006. If, in 2007, you actually receive $5,000 from the insurance company, you don't have to declare any of it as income.

Calculating the Tax Deduction

For losses of trade or business property, or property used to produce rentals or royalties, once you've calculated the amount of your loss and subtracted the amount of your reimbursement, the remainder is your deductible loss (or gain).

For losses of income-producing property that is not described above (for example, investments such as stocks, bonds, gold, silver, and works of art), your casualty losses are added to your itemized miscellaneous deductions. All of these deductions are added together, 2 percent of your adjusted gross income is subtracted, and the remainder is your deductible amount.

Limits on Personal Losses

For thefts or casualties of personal or family property, your deductible loss is much more strictly limited. After calculating the amount of your loss and subtracting any reimbursements, you must subtract $100 for each casualty, theft, or accident you suffered during the year, regardless of the number of items that were damaged or destroyed during the event.

If you are married filing jointly, a single $100 reduction applies for each event, but if you are filing separately, each spouse who claims a loss must subtract $100, for a total of $200 per event for jointly owned property. If only one spouse owned the property at issue and you are filing separately, that spouse is the only one who can claim a deduction (and must apply the $100 reduction).

After the first $100 is subtracted, you're not in the clear yet. You must again reduce your deductible loss by a full 10 percent of your adjusted gross income as shown on Line 37 of your Form 1040. As a result, small personal casualty losses are unlikely to bring you any tax benefits.

Save Money

Casualty losses that arise in the Hurricane Katrina disaster area on or after August 25, 2005, and that are attributable to Hurricane Katrina are not subject to the above restrictions. Similar treatment applies to the Hurricane Rita disaster area after September 22, 2005, and the Hurricane Wilma disaster area after October 22, 2005. Essentially, such losses are treated as a separate deduction from all other casualty losses. Taxpayers in a Presidential Disaster Area have the option of deducting *the loss on the return for the year in which the loss occurred or deducting the loss on their previous-year returns. Elimination of the 10 percent/$100 limits will mean larger refunds for hurricane victims who amend previous-year returns.*

Mixed-use property. If you suffered damage to your home, part of which you were using as a home office, or to your car, which you sometimes used for business, you have mixed-use property and your loss must be proportionately divided between the two types of usage. You will actually treat the event as if it were two separate losses. The $100 and 10 percent of AGI reduction applies only to the personal portion of the loss. For more on casualty losses to home offices, see page 86.

Casualty Gains

If you receive insurance reimbursement that is more than your adjusted basis in the destroyed or damaged property, you may actually have a gain as a result of the casualty or theft. However, the fact that a gain exists does not necessarily mean that it will be taxable right away. You will probably be able to defer the gain to a later year (or perhaps indefinitely) if you purchase qualified replacement property.

First, in calculating your gain, remember that you can subtract from your reimbursement any expenses you incurred in obtaining the reimbursement, such as the expenses of hiring an independent insurance adjuster.

Then, if you spend the same amount as the remainder of the insurance money you received, either repairing or restoring the property, or in purchasing replacement property, you can postpone tax on the gain. However, you must make the replacement within two years of the end of the tax year in which you have the gain. If the loss was to your main home, and the area was declared a federal disaster area, you have more time: up to four years after the end of your tax year in which you have the gain.

The replacement property must be similar or related in use to the property that was destroyed. For instance, if your car was destroyed, you can replace it with another car, but not with a piano. If your home was destroyed, you can replace it with another main residence such as a home or a condo, but not with a store building. If the property was investment real estate, then other investment real estate will qualify as a replacement, but not a second home. However, if the property was business or income-producing property located in a federally declared disaster area, any business-use property will qualify.

You cannot postpone a casualty gain of more than $100,000 by purchasing replacement property from a related party, such as a corporation you control.

However, you can replace property and defer gain by purchasing a controlling interest in a corporation that owns similar property, as long as you own at least 80 percent of the stock.

If you purchase replacement property, you will have to reduce the tax basis of the new property to reflect the casualty gain you postponed.

Example

Daisy Tandy, an avid car collector, purchased a 1948 Packard convertible in poor condition at a garage sale for $1,000. After months of hard work and an additional $5,000 in car parts, she managed to restore most of the car's majesty, not to mention its chrome. To protect her labor of love and her investment, she insured the car for $25,000, with a $500 deductible.

After a freak auto accident involving her neighbor's fence, Miss Daisy's car was totaled. Her insurance company reimbursed her in the amount of $24,500 ($25,000 less the $500 deductible). So, Miss Daisy had $18,500 ($24,500 minus the $1,000 purchase price and $5,000 in upgrades) of realized gain on the involuntary conversion of the property.

Miss Daisy spent the entire $24,500 of insurance proceeds on a replacement car and thereby qualified for a deferral of tax on all her gain. Her basis in the replacement car is $6,000, the cost of her new car reduced by the amount of her unrecognized gain ($24,500-$18,500=$6,000). If she had spent less than the full amount of insurance proceeds she received, any amount between $6,000 (the original cost of the car plus restoration costs) and $24,500 would be recognized as taxable gain.

Reporting a Loss or Gain on Your Tax Return

If you have a loss to personal-use property, you must fill out Section A of Form 4684. Each item is reported in a separate column on this form (if a large number of items were lost or damaged, you can use reasonable categories such as "clothing," "jewelry," "furniture," etc. Separate copies of Form 4684 must be used if you suffered more than one casualty during the year; transfer the amounts from Line 12 of all the forms you used to Line 13 on one of the forms and use that as the "master" for the remainder of the questions. Ultimately, you will transfer the loss amount to Schedule A as an itemized casualty loss deduction.

If you have a taxable gain as a result of a casualty to personal-use property, use Section A of Form 4684, and transfer the gain amount to Schedule D, *Capital Gains and Losses.* The gain will be treated as short-term or long-term, depending on whether you held the property for one year or less, or for more than one year. If you elect to defer gain by purchasing qualified replacement property, you won't have to transfer the gain to Schedule D, but you must attach a statement to your tax return explaining the date and details of the casualty or theft, the amount of insurance, how you figured the gain, and that you are choosing to postpone gain by purchasing replacement property.

If you've already done the replacing, include information about the property, the postponed gain, the basis adjustment that reflects the postponed gain, and any remaining (unpostponed gain) you are reporting on Schedule D. If you make the replacement in a later year, attach a statement including this information about the replacement property to the tax return for that later year. If you expected to replace property but then didn't, or replaced at less than the full amount, you'll have to go back and amend your tax return for the year you claimed the loss.

Save Money

If you are in a position to realize a potential gain on property located in the New York Liberty Zone (essentially southern Manhattan) due to the terrorist attacks of September 11, 2001, the period in which you must purchase replacement property may be extended until five years after the end of the first tax year in which any part of the gain is realized. The five-year period only applies, though, if substantially all of the use of the replacement property occurs in the city of New York. Otherwise, the usual two-year replacement period for trade or business property applies.

Similar treatment applies to the Hurricane Katrina disaster area replacement property.

For more details on how to postpone gain in this situation, see IRS Publication 547, Casualties, Disasters, and Thefts. Business or Income Property.

Business or Income Property

If you had a loss to income-producing property, complete Section B of Form 4684, and transfer the loss to Schedule A as a miscellaneous itemized deduction.

If you had a gain to income-producing property, or if you had a gain or loss to trade or business property or rental or royalty property, complete Section B of Form 4684 and then transfer the gain or loss to Form 4797, *Sales of Business Property.* Again, you can elect to postpone tax on the gains by purchasing replacement property and attaching a statement to that effect to your tax return, as described above under "Reporting a Loss or Gain on Your Tax Return."

Timing the Deduction

Casualty losses must generally be deducted in the tax year in which the loss event occurred. However, if you suffered a loss in a presidentially declared federal disaster area, you may deduct your loss in the preceding year. To do this, you must file an amended tax return for the preceding year, and figure the loss and the change in taxes exactly as if the loss actually occurred in that preceding year. If you did not itemize your deductions in that preceding year, you can go back and add any other itemized deductions (such as mortgage interest, taxes, charitable contributions, etc.) that you would have been able to deduct in that year. You generally must make this choice by the due date (not including extensions) for the tax return of the year that the loss actually occurred.

Save Money

If your losses were very large, and exceed your income for the year, you may have a net operating loss (NOL) for the year. You can use an NOL to lower your taxes for a previous year, allowing you to get a tax refund for the earlier year. You don't have to be in business to claim an NOL due to a casualty or theft loss, but the rules for claiming NOLs are fairly complex, and we recommend that you consult your tax advisor for advice on the mechanics of amending your prior year's return to claim this deduction.

Miscellaneous Itemized Deductions

We've already discussed two categories of miscellaneous

itemized deductions: Chapter 11 covered deductible employee business expenses, and Chapter 13 discussed deductions related to investment income. For people who have them, these are usually the biggest-ticket items under the "miscellaneous" umbrella. Line 20 of Schedule A is used to report employee business expenses transferred from Form 2106 or 2106-EZ, and Line 22 is used to report investment expenses. We've also discussed hobby expenses in Chapter 4 – hobby expenses are deductible on Line 22 as well. However, there are a number of other things that count as miscellaneous itemized deductions.

Job Search Expenses

Expenses that you pay in looking for another job in your present occupation can be deducted, even if you don't find a new job. However, you can't deduct the expenses of looking for your first job or a job after you've been out of the workforce for an extended period of time. You also can't deduct expenses of seeking the first job in a new occupation.

If your job search qualifies, you can deduct costs for things like writing, printing, and distributing a resume; using an employment agency, outplacement agency or career counselor; and for traveling to interviews or to a different city to look for work. If you use the standard mileage rate to deduct car expenses, use the business rate (44.5 cents per mile in 2006; 48.5 cents per mile in 2007.

Tax Preparation Expenses

You can deduct, as a miscellaneous expense, amounts that you pay to determine the amount of any tax due, to pay the tax, or to claim a refund or contest the amount of tax due. This applies to federal income tax, as well as any other type of tax that you pay.

So, you can deduct the cost of purchasing books like this one, of copying your tax returns, and even postage costs for obtaining a return receipt when you mail your tax forms. If you pay a fee to file your tax return electronically, you can deduct that cost. If you get professional help in preparing your return or in obtaining appraisals needed to determine the amount of tax due, you can deduct those fees.

Investment-Related Deductions

You can deduct, as a miscellaneous itemized deduction, investment expenses you incurred to produce, manage, or collect income, dividends, gains, losses, etc. that are taxable to you. These expenses are discussed in more detail at the end of Chapter 13.

The Two Percent Limit

All of the miscellaneous expenses we've discussed so far are subject to the 2 percent of adjusted gross income (AGI) limit. That is, you must total up all your allowable expenses, and subtract 2 percent of your AGI as shown on Line 37 of your Form 1040. If anything remains, that is the amount you can deduct as an itemized deduction on Line 26 of Schedule A.

Items Not Subject to the Limit

There are a few types of miscellaneous deductions that are not subject to the 2 percent limit. If you have any of these, they are totaled up and reported on Line 27 of your Schedule A. They are:

- amortizable premiums on taxable bonds (see page 226)
- federal estate tax that was paid on income in respect of a decedent (see page 171)
- gambling losses, up to the amount of gambling winnings (the full amount of winnings are reported as income on Line 21 of Form 1040)
- impairment-related work expenses of persons with disabilities
- repayments you had to make of income you reported in earlier years, if more than $3,000
- unrecovered investment in a pension

The Limit on Itemized Deductions

Unfortunately, at higher levels of income, your hard-won and carefully documented itemized deductions will be phased out, and you won't be able to deduct them in the current year–or ever.

As we noted on page 169, this is true of personal exemptions as well. However, while personal exemptions can be phased out completely if your income is high enough, the situation with itemized deductions is a little better–they won't be reduced by more than 80 percent.

Save Money

Regardless of whether your itemized deductions are phased out, you always have the option of using the standard deduction for your filing status, which remains the same no matter how high your income rises.

Income Levels that Trigger the Phaseout

The adjusted gross income (AGI) levels at which the phaseout of itemized deductions begins are adjusted annually for inflation. For 2006, they are:

- $150,500 for singles, heads of households, and married people filing jointly
- $75,250 for marrieds filing separately

If your AGI as shown on Line 37 of your tax return is higher than the applicable threshold, you have to subtract the threshold amount from your income. The remaining amount of AGI is multiplied by 3 percent. The answer you get is subtracted from the total amount of affected deductions, and you can only deduct the remainder. However, in no event will your deductions be reduced by more than 80 percent of their value.

Note that whatever limits are applicable to the particular type of deduction (for example, the $100,000 limit on home equity loans, or the two percent limit for miscellaneous deductions) are applied first, before computing the amount of the phaseout.

Deductions Subject to the Phaseout

Not all deductions are affected by the phaseout, but most of the larger ones are:

- home mortgage interest
- taxes
- charitable contributions
- miscellaneous itemized deductions that are subject to the 2 percent limit, including employee business expenses
- federal estate tax in respect of a decedent
- impairment-related work expenses
- amortizable bond premiums on bonds acquired before 10/23/86
- unrecovered investment in a pension
- repayments of income previously taxed

Deductions Not Subject to the Phaseout

- medical and dental expenses
- gambling losses
- investment interest expenses
- nonbusiness casualty and theft losses

Case Study

Boris and Natasha are married taxpayers who file jointly. In 2006 they had adjusted gross income (AGI) of $339,450 and itemized deductions of $23,700. Their only allowable deductions were for home mortgage interest, real estate taxes, and charitable contributions.

Boris and Natasha can deduct only $17,797.50, computed as follows:

AGI	$339,450
Less: threshold amount	-150,500
Excess over threshold:	$188,950
Multiplier	x .03
Reduction required	$ 5,668.50
Unreduced deductions	$ 23,700
Less: reduction required	- 5,668.50
Deductions that may be claimed:	$18,031.50

Minimizing the Effect of the Phaseout

If your family income is high enough to be affected by the phaseout of itemized deductions, your marginal tax rate may actually be several percentage points higher than the rates shown on page 15. The negative effects of the phaseout can sometimes be reduced by careful tax planning.

Reduce Taxable Income

The most basic strategy, of course, would be to reduce your adjusted gross income below the threshold for your filing status. Business owners can do this more easily than other taxpayers, because their ability to plow earnings back into the business is virtually unlimited.

Some other simple ways of doing this include maximizing your contributions to any retirement plans available to you, or to a nondeductible IRA or Roth IRA. While these IRA contributions won't lower your AGI for the current year, they will lower your taxable income in the future because earnings on the accounts are tax-free.

Another simple strategy is to receive investment income in a nontaxable form, by investing in tax-free municipal bonds. You might also decide to invest more heavily in non-dividend paying growth stocks, to avoid receiving currently taxable dividends.

You may also want to consult a financial planner or tax expert who can suggest more specific ways to trim your current income, including various family income-splitting tactics, charitable remainder trusts, etc.

Reverse Planning for Deductions

If it looks as if you're going to lose some percentage of your deductions anyway, you might want to reduce some of your deductible expenses. In particular, consider paying down your home mortgage or refinancing it at a cheaper rate, since the interest deduction is less valuable to you.

If, like many business owners, your income fluctuates from year to year, you might be able to pay for more deductible expenses in years when you have lower income and the deductions are less likely to be reduced.

Example

Charitable gifts should be made in January of a low-income year, rather than in December of a high-income year.

Chapter 16

Tax Credits and Miscellaneous Issues for Families

So far, we've discussed most of the tax issues that affect you in your capacity as a business owner, an employee, an investor, a homeowner, or a retiree.

In this chapter, we're going to tie up the loose ends by discussing a number of tax issues that pertain primarily to your family situation. First, we'll discuss the treatment of alimony, which is deductible by the person who pays it and is taxable to the person who receives it.

Next, we're going to cover a number of special tax breaks based on your family situation, including the newly increased $1,000-per-child tax credit, the adoption expense exemption and credit that were added in 1997, and the credit for the elderly and the disabled.

We'll also discuss the tax breaks for education, including the Hope Scholarship credit, the Lifetime Learning credit, education IRAs, and the exclusion of interest on certain student loans. We'll conclude with a discussion of the earned income credit for lower-income families and individuals.

Tax Organizer Tip

Information regarding any alimony, separate maintenance, adoption expenses, or education expenses that qualify for the Hope Scholarship, Lifetime Learning credits or Tuition and Fees Deduction can be entered in CompleteTax on the "Miscellaneous" tab. You can also enter qualifying educator expenses on the "Miscellaneous" tab.

The Child Tax Credit and the Earned Income Credit will be automatically calculated based upon your entries for dependents and income as entered in CompleteTax.

ALIMONY

There are basically three ways in which money or property can change hands between divorced or divorcing spouses: child support, alimony, and division of property.

Two of these methods (child support payments and division of property) are generally non-events in terms of your taxes. Child support payments don't affect your taxes at all, unless you fall behind and have your tax refund confiscated to pay child support in arrears (more about that on page 303). And property transfers from one spouse to another either during a marriage, or transfers within one year after the divorce or pursuant to a divorce or separation agreement, are not taxable events for either party.

However, alimony is a different story. Although alimony (also known as spousal support) is generally out of fashion with most divorce courts, it is still afforded favorable treatment by the IRS.

Alimony is normally deductible by the person who pays it, and is taxable income to the recipient. Because the purpose of alimony is to provide support from a higher-income person to a lower-income ex-spouse, the person paying alimony will very frequently be in a higher tax bracket than the person receiving it. Thus, a tax savings occurs that, in effect, causes Uncle Sam to pay part of the alimony.

Example

John is required by the divorce decree to pay Mary $1,000 a month in alimony. John is in the 25% bracket, so he gains a $250-per-month tax deduction, and his actual out-of-pocket cost for alimony is $750 per month. If Mary is in the 15% bracket, she must pay $150 in tax on the $1,000 alimony payment, and she keeps $850. The $100 difference between what John paid out-of-pocket and what Mary got to keep is "paid" by Uncle Sam.

Because alimony is treated so favorably, the IRS has devised a set of rules that are designed to keep people from treating as alimony those payments that are really a property settlement or child support.

Definition of Alimony

In order to be treated as deductible alimony, payments made from you to your spouse (or ex-spouse) must meet all of the following requirements:

- The payments must be in cash, check, or money order.
- The payments must be received by or on behalf of your spouse under a divorce or separation document (including a final decree, a temporary court order, or a written separation agreement between the two of you). Payments you make to third parties on behalf of your spouse, such as for your spouse's medical expenses, housing costs, taxes, tuition, etc., can qualify.
- You and your spouse must not opt out of alimony treatment by stating in the divorce decree that the payments aren't to be considered alimony for federal income tax purposes.
- If you and your spouse have received a final decree of divorce or decree of separate maintenance, you may not be living in the same household when the payment is made. If the payment was made under temporary orders and the decree is not yet final, it is okay to be living in the same home.
- The payer's obligation to make payments must end when the recipient dies, and there must be no liability to make any payment in cash or property as a substitute after the death.

- You and your spouse may not file a joint tax return with each other for the year.
- If any portion of the payment is considered by the IRS to be child support, that portion can't be treated as alimony.

Distinguishing Alimony from Child Support

The IRS will treat a payment as child support to the extent that it could in the future be reduced or ended when some event happens relating to your child, such as the child's death, marriage, graduation from high school or college, getting a job, reaching a specified age or income level, etc.

Even if the divorce decree is drafted to avoid mentioning any child-related events, the payment will be presumed to be child support if it will be reduced or ended within six months before or after your child reaches age 18 or 21, or, if you have more than one child, if the payments are to be reduced on two or more occasions, and each occasion takes place not more than one year before or after a different child reaches a certain age. The "certain age" must be between 18 and 24, and must be the same for each child.

Example

Michael is to pay Lisa Marie, his former wife, $2,000 per month in alimony. However, the payments are to be reduced to $1,500 per month on January 1, 2009, and to $1,000 per month on January 1, 2012. When the first reduction is scheduled to occur, the couple's first child, Michael Jr., will be 20 years, 5 months, and one day old. The second reduction will occur when their second child, Priscilla, is 22 years, 3 months, and 9 days old.

Because each reduction will occur within 1 year of a child's attainment of the age of 21 years and 4 months, and the total reductions are equal to $1,000, $1,000 of each "alimony" payment is considered to be nondeductible child support for tax purposes.

The rules discussed above apply to alimony in most states. However, in community property states, there are some differences in the way alimony is treated if paid before the divorce is final (e.g., under a temporary order). If you live in Arizona, California, Idaho, Louisiana, Nevada, New Mexico, Texas, Washington, or Wisconsin, you'll want to check with your lawyer or tax advisor about the tax treatment of temporary alimony you pay or receive.

Recapture of Frontloaded Alimony

To prevent a property settlement from being disguised as alimony, a provision in the federal tax law requires that when large sums of alimony (over $15,000) are paid in the first or second year following the divorce, but significantly less is paid in the third year, a portion of the alimony deducted by the payer in the first two years is recaptured by being added back to the payer's taxable income in the third year. This has the effect of "recapturing" the lost tax for the IRS.

If this recapture rule applies, the spouse who received the alimony (and had initially been required to include it in income) is entitled to a corresponding deduction in the third year.

The rule does not apply to alimony paid under temporary support orders (i.e., before the final decree is issued) nor does it apply when the reason for the drop-off in alimony in the third year was that the recipient died or remarried, or that less alimony was paid because the amount of alimony was based on a fixed portion of the payer's income from a business, property, or other compensation.

If the recapture rule applies to you, you can use the following worksheet to determine the amount to be recaptured.

Worksheet for Recapture of Alimony

Note: Do not enter less than zero on any line.

1. Alimony paid in **2nd year**			
2. Alimony paid in **3rd year**			
3. Floor	$15,000		
4. Add lines 2 and 3			
5. Subtract line 4 from line 1			
6. Alimony paid in **1st year**			
7. Adjusted alimony paid in **2nd year** (line 1 less line 5)			
8. Alimony paid in **3rd year**			
9. Add lines 7 and 8			
10. Divide line 9 by 2			
11. Floor	$15,000		
12. Add lines 10 and 11			
13. Subtract line 12 from line 6			
14. **Recaptured alimony.** Add lines 5 and 13			*

Reporting Alimony Payments

Reporting alimony is simple – you don't need to file an extra tax form to do it. However, you must use the long income tax form (Form 1040) instead of Form 1040EZ or 1040A.

If you received alimony, write the amount on Line 11 of Form 1040. If you paid alimony, write the amount on Line 31a, and also write the recipient's Social Security number on Line 31b. If you paid alimony to more than one person, write one person's number on Line 31b, and attach a statement to your return showing an itemization of how much you paid to each person, and listing each recipient's SSN.

The Child Tax Credit

If you have children, you know what a blessing they can be, especially during tax time. If you have dependent children, you may be able to claim a child tax credit that is set at $1,000 per qualifying child for tax years 2005 through 2010.

A qualifying child must remain under age 17 through the end of the year and be either a U.S. citizen or resident alien. A qualifying child must also meet the dependency tests (see page 163) and be your natural or adopted child, grandchild or great-grandchild, stepchild, or a foster child. "Adopted child" includes a child placed with you for adoption even if the adoption has not been finalized. A foster child must have lived with you the entire year to qualify, unless the child was born or died during the year.

Like most of the tax credits and other breaks that have been enacted lately, there is an income limitation on the people who can claim this credit. The phaseout of the credit begins at modified adjusted gross income (AGI) of $110,000 for joint filers, $75,000 for singles and heads of household, and $55,000 for marrieds filing separately. You will lose $50 of your total child credit for each $1,000 (or fraction of $1,000) of your modified AGI that exceeds the applicable threshold. For this purpose, modified AGI includes the amount shown on Line 38 of Form 1040 or Line 22 of Form 1040A, plus any foreign earned income exclusion, foreign housing exclusion, and income from U.S. possessions, if any.

Example

Stephen Cooper and his wife Sally have three children, which would qualify them for a child tax credit of $3,000 in 2006. Their modified AGI is $119,500, which exceeds the threshold of $110,000 by $9,500. Therefore, they will lose $50 x 10 = $500 of their credit, leaving a remaining credit of $2,500.

Claiming the Credit

After you determine whether and how many of your dependents qualify for the credit, you must remember to check the box next to the names of the qualifying children on the front of your tax form (the boxes are in Column 4 of Line 6c on Form 1040 or 1040A).

The child tax credit is subtracted from your tax bill after several of the other credits; namely, the credit for child and dependent care expenses, the credit for the elderly and the disabled, and the education credits described below. You will need to compute the amounts of any of those credits that apply to you before you can determine the amount of tax that's left over, and therefore is available to be reduced by your child tax credit.

You'll need to use the worksheets that follow (taken from the 2006 Form 1040 instructions) to determine the actual amount of your child tax credit.

If you had three or more children and your tax bill is too low to allow you to claim all of your child credit, you must complete and file IRS Form 8812, *Additional Child Tax Credit,* in order to be able to claim the extra refundable amount.

Form 1040—Line 53

Line 53—Child Tax Credit

Three Steps To Take the Child Tax Credit!

Step 1. Make sure you have a qualifying child for the child tax credit (see the instructions for line 6c).

Step 2. Make sure that for each qualifying child you either checked the box on Form 1040, line 6c, column (4), or completed Form 8901 (if the child is not your dependent).

Step 3. Answer the questions on this page to see if you can use the worksheet on page 43 to figure your credit or if you must use Pub. 972.

Questions **Who Must Use Pub. 972**

1. Is the amount on Form 1040, line 38, more than the amount shown below for your filing status?
   - Married filing jointly – $110,000
   - Single, head of household, or qualifying widow(er) – $75,000
   - Married filing separately – $55,000

   ☐ **Yes.** STOP You must use Pub. 972 to figure your credit.

   ☐ **No.** Go to question 2.

2. Are you claiming any of the following credits?
   - Residential energy efficient property credit, Form 5695, Part II.
   - Adoption credit, Form 8839.
   - Mortgage interest credit, Form 8396.
   - District of Columbia first-time homebuyer credit, Form 8859.

   ☐ **Yes.** STOP You must use Pub. 972 to figure your child tax credit. You will also need the form(s) listed above for any credit(s) you are claiming.

   ☐ **No.** Continue

3. Are you excluding income from Puerto Rico or are you filing any of the following forms?
   - Form 2555 or 2555-EZ (relating to foreign earned income).
   - Form 4563 (exclusion of income for residents of American Samoa).

   ☐ **Yes.** STOP You must use Pub. 972 to figure your credit.

   ☐ **No.** Use the worksheet on page 43 to figure your credit.

Form 1040—Line 53

Child Tax Credit Worksheet—Line 53 *Keep for Your Records*

CAUTION

- To be a qualifying child for the child tax credit, the child must be **under age 17** at the end of 2006 and meet the other requirements listed on page 19.
- **Do not** use this worksheet if you answered "Yes" to question 1, 2, or 3 on page 42. Instead, use Pub. 972.

1. Number of qualifying children: ________ × $1,000. Enter the result. **1** [ ]

2. Enter the amount from Form 1040, line 46. **2** [ ]

3. Add the amounts from Form 1040:

Line 47 ________

Line 48 + ________

Line 49 + ________

Line 50 + ________

Line 51 + ________

Line 52* + ________ Enter the total. **3** [ ]

*Include only the amount, if any, from Form 5695, line 12.

4. Are the amounts on lines 2 and 3 the same?

☐ **Yes.** STOP
You cannot take this credit because there is no tax to reduce. However, you may be able to take the **additional child tax credit.** See the **TIP** below.

☐ **No.** Subtract line 3 from line 2. **4** [ ]

5. Is the amount on line 1 more than the amount on line 4?

☐ **Yes.** Enter the amount from line 4. Also, you may be able to take the **additional child tax credit.** See the **TIP** below.

☐ **No.** Enter the amount from line 1.

} **This is your child tax credit.** **5** [ ]

Enter this amount on Form 1040, line 53.

1040

TIP You may be able to take the **additional child tax credit** on Form 1040, line 68, if you answered "Yes" on line 4 **or** line 5 above.

- First, complete your Form 1040 through line 67.
- Then, use Form 8812 to figure any additional child tax credit.

- 43 - *Need more information or forms? See page 7.*

TAX BENEFITS FOR ADOPTION

There are two important tax breaks for adoptive parents in 2006: an exclusion of up to $10,960 ($11,390 in 2007) paid under an employee benefit plan that pays for adoption expenses, and a tax credit for up to $10,960 ($11,390 in 2007) for expenses that were not reimbursed by your employer. The $10,960 amount also applies for adoptions of children who are U.S. citizens or residents, and are determined to be "special needs children" by a state.

However, both tax breaks begin to be phased out for those with adjusted gross income (AGI) over $164,410 in 2006. If your AGI is $204,410 or more, you can't claim any tax benefits for adoptions.

Qualifying Expenses

For both of these tax breaks, adoption expenses are defined in the same way. They include:

- adoption fees
- court costs
- legal fees
- traveling expenses (including meals and lodging)
- other expenses directly related to the legal adoption of an eligible child

The child must be under 18 years old, or physically or mentally incapable of self-care. You can't deduct expenses for adoptions that violate state law, that involve surrogate parent arrangements, that involve adopting your spouse's child, or that are allowed as a credit or deduction under any other federal income tax rule (for example, medical expenses that can be claimed as itemized deductions are not adoption expenses).

If eligible, you can take advantage of both the employer-provided benefits and the adoption tax credit, but you can't use the same expenses to qualify for two different tax breaks.

For 2006, $10,960 is also allowed as an adoption credit and as an exclusion from income in the case of a special needs child even if there are no qualified adoption expenses.

Example

In 2006, the adoption of your son was finalized, and you had paid a total of $12,000 in qualified expenses for the adoption. Your employer reimbursed you for $10,960 of your expenses. Therefore, you can claim a tax credit for the other $1,040 in qualified expenses in 2006.

Special Needs Children

To be considered a special needs child, a state must determine that the child cannot or should not live with his or her parents, and that unless financial assistance is provided, it's unlikely that the child will be adopted because of factors such as the child's ethnic or minority background, the child's age, the fact that the child is a member of a sibling group, or the child's medical condition or mental or physical handicap.

The special needs foreign child adoption provisions expired at the end of 2001. However, the provisions for adoption of U.S. special needs children will continue without interruption.

Dollar Limits on the Exclusion and Credit

The dollar limits for both the exclusion and the credit apply "per adoption effort." Therefore, if your adoption spans two or more years, you can only claim total credits of $10,960 over all the years that you paid expenses. You could also claim an additional $10,960 in excluded employee benefits, if your employer provides an adoption assistance plan.

If the child is a U.S. citizen or resident, you can claim the tax benefits whether or not your adoption effort is successful. However, if you attempt to adopt one child and the adoption falls through, upon which you attempt to adopt another child, the entire chain of events counts as one "adoption effort." If you adopt two (or more) children, each child's adoption would count as a separate adoption effort even if you adopt the children at the same time (for example, if you adopt a sibling group).

Phaseout of Benefits at Higher Income Levels

To determine whether your income is high enough to cause you to lose some of the adoption benefits, add up your adjusted gross income as shown on Line 38 of Form 1040. Qualified adoption expenses can no longer be claimed on Form 1040A. You must add to this amount the amount of any tax-free adoption benefits you received from your employer, and also any foreign earned income exclusion, foreign housing exclusion or deduction, or excluded income from U.S. possessions.

If your AGI, as modified above, is $164,410 or less, you qualify for the entire dollar amount of the credit and/or exclusion. If your AGI is $204,410 or more in 2006, you won't qualify at all. If your AGI is in between these amounts, your credit and exclusion will both be reduced in proportion to how high your income is in relation to the $40,000 phaseout range. By working through IRS Form 8839, *Qualified Adoption Expenses,* you'll compute the limitation if one applies.

Example

If your modified AGI is $174,410, the

amount that exceeds $164,410 is $10,000. Since $10,000 is ¼ of the phaseout range, you will lose ¼ of the adoption credit and also ¼ of the exclusion, so the maximum benefit you could claim for either the exclusion or credit for a non-special-needs child would be $7,620. If you were eligible for both the credit and exclusion, you could claim a maximum of $15,240 in total benefits.

Claiming the Exclusion or Credit

If you are married, you must file a joint return with your spouse to claim either the credit or the exclusion, unless (1) you are legally separated, or (2) you have lived apart from your spouse for the last six months of the year and your home is the child's home for more than half the year, and you paid more than half the cost of keeping up your home for the year.

Both the exclusion of employer-paid adoption benefits and the tax credit for adoption must be claimed on IRS Form 8839, which must be attached to Form 1040.

The exclusion is claimed on Part III of the form. Note that any employer-paid benefits are excluded from income taxation, but are still taxable for purposes of Social Security and Medicare tax. The total amount of adoption benefits you received should be shown in Box 12 of your W-2 Form. If your employer excluded more benefits than you are entitled to (for example, because your spouse is employed, thus raising your AGI above $164,410), you may have to add some of the amount in Box 12 to your taxable wages shown in Box 1.

You should generally claim the exclusion in the year your employer pays you for the expenses, but for foreign adoptions, you must claim the exclusion in the later of the year the adoption becomes final or the year of the payment. Unsuccessful foreign adoptions don't qualify for the exclusion.

The tax credit is claimed on Part II of the form. For adoptions of children that are U.S. citizens or residents, you may claim expenses in the year after they are paid or the year the adoption is final, whichever is earlier. If you pay expenses in a year after the year the adoption is final, claim the credit for those expenses in the year you pay them. Again, if the child is a foreign child, you must claim the expenses in the later of the year the adoption becomes final, or the year you paid them. Unsuccessful foreign adoptions do not qualify for the credit.

Carryovers of Unused Credits

The adoption tax credit is subtracted from your income tax bill, after the subtraction of any credit for child and dependent care expenses, any credit for the elderly or disabled, any mortgage interest credit, and the education credits. If your tax bill is not all that large to begin with, you may find that you're not able to take full advantage of all the credits you're entitled to.

If that is the case, any unused portion of your adoption tax credit for 2006 can be carried over to the next year to be subtracted from your 2007 tax bill. If there are still unused portions of the credit, you can carry it forward for up to four more years.

Child's Identification Number

If your adoptive child can not obtain a Social Security number, or an ITIN for a resident or nonresident alien, you must obtain an adoption taxpayer identification number by completing IRS Form W-7A, which you can obtain by calling 1-800-TAX-FORM.

CREDIT FOR THE ELDERLY AND DISABLED

A tax credit is available to certain low-income individuals if they are at least age 65 or older before the close of the tax year, and to individuals under age 65 if they are retired with a permanent and total disability, and have taxable disability income from a public or private employer.

If you're married at the end of the tax year, you and your spouse must file a joint return to claim this credit, unless you did not live with your spouse at any time during the tax year. In that case, you can file either jointly or separately.

You must be a U.S. citizen or resident to claim this credit, unless you're married to a U.S. citizen or resident, and you both elect to be treated as U.S. residents (and taxed on your worldwide income).

Income Limits for the Credit

Because of the way the credit is structured, your credit will be phased out completely under the following circumstances:

- For singles, your credit will be zero if you have an adjusted gross income (AGI) for the year of $17,500 or more, or if you receive $5,000 or more in nontaxable Social Security, railroad retirement, or veteran's benefits or pension, annuity, or disability benefits that are excluded from your gross income.

- If you are married and file a joint return, and either you or your spouse (but not both) qualify for the credit, your credit will be zero if your joint return adjusted gross income is $20,000 or more, or if you or your spouse receive $5,000 or more in nontaxable Social Security, railroad retirement, or veterans' benefits or pension, annuity, or disability benefits that are excluded from gross income.

- For marrieds filing jointly, if both you and your spouse qualify for the credit, your credit will be zero if your joint return adjusted gross income is $25,000 or more, or if you or your spouse receive $7,500 or more in nontaxable Social Security, railroad retirement, or veterans' benefits or pension, annuity, or disability benefits that are excluded from gross income.

- If you are married and file a separate return, you will not be entitled to any credit unless you are living apart from your spouse for the entire tax year. Even if you qualify, your credit will be zero if you have an adjusted gross income of $12,500 or more, or receive $3,750 or more in nontaxable Social Security, railroad retirement, or veterans' benefits or pension, annuity, or disability benefit that are excluded from your gross income.

Clearly, before you can determine your credit amount, you'll have to determine how much (if any) of your Social Security benefits are taxable, as discussed on page 251.

Computing Your Credit

If you qualify and have income below the limits described above, your starting point for computing the credit is an amount that is determined by your filing status: $5,000 if you are single or married filing jointly with one spouse qualifying for the credit, $7,500 if you are filing jointly and both spouses qualify for the credit, or $3,750 if you are married filing separately.

Then, reduce this amount dollar-for-dollar for pension, annuity, or disability benefits that are excluded from your gross income and also for nontaxable Social Security, railroad retirement, or veteran's benefits payable under a VA program. If you file a joint return, you must combine all benefits paid to both you and your spouse.

Your initial credit amount is further reduced by one-half the amount by which your AGI exceeds one of the following amounts: $7,500 for singles, $10,000 if married filing jointly, or $5,000 if married filing separately.

Finally, multiply the amount that remains after all these subtractions by 15 percent to arrive at your credit amount.

Example

Assume that you are age 66 and single, have an adjusted gross income (AGI) of $8,500 for 2006, and receive $4,000 of nontaxable Social Security benefits for the year. You would determine your credit for the elderly as follows:

Initial amount	*$5,000*
Less: Social Security benefits	*-4,000*
Reduced initial amount	*1,000*
Less: one-half of AGI above $7,500	*-500*
	500

Credit: $500 x 15% = $75

Special Rules for Disabled People Under Age 65

If you are permanently and totally disabled and are under age 65, special rules apply to determine your credit. Your initial amount may not exceed your taxable disability income for the tax year. Thus, your initial amount is the lesser of your applicable initial amount based on your filing status, as described above, or your disability income for the year.

You are considered to be permanently and totally disabled if you are unable to engage in any substantial gainful activity by reason of any medically determinable physical or mental impairment that can be expected to last for not less than 12 months, or to result in death.

You must furnish proof of your disability to the IRS. Generally this means you must attach a physician's statement, certifying the disability, to your tax return, using the statement on page 4 of the instructions for either Schedule R (for Form 1040) or Schedule 3 (for Form 1040A). You don't have to attach a statement if you filed one in an earlier year and the doctor signed line B on the statement.

TAX BREAKS FOR EDUCATION

Beginning in 1998, a new group of tax benefits has become available to those who are pursuing higher education for themselves, their spouse, or their dependents.

In this section we'll describe the similarities and differences between the Hope Scholarship credit, the Lifetime Learning credit, Coverdell education savings accounts (ESAs), and the deduction for interest on qualified student loans. In most cases you have to choose among these benefits, since the same student is not permitted to use two different education tax breaks in the same year.

Save Money

For each student, in a given year you can only take advantage of one of the following: Hope Scholarship credit, Lifetime Learning credit, or withdrawal from an education IRA.

For those who qualify, the Hope Scholarship credit will generally save you the most tax money. If you don't qualify, the Lifetime Learning Credit is generally the next-best tax break. Since education IRAs only became available in 1998, they are unlikely to help current students; however they can be a useful way to start an education fund for a new baby or young child. For those who have recently graduated, the student-loan interest deduction provides a measure of relief.

The Hope Scholarship Credit

If you, your spouse, or a dependent for whom you claim an exemption was enrolled at least half-time in the first or second year of college in 2006, you may benefit from the Hope Scholarship credit.

The credit is for the first $1,100 of qualified expenses incurred by the student, and 50 percent of the next $1,100, so that the full credit of $1,650 applies if the student has at least $2,200 in expenses. Under a special tax provision in 2006, students enrolled in and paying tuition at an eligible education institution located in the Gulf Opportunity Zone (i.e., certain parishes and counties in Alabama, Louisiana and Mississippi) get to double the above credit amount.

The Hope credit is available for each student in your family who meets the qualifications:

- he or she is enrolled in the first or second year of postsecondary education
- is enrolled in a program that leads to a degree, certificate, or other recognized academic credential
- is taking at least one-half of the normal full-time load of classes, for at least one academic period beginning during the calendar year
- has not been convicted of a drug-related felony

The only expenses that count toward the credit are tuition and fees required for attendance. Generally, the expenses can be deducted in the year the class begins, if the expenses were paid during that year. However, if you prepay expenses during one year, for a course that begins in the first three months of the following year, you can count those expenses toward the credit in the year they were paid.

Eligible institutions are any accredited public, nonprofit, or for-profit postsecondary institution eligible to participate in federal student aid programs.

Income-Related Phaseout

Unfortunately, the Hope Scholarship credit (as well as the Lifetime Learning credit) is phased out for those at higher income levels.

Warning

Although either the student or the parent (but not both) can claim a Hope Scholarship or Lifetime Learning credit, you can't avoid the high-income phaseouts for either of these credits by having the student claim the credit, unless *the student is not claimed as a dependent on the parent's tax return.*

The 2006 phaseout occurs in the income range of $45,000 to $55,000 for singles and the range of $90,000 to $110,000 for marrieds filing a joint return. To determine whether your credit will be affected by the phaseout, you must consider your modified adjusted gross income; that is, your AGI as shown on Line 38 of Form 1040 (or Line 22 on Form 1040A), plus any foreign earned income exclusion, plus amounts derived from sources in American possessions if you are a resident of the possession (Guam, American Samoa, the Northern Mariana Islands, or Puerto Rico).

The phaseout is computed by reducing the amount of your credit by a fraction. The fraction is found by taking the amount of your modified AGI that exceeds $45,000 (or $90,000 if filing jointly) and dividing it by $10,000 (or by $20,000 if filing jointly).

Example

Steve and Kit are married filing jointly, and have twin sons who are both freshmen in college in 2006. For each of the boys, tuition costs exceed $2,000. Steve and Kit would normally have a Hope credit of $1,500 for each son, or $3,000 in total.

However, their AGI is $94,000 so they must reduce their credit as follows: their AGI exceeds $90,000 by $4,000, and they divide $4,000 by $20,000 to get 0.20. Therefore, 20 percent of their credit will not be allowed, and they can claim a Hope credit of only $2,400 for 2006.

Claiming the Credit

To claim the Hope Scholarship credit (or the Lifetime Learning credit described below) you must complete IRS Form 8863, *Education Credits,* and attach it to your Form 1040 or 1040A. These credits are subtracted from your tax bill after the credit for child and dependent care expenses, the credit for the elderly and the disabled, and the child tax credit – and if all these credits reduce your tax bill to zero, you will lose any unclaimed amount of the education credits, because they may not be carried over into a subsequent year.

Lifetime Learning Credit

For those who have two years of college under their belt and can't qualify for the Hope credit, the Lifetime Learning credit provides a smaller tax benefit for an unlimited number of years in which you took one or more postsecondary educational courses. The courses can apply towards an undergraduate, graduate, or professional degree, certificate program, or other academic credential. You can claim the credit for yourself, your spouse if filing jointly, and any dependents for whom you claim an exemption on your tax return.

This credit is worth 20 percent of the first $10,000 in higher education expenses *per family.* Therefore, the maximum amount of credit you can claim is $2,000. If one or more students in the family are eligible for the Hope credit, other family members may use the full $10,000 of the Lifetime Learning credit. However, a single student cannot use both credits; he or she must choose between them.

For tax years beginning in 2005 and 2006, students enrolled in and paying tuition at an eligible education institution located in the Gulf Opportunity Zone (i.e., certain parishes and counties in Alabama, Louisiana and Mississippi) may be eligible for a Lifetime

Learning credit of 40 percent of up to $10,000 of qualified tuition and related expenses.

The Lifetime Learning credit applies to tuition and fees (as with the Hope credit) and the same higher-income phaseout methods apply. To claim the credit, you must use Form 8863, *Education Credits,* and attach it to your tax return. Don't forget that if the education was job- or business-related, you might be able to deduct it instead of claiming the credit. See page 184.

Coverdell ESAs

A third type of tax break to help pay for education (including elementary and secondary education) is the Coverdell education savings account (ESA), formerly known as the education IRA. "IRA" was something of a misnomer because this type of account is not designed to survive into the beneficiary's retirement. However, the account works similarly to a Roth IRA in that contributions are not deductible, but interest and dividends that build up within the account are tax-free, and amounts withdrawn from the account under proper circumstances will not be taxed.

An ESA is set up on a per-child basis with a bank or other financial institution approved by the IRS. Each child must have one or more separate accounts, and the child, a parent, grandparent or friend may contribute up to $2,000 to the account in 2002 and later years. More than one person can contribute on behalf of the same child, but the total contributions for that child cannot exceed $2,000. No contributions can be after the child turns 18, and no contributions can be made in the same year that a contribution is made to a qualified state tuition program on behalf of the child.

Income Restrictions

As you might expect, there is a phaseout range for contributions from $95,000 to $110,000 for singles and from $190,000 to $220,000 for joint filers. If you fall within the range, your contribution is limited as follows: Take the amount by which your modified AGI exceeds the lower limit of the phaseout range that applies to you, and divide it by $15,000 (or by $10,000 in the case of a joint return). The result will be a decimal number that should be multiplied by $500 to determine the amount of the contribution you can't make.

Work Smart

If your income is high enough to fall within the phaseout range, you can avoid losing any of the contribution by having someone with lower income, such as a grandparent or family friend, make a contribution for the child.

Distributions from ESAs

If a distribution is taken from an ESA, the amount will not be taxed to the extent that it does not exceed the beneficiary's qualified higher education expenses. For this purpose, qualified expenses include tuition, fees, books, supplies and equipment, and if the child is at least a half-time student, up to $2,500 each year for room and board. Virtually any accredited postsecondary educational institution will qualify. Beginning in 2002, ESAs may also be used for elementary and secondary education expenses as well.

If the distribution does exceed the child's educational expenses, the excess portion of the distribution will be taxable to the child to the extent that it represents the tax-free earnings on the account (the original contributions will be recovered tax-free). In addition, a 10 percent additional tax will apply to the taxable portion of the distribution, unless the distribution was made because of the beneficiary's death, disability, or because the beneficiary received a scholarship or some other nontaxable education benefit (such as employer-paid benefits). If the beneficiary dies, the balance must be distributed to his or her estate within 30 days.

An ESA can be rolled over to a different trustee, so long as the rollover occurs within 60 days of the withdrawal from the original account. Once a rollover is made, you must wait at least 12 months before making another one.

The balance remaining in an ESA must be distributed within 30 days after a beneficiary reaches age 30. To avoid tax on the distribution at age 30 (or indeed at any time) the beneficiary on the account can be changed, with no tax consequences, if the new beneficiary is the child's child or descendent, stepchildren or descendent, sibling or their descendent, parent or grandparent, stepparent, the spouse of any of these family members, or first cousin (starting in 2002). Beginning in 2002, the age limit is waived for beneficiaries with special needs (i.e., those with physical, mental, or emotional conditions, including learning disabilities).

Student Loan Interest

If you paid interest on a student loan in 2006, you may be eligible to deduct up to $2,500 of the interest you paid, whether the loan was for your own education, your spouse's, or that of a child or anyone else who was your dependent at the time the education was undertaken.

All student loan interest payments made in 2003 and later years are eligible for the deduction. The 60-month loan limitation in effect prior to 2002 no longer applies.

In 2006, the deduction is phased out for those with modified adjusted gross income between $50,000 ($55,000 in 2007) and $65,000 ($70,000 in 2007) if you are single, or between $105,000 ($110,000 in 2007) and $135,000 ($40,000 in 2007) if filing a joint return (these rates may be adjusted annually for inflation). You can't claim this deduction at all if you are married filing separately, or if you can be claimed as a dependent on someone else's return.

For purposes of this deduction, "modified adjusted gross income" is computed by taking the AGI amount from Line 38 of Form 1040, and adding back any foreign earned income exclusion, foreign housing exclusion or deduction, and the exclusion of income for residents of American possessions.

To figure the limit, take the portion of your modified AGI that exceeds $50,000 (or $105,000 if you are married filing jointly) and divide it by $15,000 ($30,000 if filing jointly). The resulting decimal should be multiplied by your interest deduction to determine the amount that you will lose due to your high level of income.

Which Loans Qualify?

Beyond the dollar amount of the interest ($1,000) and the AGI restrictions, this tax break also places some limits on the types of loan, the expenses that the loan had to be used for, and the type of education the student was pursuing.

The loan must have been taken out to pay qualified higher education expenses, which include the costs of tuition, fees, room and board, books, equipment, and other necessary expenses such as transportation. However, you must reduce these costs by any employer-provided educational benefits received by the student, any nontaxable distributions from a Coverdell ESA, any savings bond interest that was nontaxable because it was used for education expenses, any nontaxable scholarships or veteran's education benefits, or any other nontaxable payments other than gifts, bequests or inheritances.

Qualified educational institutions for this purpose include virtually any accredited postsecondary institution, including those conducting internship or residency programs in hospitals or health care facilities. However, to be eligible the student must have been enrolled in a degree, certificate or similar program, and must have been carrying at least one-half the normal full-time load.

Claiming the Deduction

You don't need to fill out any special forms to claim the student loan interest deduction, and you don't need to itemize your deductions to take advantage of it. The deductible amount is simply written on Line 33 of Form 1040, or Line 18 of Form 1040A, and subtracted from your income.

THE EARNED INCOME CREDIT

A special tax credit, known as the earned income credit or EIC, is available to lower-income taxpayers who have at least some earnings from personal services during the year. For 2006, the credit is available to most workers between the ages of 25 and 64 with an adjusted gross income (AGI) of less than $12,120 ($14,140 if married filing jointly) if they have no qualifying children. Workers with one qualifying child may get the credit if their AGI is less than $32,001 ($34,001 if filing jointly), or less than $36,348 ($38,348 if filing jointly) if they have more than one qualifying child.

However, if you have investment income over $2,800 in 2006, you won't qualify for the credit. Investment income includes taxable and nontaxable interest and dividends, capital gains, net income from rental of personal property, net royalty income, and net income from passive activities shown on Schedule E, including real estate rentals (see IRS Publication 596, *Earned Income Credit,* if you are on the borderline and need to know exactly which lines on Schedule E to look at in determining your passive income).

All of these ceiling amounts are adjusted for inflation each year.

Work Smart

The extraordinary thing about the EIC is that if your credit is higher than the tax you'd otherwise owe, you will get the difference as a "refund" from the IRS. This extra payment from the federal government is intended to reward lower-income persons for working.

Are You Eligible for the Credit?

In order to be eligible for the EIC in 2006, you must earn at least $1 during the year at a job or self-employment, and meet the income requirements discussed above.

If you are claiming the higher credit based on having one or two children, each child must meet certain requirements. The child may be your natural child, grandchild, stepchild, sibling, stepsibling, any descendent of the above treated as the taxpayer's own child, foster child, or adopted child.

The child must be under the age of 19, and must live with you for more than half your tax year. However, if the child is a student he or she may be up to 23 years old. If the child is permanently and totally disabled, age doesn't matter. A child who is married does not qualify you for the EIC, unless you can claim a dependency exemption for the child. Also, if a child qualifies you for the EIC, that child cannot claim the EIC himself or herself.

If you're married, you must file a joint tax return with your spouse to claim the EIC. Both spouses' income counts in determining the amount of the credit. There's an exception for persons who are treated as unmarried because their spouses have not been a member of the household during the last six months of the tax year; these people can still claim the EIC when they file their tax returns as single or as a head of household.

If two or more taxpayers seek to claim the same child in their bid for the EIC (e.g., a parent and grandparent living in the same household with a child) only the person with the highest AGI may claim the credit. If the child spends exactly half the year in each of two households, nobody can claim an EIC based on that child.

How the Credit Is Computed

The basic EIC is computed in two stages. First, you start with a certain percentage of your earned income up to a certain amount. This is the maximum basic EIC. For 2006, the maximum is $412 if you have no children, $2,747 with one qualifying child, and $4,536 if you have two or more.

Then, you subtract a percentage of the portion of your AGI that exceeds a specified level. For this part of the computation, you must count all your taxable income, whatever the source – not just earned income. What's more, you must also add in any nontaxable interest you received, any capital losses, any nontaxable retirement plan payments unless they were rolled over into an IRA, and 75 percent of any losses you had in your business or farm. You must also include certain nontaxable earned income, such as 401(k) contributions, nontaxable dependent care and adoption benefits, and the value of food and lodging provided for the convenience of the employer.

The EIC amount is phased down as your income gets higher, and at a certain point it's phased out completely. To find the actual amount of your EIC, you must complete the EIC worksheets reproduced below. The EIC tables referred to in the worksheet are those at the end of this chapter.

Also, if you are claiming a higher EIC amount because you have one or more qualifying children, you must also complete Schedule EIC and attach it to your tax return. The credit amount will be transferred to Line 66a on Form 1040, or Line 40a of Form 1040A.

Worksheet B—Earned Income Credit (EIC)—Lines 66a and 66b *Keep for Your Records*

Use this worksheet if you answered "Yes" to Step 5, question 3, on page 48.

√ Complete the parts below (Parts 1 through 3) that apply to you. Then, continue to Part 4.

√ If you are married filing a joint return, include your spouse's amounts, if any, with yours to figure the amounts to enter in Parts 1 through 3.

Part 1

Self-Employed, Members of the Clergy, and People With Church Employee Income Filing Schedule SE

1a. Enter the amount from Schedule SE, Section A, line 3, or Section B, line 3, whichever applies.		1a	
b. Enter any amount from Schedule SE, Section B, line 4b, and line 5a.	+	1b	
c. Combine lines 1a and 1b.	=	1c	
d. Enter the amount from Schedule SE, Section A, line 6, or Section B, line 13, whichever applies.	–	1d	
e. Subtract line 1d from 1c.	=	1e	

Part 2

Self-Employed NOT Required To File Schedule SE

For example, your net earnings from self-employment were less than $400.

2. Do not include on these lines any statutory employee income, any net profit from services performed as a notary public, or any amount exempt from self-employment tax as the result of the filing and approval of Form 4029 or Form 4361.

a. Enter any net farm profit or (loss) from Schedule F, line 36, and from farm partnerships, Schedule K-1 (Form 1065), box 14, code A*.		2a	
b. Enter any net profit or (loss) from Schedule C, line 31; Schedule C-EZ, line 3; Schedule K-1 (Form 1065), box 14, code A (other than farming); and Schedule K-1 (Form 1065-B), box 9, code J1*.	+	2b	
c. Combine lines 2a and 2b.	=	2c	

*Reduce any Schedule K-1 amounts by any partnership section 179 expense deduction claimed, unreimbursed partnership expenses claimed, and depletion claimed on oil and gas properties. If you have any Schedule K-1 amounts, complete the appropriate line(s) of Schedule SE, Section A. Enter your name and social security number on Schedule SE and attach it to your return.

Part 3

Statutory Employees Filing Schedule C or C-EZ

3. Enter the amount from Schedule C, line 1, or Schedule C-EZ, line 1, that you are filing as a statutory employee.	3	

Part 4

All Filers Using Worksheet B

Note. If line 4b includes income on which you should have paid self-employment tax but did not, we may reduce your credit by the amount of self-employment tax not paid.

4a. Enter your earned income from Step 5 on page 48.	4a	
b. Combine lines 1e, 2c, 3, and 4a. **This is your total earned income.**	4b	

If line 4b is zero or less, STOP You cannot take the credit. Enter "No" on the dotted line next to line 66a.

5. If you have:

- 2 or more qualifying children, is line 4b less than $36,348 ($38,348 if married filing jointly)?
- 1 qualifying child, is line 4b less than $32,001 ($34,001 if married filing jointly)?
- No qualifying children, is line 4b less than $12,120 ($14,120 if married filing jointly)?

☐ **Yes.** If you want the IRS to figure your credit, see page 48. If you want to figure the credit yourself, enter the amount from line 4b on line 6 (page 52).

☐ **No.** STOP You cannot take the credit. Enter "No" on the dotted line next to line 66a.

- 51 - *Need more information or forms? See page*

Worksheet B—Continued from page 51

Keep for Your Records

Part 5

All Filers Using Worksheet B

6. Enter your total earned income from Part 4, line 4b, on page 51. **6** ______

7. Look up the amount on line 6 above in the EIC Table on pages 53–59 to find the credit. Be sure you use the correct column for your filing status and the number of children you have. Enter the credit here. **7** ______

If line 7 is zero, STOP You cannot take the credit. Enter "No" on the dotted line next to line 66a.

8. Enter the amount from Form 1040, line 38. **8** ______

9. Are the amounts on lines 8 and 6 the same?

☐ **Yes.** Skip line 10; enter the amount from line 7 on line 11.

☐ **No.** Go to line 10.

Part 6

Filers Who Answered "No" on Line 9

10. If you have:

- No qualifying children, is the amount on line 8 less than $6,750 ($8,750 if married filing jointly)?
- 1 or more qualifying children, is the amount on line 8 less than $14,850 ($16,850 if married filing jointly)?

☐ **Yes.** Leave line 10 blank; enter the amount from line 7 on line 11.

☐ **No.** Look up the amount on line 8 in the EIC Table on pages 53–59 to find the credit. Be sure you use the correct column for your filing status and the number of children you have. Enter the credit here. **10** ______
Look at the amounts on lines 10 and 7.
Then, enter the **smaller** amount on line 11.

Part 7

Your Earned Income Credit

11. This is your earned income credit. **11** ______

Enter this amount on Form 1040, line 66a.

Reminder—

√ If you have a qualifying child, complete and attach Schedule EIC.

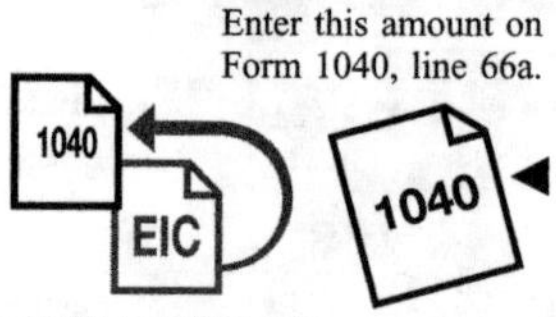

CAUTION *If your EIC for a year after 1996 was reduced or disallowed, see page 49 to find out if you must file Form 8862 to take the credit for 2006.*

2006 Earned Income Credit (EIC) Table

Caution. This is **not** a tax table.

1. To find your credit, read down the "At least - But less than" columns and find the line that includes the amount you were told to look up from your EIC Worksheet.

2. Then, go to the column that includes your filing status and the number of qualifying children you have. Enter the credit from that column on your EIC Worksheet.

Example. If your filing status is single, you have one qualifying child, and the amount you are looking up from your EIC Worksheet is $2,455, you would enter $842.

If the amount you are looking up from the worksheet is—		And your filing status is— Single, head of household, or qualifying widow(er) and you have—		
		No children	One child	Two children
At least	But less than	Your credit is—		
2,400	2,450	186	825	970
2,450	2,500	189	842	990

If the amount you are looking up from the worksheet is–		And your filing status is– Single, head of household, or qualifying widow(er) and you have–			Married filing jointly and you have–		
		No children	One child	Two children	No children	One child	Two children
At least	But less than	Your credit is–			Your credit is–		
$1	**$50**	$2	$9	$10	$2	$9	$10
50	**100**	6	26	30	6	26	30
100	**150**	10	43	50	10	43	50
150	**200**	13	60	70	13	60	70
200	**250**	17	77	90	17	77	90
250	**300**	21	94	110	21	94	110
300	**350**	25	111	130	25	111	130
350	**400**	29	128	150	29	128	150
400	**450**	33	145	170	33	145	170
450	**500**	36	162	190	36	162	190
500	**550**	40	179	210	40	179	210
550	**600**	44	196	230	44	196	230
600	**650**	48	213	250	48	213	250
650	**700**	52	230	270	52	230	270
700	**750**	55	247	290	55	247	290
750	**800**	59	264	310	59	264	310
800	**850**	63	281	330	63	281	330
850	**900**	67	298	350	67	298	350
900	**950**	71	315	370	71	315	370
950	**1,000**	75	332	390	75	332	390
1,000	**1,050**	78	349	410	78	349	410
1,050	**1,100**	82	366	430	82	366	430
1,100	**1,150**	86	383	450	86	383	450
1,150	**1,200**	90	400	470	90	400	470
1,200	**1,250**	94	417	490	94	417	490
1,250	**1,300**	98	434	510	98	434	510
1,300	**1,350**	101	451	530	101	451	530
1,350	**1,400**	105	468	550	105	468	550
1,400	**1,450**	109	485	570	109	485	570
1,450	**1,500**	113	502	590	113	502	590
1,500	**1,550**	117	519	610	117	519	610
1,550	**1,600**	120	536	630	120	536	630
1,600	**1,650**	124	553	650	124	553	650
1,650	**1,700**	128	570	670	128	570	670
1,700	**1,750**	132	587	690	132	587	690
1,750	**1,800**	136	604	710	136	604	710
1,800	**1,850**	140	621	730	140	621	730
1,850	**1,900**	143	638	750	143	638	750
1,900	**1,950**	147	655	770	147	655	770
1,950	**2,000**	151	672	790	151	672	790
2,000	**2,050**	155	689	810	155	689	810
2,050	**2,100**	159	706	830	159	706	830
2,100	**2,150**	163	723	850	163	723	850
2,150	**2,200**	166	740	870	166	740	870
2,200	**2,250**	170	757	890	170	757	890
2,250	**2,300**	174	774	910	174	774	910
2,300	**2,350**	178	791	930	178	791	930
2,350	**2,400**	182	808	950	182	808	950
2,400	**2,450**	186	825	970	186	825	970
2,450	**2,500**	189	842	990	189	842	990

If the amount you are looking up from the worksheet is–		And your filing status is– Single, head of household, or qualifying widow(er) and you have–			Married filing jointly and you have–		
		No children	One child	Two children	No children	One child	Two children
At least	But less than	Your credit is–			Your credit is–		
2,500	**2,550**	193	859	1,010	193	859	1,010
2,550	**2,600**	197	876	1,030	197	876	1,030
2,600	**2,650**	201	893	1,050	201	893	1,050
2,650	**2,700**	205	910	1,070	205	910	1,070
2,700	**2,750**	208	927	1,090	208	927	1,090
2,750	**2,800**	212	944	1,110	212	944	1,110
2,800	**2,850**	216	961	1,130	216	961	1,130
2,850	**2,900**	220	978	1,150	220	978	1,150
2,900	**2,950**	224	995	1,170	224	995	1,170
2,950	**3,000**	228	1,012	1,190	228	1,012	1,190
3,000	**3,050**	231	1,029	1,210	231	1,029	1,210
3,050	**3,100**	235	1,046	1,230	235	1,046	1,230
3,100	**3,150**	239	1,063	1,250	239	1,063	1,250
3,150	**3,200**	243	1,080	1,270	243	1,080	1,270
3,200	**3,250**	247	1,097	1,290	247	1,097	1,290
3,250	**3,300**	251	1,114	1,310	251	1,114	1,310
3,300	**3,350**	254	1,131	1,330	254	1,131	1,330
3,350	**3,400**	258	1,148	1,350	258	1,148	1,350
3,400	**3,450**	262	1,165	1,370	262	1,165	1,370
3,450	**3,500**	266	1,182	1,390	266	1,182	1,390
3,500	**3,550**	270	1,199	1,410	270	1,199	1,410
3,550	**3,600**	273	1,216	1,430	273	1,216	1,430
3,600	**3,650**	277	1,233	1,450	277	1,233	1,450
3,650	**3,700**	281	1,250	1,470	281	1,250	1,470
3,700	**3,750**	285	1,267	1,490	285	1,267	1,490
3,750	**3,800**	289	1,284	1,510	289	1,284	1,510
3,800	**3,850**	293	1,301	1,530	293	1,301	1,530
3,850	**3,900**	296	1,318	1,550	296	1,318	1,550
3,900	**3,950**	300	1,335	1,570	300	1,335	1,570
3,950	**4,000**	304	1,352	1,590	304	1,352	1,590
4,000	**4,050**	308	1,369	1,610	308	1,369	1,610
4,050	**4,100**	312	1,386	1,630	312	1,386	1,630
4,100	**4,150**	316	1,403	1,650	316	1,403	1,650
4,150	**4,200**	319	1,420	1,670	319	1,420	1,670
4,200	**4,250**	323	1,437	1,690	323	1,437	1,690
4,250	**4,300**	327	1,454	1,710	327	1,454	1,710
4,300	**4,350**	331	1,471	1,730	331	1,471	1,730
4,350	**4,400**	335	1,488	1,750	335	1,488	1,750
4,400	**4,450**	339	1,505	1,770	339	1,505	1,770
4,450	**4,500**	342	1,522	1,790	342	1,522	1,790
4,500	**4,550**	346	1,539	1,810	346	1,539	1,810
4,550	**4,600**	350	1,556	1,830	350	1,556	1,830
4,600	**4,650**	354	1,573	1,850	354	1,573	1,850
4,650	**4,700**	358	1,590	1,870	358	1,590	1,870
4,700	**4,750**	361	1,607	1,890	361	1,607	1,890
4,750	**4,800**	365	1,624	1,910	365	1,624	1,910
4,800	**4,850**	369	1,641	1,930	369	1,641	1,930
4,850	**4,900**	373	1,658	1,950	373	1,658	1,950
4,900	**4,950**	377	1,675	1,970	377	1,675	1,970
4,950	**5,000**	381	1,692	1,990	381	1,692	1,990

(Continued on page 54)

Need more information or forms? See page 7.

2006 Earned Income Credit (EIC) Table–*Continued* (**Caution.** This is **not** a tax table.)

If the amount you are looking up from the worksheet is–		And your filing status is–					
		Single, head of household, or qualifying widow(er) and you have–			Married filing jointly and you have–		
		No children	One child	Two children	No children	One child	Two children
At least	But less than	Your credit is–			Your credit is–		
5,000	**5,050**	384	1,709	2,010	384	1,709	2,010
5,050	**5,100**	388	1,726	2,030	388	1,726	2,030
5,100	**5,150**	392	1,743	2,050	392	1,743	2,050
5,150	**5,200**	396	1,760	2,070	396	1,760	2,070
5,200	**5,250**	400	1,777	2,090	400	1,777	2,090
5,250	**5,300**	404	1,794	2,110	404	1,794	2,110
5,300	**5,350**	407	1,811	2,130	407	1,811	2,130
5,350	**5,400**	412	1,828	2,150	412	1,828	2,150
5,400	**5,450**	412	1,845	2,170	412	1,845	2,170
5,450	**5,500**	412	1,862	2,190	412	1,862	2,190
5,500	**5,550**	412	1,879	2,210	412	1,879	2,210
5,550	**5,600**	412	1,896	2,230	412	1,896	2,230
5,600	**5,650**	412	1,913	2,250	412	1,913	2,250
5,650	**5,700**	412	1,930	2,270	412	1,930	2,270
5,700	**5,750**	412	1,947	2,290	412	1,947	2,290
5,750	**5,800**	412	1,964	2,310	412	1,964	2,310
5,800	**5,850**	412	1,981	2,330	412	1,981	2,330
5,850	**5,900**	412	1,998	2,350	412	1,998	2,350
5,900	**5,950**	412	2,015	2,370	412	2,015	2,370
5,950	**6,000**	412	2,032	2,390	412	2,032	2,390
6,000	**6,050**	412	2,049	2,410	412	2,049	2,410
6,050	**6,100**	412	2,066	2,430	412	2,066	2,430
6,100	**6,150**	412	2,083	2,450	412	2,083	2,450
6,150	**6,200**	412	2,100	2,470	412	2,100	2,470
6,200	**6,250**	412	2,117	2,490	412	2,117	2,490
6,250	**6,300**	412	2,134	2,510	412	2,134	2,510
6,300	**6,350**	412	2,151	2,530	412	2,151	2,530
6,350	**6,400**	412	2,168	2,550	412	2,168	2,550
6,400	**6,450**	412	2,185	2,570	412	2,185	2,570
6,450	**6,500**	412	2,202	2,590	412	2,202	2,590
6,500	**6,550**	412	2,219	2,610	412	2,219	2,610
6,550	**6,600**	412	2,236	2,630	412	2,236	2,630
6,600	**6,650**	412	2,253	2,650	412	2,253	2,650
6,650	**6,700**	412	2,270	2,670	412	2,270	2,670
6,700	**6,750**	412	2,287	2,690	412	2,287	2,690
6,750	**6,800**	409	2,304	2,710	412	2,304	2,710
6,800	**6,850**	405	2,321	2,730	412	2,321	2,730
6,850	**6,900**	401	2,338	2,750	412	2,338	2,750
6,900	**6,950**	397	2,355	2,770	412	2,355	2,770
6,950	**7,000**	394	2,372	2,790	412	2,372	2,790
7,000	**7,050**	390	2,389	2,810	412	2,389	2,810
7,050	**7,100**	386	2,406	2,830	412	2,406	2,830
7,100	**7,150**	382	2,423	2,850	412	2,423	2,850
7,150	**7,200**	378	2,440	2,870	412	2,440	2,870
7,200	**7,250**	374	2,457	2,890	412	2,457	2,890
7,250	**7,300**	371	2,474	2,910	412	2,474	2,910
7,300	**7,350**	367	2,491	2,930	412	2,491	2,930
7,350	**7,400**	363	2,508	2,950	412	2,508	2,950
7,400	**7,450**	359	2,525	2,970	412	2,525	2,970
7,450	**7,500**	355	2,542	2,990	412	2,542	2,990
7,500	**7,550**	352	2,559	3,010	412	2,559	3,010
7,550	**7,600**	348	2,576	3,030	412	2,576	3,030
7,600	**7,650**	344	2,593	3,050	412	2,593	3,050
7,650	**7,700**	340	2,610	3,070	412	2,610	3,070
7,700	**7,750**	336	2,627	3,090	412	2,627	3,090
7,750	**7,800**	332	2,644	3,110	412	2,644	3,110
7,800	**7,850**	329	2,661	3,130	412	2,661	3,130
7,850	**7,900**	325	2,678	3,150	412	2,678	3,150
7,900	**7,950**	321	2,695	3,170	412	2,695	3,170
7,950	**8,000**	317	2,712	3,190	412	2,712	3,190

If the amount you are looking up from the worksheet is–		And your filing status is–					
		Single, head of household, or qualifying widow(er) and you have–			Married filing jointly and you have–		
		No children	One child	Two children	No children	One child	Two children
At least	But less than	Your credit is–			Your credit is–		
8,000	**8,050**	313	2,729	3,210	412	2,729	3,210
8,050	**8,100**	309	2,747	3,230	412	2,747	3,230
8,100	**8,150**	306	2,747	3,250	412	2,747	3,250
8,150	**8,200**	302	2,747	3,270	412	2,747	3,270
8,200	**8,250**	298	2,747	3,290	412	2,747	3,290
8,250	**8,300**	294	2,747	3,310	412	2,747	3,310
8,300	**8,350**	290	2,747	3,330	412	2,747	3,330
8,350	**8,400**	286	2,747	3,350	412	2,747	3,350
8,400	**8,450**	283	2,747	3,370	412	2,747	3,370
8,450	**8,500**	279	2,747	3,390	412	2,747	3,390
8,500	**8,550**	275	2,747	3,410	412	2,747	3,410
8,550	**8,600**	271	2,747	3,430	412	2,747	3,430
8,600	**8,650**	267	2,747	3,450	412	2,747	3,450
8,650	**8,700**	264	2,747	3,470	412	2,747	3,470
8,700	**8,750**	260	2,747	3,490	412	2,747	3,490
8,750	**8,800**	256	2,747	3,510	409	2,747	3,510
8,800	**8,850**	252	2,747	3,530	405	2,747	3,530
8,850	**8,900**	248	2,747	3,550	401	2,747	3,550
8,900	**8,950**	244	2,747	3,570	397	2,747	3,570
8,950	**9,000**	241	2,747	3,590	394	2,747	3,590
9,000	**9,050**	237	2,747	3,610	390	2,747	3,610
9,050	**9,100**	233	2,747	3,630	386	2,747	3,630
9,100	**9,150**	229	2,747	3,650	382	2,747	3,650
9,150	**9,200**	225	2,747	3,670	378	2,747	3,670
9,200	**9,250**	221	2,747	3,690	374	2,747	3,690
9,250	**9,300**	218	2,747	3,710	371	2,747	3,710
9,300	**9,350**	214	2,747	3,730	367	2,747	3,730
9,350	**9,400**	210	2,747	3,750	363	2,747	3,750
9,400	**9,450**	206	2,747	3,770	359	2,747	3,770
9,450	**9,500**	202	2,747	3,790	355	2,747	3,790
9,500	**9,550**	199	2,747	3,810	352	2,747	3,810
9,550	**9,600**	195	2,747	3,830	348	2,747	3,830
9,600	**9,650**	191	2,747	3,850	344	2,747	3,850
9,650	**9,700**	187	2,747	3,870	340	2,747	3,870
9,700	**9,750**	183	2,747	3,890	336	2,747	3,890
9,750	**9,800**	179	2,747	3,910	332	2,747	3,910
9,800	**9,850**	176	2,747	3,930	329	2,747	3,930
9,850	**9,900**	172	2,747	3,950	325	2,747	3,950
9,900	**9,950**	168	2,747	3,970	321	2,747	3,970
9,950	**10,000**	164	2,747	3,990	317	2,747	3,990
10,000	**10,050**	160	2,747	4,010	313	2,747	4,010
10,050	**10,100**	156	2,747	4,030	309	2,747	4,030
10,100	**10,150**	153	2,747	4,050	306	2,747	4,050
10,150	**10,200**	149	2,747	4,070	302	2,747	4,070
10,200	**10,250**	145	2,747	4,090	298	2,747	4,090
10,250	**10,300**	141	2,747	4,110	294	2,747	4,110
10,300	**10,350**	137	2,747	4,130	290	2,747	4,130
10,350	**10,400**	133	2,747	4,150	286	2,747	4,150
10,400	**10,450**	130	2,747	4,170	283	2,747	4,170
10,450	**10,500**	126	2,747	4,190	279	2,747	4,190
10,500	**10,550**	122	2,747	4,210	275	2,747	4,210
10,550	**10,600**	118	2,747	4,230	271	2,747	4,230
10,600	**10,650**	114	2,747	4,250	267	2,747	4,250
10,650	**10,700**	111	2,747	4,270	264	2,747	4,270
10,700	**10,750**	107	2,747	4,290	260	2,747	4,290
10,750	**10,800**	103	2,747	4,310	256	2,747	4,310
10,800	**10,850**	99	2,747	4,330	252	2,747	4,330
10,850	**10,900**	95	2,747	4,350	248	2,747	4,350
10,900	**10,950**	91	2,747	4,370	244	2,747	4,370
10,950	**11,000**	88	2,747	4,390	241	2,747	4,390

(Continued on page 55)

2006 Earned Income Credit (EIC) Table–*Continued* (**Caution.** This is **not** a tax table.)

If the amount you are looking up from the worksheet is– At least	But less than	Single, head of household, or qualifying widow(er) and you have– No children	One child	Two children	Married filing jointly and you have– No children	One child	Two children
		Your credit is–			Your credit is–		
11,000	**11,050**	84	2,747	4,410	237	2,747	4,410
11,050	**11,100**	80	2,747	4,430	233	2,747	4,430
11,100	**11,150**	76	2,747	4,450	229	2,747	4,450
11,150	**11,200**	72	2,747	4,470	225	2,747	4,470
11,200	**11,250**	68	2,747	4,490	221	2,747	4,490
11,250	**11,300**	65	2,747	4,510	218	2,747	4,510
11,300	**11,350**	61	2,747	4,536	214	2,747	4,536
11,350	**11,400**	57	2,747	4,536	210	2,747	4,536
11,400	**11,450**	53	2,747	4,536	206	2,747	4,536
11,450	**11,500**	49	2,747	4,536	202	2,747	4,536
11,500	**11,550**	46	2,747	4,536	199	2,747	4,536
11,550	**11,600**	42	2,747	4,536	195	2,747	4,536
11,600	**11,650**	38	2,747	4,536	191	2,747	4,536
11,650	**11,700**	34	2,747	4,536	187	2,747	4,536
11,700	**11,750**	30	2,747	4,536	183	2,747	4,536
11,750	**11,800**	26	2,747	4,536	179	2,747	4,536
11,800	**11,850**	23	2,747	4,536	176	2,747	4,536
11,850	**11,900**	19	2,747	4,536	172	2,747	4,536
11,900	**11,950**	15	2,747	4,536	168	2,747	4,536
11,950	**12,000**	11	2,747	4,536	164	2,747	4,536
12,000	**12,050**	7	2,747	4,536	160	2,747	4,536
12,050	**12,100**	3	2,747	4,536	156	2,747	4,536
12,100	**12,150**	*	2,747	4,536	153	2,747	4,536
12,150	**12,200**	0	2,747	4,536	149	2,747	4,536
12,200	**12,250**	0	2,747	4,536	145	2,747	4,536
12,250	**12,300**	0	2,747	4,536	141	2,747	4,536
12,300	**12,350**	0	2,747	4,536	137	2,747	4,536
12,350	**12,400**	0	2,747	4,536	133	2,747	4,536
12,400	**12,450**	0	2,747	4,536	130	2,747	4,536
12,450	**12,500**	0	2,747	4,536	126	2,747	4,536
12,500	**12,550**	0	2,747	4,536	122	2,747	4,536
12,550	**12,600**	0	2,747	4,536	118	2,747	4,536
12,600	**12,650**	0	2,747	4,536	114	2,747	4,536
12,650	**12,700**	0	2,747	4,536	111	2,747	4,536
12,700	**12,750**	0	2,747	4,536	107	2,747	4,536
12,750	**12,800**	0	2,747	4,536	103	2,747	4,536
12,800	**12,850**	0	2,747	4,536	99	2,747	4,536
12,850	**12,900**	0	2,747	4,536	95	2,747	4,536
12,900	**12,950**	0	2,747	4,536	91	2,747	4,536
12,950	**13,000**	0	2,747	4,536	88	2,747	4,536
13,000	**13,050**	0	2,747	4,536	84	2,747	4,536
13,050	**13,100**	0	2,747	4,536	80	2,747	4,536
13,100	**13,150**	0	2,747	4,536	76	2,747	4,536
13,150	**13,200**	0	2,747	4,536	72	2,747	4,536
13,200	**13,250**	0	2,747	4,536	68	2,747	4,536
13,250	**13,300**	0	2,747	4,536	65	2,747	4,536
13,300	**13,350**	0	2,747	4,536	61	2,747	4,536
13,350	**13,400**	0	2,747	4,536	57	2,747	4,536
13,400	**13,450**	0	2,747	4,536	53	2,747	4,536
13,450	**13,500**	0	2,747	4,536	49	2,747	4,536

If the amount you are looking up from the worksheet is– At least	But less than	Single, head of household, or qualifying widow(er) and you have– No children	One child	Two children	Married filing jointly and you have– No children	One child	Two children
		Your credit is–			Your credit is–		
13,500	**13,550**	0	2,747	4,536	46	2,747	4,536
13,550	**13,600**	0	2,747	4,536	42	2,747	4,536
13,600	**13,650**	0	2,747	4,536	38	2,747	4,536
13,650	**13,700**	0	2,747	4,536	34	2,747	4,536
13,700	**13,750**	0	2,747	4,536	30	2,747	4,536
13,750	**13,800**	0	2,747	4,536	26	2,747	4,536
13,800	**13,850**	0	2,747	4,536	23	2,747	4,536
13,850	**13,900**	0	2,747	4,536	19	2,747	4,536
13,900	**13,950**	0	2,747	4,536	15	2,747	4,536
13,950	**14,000**	0	2,747	4,536	11	2,747	4,536
14,000	**14,050**	0	2,747	4,536	7	2,747	4,536
14,050	**14,100**	0	2,747	4,536	3	2,747	4,536
14,100	**14,150**	0	2,747	4,536	*	2,747	4,536
14,150	**14,200**	0	2,747	4,536	0	2,747	4,536
14,200	**14,250**	0	2,747	4,536	0	2,747	4,536
14,250	**14,300**	0	2,747	4,536	0	2,747	4,536
14,300	**14,350**	0	2,747	4,536	0	2,747	4,536
14,350	**14,400**	0	2,747	4,536	0	2,747	4,536
14,400	**14,450**	0	2,747	4,536	0	2,747	4,536
14,450	**14,500**	0	2,747	4,536	0	2,747	4,536
14,500	**14,550**	0	2,747	4,536	0	2,747	4,536
14,550	**14,600**	0	2,747	4,536	0	2,747	4,536
14,600	**14,650**	0	2,747	4,536	0	2,747	4,536
14,650	**14,700**	0	2,747	4,536	0	2,747	4,536
14,700	**14,750**	0	2,747	4,536	0	2,747	4,536
14,750	**14,800**	0	2,747	4,536	0	2,747	4,536
14,800	**14,850**	0	2,747	4,536	0	2,747	4,536
14,850	**14,900**	0	2,737	4,522	0	2,747	4,536
14,900	**14,950**	0	2,729	4,512	0	2,747	4,536
14,950	**15,000**	0	2,721	4,501	0	2,747	4,536
15,000	**15,050**	0	2,713	4,491	0	2,747	4,536
15,050	**15,100**	0	2,705	4,480	0	2,747	4,536
15,100	**15,150**	0	2,697	4,470	0	2,747	4,536
15,150	**15,200**	0	2,689	4,459	0	2,747	4,536
15,200	**15,250**	0	2,681	4,449	0	2,747	4,536
15,250	**15,300**	0	2,673	4,438	0	2,747	4,536
15,300	**15,350**	0	2,665	4,428	0	2,747	4,536
15,350	**15,400**	0	2,657	4,417	0	2,747	4,536
15,400	**15,450**	0	2,649	4,406	0	2,747	4,536
15,450	**15,500**	0	2,641	4,396	0	2,747	4,536
15,500	**15,550**	0	2,633	4,385	0	2,747	4,536
15,550	**15,600**	0	2,625	4,375	0	2,747	4,536
15,600	**15,650**	0	2,617	4,364	0	2,747	4,536
15,650	**15,700**	0	2,609	4,354	0	2,747	4,536
15,700	**15,750**	0	2,601	4,343	0	2,747	4,536
15,750	**15,800**	0	2,593	4,333	0	2,747	4,536
15,800	**15,850**	0	2,585	4,322	0	2,747	4,536
15,850	**15,900**	0	2,577	4,312	0	2,747	4,536
15,900	**15,950**	0	2,569	4,301	0	2,747	4,536
15,950	**16,000**	0	2,561	4,291	0	2,747	4,536

(Continued on page 56)

*If the amount you are looking up from the worksheet is at least $12,100 ($14,100 if married filing jointly) but less than $12,120 ($14,120 if married filing jointly), your credit is $1. Otherwise, you cannot take the credit.

 Need more information or forms? See page 7.

2006 Earned Income Credit (EIC) Table–*Continued* **(Caution.** This is **not** a tax table.)

If the amount you are looking up from the worksheet is–		And your filing status is–					
		Single, head of household, or qualifying widow(er) and you have–			Married filing jointly and you have–		
		No children	One child	Two children	No children	One child	Two children
At least	But less than	Your credit is–			Your credit is–		
16,000	**16,050**	0	2,553	4,280	0	2,747	4,536
16,050	**16,100**	0	2,545	4,270	0	2,747	4,536
16,100	**16,150**	0	2,537	4,259	0	2,747	4,536
16,150	**16,200**	0	2,529	4,249	0	2,747	4,536
16,200	**16,250**	0	2,521	4,238	0	2,747	4,536
16,250	**16,300**	0	2,513	4,227	0	2,747	4,536
16,300	**16,350**	0	2,505	4,217	0	2,747	4,536
16,350	**16,400**	0	2,497	4,206	0	2,747	4,536
16,400	**16,450**	0	2,489	4,196	0	2,747	4,536
16,450	**16,500**	0	2,481	4,185	0	2,747	4,536
16,500	**16,550**	0	2,473	4,175	0	2,747	4,536
16,550	**16,600**	0	2,465	4,164	0	2,747	4,536
16,600	**16,650**	0	2,457	4,154	0	2,747	4,536
16,650	**16,700**	0	2,449	4,143	0	2,747	4,536
16,700	**16,750**	0	2,441	4,133	0	2,747	4,536
16,750	**16,800**	0	2,433	4,122	0	2,747	4,536
16,800	**16,850**	0	2,425	4,112	0	2,747	4,536
16,850	**16,900**	0	2,417	4,101	0	2,737	4,522
16,900	**16,950**	0	2,409	4,091	0	2,729	4,512
16,950	**17,000**	0	2,401	4,080	0	2,721	4,501
17,000	**17,050**	0	2,393	4,070	0	2,713	4,491
17,050	**17,100**	0	2,385	4,059	0	2,705	4,480
17,100	**17,150**	0	2,377	4,048	0	2,697	4,470
17,150	**17,200**	0	2,369	4,038	0	2,689	4,459
17,200	**17,250**	0	2,361	4,027	0	2,681	4,449
17,250	**17,300**	0	2,353	4,017	0	2,673	4,438
17,300	**17,350**	0	2,345	4,006	0	2,665	4,428
17,350	**17,400**	0	2,337	3,996	0	2,657	4,417
17,400	**17,450**	0	2,329	3,985	0	2,649	4,406
17,450	**17,500**	0	2,321	3,975	0	2,641	4,396
17,500	**17,550**	0	2,313	3,964	0	2,633	4,385
17,550	**17,600**	0	2,305	3,954	0	2,625	4,375
17,600	**17,650**	0	2,297	3,943	0	2,617	4,364
17,650	**17,700**	0	2,289	3,933	0	2,609	4,354
17,700	**17,750**	0	2,281	3,922	0	2,601	4,343
17,750	**17,800**	0	2,273	3,912	0	2,593	4,333
17,800	**17,850**	0	2,265	3,901	0	2,585	4,322
17,850	**17,900**	0	2,257	3,891	0	2,577	4,312
17,900	**17,950**	0	2,249	3,880	0	2,569	4,301
17,950	**18,000**	0	2,241	3,869	0	2,561	4,291
18,000	**18,050**	0	2,233	3,859	0	2,553	4,280
18,050	**18,100**	0	2,225	3,848	0	2,545	4,270
18,100	**18,150**	0	2,217	3,838	0	2,537	4,259
18,150	**18,200**	0	2,209	3,827	0	2,529	4,249
18,200	**18,250**	0	2,201	3,817	0	2,521	4,238
18,250	**18,300**	0	2,193	3,806	0	2,513	4,227
18,300	**18,350**	0	2,186	3,796	0	2,505	4,217
18,350	**18,400**	0	2,178	3,785	0	2,497	4,206
18,400	**18,450**	0	2,170	3,775	0	2,489	4,196
18,450	**18,500**	0	2,162	3,764	0	2,481	4,185
18,500	**18,550**	0	2,154	3,754	0	2,473	4,175
18,550	**18,600**	0	2,146	3,743	0	2,465	4,164
18,600	**18,650**	0	2,138	3,733	0	2,457	4,154
18,650	**18,700**	0	2,130	3,722	0	2,449	4,143
18,700	**18,750**	0	2,122	3,712	0	2,441	4,133
18,750	**18,800**	0	2,114	3,701	0	2,433	4,122
18,800	**18,850**	0	2,106	3,690	0	2,425	4,112
18,850	**18,900**	0	2,098	3,680	0	2,417	4,101
18,900	**18,950**	0	2,090	3,669	0	2,409	4,091
18,950	**19,000**	0	2,082	3,659	0	2,401	4,080

If the amount you are looking up from the worksheet is–		And your filing status is–					
		Single, head of household, or qualifying widow(er) and you have–			Married filing jointly and you have–		
		No children	One child	Two children	No children	One child	Two children
At least	But less than	Your credit is–			Your credit is–		
19,000	**19,050**	0	2,074	3,648	0	2,393	4,070
19,050	**19,100**	0	2,066	3,638	0	2,385	4,059
19,100	**19,150**	0	2,058	3,627	0	2,377	4,048
19,150	**19,200**	0	2,050	3,617	0	2,369	4,038
19,200	**19,250**	0	2,042	3,606	0	2,361	4,027
19,250	**19,300**	0	2,034	3,596	0	2,353	4,017
19,300	**19,350**	0	2,026	3,585	0	2,345	4,006
19,350	**19,400**	0	2,018	3,575	0	2,337	3,996
19,400	**19,450**	0	2,010	3,564	0	2,329	3,985
19,450	**19,500**	0	2,002	3,554	0	2,321	3,975
19,500	**19,550**	0	1,994	3,543	0	2,313	3,964
19,550	**19,600**	0	1,986	3,532	0	2,305	3,954
19,600	**19,650**	0	1,978	3,522	0	2,297	3,943
19,650	**19,700**	0	1,970	3,511	0	2,289	3,933
19,700	**19,750**	0	1,962	3,501	0	2,281	3,922
19,750	**19,800**	0	1,954	3,490	0	2,273	3,912
19,800	**19,850**	0	1,946	3,480	0	2,265	3,901
19,850	**19,900**	0	1,938	3,469	0	2,257	3,891
19,900	**19,950**	0	1,930	3,459	0	2,249	3,880
19,950	**20,000**	0	1,922	3,448	0	2,241	3,869
20,000	**20,050**	0	1,914	3,438	0	2,233	3,859
20,050	**20,100**	0	1,906	3,427	0	2,225	3,848
20,100	**20,150**	0	1,898	3,417	0	2,217	3,838
20,150	**20,200**	0	1,890	3,406	0	2,209	3,827
20,200	**20,250**	0	1,882	3,396	0	2,201	3,817
20,250	**20,300**	0	1,874	3,385	0	2,193	3,806
20,300	**20,350**	0	1,866	3,375	0	2,186	3,796
20,350	**20,400**	0	1,858	3,364	0	2,178	3,785
20,400	**20,450**	0	1,850	3,353	0	2,170	3,775
20,450	**20,500**	0	1,842	3,343	0	2,162	3,764
20,500	**20,550**	0	1,834	3,332	0	2,154	3,754
20,550	**20,600**	0	1,826	3,322	0	2,146	3,743
20,600	**20,650**	0	1,818	3,311	0	2,138	3,733
20,650	**20,700**	0	1,810	3,301	0	2,130	3,722
20,700	**20,750**	0	1,802	3,290	0	2,122	3,712
20,750	**20,800**	0	1,794	3,280	0	2,114	3,701
20,800	**20,850**	0	1,786	3,269	0	2,106	3,690
20,850	**20,900**	0	1,778	3,259	0	2,098	3,680
20,900	**20,950**	0	1,770	3,248	0	2,090	3,669
20,950	**21,000**	0	1,762	3,238	0	2,082	3,659
21,000	**21,050**	0	1,754	3,227	0	2,074	3,648
21,050	**21,100**	0	1,746	3,217	0	2,066	3,638
21,100	**21,150**	0	1,738	3,206	0	2,058	3,627
21,150	**21,200**	0	1,730	3,196	0	2,050	3,617
21,200	**21,250**	0	1,722	3,185	0	2,042	3,606
21,250	**21,300**	0	1,714	3,174	0	2,034	3,596
21,300	**21,350**	0	1,706	3,164	0	2,026	3,585
21,350	**21,400**	0	1,698	3,153	0	2,018	3,575
21,400	**21,450**	0	1,690	3,143	0	2,010	3,564
21,450	**21,500**	0	1,682	3,132	0	2,002	3,554
21,500	**21,550**	0	1,674	3,122	0	1,994	3,543
21,550	**21,600**	0	1,666	3,111	0	1,986	3,532
21,600	**21,650**	0	1,658	3,101	0	1,978	3,522
21,650	**21,700**	0	1,650	3,090	0	1,970	3,511
21,700	**21,750**	0	1,642	3,080	0	1,962	3,501
21,750	**21,800**	0	1,634	3,069	0	1,954	3,490
21,800	**21,850**	0	1,626	3,059	0	1,946	3,480
21,850	**21,900**	0	1,618	3,048	0	1,938	3,469
21,900	**21,950**	0	1,610	3,038	0	1,930	3,459
21,950	**22,000**	0	1,602	3,027	0	1,922	3,448

(Continued on page 57)

2006 Earned Income Credit (EIC) Table–*Continued* (**Caution.** This is **not** a tax table.)

If the amount you are looking up from the worksheet is–		And your filing status is–					
		Single, head of household, or qualifying widow(er) and you have–			Married filing jointly and you have–		
		No children	One child	Two children	No children	One child	Two children
At least	But less than	Your credit is–			Your credit is–		
22,000	22,050	0	1,594	3,017	0	1,914	3,438
22,050	22,100	0	1,586	3,006	0	1,906	3,427
22,100	22,150	0	1,578	2,995	0	1,898	3,417
22,150	22,200	0	1,570	2,985	0	1,890	3,406
22,200	22,250	0	1,562	2,974	0	1,882	3,396
22,250	22,300	0	1,554	2,964	0	1,874	3,385
22,300	22,350	0	1,546	2,953	0	1,866	3,375
22,350	22,400	0	1,538	2,943	0	1,858	3,364
22,400	22,450	0	1,530	2,932	0	1,850	3,353
22,450	22,500	0	1,522	2,922	0	1,842	3,343
22,500	22,550	0	1,514	2,911	0	1,834	3,332
22,550	22,600	0	1,506	2,901	0	1,826	3,322
22,600	22,650	0	1,498	2,890	0	1,818	3,311
22,650	22,700	0	1,490	2,880	0	1,810	3,301
22,700	22,750	0	1,482	2,869	0	1,802	3,290
22,750	22,800	0	1,474	2,859	0	1,794	3,280
22,800	22,850	0	1,466	2,848	0	1,786	3,269
22,850	22,900	0	1,458	2,838	0	1,778	3,259
22,900	22,950	0	1,450	2,827	0	1,770	3,248
22,950	23,000	0	1,442	2,816	0	1,762	3,238
23,000	23,050	0	1,434	2,806	0	1,754	3,227
23,050	23,100	0	1,426	2,795	0	1,746	3,217
23,100	23,150	0	1,418	2,785	0	1,738	3,206
23,150	23,200	0	1,410	2,774	0	1,730	3,196
23,200	23,250	0	1,402	2,764	0	1,722	3,185
23,250	23,300	0	1,394	2,753	0	1,714	3,174
23,300	23,350	0	1,387	2,743	0	1,706	3,164
23,350	23,400	0	1,379	2,732	0	1,698	3,153
23,400	23,450	0	1,371	2,722	0	1,690	3,143
23,450	23,500	0	1,363	2,711	0	1,682	3,132
23,500	23,550	0	1,355	2,701	0	1,674	3,122
23,550	23,600	0	1,347	2,690	0	1,666	3,111
23,600	23,650	0	1,339	2,680	0	1,658	3,101
23,650	23,700	0	1,331	2,669	0	1,650	3,090
23,700	23,750	0	1,323	2,659	0	1,642	3,080
23,750	23,800	0	1,315	2,648	0	1,634	3,069
23,800	23,850	0	1,307	2,637	0	1,626	3,059
23,850	23,900	0	1,299	2,627	0	1,618	3,048
23,900	23,950	0	1,291	2,616	0	1,610	3,038
23,950	24,000	0	1,283	2,606	0	1,602	3,027
24,000	24,050	0	1,275	2,595	0	1,594	3,017
24,050	24,100	0	1,267	2,585	0	1,586	3,006
24,100	24,150	0	1,259	2,574	0	1,578	2,995
24,150	24,200	0	1,251	2,564	0	1,570	2,985
24,200	24,250	0	1,243	2,553	0	1,562	2,974
24,250	24,300	0	1,235	2,543	0	1,554	2,964
24,300	24,350	0	1,227	2,532	0	1,546	2,953
24,350	24,400	0	1,219	2,522	0	1,538	2,943
24,400	24,450	0	1,211	2,511	0	1,530	2,932
24,450	24,500	0	1,203	2,501	0	1,522	2,922
24,500	24,550	0	1,195	2,490	0	1,514	2,911
24,550	24,600	0	1,187	2,479	0	1,506	2,901
24,600	24,650	0	1,179	2,469	0	1,498	2,890
24,650	24,700	0	1,171	2,458	0	1,490	2,880
24,700	24,750	0	1,163	2,448	0	1,482	2,869
24,750	24,800	0	1,155	2,437	0	1,474	2,859
24,800	24,850	0	1,147	2,427	0	1,466	2,848
24,850	24,900	0	1,139	2,416	0	1,458	2,838
24,900	24,950	0	1,131	2,406	0	1,450	2,827
24,950	25,000	0	1,123	2,395	0	1,442	2,816
25,000	25,050	0	1,115	2,385	0	1,434	2,806
25,050	25,100	0	1,107	2,374	0	1,426	2,795
25,100	25,150	0	1,099	2,364	0	1,418	2,785
25,150	25,200	0	1,091	2,353	0	1,410	2,774
25,200	25,250	0	1,083	2,343	0	1,402	2,764
25,250	25,300	0	1,075	2,332	0	1,394	2,753
25,300	25,350	0	1,067	2,322	0	1,387	2,743
25,350	25,400	0	1,059	2,311	0	1,379	2,732
25,400	25,450	0	1,051	2,300	0	1,371	2,722
25,450	25,500	0	1,043	2,290	0	1,363	2,711
25,500	25,550	0	1,035	2,279	0	1,355	2,701
25,550	25,600	0	1,027	2,269	0	1,347	2,690
25,600	25,650	0	1,019	2,258	0	1,339	2,680
25,650	25,700	0	1,011	2,248	0	1,331	2,669
25,700	25,750	0	1,003	2,237	0	1,323	2,659
25,750	25,800	0	995	2,227	0	1,315	2,648
25,800	25,850	0	987	2,216	0	1,307	2,637
25,850	25,900	0	979	2,206	0	1,299	2,627
25,900	25,950	0	971	2,195	0	1,291	2,616
25,950	26,000	0	963	2,185	0	1,283	2,606
26,000	26,050	0	955	2,174	0	1,275	2,595
26,050	26,100	0	947	2,164	0	1,267	2,585
26,100	26,150	0	939	2,153	0	1,259	2,574
26,150	26,200	0	931	2,143	0	1,251	2,564
26,200	26,250	0	923	2,132	0	1,243	2,553
26,250	26,300	0	915	2,121	0	1,235	2,543
26,300	26,350	0	907	2,111	0	1,227	2,532
26,350	26,400	0	899	2,100	0	1,219	2,522
26,400	26,450	0	891	2,090	0	1,211	2,511
26,450	26,500	0	883	2,079	0	1,203	2,501
26,500	26,550	0	875	2,069	0	1,195	2,490
26,550	26,600	0	867	2,058	0	1,187	2,479
26,600	26,650	0	859	2,048	0	1,179	2,469
26,650	26,700	0	851	2,037	0	1,171	2,458
26,700	26,750	0	843	2,027	0	1,163	2,448
26,750	26,800	0	835	2,016	0	1,155	2,437
26,800	26,850	0	827	2,006	0	1,147	2,427
26,850	26,900	0	819	1,995	0	1,139	2,416
26,900	26,950	0	811	1,985	0	1,131	2,406
26,950	27,000	0	803	1,974	0	1,123	2,395
27,000	27,050	0	795	1,964	0	1,115	2,385
27,050	27,100	0	787	1,953	0	1,107	2,374
27,100	27,150	0	779	1,942	0	1,099	2,364
27,150	27,200	0	771	1,932	0	1,091	2,353
27,200	27,250	0	763	1,921	0	1,083	2,343
27,250	27,300	0	755	1,911	0	1,075	2,332
27,300	27,350	0	747	1,900	0	1,067	2,322
27,350	27,400	0	739	1,890	0	1,059	2,311
27,400	27,450	0	731	1,879	0	1,051	2,300
27,450	27,500	0	723	1,869	0	1,043	2,290
27,500	27,550	0	715	1,858	0	1,035	2,279
27,550	27,600	0	707	1,848	0	1,027	2,269
27,600	27,650	0	699	1,837	0	1,019	2,258
27,650	27,700	0	691	1,827	0	1,011	2,248
27,700	27,750	0	683	1,816	0	1,003	2,237
27,750	27,800	0	675	1,806	0	995	2,227
27,800	27,850	0	667	1,795	0	987	2,216
27,850	27,900	0	659	1,785	0	979	2,206
27,900	27,950	0	651	1,774	0	971	2,195
27,950	28,000	0	643	1,763	0	963	2,185

(Continued on page 58)

Need more information or forms? See page 7.

2006 Earned Income Credit (EIC) Table–*Continued* (**Caution.** This is **not** a tax table.)

If the amount you are looking up from the worksheet is–		And your filing status is– Single, head of household, or qualifying widow(er) and you have–			Married filing jointly and you have–		
		No children	One child	Two children	No children	One child	Two children
At least	But less than	Your credit is–			Your credit is–		
28,000	28,050	0	635	1,753	0	955	2,174
28,050	28,100	0	627	1,742	0	947	2,164
28,100	28,150	0	619	1,732	0	939	2,153
28,150	28,200	0	611	1,721	0	931	2,143
28,200	28,250	0	603	1,711	0	923	2,132
28,250	28,300	0	595	1,700	0	915	2,121
28,300	28,350	0	588	1,690	0	907	2,111
28,350	28,400	0	580	1,679	0	899	2,100
28,400	28,450	0	572	1,669	0	891	2,090
28,450	28,500	0	564	1,658	0	883	2,079
28,500	28,550	0	556	1,648	0	875	2,069
28,550	28,600	0	548	1,637	0	867	2,058
28,600	28,650	0	540	1,627	0	859	2,048
28,650	28,700	0	532	1,616	0	851	2,037
28,700	28,750	0	524	1,606	0	843	2,027
28,750	28,800	0	516	1,595	0	835	2,016
28,800	28,850	0	508	1,584	0	827	2,006
28,850	28,900	0	500	1,574	0	819	1,995
28,900	28,950	0	492	1,563	0	811	1,985
28,950	29,000	0	484	1,553	0	803	1,974
29,000	29,050	0	476	1,542	0	795	1,964
29,050	29,100	0	468	1,532	0	787	1,953
29,100	29,150	0	460	1,521	0	779	1,942
29,150	29,200	0	452	1,511	0	771	1,932
29,200	29,250	0	444	1,500	0	763	1,921
29,250	29,300	0	436	1,490	0	755	1,911
29,300	29,350	0	428	1,479	0	747	1,900
29,350	29,400	0	420	1,469	0	739	1,890
29,400	29,450	0	412	1,458	0	731	1,879
29,450	29,500	0	404	1,448	0	723	1,869
29,500	29,550	0	396	1,437	0	715	1,858
29,550	29,600	0	388	1,426	0	707	1,848
29,600	29,650	0	380	1,416	0	699	1,837
29,650	29,700	0	372	1,405	0	691	1,827
29,700	29,750	0	364	1,395	0	683	1,816
29,750	29,800	0	356	1,384	0	675	1,806
29,800	29,850	0	348	1,374	0	667	1,795
29,850	29,900	0	340	1,363	0	659	1,785
29,900	29,950	0	332	1,353	0	651	1,774
29,950	30,000	0	324	1,342	0	643	1,763
30,000	30,050	0	316	1,332	0	635	1,753
30,050	30,100	0	308	1,321	0	627	1,742
30,100	30,150	0	300	1,311	0	619	1,732
30,150	30,200	0	292	1,300	0	611	1,721
30,200	30,250	0	284	1,290	0	603	1,711
30,250	30,300	0	276	1,279	0	595	1,700
30,300	30,350	0	268	1,269	0	588	1,690
30,350	30,400	0	260	1,258	0	580	1,679
30,400	30,450	0	252	1,247	0	572	1,669
30,450	30,500	0	244	1,237	0	564	1,658
30,500	30,550	0	236	1,226	0	556	1,648
30,550	30,600	0	228	1,216	0	548	1,637
30,600	30,650	0	220	1,205	0	540	1,627
30,650	30,700	0	212	1,195	0	532	1,616
30,700	30,750	0	204	1,184	0	524	1,606
30,750	30,800	0	196	1,174	0	516	1,595
30,800	30,850	0	188	1,163	0	508	1,584
30,850	30,900	0	180	1,153	0	500	1,574
30,900	30,950	0	172	1,142	0	492	1,563
30,950	31,000	0	164	1,132	0	484	1,553

If the amount you are looking up from the worksheet is–		And your filing status is– Single, head of household, or qualifying widow(er) and you have–			Married filing jointly and you have–		
		No children	One child	Two children	No children	One child	Two children
At least	But less than	Your credit is–			Your credit is–		
31,000	31,050	0	156	1,121	0	476	1,542
31,050	31,100	0	148	1,111	0	468	1,532
31,100	31,150	0	140	1,100	0	460	1,521
31,150	31,200	0	132	1,090	0	452	1,511
31,200	31,250	0	124	1,079	0	444	1,500
31,250	31,300	0	116	1,068	0	436	1,490
31,300	31,350	0	108	1,058	0	428	1,479
31,350	31,400	0	100	1,047	0	420	1,469
31,400	31,450	0	92	1,037	0	412	1,458
31,450	31,500	0	84	1,026	0	404	1,448
31,500	31,550	0	76	1,016	0	396	1,437
31,550	31,600	0	68	1,005	0	388	1,426
31,600	31,650	0	60	995	0	380	1,416
31,650	31,700	0	52	984	0	372	1,405
31,700	31,750	0	44	974	0	364	1,395
31,750	31,800	0	36	963	0	356	1,384
31,800	31,850	0	28	953	0	348	1,374
31,850	31,900	0	20	942	0	340	1,363
31,900	31,950	0	12	932	0	332	1,353
31,950	32,000	0	4	921	0	324	1,342
32,000	32,050	0	0	911	0	316	1,332
32,050	32,100	0	0	900	0	308	1,321
32,100	32,150	0	0	889	0	300	1,311
32,150	32,200	0	0	879	0	292	1,300
32,200	32,250	0	0	868	0	284	1,290
32,250	32,300	0	0	858	0	276	1,279
32,300	32,350	0	0	847	0	268	1,269
32,350	32,400	0	0	837	0	260	1,258
32,400	32,450	0	0	826	0	252	1,247
32,450	32,500	0	0	816	0	244	1,237
32,500	32,550	0	0	805	0	236	1,226
32,550	32,600	0	0	795	0	228	1,216
32,600	32,650	0	0	784	0	220	1,205
32,650	32,700	0	0	774	0	212	1,195
32,700	32,750	0	0	763	0	204	1,184
32,750	32,800	0	0	753	0	196	1,174
32,800	32,850	0	0	742	0	188	1,163
32,850	32,900	0	0	732	0	180	1,153
32,900	32,950	0	0	721	0	172	1,142
32,950	33,000	0	0	710	0	164	1,132
33,000	33,050	0	0	700	0	156	1,121
33,050	33,100	0	0	689	0	148	1,111
33,100	33,150	0	0	679	0	140	1,100
33,150	33,200	0	0	668	0	132	1,090
33,200	33,250	0	0	658	0	124	1,079
33,250	33,300	0	0	647	0	116	1,068
33,300	33,350	0	0	637	0	108	1,058
33,350	33,400	0	0	626	0	100	1,047
33,400	33,450	0	0	616	0	92	1,037
33,450	33,500	0	0	605	0	84	1,026
33,500	33,550	0	0	595	0	76	1,016
33,550	33,600	0	0	584	0	68	1,005
33,600	33,650	0	0	574	0	60	995
33,650	33,700	0	0	563	0	52	984
33,700	33,750	0	0	553	0	44	974
33,750	33,800	0	0	542	0	36	963
33,800	33,850	0	0	531	0	28	953
33,850	33,900	0	0	521	0	20	942
33,900	33,950	0	0	510	0	12	932
33,950	34,000	0	0	500	0	4	921

(Continued on page 59)

2006 Earned Income Credit (EIC) Table—*Continued* (**Caution.** This is **not** a tax table.)

If the amount you are looking up from the worksheet is—		And your filing status is— Single, head of household, or qualifying widow(er) and you have—			Married filing jointly and you have—		
At least	But less than	No children	One child	Two children	No children	One child	Two children
		Your credit is—			Your credit is—		
34,000	**34,050**	0	0	489	0	0	911
34,050	**34,100**	0	0	479	0	0	900
34,100	**34,150**	0	0	468	0	0	889
34,150	**34,200**	0	0	458	0	0	879
34,200	**34,250**	0	0	447	0	0	868
34,250	**34,300**	0	0	437	0	0	858
34,300	**34,350**	0	0	426	0	0	847
34,350	**34,400**	0	0	416	0	0	837
34,400	**34,450**	0	0	405	0	0	826
34,450	**34,500**	0	0	395	0	0	816
34,500	**34,550**	0	0	384	0	0	805
34,550	**34,600**	0	0	373	0	0	795
34,600	**34,650**	0	0	363	0	0	784
34,650	**34,700**	0	0	352	0	0	774
34,700	**34,750**	0	0	342	0	0	763
34,750	**34,800**	0	0	331	0	0	753
34,800	**34,850**	0	0	321	0	0	742
34,850	**34,900**	0	0	310	0	0	732
34,900	**34,950**	0	0	300	0	0	721
34,950	**35,000**	0	0	289	0	0	710
35,000	**35,050**	0	0	279	0	0	700
35,050	**35,100**	0	0	268	0	0	689
35,100	**35,150**	0	0	258	0	0	679
35,150	**35,200**	0	0	247	0	0	668
35,200	**35,250**	0	0	237	0	0	658
35,250	**35,300**	0	0	226	0	0	647
35,300	**35,350**	0	0	216	0	0	637
35,350	**35,400**	0	0	205	0	0	626
35,400	**35,450**	0	0	194	0	0	616
35,450	**35,500**	0	0	184	0	0	605
35,500	**35,550**	0	0	173	0	0	595
35,550	**35,600**	0	0	163	0	0	584
35,600	**35,650**	0	0	152	0	0	574
35,650	**35,700**	0	0	142	0	0	563
35,700	**35,750**	0	0	131	0	0	553
35,750	**35,800**	0	0	121	0	0	542
35,800	**35,850**	0	0	110	0	0	531
35,850	**35,900**	0	0	100	0	0	521
35,900	**35,950**	0	0	89	0	0	510
35,950	**36,000**	0	0	79	0	0	500
36,000	**36,050**	0	0	68	0	0	489
36,050	**36,100**	0	0	58	0	0	479
36,100	**36,150**	0	0	47	0	0	468
36,150	**36,200**	0	0	37	0	0	458
36,200	**36,250**	0	0	26	0	0	447
36,250	**36,300**	0	0	15	0	0	437
36,300	**36,350**	0	0	**	0	0	426
36,350	**36,400**	0	0	0	0	0	416
36,400	**36,450**	0	0	0	0	0	405
36,450	**36,500**	0	0	0	0	0	395

If the amount you are looking up from the worksheet is—		And your filing status is— Single, head of household, or qualifying widow(er) and you have—			Married filing jointly and you have—		
At least	But less than	No children	One child	Two children	No children	One child	Two children
		Your credit is—			Your credit is—		
36,500	**36,550**	0	0	0	0	0	384
36,550	**36,600**	0	0	0	0	0	373
36,600	**36,650**	0	0	0	0	0	363
36,650	**36,700**	0	0	0	0	0	352
36,700	**36,750**	0	0	0	0	0	342
36,750	**36,800**	0	0	0	0	0	331
36,800	**36,850**	0	0	0	0	0	321
36,850	**36,900**	0	0	0	0	0	310
36,900	**36,950**	0	0	0	0	0	300
36,950	**37,000**	0	0	0	0	0	289
37,000	**37,050**	0	0	0	0	0	279
37,050	**37,100**	0	0	0	0	0	268
37,100	**37,150**	0	0	0	0	0	258
37,150	**37,200**	0	0	0	0	0	247
37,200	**37,250**	0	0	0	0	0	237
37,250	**37,300**	0	0	0	0	0	226
37,300	**37,350**	0	0	0	0	0	216
37,350	**37,400**	0	0	0	0	0	205
37,400	**37,450**	0	0	0	0	0	194
37,450	**37,500**	0	0	0	0	0	184
37,500	**37,550**	0	0	0	0	0	173
37,550	**37,600**	0	0	0	0	0	163
37,600	**37,650**	0	0	0	0	0	152
37,650	**37,700**	0	0	0	0	0	142
37,700	**37,750**	0	0	0	0	0	131
37,750	**37,800**	0	0	0	0	0	121
37,800	**37,850**	0	0	0	0	0	110
37,850	**37,900**	0	0	0	0	0	100
37,900	**37,950**	0	0	0	0	0	89
37,950	**38,000**	0	0	0	0	0	79
38,000	**38,050**	0	0	0	0	0	68
38,050	**38,100**	0	0	0	0	0	58
38,100	**38,150**	0	0	0	0	0	47
38,150	**38,200**	0	0	0	0	0	37
38,200	**38,250**	0	0	0	0	0	26
38,250	**38,300**	0	0	0	0	0	15
38,300	**38,348**	0	0	0	0	0	5
38,348	**or more**	0	0	0	0	0	0

**If the amount you are looking up from the worksheet is at least $36,300 but less than $36,348, your credit is $5. Otherwise, you cannot take the credit.

RESIDENTIAL ENERGY CREDITS

Homeowners will be happy to learn of two new credits for 2006 and 2007: the nonbusiness energy property credit and residential energy efficient property credit. These credits are claimed on Line 52 of Form 1040 after completing Form 5695, *Residential Energy Credits.*

Nonbusiness Energy Property Credit

For 2006 and 2007, a tax credit of up to $500 is available to individuals for nonbusiness energy property, such as residential exterior doors and windows, insulation, heat pumps, furnaces, central air conditioners and water heaters. The nonbusiness energy property must be installed in or on a dwelling unit in the United States that is owned and used by the taxpayer as the taxpayer's principal residence and originally placed in service by the taxpayer.

There must be a reasonable expectation that the qualified energy efficiency improvements (exterior doors and windows, insulation, and certain metal roofs) will remain in use for at least 5 years. Residential energy property expenditures (heat pumps, furnaces, central air conditioners and water heaters) include labor costs.

The credit is equal to the residential energy property expenditure plus 10 percent of the cost of qualified energy efficiency improvements.

The residential energy property credit is limited to a maximum of $500 for all tax years and no more than $200 of the credit can be based on expenditures for windows. The residential energy property credit applies to qualified energy efficiency improvements and qualified energy property placed in service in 2006 and 2007.

Eligible improvements include:

- insulation materials
- exterior windows, including skylights
- exterior doors;
- metal roofs with special pigmented coatings
- electric heat pump water heaters
- electric and geothermal heat pumps
- central air conditioners
- natural gas, propane, or oil water heaters or furnaces
- hot water boilers
- advanced main air circulating fans

Residential Energy Efficient Property Credit

For 2006 and 2007, a tax credit is available to help individual taxpayers pay for residential alternative energy equipment. The credit is 30 percent of the cost of eligible solar water heaters, solar electricity equipment (photovoltaics) and fuel cell plants. The maximum credit is $2,000 per tax year for *each* category of solar equipment, and $500 for each half kilowatt of capacity of fuel cell plants installed per tax year.

The annual dollar limitations applicable to the residential alternative energy credit ($2,000 per tax year for each category of solar equipment, and $500 for each half kilowatt of capacity of fuel cell plants installed per tax year) are applied without regard to any carryover of the credit from the prior tax year. Cooperative and condominium dwellers can claim the credit by splitting the cost of installing equipment with other unit owners. Eligible equipment must be placed in service during 2006 and 2007.

Credit for Federal Excise Tax Paid

In 2006, the IRS finally conceded that long distance telephone charges that vary only by elapsed time (and not by distance) are not taxable. This is good news for taxpayers because of its related decision to issue credits or refunds of all excise taxes paid on long distance service billed after February 28, 2003, and before August 1, 2006, along with interest.

The standard refund amount, based on the total number of exemptions claimed on the 2006 federal income tax return, allows individual taxpayers to request the telephone tax refund without having to examine old phone bills. The standard amounts are $30 for a person filing a return with one exemption, $40 for two exemptions, $50 for three exemptions, and $60 for four of more exemptions.

Any individual, business, or nonprofit organization that paid the long distance telephone tax is entitled to the refund on their 2006 federal income tax return, but only individuals can use the standard amount. To get the standard amount, eligible taxpayers must fill in Line 71 of Form 1040 after completing Form 8913, *Credit for Federal Telephone Excise Tax Paid.* For those who do not need to file a regular return, the IRS is creating a special short form (Form 1040EZ-T). As a more difficult alternative, individuals can chose to figure their refund using the actual amount of tax paid.

Chapter 17

Calculating Your Tax

Now that you know how to report your income, deductions, exemptions, and the special tax breaks and credits you might be entitled to in your business or personal life, it's time to pull the whole thing together and calculate the amount of tax you owe.

In this chapter we'll explain how to compute your income taxes, and we'll also discuss a couple of other types of tax you may have to report and pay on your tax return: the alternative minimum tax (AMT), and payroll taxes on household employees.

COMPUTING AND PAYING INCOME TAX

To review what we've covered so far, the basic formula for federal income taxes is:

total income – adjustments = adjusted gross income

AGI – deductions and exemptions = taxable income

Taxes are then calculated based on the amount of your taxable income. From this initial tax bill, your allowable credits are subtracted, and any additional taxes (like AMT, self-employment taxes, and payroll taxes on household help) are added, to arrive at the amount of taxes you actually owe for the year.

Many people can calculate their taxes using the tax tables provided at the end of this book. Simply take the taxable income amount from Line 43 of Form 1040, Line 27 of Form 1040A, or Line 6 of Form 1040EZ, go to the tax tables and find the line in the bold-faced column that includes your income amount, and read across to the right to find the column that pertains to your filing status. The amount shown at the intersection between the income line and the filing status column will be your tax.

If your taxable income is $100,000 or more, you can't use the tables. Instead, you must use the tax rate schedules that follow the end of the tables.

Some taxpayers must use other forms to calculate their initial tax bills. If you have a net capital gain shown on Schedule D, you must calculate your tax by following the directions for each line on the back of Schedule D, to take advantage of the lower rates on long-term capital gains. If you have farm income and choose to use income averaging, calculate your tax using Schedule J, *Farm Income Averaging.*

After you've determined your tax amount using one of the methods described above, add to it any tax amount shown on Form 8814, *Parents' Election to Report Child's Interest and Dividends,* or on Form 4972, *Tax on Lump-Sum Distributions.* Write the total amount of your tax on Line 44 of Form 1040, Line 28 of Form 1040A, or Line 10 of Form 1040EZ.

Claiming Your Credits

From your initial tax bill, you will subtract any of the tax credits that apply to you in 2006:

1. the credit for child and dependent care expenses (see page 191)
2. the credit for the elderly or the disabled (see page 286)
3. the child tax credit (see page 282)
4. the education credits (see page 288)
5. the adoption credit (see page 284)
6. the foreign tax credit (see page 229)
7. the mortgage interest credit, claimed on Form 8396 (see page 205)
8. the residential energy credits, claimed on Form 5695
9. the credit for prior year's minimum tax, claimed on Form 8801 (see page 305)
10. the credit for a qualified electric vehicle, claimed on Form 8834 (see page 145)
11. the general business credit (see page 149)
12. the empowerment zone employment credit (see page 144)

Note that none of these credits can be claimed on Form 1040EZ, and only the first five can be claimed on Form 1040A. The full list of credits may be claimed on Form 1040.

Add Your Other Taxes

Now that you've calculated your income tax bill, you must add in any other taxes that you owe:

- the self-employment tax, as shown on Schedule SE (see page 135)
- the AMT, as shown on Form 6251 (see page 305)
- any Social Security and Medicare tax on tip income not reported to your employer, as shown on Form 4137
- additional tax on improper distributions or excess contributions to IRAs, other retirement plans, or medical savings accounts, as shown on Form 5329 (see pages 251 and 92, respectively)
- advance earned income credit payments you received, as shown on your W-2 (although this is not, strictly speaking, a tax, it's treated as one for purposes of the computation)
- employment taxes on household help, as shown on Schedule H (see page 306)
- any recapture of the investment tax credit on Form 4255, low-income housing credit on Form 8611, qualified electric vehicle credit on Form 8611, or Indian employment credit on Form 8845
- any recapture of federal mortgage subsidies on Form 8828, the 10 percent tax on retirement benefits that exceed plan formulas for business owners, and the tax on accumulation distributions of trusts on Form 4970

Note that none of these are reported on Form 1040EZ, and only the advance earned income credit may be reported on Form 1040A. If you owe any of the other listed taxes, you must file Form 1040.

Subtract Your Payments

After you've determined the dollar amount of all the tax that you owe, you must subtract the amounts of the payments you've made during the year. This includes both tax that was withheld on a paycheck, as shown in Box 2 of any W-2 forms you (or your spouse, if filing jointly) received, and any estimated tax payments you made during the year.

Save Money

Don't forget to add in any income tax withheld from pension checks or investment income such as interest and dividends, as shown on your 1099 forms.

Refundable tax credits are treated as if they were payments that you made. Therefore, if you had an earned income credit (EIC) amount for 2006, or if you claimed the additional child credit (see page 283), it will be added to your other tax payments. In effect, the credit will increase the refund you get (or at least reduce your tax bill).

If you are filing after April 15th because you requested an extension on Form 4868 (see page 309), include any amount you sent in with that form on Line 69 of Form 1040. If you overpaid your Social Security tax (see page 138), report the overpaid amount on Line 67. And if you have any credit on Form 2439, *Notice to Shareholder of Undistributed Long-Term Capital Gains,* or Form 4136, *Credit for Federal Tax Paid on Fuels,* include those amounts on Line 70 since they are treated as tax payments.

Refunds and Payments

Your total tax payments are subtracted from your total tax owed, to see whether you are due a refund, or must pay more when you file your tax return.

If you're due a refund, you have a couple of choices. You can ask the IRS to electronically deposit the amount in your bank account, by using the space provided to write down your bank routing number (the first nine-digit number that appears on the last line of your check) and your bank account number (the number that immediately follows the routing number).

If you prefer, you can have some or all of your refund applied to your 2007 estimated tax, by writing the amount you want to apply on Line 75 of Form 1040, or on Line 46 of Form 1040A.

Save Time

For those who will owe estimated tax for 2007 and are filing by April 15th, applying your refund to 2007 can be a good solution because your first estimated payment is also due on April 15th. Simply rolling the amount due you for 2006 into the account for 2007 saves you the time and trouble of writing an additional check to the IRS.

If you don't elect to receive an electronic deposit or to have your refund applied to your 2007 taxes, you will receive a paper check from the government, generally within six weeks.

Offset of Refunds for Debts

If you owe certain types of debts, the IRS will keep your refund and apply it to the amount you owe. This applies to those who owe back child support, a previous year's taxes, or a federal nontax debt such as a student loan. If an offset occurs, you will get a notice from a federal agency known as Financial Management Service. FMS will provide information to you about the amount, date, and nature of the offset. If the debt is back child support, the notice will indicate the state to which the offset amount was paid, and give you a contact in the state that would handle concerns or questions regarding the delinquent debt that resulted in the tax refund offset.

If you file jointly and it is your spouse who owes the debt, the IRS may keep the entire refund. However, you can get your portion of the refund by filing IRS Form 8379, *Injured Spouse Claim and Allocation.*

Paying Your Taxes

If your tax return shows that your prepaid taxes are less than the taxes you actually owe, you'll have to send some money in with your tax forms. If you owe more than $1,000 and more than 10 percent of the tax shown on your return, you may also owe a penalty (see page 313 for a discussion of the tax penalties). You can, if you wish, send in the amount you owe without the penalties – the IRS will compute the penalties and interest you owe and send you a bill later.

We generally recommend that you let the IRS compute your penalty, since the computation is extremely complicated and time consuming.

However, the standard IRS computation assumes that you received your income evenly over the year. If in fact you received most of your income in one or two quarters, you will have to file IRS Form 2210 in order to show that.

Make your check payable to the United States Treasury, and be sure to write the year and the tax form (e.g., "2006 Form 1040"), and your Social Security number on the check.

Work Smart

If you are filing jointly, write the name and Social Security number of the spouse whose name appears first on the front of your tax form. Otherwise the IRS might not apply the payment to the correct account.

If you send in a check, you must also complete Form 1040-V, *Payment Voucher,* and include it with your tax return. The IRS requests that you don't staple the check to your return, but simply enclose it in your envelope.

Signing Your Return

You must sign your tax return before the IRS will accept it – if you don't, the document will probably be returned to you so you can sign it. Make sure that both spouses sign the return if you're filing jointly.

If you are filing a return for a minor child, sign the child's name, and add "By (your signature), parent (or guardian) for minor child." The parent who signs the child's return will be authorized to deal with the IRS if any questions arise about the return.

Assembling and Mailing Your Tax Return

Each form that you need to attach to your Form 1040 or 1040A has an "attachment sequence number"

Where Do You File? If an envelope addressed to "Internal Revenue Service Center" came with this booklet, please use it. If you do not have one or if you moved during the year, mail your return to the Internal Revenue Service Center shown below that applies to you.

TIP *Envelopes without enough postage will be returned to you by the post office. Your envelope may need additional postage if it contains more than five pages or is oversized (for example, it is over ¼" thick). Also, include your complete return address.*

	THEN use this address if you:	
IF you live in...	**Are not enclosing a check or money order...**	**Are enclosing a check or money order...**
Alabama, Delaware, Florida, Georgia, North Carolina, Rhode Island, South Carolina, Virginia	Internal Revenue Service Center Atlanta, GA 39901-0002	Internal Revenue Service Center Atlanta, GA 39901-0102
District of Columbia, Maine, Maryland, Massachusetts, New Hampshire, New York, Vermont	Internal Revenue Service Center Andover, MA 05501-0002	Internal Revenue Service Center Andover, MA 05501-0102
Arkansas, Connecticut, Illinois, Indiana, Iowa, Michigan, Missouri, New Jersey, Ohio, Wisconsin	Internal Revenue Service Center Kansas City, MO 64999-0002	Internal Revenue Service Center Kansas City, MO 64999-0102
Kentucky*, Pennsylvania*	Internal Revenue Service Center Philadelphia, PA 19255-0002	Internal Revenue Service Center Philadelphia, PA 19255-0102
Kansas, Louisiana, Mississippi, Oklahoma, Tennessee, Texas, West Virginia, APO, FPO	Internal Revenue Service Center Austin, TX 73301-0002	Internal Revenue Service Center Austin, TX 73301-0102
Alaska, Arizona, California, Colorado, Hawaii, Idaho, Minnesota, Montana, Nebraska, Nevada, New Mexico, North Dakota, Oregon, South Dakota, Utah, Washington, Wyoming	Internal Revenue Service Center Fresno, CA 93888-0002	Internal Revenue Service Center Fresno, CA 93888-0102
American Samoa, nonpermanent residents of Guam or the Virgin Islands**, Puerto Rico (or if excluding income under Internal Revenue Code section 933), dual-status aliens, a foreign country: U.S. citizens and those filing Form 2555, 2555-EZ, or Form 4563	Internal Revenue Service Center Austin, TX 73301-0215 USA	Internal Revenue Service Center Austin, TX 73301-0215 USA

* If you live in Kentucky or Pennsylvania and file your return after June 30, 2007, use: Internal Revenue Service Center, Kansas City, MO 64999-0002 (if you are not enclosing a check or money order); or Internal Revenue Service Center, Kansas City, MO 64999-0102 (if you are enclosing a check or money order).

** Permanent residents of Guam should use: Department of Revenue and Taxation, Government of Guam, P.O. Box 23607, GMF, GU 96921; permanent residents of the Virgin Islands should use: V.I. Bureau of Internal Revenue, 9601 Estate Thomas, Charlotte Amalie, St. Thomas, VI 00802.

printed in its upper right-hand corner. When assembling your tax return, place the forms in order of their sequence, with Form 1040 (or 1040A) on top. If you have any supporting statements or schedules, attach them all at the end, in the same order as the forms or schedules they refer to.

Be sure to write your name and Social Security number on the top of each tax form, just in case they are separated. And staple a copy of any W-2 forms you received to the front of the return.

Work Smart

Whenever you send a tax form or, for that matter, any other correspondence to the IRS, we recommend that you use certified or registered mail so that you get a return receipt. If you ever need proof that you mailed your documents on time, and that the IRS received them, you'll have it.

If you're filing close to the deadline, you can also use next-day or second-day service from Airborne Express, DHL Worldwide Express, Federal Express, or United Parcel Service. Any of these services can tell you how to get written proof of the mailing date.

THE AMT

In a twisted plot to take back the tax breaks it provides, Congress created the alternative minimum tax (AMT). Initially, the AMT was intended to prevent higher-income taxpayers from substantially reducing or eliminating their tax liabilities through incentives offered by the tax code. In practice, however, the AMT affects even middle-income taxpayers because the AMT exemption amounts have traditionally not kept up with inflation. For example, the exemption rates set in 1992 were not increased until 2001.

Because some taxpayers — particularly wealthy taxpayers — have been so successful in their efforts to legally minimize their tax bills, Congress came up with another way to tax them: the alternative minimum tax (AMT). The AMT provides a formula for computing tax that ignores certain preferential tax treatments and deductions that taxpayers would otherwise be entitled to claim.

As a result, many taxpayers are required to compute their income tax liability twice: once under the regular method and once again under the AMT method. An individual will be subject to the AMT if his or her AMT liability is more than the regular tax liability for the year.

What types of things can trigger the AMT? The most common items that can cause you to become subject to the AMT are listed below. These items must be added back to your taxable income in order to compute your AMT:

- all personal exemptions
- the standard deduction, if you claimed it
- itemized deductions for state and local income taxes, and real estate taxes
- itemized deductions for home equity loan interest (this does not include interest on a loan to buy, build, or improve your home)
- itemized deductions for miscellaneous deductions
- itemized deductions for any portion of medical expenses that exceed 7.5 percent of AGI but not 10 percent of AGI
- deductions you claimed for accelerated depreciation that exceed what you could have claimed under straight-line depreciation
- differences between gain or loss on the sale of property for AMT purposes and for regular tax purposes; these differences most commonly occur as a result of the different depreciation methods required under AMT, as described above
- addition of certain income from incentive stock options
- changes in income from installment sales, since the installment sale method generally can't be used for AMT purposes
- changes in certain passive activity loss deductions
- deductions relating to oil and gas investments, or drilling or mining operations

- interest on certain private activity bonds that would otherwise be tax-exempt

If you have large amounts of any items on this list, and your adjusted gross income exceeds the exemption amounts discussed below, you (or your accountant) should compute your AMT liability on IRS Form 6251, *Alternative Minimum Tax—Individuals,* to determine whether you must actually pay any AMT. We've reproduced this form at the end of the book for reference, to allow you to decide whether you need to complete it or not. If you do need to complete it, you can get a free copy of the form's instructions by calling 1-800-TAX-FORM, or by downloading them from the Internet at www.irs.gov/forms_pubs/forms.html.

Children under age 18 who have investment income of more than $6,050 in 2005 should also complete Form 6251 to see whether they owe any AMT.

AMT Rates and Exemptions

The AMT method does provide each taxpayer with a flat dollar amount that is completely exempt from tax. The dollar amount of your exemption depends on your filing status. The exemption amounts for 2006 are:

- $62,550 if married filing jointly
- $42,500 if single or head of household
- $31,275 if married filing separately

Although the exemption amounts above have been increased, the AMT rates remain the same for 2001 and beyond. If your taxable income for AMT purposes (called AMTI) exceeds the exemption amount, you will be subject to a 26 percent AMT rate on the first $175,000 of AMTI ($87,500 for married taxpayers filing separately) that exceeds the exemption amount, and a 28 percent rate on any AMTI above this $175,000 amount.

The AMT exemption amounts are phased out for taxpayers having AMTI exceeding the specified income levels. Under these rules, the exemption available to married couples filing jointly is eliminated entirely if AMTI exceeds $382,000. The amount where the exemption is reduced to zero is $273,500 for single individuals and heads of households, and $191,000 for married taxpayers filing separately.

Work Smart

There's no doubt about it — the AMT can play havoc with your tax planning. If your AMT liability and your regular tax liability tend to be approximately equal from year to year, your best bet is to maintain this stability. If your deductions are not so evenly spaced and you tend to have great fluctuations in income from year to year, you may be able to shift some AMT-triggering items from an AMT year to a non-AMT year, so as to reduce your liability in a non-AMT year almost to the point at which you would become subject to the AMT. Your tax professional can tell you whether this might be possible in your individual situation.

Credit for Prior Year's Minimum Tax

If you paid AMT last year, or you had a minimum tax credit carryforward from last year, you may be able to claim a tax credit on Form 8801, *Credit for Prior Year Minimum Tax.* You can get a copy of this form by calling 1-800-TAX-FORM or downloading it from the Internet at www.irs.gov/ forms_pubs/forms.html.

Payroll Taxes on Household Employees

If you are a working parent or, for that matter, anyone who sets out to hire a maid, babysitter, caregiver for an elderly relative, or some other kind of domestic help, it may come as a surprise to discover that you'll be required to pay significant amounts in employment taxes.

Warning

For various reasons, the person you hire may not want you to withhold taxes, preferring to be paid "under the table" in cash. However, the tax laws provide penalties, sometimes substantial ones, for noncompliance. If you went for several years without paying Social Security and Medicare taxes, for example, the back taxes, interest, and penalties you'd owe could add up to hundreds or even thousands of dollars. Employers who have paid their domestic workers in cash, without paying payroll taxes, have been surprised to find that if a former employee files for unemployment benefits, the state will report them to the IRS, triggering an audit that goes back many years.

Are You an Employer?

You don't have to pay taxes on payments that you make to independent contractors, because they are treated as business owners themselves, and they're responsible for paying their own self-employment taxes. If you get domestic workers through an agency, the agency is generally considered the employer. But if you use independent workers and your arrangement gives you the right to control not only the type of work that must be done, but how it must be done (such as what specific tasks must be done by a maid, what cleaning products should be used, etc.), you will be considered an employer.

Generally, you must pay employment taxes if you paid any one employee cash wages of $1,400 or more in 2006 (unless the worker was a student under age 18 at any time during the year). You must also pay if you paid total cash wages of $1,000 or more in any calendar quarter of 2005 or 2006 to any number of household employees. However, if you hire your spouse or your child under age 21, you don't need to pay any payroll taxes. If you hire your parent, you don't pay federal unemployment tax, and you don't need to pay Social Security or Medicare tax unless your parent cares for a child who lives with you and is under 18 or disabled, and you are divorced and not remarried, you are widowed, or you're married to a person whose physical or mental condition prevents him or her from caring for the child.

Payroll Tax Rates and Forms

If you are required to pay employment taxes on domestic help, you can pay them along with your regular income tax on Form 1040. However, you will need to complete Schedule H, *Household Employment Taxes,* and attach it to your tax return. Call 1-800-TAX-FORM to get a copy of this form and its instructions, which will walk you through the procedures for completing the form. Also ask for a copy of IRS Publication 926, *Household Employer's Tax Guide,* which explains more about the responsibilities of employers, including the need to file annual W-2 forms for each employee.

If you are required to pay payroll taxes on your employee's paycheck, the FICA tax rate that you'll pay is 7.65 percent of the employee's paycheck, and you should withhold an equal amount (7.65 percent of pay) from the amount you give your employee. FICA taxes include Social Security and Medicare. You may choose to pay your employee's portion of the tax, if you wish. You will also have to pay federal unemployment taxes, generally at a 0.8 percent rate (be sure to check with your state department of labor for the rules on state unemployment tax, since you will generally have to pay that tax as well).

You don't have to withhold income tax from your household employee's paycheck unless you want to. However, you may have to make advance payments of the employee's earned income credit, if the employee asks you to. See IRS Publication 926 for more details.

As mentioned above, you can report all the employment taxes you owe for domestic workers during 2006 on your 2006 tax return. However, you may have to pay an estimated tax penalty if your total tax bill, including taxes on household workers, is over $1,000 more than the tax you prepaid throughout the year through estimated tax payments or payroll withholding.

To avoid this penalty, it's generally necessary to estimate the household taxes you'll be liable for during the year, and use your estimate to increase the withholding amount on any paychecks you receive, or add the amount to your quarterly estimated tax payments during the year (see page 310).

Chapter 18

Dealing with the IRS

As a small business owner, it's important for you to be aware of what your tax payment obligations are and when they are due.

There's no sinking feeling like the one you have when you thought you had a cash surplus on your books, and then suddenly you have to make a payment to the IRS that depletes your entire balance. Worse yet is the scenario where the funds have been spent elsewhere because you didn't realize a tax payment was due. With a good awareness of your filing and payment obligations, you won't find yourself in this situation or subject to penalties for late filing or payments.

So, this chapter includes information on:

- due dates for regular returns and payments
- estimated tax payment information
- penalties for underpayments or late returns

Finally, we'll end with a discussion of other situations in which you may need to deal with the IRS. We'll give you a list of common errors that trigger IRS letters, and we'll provide some advice on what to expect if you are audited.

DUE DATES FOR TAX RETURNS

For calendar year taxpayers, the due date for filing and payment of tax due on individual income tax returns is April 15.

Work Smart

As a general rule, if a due date that is set by law falls on a Saturday, Sunday, or federal legal holiday, it is delayed until the next day that isn't a Saturday, Sunday, or legal holiday. However, a statewide legal holiday delays a due date only if the IRS office where you are required to file your returns is located in that state.

If you want an automatic six-month extension to file your 2006 return, you can file Form 4868, *Application For Automatic Extension of Time To File U.S. Individual Income Tax Return,* by April 16. Your actual return would then be due on October 16.

Warning

It's important to realize that the automatic extension only applies to the filing of your return, not to the payment of any tax that may be due. You must pay any tax that you estimate will be due for 2006 by April 16 of 2007, or you may be subject to interest and penalties on overdue taxes, as discussed below.

Fiscal Year Taxpayers

If you are a sole proprietor who uses a fiscal year rather than a calendar year, you must file your individual income tax return (including all the applicable schedules) no later than the 15th day of the fourth month after the end of your tax year.

You are entitled to the same automatic six-month extension to file your return that a calendar year taxpayer is entitled to, but you must file for the extension on Form 4868 by the due date for filing the return. The due date for the filing of your return is then the 15th day of the sixth month after the original due date of your return.

ESTIMATED TAX PAYMENTS

If you are a small business owner, chances are good that you will have to make estimated tax payments.

Estimated tax payments are used to pay tax on income that is not subject to withholding. This, of course, includes income from self-employment (estimated tax payments cover both income tax and self-employment tax). Even if you receive a salary from a job you hold in addition to running your own business, you may still have to make estimated tax payments if the amount of tax being withheld from your salary is insufficient.

Who Must Make Estimated Tax Payments?

You're probably asking yourself, "do I have to make estimated tax payments for 2007?" By answering "yes" or "no" to these three questions, you'll have your answer:

1. Do you expect to owe $1,000 or more for 2006, after subtracting any income tax withholding and credits from your total tax? If the answer is no, you are not required to pay estimated tax. If the answer is yes, go on to the next question.

2. Do you expect your income tax withholding and credits to be at least 90 percent of the tax you'll owe for 2007? If the answer is yes, you are not required to pay estimated tax. If the answer is no, go on to the next question.

3. Do you expect your income tax withholding and credits to be at least 100 percent of the tax shown on your 2006 return? (If your 2006 adjusted gross income was more than $150,000, or more than $75,000 for marrieds filing separately, substitute 110 percent in the preceding sentence). If the answer is yes, you are not required to pay estimated tax. If the answer is no, you must make estimated tax payments.

Save Money

The IRS treats tax payments that are made through payroll withholding as being made evenly through the year, regardless of when the withholding is actually done. If you or your spouse is receiving a paycheck, you can avoid the need to make estimated tax payments and retain the use of more money throughout the year, if you arrange to have extra tax withheld from your paycheck during the last month of the year.

You can do this by filing a revised Form W-4 with your employer (or your spouse's employer) at the end of the year. To avoid penalties, the extra withholding must be a dollar amount that brings your total tax withholding for the year at least up to the lesser of (a) 100 percent of the amount you expect to owe minus $1,000, (b) 90 percent of the amount you expect to owe, or (c) 100 percent of the amount you owed last year (110 percent for high-income taxpayers).

Calculating Your Estimated Tax Payments

If you are required to make estimated tax payments, how much do you have to pay?

Your total tax payments during the year (that is, before January 15th of the next year) must add up to the lower of these two amounts: (1) 90 percent of the tax you owe for the current year, or (2) 100 percent of the tax you owed for last year. (If your 2006 adjusted gross income was more than $150,000, or more than $75,000 for marrieds filing separately, substitute 110 percent in the preceding sentence.) "Tax you owe for the year" includes federal income tax and any self-employment (SECA) tax due on your business income.

"Total tax payments" includes any tax withholding on any paychecks, investment income, pensions, or any other income you receive (or that your spouse receives, if filing jointly). If the difference between any withholding during the year and the amount computed in the paragraph above is $1,000 or more, it must be made up with estimated tax payments.

The best way to do this is to look at each major item on each tax form and schedule that you filed this year, and make a guess as to whether it will change for next year. If you think there will be a change, estimate what the change will be (for instance if your real estate tax bill on your office will rise by 10 percent, that will reduce the amount of net income from your business on Schedule C, and increase the amount of itemized real estate taxes deductible on Schedule A). Then, determine how the cumulative changes will affect your tax bill to arrive at a ballpark estimated bill. From this expected tax bill, subtract any withholding that will be done, and the amount remaining, minus $1,000, is what you need to pay in estimated taxes. Many business owners go through this exercise at least twice a year: around April 15th, and then again sometime in the third quarter of the year.

The IRS provides a worksheet on which you can make this calculation, as part of the instructions to Form 1040-ES. This form and its instructions were not available when we went to press, but you can get a copy by calling 1-800-TAX-FORM.

Regular or Annualized Method

Once you know the total amount of estimated tax payments you'll have to make during the year, there are two ways to compute the dollar amount you must pay for each quarter: the regular installment method and the annualized income installment method.

The regular installment method works by dividing your total amount of estimated payments for the year by four. On each payment due date, you pay one-fourth of the total tax due for the year. The IRS prefers this method, and it's by far the simplest to use.

If your business is of the type that doesn't receive income evenly throughout the year (for example, you sell surfboards year-round in the Northeast), you may want to use the second method. Under this method, your required estimated tax payment for one or more periods may be less than the amount figured using the regular installment method.

If you elect to use this method, you will have to file Form 2210, *Underpayment of Estimated Tax by Individuals, Estates, and Trusts,* with your regular individual income tax return for 2006. Using this method is more complicated than simply determining your net income for each quarter, and figuring the tax on it. For complete instructions, talk to your tax advisor or get a copy of the IRS's free Publication 505, *Tax Withholding and Estimated Tax.*

How to Make Estimated Tax Payments

You can make your estimated tax payments in two ways:

- by crediting all or part of any overpayment on your annual tax return towards your next year's estimated tax (rather than getting a refund)
- by sending in your estimated tax payments with payment vouchers using Form 1040-ES, *Estimated Tax For Individuals*

When to Make Estimated Tax Payments

For estimated tax payment purposes, a year is divided into four payment periods. Each period has a specific payment due date. If you don't pay enough tax by the due date of each of the payment periods, you may be charged a penalty for underpayment of tax until the underpayment is made up. This means that you may be charged a penalty for a particular quarter even if you're due a refund when you file your income tax return for the entire year! For calendar year taxpayers, your estimated tax payment due dates are:

For the Period	Due Date
January 1-March 31	April 15
April 1-May 31	June 15
June 1-August 31	September 15
September 1-December 31	January 15 (of the following year)

If at least two-thirds of your annual income comes from farming or fishing, you have only one payment due date for your estimated taxes — January 15. The first three payment periods don't apply.

Fiscal Year Filers

If you operate your business on a fiscal year, your estimated tax payment due dates are:

- the 15th day of the fourth month of your fiscal year
- the 15th day of the sixth month of your fiscal year
- the 15th day of the ninth month of your fiscal year
- the 15th day of the first month after the end of your fiscal year

Again, if at least two-thirds of your annual income comes from farming or fishing, and your operate on a fiscal tax year, you have only one payment due date for your estimated taxes — the 15th day of the first month after the end of your fiscal year. The first three payment periods don't apply.

If the due date for making an estimated tax payment falls on a Saturday, Sunday, or legal holiday, the payment must be made on the next day that is not a Saturday, Sunday, or legal holiday.

Filing Early in Lieu of Making Last Payment

There is a special rule in the tax law that excuses you from filing fourth quarter estimated taxes if you file your annual tax return (Form 1040, etc.), and pay any tax due by January 31. If you are a fiscal year taxpayer, you don't have to make the last quarterly estimated tax payment if you file your income tax return by the last day of the first month after the end of your fiscal year and pay all the tax you owe with your return.

Example

Stella, a self-employed individual with no tax withheld, does not make an estimated tax payment for the fourth quarter of 2006 but files a Form 1040 and pays the tax due as shown on the return on January 20, 2007. Although she did not make a fourth quarter payment of tax, she is excused from doing so because she filed her return on or before January 31, 2007, and paid the full estimated tax amount due. Otherwise, she would have to make a fourth quarter estimated tax payment by January 15, 2007.

Some of the advantages of filing your annual return by January 31 include:

- an 16-day (from January 15 to January 31) interest-free loan from the IRS
- one less payment that can be potentially lost in the mail — of course, it remains good practice to send estimated payments or final returns via certified or registered mail, to make sure the mail is received by the IRS

However, there are pitfalls to filing early:

- It's difficult to be accurate on your final tax return when you might not have received all the 1099s and other information you need to complete the forms.
- If you have computed your estimated tax payments based on a figure of less than 100 percent of the final tax amount shown on the return (i.e., the lesser of 90 percent of the final amount shown on the return or 100 percent of the tax shown on the preceding year's return) you will have to come up with the balance by January 31, rather than having the luxury of waiting until April 15.

Of course even if you think it's a good idea, filing early isn't always possible due to factors beyond your control. You may not have received documents that must be attached to your final tax return (Form W-2 for example). Or, if you are a partner or S corporation shareholder, you may not have received Schedule K-1s containing important tax information needed to complete your annual return. Finally, as a business owner, you simply may not have had sufficient time to compile the tax information needed to complete your Schedule C, *Profit or Loss From Business.*

INTEREST AND PENALTIES FOR UNDERPAYMENT OR LATE RETURNS

What happens if you don't file a tax return or pay taxes that you owe by their due date? Generally, in this situation the IRS will send you a notice hitting you with interest and penalties.

Interest

The IRS will charge you interest on taxes not paid by their due date, even if you've been granted an extension of time to file your return. The interest rates, for most taxpayers, are based on the federal short-term rate plus 3 percentage points. As we go to press, the most recently announced interest rate on underpayments of tax is 5 percent.

Interest is also charged on the penalties imposed for failure to file a return, as well as other penalties imposed for inaccuracy, fraud, etc. This interest is charged on the penalty from the due date of the return, including extensions.

Penalties

If you pay your taxes late, the penalty is usually 0.5 percent of the unpaid amount for each month or part of a month the tax is not paid. The penalty can't be more than 25 percent of the unpaid amount and applies to any unpaid tax on the return. Please note, this penalty is *in addition* to the interest charged for late payments.

The IRS will also hit you with a penalty if you file your return late. In that case, the penalty is usually 5 percent of the amount due for each month or part of a month your return is late, unless you have a reasonable explanation. If you think you have a reasonable explanation, write it down in a statement and attach it to your return, and you might be able to avoid the penalty. In any case, the penalty usually can't be more than 25 percent of the tax due. However, if your return is more than 60 days late, the minimum penalty will be $100 or the amount of any tax you owe, whichever is smaller.

Estimated Tax Penalty

What happens if you underpay your estimated tax? You may have to pay a penalty in the form of interest on the underpayment for the period when the underpayment occurred. The penalty is figured separately for each payment period, and you may owe a penalty for an earlier payment period even if you later paid enough to make up the underpayment.

As a matter of fact, if you didn't pay enough tax by the due date of each of the payment periods, you may owe a penalty even if you are due a refund from the IRS when you file your income tax return.

Example

Cherilyn is employed as a teacher and runs her own tutoring business as well. She didn't make any estimated tax payments during 2006 because she thought she had enough tax withheld from her teaching wages. Early in January 2007, she estimated her total 2005 tax and realized that her withholding was $2,000 less than the amount needed to avoid a penalty for underpayment of estimated tax. So on January 11, Cherilyn made an estimated tax payment of $2,000, the difference between her withholding and her estimate of her total tax.

When she files her final return, Cherilyn's total tax is $50 less than she originally figured, so she is due a refund from the IRS. However, Cherilyn will owe a penalty through January 11 for her underpayments for the first three quarterly payment periods. She won't owe a penalty for the fourth quarter because she made a payment for that quarter by the January 15 due date.)

You can request a waiver of the penalty if the underpayment was caused by a casualty, disaster, or some other unusual circumstance that would make its imposition unfair. The IRS may also waive the penalty for reasonable cause during the first two years after a taxpayer retires upon reaching age 62 or becomes disabled. Form 2210, *Underpayment of Estimated Tax by Individuals, Estates, and Trusts,* must be filed to request a waiver.

You can use Form 2210 to calculate your estimated tax penalty. But this form is very complicated, and generally, you aren't required to complete it. When you file your tax return, the IRS will usually figure the penalty for you and send you a bill. Depending on what you pay your tax pro, it may be more beneficial to you to let the IRS do the calculations.

What other situations might require you to file Form 2210? Other than when you request a waiver, you must file Form 2210 when:

- You use the annualized income installment method.
- You use your actual withholding for each payment period for estimated tax purposes.
- You base any of your required installments on the tax shown on the previous year's return and you filed or are filing a joint return for either that previous year or the present year, but not for both years.

How to Handle an Audit

There are two pieces of advice that you should keep in mind about audits:

- If you've done your homework, kept good records, and your return is truthful, you don't have anything to worry about.
- It's better not to be audited.

Minimize the Risk of Being Audited

First, let's talk about the second point.

The average taxpayer has a very small chance of being audited. But if you are self-employed, your return is definitely not typical of the millions of returns filed by employees. You may be waving some red flags at the IRS and increasing your chances of being audited.

What to Expect if You Are Audited

The IRS has several different levels of audits. If questions arise about your math, items seem to be omitted from your return, or your figures don't match those on your W-2s, 1099s, or 1098s, the IRS may simply request a correction or explanation by mail.

Respond to the request as quickly as possible and, if you have doubts about the answer, consult your tax professional if you have one.

Work Smart

The IRS makes mistakes, too. Don't assume the IRS notice is correct. Check things out. Computer-generated forms, which include the forms most commonly sent out to deal with small errors, are notorious for automatically adding penalties that may not apply in your situation. If you are in doubt, call the IRS and ask them about anything you don't understand.

The first level of inquiry that can truly be considered an "audit" occurs when you get a letter requesting that you come into the IRS office to review one or more areas on your return. This is a true audit because the IRS is asking for proof of items on your return that goes beyond your word.

Work Smart

You can attend an audit yourself, but you don't have to. You can authorize your accountant, lawyer, or other tax professional to handle it without you. Often this is the best way to prevent the audit from escalating beyond the original areas that piqued the IRS's interest. Experienced professional advisors are less likely to become emotional or to make statements that lead to more IRS questioning.

If you have kept records, including bills, receipts, and canceled checks (see Chapter 2), you shouldn't worry. The IRS may end up interpreting your situation differently than you, but there is no crime in having differences of opinion. Nevertheless, professional help may be in order with an office audit, particularly if you yourself suspect that there are errors or omissions in your tax return.

As rare as audits are, the dreaded knock on the door from the IRS agent is even rarer. Individuals are almost never audited in this way. On-site or "field audits" are used mainly for larger businesses, particularly when records are not portable. If you do get a notice of a field audit, professional help is definitely recommended.

Suggestions for Minimizing Audit Risk

The IRS does not provide details on its audit criteria – in fact, they are a closely guarded secret. However, we offer the following suggestions for minimizing your risk:

- Make sure that the information provided on any W-2 forms you receive from employers, and 1099s or 1098s you receive from banks, mutual funds, brokerages, retirement plans, or any other source, are accurately reflected on your return. If there is a mistake, get the issuer of the form to correct it. The IRS computer matches these figures with the figures on your return, and it will question any mismatch. If you have many of these forms, report each one separately somewhere on your tax return. The computer will not catch it if you lump the numbers together.
- If you are claiming an unusual deduction or there is something confusing on your return, attach a written explanation. Any statements should be as brief and to the point as possible – don't ramble or provide unessential details.
- If you are claiming home office expenses or significant travel or entertainment expenses, make sure you have the records. The IRS scrutinizes these expenses very carefully. The same is true of all business expenses if you haven't yet established a track record, and especially if your business is not profitable.
- Sign your return. Fill out all the information required. For example, it's common to omit the Social Security number of an ex-spouse from a return, but you are required to supply it if you are paying alimony. Make sure your return is complete.
- Make sure your math is correct. Arithmetic errors are the most common errors turned up by the IRS. If you are doing your own return with a calculator, after you've done all the computations, we suggest you start at the amount of your refund (or tax you owe) and work backwards to check your work (e.g., add back your payments, subtract your other taxes, and add back your credits to see whether you arrive at the same tax amount; continue in this vein for the rest of the return).
- Make sure that all Social Security numbers for your dependents are correct.

Glossary of Tax Terms

Accelerated depreciation. A depreciation method that allows larger deductions in the early years of an asset's "life" and smaller deductions at the end of the period. (See "Straight-line depreciation.")

Accrual method (or accrual basis). One of two main accounting methods for determining when a transaction has tax significance. The accrual method says that a transaction is taxed when an obligation to pay or a right to receive payment is created (for example, at the time products are delivered, services rendered, billings sent, etc.). This method is used by all but the smallest businesses. (See "Cash method (or cash basis).")

Adjusted basis. The cost of property (or a substitute figure—see "Basis") with adjustments made to account for depreciation (in the case of business property), improvements (in the case of real estate), withdrawals or reinvestment (in the case of securities, funds, accounts, insurance or annuities), etc. Adjusted basis is part of the computation for determining gain or loss on a sale or exchange and for depreciation.

Adjusted gross income. The amount of income considered actually "available" to be taxed. Adjusted gross income is gross income reduced principally by business expenses incurred to earn the income and other specified reductions (such as alimony).

Alternative minimum tax. An alternative tax system that says: your tax shall not go below this level. The alternative minimum tax works by negating (or minimizing) the effects of tax preferences or loopholes.

Amortization. The write-off of an amount spent for certain capital assets, similar to depreciation. This tax meaning is different from the common meaning of the term that describes, for example, payment schedules of loans.

Applicable Federal Rates (AFRs). Minimum interest rates that must be charged on various transactions that involve payments over a number of years. If the parties to a transaction do not adhere to these rates, the IRS will impute the interest. (See "Imputed interest.")

At-risk rules. Rules that limit an investor's deductible losses from an investment to the amount invested. Complications arise when investors finance their investment through loans that they are not personally on the hook for (nonrecourse financing). Without these rules, investors could raise their deduction limit considerably without being at-risk for the actual loss.

Basis. The starting point for computing gain or loss on a sale or exchange of property or for depreciation. (See "Adjusted basis.") For property that is purchased, basis is its cost. The basis of inherited property is its value at the date of death (or alternative valuation date). The basis of property received as a gift or a nontaxable transaction is based on the adjusted basis of the transferor (with some adjustments). Special rules govern property transferred between corporations and their shareholders, partners and their partnership, etc.

Cafeteria plan. A plan maintained by an employer that allows employees to select from a menu of taxable and nontaxable benefits.

Capital expenditures. Amounts spent to acquire or improve assets with useful lives of more than one year. These expenditures may not be deducted, but are added to the basis of the property (See "Adjusted basis.") and, for business property, may be converted into deductions through depreciation or amortization.

Capital gain or loss. Gain or loss from the sale or exchange of investment property, personal property (such as a home) or other "capital asset," which is often entitled to preferential tax treatment.

Carrybacks and carryforwards. Deductions that may be transferred to a year other than the current year because they exceeded certain limits. These deductions are typically carried back to earlier years first and, if they exceed the limits for those years, are then carried forward to later years until the deduction is used up. Charitable contributions and net operating losses are examples of deductions that may be carried back or forward.

Cash method (or cash basis). One of two main accounting methods for determining when a transaction has tax significance. The cash method says that a transaction is taxed when payment is made. This method is used by most individuals. (See "Accrual method (or accrual basis).")

Community property. A system governing spousal ownership of property and income that is the law in certain western and southern states and Wisconsin. The differences between community property and "common law" can change how federal tax law applies to spouses. For example: married taxpayers filing separately in a common law state do not have to report income earned by the other spouse. They do have to report income earned in a community property state.

Deferred compensation. An arrangement that allows an employee to receive part of a year's pay in a later year and not be taxed in the year the money was earned.

Depletion. A system similar to depreciation that allows the owner of natural resources (for example: a coal mine or an oil well) to deduct a portion of the cost of the asset during each year of its presumed productive life.

Depreciation. A system that allows a business or individual to deduct a portion of the cost of an asset ("recover its cost") during each year of its predetermined "life" (or "recovery period").

Earned income. Income earned by working for it. Interest, dividends and other kinds of profits are examples of *un*earned income.

Earned income credit. A tax credit available to individuals with low earned income. An individual is entitled to the full amount of this credit even if it exceeds the amount of tax otherwise due.

Employee stock ownership plan (ESOP). A type of profit-sharing plan in which benefits come in the form of stock in the employer.

Estimated tax. Quarterly down payments on a year's taxes that are required (on April 15, June 15, September 15, and January 15) if the total year's taxes will exceed $1,000 and the amount is not covered by withholding.

Federal Insurance Contributions Act (FICA). Social security taxes (for both old-age, survivors and disability insurance—OASDI—and Medicare).

Federal Unemployment Tax Act (FUTA). Unemployment taxes.

Filing status. One of four tax ranks determined by your marital status, your dependents and the way you file your tax return: (1) single, (2) married filing jointly, (3) married filing separately and (4) head of household. Filing status determines your tax rates and your eligibility for various tax benefits (for example: alimony deduction, IRA deduction, standard deduction, etc.).

First-in, first-out (FIFO). A rule that applies to the sale of part of a group of similar items (such as inventory, shares of the same stock, etc.) that assumes the first ones acquired were the first ones sold. This is important if the items in the group were acquired or manufactured at different times or for different costs. The rule may be overridden by identifying the specific item sold, if possible. (See "Last-in, first-out (LIFO).")

Generation-skipping transfer tax. An extra tax on gifts or on-death transfers of money or property that would otherwise escape the once-per-generation transfer taxes that apply to gifts and estates. For example: a gift from a grandfather to a granddaughter skips a generation and might be subject to this tax.

Golden parachutes. Bonuses payable to key executives in the event control of their corporation changes, as in the case of a takeover. "Excess" golden parachute payments are subject to tax penalties.

Gross income. All income that might be subject to tax. Most "realized" increases in wealth are considered income. The main exceptions for individuals are gifts, inheritances, increases in value of property *prior* to sale, loan repayments and some personal injury awards. For businesses, investments in their capital are not considered income.

Head of household. A filing status available to qualifying single parents (or others supporting certain dependents) that allows lower taxes than the normal rates for singles.

Imputed interest. A portion of a future payment that is treated as interest if parties to the transaction do not provide a stated amount of interest at a rate acceptable to the IRS. (See "Applicable Federal Rates (AFRs).") This prevents improper use of certain tax advantages (capital gains rates or tax deferral). For example: if a business sells an asset on the installment basis, part of all future payments is treated as interest whether the transaction states it or not.

Incentive stock option. A stock option that may be granted to an employee under tax-favored terms.

Itemized deductions. Personal deductions that may be taken if they total more than the standard deduction. (See "Standard deduction.") The following deductions are then itemized or listed on Schedule A of Form 1040: medical expenses, charitable contributions, state and local taxes, home mortgage interest, real estate taxes, casualty losses, unreimbursed employee expenses, investment expenses and others.

Investment credit. A credit against tax available for investment in a limited range of business property. The *general* investment credit was repealed in 1986, but this type of credit has been enacted and repealed repeatedly throughout history.

Involuntary conversion. The conversion of property into money under circumstances beyond the control of the owner. For example: (1) property that is destroyed and "converted" into an insurance settlement or (2) property that is seized by the government and "converted" into a condemnation award. Owners may avoid tax on any gain that may result (if the insurance settlement or condemnation award exceeds the adjusted basis of the property) by reinvesting in similar property within certain time limits.

Joint return. An optional filing status available to married taxpayers that offers generally (but not always) lower taxes than "married filing separately."

Keogh plan. A retirement plan available to self-employed individuals.

Last-in, first-out (LIFO). A rule that applies to the sale of part of a group of similar items in an inventory that assumes the last ones acquired were the first ones sold. This is important if the items in the group were acquired or manufactured at different times or for different costs. (See "First-in, first-out (FIFO).")

Like-kind exchanges. Tax-free swaps of investment property. Commonly used for real estate.

Limited liability company (LLC). A legal structure that allows a business to be taxed like a partnership but function generally like a corporation. An LLC offers members (among other things) protection against liability for claims against the business that is not available in a partnership.

Listed property. Property listed in the tax code or by the IRS that must comply with special rules before depreciation may be claimed. Cars and personal computers are examples of listed property. The special rules are designed to prevent deductions where the property is used for personal rather than business purposes.

Modified Accelerated Cost Recovery System (MACRS). The system for computing depreciation for most business assets.

Net operating loss. The excess of business expenses over income. A business may apply a net operating loss to get a refund of past taxes (or a reduction of future taxes) by carrying it back to profitable years as an additional deduction (or by carrying it forward as a deduction to future years).

Original issue discount (OID). The purchase discount offered on some bonds (and similar obligations) in lieu of interest. For example: zero-coupon bonds. OID is generally treated as interest income to the holder rather than as a capital gain.

Passive activity loss (PAL). Loss on an investment that is deductible only up to the limit of gains from similar investments. The limit mainly affects tax shelters and does not apply to stocks, bonds or investments in businesses in which the investor materially participates. Special rules apply to investments in real estate.

Qualified plan. A retirement or profit-sharing plan that meets requirements about who must be covered, the amount of benefits that are paid, information that must be given to plan participants, etc. Qualified plans are entitled to tax benefits unavailable to nonqualified plans.

Real estate investment trust (REIT). A kind of "mutual fund" that invests in real estate rather than stocks and bonds.

Real estate mortgage investment conduit (REMIC). A kind of "mutual fund" that invests in real estate mortgages rather than stocks and bonds.

Recapture. The undoing of a tax benefit if certain requirements are not met in future years. For example: (1) The low-income housing credit may be recaptured or added back to tax if the credit property ceases to be used as low-income housing for a minimum number of years. (2) The alimony deduction may be retroactively lost or recaptured if payments do not continue at the requisite level for a minimum number of years.

Regulated investment company (RIC). A mutual fund.

Rollover. The tax-free termination of one investment and reinvestment of the proceeds. For example: An individual may roll over a lump-sum distribution from an employer's retirement plan into an IRA.

S corporation. A corporation with no more than 100 shareholders that is not taxed, but treated similarly to a partnership, if other requirements are met.

Savings Incentive Match Plan for Employees (SIMPLE plans). A simplified retirement arrangement for small businesses that comes in two varieties: one similar to a 401(k) plan and one that funds IRAs for employees.

Standard deduction. A deduction allowed individuals instead of listing or itemizing deductible personal expenses. (See "Itemized deductions.") The amount depends on the individual's filing status. Additional amounts are available for taxpayers who are blind or are age 65 or over. Individuals may deduct either their standard deduction or the total of their itemized deductions, whichever is greater.

Straight-line depreciation. A depreciation method that allows equal deductions in each year of an asset's "life" or recovery period. (See "Accelerated depreciation.")

Swaps, tax-free. (1) Exchanges of like-kind property that result in no capital gains tax (commonly used for real estate). (2) Sales and repurchases of stock (or other securities) designed to realize a tax loss without discontinuing the investment. Transactions must comply with the wash sale rules to be effective. (See "Wash sales.")

Taxable income. What is left after all deductions are taken. This is the amount upon which tax is computed.

Taxpayer identification number (TIN). In the case of an individual, the Social Security number. In the case of a business (even an individual in business), the employer identification number.

Top-heavy plan. An employee retirement or profit-sharing plan that disproportionately benefits top executives.

Uniform capitalization rules (Unicap). A set of uniform rules for computing the cost of goods produced by a business that prevents current deductions for costs that must be capitalized (See "Capital expenditures.") or added to inventory.

Wash sales. Simultaneous or near-simultaneous purchases and sales of the same property, usually stocks or bonds, made to generate deductible tax losses without discontinuing the investment. Losses on the transactions are ignored for tax purposes, however, unless a 30-day waiting period is observed between them.

Withholding allowances. Adjustments made to assure correct withholding on wages for individuals who may have unusually large deductions or who may be subject to other special circumstances.

2006 Tax Forms

The blank forms included in this section are ready for you to photocopy, or to use "as is."

As we go to press, the IRS has not yet released the final version of all of the forms you might need. If you need a form that is not included here, there are a number of other ways to obtain free copies.

Many forms are available at local libraries, post offices, and banks. You can also obtain a copy of any form by stopping by a local IRS office, or by calling the IRS at 1-800-TAX-FORM. If you call, allow at least a week for the form to arrive.

If you have a fax machine, you can call the IRS at 703-368-9694 to obtain a free copy of most forms by fax. However, you'll need to know the fax order numbers of the forms you need, which are listed on page 8 of the 2006 Form 1040 Instructions.

You can also obtain most forms by downloading them from the IRS's Internet site, at www.irs.gov. While not all forms and instructions are available, the IRS has made a concerted effort to increase the number of the forms that are posted.

Tax Forms Included

- SS-4
- Form 1040EZ
- Form 1040A
  - Schedule 1
  - Schedule 2
  - Schedule 3
- Form 1040
  - Schedules A&B
  - Schedule C
  - Schedule C-EZ
  - Schedule D
  - Schedule E
  - Schedule EIC
  - Schedule F
  - Schedule H
  - Schedule R
  - Schedule SE
- Form 1040-V
- Form 1040X
- Form 1116
- Form 2106
- Form 2106-EZ
- Form 2441
- Form 3903
- Form 4562
- Form 4684
- Form 4797
- Form 4868
- Form 5213
- Form 6251
- Form 6252
- Form 8283
- Form 8582
- Form 8615
- Form 8812
- Form 8814
- Form 8829
- Form 8839
- 2006 Tax Table
- 2006 Tax Rate Schedules

Form **SS-4**

(Rev. February 2006)

Department of the Treasury
Internal Revenue Service

Application for Employer Identification Number

(For use by employers, corporations, partnerships, trusts, estates, churches, government agencies, Indian tribal entities, certain individuals, and others.)

▶ See separate instructions for each line. **▶ Keep a copy for your records.**

OMB No. 1545-0003

EIN

Type or print clearly.

1 Legal name of entity (or individual) for whom the EIN is being requested

2 Trade name of business (if different from name on line 1)

3 Executor, administrator, trustee, "care of" name

4a Mailing address (room, apt., suite no. and street, or P.O. box)

5a Street address (if different) (Do not enter a P.O. box.)

4b City, state, and ZIP code

5b City, state, and ZIP code

6 County and state where principal business is located

7a Name of principal officer, general partner, grantor, owner, or trustor

7b SSN, ITIN, or EIN

8a **Type of entity** (check only one box)

☐ Sole proprietor (SSN) ______

☐ Partnership

☐ Corporation (enter form number to be filed) ▶ ______

☐ Personal service corporation

☐ Church or church-controlled organization

☐ Other nonprofit organization (specify) ▶ ______

☐ Other (specify) ▶

☐ Estate (SSN of decedent) ______

☐ Plan administrator (SSN) ______

☐ Trust (SSN of grantor) ______

☐ National Guard ☐ State/local government

☐ Farmers' cooperative ☐ Federal government/military

☐ REMIC ☐ Indian tribal governments/enterprises

Group Exemption Number (GEN) ▶ ______

8b If a corporation, name the state or foreign country (if applicable) where incorporated | State | Foreign country

9 **Reason for applying** (check only one box)

☐ Started new business (specify type) ▶ ______

☐ Hired employees (Check the box and see line 12.)

☐ Compliance with IRS withholding regulations

☐ Other (specify) ▶

☐ Banking purpose (specify purpose) ▶ ______

☐ Changed type of organization (specify new type) ▶ ______

☐ Purchased going business

☐ Created a trust (specify type) ▶ ______

☐ Created a pension plan (specify type) ▶ ______

10 Date business started or acquired (month, day, year). See instructions.

11 Closing month of accounting year

12 First date wages or annuities were paid (month, day, year). **Note.** If applicant is a withholding agent, enter date income will first be paid to nonresident alien. (month, day, year) . . . . ▶

13 Highest number of employees expected in the next 12 months (enter -0- if none).

Agricultural	Household	Other

Do you expect to have $1,000 or less in employment tax liability for the calendar year? ☐ **Yes** ☐ **No.** (If you expect to pay $4,000 or less in wages, you can mark yes.)

14 Check **one** box that best describes the principal activity of your business.

☐ Construction ☐ Rental & leasing ☐ Transportation & warehousing ☐ Health care & social assistance ☐ Wholesale–agent/broker

☐ Real estate ☐ Manufacturing ☐ Finance & insurance ☐ Accommodation & food service ☐ Wholesale–other ☐ Retail

☐ Other (specify)

15 Indicate principal line of merchandise sold, specific construction work done, products produced, or services provided.

16a Has the applicant ever applied for an employer identification number for this or any other business? . . . . ☐ **Yes** ☐ **No**

Note. If "Yes," please complete lines 16b and 16c.

16b If you checked "Yes" on line 16a, give applicant's legal name and trade name shown on prior application if different from line 1 or 2 above.

Legal name ▶ Trade name ▶

16c Approximate date when, and city and state where, the application was filed. Enter previous employer identification number if known.

Approximate date when filed (mo., day, year)	City and state where filed	Previous EIN

Third Party Designee

Complete this section **only** if you want to authorize the named individual to receive the entity's EIN and answer questions about the completion of this form.

Designee's name | Designee's telephone number (include area code) ( )

Address and ZIP code | Designee's fax number (include area code) ( )

Under penalties of perjury, I declare that I have examined this application, and to the best of my knowledge and belief, it is true, correct, and complete.

Applicant's telephone number (include area code) ( )

Name and title (type or print clearly) ▶

Applicant's fax number (include area code) ( )

Signature ▶ Date ▶

Form **1040EZ**

Department of the Treasury—Internal Revenue Service

Income Tax Return for Single and Joint Filers With No Dependents (99) 2006

OMB No. 1545-0074

Label (See page 11.) **Use the IRS label.** Otherwise, please print or type.

LABEL HERE

Your first name and initial	Last name		Your social security number
If a joint return, spouse's first name and initial	Last name		Spouse's social security number
Home address (number and street). If you have a P.O. box, see page 11.		Apt. no.	▲ You **must** enter your SSN(s) above. ▲
City, town or post office, state, and ZIP code. If you have a foreign address, see page 11.			Checking a box below will not change your tax or refund.

Presidential Election Campaign (page 11) ▶ Check here if you, or your spouse if a joint return, want $3 to go to this fund . . . . ▶ ☐ **You** ☐ **Spouse**

Income

Attach Form(s) W-2 here.

Enclose, but do not attach, any payment.

1 Wages, salaries, and tips. This should be shown in box 1 of your Form(s) W-2. Attach your Form(s) W-2. 1

2 Taxable interest. If the total is over $1,500, you cannot use Form 1040EZ. 2

3 Unemployment compensation and Alaska Permanent Fund dividends (see page 13). 3

4 Add lines 1, 2, and 3. This is your **adjusted gross income.** 4

5 If someone can claim you (or your spouse if a joint return) as a dependent, check the applicable box(es) below and enter the amount from the worksheet on back.

☐ **You** ☐ **Spouse**

If no one can claim you (or your spouse if a joint return), enter $8,450 if **single;** $16,900 if **married filing jointly.** See back for explanation. 5

6 Subtract line 5 from line 4. If line 5 is larger than line 4, enter -0-. This is your **taxable income.** ▶ 6

Payments and tax

7 Federal income tax withheld from box 2 of your Form(s) W-2. 7

8a **Earned income credit (EIC).** 8a

b Nontaxable combat pay election. 8b

9 Credit for federal telephone excise tax paid. Attach Form 8913 if required. 9

10 Add lines 7, 8a, and 9. These are your **total payments.** ▶ 10

11 **Tax.** Use the amount on **line 6 above** to find your tax in the tax table on pages 24–32 of the booklet. Then, enter the tax from the table on this line. 11

Refund

Have it directly deposited! See page 18 and fill in 12b, 12c, and 12d or Form 8888.

12a If line 10 is larger than line 11, subtract line 11 from line 10. This is your **refund.** If Form 8888 is attached, check here ▶ ☐ 12a

▶ b Routing number ☐☐☐☐☐☐☐☐☐ ▶ c Type: ☐ Checking ☐ Savings

▶ d Account number ☐☐☐☐☐☐☐☐☐☐☐☐☐☐☐☐☐

Amount you owe

13 If line 11 is larger than line 10, subtract line 10 from line 11. This is the **amount you owe.** For details on how to pay, see page 19. ▶ 13

Third party designee

Do you want to allow another person to discuss this return with the IRS (see page 20)? ☐ **Yes.** Complete the following. ☐ **No**

Designee's name ▶ Phone no. ▶ ( ) Personal identification number (PIN) ▶ ☐☐☐☐☐

Sign here

Joint return? See page 11. Keep a copy for your records.

Under penalties of perjury, I declare that I have examined this return, and to the best of my knowledge and belief, it is true, correct, and accurately lists all amounts and sources of income I received during the tax year. Declaration of preparer (other than the taxpayer) is based on all information of which the preparer has any knowledge.

Your signature	Date	Your occupation	Daytime phone number ( )
Spouse's signature. If a joint return, **both** must sign.	Date	Spouse's occupation	

Paid preparer's use only

Preparer's signature ▶	Date	Check if self-employed ☐	Preparer's SSN or PTIN
Firm's name (or yours if self-employed), address, and ZIP code ▶		EIN	
		Phone no. ( )	

Use this form if

- Your filing status is single or married filing jointly. If you are not sure about your filing status, see page 11.
- You (and your spouse if married filing jointly) were under age 65 and not blind at the end of 2006. If you were born on January 1, 1942, you are considered to be age 65 at the end of 2006.
- You do not claim any dependents. For information on dependents, use TeleTax topic 354 (see page 6).
- Your taxable income (line 6) is less than $100,000.
- You do not claim any adjustments to income. For information on adjustments to income, use TeleTax topics 451-453, 455, and 456 (see page 6).
- The only tax credits you can claim are the earned income credit and the credit for the federal telephone excise tax. For information on credits, use TeleTax topics 601-608 and 610 (see page 6).
- You had only wages, salaries, tips, taxable scholarship or fellowship grants, unemployment compensation, or Alaska Permanent Fund dividends, and your taxable interest was not over $1,500. But if you earned tips, including allocated tips, that are not included in box 5 and box 7 of your Form W-2, you may not be able to use Form 1040EZ (see page 12). If you are planning to use Form 1040EZ for a child who received Alaska Permanent Fund dividends, see page 13.
- You did not receive any advance earned income credit payments. If you cannot use this form, use TeleTax topic 352 (see page 6).

Filling in your return

If you received a scholarship or fellowship grant or tax-exempt interest income, such as on municipal bonds, see the booklet before filling in the form. Also, see the booklet if you received a Form 1099-INT showing federal income tax withheld or if federal income tax was withheld from your unemployment compensation or Alaska Permanent Fund dividends.

For tips on how to avoid common mistakes, see page 20.

Remember, you must report all wages, salaries, and tips even if you do not get a Form W-2 from your employer. You must also report all your taxable interest, including interest from banks, savings and loans, credit unions, etc., even if you do not get a Form 1099-INT.

Worksheet for dependents who checked one or both boxes on line 5

(keep a copy for your records)

Use this worksheet to figure the amount to enter on line 5 if someone can claim you (or your spouse if married filing jointly) as a dependent, even if that person chooses not to do so. To find out if someone can claim you as a dependent, use TeleTax topic 354 (see page 6).

A. Amount, if any, from line 1 on front . ______________

\+ 300.00 Enter total ▶ **A.** ______________

B. Minimum standard deduction . . . . **B.** 850.00

C. Enter the **larger** of line A or line B here . . . . **C.** ______________

D. Maximum standard deduction. If **single,** enter $5,150; if **married filing jointly,** enter $10,300 . . . . **D.** ______________

E. Enter the **smaller** of line C or line D here. This is your standard deduction **E.** ______________

F. Exemption amount.

- If single, enter -0-.
- If married filing jointly and—
  - —both you and your spouse can be claimed as dependents, enter -0-.
  - —only one of you can be claimed as a dependent, enter $3,300.

F. ______________

G. Add lines E and F. Enter the total here and on line 5 on the front . . . **G.** ______________

If you did not check any boxes on line 5, enter on line 5 the amount shown below that applies to you.

- Single, enter $8,450. This is the total of your standard deduction ($5,150) and your exemption ($3,300).
- Married filing jointly, enter $16,900. This is the total of your standard deduction ($10,300), your exemption ($3,300), and your spouse's exemption ($3,300).

Mailing return

Mail your return by **April 16, 2007.** If you live in Maine, Maryland, Massachusetts, New Hampshire, New York, Vermont, or the District of Columbia, you have until April 17, 2007. Use the envelope that came with your booklet. If you do not have that envelope or if you moved during the year, see the back cover for the address to use.

Form **1040A** Department of the Treasury—Internal Revenue Service

U.S. Individual Income Tax Return (99) 2006

IRS Use Only—Do not write or staple in this space. OMB No. 1545-0074

Label

(See page 18.)

Use the IRS label. Otherwise, please print or type.

LABEL HERE

Your first name and initial	Last name	Your social security number
If a joint return, spouse's first name and initial	Last name	Spouse's social security number
Home address (number and street). If you have a P.O. box, see page 18.	Apt. no.	▲ You **must** enter your SSN(s) above. ▲
City, town or post office, state, and ZIP code. If you have a foreign address, see page 18.		Checking a box below will not change your tax or refund.

Presidential Election Campaign ▶ Check here if you, or your spouse if filing jointly, want $3 to go to this fund (see page 18) ▶ ☐ **You** ☐ **Spouse**

Filing status

Check only one box.

1 ☐ Single
2 ☐ Married filing jointly (even if only one had income)
3 ☐ Married filing separately. Enter spouse's SSN above and full name here. ▶
4 ☐ Head of household (with qualifying person). (See page 19.) If the qualifying person is a child but not your dependent, enter this child's name here. ▶ ________
5 ☐ Qualifying widow(er) with dependent child (see page 20)

Exemptions

6a ☐ **Yourself.** If someone can claim you as a dependent, **do not** check box 6a.
b ☐ **Spouse**

Boxes checked on 6a and 6b ____

c **Dependents:**

If more than six dependents, see page 21.

(1) First name Last name	(2) Dependent's social security number	(3) Dependent's relationship to you	(4) ✓ if qualifying child for child tax credit (see page 21)
			☐
			☐
			☐
			☐
			☐
			☐

No. of children on 6c who:
- **lived with you** ____
- **did not live with you due to divorce or separation (see page 22)** ____

Dependents on 6c not entered above ____

d Total number of exemptions claimed.

Add numbers on lines above ▶ ☐

Income

Attach Form(s) W-2 here. Also attach Form(s) 1099-R if tax was withheld.

If you did not get a W-2, see page 24.

Enclose, but do not attach, any payment.

7	Wages, salaries, tips, etc. Attach Form(s) W-2.		7
8a	**Taxable** interest. Attach Schedule 1 if required.		8a
b	**Tax-exempt** interest. **Do not** include on line 8a.	8b	
9a	Ordinary dividends. Attach Schedule 1 if required.		9a
b	Qualified dividends (see page 25).	9b	
10	Capital gain distributions (see page 25).		10
11a	IRA distributions. 11a	**11b** Taxable amount (see page 25).	11b
12a	Pensions and annuities. 12a	**12b** Taxable amount (see page 26).	12b
13	Unemployment compensation, Alaska Permanent Fund dividends, and jury duty pay.		13
14a	Social security benefits. 14a	**14b** Taxable amount (see page 28).	14b
15	Add lines 7 through 14b (far right column). This is your **total income.** ▶		15

Adjusted gross income

16	Penalty on early withdrawal of savings (see page 28).	16	
17	IRA deduction (see page 28).	17	
18	Student loan interest deduction (see page 31).	18	
19	Jury duty pay you gave your employer (see page 31).	19	
20	Add lines 16 through 19. These are your **total adjustments.**		20
21	Subtract line 20 from line 15. This is your **adjusted gross income.** ▶		21

For Disclosure, Privacy Act, and Paperwork Reduction Act Notice, see page 58. Cat. No. 11327A Form **1040A** (2006)

Tax, credits, and payments

Standard Deduction for—
- People who checked any box on line 23a or 23b **or** who can be claimed as a dependent, see page 32.
- All others:

Single or Married filing separately, $5,150

Married filing jointly or Qualifying widow(er), $10,300

Head of household, $7,550

22 Enter the amount from line 21 (adjusted gross income). 22

23a Check if: ☐ **You** were born before January 2, 1942, ☐ Blind; ☐ **Spouse** was born before January 2, 1942, ☐ Blind } **Total boxes checked** ▶ 23a ☐

b If you are married filing separately and your spouse itemizes deductions, see page 32 and check here ▶ 23b ☐

24 Enter your **standard deduction** (see left margin). 24

25 Subtract line 24 from line 22. If line 24 is more than line 22, enter -0-. 25

26 If line 22 is over $112,875, or you provided housing to a person displaced by Hurricane Katrina, see page 32. Otherwise, multiply $3,300 by the total number of exemptions claimed on line 6d. 26

27 Subtract line 26 from line 25. If line 26 is more than line 25, enter -0-. This is your **taxable income.** ▶ 27

28 **Tax,** including any alternative minimum tax (see page 32). 28

29 Credit for child and dependent care expenses. Attach Schedule 2. 29

30 Credit for the elderly or the disabled. Attach Schedule 3. 30

31 Education credits. Attach Form 8863. 31

32 Retirement savings contributions credit. Attach Form 8880. 32

33 Child tax credit (see page 37). Attach Form 8901 if required. 33

34 Add lines 29 through 33. These are your **total credits.** 34

35 Subtract line 34 from line 28. If line 34 is more than line 28, enter -0-. 35

36 Advance earned income credit payments from Form(s) W-2, box 9. 36

37 Add lines 35 and 36. This is your **total tax.** ▶ 37

38 Federal income tax withheld from Forms W-2 and 1099. 38

39 2006 estimated tax payments and amount applied from 2005 return. 39

If you have a qualifying child, attach Schedule EIC.

40a **Earned income credit (EIC).** 40a

b Nontaxable combat pay election. 40b

41 Additional child tax credit. Attach Form 8812. 41

42 Credit for federal telephone excise tax paid. Attach Form 8913 if required. 42

43 Add lines 38, 39, 40a, 41, and 42. These are your **total payments.** ▶ 43

Refund

Direct deposit? See page 53 and fill in 45b, 45c, and 45d or Form 8888.

44 If line 43 is more than line 37, subtract line 37 from line 43. This is the amount you **overpaid.** 44

45a Amount of line 44 you want **refunded to you.** If Form 8888 is attached, check here ▶ ☐ 45a

▶ b Routing number ☐☐☐☐☐☐☐☐☐ ▶ c Type: ☐ Checking ☐ Savings

▶ d Account number ☐☐☐☐☐☐☐☐☐☐☐☐☐☐☐☐☐

46 Amount of line 44 you want **applied to your 2007 estimated tax.** 46

Amount you owe

47 **Amount you owe.** Subtract line 43 from line 37. For details on how to pay, see page 54. ▶ 47

48 Estimated tax penalty (see page 54). 48

Third party designee

Do you want to allow another person to discuss this return with the IRS (see page 55)? ☐ **Yes.** Complete the following. ☐ **No**

Designee's name ▶ Phone no. ▶ ( ) Personal identification number (PIN) ▶ ☐☐☐☐☐

Sign here

Joint return? See page 18. Keep a copy for your records.

Under penalties of perjury, I declare that I have examined this return and accompanying schedules and statements, and to the best of my knowledge and belief, they are true, correct, and accurately list all amounts and sources of income I received during the tax year. Declaration of preparer (other than the taxpayer) is based on all information of which the preparer has any knowledge.

Your signature	Date	Your occupation	Daytime phone number ( )
Spouse's signature. If a joint return, **both** must sign.	Date	Spouse's occupation	

Paid preparer's use only

Preparer's signature ▶	Date	Check if self-employed ☐	Preparer's SSN or PTIN
Firm's name (or yours if self-employed), address, and ZIP code ▶		EIN	
		Phone no. ( )	

Schedule 1 (Form 1040A)

Department of the Treasury—Internal Revenue Service

Interest and Ordinary Dividends for Form 1040A Filers

(99) **2006** OMB No. 1545-0074

Name(s) shown on Form 1040A	Your social security number

Part I

Interest

(See back of schedule and the instructions for Form 1040A, line 8a.)

Note. If you received a Form 1099-INT, Form 1099-OID, or substitute statement from a brokerage firm, enter the firm's name and the total interest shown on that form.

			Amount
1	List name of payer. If any interest is from a seller-financed mortgage and the buyer used the property as a personal residence, see back of schedule and list this interest first. Also, show that buyer's social security number and address.	1	
2	Add the amounts on line 1.	2	
3	Excludable interest on series EE and I U.S. savings bonds issued after 1989. Attach Form 8815.	3	
4	Subtract line 3 from line 2. Enter the result here and on Form 1040A, line 8a.	4	

Part II

Ordinary dividends

(See back of schedule and the instructions for Form 1040A, line 9a.)

Note. If you received a Form 1099-DIV or substitute statement from a brokerage firm, enter the firm's name and the ordinary dividends shown on that form.

			Amount
5	List name of payer.	5	
6	Add the amounts on line 5. Enter the total here and on Form 1040A, line 9a.	6	

Purpose of Schedule

Use Schedule 1 if any of the following apply.

- You had over $1,500 of taxable interest (fill in Part I).
- You received interest from a seller-financed mortgage and the buyer used the property as a personal residence (fill in Part I).
- You are claiming the exclusion of interest from series EE or I U.S. savings bonds issued after 1989 (fill in Part I).
- You received interest as a nominee (fill in Part I).
- You had over $1,500 of ordinary dividends or you received ordinary dividends as a nominee (fill in Part II).

TIP *If you need more space to list your interest or ordinary dividends, attach separate statements that are the same size as Schedule 1. Use the same format as lines 1 and 5, but show your totals on Schedule 1. Be sure to put your name and social security number on the statements and attach them at the end of your return.*

Part I

Interest

Line 1

Report on line 1 all of your taxable interest. Interest should be shown on your Forms 1099-INT, Forms 1099-OID, or substitute statements. Include interest from series EE and I U.S. savings bonds. List each payer's name and show the amount.

Seller-financed mortgages. If you sold your home or other property and the buyer used the property as a personal residence, list first any interest the buyer paid you on a mortgage or other form of seller financing. Be sure to show the buyer's name, address, and social security number (SSN). You must also let the buyer know your SSN. If you do not show the buyer's name, address, and SSN, or let the buyer know your SSN, you may have to pay a $50 penalty.

Nominees. If you received a Form 1099-INT that includes interest you received as a nominee (that is, in your name, but the interest actually belongs to someone else), report the total on line 1. Do this even if you later distributed some or all of this income to others. Under your last entry on line 1, put a subtotal of all interest listed on line 1. Below this subtotal, enter "Nominee Distribution" and show the total interest you received as a nominee. Subtract this amount from the subtotal and enter the result on line 2.

TIP *If you received interest as a nominee, you must give the actual owner a Form 1099-INT unless the owner is your spouse. You must also file a Form 1096 and a Form 1099-INT with the IRS. For more details, see the General Instructions for Forms 1099, 1098, 5498, and W-2G and Instructions for Forms 1099-INT and 1099-OID.*

Line 3

Did you cash series EE or I U.S. savings bonds in 2006 that were issued after 1989? If you did and you paid qualified higher education expenses in 2006 for yourself, your spouse, or your dependents, you may be able to exclude part or all of the interest on those bonds. See Form 8815 for details.

Part II

Ordinary Dividends

Line 5

Report on line 5 all of your ordinary dividends. Ordinary dividends should be shown in box 1a of your Forms 1099-DIV or substitute statements. List each payer's name and show the amount.

Nominees. If you received a Form 1099-DIV that includes ordinary dividends you received as a nominee (that is, in your name, but the ordinary dividends actually belong to someone else), report the total on line 5. Do this even if you later distributed some or all of this income to others. Under your last entry on line 5, put a subtotal of all ordinary dividends listed on line 5. Below this subtotal, enter "Nominee Distribution" and show the total ordinary dividends you received as a nominee. Subtract this amount from the subtotal and enter the result on line 6.

TIP *If you received dividends as a nominee, you must give the actual owner a Form 1099-DIV unless the owner is your spouse. You must also file a Form 1096 and a Form 1099-DIV with the IRS. For more details, see the General Instructions for Forms 1099, 1098, 5498, and W-2G and Instructions for Form 1099-DIV.*

Schedule 2 (Form 1040A)

Department of the Treasury—Internal Revenue Service

Child and Dependent Care Expenses for Form 1040A Filers (99) 2006

OMB No. 1545-0074

Name(s) shown on Form 1040A | Your social security number

Before you begin: You need to understand the following terms. See **Definitions** on page 1 of the separate instructions.
- **Dependent care benefits**
- **Qualifying person(s)**
- **Qualified expenses**

Part I

Persons or organizations who provided the care

You **must** complete this part.

1

(a) Care provider's name	(b) Address (number, street, apt. no., city, state, and ZIP code)	(c) Identifying number (SSN or EIN)	(d) Amount paid (see instructions)

(If you need more space, use the bottom of page 2.)

Did you receive **dependent care benefits?**
- **No** → Complete only Part II below.
- **Yes** → Complete Part III on the back next.

Caution. If the care was provided in your home, you may owe employment taxes. If you do, you must use Form 1040. See **Schedule H** and its instructions for details.

Part II

Credit for child and dependent care expenses

2 Information about your **qualifying person(s).** If you have more than two qualifying persons, see the instructions.

(a) Qualifying person's name — First	Last	(b) Qualifying person's social security number	(c) Qualified expenses you incurred and paid in 2006 for the person listed in column (a)

3 Add the amounts in column (c) of line 2. **Do not** enter more than $3,000 for one qualifying person or $6,000 for two or more persons. If you completed Part III, enter the amount from line 27. **3**

4 Enter your **earned income.** See the instructions. **4**

5 If married filing jointly, enter your spouse's earned income (if your spouse was a student or was disabled, see the instructions); **all others,** enter the amount from line 4. **5**

6 Enter the **smallest** of line 3, 4, or 5. **6**

7 Enter the amount from Form 1040A, line 22. **7**

8 Enter on line 8 the decimal amount shown below that applies to the amount on line 7.

If line 7 is: Over	But not over	Decimal amount is	If line 7 is: Over	But not over	Decimal amount is
$0	15,000	.35	$29,000	31,000	.27
15,000	17,000	.34	31,000	33,000	.26
17,000	19,000	.33	33,000	35,000	.25
19,000	21,000	.32	35,000	37,000	.24
21,000	23,000	.31	37,000	39,000	.23
23,000	25,000	.30	39,000	41,000	.22
25,000	27,000	.29	41,000	43,000	.21
27,000	29,000	.28	43,000	No limit	.20

8 × .

9 Multiply **line 6** by the decimal amount on line 8. If you paid 2005 expenses in 2006, see the instructions. **9**

10 Enter the amount from Form 1040A, line 28. **10**

11 **Credit for child and dependent care expenses.** Enter the **smaller** of line 9 or line 10 here and on Form 1040A, line 29. **11**

Part III

Dependent care benefits

12 Enter the total amount of **dependent care benefits** you received for 2006. This amount should be shown in box 10 of your Form(s) W-2. **Do not** include amounts that were reported to you as wages in box 1 of Form(s) W-2.	12	
13 Enter the amount, if any, you carried over from 2005 and used in 2006 during the grace period. See the instructions.	13	
14 Enter the amount, if any, you forfeited or carried forward to 2007. See the instructions.	14	( )
15 Combine lines 12 through 14. See the instructions.	15	
16 Enter the total amount of **qualified expenses** incurred in 2006 for the care of the qualifying person(s).	16	
17 Enter the **smaller** of line 15 or 16.	17	
18 Enter your **earned income.** See the instructions.	18	
19 Enter the amount shown below that applies to you. • If married filing jointly, enter your spouse's earned income (if your spouse was a student or was disabled, see the instructions for line 5). • If married filing separately, see the instructions for the amount to enter. • All others, enter the amount from line 18.	19	
20 Enter the **smallest** of line 17, 18, or 19.	20	
21 **Excluded benefits.** Enter here the **smaller** of the following: • The amount from line 20, or • $5,000 ($2,500 if married filing separately **and** you were required to enter your spouse's earned income on line 19).	21	
22 **Taxable benefits.** Subtract line 21 from line 15. Also, include this amount on Form 1040A, line 7. In the space to the left of line 7, enter "DCB."	22	

To claim the child and dependent care credit, complete lines 23–27 below.

23 Enter $3,000 ($6,000 if two or more qualifying persons).	23	
24 Enter the amount from line 21.	24	
25 Subtract line 24 from line 23. If zero or less, **stop.** You cannot take the credit. **Exception.** If you paid 2005 expenses in 2006, see the instructions for line 9.	25	
26 Complete line 2 on the front of this schedule. **Do not** include in column (c) any benefits shown on line 21 above. Then, add the amounts in column (c) and enter the total here.	26	
27 Enter the **smaller** of line 25 or 26. Also, enter this amount on line 3 on the front of this schedule and complete lines 4–11.	27	

Schedule 3 (Form 1040A)

Department of the Treasury—Internal Revenue Service

Credit for the Elderly or the Disabled for Form 1040A Filers

(99) **2006**

OMB No. 1545-0074

Name(s) shown on Form 1040A	Your social security number

You may be able to take this credit and reduce your tax if by the end of 2006:

- You were age 65 or older **or**
- You were under age 65, you retired on **permanent and total** disability, and you received taxable disability income.

But you must also meet other tests. See the separate instructions for Schedule 3.

TIP In most cases, the IRS can figure the credit for you. See the instructions.

Part I Check the box for your filing status and age

If your filing status is:	And by the end of 2006:	Check only one box:
Single, Head of household, or Qualifying widow(er)	**1** You were 65 or older	1 ☐
	2 You were under 65 and you retired on permanent and total disability	2 ☐
Married filing jointly	**3** Both spouses were 65 or older	3 ☐
	4 Both spouses were under 65, but only one spouse retired on permanent and total disability	4 ☐
	5 Both spouses were under 65, and both retired on permanent and total disability.	5 ☐
	6 One spouse was 65 or older, and the other spouse was under 65 and retired on permanent and total disability	6 ☐
	7 One spouse was 65 or older, and the other spouse was under 65 and **not** retired on permanent and total disability	7 ☐
Married filing separately	**8** You were 65 or older and you lived apart from your spouse for all of 2006	8 ☐
	9 You were under 65, you retired on permanent and total disability, and you lived apart from your spouse for all of 2006	9 ☐

Did you check box 1, 3, 7, or 8?

- **Yes** ▶ Skip Part II and complete Part III on the back.
- **No** ▶ Complete Parts II and III.

Part II Statement of permanent and total disability

Complete this part **only** if you checked box 2, 4, 5, 6, or 9 above.

If: **1** You filed a physician's statement for this disability for 1983 or an earlier year, or you filed or got a statement for tax years after 1983 and your physician signed line B on the statement, **and**

2 Due to your continued disabled condition, you were unable to engage in any substantial gainful activity in 2006, check this box . . . . ▶ ☐

- If you checked this box, you do not have to get another statement for 2006.
- If you **did not** check this box, have your physician complete the statement on page 4 of the instructions. You **must** keep the statement for your records.

Part III
Figure your credit

10 **If you checked (in Part I):** **Enter:**
Box 1, 2, 4, or 7 . . . . $5,000
Box 3, 5, or 6 . . . . $7,500
Box 8 or 9 . . . . $3,750 **10**

Did you check box 2, 4, 5, 6, or 9 in Part I?
- **Yes** → You **must** complete line 11.
- **No** → Enter the amount from line 10 on line 12 and go to line 13.

11 **If you checked (in Part I):**
- Box 6, add $5,000 to the taxable disability income of the spouse who was under age 65. Enter the total.
- Box 2, 4, or 9, enter your taxable disability income.
- Box 5, add your taxable disability income to your spouse's taxable disability income. Enter the total.

TIP For more details on what to include on line 11, see the instructions. **11**

12 If you completed line 11, enter the **smaller** of line 10 or line 11; **all others,** enter the amount from line 10. **12**

13 Enter the following pensions, annuities, or disability income that you (and your spouse if filing a joint return) received in 2006.

a Nontaxable part of social security benefits and Nontaxable part of railroad retirement benefits treated as social security (see the instructions). **13a**

b Nontaxable veterans' pensions and Any other pension, annuity, or disability benefit that is excluded from income under any other provision of law (see the instructions). **13b**

c Add lines 13a and 13b. (Even though these income items are not taxable, they **must** be included here to figure your credit.) If you did not receive any of the types of nontaxable income listed on line 13a or 13b, enter -0- on line 13c. **13c**

14 Enter the amount from Form 1040A, line 22. **14**

15 **If you checked (in Part I):** **Enter:**
Box 1 or 2 . . . . $7,500
Box 3, 4, 5, 6, or 7 . . . . . . $10,000
Box 8 or 9 . . . . $5,000 **15**

16 Subtract line 15 from line 14. If zero or less, enter -0-. **16**

17 Enter one-half of line 16. **17**

18 Add lines 13c and 17. **18**

19 Subtract line 18 from line 12. If zero or less, **stop;** you **cannot** take the credit. Otherwise, go to line 20. **19**

20 Multiply line 19 by 15% (.15). **20**

21 Enter the amount from Form 1040A, line 28, minus any amount on Form 1040A, line 29. **21**

22 **Credit for the elderly or the disabled.** Enter the **smaller** of line 20 or line 21 here and on Form 1040A, line 30. **22**

Form **1040** Department of the Treasury—Internal Revenue Service
U.S. Individual Income Tax Return 2006 (99) IRS Use Only—Do not write or staple in this space.

For the year Jan. 1–Dec. 31, 2006, or other tax year beginning , 2006, ending , 20 OMB No. 1545-0074

Label (See instructions on page 16.) **Use the IRS label.** Otherwise, please print or type.

LABEL HERE

Your first name and initial	Last name	**Your social security number**
If a joint return, spouse's first name and initial	Last name	**Spouse's social security number**
Home address (number and street). If you have a P.O. box, see page 16.	Apt. no.	▲ You **must** enter your SSN(s) above. ▲
City, town or post office, state, and ZIP code. If you have a foreign address, see page 16.		Checking a box below will not change your tax or refund.

Presidential Election Campaign ▶ Check here if you, or your spouse if filing jointly, want $3 to go to this fund (see page 16) ▶ ☐ **You** ☐ **Spouse**

Filing Status

Check only one box.

1 ☐ Single
2 ☐ Married filing jointly (even if only one had income)
3 ☐ Married filing separately. Enter spouse's SSN above and full name here. ▶
4 ☐ Head of household (with qualifying person). (See page 17.) If the qualifying person is a child but not your dependent, enter this child's name here. ▶
5 ☐ Qualifying widow(er) with dependent child (see page 17)

Exemptions

6a ☐ **Yourself.** If someone can claim you as a dependent, **do not** check box 6a . . . .
b ☐ **Spouse** . . . .

Boxes checked on 6a and 6b ____

c **Dependents:**

(1) First name Last name	(2) Dependent's social security number	(3) Dependent's relationship to you	(4) ✓ if qualifying child for child tax credit (see page 19)
			☐
			☐
			☐
			☐

If more than four dependents, see page 19.

No. of children on 6c who:
- **lived with you** ____
- **did not live with you due to divorce or separation (see page 20)** ____

Dependents on 6c not entered above ____

d Total number of exemptions claimed . . . . **Add numbers on lines above ▶** ☐

Income

Attach Form(s) W-2 here. Also attach Forms W-2G and 1099-R if tax was withheld.

If you did not get a W-2, see page 23.

Enclose, but do not attach, any payment. Also, please use **Form 1040-V.**

7	Wages, salaries, tips, etc. Attach Form(s) W-2 . . .		7	
8a	**Taxable** interest. Attach Schedule B if required . . .		8a	
b	**Tax-exempt** interest. **Do not** include on line 8a . . .	8b		
9a	Ordinary dividends. Attach Schedule B if required . . .		9a	
b	Qualified dividends (see page 23) . . .	9b		
10	Taxable refunds, credits, or offsets of state and local income taxes (see page 24) . .		10	
11	Alimony received . . .		11	
12	Business income or (loss). Attach Schedule C or C-EZ . . .		12	
13	Capital gain or (loss). Attach Schedule D if required. If not required, check here ▶ ☐		13	
14	Other gains or (losses). Attach Form 4797 . . .		14	
15a	IRA distributions . . 15a	**b** Taxable amount (see page 25)	15b	
16a	Pensions and annuities 16a	**b** Taxable amount (see page 26)	16b	
17	Rental real estate, royalties, partnerships, S corporations, trusts, etc. Attach Schedule E		17	
18	Farm income or (loss). Attach Schedule F . . .		18	
19	Unemployment compensation . . .		19	
20a	Social security benefits . 20a	**b** Taxable amount (see page 27)	20b	
21	Other income. List type and amount (see page 29)		21	
22	Add the amounts in the far right column for lines 7 through 21. This is your **total income** ▶		22	

Adjusted Gross Income

23	Archer MSA deduction. Attach Form 8853 . . .	23		
24	Certain business expenses of reservists, performing artists, and fee-basis government officials. Attach Form 2106 or 2106-EZ	24		
25	Health savings account deduction. Attach Form 8889. .	25		
26	Moving expenses. Attach Form 3903 . . .	26		
27	One-half of self-employment tax. Attach Schedule SE . .	27		
28	Self-employed SEP, SIMPLE, and qualified plans . . .	28		
29	Self-employed health insurance deduction (see page 29)	29		
30	Penalty on early withdrawal of savings . . .	30		
31a	Alimony paid **b** Recipient's SSN ▶	31a		
32	IRA deduction (see page 31) . . .	32		
33	Student loan interest deduction (see page 33) . . .	33		
34	Jury duty pay you gave to your employer . . .	34		
35	Domestic production activities deduction. Attach Form 8903	35		
36	Add lines 23 through 31a and 32 through 35 . . .		36	
37	Subtract line 36 from line 22. This is your **adjusted gross income** . . . ▶		37	

Tax and Credits

38	Amount from line 37 (adjusted gross income)		38
39a	Check if: ☐ **You** were born before January 2, 1942, ☐ Blind. ☐ **Spouse** was born before January 2, 1942, ☐ Blind. **Total boxes checked ▶ 39a**		
b	If your spouse itemizes on a separate return or you were a dual-status alien, see page 34 and check here ▶39b ☐		
40	**Itemized deductions** (from Schedule A) **or** your **standard deduction** (see left margin)		40
41	Subtract line 40 from line 38		41
42	If line 38 is over $112,875, or you provided housing to a person displaced by Hurricane Katrina, see page 36. Otherwise, multiply $3,300 by the total number of exemptions claimed on line 6d		42
43	**Taxable income.** Subtract line 42 from line 41. If line 42 is more than line 41, enter -0-		43
44	**Tax** (see page 36). Check if any tax is from: **a** ☐ Form(s) 8814 **b** ☐ Form 4972		44
45	**Alternative minimum tax** (see page 39). Attach Form 6251		45
46	Add lines 44 and 45 ▶		46
47	Foreign tax credit. Attach Form 1116 if required	47	
48	Credit for child and dependent care expenses. Attach Form 2441	48	
49	Credit for the elderly or the disabled. Attach Schedule R	49	
50	Education credits. Attach Form 8863	50	
51	Retirement savings contributions credit. Attach Form 8880	51	
52	Residential energy credits. Attach Form 5695	52	
53	Child tax credit (see page 42). Attach Form 8901 if required	53	
54	Credits from: **a** ☐ Form 8396 **b** ☐ Form 8839 **c** ☐ Form 8859	54	
55	Other credits: **a** ☐ Form 3800 **b** ☐ Form 8801 **c** ☐ Form______	55	
56	Add lines 47 through 55. These are your **total credits**		56
57	Subtract line 56 from line 46. If line 56 is more than line 46, enter -0- ▶		57

Standard Deduction for—

- People who checked any box on line 39a or 39b **or** who can be claimed as a dependent, see page 34.
- All others:

Single or Married filing separately, $5,150

Married filing jointly or Qualifying widow(er), $10,300

Head of household, $7,550

Other Taxes

58	Self-employment tax. Attach Schedule SE	58
59	Social security and Medicare tax on tip income not reported to employer. Attach Form 4137	59
60	Additional tax on IRAs, other qualified retirement plans, etc. Attach Form 5329 if required	60
61	Advance earned income credit payments from Form(s) W-2, box 9	61
62	Household employment taxes. Attach Schedule H	62
63	Add lines 57 through 62. This is your **total tax** ▶	63

Payments

64	Federal income tax withheld from Forms W-2 and 1099	64	
65	2006 estimated tax payments and amount applied from 2005 return	65	
66a	**Earned income credit (EIC)**	66a	
b	Nontaxable combat pay election ▶ 66b		
67	Excess social security and tier 1 RRTA tax withheld (see page 60)	67	
68	Additional child tax credit. Attach Form 8812	68	
69	Amount paid with request for extension to file (see page 60)	69	
70	Payments from: **a** ☐ Form 2439 **b** ☐ Form 4136 **c** ☐ Form 8885	70	
71	Credit for federal telephone excise tax paid. Attach Form 8913 if required	71	
72	Add lines 64, 65, 66a, and 67 through 71. These are your **total payments** ▶		72

If you have a qualifying child, attach Schedule EIC.

Refund

Direct deposit? See page 61 and fill in 74b, 74c, and 74d, or Form 8888.

73	If line 72 is more than line 63, subtract line 63 from line 72. This is the amount you **overpaid**		73
74a	Amount of line 73 you want **refunded to you.** If Form 8888 is attached, check here ▶ ☐		74a
▶ b	Routing number ▶ **c** Type: ☐ Checking ☐ Savings		
▶ d	Account number		
75	Amount of line 73 you want **applied to your 2007 estimated tax** ▶	75	

Amount You Owe

76	**Amount you owe.** Subtract line 72 from line 63. For details on how to pay, see page 62 ▶		76
77	Estimated tax penalty (see page 62)	77	

Third Party Designee

Do you want to allow another person to discuss this return with the IRS (see page 63)? ☐ **Yes.** Complete the following. ☐ **No**

Designee's name ▶ Phone no. ▶ (   ) Personal identification number (PIN) ▶

Sign Here

Joint return? See page 17. Keep a copy for your records.

Under penalties of perjury, I declare that I have examined this return and accompanying schedules and statements, and to the best of my knowledge and belief, they are true, correct, and complete. Declaration of preparer (other than taxpayer) is based on all information of which preparer has any knowledge.

Your signature	Date	Your occupation	Daytime phone number ( )
Spouse's signature. If a joint return, **both** must sign.	Date	Spouse's occupation	

Paid Preparer's Use Only

Preparer's signature ▶	Date	Check if self-employed ☐	Preparer's SSN or PTIN
Firm's name (or yours if self-employed), address, and ZIP code ▶		EIN	
		Phone no.	( )

SCHEDULES A&B (Form 1040)

Department of the Treasury Internal Revenue Service (99)

Schedule A—Itemized Deductions

(Schedule B is on back)

▶ **Attach to Form 1040.** ▶ **See Instructions for Schedules A&B (Form 1040).**

OMB No. 1545-0074

2006

Attachment Sequence No. **07**

Name(s) shown on Form 1040 | **Your social security number**

Medical and Dental Expenses		**Caution.** Do not include expenses reimbursed or paid by others.				
	1	Medical and dental expenses (see page A-1)	1			
	2	Enter amount from Form 1040, line 38 [2]				
	3	Multiply line 2 by 7.5% (.075)	3			
	4	Subtract line 3 from line 1. If line 3 is more than line 1, enter -0-			4	
Taxes You Paid (See page A-3.)	5	State and local income taxes	5			
	6	Real estate taxes (see page A-3)	6			
	7	Personal property taxes	7			
	8	Other taxes. List type and amount ▶	8			
	9	Add lines 5 through 8			9	
Interest You Paid (See page A-3.)	10	Home mortgage interest and points reported to you on Form 1098	10			
	11	Home mortgage interest not reported to you on Form 1098. If paid to the person from whom you bought the home, see page A-3 and show that person's name, identifying no., and address ▶	11			
Note. Personal interest is not deductible.	12	Points not reported to you on Form 1098. See page A-4 for special rules	12			
	13	Investment interest. Attach Form 4952 if required. (See page A-4.)	13			
	14	Add lines 10 through 13			14	
Gifts to Charity If you made a gift and got a benefit for it, see page A-4.	15	Gifts by cash or check. If you made any gift of $250 or more, see page A-5	15			
	16	Other than by cash or check. If any gift of $250 or more, see page A-5. You **must** attach Form 8283 if over $500	16			
	17	Carryover from prior year	17			
	18	Add lines 15 through 17			18	
Casualty and Theft Losses	19	Casualty or theft loss(es). Attach Form 4684. (See page A-6.)			19	
Job Expenses and Certain Miscellaneous Deductions (See page A-6.)	20	Unreimbursed employee expenses—job travel, union dues, job education, etc. Attach Form 2106 or 2106-EZ if required. (See page A-6.) ▶	20			
	21	Tax preparation fees	21			
	22	Other expenses—investment, safe deposit box, etc. List type and amount ▶	22			
	23	Add lines 20 through 22	23			
	24	Enter amount from Form 1040, line 38 [24]				
	25	Multiply line 24 by 2% (.02)	25			
	26	Subtract line 25 from line 23. If line 25 is more than line 23, enter -0-			26	
Other Miscellaneous Deductions	27	Other—from list on page A-7. List type and amount ▶			27	
Total Itemized Deductions	28	Is Form 1040, line 38, over $150,500 (over $75,250 if married filing separately)? ☐ **No.** Your deduction is not limited. Add the amounts in the far right column for lines 4 through 27. Also, enter this amount on Form 1040, line 40. ☐ **Yes.** Your deduction may be limited. See page A-7 for the amount to enter. ▶			28	
	29	If you elect to itemize deductions even though they are less than your standard deduction, check here ▶ ☐				

Name(s) shown on Form 1040. Do not enter name and social security number if shown on other side. | **Your social security number**

Schedule B—Interest and Ordinary Dividends

Attachment Sequence No. **08**

Part I Interest

(See page B-1 and the instructions for Form 1040, line 8a.)

Note. If you received a Form 1099-INT, Form 1099-OID, or substitute statement from a brokerage firm, list the firm's name as the payer and enter the total interest shown on that form.

			Amount
1	List name of payer. If any interest is from a seller-financed mortgage and the buyer used the property as a personal residence, see page B-1 and list this interest first. Also, show that buyer's social security number and address ▶	1	
2	Add the amounts on line 1	2	
3	Excludable interest on series EE and I U.S. savings bonds issued after 1989. Attach Form 8815	3	
4	Subtract line 3 from line 2. Enter the result here and on Form 1040, line 8a ▶	4	

Note. If line 4 is over $1,500, you must complete Part III.

Part II Ordinary Dividends

(See page B-1 and the instructions for Form 1040, line 9a.)

Note. If you received a Form 1099-DIV or substitute statement from a brokerage firm, list the firm's name as the payer and enter the ordinary dividends shown on that form.

			Amount
5	List name of payer ▶	5	
6	Add the amounts on line 5. Enter the total here and on Form 1040, line 9a . ▶	6	

Note. If line 6 is over $1,500, you must complete Part III.

Part III Foreign Accounts and Trusts

(See page B-2.)

	You must complete this part if you **(a)** had over $1,500 of taxable interest or ordinary dividends; or **(b)** had a foreign account; or **(c)** received a distribution from, or were a grantor of, or a transferor to, a foreign trust.	Yes	No
7a	At any time during 2006, did you have an interest in or a signature or other authority over a financial account in a foreign country, such as a bank account, securities account, or other financial account? See page B-2 for exceptions and filing requirements for Form TD F 90-22.1		
b	If "Yes," enter the name of the foreign country ▶		
8	During 2006, did you receive a distribution from, or were you the grantor of, or transferor to, a foreign trust? If "Yes," you may have to file Form 3520. See page B-2		

SCHEDULE C (Form 1040)

Department of the Treasury Internal Revenue Service (99)

Profit or Loss From Business

(Sole Proprietorship)

▶ Partnerships, joint ventures, etc., must file Form 1065 or 1065-B.

▶ Attach to Form 1040, 1040NR, or 1041. ▶ See Instructions for Schedule C (Form 1040).

OMB No. 1545-0074

2006

Attachment Sequence No. **09**

Name of proprietor | Social security number (SSN)

A Principal business or profession, including product or service (see page C-2 of the instructions) | **B Enter code from pages C-8, 9, & 10** ▶

C Business name. If no separate business name, leave blank. | **D Employer ID number (EIN), if any**

E Business address (including suite or room no.) ▶
City, town or post office, state, and ZIP code

F Accounting method: (1) ☐ Cash (2) ☐ Accrual (3) ☐ Other (specify) ▶

G Did you "materially participate" in the operation of this business during 2006? If "No," see page C-3 for limit on losses ☐ Yes ☐ No

H If you started or acquired this business during 2006, check here ▶ ☐

Part I Income

1	Gross receipts or sales. **Caution.** If this income was reported to you on Form W-2 and the "Statutory employee" box on that form was checked, see page C-3 and check here ▶ ☐	1	
2	Returns and allowances	2	
3	Subtract line 2 from line 1	3	
4	Cost of goods sold (from line 42 on page 2)	4	
5	**Gross profit.** Subtract line 4 from line 3	5	
6	Other income, including federal and state gasoline or fuel tax credit or refund (see page C-3)	6	
7	**Gross income.** Add lines 5 and 6 ▶	7	

Part II Expenses. Enter expenses for business use of your home only on line 30.

8	Advertising	8		18	Office expense	18	
9	Car and truck expenses (see page C-4)	9		19	Pension and profit-sharing plans	19	
10	Commissions and fees	10		20	Rent or lease (see page C-5):		
11	Contract labor (see page C-4)	11		a	Vehicles, machinery, and equipment	20a	
12	Depletion	12		b	Other business property	20b	
13	Depreciation and section 179 expense deduction (not included in Part III) (see page C-4)	13		21	Repairs and maintenance	21	
				22	Supplies (not included in Part III)	22	
				23	Taxes and licenses	23	
				24	Travel, meals, and entertainment:		
				a	Travel	24a	
14	Employee benefit programs (other than on line 19)	14		b	Deductible meals and entertainment (see page C-6)	24b	
15	Insurance (other than health)	15		25	Utilities	25	
16	Interest:			26	Wages (less employment credits)	26	
a	Mortgage (paid to banks, etc.)	16a		27	Other expenses (from line 48 on page 2)	27	
b	Other	16b					
17	Legal and professional services	17					

28	**Total expenses** before expenses for business use of home. Add lines 8 through 27 in columns ▶	28	
29	Tentative profit (loss). Subtract line 28 from line 7	29	
30	Expenses for business use of your home. Attach **Form 8829**	30	
31	**Net profit or (loss).** Subtract line 30 from line 29. • If a profit, enter on both **Form 1040, line 12,** and **Schedule SE, line 2,** or on **Form 1040NR, line 13** (statutory employees, see page C-6). Estates and trusts, enter on Form 1041, line 3. • If a loss, you **must** go to line 32.	31	

32 If you have a loss, check the box that describes your investment in this activity (see page C-6).

- If you checked 32a, enter the loss on both **Form 1040, line 12,** and **Schedule SE, line 2,** or on **Form 1040NR, line 13** (statutory employees, see page C-6). Estates and trusts, enter on Form 1041, line 3.
- If you checked 32b, you **must** attach **Form 6198.** Your loss may be limited.

32a ☐ All investment is at risk.
32b ☐ Some investment is not at risk.

Part III Cost of Goods Sold (see page C-7)

33 Method(s) used to value closing inventory: a ☐ Cost b ☐ Lower of cost or market c ☐ Other (attach explanation)

34 Was there any change in determining quantities, costs, or valuations between opening and closing inventory? If "Yes," attach explanation . . . ☐ Yes ☐ No

35	Inventory at beginning of year. If different from last year's closing inventory, attach explanation	35	
36	Purchases less cost of items withdrawn for personal use	36	
37	Cost of labor. Do not include any amounts paid to yourself	37	
38	Materials and supplies	38	
39	Other costs	39	
40	Add lines 35 through 39	40	
41	Inventory at end of year	41	
42	**Cost of goods sold.** Subtract line 41 from line 40. Enter the result here and on page 1, line 4	42	

Part IV Information on Your Vehicle.

Complete this part **only** if you are claiming car or truck expenses on line 9 and are not required to file Form 4562 for this business. See the instructions for line 13 on page C-4 to find out if you must file Form 4562.

43 When did you place your vehicle in service for business purposes? (month, day, year) ▶ ______ / ______ / ______

44 Of the total number of miles you drove your vehicle during 2006, enter the number of miles you used your vehicle for:

a Business ______________ b Commuting (see instructions) ______________ c Other ______________

45 Do you (or your spouse) have another vehicle available for personal use? . . . ☐ Yes ☐ No

46 Was your vehicle available for personal use during off-duty hours? . . . ☐ Yes ☐ No

47a Do you have evidence to support your deduction? . . . ☐ Yes ☐ No

b If "Yes," is the evidence written? . . . ☐ Yes ☐ No

Part V Other Expenses.

List below business expenses not included on lines 8–26 or line 30.

48 **Total other expenses.** Enter here and on page 1, line 27	48	

SCHEDULE C-EZ (Form 1040)

Department of the Treasury
Internal Revenue Service

Net Profit From Business

(Sole Proprietorship)

▶ Partnerships, joint ventures, etc., must file Form 1065 or 1065-B.
▶ Attach to Form 1040, 1040NR, or 1041. ▶ See instructions on back.

OMB No. 1545-0074

2006

Attachment Sequence No. **09A**

Name of proprietor	Social security number (SSN)

Part I General Information

You May Use Schedule C-EZ Instead of Schedule C Only If You:

- Had business expenses of $5,000 or less.
- Use the cash method of accounting.
- Did not have an inventory at any time during the year.
- Did not have a net loss from your business.
- Had only one business as either a sole proprietor or statutory employee.

And You:

- Had no employees during the year.
- Are not required to file **Form 4562,** Depreciation and Amortization, for this business. See the instructions for Schedule C, line 13, on page C-4 to find out if you must file.
- Do not deduct expenses for business use of your home.
- Do not have prior year unallowed passive activity losses from this business.

A	Principal business or profession, including product or service	**B** Enter code from pages C-8, 9, & 10 ▶
C	Business name. If no separate business name, leave blank.	**D** Employer ID number (EIN), if any
E	Business address (including suite or room no.). Address not required if same as on page 1 of your tax return.	
	City, town or post office, state, and ZIP code	

Part II Figure Your Net Profit

1	**Gross receipts. Caution.** If this income was reported to you on Form W-2 and the "Statutory employee" box on that form was checked, see **Statutory Employees** in the instructions for Schedule C, line 1, on page C-3 and check here . . . . ▶ ☐	**1**	
2	**Total expenses** (see instructions). If more than $5,000, you **must** use Schedule C	**2**	
3	**Net profit.** Subtract line 2 from line 1. If less than zero, you **must** use Schedule C. Enter on both **Form 1040, line 12,** and **Schedule SE, line 2,** or on **Form 1040NR, line 13.** (Statutory employees **do not** report this amount on Schedule SE, line 2. Estates and trusts, enter on Form 1041, line 3.)	**3**	

Part III Information on Your Vehicle. Complete this part **only** if you are claiming car or truck expenses on line 2.

4 When did you place your vehicle in service for business purposes? (month, day, year) ▶ ..../........./........ .

5 Of the total number of miles you drove your vehicle during 2006, enter the number of miles you used your vehicle for:

a Business .... **b** Commuting (see instructions) .... **c** Other ....

6 Do you (or your spouse) have another vehicle available for personal use? . . . . ☐ **Yes** ☐ **No**

7 Was your vehicle available for personal use during off-duty hours? . . . . ☐ **Yes** ☐ **No**

8a Do you have evidence to support your deduction? . . . . ☐ **Yes** ☐ **No**

b If "Yes," is the evidence written? . . . . ☐ **Yes** ☐ **No**

Instructions

You can use Schedule C-EZ instead of Schedule C if you operated a business or practiced a profession as a sole proprietorship or you were a statutory employee and you have met all the requirements listed in Schedule C-EZ, Part I.

Line A

Describe the business or professional activity that provided your principal source of income reported on line 1. Give the general field or activity and the type of product or service.

Line B

Enter the six-digit code that identifies your principal business or professional activity. See pages C-8 through C-10 of the Instructions for Schedule C for the list of codes.

Line D

You need an employer identification number (EIN) only if you had a qualified retirement plan or were required to file an employment, excise, estate, trust, or alcohol, tobacco, and firearms tax return. If you need an EIN, see the Instructions for Form SS-4. If you do not have an EIN, leave line D blank. Do not enter your SSN.

Line E

Enter your business address. Show a street address instead of a box number. Include the suite or room number, if any.

Line 1

Enter gross receipts from your trade or business. Include amounts you received in your trade or business that were properly shown on Forms 1099-MISC. If the total amounts that were reported in box 7 of Forms 1099-MISC are more than the total you are reporting on line 1, attach a statement explaining the difference. You must show all items of taxable income actually or constructively received during the year (in cash, property, or services). Income is constructively received when it is credited to your account or set aside for you to use. Do not offset this amount by any losses.

Line 2

Enter the total amount of all deductible business expenses you actually paid during the year. Examples of these expenses include advertising, car and truck expenses, commissions and fees, insurance, interest, legal and professional services, office expenses, rent or lease expenses, repairs and maintenance, supplies, taxes, travel, the allowable percentage of business meals and entertainment, and utilities (including telephone). For details, see the Instructions for Schedule C, Parts II and V, on pages C-3 through C-8. If you wish, you can use the optional worksheet below to record your expenses. Enter on lines **b** through **g** the type and amount of expenses not included on line **a.**

If you claim car or truck expenses, be sure to complete Schedule C-EZ, Part III.

Line 5b

Generally, commuting is travel between your home and a work location. If you converted your vehicle during the year from personal to business use (or vice versa), enter your commuting miles only for the period you drove your vehicle for business. For information on certain travel that is considered a business expense rather than commuting, see the Instructions for Form 2106.

Paperwork Reduction Act Notice. We ask for the information on this form to carry out the Internal Revenue laws of the United States. You are required to give us the information. We need it to ensure that you are complying with these laws and to allow us to figure and collect the right amount of tax.

You are not required to provide the information requested on a form that is subject to the Paperwork Reduction Act unless the form displays a valid OMB control number. Books or records relating to a form or its instructions must be retained as long as their contents may become material in the administration of any Internal Revenue law. Generally, tax returns and return information are confidential, as required by Internal Revenue Code section 6103.

The time needed to complete and file this form will vary depending on individual circumstances. The estimated burden for individual taxpayers filing this form is included in the estimates shown in the instructions for their individual income tax return. The estimated burden for all other taxpayers who file this form is approved under OMB control number 1545-1973 and is shown below.

Recordkeeping	45 min.
Learning about the law or the form	4 min.
Preparing the form	35 min.
Copying, assembling, and sending the form to the IRS	20 min.

If you have comments concerning the accuracy of these time estimates or suggestions for making this form simpler, we would be happy to hear from you. See the instructions for the tax return with which this form is filed.

Optional Worksheet for Line 2 (keep a copy for your records)

a	Deductible business meals and entertainment (see pages C-5 and C-6)	**a**	
b		**b**	
c		**c**	
d		**d**	
e		**e**	
f		**f**	
g		**g**	
h	**Total.** Add lines **a** through **g.** Enter here and on line 2	**h**	

SCHEDULE D (Form 1040)

Department of the Treasury Internal Revenue Service (99)

Capital Gains and Losses

▶ Attach to Form 1040 or Form 1040NR. ▶ See Instructions for Schedule D (Form 1040).

▶ Use Schedule D-1 to list additional transactions for lines 1 and 8.

OMB No. 1545-0074

2006

Attachment Sequence No. 12

Name(s) shown on return | Your social security number

Part I Short-Term Capital Gains and Losses—Assets Held One Year or Less

	(a) Description of property (Example: 100 sh. XYZ Co.)	(b) Date acquired (Mo., day, yr.)	(c) Date sold (Mo., day, yr.)	(d) Sales price (see page D-6 of the instructions)	(e) Cost or other basis (see page D-7 of the instructions)	(f) Gain or (loss) Subtract (e) from (d)
1						

2	Enter your short-term totals, if any, from Schedule D-1, line 2	2		
3	**Total short-term sales price amounts.** Add lines 1 and 2 in column (d)	3		
4	Short-term gain from Form 6252 and short-term gain or (loss) from Forms 4684, 6781, and 8824		4	
5	Net short-term gain or (loss) from partnerships, S corporations, estates, and trusts from Schedule(s) K-1		5	
6	Short-term capital loss carryover. Enter the amount, if any, from line 10 of your **Capital Loss Carryover Worksheet** on page D-7 of the instructions		6	( )
7	**Net short-term capital gain or (loss).** Combine lines 1 through 6 in column (f)		7	

Part II Long-Term Capital Gains and Losses—Assets Held More Than One Year

	(a) Description of property (Example: 100 sh. XYZ Co.)	(b) Date acquired (Mo., day, yr.)	(c) Date sold (Mo., day, yr.)	(d) Sales price (see page D-6 of the instructions)	(e) Cost or other basis (see page D-7 of the instructions)	(f) Gain or (loss) Subtract (e) from (d)
8						

9	Enter your long-term totals, if any, from Schedule D-1, line 9	9		
10	**Total long-term sales price amounts.** Add lines 8 and 9 in column (d)	10		
11	Gain from Form 4797, Part I; long-term gain from Forms 2439 and 6252; and long-term gain or (loss) from Forms 4684, 6781, and 8824		11	
12	Net long-term gain or (loss) from partnerships, S corporations, estates, and trusts from Schedule(s) K-1		12	
13	Capital gain distributions. See page D-2 of the instructions		13	
14	Long-term capital loss carryover. Enter the amount, if any, from line 15 of your **Capital Loss Carryover Worksheet** on page D-7 of the instructions		14	( )
15	**Net long-term capital gain or (loss).** Combine lines 8 through 14 in column (f). Then go to Part III on the back		15	

Part III **Summary**

16 Combine lines 7 and 15 and enter the result. If line 16 is a loss, skip lines 17 through 20, and go to line 21. If a gain, enter the gain on Form 1040, line 13, or Form 1040NR, line 14. Then go to line 17 below 16

17 Are lines 15 and 16 **both** gains?

☐ **Yes.** Go to line 18.

☐ **No.** Skip lines 18 through 21, and go to line 22.

18 Enter the amount, if any, from line 7 of the **28% Rate Gain Worksheet** on page D-8 of the instructions . . . . ▶ 18

19 Enter the amount, if any, from line 18 of the **Unrecaptured Section 1250 Gain Worksheet** on page D-9 of the instructions . . . . ▶ 19

20 Are lines 18 and 19 **both** zero or blank?

☐ **Yes.** Complete Form 1040 through line 43, or Form 1040NR through line 40. Then complete the **Qualified Dividends and Capital Gain Tax Worksheet** on page 38 of the Instructions for Form 1040 (or in the Instructions for Form 1040NR). **Do not** complete lines 21 and 22 below.

☐ **No.** Complete Form 1040 through line 43, or Form 1040NR through line 40. Then complete the **Schedule D Tax Worksheet** on page D-10 of the instructions. **Do not** complete lines 21 and 22 below.

21 If line 16 is a loss, enter here and on Form 1040, line 13, or Form 1040NR, line 14, the **smaller** of:

- The loss on line 16 or
- ($3,000), or if married filing separately, ($1,500)

} . . . . 21 ( )

Note. When figuring which amount is smaller, treat both amounts as positive numbers.

22 Do you have qualified dividends on Form 1040, line 9b, or Form 1040NR, line 10b?

☐ **Yes.** Complete Form 1040 through line 43, or Form 1040NR through line 40. Then complete the **Qualified Dividends and Capital Gain Tax Worksheet** on page 38 of the Instructions for Form 1040 (or in the Instructions for Form 1040NR).

☐ **No.** Complete the rest of Form 1040 or Form 1040NR.

SCHEDULE E (Form 1040) Department of the Treasury Internal Revenue Service (99)	**Supplemental Income and Loss** (From rental real estate, royalties, partnerships, S corporations, estates, trusts, REMICs, etc.) ▶ Attach to Form 1040, 1040NR, or Form 1041. ▶ See Instructions for Schedule E (Form 1040).	OMB No. 1545-0074 2006 Attachment Sequence No. 13

Name(s) shown on return | Your social security number

Part I **Income or Loss From Rental Real Estate and Royalties** **Note.** If you are in the business of renting personal property, use **Schedule C** or **C-EZ** (see page E-3). Report farm rental income or loss from **Form 4835** on page 2, line 40.

1	List the type and location of each **rental real estate property:**	2 For each rental real estate property listed on line 1, did you or your family use it during the tax year for personal purposes for more than the greater of: • 14 days **or** • 10% of the total days rented at fair rental value? (See page E-3.)		Yes	No
A			A		
B			B		
C			C		

		Properties A	Properties B	Properties C		Totals (Add columns A, B, and C.)
Income:						
3 Rents received	3				3	
4 Royalties received	4				4	
Expenses:						
5 Advertising	5					
6 Auto and travel (see page E-4)	6					
7 Cleaning and maintenance	7					
8 Commissions	8					
9 Insurance	9					
10 Legal and other professional fees	10					
11 Management fees	11					
12 Mortgage interest paid to banks, etc. (see page E-4)	12				12	
13 Other interest	13					
14 Repairs	14					
15 Supplies	15					
16 Taxes	16					
17 Utilities	17					
18 Other (list) ▶	18					
19 Add lines 5 through 18	19				19	
20 Depreciation expense or depletion (see page E-4)	20				20	
21 Total expenses. Add lines 19 and 20	21					
22 Income or (loss) from rental real estate or royalty properties. Subtract line 21 from line 3 (rents) or line 4 (royalties). If the result is a (loss), see page E-5 to find out if you must file **Form 6198**	22					
23 Deductible rental real estate loss. **Caution.** Your rental real estate loss on line 22 may be limited. See page E-5 to find out if you must file **Form 8582.** Real estate professionals must complete line 43 on page 2	23	( )	( )	( )		
24 **Income.** Add positive amounts shown on line 22. **Do not** include any losses					24	
25 **Losses.** Add royalty losses from line 22 and rental real estate losses from line 23. Enter total losses here					25	( )
26 **Total rental real estate and royalty income or (loss).** Combine lines 24 and 25. Enter the result here. If Parts II, III, IV, and line 40 on page 2 do not apply to you, also enter this amount on Form 1040, line 17, or Form 1040NR, line 18. Otherwise, include this amount in the total on line 41 on page 2					26	

Name(s) shown on return. Do not enter name and social security number if shown on other side. | Your social security number

Caution. The IRS compares amounts reported on your tax return with amounts shown on Schedule(s) K-1.

Part II Income or Loss From Partnerships and S Corporations

Note. If you report a loss from an at-risk activity for which **any** amount is **not** at risk, you **must** check the box in column **(e)** on line 28 and attach **Form 6198.** See page E-1.

27 Are you reporting any loss not allowed in a prior year due to the at-risk or basis limitations, a prior year unallowed loss from a passive activity (if that loss was not reported on Form 8582), or unreimbursed partnership expenses? ☐ Yes ☐ No
If you answered "Yes," see page E-6 before completing this section.

28	(a) Name	(b) Enter P for partnership; S for S corporation	(c) Check if foreign partnership	(d) Employer identification number	(e) Check if any amount is not at risk
A			☐		☐
B			☐		☐
C			☐		☐
D			☐		☐

	Passive Income and Loss		Nonpassive Income and Loss		
	(f) Passive loss allowed (attach Form 8582 if required)	(g) Passive income from Schedule K-1	(h) Nonpassive loss from Schedule K-1	(i) Section 179 expense deduction from Form 4562	(j) Nonpassive income from Schedule K-1
A					
B					
C					
D					
29a Totals					
b Totals					

30 Add columns (g) and (j) of line 29a	30	
31 Add columns (f), (h), and (i) of line 29b	31	( )
32 **Total partnership and S corporation income or (loss).** Combine lines 30 and 31. Enter the result here and include in the total on line 41 below	32	

Part III Income or Loss From Estates and Trusts

33	(a) Name	(b) Employer identification number
A		
B		

	Passive Income and Loss		Nonpassive Income and Loss	
	(c) Passive deduction or loss allowed (attach Form 8582 if required)	(d) Passive income from Schedule K-1	(e) Deduction or loss from Schedule K-1	(f) Other income from Schedule K-1
A				
B				
34a Totals				
b Totals				

35 Add columns (d) and (f) of line 34a	35	
36 Add columns (c) and (e) of line 34b	36	( )
37 **Total estate and trust income or (loss).** Combine lines 35 and 36. Enter the result here and include in the total on line 41 below	37	

Part IV Income or Loss From Real Estate Mortgage Investment Conduits (REMICs)—Residual Holder

38 (a) Name	(b) Employer identification number	(c) Excess inclusion from Schedules Q, line 2c (see page E-7)	(d) Taxable income (net loss) from Schedules Q, line 1b	(e) Income from Schedules Q, line 3b

39 Combine columns (d) and (e) only. Enter the result here and include in the total on line 41 below	39	

Part V Summary

40 Net farm rental income or (loss) from **Form 4835**. Also, complete line 42 below	40	
41 **Total income or (loss).** Combine lines 26, 32, 37, 39, and 40. Enter the result here and on Form 1040, line 17, or Form 1040NR, line 18 ▶	41	

42 **Reconciliation of farming and fishing income.** Enter your **gross** farming and fishing income reported on Form 4835, line 7; Schedule K-1 (Form 1065), box 14, code B; Schedule K-1 (Form 1120S), box 17, code T; and Schedule K-1 (Form 1041), line 14, code F (see page E-7)	42	
43 **Reconciliation for real estate professionals.** If you were a real estate professional (see page E-1), enter the net income or (loss) you reported anywhere on Form 1040 or Form 1040NR from all rental real estate activities in which you materially participated under the passive activity loss rules	43	

SCHEDULE EIC
(Form 1040A or 1040)

Department of the Treasury
Internal Revenue Service (99)

Earned Income Credit

Qualifying Child Information

Complete and attach to Form 1040A or 1040 only if you have a qualifying child.

1040A
1040
EIC

OMB No. 1545-0074

2006

Attachment Sequence No. 43

Name(s) shown on return | Your social security number

Before you begin: See the instructions for Form 1040A, lines 40a and 40b, or Form 1040, lines 66a and 66b, to make sure that **(a)** you can take the EIC, and **(b)** you have a qualifying child.

CAUTION

- If you take the EIC even though you are not eligible, you may not be allowed to take the credit for up to 10 years. See back of schedule for details.
- It will take us longer to process your return and issue your refund if you do not fill in all lines that apply for each qualifying child.
- Be sure the child's name on line 1 and social security number (SSN) on line 2 agree with the child's social security card. Otherwise, at the time we process your return, we may reduce or disallow your EIC. If the name or SSN on the child's social security card is not correct, call the Social Security Administration at 1-800-772-1213.

Qualifying Child Information	Child 1		Child 2	
1 Child's name If you have more than two qualifying children, you only have to list two to get the maximum credit.	First name	Last name	First name	Last name
2 Child's SSN The child must have an SSN as defined on page 43 of the Form 1040A instructions or page 49 of the Form 1040 instructions unless the child was born and died in 2006. If your child was born and died in 2006 and did not have an SSN, enter "Died" on this line and attach a copy of the child's birth certificate.				
3 Child's year of birth	Year ____ *If born after 1987, skip lines 4a and 4b; go to line 5.*		Year ____ *If born after 1987, skip lines 4a and 4b; go to line 5.*	
4 If the child was born before 1988—				
a Was the child under age 24 at the end of 2006 and a student?	☐ **Yes.** ***Go to line 5.***	☐ **No.** ***Continue.***	☐ **Yes.** ***Go to line 5.***	☐ **No.** ***Continue.***
b Was the child permanently and totally disabled during any part of 2006?	☐ **Yes.** ***Continue.***	☐ **No.** The child is not a qualifying child.	☐ **Yes.** ***Continue.***	☐ **No.** The child is not a qualifying child.
5 Child's relationship to you (for example, son, daughter, grandchild, niece, nephew, foster child, etc.)				
6 Number of months child lived with you in the United States during 2006 • If the child lived with you for more than half of 2006 but less than 7 months, enter "7." • If the child was born or died in 2006 and your home was the child's home for the entire time he or she was alive during 2006, enter "12."	____ months *Do not enter more than 12 months.*		____ months *Do not enter more than 12 months.*	

TIP

You may also be able to take the additional child tax credit if your child **(a)** was under age 17 at the end of 2006, **and (b)** is a U.S. citizen or resident alien. For more details, see the instructions for line 41 of Form 1040A or line 68 of Form 1040.

Purpose of Schedule

After you have figured your earned income credit (EIC), use Schedule EIC to give the IRS information about your qualifying child(ren).

To figure the amount of your credit or to have the IRS figure it for you, see the instructions for Form 1040A, lines 40a and 40b, or Form 1040, lines 66a and 66b.

Taking the EIC when not eligible. If you take the EIC even though you are not eligible and it is determined that your error is due to reckless or intentional disregard of the EIC rules, you will not be allowed to take the credit for 2 years even if you are otherwise eligible to do so. If you fraudulently take the EIC, you will not be allowed to take the credit for 10 years. You may also have to pay penalties.

Qualifying Child

A qualifying child for the EIC is a child who is your . . .

Son, daughter, stepchild, foster child, brother, sister, stepbrother, stepsister, or a descendant of any of them (for example, your grandchild, niece, or nephew)

AND

was . . .

Under age 19 at the end of 2006

or

Under age 24 at the end of 2006 and a student

or

Any age and permanently and totally disabled

AND

who . . .

Lived with you in the United States for more than half of 2006. If the child did not live with you for the required time, see *Exception to time lived with you* beginning on page 42 of the Form 1040A instructions or page 49 of the Form 1040 instructions.

CAUTION

If the child was married or meets the conditions to be a qualifying child of another person (other than your spouse if filing a joint return), special rules apply. For details, see page 43 of the Form 1040A instructions or page 49 of the Form 1040 instructions.

Do you want part of the EIC added to your take-home pay in 2007? To see if you qualify, get Form W-5 from your employer, call the IRS at 1-800-TAX-FORM (1-800-829-3676), or go to *www.irs.gov.*

SCHEDULE F (Form 1040)

Department of the Treasury
Internal Revenue Service (99)

Profit or Loss From Farming

▶ Attach to Form 1040, Form 1040NR, Form 1041, Form 1065, or Form 1065-B.

▶ See Instructions for Schedule F (Form 1040).

OMB No. 1545-0074

2006

Attachment Sequence No. **14**

Name of proprietor | **Social security number (SSN)**

A Principal product. Describe in one or two words your principal crop or activity for the current tax year. | **B Enter code from Part IV** ▶

C Accounting method: (1) ☐ Cash (2) ☐ Accrual | **D Employer ID number (EIN), if any**

E Did you "materially participate" in the operation of this business during 2006? If "No," see page F-2 for limit on passive losses. ☐ Yes ☐ No

Part I Farm Income—Cash Method.

Complete Parts I and II (Accrual method. Complete Parts II and III, and Part I, line 11.)
Do not include sales of livestock held for draft, breeding, sport, or dairy purposes. Report these sales on Form 4797.

1	Sales of livestock and other items you bought for resale	1		
2	Cost or other basis of livestock and other items reported on line 1	2		
3	Subtract line 2 from line 1		3	
4	Sales of livestock, produce, grains, and other products you raised		4	
5a	Cooperative distributions (Form(s) 1099-PATR)	5a	5b Taxable amount 5b	
6a	Agricultural program payments (see page F-3)	6a	6b Taxable amount 6b	
7	Commodity Credit Corporation (CCC) loans (see page F-3):			
a	CCC loans reported under election		7a	
b	CCC loans forfeited	7b	7c Taxable amount 7c	
8	Crop insurance proceeds and federal crop disaster payments (see page F-3):			
a	Amount received in 2006	8a	8b Taxable amount 8b	
c	If election to defer to 2007 is attached, check here ▶ ☐		8d Amount deferred from 2005 8d	
9	Custom hire (machine work) income		9	
10	Other income, including federal and state gasoline or fuel tax credit or refund (see page F-3)		10	
11	**Gross income.** Add amounts in the right column for lines 3 through 10. If you use the accrual method, enter the amount from Part III, line 51 ▶		11	

Part II Farm Expenses—Cash and Accrual Method.

Do not include personal or living expenses such as taxes, insurance, or repairs on your home.

12	Car and truck expenses (see page F-4). Also attach **Form 4562**	12		25	Pension and profit-sharing plans	25	
13	Chemicals	13		26	Rent or lease (see page F-5):		
14	Conservation expenses (see page F-4)	14		a	Vehicles, machinery, and equipment	26a	
15	Custom hire (machine work)	15		b	Other (land, animals, etc.)	26b	
16	Depreciation and section 179 expense deduction not claimed elsewhere (see page F-4)	16		27	Repairs and maintenance	27	
				28	Seeds and plants	28	
				29	Storage and warehousing	29	
17	Employee benefit programs other than on line 25	17		30	Supplies	30	
				31	Taxes	31	
18	Feed	18		32	Utilities	32	
19	Fertilizers and lime	19		33	Veterinary, breeding, and medicine	33	
20	Freight and trucking	20		34	Other expenses (specify):		
21	Gasoline, fuel, and oil	21		a		34a	
22	Insurance (other than health)	22		b		34b	
23	Interest:			c		34c	
a	Mortgage (paid to banks, etc.)	23a		d		34d	
b	Other	23b		e		34e	
24	Labor hired (less employment credits)	24		f		34f	

35	**Total expenses.** Add lines 12 through 34f. If line 34f is negative, see instructions ▶	35	
36	**Net farm profit or (loss).** Subtract line 35 from line 11. • If a profit, enter the profit on **Form 1040, line 18,** and **also** on **Schedule SE, line 1.** If you file Form 1040NR, enter the profit on **Form 1040NR, line 19.** • If a loss, you **must** go to line 37. Estates, trusts, and partnerships, see page F-6.	36	
37	If you have a loss, you **must** check the box that describes your investment in this activity (see page F-6). • If you checked 37a, enter the loss on **Form 1040, line 18,** and **also** on **Schedule SE, line 1.** If you file Form 1040NR, enter the loss on **Form 1040NR, line 19.** • If you checked 37b, you **must** attach **Form 6198.** Your loss may be limited.	**37a** ☐ All investment is at risk. **37b** ☐ Some investment is not at risk.	

Part III Farm Income—Accrual Method (see page F-7).

Do not include sales of livestock held for draft, breeding, sport, or dairy purposes. Report these sales on Form 4797 and do not include this livestock on line 46 below.

38	Sales of livestock, produce, grains, and other products	38	
39a	Cooperative distributions (Form(s) 1099-PATR) 39a ______ 39b Taxable amount	39b	
40a	Agricultural program payments 40a ______ 40b Taxable amount	40b	
41	Commodity Credit Corporation (CCC) loans:		
a	CCC loans reported under election	41a	
b	CCC loans forfeited 41b ______ 41c Taxable amount	41c	
42	Crop insurance proceeds	42	
43	Custom hire (machine work) income	43	
44	Other income, including federal and state gasoline or fuel tax credit or refund	44	
45	Add amounts in the right column for lines 38 through 44	45	
46	Inventory of livestock, produce, grains, and other products at beginning of the year 46 ______		
47	Cost of livestock, produce, grains, and other products purchased during the year 47 ______		
48	Add lines 46 and 47 48 ______		
49	Inventory of livestock, produce, grains, and other products at end of year 49 ______		
50	Cost of livestock, produce, grains, and other products sold. Subtract line 49 from line 48*	50	
51	**Gross income.** Subtract line 50 from line 45. Enter the result here and on Part I, line 11 ▶	51	

*If you use the unit-livestock-price method or the farm-price method of valuing inventory and the amount on line 49 is larger than the amount on line 48, subtract line 48 from line 49. Enter the result on line 50. Add lines 45 and 50. Enter the total on line 51 and on Part I, line 11.

Part IV Principal Agricultural Activity Codes

CAUTION *File Schedule C (Form 1040) or Schedule C-EZ (Form 1040) instead of Schedule F if **(a)** your principal source of income is from providing agricultural services such as soil preparation, veterinary, farm labor, horticultural, or management for a fee or on a contract basis, or **(b)** you are engaged in the business of breeding, raising, and caring for dogs, cats, or other pet animals.*

These codes for the Principal Agricultural Activity classify farms by their primary activity to facilitate the administration of the Internal Revenue Code. These six-digit codes are based on the North American Industry Classification System (NAICS).

Select the code that best identifies your primary farming activity and enter the six digit number on page 1, line B.

Crop Production

111100 Oilseed and grain farming
111210 Vegetable and melon farming
111300 Fruit and tree nut farming
111400 Greenhouse, nursery, and floriculture production
111900 Other crop farming

Animal Production

112111 Beef cattle ranching and farming
112112 Cattle feedlots
112120 Dairy cattle and milk production
112210 Hog and pig farming
112300 Poultry and egg production
112400 Sheep and goat farming
112510 Animal aquaculture
112900 Other animal production

Forestry and Logging

113000 Forestry and logging (including forest nurseries and timber tracts)

SCHEDULE H (Form 1040)

Department of the Treasury Internal Revenue Service (99)

Household Employment Taxes

(For Social Security, Medicare, Withheld Income, and Federal Unemployment (FUTA) Taxes)

▶ **Attach to Form 1040, 1040NR, 1040-SS, or 1041.**

▶ **See separate instructions.**

OMB No. 1545-1971

2006

Attachment Sequence No. **44**

Name of employer | **Social security number** | **Employer identification number**

A Did you pay **any one** household employee cash wages of $1,500 or more in 2006? (If any household employee was your spouse, your child under age 21, your parent, or anyone under age 18, see the line A instructions on page H-3 before you answer this question.)

- ☐ **Yes.** Skip lines B and C and go to line 1.
- ☐ **No.** Go to line B.

B Did you withhold federal income tax during 2006 for any household employee?

- ☐ **Yes.** Skip line C and go to line 5.
- ☐ **No.** Go to line C.

C Did you pay **total** cash wages of $1,000 or more in **any** calendar **quarter** of 2005 or 2006 to **all** household employees? (**Do not** count cash wages paid in 2005 or 2006 to your spouse, your child under age 21, or your parent.)

- ☐ **No. Stop.** Do not file this schedule.
- ☐ **Yes.** Skip lines 1-9 and go to line 10 on the back. (Calendar year taxpayers having no household employees in 2006 **do not** have to complete this form for 2006.)

Part I Social Security, Medicare, and Income Taxes

1	Total cash wages subject to social security taxes (see page H-4)	1		
2	Social security taxes. Multiply line 1 by 12.4% (.124)		2	
3	Total cash wages subject to Medicare taxes (see page H-4) . .	3		
4	Medicare taxes. Multiply line 3 by 2.9% (.029)		4	
5	Federal income tax withheld, if any		5	
6	**Total social security, Medicare, and income taxes.** Add lines 2, 4, and 5		6	
7	Advance earned income credit (EIC) payments, if any		7	
8	**Net taxes** (subtract line 7 from line 6)		8	

9 Did you pay **total** cash wages of $1,000 or more in **any** calendar **quarter** of 2005 or 2006 to household employees? (**Do not** count cash wages paid in 2005 or 2006 to your spouse, your child under age 21, or your parent.)

- ☐ **No. Stop.** Enter the amount from line 8 above on Form 1040, line 62. If you are not required to file Form 1040, see the line 9 instructions on page H-4.
- ☐ **Yes.** Go to line 10 on the back.

Part II Federal Unemployment (FUTA) Tax

			Yes	No
10	Are you required to pay unemployment contributions to only one state?	10		
11	Did you pay all state unemployment contributions for 2006 by April 16, 2007? Fiscal year filers, see page H-4.	11		
12	Were all wages that are taxable for FUTA tax also taxable for your state's unemployment tax?	12		

Next: If you checked the **"Yes"** box on **all** the lines above, complete Section A.
If you checked the **"No"** box on **any** of the lines above, skip Section A and complete Section B.

Section A

13 Name of the state where you paid unemployment contributions ▶ ____________

14 State reporting number as shown on state unemployment tax return ▶ ____________

15 Contributions paid to your state unemployment fund (see page H-4) | 15 | |

16 Total cash wages subject to FUTA tax (see page H-4) . . . | 16 | |

17 **FUTA tax.** Multiply line 16 by .008. Enter the result here, skip Section B, and go to line 26 . | 17 | |

Section B

18 Complete all columns below that apply (if you need more space, see page H-5):

(a) Name of state	(b) State reporting number as shown on state unemployment tax return	(c) Taxable wages (as defined in state act)	(d) State experience rate period From	To	(e) State experience rate	(f) Multiply col. (c) by .054	(g) Multiply col. (c) by col. (e)	(h) Subtract col. (g) from col. (f). If zero or less, enter -0-.	(i) Contributions paid to state unemployment fund

19 Totals . . . | 19 | |

20 Add columns (h) and (i) of line 19 . . . | 20 | |

21 Total cash wages subject to FUTA tax (see the line 16 instructions on page H-4) . . . | 21 | |

22 Multiply line 21 by 6.2% (.062) . . . | 22 | |

23 Multiply line 21 by 5.4% (.054) . . . | 23 | |

24 Enter the **smaller** of line 20 or line 23 . . . | 24 | |

25 **FUTA tax.** Subtract line 24 from line 22. Enter the result here and go to line 26 . . . | 25 | |

Part III Total Household Employment Taxes

26 Enter the amount from line 8. If you checked the "Yes" box on line C of page 1, enter -0- . . | 26 | |

27 Add line 17 (or line 25) and line 26 . . . | 27 | |

28 Are you required to file Form 1040?

☐ **Yes.** **Stop.** Enter the amount from line 27 above on Form 1040, line 62. **Do not** complete Part IV below.

☐ **No.** You may have to complete Part IV. See page H-5 for details.

Part IV Address and Signature—Complete this part **only** if required. See the line 28 instructions on page H-5.

Address (number and street) or P.O. box if mail is not delivered to street address | Apt., room, or suite no.

City, town or post office, state, and ZIP code

Under penalties of perjury, I declare that I have examined this schedule, including accompanying statements, and to the best of my knowledge and belief, it is true, correct, and complete. No part of any payment made to a state unemployment fund claimed as a credit was, or is to be, deducted from the payments to employees.

▶ Employer's signature ▶ Date

Schedule R (Form 1040)	Credit for the Elderly or the Disabled	OMB No. 1545-0074
Department of the Treasury Internal Revenue Service (99)	▶ Attach to Form 1040. ▶ See Instructions for Schedule R (Form 1040).	2006 Attachment Sequence No. 16

Name(s) shown on Form 1040 | Your social security number

You may be able to take this credit and reduce your tax if by the end of 2006:

- You were age 65 or older **or**
- You were under age 65, you retired on **permanent and total** disability, and you received taxable disability income.

But you must also meet other tests. See page R-1.

TIP In most cases, the IRS can figure the credit for you. See page R-1.

Part I **Check the Box for Your Filing Status and Age**

If your filing status is:	And by the end of 2006:	Check only one box:
Single, Head of household, or Qualifying widow(er)	1 You were 65 or older 1	☐
	2 You were under 65 and you retired on permanent and total disability 2	☐
Married filing jointly	3 Both spouses were 65 or older 3	☐
	4 Both spouses were under 65, but only one spouse retired on permanent and total disability 4	☐
	5 Both spouses were under 65, and both retired on permanent and total disability 5	☐
	6 One spouse was 65 or older, and the other spouse was under 65 and retired on permanent and total disability 6	☐
	7 One spouse was 65 or older, and the other spouse was under 65 and **not** retired on permanent and total disability 7	☐
Married filing separately	8 You were 65 or older and you lived apart from your spouse for all of 2006 8	☐
	9 You were under 65, you retired on permanent and total disability, and you lived apart from your spouse for all of 2006 9	☐

Did you check box 1, 3, 7, or 8?

- **Yes** ▶ Skip Part II and complete Part III on back.
- **No** ▶ Complete Parts II and III.

Part II **Statement of Permanent and Total Disability** (Complete **only** if you checked box 2, 4, 5, 6, or 9 above.)

If: **1** You filed a physician's statement for this disability for 1983 or an earlier year, or you filed or got a statement for tax years after 1983 and your physician signed line B on the statement, **and**

2 Due to your continued disabled condition, you were unable to engage in any substantial gainful activity in 2006, check this box . . . . ▶ ☐

- If you checked this box, you do not have to get another statement for 2006.
- If you **did not** check this box, have your physician complete the statement on page R-4. You **must** keep the statement for your records.

Part III Figure Your Credit

10 **If you checked (in Part I):** **Enter:**
Box 1, 2, 4, or 7 . . . . $5,000
Box 3, 5, or 6 . . . . $7,500
Box 8 or 9 . . . . $3,750 . . . . **10**

Did you check box 2, 4, 5, 6, or 9 in Part I?
Yes → You **must** complete line 11.
No → Enter the amount from line 10 on line 12 and go to line 13.

11 **If you checked (in Part I):**
- Box 6, add $5,000 to the taxable disability income of the spouse who was under age 65. Enter the total.
- Box 2, 4, or 9, enter your taxable disability income.
- Box 5, add your taxable disability income to your spouse's taxable disability income. Enter the total. **11**

TIP For more details on what to include on line 11, see page R-3.

12 If you completed line 11, enter the **smaller** of line 10 or line 11; **all others,** enter the amount from line 10 . . . . **12**

13 Enter the following pensions, annuities, or disability income that you (and your spouse if filing a joint return) received in 2006.

a Nontaxable part of social security benefits and Nontaxable part of railroad retirement benefits treated as social security (see page R-3). . . **13a**

b Nontaxable veterans' pensions and Any other pension, annuity, or disability benefit that is excluded from income under any other provision of law (see page R-3). . . **13b**

c Add lines 13a and 13b. (Even though these income items are not taxable, they **must** be included here to figure your credit.) If you did not receive any of the types of nontaxable income listed on line 13a or 13b, enter -0- on line 13c **13c**

14 Enter the amount from Form 1040, line 38 . . . . **14**

15 **If you checked (in Part I):** **Enter:**
Box 1 or 2 . . . . . . $7,500
Box 3, 4, 5, 6, or 7 . . . $10,000
Box 8 or 9 . . . . . . $5,000 **15**

16 Subtract line 15 from line 14. If zero or less, enter -0- **16**

17 Enter one-half of line 16 . . . . **17**

18 Add lines 13c and 17 . . . . **18**

19 Subtract line 18 from line 12. If zero or less, **stop;** you **cannot** take the credit. Otherwise, go to line 20 . . . . **19**

20 Multiply line 19 by 15% (.15) **20**

21 Enter the amount from Form 1040, line 46 . . . . **21**

22 Add the amounts from Form 1040, lines 47 and 48, and enter the total **22**

23 Subtract line 22 from line 21 . . . . **23**

24 **Credit for the elderly or the disabled.** Enter the **smaller** of line 20 or line 23 here and on Form 1040, line 49 . . . . **24**

SCHEDULE SE (Form 1040) Department of the Treasury Internal Revenue Service (99)	**Self-Employment Tax** ▶ Attach to Form 1040. ▶ See Instructions for Schedule SE (Form 1040).	OMB No. 1545-0074 **2006** Attachment Sequence No. **17**

Name of person with **self-employment** income (as shown on Form 1040)	Social security number of person with **self-employment** income ▶	

Who Must File Schedule SE

You must file Schedule SE if:

- You had net earnings from self-employment from **other than** church employee income (line 4 of Short Schedule SE or line 4c of Long Schedule SE) of $400 or more, **or**
- You had church employee income of $108.28 or more. Income from services you performed as a minister or a member of a religious order **is not** church employee income (see page SE-1).

Note. Even if you had a loss or a small amount of income from self-employment, it may be to your benefit to file Schedule SE and use either "optional method" in Part II of Long Schedule SE (see page SE-3).

Exception. If your only self-employment income was from earnings as a minister, member of a religious order, or Christian Science practitioner **and** you filed Form 4361 and received IRS approval not to be taxed on those earnings, **do not** file Schedule SE. Instead, write "Exempt–Form 4361" on Form 1040, line 58.

May I Use Short Schedule SE or Must I Use Long Schedule SE?

Note. Use this flowchart **only if** you must file Schedule SE. If unsure, see Who Must File Schedule SE, above.

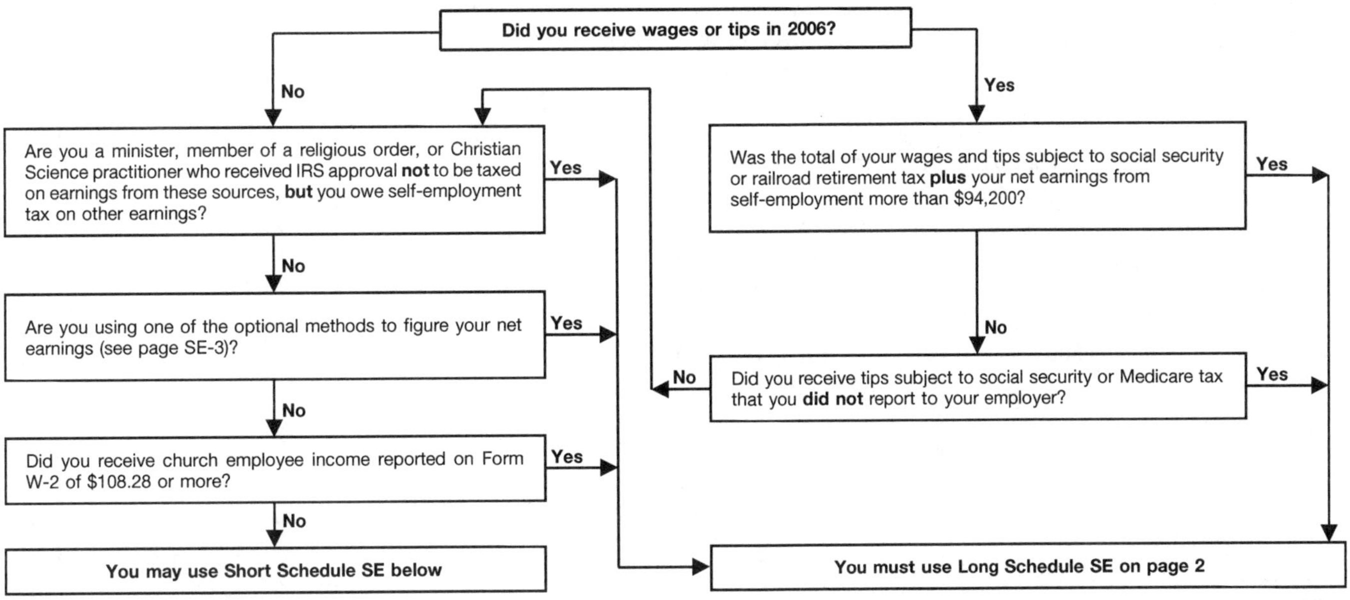

Section A—Short Schedule SE. Caution. Read above to see if you can use Short Schedule SE.

1	Net farm profit or (loss) from Schedule F, line 36, and farm partnerships, Schedule K-1 (Form 1065), box 14, code A	1		
2	Net profit or (loss) from Schedule C, line 31; Schedule C-EZ, line 3; Schedule K-1 (Form 1065), box 14, code A (other than farming); and Schedule K-1 (Form 1065-B), box 9, code J1. Ministers and members of religious orders, see page SE-1 for amounts to report on this line. See page SE-3 for other income to report	2		
3	Combine lines 1 and 2	3		
4	**Net earnings from self-employment.** Multiply line 3 by 92.35% (.9235). If less than $400, **do not** file this schedule; you do not owe self-employment tax . . . . ▶	4		
5	**Self-employment tax.** If the amount on line 4 is: • $94,200 or less, multiply line 4 by 15.3% (.153). Enter the result here and on **Form 1040, line 58.** • More than $94,200, multiply line 4 by 2.9% (.029). Then, add $11,680.80 to the result. Enter the total here and on **Form 1040, line 58.**	5		
6	**Deduction for one-half of self-employment tax.** Multiply line 5 by 50% (.5). Enter the result here and on **Form 1040, line 27** . . .	6				

Name of person with **self-employment** income (as shown on Form 1040)	Social security number of person with **self-employment** income ▶

Section B—Long Schedule SE

Part I Self-Employment Tax

Note. If your only income subject to self-employment tax is **church employee income,** skip lines 1 through 4b. Enter -0- on line 4c and go to line 5a. Income from services you performed as a minister or a member of a religious order **is not** church employee income. See page SE-1.

A If you are a minister, member of a religious order, or Christian Science practitioner **and** you filed Form 4361, but you had $400 or more of **other** net earnings from self-employment, check here and continue with Part I . . . . ▶ ☐

1	Net farm profit or (loss) from Schedule F, line 36, and farm partnerships, Schedule K-1 (Form 1065), box 14, code A. **Note.** Skip this line if you use the farm optional method (see page SE-4)			1		
2	Net profit or (loss) from Schedule C, line 31; Schedule C-EZ, line 3; Schedule K-1 (Form 1065), box 14, code A (other than farming); and Schedule K-1 (Form 1065-B), box 9, code J1. Ministers and members of religious orders, see page SE-1 for amounts to report on this line. See page SE-3 for other income to report. **Note.** Skip this line if you use the nonfarm optional method (see page SE-4)			2		
3	Combine lines 1 and 2			3		
4a	If line 3 is more than zero, multiply line 3 by 92.35% (.9235). Otherwise, enter amount from line 3			4a		
b	If you elect one or both of the optional methods, enter the total of lines 15 and 17 here . . .			4b		
c	Combine lines 4a and 4b. If less than $400, **stop**; you do not owe self-employment tax. **Exception.** If less than $400 and you had **church employee income,** enter -0- and continue. . . . . . ▶			4c		
5a	Enter your **church employee income** from Form W-2. See page SE-1 for definition of church employee income	5a				
b	Multiply line 5a by 92.35% (.9235). If less than $100, enter -0-			5b		
6	**Net earnings from self-employment.** Add lines 4c and 5b			6		
7	Maximum amount of combined wages and self-employment earnings subject to social security tax or the 6.2% portion of the 7.65% railroad retirement (tier 1) tax for 2006			7	94,200	00
8a	Total social security wages and tips (total of boxes 3 and 7 on Form(s) W-2) and railroad retirement (tier 1) compensation. If $94,200 or more, skip lines 8b through 10, and go to line 11	8a				
b	Unreported tips subject to social security tax (from Form 4137, line 9)	8b				
c	Add lines 8a and 8b			8c		
9	Subtract line 8c from line 7. If zero or less, enter -0- here and on line 10 and go to line 11 . ▶			9		
10	Multiply the **smaller** of line 6 or line 9 by 12.4% (.124)			10		
11	Multiply line 6 by 2.9% (.029)			11		
12	**Self-employment tax.** Add lines 10 and 11. Enter here and on **Form 1040, line 58**			12		
13	**Deduction for one-half of self-employment tax.** Multiply line 12 by 50% (.5). Enter the result here and on **Form 1040, line 27**	13				

Part II Optional Methods To Figure Net Earnings (see page SE-3)

Farm Optional Method. You may use this method **only** if **(a)** your gross farm income[1] was not more than $2,400, **or (b)** your net farm profits[2] were less than $1,733.

14	Maximum income for optional methods	14	1,600	00
15	Enter the **smaller** of: two-thirds (⅔) of gross farm income[1] (not less than zero) **or** $1,600. Also include this amount on line 4b above	15		

Nonfarm Optional Method. You may use this method **only** if **(a)** your net nonfarm profits[3] were less than $1,733 and also less than 72.189% of your gross nonfarm income,[4] **and (b)** you had net earnings from self-employment of at least $400 in 2 of the prior 3 years.

Caution. You may use this method no more than five times.

16	Subtract line 15 from line 14	16		
17	Enter the **smaller** of: two-thirds (⅔) of gross nonfarm income[4] (not less than zero) **or** the amount on line 16. Also include this amount on line 4b above	17		

[1] From Sch. F, line 11, and Sch. K-1 (Form 1065), box 14, code B.

[2] From Sch. F, line 36, and Sch. K-1 (Form 1065), box 14, code A.

[3] From Sch. C, line 31; Sch. C-EZ, line 3; Sch. K-1 (Form 1065), box 14, code A; and Sch. K-1 (Form 1065-B), box 9, code J1.

[4] From Sch. C, line 7; Sch. C-EZ, line 1; Sch. K-1 (Form 1065), box 14, code C; and Sch. K-1 (Form 1065-B), box 9, code J2.

2006 Form 1040-V

Department of the Treasury
Internal Revenue Service

What Is Form 1040-V and Do You Have To Use It?

It is a statement you send with your check or money order for any balance due on the "Amount you owe" line of your 2006 Form 1040. Using Form 1040-V allows us to process your payment more accurately and efficiently. We strongly encourage you to use Form 1040-V, but there is no penalty if you do not.

How To Fill In Form 1040-V

Line 1. Enter your social security number (SSN). If you are filing a joint return, enter the SSN shown first on your return.

Line 2. If you are filing a joint return, enter the SSN shown second on your return.

Line 3. Enter the amount you are paying by check or money order.

Line 4. Enter your name(s) and address exactly as shown on your return. Please print clearly.

How To Prepare Your Payment

- Make your check or money order payable to the "United States Treasury." Do not send cash.
- Make sure your name and address appear on your check or money order.
- Enter "2006 Form 1040," your daytime phone number, and your SSN on your check or money order. If you are filing a joint return, enter the SSN shown first on your return.
- To help process your payment, enter the amount on the right side of your check like this: $ XXX.XX. Do not use dashes or lines (for example, do not enter "$ XXX—" or "$ XXX $\frac{xx}{100}$").

How To Send In Your 2006 Tax Return, Payment, and Form 1040-V

- Detach Form 1040-V along the dotted line.
- Do not staple or otherwise attach your payment or Form 1040-V to your return or to each other. Instead, just put them loose in the envelope.
- Mail your 2006 tax return, payment, and Form 1040-V in the envelope that came with your 2006 Form 1040 instruction booklet.

Note. If you do not have that envelope or you moved or used a paid preparer, mail your return, payment, and Form 1040-V to the Internal Revenue Service at the address shown on the back that applies to you.

Paperwork Reduction Act Notice. We ask for the information on Form 1040-V to help us carry out the Internal Revenue laws of the United States. If you use Form 1040-V, you must provide the requested information. Your cooperation will help us ensure that we are collecting the right amount of tax.

You are not required to provide the information requested on a form that is subject to the Paperwork Reduction Act unless the form displays a valid OMB control number. Books or records relating to a form or its instructions must be retained as long as their contents may become material in the administration of any Internal Revenue law. Generally, tax returns and return information are confidential, as required by Internal Revenue Code section 6103.

The average time and expenses required to complete and file this form will vary depending on individual circumstances. For the estimated averages, see the instructions for your income tax return. If you have suggestions for making this form simpler, we would be happy to hear from you. See the instructions for your income tax return.

▼ Detach Here and Mail With Your Payment and Return ▼

Form **1040-V** Department of the Treasury Internal Revenue Service (99)	**Payment Voucher** ▶ **Do not staple or attach this voucher to your payment or return.**	OMB No. 1545-0074 **2006**

1 Your social security number (SSN)	2 If a joint return, SSN shown second on your return	3 **Amount you are paying by check or money order**	Dollars	Cents

4 Your first name and initial	Last name
If a joint return, spouse's first name and initial	Last name
Home address (number and street)	Apt. no.
City, town or post office, state, and ZIP code	

Cat. No. 20975C

IF you live in . . .	THEN use this address if you: Prepared your own return . . .	Used a paid preparer . . .
Alabama, Delaware, Florida, Georgia, North Carolina, Rhode Island, South Carolina, Virginia	Atlanta, GA 39901-0102	P.O. Box 105017 Atlanta, GA 30348-5017
District of Columbia, Maine, Maryland, Massachusetts, New Hampshire, New York, Vermont	Andover, MA 05501-0102	P.O. Box 37002 Hartford, CT 06176-7002
Kentucky*, Pennsylvania*	Philadelphia, PA 19255-0102	P.O. Box 80101 Cincinnati, OH 45280-0001
Kansas, Louisiana, Mississippi, Oklahoma, Tennessee, Texas, West Virginia, APO and FPO addresses	Austin, TX 73301-0102	P.O. Box 660308 Dallas, TX 75266-0308
Colorado, Idaho, Minnesota, Montana, Nebraska, New Mexico, North Dakota, South Dakota, Utah, Washington, Wyoming	Fresno, CA 93888-0102	P.O. Box 802501 Cincinnati, OH 45280-2501
Alaska, Arizona, California, Hawaii, Nevada, Oregon	Fresno, CA 93888-0102	P.O. Box 7704 San Francisco, CA 94120-7704
Arkansas, Connecticut, Illinois, Indiana, Iowa, Michigan, Missouri, New Jersey, Ohio, Wisconsin	Kansas City, MO 64999-0102	P.O. Box 970011 St. Louis, MO 63197-0011
American Samoa, nonpermanent residents of Guam or the Virgin Islands**, Puerto Rico (or if excluding income under Internal Revenue Code section 933), dual-status aliens, a foreign country: U.S. citizens and those filing Form 2555, 2555-EZ, or 4563	Austin, TX 73301-0215 USA	P.O. Box 660335 Dallas, TX 75266-0335 USA

* If you live in Kentucky or Pennsylvania and file your return after June 30, 2007, use: Internal Revenue Service Center, Kansas City, MO 64999-0102 (if you prepared your own return); or Internal Revenue Service Center, P.O. Box 970011, St. Louis, MO 63197-0011 (if you used a paid preparer).

** Permanent residents of Guam or the Virgin Islands should not use Form 1040-V.

Form **1040X** (Rev. November 2005)

Department of the Treasury—Internal Revenue Service

Amended U.S. Individual Income Tax Return

► See separate instructions.

OMB No. 1545-0074

This return is for calendar year ► , or fiscal year ended ► ,

Please print or type

Your first name and initial	Last name		Your social security number
If a joint return, spouse's first name and initial	Last name		Spouse's social security number
Home address (no. and street) or P.O. box if mail is not delivered to your home		Apt. no.	Phone number ( )
City, town or post office, state, and ZIP code. If you have a foreign address, see page 2 of the instructions.			**For Paperwork Reduction Act Notice, see page 6.**

A If the address shown above is different from that shown on your last return filed with the IRS and you would like us to change it, check here . . . . . ► ☐

B Filing status. Be sure to complete this line. **Note.** You cannot change from joint to separate returns after the due date.

On original return ► ☐ Single ☐ Married filing jointly ☐ Married filing separately ☐ Head of household ☐ Qualifying widow(er)

On this return ► ☐ Single ☐ Married filing jointly ☐ Married filing separately ☐ Head of household* ☐ Qualifying widow(er)

* If the qualifying person is a child but not your dependent, see page 2 of the instructions.

Use Part II on the back to explain any changes		A. Original amount or as previously adjusted (see page 3)	B. Net change—amount of increase or (decrease)—explain in Part II	C. Correct amount
Income and Deductions (see instructions)				
1 Adjusted gross income (see page 3)	1			
2 Itemized deductions or standard deduction (see page 3)	2			
3 Subtract line 2 from line 1	3			
4 Exemptions. If changing, fill in Parts I and II on the back (see page 3)	4			
5 Taxable income. Subtract line 4 from line 3	5			
Tax Liability				
6 Tax (see page 4). Method used in col. C ________	6			
7 Credits (see page 4)	7			
8 Subtract line 7 from line 6. Enter the result but not less than zero	8			
9 Other taxes (see page 4)	9			
10 Total tax. Add lines 8 and 9	10			
Payments				
11 Federal income tax withheld and excess social security and tier 1 RRTA tax withheld. If changing, see page 4	11			
12 Estimated tax payments, including amount applied from prior year's return	12			
13 Earned income credit (EIC)	13			
14 Additional child tax credit from Form 8812	14			
15 Credits from Form 2439, Form 4136, or Form 8885	15			
16 Amount paid with request for extension of time to file (see page 4)			16	
17 Amount of tax paid with original return plus additional tax paid after it was filed			17	
18 Total payments. Add lines 11 through 17 in column C			18	
Refund or Amount You Owe				
19 Overpayment, if any, as shown on original return or as previously adjusted by the IRS			19	
20 Subtract line 19 from line 18 (see page 5)			20	
21 **Amount you owe.** If line 10, column C, is more than line 20, enter the difference and see page 5			21	
22 If line 10, column C, is less than line 20, enter the difference			22	
23 Amount of line 22 you want **refunded to you**			23	
24 Amount of line 22 you want **applied to your** **estimated tax**	24			

Sign Here

Joint return? See page 2. Keep a copy for your records.

Under penalties of perjury, I declare that I have filed an original return and that I have examined this amended return, including accompanying schedules and statements, and to the best of my knowledge and belief, this amended return is true, correct, and complete. Declaration of preparer (other than taxpayer) is based on all information of which the preparer has any knowledge.

► Your signature Date ► Spouse's signature. If a joint return, **both** must sign. Date

Paid Preparer's Use Only

Preparer's signature ►	Date	Check if self-employed ☐	Preparer's SSN or PTIN
Firm's name (or yours if self-employed), address, and ZIP code ►		EIN	
		Phone no. ( )	

Part I **Exemptions.** See Form 1040 or 1040A instructions.

Complete this part **only** if you are:

- Increasing or decreasing the number of exemptions claimed on line 6d of the return you are amending, or
- Increasing or decreasing the exemption amount for housing individuals displaced by Hurricane Katrina.

			A. Original number of exemptions reported or as previously adjusted	B. Net change	C. Correct number of exemptions
25	Yourself and spouse . . . . **Caution.** If someone can claim you as a dependent, you cannot claim an exemption for yourself.	25			
26	Your dependent children who lived with you	26			
27	Your dependent children who did not live with you due to divorce or separation	27			
28	Other dependents	28			
29	Total number of exemptions. Add lines 25 through 28	29			
30	Multiply the number of exemptions claimed on line 29 by the amount listed below for the tax year you are amending. Enter the result here and on line 4.	30			
31	If you are claiming an exemption amount for housing individuals displaced by Hurricane Katrina, enter the amount from Form 8914, line 2 (see instructions for line 4)	31			
32	Add lines 30 and 31. Enter the result here and on line 4	32			

Tax year	Exemption amount	But see the instructions for line 4 on page 3 if the amount on line 1 is over:
2005	$3,200	$109,475
2004	3,100	107,025
2003	3,050	104,625
2002	3,000	103,000

33 Dependents (children and other) not claimed on original (or adjusted) return:

(a) First name	Last name	(b) Dependent's social security number	(c) Dependent's relationship to you	(d) ✓ if qualifying child for child tax credit (see page 5)
				☐
				☐
				☐
				☐
				☐
				☐

No. of children on 33 who:
- lived with you . . ▶ ☐
- **did not** live with you due to divorce or separation (see page 5) . . ▶ ☐

Dependents on 33 not entered above ▶ ☐

Part II **Explanation of Changes**

Enter the line number from the front of the form for each item you are changing and give the reason for each change. Attach only the supporting forms and schedules for the items changed. If you do not attach the required information, your Form 1040X may be returned. Be sure to include your name and social security number on any attachments.

If the change relates to a net operating loss carryback or a general business credit carryback, attach the schedule or form that shows the year in which the loss or credit occurred. See page 2 of the instructions. Also, check here. . . . . . ▶ ☐

Part III **Presidential Election Campaign Fund.** Checking below will not increase your tax or reduce your refund.

If you did not previously want $3 to go to the fund but now want to, check here . . . . ▶ ☐

If a joint return and your spouse did not previously want $3 to go to the fund but now wants to, check here . . . . ▶ ☐

Form **1116**

Department of the Treasury
Internal Revenue Service (99)

Foreign Tax Credit

(Individual, Estate, or Trust)

▶ **Attach to Form 1040, 1040NR, 1041, or 990-T.**

▶ **See separate instructions.**

OMB No. 1545-0121

2006

Attachment Sequence No. **19**

Name | **Identifying number** as shown on page 1 of your tax return

Use a separate Form 1116 for each category of income listed below. See **Categories of Income** on page 3 of the instructions. Check only one box on each Form 1116. Report all amounts in U.S. dollars except where specified in Part II below.

- **a** ☐ Passive income
- **b** ☐ High withholding tax interest
- **c** ☐ Financial services income
- **d** ☐ Shipping income
- **e** ☐ Dividends from a DISC or former DISC
- **f** ☐ Certain distributions from a foreign sales corporation (FSC) or former FSC
- **g** ☐ Lump-sum distributions
- **h** ☐ Section 901(j) income
- **i** ☐ Certain income re-sourced by treaty
- **j** ☐ General limitation income

k Resident of (name of country) ▶

Note: *If you paid taxes to only one foreign country or U.S. possession, use column A in Part I and line A in Part II. If you paid taxes to* ***more than one*** *foreign country or U.S. possession, use a separate column and line for each country or possession.*

Part I Taxable Income or Loss From Sources Outside the United States (for Category Checked Above)

	Foreign Country or U.S. Possession			Total
	A	B	C	(Add cols. A, B, and C.)
i **Enter the name of the foreign country or U.S. possession** . . . . ▶				
1a Gross income from sources within country shown above and of the type checked above (see page 13 of the instructions):				**1a**
b Check if line 1a is compensation for personal services as an employee, your total compensation from all sources is $250,000 or more, and you used an alternative basis to determine its source (see instructions) ▶ ☐				
Deductions and losses (*Caution: See pages 13 and 14 of the instructions*):				
2 Expenses **definitely related** to the income on line 1a (attach statement)				
3 Pro rata share of other deductions **not definitely related:**				
a Certain itemized deductions or standard deduction (see instructions)				
b Other deductions (attach statement)				
c Add lines 3a and 3b				
d Gross foreign source income (see instructions) .				
e Gross income from all sources (see instructions)				
f Divide line 3d by line 3e (see instructions) . .				
g Multiply line 3c by line 3f				
4 Pro rata share of interest expense (see instructions):				
a Home mortgage interest (use worksheet on page 13 of the instructions)				
b Other interest expense				
5 Losses from foreign sources				
6 Add lines 2, 3g, 4a, 4b, and 5				**6**
7 Subtract line 6 from line 1a. Enter the result here and on line 14, page 2 . . . . ▶				**7**

Part II Foreign Taxes Paid or Accrued (see page 14 of the instructions)

Country	Credit is claimed for taxes (you must check one) (m) ☐ Paid (n) ☐ Accrued	Foreign taxes paid or accrued								
		In foreign currency				In U.S. dollars				
		Taxes withheld at source on:			(s) Other foreign taxes paid or accrued	Taxes withheld at source on:			(w) Other foreign taxes paid or accrued	(x) Total foreign taxes paid or accrued (add cols. (t) through (w))
	(o) Date paid or accrued	(p) Dividends	(q) Rents and royalties	(r) Interest		(t) Dividends	(u) Rents and royalties	(v) Interest		
A										
B										
C										

8 Add lines A through C, column (x). Enter the total here and on line 9, page 2 . . . . ▶ **8**

For Paperwork Reduction Act Notice, see page 18 of the instructions. Cat. No. 11440U Form **1116** (2006)

Part III Figuring the Credit

9	Enter the amount from line 8. These are your total foreign taxes paid or accrued for the category of income checked above Part I . . .	9	
10	Carryback or carryover (attach detailed computation)	10	
11	Add lines 9 and 10	11	
12	Reduction in foreign taxes (see page 15 of the instructions) . . .	12	
13	Subtract line 12 from line 11. This is the total amount of foreign taxes available for credit . . .	13	
14	Enter the amount from line 7. This is your taxable income or (loss) from sources outside the United States (before adjustments) for the category of income checked above Part I (see page 15 of the instructions) .	14	
15	Adjustments to line 14 (see pages 15 and 16 of the instructions) .	15	
16	Combine the amounts on lines 14 and 15. This is your net foreign source taxable income. (If the result is zero or less, you have no foreign tax credit for the category of income you checked above Part I. Skip lines 17 through 21. However, if you are filing more than one Form 1116, you must complete line 19.)	16	
17	**Individuals:** Enter the amount from Form 1040, line 41 (minus any amount on Form 8914, line 6). If you are a nonresident alien, enter the amount from Form 1040NR, line 38 (minus any amount on Form 8914, line 6). **Estates and trusts:** Enter your taxable income without the deduction for your exemption	17	
	Caution: *If you figured your tax using the lower rates on qualified dividends or capital gains, see page 16 of the instructions.*		
18	Divide line 16 by line 17. If line 16 is more than line 17, enter "1"	18	
19	**Individuals:** Enter the amount from Form 1040, line 44. If you are a nonresident alien, enter the amount from Form 1040NR, line 41. **Estates and trusts:** Enter the amount from Form 1041, Schedule G, line 1a, or the total of Form 990-T, lines 36 and 37	19	
	Caution: *If you are completing line 19 for separate category **g** (lump-sum distributions), see page 18 of the instructions.*		
20	Multiply line 19 by line 18 (maximum amount of credit)	20	
21	Enter the **smaller** of line 13 or line 20. If this is the only Form 1116 you are filing, skip lines 22 through 30 and enter this amount on line 31. Otherwise, complete the appropriate line in Part IV (see page 18 of the instructions) . . . . ▶	21	

Part IV Summary of Credits From Separate Parts III (see page 18 of the instructions)

22	Credit for taxes on passive income	22	
23	Credit for taxes on high withholding tax interest	23	
24	Credit for taxes on financial services income	24	
25	Credit for taxes on shipping income	25	
26	Credit for taxes on dividends from a DISC or former DISC and certain distributions from a FSC or former FSC	26	
27	Credit for taxes on lump-sum distributions	27	
28	Credit for taxes on certain income re-sourced by treaty	28	
29	Credit for taxes on general limitation income	29	
30	Add lines 22 through 29	30	
31	Enter the **smaller** of line 19 or line 30	31	
32	Reduction of credit for international boycott operations. See instructions for line 12 on page 15 .	32	
33	Subtract line 32 from line 31. This is your **foreign tax credit.** Enter here and on Form 1040, line 47; Form 1040NR, line 44; Form 1041, Schedule G, line 2a; or Form 990-T, line 40a . . . . . ▶	33	

Form **2106**

Department of the Treasury
Internal Revenue Service (99)

Employee Business Expenses

▶ See separate instructions.

▶ Attach to Form 1040 or Form 1040NR.

OMB No. 1545-0074

2006

Attachment Sequence No. **54**

Your name	Occupation in which you incurred expenses	Social security number

Part I Employee Business Expenses and Reimbursements

Step 1 Enter Your Expenses		**Column A** Other Than Meals and Entertainment	**Column B** Meals and Entertainment
1 Vehicle expense from line 22 or line 29. (Rural mail carriers: See instructions.)	1		
2 Parking fees, tolls, and transportation, including train, bus, etc., that **did not** involve overnight travel or commuting to and from work . .	2		
3 Travel expense while away from home overnight, including lodging, airplane, car rental, etc. **Do not** include meals and entertainment	3		
4 Business expenses not included on lines 1 through 3. **Do not** include meals and entertainment.	4		
5 Meals and entertainment expenses (see instructions)	5		
6 **Total expenses.** In Column A, add lines 1 through 4 and enter the result. In Column B, enter the amount from line 5	6		

Note: *If you were not reimbursed for any expenses in Step 1, skip line 7 and enter the amount from line 6 on line 8.*

Step 2 Enter Reimbursements Received From Your Employer for Expenses Listed in Step 1

		Column A	Column B
7 Enter reimbursements received from your employer that were **not** reported to you in box 1 of Form W-2. Include any reimbursements reported under code "L" in box 12 of your Form W-2 (see instructions)	7		

Step 3 Figure Expenses To Deduct on Schedule A (Form 1040)

		Column A	Column B
8 Subtract line 7 from line 6. If zero or less, enter -0-. However, if line 7 is greater than line 6 in Column A, report the excess as income on Form 1040, line 7 (or on Form 1040NR, line 8) . . .	8		
Note: *If* ***both columns*** *of line 8 are zero, you cannot deduct employee business expenses. Stop here and attach Form 2106 to your return.* **9** In Column A, enter the amount from line 8. In Column B, multiply line 8 by 50% (.50). (Employees subject to Department of Transportation (DOT) hours of service limits: Multiply meal expenses incurred while away from home on business by 75% (.75) instead of 50%. For details, see instructions.)	9		

10 Add the amounts on line 9 of both columns and enter the total here. **Also, enter the total on Schedule A (Form 1040), line 20** (or on Schedule A (Form 1040NR), line 9). (Reservists, qualified performing artists, fee-basis state or local government officials, and individuals with disabilities: See the instructions for special rules on where to enter the total.) . . . . ▶ **10** ______

Part II Vehicle Expenses

Section A—General Information (You must complete this section if you are claiming vehicle expenses.)

			(a) Vehicle 1	(b) Vehicle 2
11	Enter the date the vehicle was placed in service	11	/ /	/ /
12	Total miles the vehicle was driven during 2006	12	miles	miles
13	Business miles included on line 12	13	miles	miles
14	Percent of business use. Divide line 13 by line 12	14	%	%
15	Average daily roundtrip commuting distance	15	miles	miles
16	Commuting miles included on line 12	16	miles	miles
17	Other miles. Add lines 13 and 16 and subtract the total from line 12	17	miles	miles

18 Do you (or your spouse) have another vehicle available for personal use? ☐ Yes ☐ No

19 Was your vehicle available for personal use during off-duty hours? ☐ Yes ☐ No

20 Do you have evidence to support your deduction? ☐ Yes ☐ No

21 If "Yes," is the evidence written? ☐ Yes ☐ No

Section B—Standard Mileage Rate (See the instructions for Part II to find out whether to complete this section or Section C.)

22 Multiply line 13 by 44.5¢ (.445) . . . 22

Section C—Actual Expenses

			(a) Vehicle 1	(b) Vehicle 2
23	Gasoline, oil, repairs, vehicle insurance, etc.	23		
24a	Vehicle rentals	24a		
b	Inclusion amount (see instructions)	24b		
c	Subtract line 24b from line 24a	24c		
25	Value of employer-provided vehicle (applies only if 100% of annual lease value was included on Form W-2—see instructions)	25		
26	Add lines 23, 24c, and 25	26		
27	Multiply line 26 by the percentage on line 14	27		
28	Depreciation (see instructions)	28		
29	Add lines 27 and 28. Enter total here and on line 1	29		

Section D—Depreciation of Vehicles (Use this section only if you owned the vehicle and are completing Section C for the vehicle.)

			(a) Vehicle 1	(b) Vehicle 2
30	Enter cost or other basis (see instructions)	30		
31	Enter section 179 deduction (see instructions)	31		
32	Multiply line 30 by line 14 (see instructions if you claimed the section 179 deduction or special allowance)	32		
33	Enter depreciation method and percentage (see instructions)	33		
34	Multiply line 32 by the percentage on line 33 (see instructions)	34		
35	Add lines 31 and 34	35		
36	Enter the applicable limit explained in the line 36 instructions	36		
37	Multiply line 36 by the percentage on line 14	37		
38	Enter the **smaller** of line 35 or line 37. If you skipped lines 36 and 37, enter the amount from line 35. Also enter this amount on line 28 above	38		

Form **2106-EZ**

Department of the Treasury
Internal Revenue Service (99)

Unreimbursed Employee Business Expenses

► Attach to Form 1040 or Form 1040NR.

OMB No. 1545-0074

2006

Attachment Sequence No. **54A**

Your name	Occupation in which you incurred expenses	**Social security number**

You May Use This Form Only if All of the Following Apply.

- You are an employee deducting ordinary and necessary expenses attributable to your job. An ordinary expense is one that is common and accepted in your field of trade, business, or profession. A necessary expense is one that is helpful and appropriate for your business. An expense does not have to be required to be considered necessary.
- You **do not** get reimbursed by your employer for any expenses (amounts your employer included in box 1 of your Form W-2 are not considered reimbursements for this purpose).
- If you are claiming vehicle expense, you are using the standard mileage rate for 2006.

Caution: *You can use the standard mileage rate for 2006* ***only if: (a)*** *you owned the vehicle and used the standard mileage rate for the first year you placed the vehicle in service,* ***or (b)*** *you leased the vehicle and used the standard mileage rate for the portion of the lease period after 1997.*

Part I Figure Your Expenses

1	Vehicle expense using the standard mileage rate. Complete Part II and multiply line 8a by 44.5¢ (.445)	1	
2	Parking fees, tolls, and transportation, including train, bus, etc., that **did not** involve overnight travel or commuting to and from work	2	
3	Travel expense while away from home overnight, including lodging, airplane, car rental, etc. **Do not** include meals and entertainment	3	
4	Business expenses not included on lines 1 through 3. **Do not** include meals and entertainment	4	
5	Meals and entertainment expenses: $______ × 50% (.50) (Employees subject to Department of Transportation (DOT) hours of service limits: Multiply meal expenses incurred while away from home on business by 75% (.75) instead of 50%. For details, see instructions.)	5	
6	**Total expenses.** Add lines 1 through 5. Enter here and on **Schedule A (Form 1040), line 20** (or on **Schedule A (Form 1040NR, line 9).** (Armed Forces reservists, fee-basis state or local government officials, qualified performing artists, and individuals with disabilities: See the instructions for special rules on where to enter this amount.)	6	

Part II Information on Your Vehicle. Complete this part **only** if you are claiming vehicle expense on line 1.

7 When did you place your vehicle in service for business use? (month, day, year) ► ________ / ________ / ________

8 Of the total number of miles you drove your vehicle during 2006, enter the number of miles you used your vehicle for:

a Business ____________ **b** Commuting (see instructions) ____________ **c** Other ____________

9 Do you (or your spouse) have another vehicle available for personal use? . . . . . ☐ **Yes** ☐ **No**

10 Was your vehicle available for personal use during off-duty hours? . . . . . ☐ **Yes** ☐ **No**

11a Do you have evidence to support your deduction?. . . . . ☐ **Yes** ☐ **No**

b If "Yes," is the evidence written?. . . . . ☐ **Yes** ☐ **No**

Instructions for Form 2106-EZ

Section references are to the Internal Revenue Code.

What's New

Standard mileage rate. For 2006, the standard mileage rate for each mile of business use is 44.5 cents.

Purpose of Form

You may use Form 2106-EZ instead of Form 2106 to claim your unreimbursed employee business expenses if you meet all the requirements listed above Part I of the form.

Recordkeeping

You cannot deduct expenses for travel (including meals, unless you used the standard meal allowance), entertainment, gifts, or use of a car or other listed property, unless you keep records to prove the time, place, business purpose, business relationship (for entertainment and gifts), and amounts of these expenses. Generally, you must also have receipts for all lodging expenses (regardless of the amount) and any other expense of $75 or more.

Additional Information

For more details about employee business expenses, see:

Pub. 463, Travel, Entertainment, Gift, and Car Expenses

Pub. 529, Miscellaneous Deductions

Pub. 587, Business Use of Your Home (Including Use by Daycare Providers)

Pub. 946, How To Depreciate Property

Specific Instructions

Part I—Figure Your Expenses

Line 2. See the line 8b instructions for the definition of commuting.

Line 3. Enter lodging and transportation expenses connected with overnight travel away from your tax home (defined on this page). You cannot deduct expenses for travel away from your tax home for any period of temporary employment of more than 1 year. Do not include expenses for meals and entertainment on this line. For more details, including limits, see Pub. 463.

If you did not pay or incur meal expenses on a day you were traveling away from your tax home, you can use an optional method for deducting incidental expenses instead of keeping records of your actual incidental expenses. The amount of the deduction is $3 a day. Incidental expenses include fees and tips given to porters, baggage carriers, bellhops, hotel maids, stewards or stewardesses and others on ships, and hotel servants in foreign countries. They do not include expenses for laundry, cleaning and pressing of clothing, lodging taxes, or the costs of telegrams or telephone calls. You cannot use this method on any day that you use the standard meal allowance (as explained in the instructions for line 5).

Tax home. Generally, your tax home is your main place of business or post of duty regardless of where you maintain your family home. If you do not have a regular or main place of business because of the nature of your work, then your tax home is the place where you regularly live. If you do not fit in either of these categories, you are considered an itinerant and your tax home is wherever you work. As an itinerant, you are never away from home and cannot claim a travel expense deduction. For more information about determining your tax home, see Pub. 463.

Line 4. Enter other job-related expenses not listed on any other line of this form. Include expenses for business gifts, education (tuition and books), home office, trade publications, etc. For details, including limits, see Pub. 463 and Pub. 529.

CAUTION *At the time these instructions went to print, Congress was considering legislation that would extend the deductions for educator expenses and tuition and fees that expired at the end of 2005. While certain of these expenses may be deductible on Form 2106-EZ, it may be to your benefit to deduct them on your tax return as adjustments to your total income.*

To find out if this legislation was enacted, and for more details, go to www.irs.gov, *click on More Forms and Publications, and then on What's Hot in forms and publications, or see Pub. 553, Highlights of 2006 Tax Changes.*

If you are deducting home office expenses, see Pub. 587 for special instructions on how to report these expenses.

If you are deducting depreciation or claiming a section 179 deduction on a cellular telephone or other similar telecommunications equipment, a home computer, etc., see Form 4562, Depreciation and Amortization, to figure the depreciation and section 179 deduction to enter on line 4.

TIP *You may be able to take a credit for your educational expenses instead of a deduction. See Form 8863, Education Credits, for details.*

Do not include expenses for meals and entertainment, taxes, or interest on line 4. Deductible taxes are entered on Schedule A (Form 1040), lines 5 through 9 (or Schedule A (Form 1040NR), lines 1 through 3). Employees cannot deduct car loan interest.

Note. If line 4 is your only entry, do not complete Form 2106-EZ unless you are claiming:

- Expenses for performing your job as a fee-basis state or local government official,
- Performing-arts-related business expenses as a qualified performing artist, or
- Impairment-related work expenses as an individual with a disability.

See the line 6 instructions for definitions. If you are not required to file Form 2106-EZ, enter your expenses directly on Schedule A (Form 1040), line 20 (or on Schedule A (Form 1040NR), line 9).

Line 5. Generally, you can deduct only 50% of your business meal and entertainment expenses, including meals incurred while away from home on business. If you were an employee subject to the Department of Transportation (DOT) hours of service limits, that percentage is 75% for business meals consumed during, or incident to, any period of duty for which those limits are in effect.

Employees subject to the DOT hours of service limits include certain air transportation employees, such as pilots, crew, dispatchers, mechanics, and control tower operators; interstate truck operators and interstate bus drivers; certain railroad employees, such as engineers, conductors, train crews, dispatchers, and control operations personnel; and certain merchant mariners.

Instead of actual cost, you may be able to claim the standard meal allowance for your daily meals and incidental expenses (M&IE) while away from your tax home overnight. Under this method, you deduct a specified amount, depending on where you travel, instead of keeping records of your actual meal expenses. However, you must still keep records to prove the time, place, and business purpose of your travel.

The standard meal allowance is the federal M&IE rate. For most small localities in the United States, this rate is $39 a day for the period from January 1 through December 31, 2006. Most major cities and many other localities in the United States qualify for higher rates. You can find these rates on the Internet at *www.gsa.gov.*

For locations outside the continental United States, the applicable rates are published each month. You can find these rates on the Internet at *www.state.gov.*

Form **2441**

Department of the Treasury
Internal Revenue Service (99)

Child and Dependent Care Expenses

▶ **Attach to Form 1040 or Form 1040NR.**

▶ **See separate instructions.**

OMB No. 1545-0074

2006

Attachment Sequence No. **21**

Name(s) shown on return	**Your social security number**

Before you begin: You need to understand the following terms. See **Definitions** on page 1 of the instructions.

- **Dependent Care Benefits**
- **Qualifying Person(s)**
- **Qualified Expenses**

Part I **Persons or Organizations Who Provided the Care**—You **must** complete this part.
(If you need more space, use the bottom of page 2.)

1 (a) Care provider's name	(b) Address (number, street, apt. no., city, state, and ZIP code)	(c) Identifying number (SSN or EIN)	(d) Amount paid (see instructions)

Did you receive **dependent care benefits?**
- **No** → Complete only Part II below.
- **Yes** → Complete Part III on the back next.

Caution. If the care was provided in your home, you may owe employment taxes. See the instructions for Form 1040, line 62, or Form 1040NR, line 57.

Part II **Credit for Child and Dependent Care Expenses**

2 Information about your **qualifying person(s).** If you have more than two qualifying persons, see the instructions.

(a) Qualifying person's name — First	Last	(b) Qualifying person's social security number	(c) **Qualified expenses** you incurred and paid in 2006 for the person listed in column (a)

3 Add the amounts in column (c) of line 2. **Do not** enter more than $3,000 for one qualifying person or $6,000 for two or more persons. If you completed Part III, enter the amount from line 33 . . . **3**

4 Enter your **earned income.** See instructions . . . **4**

5 If married filing jointly, enter your spouse's earned income (if your spouse was a student or was disabled, see the instructions); **all others,** enter the amount from line 4 . . . **5**

6 Enter the **smallest** of line 3, 4, or 5 . . . **6**

7 Enter the amount from Form 1040, line 38, or Form 1040NR, line 36 . . . **7**

8 Enter on line 8 the decimal amount shown below that applies to the amount on line 7

If line 7 is:

Over	But not over	Decimal amount is
$0—	15,000	.35
15,000—	17,000	.34
17,000—	19,000	.33
19,000—	21,000	.32
21,000—	23,000	.31
23,000—	25,000	.30
25,000—	27,000	.29
27,000—	29,000	.28

If line 7 is:

Over	But not over	Decimal amount is
$29,000—	31,000	.27
31,000—	33,000	.26
33,000—	35,000	.25
35,000—	37,000	.24
37,000—	39,000	.23
39,000—	41,000	.22
41,000—	43,000	.21
43,000—	No limit	.20

8 X .

9 Multiply line 6 by the decimal amount on line 8. If you paid 2005 expenses in 2006, see the instructions . . . **9**

10 Enter the amount from Form 1040, line 46, minus any amount on Form 1040, line 47, or Form 1040NR, line 43, minus any amount on Form 1040NR, line 44 . . . **10**

11 **Credit for child and dependent care expenses.** Enter the **smaller** of line 9 or line 10 here and on Form 1040, line 48, or Form 1040NR, line 45 . . . **11**

Part III Dependent Care Benefits

12	Enter the total amount of **dependent care benefits** you received in 2006. Amounts you received as an employee should be shown in box 10 of your Form(s) W-2. **Do not** include amounts reported as wages in box 1 of Form(s) W-2. If you were self-employed or a partner, include amounts you received under a dependent care assistance program from your sole proprietorship or partnership			12	
13	Enter the amount, if any, you carried over from 2005 and used in 2006 during the grace period. See instructions			13	
14	Enter the amount, if any, you forfeited or carried forward to 2007. See instructions			14	( )
15	Combine lines 12 through 14. See instructions			15	
16	Enter the total amount of **qualified expenses** incurred in 2006 for the care of the **qualifying person(s)**	16			
17	Enter the **smaller** of line 15 or 16	17			
18	Enter your **earned income.** See instructions	18			
19	Enter the amount shown below that applies to you. • If married filing jointly, enter your spouse's earned income (if your spouse was a student or was disabled, see the instructions for line 5). • If married filing separately, see the instructions for the amount to enter. • All others, enter the amount from line 18.	19			
20	Enter the **smallest** of line 17, 18, or 19	20			
21	Enter the amount from line 12 that you received from your sole proprietorship or partnership. If you did not receive any such amounts, enter -0-			21	
22	Subtract line 21 from line 15	22			
23	Enter $5,000 ($2,500 if married filing separately **and** you were required to enter your spouse's earned income on line 19)			23	
24	**Deductible benefits.** Enter the **smallest** of line 20, 21, or 23. Also, include this amount on the appropriate line(s) of your return. See instructions			24	
25	Enter the **smaller** of line 20 or 23	25			
26	Enter the amount from line 24	26			
27	**Excluded benefits.** Subtract line 26 from line 25. If zero or less, enter -0-			27	
28	**Taxable benefits.** Subtract line 27 from line 22. If zero or less, enter -0-. Also, include this amount on Form 1040, line 7, or Form 1040NR, line 8. On the dotted line next to Form 1040, line 7, or Form 1040NR, line 8, enter "DCB".			28	

To claim the child and dependent care credit, complete lines 29–33 below.

29	Enter $3,000 ($6,000 if two or more qualifying persons)	29	
30	Add lines 24 and 27	30	
31	Subtract line 30 from line 29. If zero or less, **stop.** You cannot take the credit. **Exception.** If you paid 2005 expenses in 2006, see the instructions for line 9	31	
32	Complete line 2 on the front of this form. **Do not** include in column (c) any benefits shown on line 30 above. Then, add the amounts in column (c) and enter the total here	32	
33	Enter the **smaller** of line 31 or 32. Also, enter this amount on line 3 on the front of this form and complete lines 4–11	33	

Form **3903**

Department of the Treasury
Internal Revenue Service

Moving Expenses

▶ **Attach to Form 1040 or Form 1040NR.**

OMB No. 1545-0074

2006

Attachment Sequence No. **62**

Name(s) shown on return | **Your social security number**

Before you begin: √ See the **Distance Test** and **Time Test** in the instructions to find out if you can deduct your moving expenses.

√ See **Members of the Armed Forces** on the back, if applicable.

1 Transportation and storage of household goods and personal effects (see instructions) . .	**1**		
2 Travel (including lodging) from your old home to your new home (see instructions). **Do not** include the cost of meals	**2**		
3 Add lines 1 and 2	**3**		
4 Enter the total amount your employer paid you for the expenses listed on lines 1 and 2 that is **not** included in box 1 of your Form W-2 (wages). This amount should be shown in box 12 of your Form W-2 with code **P**	**4**		
5 Is line 3 **more than** line 4? ☐ **No.** You **cannot** deduct your moving expenses. If line 3 is less than line 4, subtract line 3 from line 4 and include the result on Form 1040, line 7, or Form 1040NR, line 8. ☐ **Yes.** Subtract line 4 from line 3. Enter the result here and on Form 1040, line 26, or Form 1040NR, line 26. This is your **moving expense deduction**	**5**		

General Instructions

What's New

For 2006, the standard mileage rate for using your vehicle to move to a new home is 18 cents a mile.

Purpose of Form

Use Form 3903 to figure your moving expense deduction for a move related to the start of work at a new principal place of work (workplace). If the new workplace is outside the United States or its possessions, you must be a U.S. citizen or resident alien to deduct your expenses.

If you qualify to deduct expenses for more than one move, use a separate Form 3903 for each move.

For more details, see Pub. 521, Moving Expenses.

Moving Expenses You Can Deduct

You can deduct the reasonable expenses of moving your household goods and personal effects and of traveling from your old home to your new home. Reasonable expenses can include the cost of lodging (but not meals) while traveling to your new home. You cannot deduct the cost of sightseeing trips.

Who Can Deduct Moving Expenses

If you move to a new home because of a new principal workplace, you may be able to deduct your moving expenses whether you are self-employed or an employee. But you must meet both the distance test and time test that follow.

TIP *Members of the Armed Forces may not have to meet the distance test and time test. See instructions on the back.*

Distance Test

Your new principal workplace must be at least 50 miles farther from your old home than your old workplace was. For example, if your old workplace was 3 miles from your old home, your new workplace must be at least 53 miles from that home. If you did not have an old workplace, your new workplace must be at least 50 miles from your old home. The distance between the two points is the shortest of the more commonly traveled routes between them.

TIP *To see if you meet the distance test, you can use the worksheet below.*

Distance Test Worksheet

Keep a Copy for Your Records

1. Number of miles from your **old home** to your **new workplace** . . . . **1.** ________ miles

2. Number of miles from your **old home** to your **old workplace** . . . . **2.** ________ miles

3. Subtract line 2 from line 1. If zero or less, enter -0-. . . . . **3.** ________ miles

Is line 3 at least 50 miles?

☐ **Yes.** You meet this test.

☐ **No.** You do not meet this test. You **cannot** deduct your moving expenses. **Do not** complete Form 3903.

Time Test

If you are an employee, you must work full time in the general area of your new workplace for at least 39 weeks during the 12 months right after you move. If you are self-employed, you must work full time in the general area of your new workplace for at least 39 weeks during the first 12 months and a total of at least 78 weeks during the 24 months right after you move.

What if you do not meet the time test before your return is due? If you expect to meet the time test, you can deduct your moving expenses in the year you move. Later, if you do not meet the time test, you must either:

- Amend your tax return for the year you claimed the deduction by filing Form 1040X, Amended U.S. Individual Income Tax Return, or
- For the year you cannot meet the time test, report as income the amount of your moving expense deduction that reduced your income tax for the year you moved.

If you did not deduct your moving expenses in the year you moved and you later meet the time test, you can take the deduction by filing an amended return for the year you moved. To do this, use Form 1040X.

Exceptions to the time test. You do not have to meet the time test if any of the following apply.

- Your job ends because of disability.
- You are transferred for your employer's benefit.
- You are laid off or discharged for a reason other than willful misconduct.
- You are in the Armed Forces and the move is due to a permanent change of station (see below).
- You meet the requirements (explained later) for retirees or survivors living outside the United States.
- You are filing this form for a decedent.

Members of the Armed Forces

If you are in the Armed Forces, you do not have to meet the distance and time tests if the move is due to a permanent change of station. A permanent change of station includes a move in connection with and within 1 year of retirement or other termination of active duty.

How To Complete This Form If You Are In the Armed Forces

Do not include on lines 1 and 2 any expenses for moving services that were provided by the government. If you and your spouse and dependents are moved to or from different locations, treat the moves as a single move.

On line 4, enter the total reimbursements and allowances you received from the government in connection with the expenses you claimed on lines 1 and 2. Do not include the value of moving services provided by the government. Complete line 5 if applicable.

Retirees or Survivors Living Outside the United States

If you are a retiree or survivor who moved to a home in the United States or its possessions and you meet the following requirements, you are treated as if you moved to a new principal workplace located in the United States. You are subject only to the distance test.

Retirees

You can deduct moving expenses for a move to a new home in the United States when you permanently retire if both your old principal workplace and your old home were outside the United States.

Survivors

You can deduct moving expenses for a move to a home in the United States if you are the spouse or dependent of a person whose principal workplace at the time of death was outside the United States. The expenses must be for a move (a) that begins within 6 months after the decedent's death, and (b) from a former home outside the United States that you lived in with the decedent at the time of death.

Reimbursements

You can choose to deduct moving expenses in the year you are reimbursed by your employer, even though you paid the expenses in a different year. However, special rules apply. See *When To Deduct Expenses* in Pub. 521.

Filers of Form 2555

If you file Form 2555, Foreign Earned Income, to exclude any of your income or housing costs, report the full amount of your deductible moving expenses on Form 3903 and on Form 1040. Report the part of your moving expenses that is not allowed because it is allocable to the excluded income on the appropriate line of Form 2555. For details on how to figure the part allocable to the excluded income, see Pub. 54, Tax Guide for U.S. Citizens and Resident Aliens Abroad.

Specific Instructions

You can deduct the following expenses you paid to move your family and dependent household members. Do not deduct expenses for employees such as a maid, nanny, or nurse.

Line 1

Moves within or to the United States or its possessions. Enter the amount you paid to pack, crate, and move your household goods and personal effects. You can also include the amount you paid to store and insure household goods and personal effects within any period of 30 days in a row after the items were moved from your old home and before they were delivered to your new home.

Moves outside the United States or its possessions. Enter the amount you paid to pack, crate, move, store, and insure your household goods and personal effects. Also, include the amount you paid to move your personal effects to and from storage and to store them for all or part of the time the new workplace continues to be your principal workplace.

TIP *You do not have to complete this form if (a) you moved in an earlier year, (b) you are claiming only storage fees during your absence from the United States, and (c) any amount your employer paid for the storage fees is included in box 1 of your Form W-2 (wages). Instead, enter the storage fees on Form 1040, line 26, or Form 1040NR, line 26, and write "Storage" on the dotted line next to line 26.*

Line 2

Enter the amount you paid to travel from your old home to your new home. This includes transportation and lodging on the way. Include costs for the day you arrive. The members of your household do not have to travel together or at the same time. But you can only include expenses for one trip per person. Do not include any househunting expenses.

If you use your own vehicle(s), you can figure the expenses by using either:

- Actual out-of-pocket expenses for gas and oil, or
- Mileage at the rate of 18 cents a mile.

You can add parking fees and tolls to the amount claimed under either method.

Form **4562**

Department of the Treasury
Internal Revenue Service

Depreciation and Amortization
(Including Information on Listed Property)

▶ See separate instructions. ▶ Attach to your tax return.

OMB No. 1545-0172

2006

Attachment Sequence No. **67**

Name(s) shown on return	Business or activity to which this form relates	Identifying number

Part I **Election To Expense Certain Property Under Section 179**
Note: *If you have any listed property, complete Part V before you complete Part I.*

1	Maximum amount. See the instructions for a higher limit for certain businesses	1	$108,000
2	Total cost of section 179 property placed in service (see instructions)	2	
3	Threshold cost of section 179 property before reduction in limitation	3	$430,000
4	Reduction in limitation. Subtract line 3 from line 2. If zero or less, enter -0-	4	
5	Dollar limitation for tax year. Subtract line 4 from line 1. If zero or less, enter -0-. If married filing separately, see instructions	5	

	(a) Description of property	(b) Cost (business use only)	(c) Elected cost
6			

7	Listed property. Enter the amount from line 29	7	
8	Total elected cost of section 179 property. Add amounts in column (c), lines 6 and 7	8	
9	Tentative deduction. Enter the **smaller** of line 5 or line 8	9	
10	Carryover of disallowed deduction from line 13 of your 2005 Form 4562	10	
11	Business income limitation. Enter the smaller of business income (not less than zero) or line 5 (see instructions)	11	
12	Section 179 expense deduction. Add lines 9 and 10, but do not enter more than line 11	12	
13	Carryover of disallowed deduction to 2007. Add lines 9 and 10, less line 12 ▶	13	

Note: *Do not use Part II or Part III below for listed property. Instead, use Part V.*

Part II **Special Depreciation Allowance and Other Depreciation (Do not** include listed property.) (See instructions.)

14	Special allowance for qualified New York Liberty or Gulf Opportunity Zone property (other than listed property) placed in service during the tax year (see instructions)	14	
15	Property subject to section 168(f)(1) election	15	
16	Other depreciation (including ACRS)	16	

Part III **MACRS Depreciation (Do not** include listed property.) (See instructions.)

Section A

17	MACRS deductions for assets placed in service in tax years beginning before 2006	17	
18	If you are electing to group any assets placed in service during the tax year into one or more general asset accounts, check here ▶ ☐		

Section B—Assets Placed in Service During 2006 Tax Year Using the General Depreciation System

(a) Classification of property	(b) Month and year placed in service	(c) Basis for depreciation (business/investment use only—see instructions)	(d) Recovery period	(e) Convention	(f) Method	(g) Depreciation deduction
19a 3-year property						
b 5-year property						
c 7-year property						
d 10-year property						
e 15-year property						
f 20-year property						
g 25-year property			25 yrs.		S/L	
h Residential rental property			27.5 yrs.	MM	S/L	
			27.5 yrs.	MM	S/L	
i Nonresidential real property			39 yrs.	MM	S/L	
				MM	S/L	

Section C—Assets Placed in Service During 2006 Tax Year Using the Alternative Depreciation System

20a Class life					S/L	
b 12-year			12 yrs.		S/L	
c 40-year			40 yrs.	MM	S/L	

Part IV **Summary** (see instructions)

21	Listed property. Enter amount from line 28	21	
22	**Total.** Add amounts from line 12, lines 14 through 17, lines 19 and 20 in column (g), and line 21. Enter here and on the appropriate lines of your return. Partnerships and S corporations—see instr.	22	
23	For assets shown above and placed in service during the current year, enter the portion of the basis attributable to section 263A costs	23	

Part V **Listed Property** (Include automobiles, certain other vehicles, cellular telephones, certain computers, and property used for entertainment, recreation, or amusement.)

Note: *For any vehicle for which you are using the standard mileage rate or deducting lease expense, complete* ***only*** *24a, 24b, columns (a) through (c) of Section A, all of Section B, and Section C if applicable.*

Section A—Depreciation and Other Information (Caution: *See the instructions for limits for passenger automobiles.***)**

24a Do you have evidence to support the business/investment use claimed? ☐ **Yes** ☐ **No** **24b** If "Yes," is the evidence written? ☐ **Yes** ☐ **No**

(a) Type of property (list vehicles first)	(b) Date placed in service	(c) Business/ investment use percentage	(d) Cost or other basis	(e) Basis for depreciation (business/investment use only)	(f) Recovery period	(g) Method/ Convention	(h) Depreciation deduction	(i) Elected section 179 cost
25 Special allowance for qualified New York Liberty or Gulf Opportunity Zone property placed in service during the tax year and used more than 50% in a qualified business use (see instructions)						**25**		
26 Property used more than 50% in a qualified business use:								
		%						
		%						
		%						
27 Property used 50% or less in a qualified business use:								
		%				S/L –		
		%				S/L –		
		%				S/L –		
28 Add amounts in column (h), lines 25 through 27. Enter here and on line 21, page 1. .						**28**		
29 Add amounts in column (i), line 26. Enter here and on line 7, page 1.							**29**	

Section B—Information on Use of Vehicles

Complete this section for vehicles used by a sole proprietor, partner, or other "more than 5% owner," or related person. If you provided vehicles to your employees, first answer the questions in Section C to see if you meet an exception to completing this section for those vehicles.

	(a) Vehicle 1		(b) Vehicle 2		(c) Vehicle 3		(d) Vehicle 4		(e) Vehicle 5		(f) Vehicle 6	
30 Total business/investment miles driven during the year (**do not** include commuting miles)												
31 Total commuting miles driven during the year												
32 Total other personal (noncommuting) miles driven												
33 Total miles driven during the year. Add lines 30 through 32												
	Yes	**No**	**Yes**	**No**	**Yes**	**No**	**Yes**	**No**	**Yes**	**No**	**Yes**	**No**
34 Was the vehicle available for personal use during off-duty hours?												
35 Was the vehicle used primarily by a more than 5% owner or related person?												
36 Is another vehicle available for personal use?												

Section C—Questions for Employers Who Provide Vehicles for Use by Their Employees

Answer these questions to determine if you meet an exception to completing Section B for vehicles used by employees who **are not** more than 5% owners or related persons (see instructions).

	Yes	**No**
37 Do you maintain a written policy statement that prohibits all personal use of vehicles, including commuting, by your employees?		
38 Do you maintain a written policy statement that prohibits personal use of vehicles, except commuting, by your employees? See the instructions for vehicles used by corporate officers, directors, or 1% or more owners		
39 Do you treat all use of vehicles by employees as personal use?		
40 Do you provide more than five vehicles to your employees, obtain information from your employees about the use of the vehicles, and retain the information received?		
41 Do you meet the requirements concerning qualified automobile demonstration use? (See instructions.)		
Note: *If your answer to 37, 38, 39, 40, or 41 is "Yes," do not complete Section B for the covered vehicles.*		

Part VI **Amortization**

(a) Description of costs	(b) Date amortization begins	(c) Amortizable amount	(d) Code section	(e) Amortization period or percentage	(f) Amortization for this year
42 Amortization of costs that begins during your 2006 tax year (see instructions):					
43 Amortization of costs that began before your 2006 tax year.				**43**	
44 **Total.** Add amounts in column (f). See the instructions for where to report				**44**	

Form **4684**

Department of the Treasury
Internal Revenue Service

Casualties and Thefts

▶ See separate instructions.
▶ Attach to your tax return.
▶ Use a separate Form 4684 for each casualty or theft.

OMB No. 1545-0177

2006

Attachment Sequence No. **26**

Name(s) shown on tax return | **Identifying number**

SECTION A—Personal Use Property (Use this section to report casualties and thefts of property **not** used in a trade or business or for income-producing purposes.)

1 Description of properties (show type, location, and date acquired for each property). Use a separate line for each property lost or damaged from the same casualty or theft.

Property **A** ____________________
Property **B** ____________________
Property **C** ____________________
Property **D** ____________________

		Properties			
		A	B	C	D
2 Cost or other basis of each property	2				
3 Insurance or other reimbursement (whether or not you filed a claim) (see instructions)	3				
Note: *If line 2 is **more** than line 3, skip line 4.*					
4 Gain from casualty or theft. If line 3 is **more** than line 2, enter the difference here and skip lines 5 through 9 for that column. See instructions if line 3 includes insurance or other reimbursement you did not claim, or you received payment for your loss in a later tax year.	4				
5 Fair market value **before** casualty or theft	5				
6 Fair market value **after** casualty or theft	6				
7 Subtract line 6 from line 5	7				
8 Enter the **smaller** of line 2 or line 7	8				
9 Subtract line 3 from line 8. If zero or less, enter -0-	9				

10 Casualty or theft loss. Add the amounts on line 9 in columns A through D . . . **10**

11 Enter the **smaller** of line 10 or $100. But if the loss arose in the Hurricane Katrina disaster area after August 24, 2005; Hurricane Rita disaster area after September 22, 2005; or Hurricane Wilma disaster area after October 22, 2005, and was caused by that particular hurricane, enter -0- . . . **11**

12 Subtract line 11 from line 10 . . . **12**

Caution: *Use only one Form 4684 for lines 13 through 21.*

13 Add the amounts on line 12 of all Forms 4684 . . . **13**

14 Add the amounts on line 4 of all Forms 4684 . . . **14**

15
- If line 14 is **more** than line 13, enter the difference here and on Schedule D. **Do not** complete the rest of this section (see instructions).
- If line 14 is **less** than line 13, enter -0- here and go to line 16.
- If line 14 is **equal** to line 13, enter -0- here. **Do not** complete the rest of this section.

. . . **15**

16 If line 14 is **less** than line 13, enter the difference . . . **16**

17 Add the amounts on line 12 of all Forms 4684 on which you entered -0- on line 11. . . . **17**

18 Is line 17 less than line 16?

☐ **No.** Stop. Enter the amount from line 16 on Schedule A (Form 1040), line 19, or Schedule A (Form 1040NR), line 8. Estates and trusts, enter the amount from line 16 on the "Other deductions" line of your tax return.

☐ **Yes.** Subtract line 17 from line 16. **18**

19 Enter 10% of your adjusted gross income from Form 1040, line 38, or Form 1040NR, line 36. Estates and trusts, see instructions . . . **19**

20 Subtract line 19 from line 18. If zero or less, enter -0- . . . **20**

21 Add lines 17 and 20. Also enter the result on Schedule A (Form 1040), line 19, or Schedule A (Form 1040NR), line 8. Estates and trusts, enter the result on the "Other deductions" line of your tax return . . . **21**

Name(s) shown on tax return. Do not enter name and identifying number if shown on other side. | **Identifying number**

SECTION B—Business and Income-Producing Property

Part I Casualty or Theft Gain or Loss (Use a separate Part I for each casualty or theft.)

22 Description of properties (show type, location, and date acquired for each property). Use a separate line for each property lost or damaged from the same casualty or theft.

Property **A** ______

Property **B** ______

Property **C** ______

Property **D** ______

		Properties A		B		C		D	
23 Cost or adjusted basis of each property	23								
24 Insurance or other reimbursement (whether or not you filed a claim). See the instructions for line 3 **Note:** *If line 23 is **more** than line 24, skip line 25.*	24								
25 Gain from casualty or theft. If line 24 is **more** than line 23, enter the difference here and on line 32 or line 37, column (c), except as provided in the instructions for line 36. Also, skip lines 26 through 30 for that column. See the instructions for line 4 if line 24 includes insurance or other reimbursement you did not claim, or you received payment for your loss in a later tax year.	25								
26 Fair market value **before** casualty or theft	26								
27 Fair market value **after** casualty or theft	27								
28 Subtract line 27 from line 26	28								
29 Enter the **smaller** of line 23 or line 28 **Note:** *If the property was totally destroyed by casualty or lost from theft, enter on line 29 the amount from line 23.*	29								
30 Subtract line 24 from line 29. If zero or less, enter -0-	30								

31 Casualty or theft loss. Add the amounts on line 30. Enter the total here and on line 32 **or** line 37 (see instructions). | 31 |

Part II Summary of Gains and Losses (from separate Parts I)

	(a) Identify casualty or theft		(b) Losses from casualties or thefts (i) Trade, business, rental or royalty property	(ii) Income-producing and employee property	(c) Gains from casualties or thefts includible in income
	Casualty or Theft of Property Held One Year or Less				
32			( )	( )	
			( )	( )	
33	Totals. Add the amounts on line 32	33	( )	( )	
34	Combine line 33, columns (b)(i) and (c). Enter the net gain or (loss) here and on Form 4797, line 14. If Form 4797 is not otherwise required, see instructions			34	
35	Enter the amount from line 33, column (b)(ii) here. Individuals, enter the amount from income-producing property on Schedule A (Form 1040), line 27, or Schedule A (Form 1040NR), line 16, and enter the amount from property used as an employee on Schedule A (Form 1040), line 22, or Schedule A (Form 1040NR), line 11. Estates and trusts, partnerships, and S corporations, see instructions.			35	
	Casualty or Theft of Property Held More Than One Year				
36	Casualty or theft gains from Form 4797, line 32			36	
37			( )	( )	
			( )	( )	
38	Total losses. Add amounts on line 37, columns (b)(i) and (b)(ii)	38	( )	( )	
39	Total gains. Add lines 36 and 37, column (c)			39	
40	Add amounts on line 38, columns (b)(i) and (b)(ii)			40	
41	If the loss on line 40 is **more** than the gain on line 39:				
a	Combine line 38, column (b)(i) and line 39, and enter the net gain or (loss) here. Partnerships (except electing large partnerships) and S corporations, see the note below. All others, enter this amount on Form 4797, line 14. If Form 4797 is not otherwise required, see instructions			41a	
b	Enter the amount from line 38, column (b)(ii) here. Individuals, enter the amount from income-producing property on Schedule A (Form 1040), line 27, or Schedule A (Form 1040NR), line 16, and enter the amount from property used as an employee on Schedule A (Form 1040), line 22 or Schedule A (Form 1040NR), line 11. Estates and trusts, enter on the "Other deductions" line of your tax return. Partnerships (except electing large partnerships) and S corporations, see the note below. Electing large partnerships, enter on Form 1065-B, Part II, line 11			41b	
42	If the loss on line 40 is **less** than or **equal** to the gain on line 39, combine lines 39 and 40 and enter here. Partnerships (except electing large partnerships), see the note below. All others, enter this amount on Form 4797, line 3			42	

Note: *Partnerships, enter the amount from line 41a, 41b, or line 42 on Form 1065, Schedule K, line 11. S corporations, enter the amount from line 41a or 41b on Form 1120S, Schedule K, line 10.*

Form **4797**

Department of the Treasury
Internal Revenue Service (99)

Sales of Business Property

(Also Involuntary Conversions and Recapture Amounts Under Sections 179 and 280F(b)(2))

▶Attach to your tax return. ▶See separate instructions.

OMB No. 1545-0184

2006

Attachment Sequence No. 27

Name(s) shown on return | Identifying number

1 Enter the gross proceeds from sales or exchanges reported to you for 2006 on Form(s) 1099-B or 1099-S (or substitute statement) that you are including on line 2, 10, or 20 (see instructions) 1

Part I Sales or Exchanges of Property Used in a Trade or Business and Involuntary Conversions From Other Than Casualty or Theft—Most Property Held More Than 1 Year (see instructions)

	(a) Description of property	(b) Date acquired (mo., day, yr.)	(c) Date sold (mo., day, yr.)	(d) Gross sales price	(e) Depreciation allowed or allowable since acquisition	(f) Cost or other basis, plus improvements and expense of sale	(g) Gain or (loss) Subtract (f) from the sum of (d) and (e)
2							

3 Gain, if any, from Form 4684, line 42 3

4 Section 1231 gain from installment sales from Form 6252, line 26 or 37 4

5 Section 1231 gain or (loss) from like-kind exchanges from Form 8824 5

6 Gain, if any, from line 32, from other than casualty or theft 6

7 Combine lines 2 through 6. Enter the gain or (loss) here and on the appropriate line as follows: 7

Partnerships (except electing large partnerships) and S corporations. Report the gain or (loss) following the instructions for Form 1065, Schedule K, line 10, or Form 1120S, Schedule K, line 9. Skip lines 8, 9, 11, and 12 below.

Individuals, partners, S corporation shareholders, and all others. If line 7 is zero or a loss, enter the amount from line 7 on line 11 below and skip lines 8 and 9. If line 7 is a gain and you did not have any prior year section 1231 losses, or they were recaptured in an earlier year, enter the gain from line 7 as a long-term capital gain on the Schedule D filed with your return and skip lines 8, 9, 11, and 12 below.

8 Nonrecaptured net section 1231 losses from prior years (see instructions) 8

9 Subtract line 8 from line 7. If zero or less, enter -0-. If line 9 is zero, enter the gain from line 7 on line 12 below. If line 9 is more than zero, enter the amount from line 8 on line 12 below and enter the gain from line 9 as a long-term capital gain on the Schedule D filed with your return (see instructions) 9

Part II Ordinary Gains and Losses (see instructions)

10 Ordinary gains and losses not included on lines 11 through 16 (include property held 1 year or less):

11 Loss, if any, from line 7 . . . . . 11 ( )

12 Gain, if any, from line 7 or amount from line 8, if applicable 12

13 Gain, if any, from line 31 13

14 Net gain or (loss) from Form 4684, lines 34 and 41a 14

15 Ordinary gain from installment sales from Form 6252, line 25 or 36 15

16 Ordinary gain or (loss) from like-kind exchanges from Form 8824 16

17 Combine lines 10 through 16 17

18 For all except individual returns, enter the amount from line 17 on the appropriate line of your return and skip lines a and b below. For individual returns, complete lines a and b below:

a If the loss on line 11 includes a loss from Form 4684, line 38, column (b)(ii), enter that part of the loss here. Enter the part of the loss from income-producing property on Schedule A (Form 1040), line 27, and the part of the loss from property used as an employee on Schedule A (Form 1040), line 22. Identify as from "Form 4797, line 18a." See instructions 18a

b Redetermine the gain or (loss) on line 17 excluding the loss, if any, on line 18a. Enter here and on Form 1040, line 14 . . . . . 18b

Part III Gain From Disposition of Property Under Sections 1245, 1250, 1252, 1254, and 1255 (see instructions)

19 (a) Description of section 1245, 1250, 1252, 1254, or 1255 property:	(b) Date acquired (mo., day, yr.)	(c) Date sold (mo., day, yr.)
A		
B		
C		
D		

These columns relate to the properties on lines 19A through 19D. ▶		Property A	Property B	Property C	Property D
20 Gross sales price (**Note:** *See line 1 before completing.*)	20				
21 Cost or other basis plus expense of sale	21				
22 Depreciation (or depletion) allowed or allowable	22				
23 Adjusted basis. Subtract line 22 from line 21	23				
24 Total gain. Subtract line 23 from line 20	24				
25 **If section 1245 property:**					
a Depreciation allowed or allowable from line 22	25a				
b Enter the **smaller** of line 24 or 25a	25b				
26 **If section 1250 property:** If straight line depreciation was used, enter -0- on line 26g, except for a corporation subject to section 291.					
a Additional depreciation after 1975 (see instructions)	26a				
b Applicable percentage multiplied by the **smaller** of line 24 or line 26a (see instructions)	26b				
c Subtract line 26a from line 24. If residential rental property **or** line 24 is not more than line 26a, skip lines 26d and 26e	26c				
d Additional depreciation after 1969 and before 1976	26d				
e Enter the **smaller** of line 26c or 26d	26e				
f Section 291 amount (corporations only)	26f				
g Add lines 26b, 26e, and 26f	26g				
27 **If section 1252 property:** Skip this section if you did not dispose of farmland or if this form is being completed for a partnership (other than an electing large partnership).					
a Soil, water, and land clearing expenses	27a				
b Line 27a multiplied by applicable percentage (see instructions)	27b				
c Enter the **smaller** of line 24 or 27b	27c				
28 **If section 1254 property:**					
a Intangible drilling and development costs, expenditures for development of mines and other natural deposits, and mining exploration costs (see instructions)	28a				
b Enter the **smaller** of line 24 or 28a	28b				
29 **If section 1255 property:**					
a Applicable percentage of payments excluded from income under section 126 (see instructions)	29a				
b Enter the **smaller** of line 24 or 29a (see instructions)	29b				

Summary of Part III Gains. Complete property columns A through D through line 29b before going to line 30.

30 Total gains for all properties. Add property columns A through D, line 24	30	
31 Add property columns A through D, lines 25b, 26g, 27c, 28b, and 29b. Enter here and on line 13	31	
32 Subtract line 31 from line 30. Enter the portion from casualty or theft on Form 4684, line 36. Enter the portion from other than casualty or theft on Form 4797, line 6	32	

Part IV Recapture Amounts Under Sections 179 and 280F(b)(2) When Business Use Drops to 50% or Less (see instructions)

		(a) Section 179	(b) Section 280F(b)(2)
33 Section 179 expense deduction or depreciation allowable in prior years	33		
34 Recomputed depreciation (see instructions)	34		
35 Recapture amount. Subtract line 34 from line 33. See the instructions for where to report	35		

Form **4868**
Department of the Treasury
Internal Revenue Service

Application for Automatic Extension of Time To File U.S. Individual Income Tax Return

OMB No. 1545-0074

2006

IRS e-file — It's Convenient, Safe, and Secure

IRS *e-file* is the IRS's electronic filing program. You can get an automatic extension of time to file your tax return by filing Form 4868 electronically. You will receive an electronic acknowledgment once you complete the transaction. Keep it with your records. Do not send in Form 4868 if you file electronically.

Complete Form 4868 to use as a worksheet. If you think you may owe tax when you file your return, you will need to estimate your total tax liability and subtract how much you have already paid (lines 4, 5, and 6 below).

For more information about e-filing the Form 4868, go to *www.irs.gov.*

If you think you may owe tax and wish to make a payment, you can pay by electronic funds withdrawal using option 1 or you can pay by credit card using option 2. See *1* and *2* on this page for details.

1 *E-file* Using Your Personal Computer or Through a Tax Professional

Refer to your tax software package or tax preparer for ways to file electronically. Be sure to have a copy of your 2005 tax return—you will be asked to provide information from the return for taxpayer verification. If you wish to make a payment, you can pay by electronic funds withdrawal (see page 4) or send your payment to the address shown in the middle column under *Where To File a Paper Form 4868* on page 4.

2 *E-file* and Pay by Credit Card

You can get an extension if you pay part or all of your estimate of income tax due by using a credit card (American Express® Card, Discover® Card, MasterCard® card, or Visa® card). Your payment must be at least $1. You can pay by phone or over the Internet through one of the service providers listed below.

Each service provider will charge a convenience fee based on the amount of the tax payment you are making. Fees may vary between service providers. You will be told what the fee is during the transaction and will have the option to continue or cancel the transaction. You can also obtain the convenience fee by calling the providers' toll-free automated customer service numbers or visiting their websites. Do not add the convenience fee to your tax payment.

Official Payments Corporation	**Link2Gov Corporation**
1-800-2PAY-TAX[sm]	1-888-PAY-1040[sm]
(1-800-272-9829)	(1-888-729-1040)
1-877-754-4413 (Customer Service)	1-888-658-5465 (Customer Service)
www.officialpayments.com	*www.PAY1040.com*

Confirmation number. You will receive a confirmation number when you pay by credit card. Enter the confirmation number below and keep for your records.

Enter confirmation number here ▶ ....

File a Paper Form 4868

If you wish to file on paper instead of electronically, fill in the Form 4868 below and mail it to the address shown on page 4. If you are a fiscal year taxpayer, you must file a paper Form 4868.

▼ DETACH HERE ▼

Form **4868**
Department of the Treasury
Internal Revenue Service

Application for Automatic Extension of Time To File U.S. Individual Income Tax Return

For calendar year 2006, or other tax year beginning , 2006, ending , 200 .

OMB No. 1545-0074

2006

Part I Identification			**Part II** Individual Income Tax
1 Your name(s) (see instructions)			**4** Estimate of total tax liability for 2006 . . $
			5 Total 2006 payments . . . . . .
Address (see instructions)			**6** **Balance due.** Subtract line 5 from line 4 (see instructions) . . . .
			7 Amount you are paying (see instructions) . ▶
City, town, or post office	State	ZIP code	**8** Check here if you are "out of the country" and a U.S. citizen or resident (see instructions) . . . . . . ▶ ☐
2 Your social security number	**3** Spouse's social security number		**9** Check here if you file Form 1040NR or 1040NR-EZ and did not receive wages as an employee subject to U.S. income tax withholding . . . . ▶ ☐

For Privacy Act and Paperwork Reduction Act Notice, see page 4. Cat. No. 13141W Form **4868** (2006)

General Instructions

Purpose of Form

Use Form 4868 to apply for 6 more months (4 if "out of the country" (defined later on this page) and a U.S. citizen or resident) to file Form 1040, 1040A, 1040EZ, 1040NR, or 1040NR-EZ.

To get the extra time you must:

- Properly estimate your 2006 tax liability using the information available to you,
- Enter your total tax liability on line 4 of Form 4868, and
- File Form 4868 by the regular due date of your return.

CAUTION *Although you are not required to make a payment of the tax you estimate as due, Form 4868 does not extend the time to pay taxes. If you do not pay the amount due by the regular due date, you will owe interest. You may also be charged penalties. For more details, see* Interest *and* Late Payment Penalty *on this page. Any remittance you make with your application for extension will be treated as a payment of tax.*

You do not have to explain why you are asking for the extension. We will contact you only if your request is denied.

Do not file Form 4868 if you want the IRS to figure your tax or you are under a court order to file your return by the regular due date.

Gift or generation-skipping transfer (GST) tax return (Form 709). An extension of time to file your 2006 calendar year income tax return also extends the time to file Form 709 for 2006. However, it does not extend the time to pay any gift or GST tax you may owe for 2006. To make a payment of gift or GST tax, see Form 8892. If you do not pay the amount due by the regular due date for Form 709, you will owe interest and may also be charged penalties. If the donor died during 2006, see the instructions for Forms 709 and 8892.

When To File Form 4868

File Form 4868 by April 16, 2007. If you live in Maine, Maryland, Massachusetts, New Hampshire, New York, Vermont, or the District of Columbia, you have until April 17, 2007. Fiscal year taxpayers, file Form 4868 by the regular due date of the return.

Taxpayers "out of the country." If, on the regular due date of your return, you are "out of the country" and a U.S. citizen or resident, you are allowed 2 extra months to file your return and pay any amount due without requesting an extension. For a calendar year return, this is June 15, 2007. File this form and be sure to check the box on line 8 if you need an additional 4 months to file your return.

If you are "out of the country" and are a U.S. citizen or resident, you may qualify for special tax treatment if you meet the foreign residence or presence tests. If you do not expect to meet either of those tests by the due date of your return, request an extension to a date after you expect to qualify using Form 2350, Application for Extension of Time To File U.S. Income Tax Return. See Pub. 54, Tax Guide for U.S. Citizens and Resident Aliens Abroad.

"Out of the country" means either:

1. You live outside the United States and Puerto Rico and your main place of work is outside the United States and Puerto Rico, or

2. You are in military or naval service outside the United States and Puerto Rico.

If you qualify as being "out of the country," you will still be eligible for the extension even if you are physically present in the United States or Puerto Rico on the regular due date of the return.

Form 1040NR or 1040NR-EZ filers. If you cannot file your return by the due date, you should file Form 4868. You must file Form 4868 by the regular due date of the return.

If you did not receive wages as an employee subject to U.S. income tax withholding, and your return is due June 15, 2007, check the box on line 9.

Total Time Allowed

Generally, we cannot extend the due date of your return for more than 6 months (October 15, 2007, for most calendar year taxpayers). There may be an exception if you are living "out of the country." See *Taxpayers "out of the country"* on this page.

Filing Your Tax Return

You can file your tax return any time before the extension expires.

Do not attach a copy of Form 4868 to your return.

Interest

You will owe interest on any tax not paid by the regular due date of your return. The interest runs until you pay the tax. Even if you had a good reason for not paying on time, you will still owe interest.

Late Payment Penalty

The late payment penalty is usually ½ of 1% of any tax (other than estimated tax) not paid by the regular due date. It is charged for each month or part of a month the tax is unpaid. The maximum penalty is 25%.

Form **5213**
(Rev. February 2006)
Department of the Treasury
Internal Revenue Service

Election To Postpone Determination as To Whether the Presumption Applies That an Activity Is Engaged in for Profit

▶ **To be filed by individuals, estates, trusts, partnerships, and S corporations.**

OMB No. 1545-0195

Name(s) as shown on tax return	**Identifying number as shown on tax return**

Address (number and street, apt. no., rural route) (or P.O. box number if mail is not delivered to street address)

City, town or post office, state, and ZIP code

The taxpayer named above elects to postpone a determination as to whether the presumption applies that the activity described below is engaged in for profit. The determination is postponed until the close of:

- The 6th tax year, for an activity that consists mainly of breeding, training, showing, or racing horses or
- The 4th tax year for any other activity,

after the tax year in which the taxpayer first engaged in the activity.

1 Type of taxpayer engaged in the activity (check the box that applies):

☐ Individual ☐ Partnership ☐ S corporation ☐ Estate or trust

2a Description of activity for which you elect to postpone a determination

2b First tax year you engaged in activity described in 2a

Under penalties of perjury, I declare that I have examined this election, including accompanying schedules, and to the best of my knowledge and belief, it is true, correct, and complete.

(Signature of taxpayer or fiduciary) (Date)

(Signature of taxpayer's spouse, if joint return was filed) (Date)

(Signature of general partner authorized to sign partnership return) (Date)

(Signature and title of officer, if an S corporation) (Date)

General Instructions

Purpose of Form

Use Form 5213 to elect to postpone an IRS determination as to whether the presumption applies that an activity is engaged in for profit.

General Information

Generally, if you are an individual, estate, trust, partnership, or S corporation in an activity not engaged in for profit, some of your deductions may not be allowed. However, an activity is presumed to be engaged in for profit (and, therefore, deductions are not limited) if the gross income exceeds the deductions:

- From an activity that consists mainly of breeding, training, showing, or racing horses for each of 2 or more of the tax years in the period of 7 consecutive tax years ending with the tax year in question or
- From any other activity for each of 3 or more of the tax years in the period of 5 consecutive tax years ending with the tax year in question.

For information on the limits on deductions in not-for-profit activities, see Pub. 535, Business Expenses.

Who Should File

Individuals, estates, trusts, partnerships (including limited liability companies or other entities that are treated as partnerships for Federal tax purposes), and S corporations should use this form if they want to postpone an IRS determination as to whether the presumption applies that they are engaged in an activity for profit. An election made by a partnership or an S corporation is binding on all persons who were partners or shareholders at any time during the presumption period.

You may not use this form if you have been engaged in:

- Breeding, training, showing, or racing horses for more than 7 years or
- Any other activity for more than 5 years.

If you elect a postponement and file this form on time, the IRS will generally postpone the determination until after the end of the 4th consecutive tax year (6th tax year for an activity that consists mainly of breeding, training, showing, or racing horses) after the tax year in which you first engaged in the activity. This period of 5 (or 7) tax years is called the "presumption period." The election to postpone covers the entire presumption period.

Joint Returns

If you and your spouse filed a joint return, both of you must elect to postpone the determination even if only one of you is engaged in the activity.

How Many Forms To File

Generally, if you want a postponement for more than one activity, you must file a separate Form 5213 for each activity. However, you may file one form for more than one activity if all of the activities have the same presumption period. Be sure to describe each activity in detail and list the first tax year in which you were engaged in the activities.

Generally, in determining whether you are engaged in more than one activity, you must consider all of the following:

- The similarity of the activities,
- The business purpose that is (or might be) served by carrying on the activities separately or together in a trade or business or investment setting, and
- The organizational and economic interrelationship of the activities.

When To File

File this form within 3 years after the due date of your return (determined without extensions) for the first tax year in which you engaged in the activity. However, if you received a written notice that the IRS proposes to disallow deductions attributable to an activity not engaged in for profit (under Internal Revenue Code section 183) and you want a postponement of the determination, you must file this form within 60 days after receiving the notice. This 60-day period does not extend the 3-year period referred to above.

Where To File

File this form with the Internal Revenue Service Center where you are required to file your return. Do not send it in with any other return because that will delay processing the election to postpone. However, if the IRS notifies you about proposing to disallow deductions for an activity not engaged in for profit, file the form with the IRS office that sent you the notification.

Automatic Extension of Period of Limitations

Generally, filing this form automatically extends the period of limitations for assessing any income tax deficiency specifically attributable to the activity during any year in the presumption period. The extension also applies to partners or shareholders in the activity.

The period is extended until 2 years after the due date for filing the return (determined without extensions) for the last tax year in the presumption period. For example, for an activity subject to a 5-year presumption period that began in 2003 and ends in 2007, the period of limitations automatically extends to April 15, 2010, for all tax years in the presumption period that would otherwise expire before that date. Periods of limitations for tax years in the 5-year period expiring after April 15, 2010, would remain open until their normal expiration date. However, early termination of the presumption period does not terminate the automatic extension of the period of limitations.

The automatic extension applies only to those deductions attributable to the activity and to any deductions (such as medical expenses or charitable contribution deductions) that are affected by changes made to adjusted gross income.

The automatic extension does not affect general waivers of the statute of limitations that may be executed.

Specific Instructions

Name and Identifying Number as Shown on Tax Return

Enter your name(s) and identifying number as shown on your tax return for the first tax year in which you engaged in the activity. If you are an individual, your identifying number is your social security number (SSN). If you are other than an individual, your identifying number is your employer identification number (EIN).

If you and your spouse filed a joint return, enter both your name and your spouse's name as they were shown on your tax return. Enter the SSN that was shown first on your return as your identifying number.

Signature and Date

Be sure to sign and date the form on the appropriate line or lines. Keep a copy for your records.

Privacy Act and Paperwork Reduction Act Notice. We ask for the information on this form to carry out the Internal Revenue laws of the United States. We need this information to determine your eligibility for making the election to postpone determination as to whether the presumption applies that an activity is engaged in for profit. If you make this election, you are required by Internal Revenue Code section 183 to provide the information requested on this form. Under section 6109, you must disclose your SSN, individual taxpayer identification number (ITIN), or EIN. Routine uses of this information include giving it to the Department of Justice for civil and criminal litigation, and to cities, states, and the District of Columbia for use in administering their tax laws. We may also disclose this information to other countries under a tax treaty, to federal and state agencies to enforce federal nontax criminal laws, or to federal law enforcement and intelligence agencies to combat terrorism. If you fail to provide this information in a timely manner, or provide incomplete or false information, you may be liable for interest and penalties.

You are not required to provide the information requested on a form that is subject to the Paperwork Reduction Act unless the form displays a valid OMB control number. Books or records relating to a form or its instructions must be retained as long as their contents may become material in the administration of any Internal Revenue law. Generally, tax returns and return information are confidential, as required by Code section 6103.

The time needed to complete and file this form will vary depending on individual circumstances. The estimated burden for individual taxpayers filing this form is approved under OMB control number 1545-0074 and is included in the estimates shown in the instructions for their individual income tax return. The estimated burden for all other taxpayers who file this form is shown below.

Recordkeeping	7 min.
Learning about the law or the form	10 min.
Preparing the form	10 min.
Copying, assembling, and sending the form to the IRS	20 min.

If you have comments concerning the accuracy of these time estimates or suggestions for making this form simpler, we would be happy to hear from you. See the instructions for the tax return with which this form is filed.

IRS Form Not Available at Press Time
See **http://www.toolkit.cch.com**
or
http://www.finance.cch.com
for the latest information

IRS Form Not Available at Press Time
See **http://www.toolkit.cch.com**
or
http://www.finance.cch.com
for the latest information

Form **6252**

Department of the Treasury
Internal Revenue Service

Installment Sale Income

▶ Attach to your tax return.

▶ Use a separate form for each sale or other disposition of property on the installment method.

OMB No. 1545-0228

2006

Attachment Sequence No. **79**

Name(s) shown on return | **Identifying number**

1 Description of property ▶

2a Date acquired (month, day, year) ▶ / / **b** Date sold (month, day, year) ▶ / /

3 Was the property sold to a related party (see instructions) after May 14, 1980? If "No," skip line 4. . . . . ☐ Yes ☐ No

4 Was the property you sold to a related party a marketable security? If "Yes," complete Part III. If "No," complete Part III for the year of sale and the 2 years after the year of sale . . . . ☐ Yes ☐ No

Part I **Gross Profit and Contract Price.** Complete this part for the year of sale only.

5	Selling price including mortgages and other debts. **Do not** include interest whether stated or unstated		5	
6	Mortgages, debts, and other liabilities the buyer assumed or took the property subject to (see instructions)	6		
7	Subtract line 6 from line 5	7		
8	Cost or other basis of property sold	8		
9	Depreciation allowed or allowable	9		
10	Adjusted basis. Subtract line 9 from line 8	10		
11	Commissions and other expenses of sale	11		
12	Income recapture from Form 4797, Part III (see instructions)	12		
13	Add lines 10, 11, and 12		13	
14	Subtract line 13 from line 5. If zero or less, **do not** complete the rest of this form (see instructions)		14	
15	If the property described on line 1 above was your main home, enter the amount of your excluded gain (see instructions). Otherwise, enter -0-		15	
16	**Gross profit.** Subtract line 15 from line 14		16	
17	Subtract line 13 from line 6. If zero or less, enter -0-		17	
18	**Contract price.** Add line 7 and line 17		18	

Part II **Installment Sale Income.** Complete this part for the year of sale **and** any year you receive a payment or have certain debts you must treat as a payment on installment obligations.

19	Gross profit percentage. Divide line 16 by line 18. For years after the year of sale, see instructions		19	
20	If this is the year of sale, enter the amount from line 17. Otherwise, enter -0-		20	
21	Payments received during year (see instructions). **Do not** include interest, whether stated or unstated		21	
22	Add lines 20 and 21		22	
23	Payments received in prior years (see instructions). **Do not** include interest, whether stated or unstated	23		
24	**Installment sale income.** Multiply line 22 by line 19		24	
25	Enter the part of line 24 that is ordinary income under the recapture rules (see instructions)		25	
26	Subtract line 25 from line 24. Enter here and on Schedule D or Form 4797 (see instructions)		26	

Part III **Related Party Installment Sale Income. Do not** complete if you received the final payment this tax year.

27 Name, address, and taxpayer identifying number of related party

28 Did the related party resell or dispose of the property ("second disposition") during this tax year? . . . . ☐ Yes ☐ No

29 **If the answer to question 28 is "Yes," complete lines 30 through 37 below unless one of the following conditions is met. Check the box that applies.**

a ☐ The second disposition was more than 2 years after the first disposition (other than dispositions of marketable securities). If this box is checked, enter the date of disposition (month, day, year) ▶ / /

b ☐ The first disposition was a sale or exchange of stock to the issuing corporation.

c ☐ The second disposition was an involuntary conversion and the threat of conversion occurred after the first disposition.

d ☐ The second disposition occurred after the death of the original seller or buyer.

e ☐ It can be established to the satisfaction of the Internal Revenue Service that tax avoidance was not a principal purpose for either of the dispositions. If this box is checked, attach an explanation (see instructions).

30	Selling price of property sold by related party (see instructions)	30	
31	Enter contract price from line 18 for year of first sale	31	
32	Enter the **smaller** of line 30 or line 31	32	
33	Total payments received by the end of your 2006 tax year (see instructions)	33	
34	Subtract line 33 from line 32. If zero or less, enter -0-	34	
35	Multiply line 34 by the gross profit percentage on line 19 for year of first sale	35	
36	Enter the part of line 35 that is ordinary income under the recapture rules (see instructions)	36	
37	Subtract line 36 from line 35. Enter here and on Schedule D or Form 4797 (see instructions)	37	

General Instructions

Section references are to the Internal Revenue Code unless otherwise noted.

Purpose of Form

Generally, use Form 6252 to report income from casual sales during this tax year of real or personal property (other than inventory) if you will receive any payments in a tax year after the year of sale. For years after the year of an installment sale, see *Which Parts To Complete* below.

Do not file Form 6252 for sales that do not result in a gain, even if you will receive a payment in a tax year after the year of sale. Instead, report the entire sale on Form 4797, Sales of Business Property, or the Schedule D for your tax return, whichever applies.

Do not file Form 6252 to report sales during the tax year of stock or securities traded on an established securities market. Instead, treat all payments as received during this tax year.

Do not file Form 6252 if you elect not to report the sale on the installment method. To elect out, report the full amount of the gain on a timely filed return (including extensions) on Form 4797 or the Schedule D for your tax return, whichever applies. If you filed your original return on time without making the election, you can make the election on an amended return filed no later than 6 months after the due date of your tax return, excluding extensions. Write "Filed pursuant to section 301.9100-2" at the top of the amended return.

Which Parts To Complete

Year of Sale

Complete lines 1 through 4, Part I, and Part II. If you sold property to a related party during the year, also complete Part III.

Later Years

Complete lines 1 through 4 and Part II for any year in which you receive a payment from an installment sale.

If you sold a marketable security to a related party after May 14, 1980, and before January 1, 1987, complete Form 6252 for each year of the installment agreement, even if you did not receive a payment. Complete lines 1 through 4. Complete Part II for any year in which you receive a payment from the sale. Complete Part III unless you received the final payment during the tax year.

After December 31, 1986, the installment method is not available for the sale of marketable securities.

If you sold property other than a marketable security to a related party after May 14, 1980, complete Form 6252 for the year of sale and for 2 years after the year of sale, even if you did not receive a payment. Complete lines 1 through 4. Complete Part II for any year during this 2-year period in which you receive a payment from the sale. Complete Part III for the 2 years after the year of sale unless you received the final payment during the tax year.

Special Rules

Interest

If any part of an installment payment you received is for interest or original issue discount, report that income on the appropriate form or schedule. Do not report interest received, carrying charges received, or unstated interest on Form 6252. See Pub. 537, Installment Sales, for details on unstated interest.

Installment Sales to Related Party

A special rule applies to a first disposition (sale or exchange) of property under the installment method to a related party who then makes a second disposition (sale, exchange, gift, or cancellation of installment note) before making all payments on the first disposition. For this purpose, a related party includes your spouse, child, grandchild, parent, brother, sister, or a related corporation, S corporation, partnership, estate, or trust. See section 453(f)(1) for more details.

Under this rule, treat part or all of the amount the related party realized (or the fair market value (FMV) if the disposed property is not sold or exchanged) from the second disposition as if you received it from the first disposition at the time of the second disposition. Figure the gain, if any, on lines 30 through 37. This rule does not apply if any of the conditions listed on line 29 are met.

Sale of Depreciable Property to Related Person

Generally, if you sell depreciable property to a related person (as defined in section 453(g)(3)), you cannot report the sale using the installment method. For this purpose, depreciable property is any property that can be depreciated by a person or entity to whom you transfer it. However, you can use the installment method if you can show to the satisfaction of the IRS that avoidance of federal income taxes was not one of the principal purposes of the sale (for example, no significant tax deferral benefits will result from the sale). If the installment method does not apply, report the sale on Schedule D or Form 4797, whichever applies. Treat all payments you will receive as if they were received in the year of sale. Use FMV for any payment that is contingent as to amount. If the FMV cannot be readily determined, basis is recovered ratably.

Pledge Rule

For certain dispositions under the installment method, if an installment obligation is pledged as security on a debt, the net proceeds of the secured debt are treated as payment on the installment obligation. However, the amount treated as payment cannot be more than the excess of the total installment contract price over any payments received under the contract before the secured debt was obtained.

An installment obligation is pledged as security on a debt to the extent that payment of principal and interest on the debt is directly secured by an interest in the installment obligation. For sales after December 16, 1999, payment on a debt is treated as directly secured by an interest in an installment obligation to the extent an arrangement allows you to satisfy all or part of the debt with the installment obligation.

The pledge rule applies to any installment sale after 1988 with a sales price of over $150,000 except:

- Personal use property disposed of by an individual,
- Farm property, and
- Timeshares and residential lots.

However, the pledge rule does not apply to pledges made after December 17, 1987, if the debt is incurred to refinance the principal amount of a debt that was outstanding on December 17, 1987, and was secured by nondealer real property installment obligations on that date and at all times after that date until the refinancing. This exception does not apply to the extent that the principal amount of the debt resulting from the refinancing exceeds the principal amount of the refinanced debt immediately before the refinancing. Also, the pledge rule does not affect refinancing due to the calling of a debt by the creditor if the debt is then refinanced by a person other than this creditor or someone related to the creditor.

Interest on Deferred Tax

Generally, you must pay interest on the deferred tax related to any obligation that arises during a tax year from the disposition of property under the installment method if:

- The property had a sales price over $150,000, and

Form **8283**

(Rev. December 2005)

Department of the Treasury
Internal Revenue Service

Noncash Charitable Contributions

▶ **Attach to your tax return if you claimed a total deduction of over $500 for all contributed property.**

▶ **See separate instructions.**

OMB No. 1545-0908

Attachment Sequence No. **155**

Name(s) shown on your income tax return | **Identifying number**

Note. Figure the amount of your contribution deduction before completing this form. See your tax return instructions.

Section A. Donated Property of $5,000 or Less and Certain Publicly Traded Securities—List in this section **only** items (or groups of similar items) for which you claimed a deduction of $5,000 or less. Also, list certain publicly traded securities even if the deduction is more than $5,000 (see instructions).

Part I Information on Donated Property—If you need more space, attach a statement.

1	**(a)** Name and address of the donee organization	**(b)** Description of donated property (For a donated vehicle, enter the year, make, model, condition, and mileage.)
A		
B		
C		
D		
E		

Note. If the amount you claimed as a deduction for an item is $500 or less, you do not have to complete columns (d), (e), and (f).

	(c) Date of the contribution	**(d)** Date acquired by donor (mo., yr.)	**(e)** How acquired by donor	**(f)** Donor's cost or adjusted basis	**(g)** Fair market value (see instructions)	**(h)** Method used to determine the fair market value
A						
B						
C						
D						
E						

Part II Partial Interests and Restricted Use Property—Complete lines 2a through 2e if you gave less than an entire interest in a property listed in Part I. Complete lines 3a through 3c if conditions were placed on a contribution listed in Part I; also attach the required statement (see instructions).

2a Enter the letter from Part I that identifies the property for which you gave less than an entire interest ▶ ______________ . If Part II applies to more than one property, attach a separate statement.

b Total amount claimed as a deduction for the property listed in Part I: **(1)** For this tax year ▶ ______________ .
(2) For any prior tax years ▶ ______________ .

c Name and address of each organization to which any such contribution was made in a prior year (complete only if different from the donee organization above):

Name of charitable organization (donee)

Address (number, street, and room or suite no.)

City or town, state, and ZIP code

d For tangible property, enter the place where the property is located or kept ▶ ______________

e Name of any person, other than the donee organization, having actual possession of the property ▶ ______________

	Yes	No
3a Is there a restriction, either temporary or permanent, on the donee's right to use or dispose of the donated property?		
b Did you give to anyone (other than the donee organization or another organization participating with the donee organization in cooperative fundraising) the right to the income from the donated property or to the possession of the property, including the right to vote donated securities, to acquire the property by purchase or otherwise, or to designate the person having such income, possession, or right to acquire?		
c Is there a restriction limiting the donated property for a particular use?		

Name(s) shown on your income tax return | **Identifying number**

Section B. Donated Property Over $5,000 (Except Certain Publicly Traded Securities)—List in this section only items (or groups of similar items) for which you claimed a deduction of more than $5,000 per item or group (except contributions of certain publicly traded securities reported in Section A). An appraisal is generally required for property listed in Section B (see instructions).

Part I Information on Donated Property—To be completed by the taxpayer and/or the appraiser.

4 Check the box that describes the type of property donated:

- ☐ Art* (contribution of $20,000 or more)
- ☐ Art* (contribution of less than $20,000)
- ☐ Collectibles**
- ☐ Qualified Conservation Contribution
- ☐ Other Real Estate
- ☐ Intellectual Property
- ☐ Equipment
- ☐ Securities
- ☐ Other

*Art includes paintings, sculptures, watercolors, prints, drawings, ceramics, antiques, decorative arts, textiles, carpets, silver, rare manuscripts, historical memorabilia, and other similar objects.

**Collectibles include coins, stamps, books, gems, jewelry, sports memorabilia, dolls, etc., but not art as defined above.

Note. If your total art contribution was $20,000 or more, you must attach a complete copy of the signed appraisal. If your deduction for any donated property was more than $500,000, you must attach a qualified appraisal of the property. See instructions.

5	(a) Description of donated property (if you need more space, attach a separate statement)	(b) If tangible property was donated, give a brief summary of the overall physical condition of the property at the time of the gift	(c) Appraised fair market value
A			
B			
C			
D			

	(d) Date acquired by donor (mo., yr.)	(e) How acquired by donor	(f) Donor's cost or adjusted basis	(g) For bargain sales, enter amount received	See instructions (h) Amount claimed as a deduction	See instructions (i) Average trading price of securities
A						
B						
C						
D						

Part II Taxpayer (Donor) Statement—List each item included in Part I above that the appraisal identifies as having a value of $500 or less. See instructions.

I declare that the following item(s) included in Part I above has to the best of my knowledge and belief an appraised value of not more than $500 (per item). Enter identifying letter from Part I and describe the specific item. See instructions. ▶ ______

Signature of taxpayer (donor) ▶ Date ▶

Part III Declaration of Appraiser

I declare that I am not the donor, the donee, a party to the transaction in which the donor acquired the property, employed by, or related to any of the foregoing persons, or married to any person who is related to any of the foregoing persons. And, if regularly used by the donor, donee, or party to the transaction, I performed the majority of my appraisals during my tax year for other persons.

Also, I declare that I hold myself out to the public as an appraiser or perform appraisals on a regular basis; and that because of my qualifications as described in the appraisal, I am qualified to make appraisals of the type of property being valued. I certify that the appraisal fees were not based on a percentage of the appraised property value. Furthermore, I understand that a false or fraudulent overstatement of the property value as described in the qualified appraisal or this Form 8283 may subject me to the penalty under section 6701(a) (aiding and abetting the understatement of tax liability). I affirm that I have not been barred from presenting evidence or testimony by the Office of Professional Responsibility.

Sign Here Signature ▶ Title ▶ Date ▶

Business address (including room or suite no.) | **Identifying number**

City or town, state, and ZIP code

Part IV Donee Acknowledgment—To be completed by the charitable organization.

This charitable organization acknowledges that it is a qualified organization under section 170(c) and that it received the donated property as described in Section B, Part I, above on the following date ▶ ______

Furthermore, this organization affirms that in the event it sells, exchanges, or otherwise disposes of the property described in Section B, Part I (or any portion thereof) within 2 years after the date of receipt, it will file **Form 8282,** Donee Information Return, with the IRS and give the donor a copy of that form. This acknowledgment does not represent agreement with the claimed fair market value.

Does the organization intend to use the property for an unrelated use? . . . . ▶ ☐ Yes ☐ No

Name of charitable organization (donee)	**Employer identification number**	
Address (number, street, and room or suite no.)	City or town, state, and ZIP code	
Authorized signature	Title	Date

Form **8582**

Department of the Treasury
Internal Revenue Service (99)

Passive Activity Loss Limitations

▶ See separate instructions.

▶ Attach to Form 1040 or Form 1041.

OMB No. 1545-1008

2006

Attachment Sequence No. **88**

Name(s) shown on return | **Identifying number**

Part I 2006 Passive Activity Loss

Caution: *Complete Worksheets 1, 2, and 3 on page 2 before completing Part I.*

Rental Real Estate Activities With Active Participation (For the definition of active participation see **Special Allowance for Rental Real Estate Activities** on page 3 of the instructions.)

1a Activities with net income (enter the amount from Worksheet 1, column (a))	**1a**		
b Activities with net loss (enter the amount from Worksheet 1, column (b))	**1b**	( )	
c Prior years unallowed losses (enter the amount from Worksheet 1, column (c))	**1c**	( )	
d Combine lines 1a, 1b, and 1c			**1d**

Commercial Revitalization Deductions From Rental Real Estate Activities

2a Commercial revitalization deductions from Worksheet 2, column (a)	**2a**	( )	
b Prior year unallowed commercial revitalization deductions from Worksheet 2, column (b)	**2b**	( )	
c Add lines 2a and 2b			**2c** ( )

All Other Passive Activities

3a Activities with net income (enter the amount from Worksheet 3, column (a))	**3a**		
b Activities with net loss (enter the amount from Worksheet 3, column (b))	**3b**	( )	
c Prior years unallowed losses (enter the amount from Worksheet 3, column (c))	**3c**	( )	
d Combine lines 3a, 3b, and 3c			**3d**

4 Combine lines 1d, 2c, and 3d. If the result is net income or zero, all losses are allowed, including any prior year unallowed losses entered on line 1c, 2b, or 3c. **Do not** complete Form 8582. Report the losses on the forms and schedules normally used . . . **4**

If line 4 is a loss and:
- Line 1d is a loss, go to Part II.
- Line 2c is a loss (and line 1d is zero or more), skip Part II and go to Part III.
- Line 3d is a loss (and lines 1d and 2c are zero or more), skip Parts II and III and go to line 15.

Caution: *If your filing status is married filing separately and you lived with your spouse at any time during the year,* **do not** *complete Part II or Part III. Instead, go to line 15.*

Part II Special Allowance for Rental Real Estate Activities With Active Participation

Note: *Enter all numbers in Part II as positive amounts. See page 8 of the instructions for an example.*

5 Enter the **smaller** of the loss on line 1d or the loss on line 4			**5**
6 Enter $150,000. If married filing separately, see page 8	**6**		
7 Enter modified adjusted gross income, but not less than zero (see page 8)	**7**		
Note: *If line 7 is greater than or equal to line 6, skip lines 8 and 9, enter -0- on line 10. Otherwise, go to line 8.*			
8 Subtract line 7 from line 6	**8**		
9 Multiply line 8 by 50% (.5). **Do not** enter more than $25,000. If married filing separately, see page 8			**9**
10 Enter the **smaller** of line 5 or line 9			**10**

If line 2c is a loss, go to Part III. Otherwise, go to line 15.

Part III Special Allowance for Commercial Revitalization Deductions From Rental Real Estate Activities

Note: *Enter all numbers in Part III as positive amounts. See the example for Part II on page 8 of the instructions.*

11 Enter $25,000 reduced by the amount, if any, on line 10. If married filing separately, see instructions	**11**
12 Enter the loss from line 4	**12**
13 Reduce line 12 by the amount on line 10	**13**
14 Enter the **smallest** of line 2c (treated as a positive amount), line 11, or line 13	**14**

Part IV Total Losses Allowed

15 Add the income, if any, on lines 1a and 3a and enter the total	**15**
16 **Total losses allowed from all passive activities for 2006.** Add lines 10, 14, and 15. See page 11 of the instructions to find out how to report the losses on your tax return	**16**

Caution: *The worksheets must be filed with your tax return. Keep a copy for your records.*

Worksheet 1—For Form 8582, Lines 1a, 1b, and 1c (See pages 7 and 8 of the instructions.)

Name of activity	Current year		Prior years	Overall gain or loss	
	(a) Net income (line 1a)	(b) Net loss (line 1b)	(c) Unallowed loss (line 1c)	(d) Gain	(e) Loss
Total. Enter on Form 8582, lines 1a, 1b, and 1c . . . . ▶					

Worksheet 2—For Form 8582, Lines 2a and 2b (See page 8 of the instructions.)

Name of activity	(a) Current year deductions (line 2a)	(b) Prior year unallowed deductions (line 2b)	(c) Overall loss
Total. Enter on Form 8582, lines 2a and 2b . . . . ▶			

Worksheet 3—For Form 8582, Lines 3a, 3b, and 3c (See page 8 of the instructions.)

Name of activity	Current year		Prior years	Overall gain or loss	
	(a) Net income (line 3a)	(b) Net loss (line 3b)	(c) Unallowed loss (line 3c)	(d) Gain	(e) Loss
Total. Enter on Form 8582, lines 3a, 3b, and 3c . . . . ▶					

Worksheet 4—Use this worksheet if an amount is shown on Form 8582, line 10 or 14 (See page 9 of the instructions.)

Name of activity	Form or schedule and line number to be reported on (see instructions)	(a) Loss	(b) Ratio	(c) Special allowance	(d) Subtract column (c) from column (a)
Total . . . . ▶			1.00		

Worksheet 5—Allocation of Unallowed Losses (See page 9 of the instructions.)

Name of activity	Form or schedule and line number to be reported on (see instructions)	(a) Loss	(b) Ratio	(c) Unallowed loss
Total . . . . ▶			1.00	

IRS Form Not Available at Press Time

See **http://www.toolkit.cch.com**

or

http://www.finance.cch.com

for the latest information

IRS Form Not Available at Press Time
See **http://www.toolkit.cch.com**
or
http://www.finance.cch.com
for the latest information

Form **8812**

Department of the Treasury
Internal Revenue Service (99)

Additional Child Tax Credit

Complete and attach to Form 1040, Form 1040A, or Form 1040NR.

OMB No. 1545-0074

2006

Attachment Sequence No. 47

Name(s) shown on return

Your social security number

Part I All Filers

1	Enter the amount from line 1 of your Child Tax Credit Worksheet on page 43 of the Form 1040 instructions, page 38 of the Form 1040A instructions, or page 20 of the Form 1040NR instructions. If you used Pub. 972, enter the amount from line 8 of the worksheet on page 4 of the publication		1
2	Enter the amount from Form 1040, line 53, Form 1040A, line 33, or Form 1040NR, line 48		2
3	Subtract line 2 from line 1. If zero, **stop**; you cannot take this credit		3
4a	Enter your total earned income (see instructions on back)	4a	
b	Nontaxable combat pay (see instructions on back) 4b		
5	Is the amount on line 4a more than $11,300? ☐ **No.** Leave line 5 blank and enter -0- on line 6. ☐ **Yes.** Subtract $11,300 from the amount on line 4a. Enter the result .	5	
6	Multiply the amount on line 5 by 15% (.15) and enter the result		6

Next. Do you have three or more qualifying children?

☐ **No.** If line 6 is zero, stop; you cannot take this credit. Otherwise, skip Part II and enter the **smaller** of line 3 or line 6 on line 13.

☐ **Yes.** If line 6 is equal to or more than line 3, skip Part II and enter the amount from line 3 on line 13. Otherwise, go to line 7.

Part II Certain Filers Who Have Three or More Qualifying Children

7	Withheld social security and Medicare taxes from Form(s) W-2, boxes 4 and 6. If married filing jointly, include your spouse's amounts with yours. If you worked for a railroad, see instructions on back	7	
8	**1040 filers:** Enter the total of the amounts from Form 1040, lines 27 and 59, plus any uncollected social security and Medicare or tier 1 RRTA taxes included on line 63. **1040A filers:** Enter -0-. **1040NR filers:** Enter the total of the amounts from Form 1040NR, line 54, plus any uncollected social security and Medicare or tier 1 RRTA taxes included on line 58.	8	
9	Add lines 7 and 8	9	
10	**1040 filers:** Enter the total of the amounts from Form 1040, lines 66a and 67. **1040A filers:** Enter the total of the amount from Form 1040A, line 40a, plus any excess social security and tier 1 RRTA taxes withheld that you entered to the left of line 43 (see instructions on back). **1040NR filers:** Enter the amount from Form 1040NR, line 61.	10	
11	Subtract line 10 from line 9. If zero or less, enter -0-		11
12	Enter the **larger** of line 6 or line 11		12

Next, enter the **smaller** of line 3 or line 12 on line 13.

Part III Additional Child Tax Credit

13	**This is your additional child tax credit**	13

Enter this amount on Form 1040, line 68, Form 1040A, line 41, or Form 1040NR, line 62.

For Paperwork Reduction Act Notice, see back of form. Cat. No. 10644E Form **8812** (2006)

Instructions

Purpose of Form

Use Form 8812 to figure your additional child tax credit. The additional child tax credit may give you a refund even if you do not owe any tax.

Who Should Use Form 8812

First, complete the Child Tax Credit Worksheet that applies to you. See the instructions for Form 1040, line 53, Form 1040A, line 33, or Form 1040NR, line 48. If you meet the condition given in the *TIP* at the end of your Child Tax Credit Worksheet, use Form 8812 to see if you can take the additional child tax credit.

Effect of Credit on Welfare Benefits

Any refund you receive as a result of taking the additional child tax credit will not be used to determine if you are eligible for the following programs, or how much you can receive from them. But if the refund you receive because of the additional child tax credit is not spent within a certain period of time, it may count as an asset (or resource) and affect your eligibility.

- Temporary Assistance for Needy Families (TANF).
- Medicaid and supplemental security income (SSI).
- Food stamps and low-income housing.

Nontaxable Combat Pay

Enter on line 4b the total amount of nontaxable combat pay that you, and your spouse if filing jointly, received in 2006. This amount should be shown in Form W-2, box 12, with code Q.

Railroad Employees

If you worked for a railroad, include the following taxes in the total on Form 8812, line 7.

- Tier 1 tax withheld from your pay. This tax should be shown in box 14 of your Form(s) W-2 and identified as "Tier 1 tax."
- If you were an employee representative, 50% of the total tier 1 tax and tier 1 Medicare tax you paid for 2006.

1040A Filers

If you, or your spouse if filing jointly, had more than one employer for 2006 and total wages of over $94,200, figure any excess social security and tier 1 railroad retirement (RRTA) taxes withheld. See Pub. 505. Include any excess on Form 8812, line 10.

Paperwork Reduction Act Notice. We ask for the information on this form to carry out the Internal Revenue laws of the United States. You are required to give us the information. We need it to ensure that you are complying with these laws and to allow us to figure and collect the right amount of tax.

You are not required to provide the information requested on a form that is subject to the Paperwork Reduction Act unless the form displays a valid OMB control number. Books or records relating to a form or its instructions must be retained as long as their contents may become material in the administration of any Internal Revenue law. Generally, tax returns and return information are confidential, as required by Internal Revenue Code section 6103.

The average time and expenses required to complete and file this form will vary depending on individual circumstances. For the estimated averages, see the instructions for your income tax return.

If you have suggestions for making this form simpler, we would be happy to hear from you. See the instructions for your income tax return.

Earned Income Chart—Line 4a

IF you...	AND you...	THEN enter on line 4a...
have net earnings from self-employment	use either optional method to figure those net earnings	the amount figured using Pub. 972.
are taking the EIC on Form 1040, line 66a, or Form 1040A, line 40a	completed Worksheet B on page 51 of your Form 1040 instructions	your earned income from Worksheet B, line 4b, plus all of your nontaxable combat pay if you did not elect to include it in earned income for the EIC. If you were a member of the clergy, subtract (a) the rental value of a home or the nontaxable portion of an allowance for a home furnished to you (including payments for utilities), and (b) the value of meals and lodging provided to you, your spouse, and your dependents for your employer's convenience.
	did not complete Worksheet B or filed Form 1040A	your earned income from Step 5 on page 48 of your 1040 instructions or page 42 of your 1040A instructions, plus all of your nontaxable combat pay if you did not elect to include it in earned income for the EIC.
are not taking the EIC	were self-employed, or you are filing Schedule SE because you were a member of the clergy or you had church employee income, or you are filing Schedule C or C-EZ as a statutory employee	the amount figured using Pub. 972.
	are not self-employed or filing Schedule SE, C, or C-EZ for the above reasons	your earned income figured as follows: Line 7 of Form 1040 or Form 1040A, or line 8 of Form 1040NR ______ Subtract, if included on line 7 (line 8 for Form 1040NR), any: • Taxable scholarship or fellowship grant not reported on a Form W-2. • Amount received for work performed while an inmate in a penal institution (put "PRI" and the amount subtracted in the space next to line 7 of Form 1040 or 1040A (line 8 for Form 1040NR)). • Amount received as a pension or annuity from a nonqualified deferred compensation plan or a nongovernmental section 457 plan (put "DFC" and the amount subtracted in the space next to line 7 of Form 1040 or Form 1040A (line 8 for Form 1040NR)). This amount may be shown in box 11 of your Form W-2. If you received such an amount but box 11 is blank, contact your employer for the amount received as a pension or annuity. • Amount from Form 2555, line 43, or Form 2555-EZ, line 18. } − ______ Add all your nontaxable combat pay from Form(s) W-2, box 12, with code Q + ______ **Earned income =** ______

Form **8814**

Department of the Treasury
Internal Revenue Service

Parents' Election To Report Child's Interest and Dividends

▶ See instructions.

▶ Attach to parents' Form 1040 or Form 1040NR.

OMB No. 1545-0074

2006

Attachment Sequence No. **40**

Name(s) shown on your return	**Your social security number**

Caution. The federal income tax on your child's income, including qualified dividends and capital gain distributions, may be less if you file a separate tax return for the child instead of making this election. This is because you cannot take certain tax benefits that your child could take on his or her own return. For details, see **Tax benefits you cannot take** on page 2.

A Child's name (first, initial, and last)	**B Child's social security number**

C If more than one Form 8814 is attached, check here . . . . . ▶ ☐

Part I Child's Interest and Dividends To Report on Your Return

1a	Enter your child's **taxable** interest. If this amount is different from the amounts shown on the child's Forms 1099-INT and 1099-OID, see the instructions . . .			1a		
b	Enter your child's **tax-exempt** interest. **Do not** include this amount on line 1a . . .	1b				
2a	Enter your child's ordinary dividends, including any Alaska Permanent Fund dividends. If your child received any ordinary dividends as a nominee, see the instructions . . .			2a		
b	Enter your child's qualified dividends included on line 2a. See the instructions . . .	2b				
3	Enter your child's capital gain distributions. If your child received any capital gain distributions as a nominee, see the instructions . . .			3		
4	Add lines 1a, 2a, and 3. If the total is $1,700 or less, skip lines 5 through 12 and go to line 13. If the total is $8,500 or more, **do not** file this form. Your child **must** file his or her own return to report the income . . .			4		
5	Base amount . . .			5	1,700	00
6	Subtract line 5 from line 4 . . .			6		
	If both lines 2b and 3 are zero or blank, skip lines 7 through 10, enter -0- on line 11, and go to line 12. Otherwise, go to line 7.					
7	Divide line 2b by line 4. Enter the result as a decimal (rounded to at least three places) . . .	7	.			
8	Divide line 3 by line 4. Enter the result as a decimal (rounded to at least three places) . . .	8	.			
9	Multiply line 6 by line 7. Enter the result here. See the instructions for where to report this amount on your return . . .	9				
10	Multiply line 6 by line 8. Enter the result here. See the instructions for where to report this amount on your return . . .	10				
11	Add lines 9 and 10 . . .			11		
12	Subtract line 11 from line 6. Include this amount in the total on Form 1040, line 21, or Form 1040NR, line 21. In the space next to line 21, enter "Form 8814" and show the amount. If you checked the box on line C above, see the instructions. Go to line 13 below . . .			12		

Part II Tax on the First $1,700 of Child's Interest and Dividends

13	Amount not taxed . . .	13	850	00
14	Subtract line 13 from line 4. If the result is zero or less, enter -0-. . .	14		
15	**Tax.** Is the amount on line 14 less than $850? ☐ **No.** Enter $85 here and see the **Note** below. ☐ **Yes.** Multiply line 14 by 10% (.10). Enter the result here and see the **Note** below.	15		

Note. If you checked the box on line C above, see the instructions. Otherwise, include the amount from line 15 in the tax you enter on Form 1040, line 44, or Form 1040NR, line 41. Be sure to check box **a** on Form 1040, line 44, or Form 1040NR, line 41.

General Instructions

What's New

- The election to report a child's income on the parents' return can be made for a child under age 18 (previously under age 14) who meets the required conditions below.
- The Child's Qualified Dividends and Capital Gain Distributions Worksheet has been eliminated. The computation previously done on that worksheet is now done on Form 8814 itself.

Purpose of Form

Use this form if you elect to report your child's income on your return. If you do, your child will not have to file a return. You can make this election if your child meets all of the following conditions.

- The child was under age 18 at the end of 2006. (A child born on January 1, 1989, is considered to be age 18 at the end of 2006. You cannot make this election for such a child.)
- The child's only income was from interest and dividends, including capital gain distributions and Alaska Permanent Fund dividends.
- The child's gross income for 2006 was less than $8,500.
- The child is required to file a 2006 return.
- The child does not file a joint return for 2006.
- There were no estimated tax payments for the child for 2006 (including any overpayment of tax from his or her 2005 return applied to 2006 estimated tax).
- There was no federal income tax withheld from the child's income.

You must also qualify. See *Parents who qualify to make the election* below.

How to make the election. To make the election, complete and attach Form(s) 8814 to your tax return and file your return by the due date (including extensions). A separate Form 8814 must be filed for each child whose income you choose to report.

Parents who qualify to make the election. You qualify to make this election if you file Form 1040 or Form 1040NR and any of the following apply.

- You are filing a joint return for 2006 with the child's other parent.
- You and the child's other parent were married to each other but file separate returns for 2006 and you had the higher taxable income.
- You were unmarried, treated as unmarried for federal income tax purposes, or separated from the child's other parent by a divorce or separate maintenance decree. The child must have lived with you for most of the year (you were the custodial parent). If you were the custodial parent and you remarried, you can make the election on a joint return with your new spouse. But if you and your new spouse do not file a joint return, you qualify to make the election only if you had higher taxable income than your new spouse.

Note. If you and the child's other parent were not married but lived together during the year with the child, you qualify to make the election only if you are the parent with the higher taxable income.

Tax benefits you cannot take. If you elect to report your child's income on your return, you cannot take any of the following deductions that your child could take on his or her own return.

- Standard deduction of $2,100 for a blind child.
- Penalty on early withdrawal of child's savings.
- Itemized deductions such as child's investment expenses or charitable contributions.

If your child received qualified dividends or capital gain distributions, you may pay up to $42.50 more tax if you make this election instead of filing a separate tax return for the child. This is because the tax rate on the child's income between $850 and $1,700 is 10% if you make this election. However, if you file a separate return for the child, the tax rate may be as low as 5% because of the preferential tax rates for qualified dividends and capital gain distributions.

If any of the above apply to your child, first figure the tax on your child's income as if he or she is filing a return. Next, figure the tax as if you are electing to report your child's income on your return. Then, compare the methods to determine which results in the lower tax.

Alternative minimum tax. If your child received tax-exempt interest (or exempt-interest dividends paid by a regulated investment company) from certain private activity bonds, you must take this into account in determining if you owe the alternative minimum tax. This type of interest may be shown in box 9 of Form 1099-INT. See Form 6251, Alternative Minimum Tax—Individuals, and its instructions for details.

Investment interest expense. Your child's income (other than qualified dividends, Alaska Permanent Fund dividends, and capital gain distributions) that you report on your return is considered to be your investment income for purposes of figuring your investment interest expense deduction. If your child received qualified dividends, Alaska Permanent Fund dividends, or capital gain distributions, see Pub. 550, Investment Income and Expenses, to figure the amount you can treat as your investment income.

Foreign accounts and trusts. Complete Schedule B (Form 1040), Part III, for your child if he or she (a) had a foreign financial account or (b) received a distribution from, or was the grantor of, or transferor to, a foreign trust. If you answer "Yes" to either question, you must file this Schedule B with your return. Enter "Form 8814" next to line 7a or line 8, whichever applies. Also, complete line 7b if applicable.

Change of address. If your child filed a return for a previous year and the address shown on the last return filed is not your child's current address, be sure to notify the IRS, in writing, of the new address. To do this, you may use Form 8822, Change of Address.

Additional information. See Pub. 929, Tax Rules for Children and Dependents, for more details.

Line Instructions

Name and social security number. If filing a joint return, include your spouse's name but enter the social security number of the person whose name is shown first on the return.

Line 1a. Enter all taxable interest income your child received in 2006. Do not include tax-exempt interest in the total for line 1a, but be sure to include it on line 1b.

If your child received, as a nominee, interest that actually belongs to another person, enter the amount and "ND" (for nominee distribution) on the dotted line next to line 1a. Do not include amounts received as a nominee in the total for line 1a.

If your child had accrued interest that was paid to the seller of a bond, amortizable bond premium (ABP) allowed as a reduction to interest income, or if any original issue discount (OID) is less than the amount shown on your child's Form 1099-OID, enter the nontaxable amount on the dotted line next to line 1a and "Accrued interest," "ABP adjustment," or "OID adjustment," whichever applies. Do not include any nontaxable amounts in the total for line 1a.

Line 1b. If your child received any tax-exempt interest income, such as from certain state and municipal bonds, report it on line 1b. Tax-exempt interest should be shown in box 8 of Form 1099-INT. Also include any exempt-interest dividends your child received as a shareholder in a mutual fund or other regulated investment company. Those amounts should also be shown in box 8 of Form 1099-INT.

(continued)

Form **8829**

Department of the Treasury
Internal Revenue Service (99)

Expenses for Business Use of Your Home

▶ File only with Schedule C (Form 1040). Use a separate Form 8829 for each home you used for business during the year.

▶ See separate instructions.

OMB No. 1545-0074

2006

Attachment Sequence No. 66

Name(s) of proprietor(s)

Your social security number

Part I Part of Your Home Used for Business

1	Area used regularly and exclusively for business, regularly for daycare, or for storage of inventory or product samples (see instructions)	1	
2	Total area of home	2	
3	Divide line 1 by line 2. Enter the result as a percentage	3	%
	For daycare facilities not used exclusively for business go to line 4. All others go to line 7.		
4	Multiply days used for daycare during year by hours used per day — 4 hr.		
5	Total hours available for use during the year (365 days × 24 hours) (see instructions) — 5 8,760 hr.		
6	Divide line 4 by line 5. Enter the result as a decimal amount — 6 .		
7	Business percentage. For daycare facilities not used exclusively for business, multiply line 6 by line 3 (enter the result as a percentage). All others, enter the amount from line 3 ▶	7	%

Part II Figure Your Allowable Deduction

			(a) Direct expenses	(b) Indirect expenses		
8	Enter the amount from Schedule C, line 29, **plus** any net gain or (loss) derived from the business use of your home and shown on Schedule D or Form 4797. If more than one place of business, see instructions				8	
	See instructions for columns (a) and (b) before completing lines 9–21.					
9	Casualty losses (see instructions)	9				
10	Deductible mortgage interest (see instructions)	10				
11	Real estate taxes (see instructions)	11				
12	Add lines 9, 10, and 11	12				
13	Multiply line 12, column (b) by line 7			13		
14	Add line 12, column (a) and line 13				14	
15	Subtract line 14 from line 8. If zero or less, enter -0-				15	
16	Excess mortgage interest (see instructions)	16				
17	Insurance	17				
18	Rent	18				
19	Repairs and maintenance	19				
20	Utilities	20				
21	Other expenses (see instructions)	21				
22	Add lines 16 through 21	22				
23	Multiply line 22, column (b) by line 7			23		
24	Carryover of operating expenses from 2005 Form 8829, line 41			24		
25	Add line 22 in column (a), line 23, and line 24				25	
26	Allowable operating expenses. Enter the **smaller** of line 15 or line 25				26	
27	Limit on excess casualty losses and depreciation. Subtract line 26 from line 15				27	
28	Excess casualty losses (see instructions)			28		
29	Depreciation of your home from Part III below			29		
30	Carryover of excess casualty losses and depreciation from 2005 Form 8829, line 42			30		
31	Add lines 28 through 30				31	
32	Allowable excess casualty losses and depreciation. Enter the **smaller** of line 27 or line 31				32	
33	Add lines 14, 26, and 32				33	
34	Casualty loss portion, if any, from lines 14 and 32. Carry amount to **Form 4684,** Section B				34	
35	Allowable expenses for business use of your home. Subtract line 34 from line 33. Enter here and on Schedule C, line 30. If your home was used for more than one business, see instructions ▶				35	

Part III Depreciation of Your Home

36	Enter the **smaller** of your home's adjusted basis or its fair market value (see instructions)	36	
37	Value of land included on line 36	37	
38	Basis of building. Subtract line 37 from line 36	38	
39	Business basis of building. Multiply line 38 by line 7	39	
40	Depreciation percentage (see instructions)	40	%
41	Depreciation allowable (see instructions). Multiply line 39 by line 40. Enter here and on line 29 above	41	

Part IV Carryover of Unallowed Expenses to 2007

42	Operating expenses. Subtract line 26 from line 25. If less than zero, enter -0-	42	
43	Excess casualty losses and depreciation. Subtract line 32 from line 31. If less than zero, enter -0-	43	

Form **8839**

Department of the Treasury
Internal Revenue Service

Qualified Adoption Expenses

▶ Attach to Form 1040 or 1040NR.
▶ See separate instructions.

OMB No. 1545-0074

2006

Attachment Sequence No. **38**

Name(s) shown on return | **Your social security number**

Before you begin: See **Definitions** on page 1 of the instructions.

Part I **Information About Your Eligible Child or Children—**You **must** complete this part. See page 2 of the instructions for details, including what to do if you need more space.

1	(a) Child's name First	Last	(b) Child's year of birth	Check if child was— (c) born **before 1989** and disabled	(d) a child with special needs	(e) a foreign child	(f) Child's identifying number
Child 1				☐	☐	☐	
Child 2				☐	☐	☐	

Caution. If the child was a foreign child, see **Special rules** in the instructions for line 1, column (e), that begin on page 2, before you complete Part II or Part III. If you received **employer-provided adoption benefits,** complete Part III on the back next.

Part II **Adoption Credit**

			Child 1	Child 2
2	Maximum adoption credit per child	2	$10,960 00	$10,960 00
3	Did you file Form 8839 for a prior year for the same child? ☐ **No.** Enter -0-. ☐ **Yes.** See page 4 of the instructions for the amount to enter.	3		
4	Subtract line 3 from line 2	4		
5	**Qualified adoption expenses** (see page 4 of the instructions)	5		
	Caution. Your qualified adoption expenses may not be equal to the adoption expenses you paid in 2006.			
6	Enter the **smaller** of line 4 or line 5	6		

7	Add the amounts on line 6. If zero, skip lines 8 through 11 and enter -0- on line 12	7	
8	Modified adjusted gross income (see page 4 of the instructions) — 8		
9	Is line 8 more than $164,410? ☐ **No.** Skip lines 9 and 10, and enter -0- on line 11. ☐ **Yes.** Subtract $164,410 from line 8 — 9		
10	Divide line 9 by $40,000. Enter the result as a decimal (rounded to at least three places). Do not enter more than 1.000	10	× .
11	Multiply line 7 by line 10	11	
12	Subtract line 11 from line 7	12	
13	Credit carryforward from prior years (line 23 of your **Credit Carryforward Worksheet** on page 5 of the **2005** Form 8839 instructions)	13	
14	Add lines 12 and 13	14	
15	Enter the amount from Form 1040, line 46, or Form 1040NR, line 43 — 15		
16	**1040 filers:** Enter the total of any amounts from Form 1040, lines 47 through 51 and line 53; Form 8396, line 11; and Form 5695, line 12. **1040NR filers:** Enter the total of any amounts from Form 1040NR, lines 44 through 46 and line 48; Form 8396, line 11; and Form 5695, line 12. — 16		
17	Subtract line 16 from line 15	17	
18	**Adoption credit.** Enter the smaller of line 14 or line 17 here and include on Form 1040, line 54, or Form 1040NR, line 49. Check box **b** on that line. If line 17 is smaller than line 14, you may have a credit carryforward (see page 4 of the instructions)	18	

Part III Employer-Provided Adoption Benefits

		Child 1		Child 2			
19 Maximum exclusion per child . . .	**19**	$10,960	00	$10,960	00		
20 Did you receive employer-provided adoption benefits for a prior year for the same child? ☐ **No.** Enter -0-. ☐ **Yes.** See page 4 of the instructions for the amount to enter.	**20**						
21 Subtract line 20 from line 19	**21**						
22 Employer-provided adoption benefits you received in 2006. This amount should be shown in box 12 of your 2006 Form(s) W-2 with code **T** . . .	**22**						
23 Add the amounts on line 22						**23**	
24 Enter the **smaller** of line 21 or line 22. But if the child was a child with special needs and the adoption became final in 2006, enter the amount from line 21 .	**24**						
25 Add the amounts on line 24. If zero, skip lines 26 through 29, enter -0- on line 30, and go to line 31			**25**				
26 Modified adjusted gross income (from the worksheet on page 6 of the instructions)	**26**						
27 Is line 26 more than $164,410? ☐ **No.** Skip lines 27 and 28, and enter -0- on line 29. ☐ **Yes.** Subtract $164,410 from line 26	**27**						
28 Divide line 27 by $40,000. Enter the result as a decimal (rounded to at least three places). Do not enter more than 1.000 . . .			**28**	× .			
29 Multiply line 25 by line 28			**29**				
30 **Excluded benefits.** Subtract line 29 from line 25						**30**	
31 **Taxable benefits.** Is line 30 more than line 23? ☐ **No.** Subtract line 30 from line 23. Also, include this amount, if more than zero, on line 7 of Form 1040 or line 8 of Form 1040NR. On the dotted line next to line 7 of Form 1040 or line 8 of Form 1040NR, enter "AB." ☐ **Yes.** Subtract line 23 from line 30. Enter the result as a negative number. Reduce the total you would enter on line 7 of Form 1040 or line 8 of Form 1040NR by the amount on Form 8839, line 31. Enter the result on line 7 of Form 1040 or line 8 of Form 1040NR. Enter "SNE" on the dotted line next to the entry line. . . .						**31**	

TIP You may be able to claim the adoption credit in Part II on the front of this form if either of the following applies.

- The total adoption expenses you paid in 2006 were not fully reimbursed by your employer and the adoption became final in 2006 or earlier.
- You adopted a child with special needs and the adoption became final in 2006.

2006 Tax Table

⚠ CAUTION

See the instructions for line 44 that begin on page 36 to see if you must use the Tax Table below to figure your tax.

Example. Mr. and Mrs. Brown are filing a joint return. Their taxable income on Form 1040, line 43, is $25,300. First, they find the $25,300–25,350 taxable income line. Next, they find the column for married filing jointly and read down the column. The amount shown where the taxable income line and filing status column meet is $3,044. This is the tax amount they should include on Form 1040, line 44.

Sample Table

At least	But less than	Single	Married filing jointly *	Married filing sepa-rately	Head of a house-hold
		Your tax is—			
25,200	**25,250**	3,406	3,029	3,406	3,246
25,250	**25,300**	3,414	3,036	3,414	3,254
25,300	**25,350**	3,421	(3,044)	3,421	3,261
25,350	**25,400**	3,429	3,051	3,429	3,269

If line 43 (taxable income) is—		And you are—			
At least	But less than	Single	Married filing jointly *	Married filing sepa-rately	Head of a house-hold
		Your tax is—			
0	**5**	0	0	0	0
5	**15**	1	1	1	1
15	**25**	2	2	2	2
25	**50**	4	4	4	4
50	**75**	6	6	6	6
75	**100**	9	9	9	9
100	**125**	11	11	11	11
125	**150**	14	14	14	14
150	**175**	16	16	16	16
175	**200**	19	19	19	19
200	**225**	21	21	21	21
225	**250**	24	24	24	24
250	**275**	26	26	26	26
275	**300**	29	29	29	29
300	**325**	31	31	31	31
325	**350**	34	34	34	34
350	**375**	36	36	36	36
375	**400**	39	39	39	39
400	**425**	41	41	41	41
425	**450**	44	44	44	44
450	**475**	46	46	46	46
475	**500**	49	49	49	49
500	**525**	51	51	51	51
525	**550**	54	54	54	54
550	**575**	56	56	56	56
575	**600**	59	59	59	59
600	**625**	61	61	61	61
625	**650**	64	64	64	64
650	**675**	66	66	66	66
675	**700**	69	69	69	69
700	**725**	71	71	71	71
725	**750**	74	74	74	74
750	**775**	76	76	76	76
775	**800**	79	79	79	79
800	**825**	81	81	81	81
825	**850**	84	84	84	84
850	**875**	86	86	86	86
875	**900**	89	89	89	89
900	**925**	91	91	91	91
925	**950**	94	94	94	94
950	**975**	96	96	96	96
975	**1,000**	99	99	99	99
1,000					
1,000	**1,025**	101	101	101	101
1,025	**1,050**	104	104	104	104
1,050	**1,075**	106	106	106	106
1,075	**1,100**	109	109	109	109
1,100	**1,125**	111	111	111	111
1,125	**1,150**	114	114	114	114
1,150	**1,175**	116	116	116	116
1,175	**1,200**	119	119	119	119
1,200	**1,225**	121	121	121	121
1,225	**1,250**	124	124	124	124
1,250	**1,275**	126	126	126	126
1,275	**1,300**	129	129	129	129

If line 43 (taxable income) is—		And you are—			
At least	But less than	Single	Married filing jointly *	Married filing sepa-rately	Head of a house-hold
		Your tax is—			
1,300	**1,325**	131	131	131	131
1,325	**1,350**	134	134	134	134
1,350	**1,375**	136	136	136	136
1,375	**1,400**	139	139	139	139
1,400	**1,425**	141	141	141	141
1,425	**1,450**	144	144	144	144
1,450	**1,475**	146	146	146	146
1,475	**1,500**	149	149	149	149
1,500	**1,525**	151	151	151	151
1,525	**1,550**	154	154	154	154
1,550	**1,575**	156	156	156	156
1,575	**1,600**	159	159	159	159
1,600	**1,625**	161	161	161	161
1,625	**1,650**	164	164	164	164
1,650	**1,675**	166	166	166	166
1,675	**1,700**	169	169	169	169
1,700	**1,725**	171	171	171	171
1,725	**1,750**	174	174	174	174
1,750	**1,775**	176	176	176	176
1,775	**1,800**	179	179	179	179
1,800	**1,825**	181	181	181	181
1,825	**1,850**	184	184	184	184
1,850	**1,875**	186	186	186	186
1,875	**1,900**	189	189	189	189
1,900	**1,925**	191	191	191	191
1,925	**1,950**	194	194	194	194
1,950	**1,975**	196	196	196	196
1,975	**2,000**	199	199	199	199
2,000					
2,000	**2,025**	201	201	201	201
2,025	**2,050**	204	204	204	204
2,050	**2,075**	206	206	206	206
2,075	**2,100**	209	209	209	209
2,100	**2,125**	211	211	211	211
2,125	**2,150**	214	214	214	214
2,150	**2,175**	216	216	216	216
2,175	**2,200**	219	219	219	219
2,200	**2,225**	221	221	221	221
2,225	**2,250**	224	224	224	224
2,250	**2,275**	226	226	226	226
2,275	**2,300**	229	229	229	229
2,300	**2,325**	231	231	231	231
2,325	**2,350**	234	234	234	234
2,350	**2,375**	236	236	236	236
2,375	**2,400**	239	239	239	239
2,400	**2,425**	241	241	241	241
2,425	**2,450**	244	244	244	244
2,450	**2,475**	246	246	246	246
2,475	**2,500**	249	249	249	249
2,500	**2,525**	251	251	251	251
2,525	**2,550**	254	254	254	254
2,550	**2,575**	256	256	256	256
2,575	**2,600**	259	259	259	259
2,600	**2,625**	261	261	261	261
2,625	**2,650**	264	264	264	264
2,650	**2,675**	266	266	266	266
2,675	**2,700**	269	269	269	269

If line 43 (taxable income) is—		And you are—			
At least	But less than	Single	Married filing jointly *	Married filing sepa-rately	Head of a house-hold
		Your tax is—			
2,700	**2,725**	271	271	271	271
2,725	**2,750**	274	274	274	274
2,750	**2,775**	276	276	276	276
2,775	**2,800**	279	279	279	279
2,800	**2,825**	281	281	281	281
2,825	**2,850**	284	284	284	284
2,850	**2,875**	286	286	286	286
2,875	**2,900**	289	289	289	289
2,900	**2,925**	291	291	291	291
2,925	**2,950**	294	294	294	294
2,950	**2,975**	296	296	296	296
2,975	**3,000**	299	299	299	299
3,000					
3,000	**3,050**	303	303	303	303
3,050	**3,100**	308	308	308	308
3,100	**3,150**	313	313	313	313
3,150	**3,200**	318	318	318	318
3,200	**3,250**	323	323	323	323
3,250	**3,300**	328	328	328	328
3,300	**3,350**	333	333	333	333
3,350	**3,400**	338	338	338	338
3,400	**3,450**	343	343	343	343
3,450	**3,500**	348	348	348	348
3,500	**3,550**	353	353	353	353
3,550	**3,600**	358	358	358	358
3,600	**3,650**	363	363	363	363
3,650	**3,700**	368	368	368	368
3,700	**3,750**	373	373	373	373
3,750	**3,800**	378	378	378	378
3,800	**3,850**	383	383	383	383
3,850	**3,900**	388	388	388	388
3,900	**3,950**	393	393	393	393
3,950	**4,000**	398	398	398	398
4,000					
4,000	**4,050**	403	403	403	403
4,050	**4,100**	408	408	408	408
4,100	**4,150**	413	413	413	413
4,150	**4,200**	418	418	418	418
4,200	**4,250**	423	423	423	423
4,250	**4,300**	428	428	428	428
4,300	**4,350**	433	433	433	433
4,350	**4,400**	438	438	438	438
4,400	**4,450**	443	443	443	443
4,450	**4,500**	448	448	448	448
4,500	**4,550**	453	453	453	453
4,550	**4,600**	458	458	458	458
4,600	**4,650**	463	463	463	463
4,650	**4,700**	468	468	468	468
4,700	**4,750**	473	473	473	473
4,750	**4,800**	478	478	478	478
4,800	**4,850**	483	483	483	483
4,850	**4,900**	488	488	488	488
4,900	**4,950**	493	493	493	493
4,950	**5,000**	498	498	498	498

* This column must also be used by a qualifying widow(er).

(Continued on page 68)

2006 Tax Table–*Continued*

If line 43 (taxable income) is—		And you are—			
At least	But less than	Single	Married filing jointly *	Married filing separately	Head of a household
		Your tax is—			
5,000					
5,000	5,050	503	503	503	503
5,050	5,100	508	508	508	508
5,100	5,150	513	513	513	513
5,150	5,200	518	518	518	518
5,200	5,250	523	523	523	523
5,250	5,300	528	528	528	528
5,300	5,350	533	533	533	533
5,350	5,400	538	538	538	538
5,400	5,450	543	543	543	543
5,450	5,500	548	548	548	548
5,500	5,550	553	553	553	553
5,550	5,600	558	558	558	558
5,600	5,650	563	563	563	563
5,650	5,700	568	568	568	568
5,700	5,750	573	573	573	573
5,750	5,800	578	578	578	578
5,800	5,850	583	583	583	583
5,850	5,900	588	588	588	588
5,900	5,950	593	593	593	593
5,950	6,000	598	598	598	598
6,000					
6,000	6,050	603	603	603	603
6,050	6,100	608	608	608	608
6,100	6,150	613	613	613	613
6,150	6,200	618	618	618	618
6,200	6,250	623	623	623	623
6,250	6,300	628	628	628	628
6,300	6,350	633	633	633	633
6,350	6,400	638	638	638	638
6,400	6,450	643	643	643	643
6,450	6,500	648	648	648	648
6,500	6,550	653	653	653	653
6,550	6,600	658	658	658	658
6,600	6,650	663	663	663	663
6,650	6,700	668	668	668	668
6,700	6,750	673	673	673	673
6,750	6,800	678	678	678	678
6,800	6,850	683	683	683	683
6,850	6,900	688	688	688	688
6,900	6,950	693	693	693	693
6,950	7,000	698	698	698	698
7,000					
7,000	7,050	703	703	703	703
7,050	7,100	708	708	708	708
7,100	7,150	713	713	713	713
7,150	7,200	718	718	718	718
7,200	7,250	723	723	723	723
7,250	7,300	728	728	728	728
7,300	7,350	733	733	733	733
7,350	7,400	738	738	738	738
7,400	7,450	743	743	743	743
7,450	7,500	748	748	748	748
7,500	7,550	753	753	753	753
7,550	7,600	759	758	759	758
7,600	7,650	766	763	766	763
7,650	7,700	774	768	774	768
7,700	7,750	781	773	781	773
7,750	7,800	789	778	789	778
7,800	7,850	796	783	796	783
7,850	7,900	804	788	804	788
7,900	7,950	811	793	811	793
7,950	8,000	819	798	819	798

If line 43 (taxable income) is—		And you are—			
At least	But less than	Single	Married filing jointly *	Married filing separately	Head of a household
		Your tax is—			
8,000					
8,000	8,050	826	803	826	803
8,050	8,100	834	808	834	808
8,100	8,150	841	813	841	813
8,150	8,200	849	818	849	818
8,200	8,250	856	823	856	823
8,250	8,300	864	828	864	828
8,300	8,350	871	833	871	833
8,350	8,400	879	838	879	838
8,400	8,450	886	843	886	843
8,450	8,500	894	848	894	848
8,500	8,550	901	853	901	853
8,550	8,600	909	858	909	858
8,600	8,650	916	863	916	863
8,650	8,700	924	868	924	868
8,700	8,750	931	873	931	873
8,750	8,800	939	878	939	878
8,800	8,850	946	883	946	883
8,850	8,900	954	888	954	888
8,900	8,950	961	893	961	893
8,950	9,000	969	898	969	898
9,000					
9,000	9,050	976	903	976	903
9,050	9,100	984	908	984	908
9,100	9,150	991	913	991	913
9,150	9,200	999	918	999	918
9,200	9,250	1,006	923	1,006	923
9,250	9,300	1,014	928	1,014	928
9,300	9,350	1,021	933	1,021	933
9,350	9,400	1,029	938	1,029	938
9,400	9,450	1,036	943	1,036	943
9,450	9,500	1,044	948	1,044	948
9,500	9,550	1,051	953	1,051	953
9,550	9,600	1,059	958	1,059	958
9,600	9,650	1,066	963	1,066	963
9,650	9,700	1,074	968	1,074	968
9,700	9,750	1,081	973	1,081	973
9,750	9,800	1,089	978	1,089	978
9,800	9,850	1,096	983	1,096	983
9,850	9,900	1,104	988	1,104	988
9,900	9,950	1,111	993	1,111	993
9,950	10,000	1,119	998	1,119	998
10,000					
10,000	10,050	1,126	1,003	1,126	1,003
10,050	10,100	1,134	1,008	1,134	1,008
10,100	10,150	1,141	1,013	1,141	1,013
10,150	10,200	1,149	1,018	1,149	1,018
10,200	10,250	1,156	1,023	1,156	1,023
10,250	10,300	1,164	1,028	1,164	1,028
10,300	10,350	1,171	1,033	1,171	1,033
10,350	10,400	1,179	1,038	1,179	1,038
10,400	10,450	1,186	1,043	1,186	1,043
10,450	10,500	1,194	1,048	1,194	1,048
10,500	10,550	1,201	1,053	1,201	1,053
10,550	10,600	1,209	1,058	1,209	1,058
10,600	10,650	1,216	1,063	1,216	1,063
10,650	10,700	1,224	1,068	1,224	1,068
10,700	10,750	1,231	1,073	1,231	1,073
10,750	10,800	1,239	1,078	1,239	1,079
10,800	10,850	1,246	1,083	1,246	1,086
10,850	10,900	1,254	1,088	1,254	1,094
10,900	10,950	1,261	1,093	1,261	1,101
10,950	11,000	1,269	1,098	1,269	1,109

If line 43 (taxable income) is—		And you are—			
At least	But less than	Single	Married filing jointly *	Married filing separately	Head of a household
		Your tax is—			
11,000					
11,000	11,050	1,276	1,103	1,276	1,116
11,050	11,100	1,284	1,108	1,284	1,124
11,100	11,150	1,291	1,113	1,291	1,131
11,150	11,200	1,299	1,118	1,299	1,139
11,200	11,250	1,306	1,123	1,306	1,146
11,250	11,300	1,314	1,128	1,314	1,154
11,300	11,350	1,321	1,133	1,321	1,161
11,350	11,400	1,329	1,138	1,329	1,169
11,400	11,450	1,336	1,143	1,336	1,176
11,450	11,500	1,344	1,148	1,344	1,184
11,500	11,550	1,351	1,153	1,351	1,191
11,550	11,600	1,359	1,158	1,359	1,199
11,600	11,650	1,366	1,163	1,366	1,206
11,650	11,700	1,374	1,168	1,374	1,214
11,700	11,750	1,381	1,173	1,381	1,221
11,750	11,800	1,389	1,178	1,389	1,229
11,800	11,850	1,396	1,183	1,396	1,236
11,850	11,900	1,404	1,188	1,404	1,244
11,900	11,950	1,411	1,193	1,411	1,251
11,950	12,000	1,419	1,198	1,419	1,259
12,000					
12,000	12,050	1,426	1,203	1,426	1,266
12,050	12,100	1,434	1,208	1,434	1,274
12,100	12,150	1,441	1,213	1,441	1,281
12,150	12,200	1,449	1,218	1,449	1,289
12,200	12,250	1,456	1,223	1,456	1,296
12,250	12,300	1,464	1,228	1,464	1,304
12,300	12,350	1,471	1,233	1,471	1,311
12,350	12,400	1,479	1,238	1,479	1,319
12,400	12,450	1,486	1,243	1,486	1,326
12,450	12,500	1,494	1,248	1,494	1,334
12,500	12,550	1,501	1,253	1,501	1,341
12,550	12,600	1,509	1,258	1,509	1,349
12,600	12,650	1,516	1,263	1,516	1,356
12,650	12,700	1,524	1,268	1,524	1,364
12,700	12,750	1,531	1,273	1,531	1,371
12,750	12,800	1,539	1,278	1,539	1,379
12,800	12,850	1,546	1,283	1,546	1,386
12,850	12,900	1,554	1,288	1,554	1,394
12,900	12,950	1,561	1,293	1,561	1,401
12,950	13,000	1,569	1,298	1,569	1,409
13,000					
13,000	13,050	1,576	1,303	1,576	1,416
13,050	13,100	1,584	1,308	1,584	1,424
13,100	13,150	1,591	1,313	1,591	1,431
13,150	13,200	1,599	1,318	1,599	1,439
13,200	13,250	1,606	1,323	1,606	1,446
13,250	13,300	1,614	1,328	1,614	1,454
13,300	13,350	1,621	1,333	1,621	1,461
13,350	13,400	1,629	1,338	1,629	1,469
13,400	13,450	1,636	1,343	1,636	1,476
13,450	13,500	1,644	1,348	1,644	1,484
13,500	13,550	1,651	1,353	1,651	1,491
13,550	13,600	1,659	1,358	1,659	1,499
13,600	13,650	1,666	1,363	1,666	1,506
13,650	13,700	1,674	1,368	1,674	1,514
13,700	13,750	1,681	1,373	1,681	1,521
13,750	13,800	1,689	1,378	1,689	1,529
13,800	13,850	1,696	1,383	1,696	1,536
13,850	13,900	1,704	1,388	1,704	1,544
13,900	13,950	1,711	1,393	1,711	1,551
13,950	14,000	1,719	1,398	1,719	1,559

* This column must also be used by a qualifying widow(er).

(Continued on page 69)

If line 43 (taxable income) is—		And you are—			
At least	But less than	Single	Married filing jointly *	Married filing separately	Head of a household
		Your tax is—			
14,000					
14,000	**14,050**	1,726	1,403	1,726	1,566
14,050	**14,100**	1,734	1,408	1,734	1,574
14,100	**14,150**	1,741	1,413	1,741	1,581
14,150	**14,200**	1,749	1,418	1,749	1,589
14,200	**14,250**	1,756	1,423	1,756	1,596
14,250	**14,300**	1,764	1,428	1,764	1,604
14,300	**14,350**	1,771	1,433	1,771	1,611
14,350	**14,400**	1,779	1,438	1,779	1,619
14,400	**14,450**	1,786	1,443	1,786	1,626
14,450	**14,500**	1,794	1,448	1,794	1,634
14,500	**14,550**	1,801	1,453	1,801	1,641
14,550	**14,600**	1,809	1,458	1,809	1,649
14,600	**14,650**	1,816	1,463	1,816	1,656
14,650	**14,700**	1,824	1,468	1,824	1,664
14,700	**14,750**	1,831	1,473	1,831	1,671
14,750	**14,800**	1,839	1,478	1,839	1,679
14,800	**14,850**	1,846	1,483	1,846	1,686
14,850	**14,900**	1,854	1,488	1,854	1,694
14,900	**14,950**	1,861	1,493	1,861	1,701
14,950	**15,000**	1,869	1,498	1,869	1,709
15,000					
15,000	**15,050**	1,876	1,503	1,876	1,716
15,050	**15,100**	1,884	1,508	1,884	1,724
15,100	**15,150**	1,891	1,514	1,891	1,731
15,150	**15,200**	1,899	1,521	1,899	1,739
15,200	**15,250**	1,906	1,529	1,906	1,746
15,250	**15,300**	1,914	1,536	1,914	1,754
15,300	**15,350**	1,921	1,544	1,921	1,761
15,350	**15,400**	1,929	1,551	1,929	1,769
15,400	**15,450**	1,936	1,559	1,936	1,776
15,450	**15,500**	1,944	1,566	1,944	1,784
15,500	**15,550**	1,951	1,574	1,951	1,791
15,550	**15,600**	1,959	1,581	1,959	1,799
15,600	**15,650**	1,966	1,589	1,966	1,806
15,650	**15,700**	1,974	1,596	1,974	1,814
15,700	**15,750**	1,981	1,604	1,981	1,821
15,750	**15,800**	1,989	1,611	1,989	1,829
15,800	**15,850**	1,996	1,619	1,996	1,836
15,850	**15,900**	2,004	1,626	2,004	1,844
15,900	**15,950**	2,011	1,634	2,011	1,851
15,950	**16,000**	2,019	1,641	2,019	1,859
16,000					
16,000	**16,050**	2,026	1,649	2,026	1,866
16,050	**16,100**	2,034	1,656	2,034	1,874
16,100	**16,150**	2,041	1,664	2,041	1,881
16,150	**16,200**	2,049	1,671	2,049	1,889
16,200	**16,250**	2,056	1,679	2,056	1,896
16,250	**16,300**	2,064	1,686	2,064	1,904
16,300	**16,350**	2,071	1,694	2,071	1,911
16,350	**16,400**	2,079	1,701	2,079	1,919
16,400	**16,450**	2,086	1,709	2,086	1,926
16,450	**16,500**	2,094	1,716	2,094	1,934
16,500	**16,550**	2,101	1,724	2,101	1,941
16,550	**16,600**	2,109	1,731	2,109	1,949
16,600	**16,650**	2,116	1,739	2,116	1,956
16,650	**16,700**	2,124	1,746	2,124	1,964
16,700	**16,750**	2,131	1,754	2,131	1,971
16,750	**16,800**	2,139	1,761	2,139	1,979
16,800	**16,850**	2,146	1,769	2,146	1,986
16,850	**16,900**	2,154	1,776	2,154	1,994
16,900	**16,950**	2,161	1,784	2,161	2,001
16,950	**17,000**	2,169	1,791	2,169	2,009

If line 43 (taxable income) is—		And you are—			
At least	But less than	Single	Married filing jointly *	Married filing separately	Head of a household
		Your tax is—			
17,000					
17,000	**17,050**	2,176	1,799	2,176	2,016
17,050	**17,100**	2,184	1,806	2,184	2,024
17,100	**17,150**	2,191	1,814	2,191	2,031
17,150	**17,200**	2,199	1,821	2,199	2,039
17,200	**17,250**	2,206	1,829	2,206	2,046
17,250	**17,300**	2,214	1,836	2,214	2,054
17,300	**17,350**	2,221	1,844	2,221	2,061
17,350	**17,400**	2,229	1,851	2,229	2,069
17,400	**17,450**	2,236	1,859	2,236	2,076
17,450	**17,500**	2,244	1,866	2,244	2,084
17,500	**17,550**	2,251	1,874	2,251	2,091
17,550	**17,600**	2,259	1,881	2,259	2,099
17,600	**17,650**	2,266	1,889	2,266	2,106
17,650	**17,700**	2,274	1,896	2,274	2,114
17,700	**17,750**	2,281	1,904	2,281	2,121
17,750	**17,800**	2,289	1,911	2,289	2,129
17,800	**17,850**	2,296	1,919	2,296	2,136
17,850	**17,900**	2,304	1,926	2,304	2,144
17,900	**17,950**	2,311	1,934	2,311	2,151
17,950	**18,000**	2,319	1,941	2,319	2,159
18,000					
18,000	**18,050**	2,326	1,949	2,326	2,166
18,050	**18,100**	2,334	1,956	2,334	2,174
18,100	**18,150**	2,341	1,964	2,341	2,181
18,150	**18,200**	2,349	1,971	2,349	2,189
18,200	**18,250**	2,356	1,979	2,356	2,196
18,250	**18,300**	2,364	1,986	2,364	2,204
18,300	**18,350**	2,371	1,994	2,371	2,211
18,350	**18,400**	2,379	2,001	2,379	2,219
18,400	**18,450**	2,386	2,009	2,386	2,226
18,450	**18,500**	2,394	2,016	2,394	2,234
18,500	**18,550**	2,401	2,024	2,401	2,241
18,550	**18,600**	2,409	2,031	2,409	2,249
18,600	**18,650**	2,416	2,039	2,416	2,256
18,650	**18,700**	2,424	2,046	2,424	2,264
18,700	**18,750**	2,431	2,054	2,431	2,271
18,750	**18,800**	2,439	2,061	2,439	2,279
18,800	**18,850**	2,446	2,069	2,446	2,286
18,850	**18,900**	2,454	2,076	2,454	2,294
18,900	**18,950**	2,461	2,084	2,461	2,301
18,950	**19,000**	2,469	2,091	2,469	2,309
19,000					
19,000	**19,050**	2,476	2,099	2,476	2,316
19,050	**19,100**	2,484	2,106	2,484	2,324
19,100	**19,150**	2,491	2,114	2,491	2,331
19,150	**19,200**	2,499	2,121	2,499	2,339
19,200	**19,250**	2,506	2,129	2,506	2,346
19,250	**19,300**	2,514	2,136	2,514	2,354
19,300	**19,350**	2,521	2,144	2,521	2,361
19,350	**19,400**	2,529	2,151	2,529	2,369
19,400	**19,450**	2,536	2,159	2,536	2,376
19,450	**19,500**	2,544	2,166	2,544	2,384
19,500	**19,550**	2,551	2,174	2,551	2,391
19,550	**19,600**	2,559	2,181	2,559	2,399
19,600	**19,650**	2,566	2,189	2,566	2,406
19,650	**19,700**	2,574	2,196	2,574	2,414
19,700	**19,750**	2,581	2,204	2,581	2,421
19,750	**19,800**	2,589	2,211	2,589	2,429
19,800	**19,850**	2,596	2,219	2,596	2,436
19,850	**19,900**	2,604	2,226	2,604	2,444
19,900	**19,950**	2,611	2,234	2,611	2,451
19,950	**20,000**	2,619	2,241	2,619	2,459

If line 43 (taxable income) is—		And you are—			
At least	But less than	Single	Married filing jointly *	Married filing separately	Head of a household
		Your tax is—			
20,000					
20,000	**20,050**	2,626	2,249	2,626	2,466
20,050	**20,100**	2,634	2,256	2,634	2,474
20,100	**20,150**	2,641	2,264	2,641	2,481
20,150	**20,200**	2,649	2,271	2,649	2,489
20,200	**20,250**	2,656	2,279	2,656	2,496
20,250	**20,300**	2,664	2,286	2,664	2,504
20,300	**20,350**	2,671	2,294	2,671	2,511
20,350	**20,400**	2,679	2,301	2,679	2,519
20,400	**20,450**	2,686	2,309	2,686	2,526
20,450	**20,500**	2,694	2,316	2,694	2,534
20,500	**20,550**	2,701	2,324	2,701	2,541
20,550	**20,600**	2,709	2,331	2,709	2,549
20,600	**20,650**	2,716	2,339	2,716	2,556
20,650	**20,700**	2,724	2,346	2,724	2,564
20,700	**20,750**	2,731	2,354	2,731	2,571
20,750	**20,800**	2,739	2,361	2,739	2,579
20,800	**20,850**	2,746	2,369	2,746	2,586
20,850	**20,900**	2,754	2,376	2,754	2,594
20,900	**20,950**	2,761	2,384	2,761	2,601
20,950	**21,000**	2,769	2,391	2,769	2,609
21,000					
21,000	**21,050**	2,776	2,399	2,776	2,616
21,050	**21,100**	2,784	2,406	2,784	2,624
21,100	**21,150**	2,791	2,414	2,791	2,631
21,150	**21,200**	2,799	2,421	2,799	2,639
21,200	**21,250**	2,806	2,429	2,806	2,646
21,250	**21,300**	2,814	2,436	2,814	2,654
21,300	**21,350**	2,821	2,444	2,821	2,661
21,350	**21,400**	2,829	2,451	2,829	2,669
21,400	**21,450**	2,836	2,459	2,836	2,676
21,450	**21,500**	2,844	2,466	2,844	2,684
21,500	**21,550**	2,851	2,474	2,851	2,691
21,550	**21,600**	2,859	2,481	2,859	2,699
21,600	**21,650**	2,866	2,489	2,866	2,706
21,650	**21,700**	2,874	2,496	2,874	2,714
21,700	**21,750**	2,881	2,504	2,881	2,721
21,750	**21,800**	2,889	2,511	2,889	2,729
21,800	**21,850**	2,896	2,519	2,896	2,736
21,850	**21,900**	2,904	2,526	2,904	2,744
21,900	**21,950**	2,911	2,534	2,911	2,751
21,950	**22,000**	2,919	2,541	2,919	2,759
22,000					
22,000	**22,050**	2,926	2,549	2,926	2,766
22,050	**22,100**	2,934	2,556	2,934	2,774
22,100	**22,150**	2,941	2,564	2,941	2,781
22,150	**22,200**	2,949	2,571	2,949	2,789
22,200	**22,250**	2,956	2,579	2,956	2,796
22,250	**22,300**	2,964	2,586	2,964	2,804
22,300	**22,350**	2,971	2,594	2,971	2,811
22,350	**22,400**	2,979	2,601	2,979	2,819
22,400	**22,450**	2,986	2,609	2,986	2,826
22,450	**22,500**	2,994	2,616	2,994	2,834
22,500	**22,550**	3,001	2,624	3,001	2,841
22,550	**22,600**	3,009	2,631	3,009	2,849
22,600	**22,650**	3,016	2,639	3,016	2,856
22,650	**22,700**	3,024	2,646	3,024	2,864
22,700	**22,750**	3,031	2,654	3,031	2,871
22,750	**22,800**	3,039	2,661	3,039	2,879
22,800	**22,850**	3,046	2,669	3,046	2,886
22,850	**22,900**	3,054	2,676	3,054	2,894
22,900	**22,950**	3,061	2,684	3,061	2,901
22,950	**23,000**	3,069	2,691	3,069	2,909

* This column must also be used by a qualifying widow(er).

(Continued on page 70)

If line 43 (taxable income) is—		And you are—			
At least	But less than	Single	Married filing jointly *	Married filing sepa-rately	Head of a house-hold
		Your tax is—			
23,000					
23,000	**23,050**	3,076	2,699	3,076	2,916
23,050	**23,100**	3,084	2,706	3,084	2,924
23,100	**23,150**	3,091	2,714	3,091	2,931
23,150	**23,200**	3,099	2,721	3,099	2,939
23,200	**23,250**	3,106	2,729	3,106	2,946
23,250	**23,300**	3,114	2,736	3,114	2,954
23,300	**23,350**	3,121	2,744	3,121	2,961
23,350	**23,400**	3,129	2,751	3,129	2,969
23,400	**23,450**	3,136	2,759	3,136	2,976
23,450	**23,500**	3,144	2,766	3,144	2,984
23,500	**23,550**	3,151	2,774	3,151	2,991
23,550	**23,600**	3,159	2,781	3,159	2,999
23,600	**23,650**	3,166	2,789	3,166	3,006
23,650	**23,700**	3,174	2,796	3,174	3,014
23,700	**23,750**	3,181	2,804	3,181	3,021
23,750	**23,800**	3,189	2,811	3,189	3,029
23,800	**23,850**	3,196	2,819	3,196	3,036
23,850	**23,900**	3,204	2,826	3,204	3,044
23,900	**23,950**	3,211	2,834	3,211	3,051
23,950	**24,000**	3,219	2,841	3,219	3,059
24,000					
24,000	**24,050**	3,226	2,849	3,226	3,066
24,050	**24,100**	3,234	2,856	3,234	3,074
24,100	**24,150**	3,241	2,864	3,241	3,081
24,150	**24,200**	3,249	2,871	3,249	3,089
24,200	**24,250**	3,256	2,879	3,256	3,096
24,250	**24,300**	3,264	2,886	3,264	3,104
24,300	**24,350**	3,271	2,894	3,271	3,111
24,350	**24,400**	3,279	2,901	3,279	3,119
24,400	**24,450**	3,286	2,909	3,286	3,126
24,450	**24,500**	3,294	2,916	3,294	3,134
24,500	**24,550**	3,301	2,924	3,301	3,141
24,550	**24,600**	3,309	2,931	3,309	3,149
24,600	**24,650**	3,316	2,939	3,316	3,156
24,650	**24,700**	3,324	2,946	3,324	3,164
24,700	**24,750**	3,331	2,954	3,331	3,171
24,750	**24,800**	3,339	2,961	3,339	3,179
24,800	**24,850**	3,346	2,969	3,346	3,186
24,850	**24,900**	3,354	2,976	3,354	3,194
24,900	**24,950**	3,361	2,984	3,361	3,201
24,950	**25,000**	3,369	2,991	3,369	3,209
25,000					
25,000	**25,050**	3,376	2,999	3,376	3,216
25,050	**25,100**	3,384	3,006	3,384	3,224
25,100	**25,150**	3,391	3,014	3,391	3,231
25,150	**25,200**	3,399	3,021	3,399	3,239
25,200	**25,250**	3,406	3,029	3,406	3,246
25,250	**25,300**	3,414	3,036	3,414	3,254
25,300	**25,350**	3,421	3,044	3,421	3,261
25,350	**25,400**	3,429	3,051	3,429	3,269
25,400	**25,450**	3,436	3,059	3,436	3,276
25,450	**25,500**	3,444	3,066	3,444	3,284
25,500	**25,550**	3,451	3,074	3,451	3,291
25,550	**25,600**	3,459	3,081	3,459	3,299
25,600	**25,650**	3,466	3,089	3,466	3,306
25,650	**25,700**	3,474	3,096	3,474	3,314
25,700	**25,750**	3,481	3,104	3,481	3,321
25,750	**25,800**	3,489	3,111	3,489	3,329
25,800	**25,850**	3,496	3,119	3,496	3,336
25,850	**25,900**	3,504	3,126	3,504	3,344
25,900	**25,950**	3,511	3,134	3,511	3,351
25,950	**26,000**	3,519	3,141	3,519	3,359
26,000					
26,000	**26,050**	3,526	3,149	3,526	3,366
26,050	**26,100**	3,534	3,156	3,534	3,374
26,100	**26,150**	3,541	3,164	3,541	3,381
26,150	**26,200**	3,549	3,171	3,549	3,389
26,200	**26,250**	3,556	3,179	3,556	3,396
26,250	**26,300**	3,564	3,186	3,564	3,404
26,300	**26,350**	3,571	3,194	3,571	3,411
26,350	**26,400**	3,579	3,201	3,579	3,419
26,400	**26,450**	3,586	3,209	3,586	3,426
26,450	**26,500**	3,594	3,216	3,594	3,434
26,500	**26,550**	3,601	3,224	3,601	3,441
26,550	**26,600**	3,609	3,231	3,609	3,449
26,600	**26,650**	3,616	3,239	3,616	3,456
26,650	**26,700**	3,624	3,246	3,624	3,464
26,700	**26,750**	3,631	3,254	3,631	3,471
26,750	**26,800**	3,639	3,261	3,639	3,479
26,800	**26,850**	3,646	3,269	3,646	3,486
26,850	**26,900**	3,654	3,276	3,654	3,494
26,900	**26,950**	3,661	3,284	3,661	3,501
26,950	**27,000**	3,669	3,291	3,669	3,509
27,000					
27,000	**27,050**	3,676	3,299	3,676	3,516
27,050	**27,100**	3,684	3,306	3,684	3,524
27,100	**27,150**	3,691	3,314	3,691	3,531
27,150	**27,200**	3,699	3,321	3,699	3,539
27,200	**27,250**	3,706	3,329	3,706	3,546
27,250	**27,300**	3,714	3,336	3,714	3,554
27,300	**27,350**	3,721	3,344	3,721	3,561
27,350	**27,400**	3,729	3,351	3,729	3,569
27,400	**27,450**	3,736	3,359	3,736	3,576
27,450	**27,500**	3,744	3,366	3,744	3,584
27,500	**27,550**	3,751	3,374	3,751	3,591
27,550	**27,600**	3,759	3,381	3,759	3,599
27,600	**27,650**	3,766	3,389	3,766	3,606
27,650	**27,700**	3,774	3,396	3,774	3,614
27,700	**27,750**	3,781	3,404	3,781	3,621
27,750	**27,800**	3,789	3,411	3,789	3,629
27,800	**27,850**	3,796	3,419	3,796	3,636
27,850	**27,900**	3,804	3,426	3,804	3,644
27,900	**27,950**	3,811	3,434	3,811	3,651
27,950	**28,000**	3,819	3,441	3,819	3,659
28,000					
28,000	**28,050**	3,826	3,449	3,826	3,666
28,050	**28,100**	3,834	3,456	3,834	3,674
28,100	**28,150**	3,841	3,464	3,841	3,681
28,150	**28,200**	3,849	3,471	3,849	3,689
28,200	**28,250**	3,856	3,479	3,856	3,696
28,250	**28,300**	3,864	3,486	3,864	3,704
28,300	**28,350**	3,871	3,494	3,871	3,711
28,350	**28,400**	3,879	3,501	3,879	3,719
28,400	**28,450**	3,886	3,509	3,886	3,726
28,450	**28,500**	3,894	3,516	3,894	3,734
28,500	**28,550**	3,901	3,524	3,901	3,741
28,550	**28,600**	3,909	3,531	3,909	3,749
28,600	**28,650**	3,916	3,539	3,916	3,756
28,650	**28,700**	3,924	3,546	3,924	3,764
28,700	**28,750**	3,931	3,554	3,931	3,771
28,750	**28,800**	3,939	3,561	3,939	3,779
28,800	**28,850**	3,946	3,569	3,946	3,786
28,850	**28,900**	3,954	3,576	3,954	3,794
28,900	**28,950**	3,961	3,584	3,961	3,801
28,950	**29,000**	3,969	3,591	3,969	3,809
29,000					
29,000	**29,050**	3,976	3,599	3,976	3,816
29,050	**29,100**	3,984	3,606	3,984	3,824
29,100	**29,150**	3,991	3,614	3,991	3,831
29,150	**29,200**	3,999	3,621	3,999	3,839
29,200	**29,250**	4,006	3,629	4,006	3,846
29,250	**29,300**	4,014	3,636	4,014	3,854
29,300	**29,350**	4,021	3,644	4,021	3,861
29,350	**29,400**	4,029	3,651	4,029	3,869
29,400	**29,450**	4,036	3,659	4,036	3,876
29,450	**29,500**	4,044	3,666	4,044	3,884
29,500	**29,550**	4,051	3,674	4,051	3,891
29,550	**29,600**	4,059	3,681	4,059	3,899
29,600	**29,650**	4,066	3,689	4,066	3,906
29,650	**29,700**	4,074	3,696	4,074	3,914
29,700	**29,750**	4,081	3,704	4,081	3,921
29,750	**29,800**	4,089	3,711	4,089	3,929
29,800	**29,850**	4,096	3,719	4,096	3,936
29,850	**29,900**	4,104	3,726	4,104	3,944
29,900	**29,950**	4,111	3,734	4,111	3,951
29,950	**30,000**	4,119	3,741	4,119	3,959
30,000					
30,000	**30,050**	4,126	3,749	4,126	3,966
30,050	**30,100**	4,134	3,756	4,134	3,974
30,100	**30,150**	4,141	3,764	4,141	3,981
30,150	**30,200**	4,149	3,771	4,149	3,989
30,200	**30,250**	4,156	3,779	4,156	3,996
30,250	**30,300**	4,164	3,786	4,164	4,004
30,300	**30,350**	4,171	3,794	4,171	4,011
30,350	**30,400**	4,179	3,801	4,179	4,019
30,400	**30,450**	4,186	3,809	4,186	4,026
30,450	**30,500**	4,194	3,816	4,194	4,034
30,500	**30,550**	4,201	3,824	4,201	4,041
30,550	**30,600**	4,209	3,831	4,209	4,049
30,600	**30,650**	4,216	3,839	4,216	4,056
30,650	**30,700**	4,226	3,846	4,226	4,064
30,700	**30,750**	4,239	3,854	4,239	4,071
30,750	**30,800**	4,251	3,861	4,251	4,079
30,800	**30,850**	4,264	3,869	4,264	4,086
30,850	**30,900**	4,276	3,876	4,276	4,094
30,900	**30,950**	4,289	3,884	4,289	4,101
30,950	**31,000**	4,301	3,891	4,301	4,109
31,000					
31,000	**31,050**	4,314	3,899	4,314	4,116
31,050	**31,100**	4,326	3,906	4,326	4,124
31,100	**31,150**	4,339	3,914	4,339	4,131
31,150	**31,200**	4,351	3,921	4,351	4,139
31,200	**31,250**	4,364	3,929	4,364	4,146
31,250	**31,300**	4,376	3,936	4,376	4,154
31,300	**31,350**	4,389	3,944	4,389	4,161
31,350	**31,400**	4,401	3,951	4,401	4,169
31,400	**31,450**	4,414	3,959	4,414	4,176
31,450	**31,500**	4,426	3,966	4,426	4,184
31,500	**31,550**	4,439	3,974	4,439	4,191
31,550	**31,600**	4,451	3,981	4,451	4,199
31,600	**31,650**	4,464	3,989	4,464	4,206
31,650	**31,700**	4,476	3,996	4,476	4,214
31,700	**31,750**	4,489	4,004	4,489	4,221
31,750	**31,800**	4,501	4,011	4,501	4,229
31,800	**31,850**	4,514	4,019	4,514	4,236
31,850	**31,900**	4,526	4,026	4,526	4,244
31,900	**31,950**	4,539	4,034	4,539	4,251
31,950	**32,000**	4,551	4,041	4,551	4,259

* This column must also be used by a qualifying widow(er).

(Continued on page 71)

If line 43 (taxable income) is—		And you are—			
At least	But less than	Single	Married filing jointly *	Married filing separately	Head of a household
		Your tax is—			
32,000					
32,000	**32,050**	4,564	4,049	4,564	4,266
32,050	**32,100**	4,576	4,056	4,576	4,274
32,100	**32,150**	4,589	4,064	4,589	4,281
32,150	**32,200**	4,601	4,071	4,601	4,289
32,200	**32,250**	4,614	4,079	4,614	4,296
32,250	**32,300**	4,626	4,086	4,626	4,304
32,300	**32,350**	4,639	4,094	4,639	4,311
32,350	**32,400**	4,651	4,101	4,651	4,319
32,400	**32,450**	4,664	4,109	4,664	4,326
32,450	**32,500**	4,676	4,116	4,676	4,334
32,500	**32,550**	4,689	4,124	4,689	4,341
32,550	**32,600**	4,701	4,131	4,701	4,349
32,600	**32,650**	4,714	4,139	4,714	4,356
32,650	**32,700**	4,726	4,146	4,726	4,364
32,700	**32,750**	4,739	4,154	4,739	4,371
32,750	**32,800**	4,751	4,161	4,751	4,379
32,800	**32,850**	4,764	4,169	4,764	4,386
32,850	**32,900**	4,776	4,176	4,776	4,394
32,900	**32,950**	4,789	4,184	4,789	4,401
32,950	**33,000**	4,801	4,191	4,801	4,409
33,000					
33,000	**33,050**	4,814	4,199	4,814	4,416
33,050	**33,100**	4,826	4,206	4,826	4,424
33,100	**33,150**	4,839	4,214	4,839	4,431
33,150	**33,200**	4,851	4,221	4,851	4,439
33,200	**33,250**	4,864	4,229	4,864	4,446
33,250	**33,300**	4,876	4,236	4,876	4,454
33,300	**33,350**	4,889	4,244	4,889	4,461
33,350	**33,400**	4,901	4,251	4,901	4,469
33,400	**33,450**	4,914	4,259	4,914	4,476
33,450	**33,500**	4,926	4,266	4,926	4,484
33,500	**33,550**	4,939	4,274	4,939	4,491
33,550	**33,600**	4,951	4,281	4,951	4,499
33,600	**33,650**	4,964	4,289	4,964	4,506
33,650	**33,700**	4,976	4,296	4,976	4,514
33,700	**33,750**	4,989	4,304	4,989	4,521
33,750	**33,800**	5,001	4,311	5,001	4,529
33,800	**33,850**	5,014	4,319	5,014	4,536
33,850	**33,900**	5,026	4,326	5,026	4,544
33,900	**33,950**	5,039	4,334	5,039	4,551
33,950	**34,000**	5,051	4,341	5,051	4,559
34,000					
34,000	**34,050**	5,064	4,349	5,064	4,566
34,050	**34,100**	5,076	4,356	5,076	4,574
34,100	**34,150**	5,089	4,364	5,089	4,581
34,150	**34,200**	5,101	4,371	5,101	4,589
34,200	**34,250**	5,114	4,379	5,114	4,596
34,250	**34,300**	5,126	4,386	5,126	4,604
34,300	**34,350**	5,139	4,394	5,139	4,611
34,350	**34,400**	5,151	4,401	5,151	4,619
34,400	**34,450**	5,164	4,409	5,164	4,626
34,450	**34,500**	5,176	4,416	5,176	4,634
34,500	**34,550**	5,189	4,424	5,189	4,641
34,550	**34,600**	5,201	4,431	5,201	4,649
34,600	**34,650**	5,214	4,439	5,214	4,656
34,650	**34,700**	5,226	4,446	5,226	4,664
34,700	**34,750**	5,239	4,454	5,239	4,671
34,750	**34,800**	5,251	4,461	5,251	4,679
34,800	**34,850**	5,264	4,469	5,264	4,686
34,850	**34,900**	5,276	4,476	5,276	4,694
34,900	**34,950**	5,289	4,484	5,289	4,701
34,950	**35,000**	5,301	4,491	5,301	4,709

If line 43 (taxable income) is—		And you are—			
At least	But less than	Single	Married filing jointly *	Married filing separately	Head of a household
		Your tax is—			
35,000					
35,000	**35,050**	5,314	4,499	5,314	4,716
35,050	**35,100**	5,326	4,506	5,326	4,724
35,100	**35,150**	5,339	4,514	5,339	4,731
35,150	**35,200**	5,351	4,521	5,351	4,739
35,200	**35,250**	5,364	4,529	5,364	4,746
35,250	**35,300**	5,376	4,536	5,376	4,754
35,300	**35,350**	5,389	4,544	5,389	4,761
35,350	**35,400**	5,401	4,551	5,401	4,769
35,400	**35,450**	5,414	4,559	5,414	4,776
35,450	**35,500**	5,426	4,566	5,426	4,784
35,500	**35,550**	5,439	4,574	5,439	4,791
35,550	**35,600**	5,451	4,581	5,451	4,799
35,600	**35,650**	5,464	4,589	5,464	4,806
35,650	**35,700**	5,476	4,596	5,476	4,814
35,700	**35,750**	5,489	4,604	5,489	4,821
35,750	**35,800**	5,501	4,611	5,501	4,829
35,800	**35,850**	5,514	4,619	5,514	4,836
35,850	**35,900**	5,526	4,626	5,526	4,844
35,900	**35,950**	5,539	4,634	5,539	4,851
35,950	**36,000**	5,551	4,641	5,551	4,859
36,000					
36,000	**36,050**	5,564	4,649	5,564	4,866
36,050	**36,100**	5,576	4,656	5,576	4,874
36,100	**36,150**	5,589	4,664	5,589	4,881
36,150	**36,200**	5,601	4,671	5,601	4,889
36,200	**36,250**	5,614	4,679	5,614	4,896
36,250	**36,300**	5,626	4,686	5,626	4,904
36,300	**36,350**	5,639	4,694	5,639	4,911
36,350	**36,400**	5,651	4,701	5,651	4,919
36,400	**36,450**	5,664	4,709	5,664	4,926
36,450	**36,500**	5,676	4,716	5,676	4,934
36,500	**36,550**	5,689	4,724	5,689	4,941
36,550	**36,600**	5,701	4,731	5,701	4,949
36,600	**36,650**	5,714	4,739	5,714	4,956
36,650	**36,700**	5,726	4,746	5,726	4,964
36,700	**36,750**	5,739	4,754	5,739	4,971
36,750	**36,800**	5,751	4,761	5,751	4,979
36,800	**36,850**	5,764	4,769	5,764	4,986
36,850	**36,900**	5,776	4,776	5,776	4,994
36,900	**36,950**	5,789	4,784	5,789	5,001
36,950	**37,000**	5,801	4,791	5,801	5,009
37,000					
37,000	**37,050**	5,814	4,799	5,814	5,016
37,050	**37,100**	5,826	4,806	5,826	5,024
37,100	**37,150**	5,839	4,814	5,839	5,031
37,150	**37,200**	5,851	4,821	5,851	5,039
37,200	**37,250**	5,864	4,829	5,864	5,046
37,250	**37,300**	5,876	4,836	5,876	5,054
37,300	**37,350**	5,889	4,844	5,889	5,061
37,350	**37,400**	5,901	4,851	5,901	5,069
37,400	**37,450**	5,914	4,859	5,914	5,076
37,450	**37,500**	5,926	4,866	5,926	5,084
37,500	**37,550**	5,939	4,874	5,939	5,091
37,550	**37,600**	5,951	4,881	5,951	5,099
37,600	**37,650**	5,964	4,889	5,964	5,106
37,650	**37,700**	5,976	4,896	5,976	5,114
37,700	**37,750**	5,989	4,904	5,989	5,121
37,750	**37,800**	6,001	4,911	6,001	5,129
37,800	**37,850**	6,014	4,919	6,014	5,136
37,850	**37,900**	6,026	4,926	6,026	5,144
37,900	**37,950**	6,039	4,934	6,039	5,151
37,950	**38,000**	6,051	4,941	6,051	5,159

If line 43 (taxable income) is—		And you are—			
At least	But less than	Single	Married filing jointly *	Married filing separately	Head of a household
		Your tax is—			
38,000					
38,000	**38,050**	6,064	4,949	6,064	5,166
38,050	**38,100**	6,076	4,956	6,076	5,174
38,100	**38,150**	6,089	4,964	6,089	5,181
38,150	**38,200**	6,101	4,971	6,101	5,189
38,200	**38,250**	6,114	4,979	6,114	5,196
38,250	**38,300**	6,126	4,986	6,126	5,204
38,300	**38,350**	6,139	4,994	6,139	5,211
38,350	**38,400**	6,151	5,001	6,151	5,219
38,400	**38,450**	6,164	5,009	6,164	5,226
38,450	**38,500**	6,176	5,016	6,176	5,234
38,500	**38,550**	6,189	5,024	6,189	5,241
38,550	**38,600**	6,201	5,031	6,201	5,249
38,600	**38,650**	6,214	5,039	6,214	5,256
38,650	**38,700**	6,226	5,046	6,226	5,264
38,700	**38,750**	6,239	5,054	6,239	5,271
38,750	**38,800**	6,251	5,061	6,251	5,279
38,800	**38,850**	6,264	5,069	6,264	5,286
38,850	**38,900**	6,276	5,076	6,276	5,294
38,900	**38,950**	6,289	5,084	6,289	5,301
38,950	**39,000**	6,301	5,091	6,301	5,309
39,000					
39,000	**39,050**	6,314	5,099	6,314	5,316
39,050	**39,100**	6,326	5,106	6,326	5,324
39,100	**39,150**	6,339	5,114	6,339	5,331
39,150	**39,200**	6,351	5,121	6,351	5,339
39,200	**39,250**	6,364	5,129	6,364	5,346
39,250	**39,300**	6,376	5,136	6,376	5,354
39,300	**39,350**	6,389	5,144	6,389	5,361
39,350	**39,400**	6,401	5,151	6,401	5,369
39,400	**39,450**	6,414	5,159	6,414	5,376
39,450	**39,500**	6,426	5,166	6,426	5,384
39,500	**39,550**	6,439	5,174	6,439	5,391
39,550	**39,600**	6,451	5,181	6,451	5,399
39,600	**39,650**	6,464	5,189	6,464	5,406
39,650	**39,700**	6,476	5,196	6,476	5,414
39,700	**39,750**	6,489	5,204	6,489	5,421
39,750	**39,800**	6,501	5,211	6,501	5,429
39,800	**39,850**	6,514	5,219	6,514	5,436
39,850	**39,900**	6,526	5,226	6,526	5,444
39,900	**39,950**	6,539	5,234	6,539	5,451
39,950	**40,000**	6,551	5,241	6,551	5,459
40,000					
40,000	**40,050**	6,564	5,249	6,564	5,466
40,050	**40,100**	6,576	5,256	6,576	5,474
40,100	**40,150**	6,589	5,264	6,589	5,481
40,150	**40,200**	6,601	5,271	6,601	5,489
40,200	**40,250**	6,614	5,279	6,614	5,496
40,250	**40,300**	6,626	5,286	6,626	5,504
40,300	**40,350**	6,639	5,294	6,639	5,511
40,350	**40,400**	6,651	5,301	6,651	5,519
40,400	**40,450**	6,664	5,309	6,664	5,526
40,450	**40,500**	6,676	5,316	6,676	5,534
40,500	**40,550**	6,689	5,324	6,689	5,541
40,550	**40,600**	6,701	5,331	6,701	5,549
40,600	**40,650**	6,714	5,339	6,714	5,556
40,650	**40,700**	6,726	5,346	6,726	5,564
40,700	**40,750**	6,739	5,354	6,739	5,571
40,750	**40,800**	6,751	5,361	6,751	5,579
40,800	**40,850**	6,764	5,369	6,764	5,586
40,850	**40,900**	6,776	5,376	6,776	5,594
40,900	**40,950**	6,789	5,384	6,789	5,601
40,950	**41,000**	6,801	5,391	6,801	5,609

* This column must also be used by a qualifying widow(er).

(Continued on page 72)

2006 Tax Table–*Continued*

If line 43 (taxable income) is— At least	But less than	And you are— Single	Married filing jointly *	Married filing sepa-rately	Head of a house-hold
		Your tax is—			
41,000					
41,000	**41,050**	6,814	5,399	6,814	5,616
41,050	**41,100**	6,826	5,406	6,826	5,626
41,100	**41,150**	6,839	5,414	6,839	5,639
41,150	**41,200**	6,851	5,421	6,851	5,651
41,200	**41,250**	6,864	5,429	6,864	5,664
41,250	**41,300**	6,876	5,436	6,876	5,676
41,300	**41,350**	6,889	5,444	6,889	5,689
41,350	**41,400**	6,901	5,451	6,901	5,701
41,400	**41,450**	6,914	5,459	6,914	5,714
41,450	**41,500**	6,926	5,466	6,926	5,726
41,500	**41,550**	6,939	5,474	6,939	5,739
41,550	**41,600**	6,951	5,481	6,951	5,751
41,600	**41,650**	6,964	5,489	6,964	5,764
41,650	**41,700**	6,976	5,496	6,976	5,776
41,700	**41,750**	6,989	5,504	6,989	5,789
41,750	**41,800**	7,001	5,511	7,001	5,801
41,800	**41,850**	7,014	5,519	7,014	5,814
41,850	**41,900**	7,026	5,526	7,026	5,826
41,900	**41,950**	7,039	5,534	7,039	5,839
41,950	**42,000**	7,051	5,541	7,051	5,851
42,000					
42,000	**42,050**	7,064	5,549	7,064	5,864
42,050	**42,100**	7,076	5,556	7,076	5,876
42,100	**42,150**	7,089	5,564	7,089	5,889
42,150	**42,200**	7,101	5,571	7,101	5,901
42,200	**42,250**	7,114	5,579	7,114	5,914
42,250	**42,300**	7,126	5,586	7,126	5,926
42,300	**42,350**	7,139	5,594	7,139	5,939
42,350	**42,400**	7,151	5,601	7,151	5,951
42,400	**42,450**	7,164	5,609	7,164	5,964
42,450	**42,500**	7,176	5,616	7,176	5,976
42,500	**42,550**	7,189	5,624	7,189	5,989
42,550	**42,600**	7,201	5,631	7,201	6,001
42,600	**42,650**	7,214	5,639	7,214	6,014
42,650	**42,700**	7,226	5,646	7,226	6,026
42,700	**42,750**	7,239	5,654	7,239	6,039
42,750	**42,800**	7,251	5,661	7,251	6,051
42,800	**42,850**	7,264	5,669	7,264	6,064
42,850	**42,900**	7,276	5,676	7,276	6,076
42,900	**42,950**	7,289	5,684	7,289	6,089
42,950	**43,000**	7,301	5,691	7,301	6,101
43,000					
43,000	**43,050**	7,314	5,699	7,314	6,114
43,050	**43,100**	7,326	5,706	7,326	6,126
43,100	**43,150**	7,339	5,714	7,339	6,139
43,150	**43,200**	7,351	5,721	7,351	6,151
43,200	**43,250**	7,364	5,729	7,364	6,164
43,250	**43,300**	7,376	5,736	7,376	6,176
43,300	**43,350**	7,389	5,744	7,389	6,189
43,350	**43,400**	7,401	5,751	7,401	6,201
43,400	**43,450**	7,414	5,759	7,414	6,214
43,450	**43,500**	7,426	5,766	7,426	6,226
43,500	**43,550**	7,439	5,774	7,439	6,239
43,550	**43,600**	7,451	5,781	7,451	6,251
43,600	**43,650**	7,464	5,789	7,464	6,264
43,650	**43,700**	7,476	5,796	7,476	6,276
43,700	**43,750**	7,489	5,804	7,489	6,289
43,750	**43,800**	7,501	5,811	7,501	6,301
43,800	**43,850**	7,514	5,819	7,514	6,314
43,850	**43,900**	7,526	5,826	7,526	6,326
43,900	**43,950**	7,539	5,834	7,539	6,339
43,950	**44,000**	7,551	5,841	7,551	6,351

If line 43 (taxable income) is— At least	But less than	And you are— Single	Married filing jointly *	Married filing sepa-rately	Head of a house-hold
		Your tax is—			
44,000					
44,000	**44,050**	7,564	5,849	7,564	6,364
44,050	**44,100**	7,576	5,856	7,576	6,376
44,100	**44,150**	7,589	5,864	7,589	6,389
44,150	**44,200**	7,601	5,871	7,601	6,401
44,200	**44,250**	7,614	5,879	7,614	6,414
44,250	**44,300**	7,626	5,886	7,626	6,426
44,300	**44,350**	7,639	5,894	7,639	6,439
44,350	**44,400**	7,651	5,901	7,651	6,451
44,400	**44,450**	7,664	5,909	7,664	6,464
44,450	**44,500**	7,676	5,916	7,676	6,476
44,500	**44,550**	7,689	5,924	7,689	6,489
44,550	**44,600**	7,701	5,931	7,701	6,501
44,600	**44,650**	7,714	5,939	7,714	6,514
44,650	**44,700**	7,726	5,946	7,726	6,526
44,700	**44,750**	7,739	5,954	7,739	6,539
44,750	**44,800**	7,751	5,961	7,751	6,551
44,800	**44,850**	7,764	5,969	7,764	6,564
44,850	**44,900**	7,776	5,976	7,776	6,576
44,900	**44,950**	7,789	5,984	7,789	6,589
44,950	**45,000**	7,801	5,991	7,801	6,601
45,000					
45,000	**45,050**	7,814	5,999	7,814	6,614
45,050	**45,100**	7,826	6,006	7,826	6,626
45,100	**45,150**	7,839	6,014	7,839	6,639
45,150	**45,200**	7,851	6,021	7,851	6,651
45,200	**45,250**	7,864	6,029	7,864	6,664
45,250	**45,300**	7,876	6,036	7,876	6,676
45,300	**45,350**	7,889	6,044	7,889	6,689
45,350	**45,400**	7,901	6,051	7,901	6,701
45,400	**45,450**	7,914	6,059	7,914	6,714
45,450	**45,500**	7,926	6,066	7,926	6,726
45,500	**45,550**	7,939	6,074	7,939	6,739
45,550	**45,600**	7,951	6,081	7,951	6,751
45,600	**45,650**	7,964	6,089	7,964	6,764
45,650	**45,700**	7,976	6,096	7,976	6,776
45,700	**45,750**	7,989	6,104	7,989	6,789
45,750	**45,800**	8,001	6,111	8,001	6,801
45,800	**45,850**	8,014	6,119	8,014	6,814
45,850	**45,900**	8,026	6,126	8,026	6,826
45,900	**45,950**	8,039	6,134	8,039	6,839
45,950	**46,000**	8,051	6,141	8,051	6,851
46,000					
46,000	**46,050**	8,064	6,149	8,064	6,864
46,050	**46,100**	8,076	6,156	8,076	6,876
46,100	**46,150**	8,089	6,164	8,089	6,889
46,150	**46,200**	8,101	6,171	8,101	6,901
46,200	**46,250**	8,114	6,179	8,114	6,914
46,250	**46,300**	8,126	6,186	8,126	6,926
46,300	**46,350**	8,139	6,194	8,139	6,939
46,350	**46,400**	8,151	6,201	8,151	6,951
46,400	**46,450**	8,164	6,209	8,164	6,964
46,450	**46,500**	8,176	6,216	8,176	6,976
46,500	**46,550**	8,189	6,224	8,189	6,989
46,550	**46,600**	8,201	6,231	8,201	7,001
46,600	**46,650**	8,214	6,239	8,214	7,014
46,650	**46,700**	8,226	6,246	8,226	7,026
46,700	**46,750**	8,239	6,254	8,239	7,039
46,750	**46,800**	8,251	6,261	8,251	7,051
46,800	**46,850**	8,264	6,269	8,264	7,064
46,850	**46,900**	8,276	6,276	8,276	7,076
46,900	**46,950**	8,289	6,284	8,289	7,089
46,950	**47,000**	8,301	6,291	8,301	7,101

If line 43 (taxable income) is— At least	But less than	And you are— Single	Married filing jointly *	Married filing sepa-rately	Head of a house-hold
		Your tax is—			
47,000					
47,000	**47,050**	8,314	6,299	8,314	7,114
47,050	**47,100**	8,326	6,306	8,326	7,126
47,100	**47,150**	8,339	6,314	8,339	7,139
47,150	**47,200**	8,351	6,321	8,351	7,151
47,200	**47,250**	8,364	6,329	8,364	7,164
47,250	**47,300**	8,376	6,336	8,376	7,176
47,300	**47,350**	8,389	6,344	8,389	7,189
47,350	**47,400**	8,401	6,351	8,401	7,201
47,400	**47,450**	8,414	6,359	8,414	7,214
47,450	**47,500**	8,426	6,366	8,426	7,226
47,500	**47,550**	8,439	6,374	8,439	7,239
47,550	**47,600**	8,451	6,381	8,451	7,251
47,600	**47,650**	8,464	6,389	8,464	7,264
47,650	**47,700**	8,476	6,396	8,476	7,276
47,700	**47,750**	8,489	6,404	8,489	7,289
47,750	**47,800**	8,501	6,411	8,501	7,301
47,800	**47,850**	8,514	6,419	8,514	7,314
47,850	**47,900**	8,526	6,426	8,526	7,326
47,900	**47,950**	8,539	6,434	8,539	7,339
47,950	**48,000**	8,551	6,441	8,551	7,351
48,000					
48,000	**48,050**	8,564	6,449	8,564	7,364
48,050	**48,100**	8,576	6,456	8,576	7,376
48,100	**48,150**	8,589	6,464	8,589	7,389
48,150	**48,200**	8,601	6,471	8,601	7,401
48,200	**48,250**	8,614	6,479	8,614	7,414
48,250	**48,300**	8,626	6,486	8,626	7,426
48,300	**48,350**	8,639	6,494	8,639	7,439
48,350	**48,400**	8,651	6,501	8,651	7,451
48,400	**48,450**	8,664	6,509	8,664	7,464
48,450	**48,500**	8,676	6,516	8,676	7,476
48,500	**48,550**	8,689	6,524	8,689	7,489
48,550	**48,600**	8,701	6,531	8,701	7,501
48,600	**48,650**	8,714	6,539	8,714	7,514
48,650	**48,700**	8,726	6,546	8,726	7,526
48,700	**48,750**	8,739	6,554	8,739	7,539
48,750	**48,800**	8,751	6,561	8,751	7,551
48,800	**48,850**	8,764	6,569	8,764	7,564
48,850	**48,900**	8,776	6,576	8,776	7,576
48,900	**48,950**	8,789	6,584	8,789	7,589
48,950	**49,000**	8,801	6,591	8,801	7,601
49,000					
49,000	**49,050**	8,814	6,599	8,814	7,614
49,050	**49,100**	8,826	6,606	8,826	7,626
49,100	**49,150**	8,839	6,614	8,839	7,639
49,150	**49,200**	8,851	6,621	8,851	7,651
49,200	**49,250**	8,864	6,629	8,864	7,664
49,250	**49,300**	8,876	6,636	8,876	7,676
49,300	**49,350**	8,889	6,644	8,889	7,689
49,350	**49,400**	8,901	6,651	8,901	7,701
49,400	**49,450**	8,914	6,659	8,914	7,714
49,450	**49,500**	8,926	6,666	8,926	7,726
49,500	**49,550**	8,939	6,674	8,939	7,739
49,550	**49,600**	8,951	6,681	8,951	7,751
49,600	**49,650**	8,964	6,689	8,964	7,764
49,650	**49,700**	8,976	6,696	8,976	7,776
49,700	**49,750**	8,989	6,704	8,989	7,789
49,750	**49,800**	9,001	6,711	9,001	7,801
49,800	**49,850**	9,014	6,719	9,014	7,814
49,850	**49,900**	9,026	6,726	9,026	7,826
49,900	**49,950**	9,039	6,734	9,039	7,839
49,950	**50,000**	9,051	6,741	9,051	7,851

* This column must also be used by a qualifying widow(er).

(Continued on page 73)

If line 43 (taxable income) is—		And you are—			
At least	But less than	Single	Married filing jointly *	Married filing separately	Head of a household
		Your tax is—			
50,000					
50,000	**50,050**	9,064	6,749	9,064	7,864
50,050	**50,100**	9,076	6,756	9,076	7,876
50,100	**50,150**	9,089	6,764	9,089	7,889
50,150	**50,200**	9,101	6,771	9,101	7,901
50,200	**50,250**	9,114	6,779	9,114	7,914
50,250	**50,300**	9,126	6,786	9,126	7,926
50,300	**50,350**	9,139	6,794	9,139	7,939
50,350	**50,400**	9,151	6,801	9,151	7,951
50,400	**50,450**	9,164	6,809	9,164	7,964
50,450	**50,500**	9,176	6,816	9,176	7,976
50,500	**50,550**	9,189	6,824	9,189	7,989
50,550	**50,600**	9,201	6,831	9,201	8,001
50,600	**50,650**	9,214	6,839	9,214	8,014
50,650	**50,700**	9,226	6,846	9,226	8,026
50,700	**50,750**	9,239	6,854	9,239	8,039
50,750	**50,800**	9,251	6,861	9,251	8,051
50,800	**50,850**	9,264	6,869	9,264	8,064
50,850	**50,900**	9,276	6,876	9,276	8,076
50,900	**50,950**	9,289	6,884	9,289	8,089
50,950	**51,000**	9,301	6,891	9,301	8,101
51,000					
51,000	**51,050**	9,314	6,899	9,314	8,114
51,050	**51,100**	9,326	6,906	9,326	8,126
51,100	**51,150**	9,339	6,914	9,339	8,139
51,150	**51,200**	9,351	6,921	9,351	8,151
51,200	**51,250**	9,364	6,929	9,364	8,164
51,250	**51,300**	9,376	6,936	9,376	8,176
51,300	**51,350**	9,389	6,944	9,389	8,189
51,350	**51,400**	9,401	6,951	9,401	8,201
51,400	**51,450**	9,414	6,959	9,414	8,214
51,450	**51,500**	9,426	6,966	9,426	8,226
51,500	**51,550**	9,439	6,974	9,439	8,239
51,550	**51,600**	9,451	6,981	9,451	8,251
51,600	**51,650**	9,464	6,989	9,464	8,264
51,650	**51,700**	9,476	6,996	9,476	8,276
51,700	**51,750**	9,489	7,004	9,489	8,289
51,750	**51,800**	9,501	7,011	9,501	8,301
51,800	**51,850**	9,514	7,019	9,514	8,314
51,850	**51,900**	9,526	7,026	9,526	8,326
51,900	**51,950**	9,539	7,034	9,539	8,339
51,950	**52,000**	9,551	7,041	9,551	8,351
52,000					
52,000	**52,050**	9,564	7,049	9,564	8,364
52,050	**52,100**	9,576	7,056	9,576	8,376
52,100	**52,150**	9,589	7,064	9,589	8,389
52,150	**52,200**	9,601	7,071	9,601	8,401
52,200	**52,250**	9,614	7,079	9,614	8,414
52,250	**52,300**	9,626	7,086	9,626	8,426
52,300	**52,350**	9,639	7,094	9,639	8,439
52,350	**52,400**	9,651	7,101	9,651	8,451
52,400	**52,450**	9,664	7,109	9,664	8,464
52,450	**52,500**	9,676	7,116	9,676	8,476
52,500	**52,550**	9,689	7,124	9,689	8,489
52,550	**52,600**	9,701	7,131	9,701	8,501
52,600	**52,650**	9,714	7,139	9,714	8,514
52,650	**52,700**	9,726	7,146	9,726	8,526
52,700	**52,750**	9,739	7,154	9,739	8,539
52,750	**52,800**	9,751	7,161	9,751	8,551
52,800	**52,850**	9,764	7,169	9,764	8,564
52,850	**52,900**	9,776	7,176	9,776	8,576
52,900	**52,950**	9,789	7,184	9,789	8,589
52,950	**53,000**	9,801	7,191	9,801	8,601
53,000					
53,000	**53,050**	9,814	7,199	9,814	8,614
53,050	**53,100**	9,826	7,206	9,826	8,626
53,100	**53,150**	9,839	7,214	9,839	8,639
53,150	**53,200**	9,851	7,221	9,851	8,651
53,200	**53,250**	9,864	7,229	9,864	8,664
53,250	**53,300**	9,876	7,236	9,876	8,676
53,300	**53,350**	9,889	7,244	9,889	8,689
53,350	**53,400**	9,901	7,251	9,901	8,701
53,400	**53,450**	9,914	7,259	9,914	8,714
53,450	**53,500**	9,926	7,266	9,926	8,726
53,500	**53,550**	9,939	7,274	9,939	8,739
53,550	**53,600**	9,951	7,281	9,951	8,751
53,600	**53,650**	9,964	7,289	9,964	8,764
53,650	**53,700**	9,976	7,296	9,976	8,776
53,700	**53,750**	9,989	7,304	9,989	8,789
53,750	**53,800**	10,001	7,311	10,001	8,801
53,800	**53,850**	10,014	7,319	10,014	8,814
53,850	**53,900**	10,026	7,326	10,026	8,826
53,900	**53,950**	10,039	7,334	10,039	8,839
53,950	**54,000**	10,051	7,341	10,051	8,851
54,000					
54,000	**54,050**	10,064	7,349	10,064	8,864
54,050	**54,100**	10,076	7,356	10,076	8,876
54,100	**54,150**	10,089	7,364	10,089	8,889
54,150	**54,200**	10,101	7,371	10,101	8,901
54,200	**54,250**	10,114	7,379	10,114	8,914
54,250	**54,300**	10,126	7,386	10,126	8,926
54,300	**54,350**	10,139	7,394	10,139	8,939
54,350	**54,400**	10,151	7,401	10,151	8,951
54,400	**54,450**	10,164	7,409	10,164	8,964
54,450	**54,500**	10,176	7,416	10,176	8,976
54,500	**54,550**	10,189	7,424	10,189	8,989
54,550	**54,600**	10,201	7,431	10,201	9,001
54,600	**54,650**	10,214	7,439	10,214	9,014
54,650	**54,700**	10,226	7,446	10,226	9,026
54,700	**54,750**	10,239	7,454	10,239	9,039
54,750	**54,800**	10,251	7,461	10,251	9,051
54,800	**54,850**	10,264	7,469	10,264	9,064
54,850	**54,900**	10,276	7,476	10,276	9,076
54,900	**54,950**	10,289	7,484	10,289	9,089
54,950	**55,000**	10,301	7,491	10,301	9,101
55,000					
55,000	**55,050**	10,314	7,499	10,314	9,114
55,050	**55,100**	10,326	7,506	10,326	9,126
55,100	**55,150**	10,339	7,514	10,339	9,139
55,150	**55,200**	10,351	7,521	10,351	9,151
55,200	**55,250**	10,364	7,529	10,364	9,164
55,250	**55,300**	10,376	7,536	10,376	9,176
55,300	**55,350**	10,389	7,544	10,389	9,189
55,350	**55,400**	10,401	7,551	10,401	9,201
55,400	**55,450**	10,414	7,559	10,414	9,214
55,450	**55,500**	10,426	7,566	10,426	9,226
55,500	**55,550**	10,439	7,574	10,439	9,239
55,550	**55,600**	10,451	7,581	10,451	9,251
55,600	**55,650**	10,464	7,589	10,464	9,264
55,650	**55,700**	10,476	7,596	10,476	9,276
55,700	**55,750**	10,489	7,604	10,489	9,289
55,750	**55,800**	10,501	7,611	10,501	9,301
55,800	**55,850**	10,514	7,619	10,514	9,314
55,850	**55,900**	10,526	7,626	10,526	9,326
55,900	**55,950**	10,539	7,634	10,539	9,339
55,950	**56,000**	10,551	7,641	10,551	9,351
56,000					
56,000	**56,050**	10,564	7,649	10,564	9,364
56,050	**56,100**	10,576	7,656	10,576	9,376
56,100	**56,150**	10,589	7,664	10,589	9,389
56,150	**56,200**	10,601	7,671	10,601	9,401
56,200	**56,250**	10,614	7,679	10,614	9,414
56,250	**56,300**	10,626	7,686	10,626	9,426
56,300	**56,350**	10,639	7,694	10,639	9,439
56,350	**56,400**	10,651	7,701	10,651	9,451
56,400	**56,450**	10,664	7,709	10,664	9,464
56,450	**56,500**	10,676	7,716	10,676	9,476
56,500	**56,550**	10,689	7,724	10,689	9,489
56,550	**56,600**	10,701	7,731	10,701	9,501
56,600	**56,650**	10,714	7,739	10,714	9,514
56,650	**56,700**	10,726	7,746	10,726	9,526
56,700	**56,750**	10,739	7,754	10,739	9,539
56,750	**56,800**	10,751	7,761	10,751	9,551
56,800	**56,850**	10,764	7,769	10,764	9,564
56,850	**56,900**	10,776	7,776	10,776	9,576
56,900	**56,950**	10,789	7,784	10,789	9,589
56,950	**57,000**	10,801	7,791	10,801	9,601
57,000					
57,000	**57,050**	10,814	7,799	10,814	9,614
57,050	**57,100**	10,826	7,806	10,826	9,626
57,100	**57,150**	10,839	7,814	10,839	9,639
57,150	**57,200**	10,851	7,821	10,851	9,651
57,200	**57,250**	10,864	7,829	10,864	9,664
57,250	**57,300**	10,876	7,836	10,876	9,676
57,300	**57,350**	10,889	7,844	10,889	9,689
57,350	**57,400**	10,901	7,851	10,901	9,701
57,400	**57,450**	10,914	7,859	10,914	9,714
57,450	**57,500**	10,926	7,866	10,926	9,726
57,500	**57,550**	10,939	7,874	10,939	9,739
57,550	**57,600**	10,951	7,881	10,951	9,751
57,600	**57,650**	10,964	7,889	10,964	9,764
57,650	**57,700**	10,976	7,896	10,976	9,776
57,700	**57,750**	10,989	7,904	10,989	9,789
57,750	**57,800**	11,001	7,911	11,001	9,801
57,800	**57,850**	11,014	7,919	11,014	9,814
57,850	**57,900**	11,026	7,926	11,026	9,826
57,900	**57,950**	11,039	7,934	11,039	9,839
57,950	**58,000**	11,051	7,941	11,051	9,851
58,000					
58,000	**58,050**	11,064	7,949	11,064	9,864
58,050	**58,100**	11,076	7,956	11,076	9,876
58,100	**58,150**	11,089	7,964	11,089	9,889
58,150	**58,200**	11,101	7,971	11,101	9,901
58,200	**58,250**	11,114	7,979	11,114	9,914
58,250	**58,300**	11,126	7,986	11,126	9,926
58,300	**58,350**	11,139	7,994	11,139	9,939
58,350	**58,400**	11,151	8,001	11,151	9,951
58,400	**58,450**	11,164	8,009	11,164	9,964
58,450	**58,500**	11,176	8,016	11,176	9,976
58,500	**58,550**	11,189	8,024	11,189	9,989
58,550	**58,600**	11,201	8,031	11,201	10,001
58,600	**58,650**	11,214	8,039	11,214	10,014
58,650	**58,700**	11,226	8,046	11,226	10,026
58,700	**58,750**	11,239	8,054	11,239	10,039
58,750	**58,800**	11,251	8,061	11,251	10,051
58,800	**58,850**	11,264	8,069	11,264	10,064
58,850	**58,900**	11,276	8,076	11,276	10,076
58,900	**58,950**	11,289	8,084	11,289	10,089
58,950	**59,000**	11,301	8,091	11,301	10,101

* This column must also be used by a qualifying widow(er).

(Continued on page 74)

2006 Tax Table–*Continued*

If line 43 (taxable income) is— At least	But less than	And you are— Single	Married filing jointly *	Married filing sepa-rately	Head of a house-hold
		Your tax is—			
59,000					
59,000	**59,050**	11,314	8,099	11,314	10,114
59,050	**59,100**	11,326	8,106	11,326	10,126
59,100	**59,150**	11,339	8,114	11,339	10,139
59,150	**59,200**	11,351	8,121	11,351	10,151
59,200	**59,250**	11,364	8,129	11,364	10,164
59,250	**59,300**	11,376	8,136	11,376	10,176
59,300	**59,350**	11,389	8,144	11,389	10,189
59,350	**59,400**	11,401	8,151	11,401	10,201
59,400	**59,450**	11,414	8,159	11,414	10,214
59,450	**59,500**	11,426	8,166	11,426	10,226
59,500	**59,550**	11,439	8,174	11,439	10,239
59,550	**59,600**	11,451	8,181	11,451	10,251
59,600	**59,650**	11,464	8,189	11,464	10,264
59,650	**59,700**	11,476	8,196	11,476	10,276
59,700	**59,750**	11,489	8,204	11,489	10,289
59,750	**59,800**	11,501	8,211	11,501	10,301
59,800	**59,850**	11,514	8,219	11,514	10,314
59,850	**59,900**	11,526	8,226	11,526	10,326
59,900	**59,950**	11,539	8,234	11,539	10,339
59,950	**60,000**	11,551	8,241	11,551	10,351
60,000					
60,000	**60,050**	11,564	8,249	11,564	10,364
60,050	**60,100**	11,576	8,256	11,576	10,376
60,100	**60,150**	11,589	8,264	11,589	10,389
60,150	**60,200**	11,601	8,271	11,601	10,401
60,200	**60,250**	11,614	8,279	11,614	10,414
60,250	**60,300**	11,626	8,286	11,626	10,426
60,300	**60,350**	11,639	8,294	11,639	10,439
60,350	**60,400**	11,651	8,301	11,651	10,451
60,400	**60,450**	11,664	8,309	11,664	10,464
60,450	**60,500**	11,676	8,316	11,676	10,476
60,500	**60,550**	11,689	8,324	11,689	10,489
60,550	**60,600**	11,701	8,331	11,701	10,501
60,600	**60,650**	11,714	8,339	11,714	10,514
60,650	**60,700**	11,726	8,346	11,726	10,526
60,700	**60,750**	11,739	8,354	11,739	10,539
60,750	**60,800**	11,751	8,361	11,751	10,551
60,800	**60,850**	11,764	8,369	11,764	10,564
60,850	**60,900**	11,776	8,376	11,776	10,576
60,900	**60,950**	11,789	8,384	11,789	10,589
60,950	**61,000**	11,801	8,391	11,801	10,601
61,000					
61,000	**61,050**	11,814	8,399	11,814	10,614
61,050	**61,100**	11,826	8,406	11,826	10,626
61,100	**61,150**	11,839	8,414	11,839	10,639
61,150	**61,200**	11,851	8,421	11,851	10,651
61,200	**61,250**	11,864	8,429	11,864	10,664
61,250	**61,300**	11,876	8,436	11,876	10,676
61,300	**61,350**	11,889	8,446	11,889	10,689
61,350	**61,400**	11,901	8,459	11,901	10,701
61,400	**61,450**	11,914	8,471	11,914	10,714
61,450	**61,500**	11,926	8,484	11,926	10,726
61,500	**61,550**	11,939	8,496	11,939	10,739
61,550	**61,600**	11,951	8,509	11,951	10,751
61,600	**61,650**	11,964	8,521	11,964	10,764
61,650	**61,700**	11,976	8,534	11,976	10,776
61,700	**61,750**	11,989	8,546	11,989	10,789
61,750	**61,800**	12,001	8,559	12,001	10,801
61,800	**61,850**	12,014	8,571	12,014	10,814
61,850	**61,900**	12,026	8,584	12,027	10,826
61,900	**61,950**	12,039	8,596	12,041	10,839
61,950	**62,000**	12,051	8,609	12,055	10,851

If line 43 (taxable income) is— At least	But less than	And you are— Single	Married filing jointly *	Married filing sepa-rately	Head of a house-hold
		Your tax is—			
62,000					
62,000	**62,050**	12,064	8,621	12,069	10,864
62,050	**62,100**	12,076	8,634	12,083	10,876
62,100	**62,150**	12,089	8,646	12,097	10,889
62,150	**62,200**	12,101	8,659	12,111	10,901
62,200	**62,250**	12,114	8,671	12,125	10,914
62,250	**62,300**	12,126	8,684	12,139	10,926
62,300	**62,350**	12,139	8,696	12,153	10,939
62,350	**62,400**	12,151	8,709	12,167	10,951
62,400	**62,450**	12,164	8,721	12,181	10,964
62,450	**62,500**	12,176	8,734	12,195	10,976
62,500	**62,550**	12,189	8,746	12,209	10,989
62,550	**62,600**	12,201	8,759	12,223	11,001
62,600	**62,650**	12,214	8,771	12,237	11,014
62,650	**62,700**	12,226	8,784	12,251	11,026
62,700	**62,750**	12,239	8,796	12,265	11,039
62,750	**62,800**	12,251	8,809	12,279	11,051
62,800	**62,850**	12,264	8,821	12,293	11,064
62,850	**62,900**	12,276	8,834	12,307	11,076
62,900	**62,950**	12,289	8,846	12,321	11,089
62,950	**63,000**	12,301	8,859	12,335	11,101
63,000					
63,000	**63,050**	12,314	8,871	12,349	11,114
63,050	**63,100**	12,326	8,884	12,363	11,126
63,100	**63,150**	12,339	8,896	12,377	11,139
63,150	**63,200**	12,351	8,909	12,391	11,151
63,200	**63,250**	12,364	8,921	12,405	11,164
63,250	**63,300**	12,376	8,934	12,419	11,176
63,300	**63,350**	12,389	8,946	12,433	11,189
63,350	**63,400**	12,401	8,959	12,447	11,201
63,400	**63,450**	12,414	8,971	12,461	11,214
63,450	**63,500**	12,426	8,984	12,475	11,226
63,500	**63,550**	12,439	8,996	12,489	11,239
63,550	**63,600**	12,451	9,009	12,503	11,251
63,600	**63,650**	12,464	9,021	12,517	11,264
63,650	**63,700**	12,476	9,034	12,531	11,276
63,700	**63,750**	12,489	9,046	12,545	11,289
63,750	**63,800**	12,501	9,059	12,559	11,301
63,800	**63,850**	12,514	9,071	12,573	11,314
63,850	**63,900**	12,526	9,084	12,587	11,326
63,900	**63,950**	12,539	9,096	12,601	11,339
63,950	**64,000**	12,551	9,109	12,615	11,351
64,000					
64,000	**64,050**	12,564	9,121	12,629	11,364
64,050	**64,100**	12,576	9,134	12,643	11,376
64,100	**64,150**	12,589	9,146	12,657	11,389
64,150	**64,200**	12,601	9,159	12,671	11,401
64,200	**64,250**	12,614	9,171	12,685	11,414
64,250	**64,300**	12,626	9,184	12,699	11,426
64,300	**64,350**	12,639	9,196	12,713	11,439
64,350	**64,400**	12,651	9,209	12,727	11,451
64,400	**64,450**	12,664	9,221	12,741	11,464
64,450	**64,500**	12,676	9,234	12,755	11,476
64,500	**64,550**	12,689	9,246	12,769	11,489
64,550	**64,600**	12,701	9,259	12,783	11,501
64,600	**64,650**	12,714	9,271	12,797	11,514
64,650	**64,700**	12,726	9,284	12,811	11,526
64,700	**64,750**	12,739	9,296	12,825	11,539
64,750	**64,800**	12,751	9,309	12,839	11,551
64,800	**64,850**	12,764	9,321	12,853	11,564
64,850	**64,900**	12,776	9,334	12,867	11,576
64,900	**64,950**	12,789	9,346	12,881	11,589
64,950	**65,000**	12,801	9,359	12,895	11,601

If line 43 (taxable income) is— At least	But less than	And you are— Single	Married filing jointly *	Married filing sepa-rately	Head of a house-hold
		Your tax is—			
65,000					
65,000	**65,050**	12,814	9,371	12,909	11,614
65,050	**65,100**	12,826	9,384	12,923	11,626
65,100	**65,150**	12,839	9,396	12,937	11,639
65,150	**65,200**	12,851	9,409	12,951	11,651
65,200	**65,250**	12,864	9,421	12,965	11,664
65,250	**65,300**	12,876	9,434	12,979	11,676
65,300	**65,350**	12,889	9,446	12,993	11,689
65,350	**65,400**	12,901	9,459	13,007	11,701
65,400	**65,450**	12,914	9,471	13,021	11,714
65,450	**65,500**	12,926	9,484	13,035	11,726
65,500	**65,550**	12,939	9,496	13,049	11,739
65,550	**65,600**	12,951	9,509	13,063	11,751
65,600	**65,650**	12,964	9,521	13,077	11,764
65,650	**65,700**	12,976	9,534	13,091	11,776
65,700	**65,750**	12,989	9,546	13,105	11,789
65,750	**65,800**	13,001	9,559	13,119	11,801
65,800	**65,850**	13,014	9,571	13,133	11,814
65,850	**65,900**	13,026	9,584	13,147	11,826
65,900	**65,950**	13,039	9,596	13,161	11,839
65,950	**66,000**	13,051	9,609	13,175	11,851
66,000					
66,000	**66,050**	13,064	9,621	13,189	11,864
66,050	**66,100**	13,076	9,634	13,203	11,876
66,100	**66,150**	13,089	9,646	13,217	11,889
66,150	**66,200**	13,101	9,659	13,231	11,901
66,200	**66,250**	13,114	9,671	13,245	11,914
66,250	**66,300**	13,126	9,684	13,259	11,926
66,300	**66,350**	13,139	9,696	13,273	11,939
66,350	**66,400**	13,151	9,709	13,287	11,951
66,400	**66,450**	13,164	9,721	13,301	11,964
66,450	**66,500**	13,176	9,734	13,315	11,976
66,500	**66,550**	13,189	9,746	13,329	11,989
66,550	**66,600**	13,201	9,759	13,343	12,001
66,600	**66,650**	13,214	9,771	13,357	12,014
66,650	**66,700**	13,226	9,784	13,371	12,026
66,700	**66,750**	13,239	9,796	13,385	12,039
66,750	**66,800**	13,251	9,809	13,399	12,051
66,800	**66,850**	13,264	9,821	13,413	12,064
66,850	**66,900**	13,276	9,834	13,427	12,076
66,900	**66,950**	13,289	9,846	13,441	12,089
66,950	**67,000**	13,301	9,859	13,455	12,101
67,000					
67,000	**67,050**	13,314	9,871	13,469	12,114
67,050	**67,100**	13,326	9,884	13,483	12,126
67,100	**67,150**	13,339	9,896	13,497	12,139
67,150	**67,200**	13,351	9,909	13,511	12,151
67,200	**67,250**	13,364	9,921	13,525	12,164
67,250	**67,300**	13,376	9,934	13,539	12,176
67,300	**67,350**	13,389	9,946	13,553	12,189
67,350	**67,400**	13,401	9,959	13,567	12,201
67,400	**67,450**	13,414	9,971	13,581	12,214
67,450	**67,500**	13,426	9,984	13,595	12,226
67,500	**67,550**	13,439	9,996	13,609	12,239
67,550	**67,600**	13,451	10,009	13,623	12,251
67,600	**67,650**	13,464	10,021	13,637	12,264
67,650	**67,700**	13,476	10,034	13,651	12,276
67,700	**67,750**	13,489	10,046	13,665	12,289
67,750	**67,800**	13,501	10,059	13,679	12,301
67,800	**67,850**	13,514	10,071	13,693	12,314
67,850	**67,900**	13,526	10,084	13,707	12,326
67,900	**67,950**	13,539	10,096	13,721	12,339
67,950	**68,000**	13,551	10,109	13,735	12,351

* This column must also be used by a qualifying widow(er).

(Continued on page 75)

If line 43 (taxable income) is—		And you are—			
At least	But less than	Single	Married filing jointly *	Married filing sepa-rately	Head of a house-hold
		Your tax is—			
68,000					
68,000	**68,050**	13,564	10,121	13,749	12,364
68,050	**68,100**	13,576	10,134	13,763	12,376
68,100	**68,150**	13,589	10,146	13,777	12,389
68,150	**68,200**	13,601	10,159	13,791	12,401
68,200	**68,250**	13,614	10,171	13,805	12,414
68,250	**68,300**	13,626	10,184	13,819	12,426
68,300	**68,350**	13,639	10,196	13,833	12,439
68,350	**68,400**	13,651	10,209	13,847	12,451
68,400	**68,450**	13,664	10,221	13,861	12,464
68,450	**68,500**	13,676	10,234	13,875	12,476
68,500	**68,550**	13,689	10,246	13,889	12,489
68,550	**68,600**	13,701	10,259	13,903	12,501
68,600	**68,650**	13,714	10,271	13,917	12,514
68,650	**68,700**	13,726	10,284	13,931	12,526
68,700	**68,750**	13,739	10,296	13,945	12,539
68,750	**68,800**	13,751	10,309	13,959	12,551
68,800	**68,850**	13,764	10,321	13,973	12,564
68,850	**68,900**	13,776	10,334	13,987	12,576
68,900	**68,950**	13,789	10,346	14,001	12,589
68,950	**69,000**	13,801	10,359	14,015	12,601
69,000					
69,000	**69,050**	13,814	10,371	14,029	12,614
69,050	**69,100**	13,826	10,384	14,043	12,626
69,100	**69,150**	13,839	10,396	14,057	12,639
69,150	**69,200**	13,851	10,409	14,071	12,651
69,200	**69,250**	13,864	10,421	14,085	12,664
69,250	**69,300**	13,876	10,434	14,099	12,676
69,300	**69,350**	13,889	10,446	14,113	12,689
69,350	**69,400**	13,901	10,459	14,127	12,701
69,400	**69,450**	13,914	10,471	14,141	12,714
69,450	**69,500**	13,926	10,484	14,155	12,726
69,500	**69,550**	13,939	10,496	14,169	12,739
69,550	**69,600**	13,951	10,509	14,183	12,751
69,600	**69,650**	13,964	10,521	14,197	12,764
69,650	**69,700**	13,976	10,534	14,211	12,776
69,700	**69,750**	13,989	10,546	14,225	12,789
69,750	**69,800**	14,001	10,559	14,239	12,801
69,800	**69,850**	14,014	10,571	14,253	12,814
69,850	**69,900**	14,026	10,584	14,267	12,826
69,900	**69,950**	14,039	10,596	14,281	12,839
69,950	**70,000**	14,051	10,609	14,295	12,851
70,000					
70,000	**70,050**	14,064	10,621	14,309	12,864
70,050	**70,100**	14,076	10,634	14,323	12,876
70,100	**70,150**	14,089	10,646	14,337	12,889
70,150	**70,200**	14,101	10,659	14,351	12,901
70,200	**70,250**	14,114	10,671	14,365	12,914
70,250	**70,300**	14,126	10,684	14,379	12,926
70,300	**70,350**	14,139	10,696	14,393	12,939
70,350	**70,400**	14,151	10,709	14,407	12,951
70,400	**70,450**	14,164	10,721	14,421	12,964
70,450	**70,500**	14,176	10,734	14,435	12,976
70,500	**70,550**	14,189	10,746	14,449	12,989
70,550	**70,600**	14,201	10,759	14,463	13,001
70,600	**70,650**	14,214	10,771	14,477	13,014
70,650	**70,700**	14,226	10,784	14,491	13,026
70,700	**70,750**	14,239	10,796	14,505	13,039
70,750	**70,800**	14,251	10,809	14,519	13,051
70,800	**70,850**	14,264	10,821	14,533	13,064
70,850	**70,900**	14,276	10,834	14,547	13,076
70,900	**70,950**	14,289	10,846	14,561	13,089
70,950	**71,000**	14,301	10,859	14,575	13,101

If line 43 (taxable income) is—		And you are—			
At least	But less than	Single	Married filing jointly *	Married filing sepa-rately	Head of a house-hold
		Your tax is—			
71,000					
71,000	**71,050**	14,314	10,871	14,589	13,114
71,050	**71,100**	14,326	10,884	14,603	13,126
71,100	**71,150**	14,339	10,896	14,617	13,139
71,150	**71,200**	14,351	10,909	14,631	13,151
71,200	**71,250**	14,364	10,921	14,645	13,164
71,250	**71,300**	14,376	10,934	14,659	13,176
71,300	**71,350**	14,389	10,946	14,673	13,189
71,350	**71,400**	14,401	10,959	14,687	13,201
71,400	**71,450**	14,414	10,971	14,701	13,214
71,450	**71,500**	14,426	10,984	14,715	13,226
71,500	**71,550**	14,439	10,996	14,729	13,239
71,550	**71,600**	14,451	11,009	14,743	13,251
71,600	**71,650**	14,464	11,021	14,757	13,264
71,650	**71,700**	14,476	11,034	14,771	13,276
71,700	**71,750**	14,489	11,046	14,785	13,289
71,750	**71,800**	14,501	11,059	14,799	13,301
71,800	**71,850**	14,514	11,071	14,813	13,314
71,850	**71,900**	14,526	11,084	14,827	13,326
71,900	**71,950**	14,539	11,096	14,841	13,339
71,950	**72,000**	14,551	11,109	14,855	13,351
72,000					
72,000	**72,050**	14,564	11,121	14,869	13,364
72,050	**72,100**	14,576	11,134	14,883	13,376
72,100	**72,150**	14,589	11,146	14,897	13,389
72,150	**72,200**	14,601	11,159	14,911	13,401
72,200	**72,250**	14,614	11,171	14,925	13,414
72,250	**72,300**	14,626	11,184	14,939	13,426
72,300	**72,350**	14,639	11,196	14,953	13,439
72,350	**72,400**	14,651	11,209	14,967	13,451
72,400	**72,450**	14,664	11,221	14,981	13,464
72,450	**72,500**	14,676	11,234	14,995	13,476
72,500	**72,550**	14,689	11,246	15,009	13,489
72,550	**72,600**	14,701	11,259	15,023	13,501
72,600	**72,650**	14,714	11,271	15,037	13,514
72,650	**72,700**	14,726	11,284	15,051	13,526
72,700	**72,750**	14,739	11,296	15,065	13,539
72,750	**72,800**	14,751	11,309	15,079	13,551
72,800	**72,850**	14,764	11,321	15,093	13,564
72,850	**72,900**	14,776	11,334	15,107	13,576
72,900	**72,950**	14,789	11,346	15,121	13,589
72,950	**73,000**	14,801	11,359	15,135	13,601
73,000					
73,000	**73,050**	14,814	11,371	15,149	13,614
73,050	**73,100**	14,826	11,384	15,163	13,626
73,100	**73,150**	14,839	11,396	15,177	13,639
73,150	**73,200**	14,851	11,409	15,191	13,651
73,200	**73,250**	14,864	11,421	15,205	13,664
73,250	**73,300**	14,876	11,434	15,219	13,676
73,300	**73,350**	14,889	11,446	15,233	13,689
73,350	**73,400**	14,901	11,459	15,247	13,701
73,400	**73,450**	14,914	11,471	15,261	13,714
73,450	**73,500**	14,926	11,484	15,275	13,726
73,500	**73,550**	14,939	11,496	15,289	13,739
73,550	**73,600**	14,951	11,509	15,303	13,751
73,600	**73,650**	14,964	11,521	15,317	13,764
73,650	**73,700**	14,976	11,534	15,331	13,776
73,700	**73,750**	14,989	11,546	15,345	13,789
73,750	**73,800**	15,001	11,559	15,359	13,801
73,800	**73,850**	15,014	11,571	15,373	13,814
73,850	**73,900**	15,026	11,584	15,387	13,826
73,900	**73,950**	15,039	11,596	15,401	13,839
73,950	**74,000**	15,051	11,609	15,415	13,851

If line 43 (taxable income) is—		And you are—			
At least	But less than	Single	Married filing jointly *	Married filing sepa-rately	Head of a house-hold
		Your tax is—			
74,000					
74,000	**74,050**	15,064	11,621	15,429	13,864
74,050	**74,100**	15,076	11,634	15,443	13,876
74,100	**74,150**	15,089	11,646	15,457	13,889
74,150	**74,200**	15,101	11,659	15,471	13,901
74,200	**74,250**	15,115	11,671	15,485	13,914
74,250	**74,300**	15,129	11,684	15,499	13,926
74,300	**74,350**	15,143	11,696	15,513	13,939
74,350	**74,400**	15,157	11,709	15,527	13,951
74,400	**74,450**	15,171	11,721	15,541	13,964
74,450	**74,500**	15,185	11,734	15,555	13,976
74,500	**74,550**	15,199	11,746	15,569	13,989
74,550	**74,600**	15,213	11,759	15,583	14,001
74,600	**74,650**	15,227	11,771	15,597	14,014
74,650	**74,700**	15,241	11,784	15,611	14,026
74,700	**74,750**	15,255	11,796	15,625	14,039
74,750	**74,800**	15,269	11,809	15,639	14,051
74,800	**74,850**	15,283	11,821	15,653	14,064
74,850	**74,900**	15,297	11,834	15,667	14,076
74,900	**74,950**	15,311	11,846	15,681	14,089
74,950	**75,000**	15,325	11,859	15,695	14,101
75,000					
75,000	**75,050**	15,339	11,871	15,709	14,114
75,050	**75,100**	15,353	11,884	15,723	14,126
75,100	**75,150**	15,367	11,896	15,737	14,139
75,150	**75,200**	15,381	11,909	15,751	14,151
75,200	**75,250**	15,395	11,921	15,765	14,164
75,250	**75,300**	15,409	11,934	15,779	14,176
75,300	**75,350**	15,423	11,946	15,793	14,189
75,350	**75,400**	15,437	11,959	15,807	14,201
75,400	**75,450**	15,451	11,971	15,821	14,214
75,450	**75,500**	15,465	11,984	15,835	14,226
75,500	**75,550**	15,479	11,996	15,849	14,239
75,550	**75,600**	15,493	12,009	15,863	14,251
75,600	**75,650**	15,507	12,021	15,877	14,264
75,650	**75,700**	15,521	12,034	15,891	14,276
75,700	**75,750**	15,535	12,046	15,905	14,289
75,750	**75,800**	15,549	12,059	15,919	14,301
75,800	**75,850**	15,563	12,071	15,933	14,314
75,850	**75,900**	15,577	12,084	15,947	14,326
75,900	**75,950**	15,591	12,096	15,961	14,339
75,950	**76,000**	15,605	12,109	15,975	14,351
76,000					
76,000	**76,050**	15,619	12,121	15,989	14,364
76,050	**76,100**	15,633	12,134	16,003	14,376
76,100	**76,150**	15,647	12,146	16,017	14,389
76,150	**76,200**	15,661	12,159	16,031	14,401
76,200	**76,250**	15,675	12,171	16,045	14,414
76,250	**76,300**	15,689	12,184	16,059	14,426
76,300	**76,350**	15,703	12,196	16,073	14,439
76,350	**76,400**	15,717	12,209	16,087	14,451
76,400	**76,450**	15,731	12,221	16,101	14,464
76,450	**76,500**	15,745	12,234	16,115	14,476
76,500	**76,550**	15,759	12,246	16,129	14,489
76,550	**76,600**	15,773	12,259	16,143	14,501
76,600	**76,650**	15,787	12,271	16,157	14,514
76,650	**76,700**	15,801	12,284	16,171	14,526
76,700	**76,750**	15,815	12,296	16,185	14,539
76,750	**76,800**	15,829	12,309	16,199	14,551
76,800	**76,850**	15,843	12,321	16,213	14,564
76,850	**76,900**	15,857	12,334	16,227	14,576
76,900	**76,950**	15,871	12,346	16,241	14,589
76,950	**77,000**	15,885	12,359	16,255	14,601

* This column must also be used by a qualifying widow(er).

(Continued on page 76)

2006 Tax Table–*Continued*

If line 43 (taxable income) is—		And you are—			
At least	But less than	Single	Married filing jointly *	Married filing sepa- rately	Head of a house- hold
		Your tax is—			
77,000					
77,000	**77,050**	15,899	12,371	16,269	14,614
77,050	**77,100**	15,913	12,384	16,283	14,626
77,100	**77,150**	15,927	12,396	16,297	14,639
77,150	**77,200**	15,941	12,409	16,311	14,651
77,200	**77,250**	15,955	12,421	16,325	14,664
77,250	**77,300**	15,969	12,434	16,339	14,676
77,300	**77,350**	15,983	12,446	16,353	14,689
77,350	**77,400**	15,997	12,459	16,367	14,701
77,400	**77,450**	16,011	12,471	16,381	14,714
77,450	**77,500**	16,025	12,484	16,395	14,726
77,500	**77,550**	16,039	12,496	16,409	14,739
77,550	**77,600**	16,053	12,509	16,423	14,751
77,600	**77,650**	16,067	12,521	16,437	14,764
77,650	**77,700**	16,081	12,534	16,451	14,776
77,700	**77,750**	16,095	12,546	16,465	14,789
77,750	**77,800**	16,109	12,559	16,479	14,801
77,800	**77,850**	16,123	12,571	16,493	14,814
77,850	**77,900**	16,137	12,584	16,507	14,826
77,900	**77,950**	16,151	12,596	16,521	14,839
77,950	**78,000**	16,165	12,609	16,535	14,851
78,000					
78,000	**78,050**	16,179	12,621	16,549	14,864
78,050	**78,100**	16,193	12,634	16,563	14,876
78,100	**78,150**	16,207	12,646	16,577	14,889
78,150	**78,200**	16,221	12,659	16,591	14,901
78,200	**78,250**	16,235	12,671	16,605	14,914
78,250	**78,300**	16,249	12,684	16,619	14,926
78,300	**78,350**	16,263	12,696	16,633	14,939
78,350	**78,400**	16,277	12,709	16,647	14,951
78,400	**78,450**	16,291	12,721	16,661	14,964
78,450	**78,500**	16,305	12,734	16,675	14,976
78,500	**78,550**	16,319	12,746	16,689	14,989
78,550	**78,600**	16,333	12,759	16,703	15,001
78,600	**78,650**	16,347	12,771	16,717	15,014
78,650	**78,700**	16,361	12,784	16,731	15,026
78,700	**78,750**	16,375	12,796	16,745	15,039
78,750	**78,800**	16,389	12,809	16,759	15,051
78,800	**78,850**	16,403	12,821	16,773	15,064
78,850	**78,900**	16,417	12,834	16,787	15,076
78,900	**78,950**	16,431	12,846	16,801	15,089
78,950	**79,000**	16,445	12,859	16,815	15,101
79,000					
79,000	**79,050**	16,459	12,871	16,829	15,114
79,050	**79,100**	16,473	12,884	16,843	15,126
79,100	**79,150**	16,487	12,896	16,857	15,139
79,150	**79,200**	16,501	12,909	16,871	15,151
79,200	**79,250**	16,515	12,921	16,885	15,164
79,250	**79,300**	16,529	12,934	16,899	15,176
79,300	**79,350**	16,543	12,946	16,913	15,189
79,350	**79,400**	16,557	12,959	16,927	15,201
79,400	**79,450**	16,571	12,971	16,941	15,214
79,450	**79,500**	16,585	12,984	16,955	15,226
79,500	**79,550**	16,599	12,996	16,969	15,239
79,550	**79,600**	16,613	13,009	16,983	15,251
79,600	**79,650**	16,627	13,021	16,997	15,264
79,650	**79,700**	16,641	13,034	17,011	15,276
79,700	**79,750**	16,655	13,046	17,025	15,289
79,750	**79,800**	16,669	13,059	17,039	15,301
79,800	**79,850**	16,683	13,071	17,053	15,314
79,850	**79,900**	16,697	13,084	17,067	15,326
79,900	**79,950**	16,711	13,096	17,081	15,339
79,950	**80,000**	16,725	13,109	17,095	15,351

If line 43 (taxable income) is—		And you are—			
At least	But less than	Single	Married filing jointly *	Married filing sepa- rately	Head of a house- hold
		Your tax is—			
80,000					
80,000	**80,050**	16,739	13,121	17,109	15,364
80,050	**80,100**	16,753	13,134	17,123	15,376
80,100	**80,150**	16,767	13,146	17,137	15,389
80,150	**80,200**	16,781	13,159	17,151	15,401
80,200	**80,250**	16,795	13,171	17,165	15,414
80,250	**80,300**	16,809	13,184	17,179	15,426
80,300	**80,350**	16,823	13,196	17,193	15,439
80,350	**80,400**	16,837	13,209	17,207	15,451
80,400	**80,450**	16,851	13,221	17,221	15,464
80,450	**80,500**	16,865	13,234	17,235	15,476
80,500	**80,550**	16,879	13,246	17,249	15,489
80,550	**80,600**	16,893	13,259	17,263	15,501
80,600	**80,650**	16,907	13,271	17,277	15,514
80,650	**80,700**	16,921	13,284	17,291	15,526
80,700	**80,750**	16,935	13,296	17,305	15,539
80,750	**80,800**	16,949	13,309	17,319	15,551
80,800	**80,850**	16,963	13,321	17,333	15,564
80,850	**80,900**	16,977	13,334	17,347	15,576
80,900	**80,950**	16,991	13,346	17,361	15,589
80,950	**81,000**	17,005	13,359	17,375	15,601
81,000					
81,000	**81,050**	17,019	13,371	17,389	15,614
81,050	**81,100**	17,033	13,384	17,403	15,626
81,100	**81,150**	17,047	13,396	17,417	15,639
81,150	**81,200**	17,061	13,409	17,431	15,651
81,200	**81,250**	17,075	13,421	17,445	15,664
81,250	**81,300**	17,089	13,434	17,459	15,676
81,300	**81,350**	17,103	13,446	17,473	15,689
81,350	**81,400**	17,117	13,459	17,487	15,701
81,400	**81,450**	17,131	13,471	17,501	15,714
81,450	**81,500**	17,145	13,484	17,515	15,726
81,500	**81,550**	17,159	13,496	17,529	15,739
81,550	**81,600**	17,173	13,509	17,543	15,751
81,600	**81,650**	17,187	13,521	17,557	15,764
81,650	**81,700**	17,201	13,534	17,571	15,776
81,700	**81,750**	17,215	13,546	17,585	15,789
81,750	**81,800**	17,229	13,559	17,599	15,801
81,800	**81,850**	17,243	13,571	17,613	15,814
81,850	**81,900**	17,257	13,584	17,627	15,826
81,900	**81,950**	17,271	13,596	17,641	15,839
81,950	**82,000**	17,285	13,609	17,655	15,851
82,000					
82,000	**82,050**	17,299	13,621	17,669	15,864
82,050	**82,100**	17,313	13,634	17,683	15,876
82,100	**82,150**	17,327	13,646	17,697	15,889
82,150	**82,200**	17,341	13,659	17,711	15,901
82,200	**82,250**	17,355	13,671	17,725	15,914
82,250	**82,300**	17,369	13,684	17,739	15,926
82,300	**82,350**	17,383	13,696	17,753	15,939
82,350	**82,400**	17,397	13,709	17,767	15,951
82,400	**82,450**	17,411	13,721	17,781	15,964
82,450	**82,500**	17,425	13,734	17,795	15,976
82,500	**82,550**	17,439	13,746	17,809	15,989
82,550	**82,600**	17,453	13,759	17,823	16,001
82,600	**82,650**	17,467	13,771	17,837	16,014
82,650	**82,700**	17,481	13,784	17,851	16,026
82,700	**82,750**	17,495	13,796	17,865	16,039
82,750	**82,800**	17,509	13,809	17,879	16,051
82,800	**82,850**	17,523	13,821	17,893	16,064
82,850	**82,900**	17,537	13,834	17,907	16,076
82,900	**82,950**	17,551	13,846	17,921	16,089
82,950	**83,000**	17,565	13,859	17,935	16,101

If line 43 (taxable income) is—		And you are—			
At least	But less than	Single	Married filing jointly *	Married filing sepa- rately	Head of a house- hold
		Your tax is—			
83,000					
83,000	**83,050**	17,579	13,871	17,949	16,114
83,050	**83,100**	17,593	13,884	17,963	16,126
83,100	**83,150**	17,607	13,896	17,977	16,139
83,150	**83,200**	17,621	13,909	17,991	16,151
83,200	**83,250**	17,635	13,921	18,005	16,164
83,250	**83,300**	17,649	13,934	18,019	16,176
83,300	**83,350**	17,663	13,946	18,033	16,189
83,350	**83,400**	17,677	13,959	18,047	16,201
83,400	**83,450**	17,691	13,971	18,061	16,214
83,450	**83,500**	17,705	13,984	18,075	16,226
83,500	**83,550**	17,719	13,996	18,089	16,239
83,550	**83,600**	17,733	14,009	18,103	16,251
83,600	**83,650**	17,747	14,021	18,117	16,264
83,650	**83,700**	17,761	14,034	18,131	16,276
83,700	**83,750**	17,775	14,046	18,145	16,289
83,750	**83,800**	17,789	14,059	18,159	16,301
83,800	**83,850**	17,803	14,071	18,173	16,314
83,850	**83,900**	17,817	14,084	18,187	16,326
83,900	**83,950**	17,831	14,096	18,201	16,339
83,950	**84,000**	17,845	14,109	18,215	16,351
84,000					
84,000	**84,050**	17,859	14,121	18,229	16,364
84,050	**84,100**	17,873	14,134	18,243	16,376
84,100	**84,150**	17,887	14,146	18,257	16,389
84,150	**84,200**	17,901	14,159	18,271	16,401
84,200	**84,250**	17,915	14,171	18,285	16,414
84,250	**84,300**	17,929	14,184	18,299	16,426
84,300	**84,350**	17,943	14,196	18,313	16,439
84,350	**84,400**	17,957	14,209	18,327	16,451
84,400	**84,450**	17,971	14,221	18,341	16,464
84,450	**84,500**	17,985	14,234	18,355	16,476
84,500	**84,550**	17,999	14,246	18,369	16,489
84,550	**84,600**	18,013	14,259	18,383	16,501
84,600	**84,650**	18,027	14,271	18,397	16,514
84,650	**84,700**	18,041	14,284	18,411	16,526
84,700	**84,750**	18,055	14,296	18,425	16,539
84,750	**84,800**	18,069	14,309	18,439	16,551
84,800	**84,850**	18,083	14,321	18,453	16,564
84,850	**84,900**	18,097	14,334	18,467	16,576
84,900	**84,950**	18,111	14,346	18,481	16,589
84,950	**85,000**	18,125	14,359	18,495	16,601
85,000					
85,000	**85,050**	18,139	14,371	18,509	16,614
85,050	**85,100**	18,153	14,384	18,523	16,626
85,100	**85,150**	18,167	14,396	18,537	16,639
85,150	**85,200**	18,181	14,409	18,551	16,651
85,200	**85,250**	18,195	14,421	18,565	16,664
85,250	**85,300**	18,209	14,434	18,579	16,676
85,300	**85,350**	18,223	14,446	18,593	16,689
85,350	**85,400**	18,237	14,459	18,607	16,701
85,400	**85,450**	18,251	14,471	18,621	16,714
85,450	**85,500**	18,265	14,484	18,635	16,726
85,500	**85,550**	18,279	14,496	18,649	16,739
85,550	**85,600**	18,293	14,509	18,663	16,751
85,600	**85,650**	18,307	14,521	18,677	16,764
85,650	**85,700**	18,321	14,534	18,691	16,776
85,700	**85,750**	18,335	14,546	18,705	16,789
85,750	**85,800**	18,349	14,559	18,719	16,801
85,800	**85,850**	18,363	14,571	18,733	16,814
85,850	**85,900**	18,377	14,584	18,747	16,826
85,900	**85,950**	18,391	14,596	18,761	16,839
85,950	**86,000**	18,405	14,609	18,775	16,851

* This column must also be used by a qualifying widow(er).

(Continued on page 77)

If line 43 (taxable income) is— At least	But less than	And you are— Single	Married filing jointly *	Married filing sepa-rately	Head of a house-hold
		Your tax is—			
86,000					
86,000	**86,050**	18,419	14,621	18,789	16,864
86,050	**86,100**	18,433	14,634	18,803	16,876
86,100	**86,150**	18,447	14,646	18,817	16,889
86,150	**86,200**	18,461	14,659	18,831	16,901
86,200	**86,250**	18,475	14,671	18,845	16,914
86,250	**86,300**	18,489	14,684	18,859	16,926
86,300	**86,350**	18,503	14,696	18,873	16,939
86,350	**86,400**	18,517	14,709	18,887	16,951
86,400	**86,450**	18,531	14,721	18,901	16,964
86,450	**86,500**	18,545	14,734	18,915	16,976
86,500	**86,550**	18,559	14,746	18,929	16,989
86,550	**86,600**	18,573	14,759	18,943	17,001
86,600	**86,650**	18,587	14,771	18,957	17,014
86,650	**86,700**	18,601	14,784	18,971	17,026
86,700	**86,750**	18,615	14,796	18,985	17,039
86,750	**86,800**	18,629	14,809	18,999	17,051
86,800	**86,850**	18,643	14,821	19,013	17,064
86,850	**86,900**	18,657	14,834	19,027	17,076
86,900	**86,950**	18,671	14,846	19,041	17,089
86,950	**87,000**	18,685	14,859	19,055	17,101
87,000					
87,000	**87,050**	18,699	14,871	19,069	17,114
87,050	**87,100**	18,713	14,884	19,083	17,126
87,100	**87,150**	18,727	14,896	19,097	17,139
87,150	**87,200**	18,741	14,909	19,111	17,151
87,200	**87,250**	18,755	14,921	19,125	17,164
87,250	**87,300**	18,769	14,934	19,139	17,176
87,300	**87,350**	18,783	14,946	19,153	17,189
87,350	**87,400**	18,797	14,959	19,167	17,201
87,400	**87,450**	18,811	14,971	19,181	17,214
87,450	**87,500**	18,825	14,984	19,195	17,226
87,500	**87,550**	18,839	14,996	19,209	17,239
87,550	**87,600**	18,853	15,009	19,223	17,251
87,600	**87,650**	18,867	15,021	19,237	17,264
87,650	**87,700**	18,881	15,034	19,251	17,276
87,700	**87,750**	18,895	15,046	19,265	17,289
87,750	**87,800**	18,909	15,059	19,279	17,301
87,800	**87,850**	18,923	15,071	19,293	17,314
87,850	**87,900**	18,937	15,084	19,307	17,326
87,900	**87,950**	18,951	15,096	19,321	17,339
87,950	**88,000**	18,965	15,109	19,335	17,351
88,000					
88,000	**88,050**	18,979	15,121	19,349	17,364
88,050	**88,100**	18,993	15,134	19,363	17,376
88,100	**88,150**	19,007	15,146	19,377	17,389
88,150	**88,200**	19,021	15,159	19,391	17,401
88,200	**88,250**	19,035	15,171	19,405	17,414
88,250	**88,300**	19,049	15,184	19,419	17,426
88,300	**88,350**	19,063	15,196	19,433	17,439
88,350	**88,400**	19,077	15,209	19,447	17,451
88,400	**88,450**	19,091	15,221	19,461	17,464
88,450	**88,500**	19,105	15,234	19,475	17,476
88,500	**88,550**	19,119	15,246	19,489	17,489
88,550	**88,600**	19,133	15,259	19,503	17,501
88,600	**88,650**	19,147	15,271	19,517	17,514
88,650	**88,700**	19,161	15,284	19,531	17,526
88,700	**88,750**	19,175	15,296	19,545	17,539
88,750	**88,800**	19,189	15,309	19,559	17,551
88,800	**88,850**	19,203	15,321	19,573	17,564
88,850	**88,900**	19,217	15,334	19,587	17,576
88,900	**88,950**	19,231	15,346	19,601	17,589
88,950	**89,000**	19,245	15,359	19,615	17,601

If line 43 (taxable income) is— At least	But less than	And you are— Single	Married filing jointly *	Married filing sepa-rately	Head of a house-hold
		Your tax is—			
89,000					
89,000	**89,050**	19,259	15,371	19,629	17,614
89,050	**89,100**	19,273	15,384	19,643	17,626
89,100	**89,150**	19,287	15,396	19,657	17,639
89,150	**89,200**	19,301	15,409	19,671	17,651
89,200	**89,250**	19,315	15,421	19,685	17,664
89,250	**89,300**	19,329	15,434	19,699	17,676
89,300	**89,350**	19,343	15,446	19,713	17,689
89,350	**89,400**	19,357	15,459	19,727	17,701
89,400	**89,450**	19,371	15,471	19,741	17,714
89,450	**89,500**	19,385	15,484	19,755	17,726
89,500	**89,550**	19,399	15,496	19,769	17,739
89,550	**89,600**	19,413	15,509	19,783	17,751
89,600	**89,650**	19,427	15,521	19,797	17,764
89,650	**89,700**	19,441	15,534	19,811	17,776
89,700	**89,750**	19,455	15,546	19,825	17,789
89,750	**89,800**	19,469	15,559	19,839	17,801
89,800	**89,850**	19,483	15,571	19,853	17,814
89,850	**89,900**	19,497	15,584	19,867	17,826
89,900	**89,950**	19,511	15,596	19,881	17,839
89,950	**90,000**	19,525	15,609	19,895	17,851
90,000					
90,000	**90,050**	19,539	15,621	19,909	17,864
90,050	**90,100**	19,553	15,634	19,923	17,876
90,100	**90,150**	19,567	15,646	19,937	17,889
90,150	**90,200**	19,581	15,659	19,951	17,901
90,200	**90,250**	19,595	15,671	19,965	17,914
90,250	**90,300**	19,609	15,684	19,979	17,926
90,300	**90,350**	19,623	15,696	19,993	17,939
90,350	**90,400**	19,637	15,709	20,007	17,951
90,400	**90,450**	19,651	15,721	20,021	17,964
90,450	**90,500**	19,665	15,734	20,035	17,976
90,500	**90,550**	19,679	15,746	20,049	17,989
90,550	**90,600**	19,693	15,759	20,063	18,001
90,600	**90,650**	19,707	15,771	20,077	18,014
90,650	**90,700**	19,721	15,784	20,091	18,026
90,700	**90,750**	19,735	15,796	20,105	18,039
90,750	**90,800**	19,749	15,809	20,119	18,051
90,800	**90,850**	19,763	15,821	20,133	18,064
90,850	**90,900**	19,777	15,834	20,147	18,076
90,900	**90,950**	19,791	15,846	20,161	18,089
90,950	**91,000**	19,805	15,859	20,175	18,101
91,000					
91,000	**91,050**	19,819	15,871	20,189	18,114
91,050	**91,100**	19,833	15,884	20,203	18,126
91,100	**91,150**	19,847	15,896	20,217	18,139
91,150	**91,200**	19,861	15,909	20,231	18,151
91,200	**91,250**	19,875	15,921	20,245	18,164
91,250	**91,300**	19,889	15,934	20,259	18,176
91,300	**91,350**	19,903	15,946	20,273	18,189
91,350	**91,400**	19,917	15,959	20,287	18,201
91,400	**91,450**	19,931	15,971	20,301	18,214
91,450	**91,500**	19,945	15,984	20,315	18,226
91,500	**91,550**	19,959	15,996	20,329	18,239
91,550	**91,600**	19,973	16,009	20,343	18,251
91,600	**91,650**	19,987	16,021	20,357	18,264
91,650	**91,700**	20,001	16,034	20,371	18,276
91,700	**91,750**	20,015	16,046	20,385	18,289
91,750	**91,800**	20,029	16,059	20,399	18,301
91,800	**91,850**	20,043	16,071	20,413	18,314
91,850	**91,900**	20,057	16,084	20,427	18,326
91,900	**91,950**	20,071	16,096	20,441	18,339
91,950	**92,000**	20,085	16,109	20,455	18,351

If line 43 (taxable income) is— At least	But less than	And you are— Single	Married filing jointly *	Married filing sepa-rately	Head of a house-hold
		Your tax is—			
92,000					
92,000	**92,050**	20,099	16,121	20,469	18,364
92,050	**92,100**	20,113	16,134	20,483	18,376
92,100	**92,150**	20,127	16,146	20,497	18,389
92,150	**92,200**	20,141	16,159	20,511	18,401
92,200	**92,250**	20,155	16,171	20,525	18,414
92,250	**92,300**	20,169	16,184	20,539	18,426
92,300	**92,350**	20,183	16,196	20,553	18,439
92,350	**92,400**	20,197	16,209	20,567	18,451
92,400	**92,450**	20,211	16,221	20,581	18,464
92,450	**92,500**	20,225	16,234	20,595	18,476
92,500	**92,550**	20,239	16,246	20,609	18,489
92,550	**92,600**	20,253	16,259	20,623	18,501
92,600	**92,650**	20,267	16,271	20,637	18,514
92,650	**92,700**	20,281	16,284	20,651	18,526
92,700	**92,750**	20,295	16,296	20,665	18,539
92,750	**92,800**	20,309	16,309	20,679	18,551
92,800	**92,850**	20,323	16,321	20,693	18,564
92,850	**92,900**	20,337	16,334	20,707	18,576
92,900	**92,950**	20,351	16,346	20,721	18,589
92,950	**93,000**	20,365	16,359	20,735	18,601
93,000					
93,000	**93,050**	20,379	16,371	20,749	18,614
93,050	**93,100**	20,393	16,384	20,763	18,626
93,100	**93,150**	20,407	16,396	20,777	18,639
93,150	**93,200**	20,421	16,409	20,791	18,651
93,200	**93,250**	20,435	16,421	20,805	18,664
93,250	**93,300**	20,449	16,434	20,819	18,676
93,300	**93,350**	20,463	16,446	20,833	18,689
93,350	**93,400**	20,477	16,459	20,847	18,701
93,400	**93,450**	20,491	16,471	20,861	18,714
93,450	**93,500**	20,505	16,484	20,875	18,726
93,500	**93,550**	20,519	16,496	20,889	18,739
93,550	**93,600**	20,533	16,509	20,903	18,751
93,600	**93,650**	20,547	16,521	20,917	18,764
93,650	**93,700**	20,561	16,534	20,931	18,776
93,700	**93,750**	20,575	16,546	20,945	18,789
93,750	**93,800**	20,589	16,559	20,959	18,801
93,800	**93,850**	20,603	16,571	20,973	18,814
93,850	**93,900**	20,617	16,584	20,987	18,826
93,900	**93,950**	20,631	16,596	21,001	18,839
93,950	**94,000**	20,645	16,609	21,015	18,851
94,000					
94,000	**94,050**	20,659	16,621	21,029	18,864
94,050	**94,100**	20,673	16,634	21,043	18,876
94,100	**94,150**	20,687	16,646	21,057	18,889
94,150	**94,200**	20,701	16,659	21,071	18,901
94,200	**94,250**	20,715	16,671	21,085	18,914
94,250	**94,300**	20,729	16,684	21,102	18,926
94,300	**94,350**	20,743	16,696	21,118	18,939
94,350	**94,400**	20,757	16,709	21,135	18,951
94,400	**94,450**	20,771	16,721	21,151	18,964
94,450	**94,500**	20,785	16,734	21,168	18,976
94,500	**94,550**	20,799	16,746	21,184	18,989
94,550	**94,600**	20,813	16,759	21,201	19,001
94,600	**94,650**	20,827	16,771	21,217	19,014
94,650	**94,700**	20,841	16,784	21,234	19,026
94,700	**94,750**	20,855	16,796	21,250	19,039
94,750	**94,800**	20,869	16,809	21,267	19,051
94,800	**94,850**	20,883	16,821	21,283	19,064
94,850	**94,900**	20,897	16,834	21,300	19,076
94,900	**94,950**	20,911	16,846	21,316	19,089
94,950	**95,000**	20,925	16,859	21,333	19,101

* This column must also be used by a qualifying widow(er).

(Continued on page 78)

2006 Tax Table–*Continued*

If line 43 (taxable income) is—		And you are—			
At least	But less than	Single	Married filing jointly *	Married filing sepa-rately	Head of a house-hold
		Your tax is—			
95,000					
95,000	**95,050**	20,939	16,871	21,349	19,114
95,050	**95,100**	20,953	16,884	21,366	19,126
95,100	**95,150**	20,967	16,896	21,382	19,139
95,150	**95,200**	20,981	16,909	21,399	19,151
95,200	**95,250**	20,995	16,921	21,415	19,164
95,250	**95,300**	21,009	16,934	21,432	19,176
95,300	**95,350**	21,023	16,946	21,448	19,189
95,350	**95,400**	21,037	16,959	21,465	19,201
95,400	**95,450**	21,051	16,971	21,481	19,214
95,450	**95,500**	21,065	16,984	21,498	19,226
95,500	**95,550**	21,079	16,996	21,514	19,239
95,550	**95,600**	21,093	17,009	21,531	19,251
95,600	**95,650**	21,107	17,021	21,547	19,264
95,650	**95,700**	21,121	17,034	21,564	19,276
95,700	**95,750**	21,135	17,046	21,580	19,289
95,750	**95,800**	21,149	17,059	21,597	19,301
95,800	**95,850**	21,163	17,071	21,613	19,314
95,850	**95,900**	21,177	17,084	21,630	19,326
95,900	**95,950**	21,191	17,096	21,646	19,339
95,950	**96,000**	21,205	17,109	21,663	19,351
96,000					
96,000	**96,050**	21,219	17,121	21,679	19,364
96,050	**96,100**	21,233	17,134	21,696	19,376
96,100	**96,150**	21,247	17,146	21,712	19,389
96,150	**96,200**	21,261	17,159	21,729	19,401
96,200	**96,250**	21,275	17,171	21,745	19,414
96,250	**96,300**	21,289	17,184	21,762	19,426
96,300	**96,350**	21,303	17,196	21,778	19,439
96,350	**96,400**	21,317	17,209	21,795	19,451
96,400	**96,450**	21,331	17,221	21,811	19,464
96,450	**96,500**	21,345	17,234	21,828	19,476
96,500	**96,550**	21,359	17,246	21,844	19,489
96,550	**96,600**	21,373	17,259	21,861	19,501
96,600	**96,650**	21,387	17,271	21,877	19,514
96,650	**96,700**	21,401	17,284	21,894	19,526
96,700	**96,750**	21,415	17,296	21,910	19,539
96,750	**96,800**	21,429	17,309	21,927	19,551
96,800	**96,850**	21,443	17,321	21,943	19,564
96,850	**96,900**	21,457	17,334	21,960	19,576
96,900	**96,950**	21,471	17,346	21,976	19,589
96,950	**97,000**	21,485	17,359	21,993	19,601

If line 43 (taxable income) is—		And you are—			
At least	But less than	Single	Married filing jointly *	Married filing sepa-rately	Head of a house-hold
		Your tax is—			
97,000					
97,000	**97,050**	21,499	17,371	22,009	19,614
97,050	**97,100**	21,513	17,384	22,026	19,626
97,100	**97,150**	21,527	17,396	22,042	19,639
97,150	**97,200**	21,541	17,409	22,059	19,651
97,200	**97,250**	21,555	17,421	22,075	19,664
97,250	**97,300**	21,569	17,434	22,092	19,676
97,300	**97,350**	21,583	17,446	22,108	19,689
97,350	**97,400**	21,597	17,459	22,125	19,701
97,400	**97,450**	21,611	17,471	22,141	19,714
97,450	**97,500**	21,625	17,484	22,158	19,726
97,500	**97,550**	21,639	17,496	22,174	19,739
97,550	**97,600**	21,653	17,509	22,191	19,751
97,600	**97,650**	21,667	17,521	22,207	19,764
97,650	**97,700**	21,681	17,534	22,224	19,776
97,700	**97,750**	21,695	17,546	22,240	19,789
97,750	**97,800**	21,709	17,559	22,257	19,801
97,800	**97,850**	21,723	17,571	22,273	19,814
97,850	**97,900**	21,737	17,584	22,290	19,826
97,900	**97,950**	21,751	17,596	22,306	19,839
97,950	**98,000**	21,765	17,609	22,323	19,851
98,000					
98,000	**98,050**	21,779	17,621	22,339	19,864
98,050	**98,100**	21,793	17,634	22,356	19,876
98,100	**98,150**	21,807	17,646	22,372	19,889
98,150	**98,200**	21,821	17,659	22,389	19,901
98,200	**98,250**	21,835	17,671	22,405	19,914
98,250	**98,300**	21,849	17,684	22,422	19,926
98,300	**98,350**	21,863	17,696	22,438	19,939
98,350	**98,400**	21,877	17,709	22,455	19,951
98,400	**98,450**	21,891	17,721	22,471	19,964
98,450	**98,500**	21,905	17,734	22,488	19,976
98,500	**98,550**	21,919	17,746	22,504	19,989
98,550	**98,600**	21,933	17,759	22,521	20,001
98,600	**98,650**	21,947	17,771	22,537	20,014
98,650	**98,700**	21,961	17,784	22,554	20,026
98,700	**98,750**	21,975	17,796	22,570	20,039
98,750	**98,800**	21,989	17,809	22,587	20,051
98,800	**98,850**	22,003	17,821	22,603	20,064
98,850	**98,900**	22,017	17,834	22,620	20,076
98,900	**98,950**	22,031	17,846	22,636	20,089
98,950	**99,000**	22,045	17,859	22,653	20,101

If line 43 (taxable income) is—		And you are—			
At least	But less than	Single	Married filing jointly *	Married filing sepa-rately	Head of a house-hold
		Your tax is—			
99,000					
99,000	**99,050**	22,059	17,871	22,669	20,114
99,050	**99,100**	22,073	17,884	22,686	20,126
99,100	**99,150**	22,087	17,896	22,702	20,139
99,150	**99,200**	22,101	17,909	22,719	20,151
99,200	**99,250**	22,115	17,921	22,735	20,164
99,250	**99,300**	22,129	17,934	22,752	20,176
99,300	**99,350**	22,143	17,946	22,768	20,189
99,350	**99,400**	22,157	17,959	22,785	20,201
99,400	**99,450**	22,171	17,971	22,801	20,214
99,450	**99,500**	22,185	17,984	22,818	20,226
99,500	**99,550**	22,199	17,996	22,834	20,239
99,550	**99,600**	22,213	18,009	22,851	20,251
99,600	**99,650**	22,227	18,021	22,867	20,264
99,650	**99,700**	22,241	18,034	22,884	20,276
99,700	**99,750**	22,255	18,046	22,900	20,289
99,750	**99,800**	22,269	18,059	22,917	20,301
99,800	**99,850**	22,283	18,071	22,933	20,314
99,850	**99,900**	22,297	18,084	22,950	20,326
99,900	**99,950**	22,311	18,096	22,966	20,339
99,950	**100,000**	22,325	18,109	22,983	20,351

$100,000 or over — use the Tax Computation Worksheet on page 79

* This column must also be used by a qualifying widow(er)

2006 Tax Rate Schedules

The Tax Rate Schedules are shown so you can see the tax rate that applies to all levels of taxable income. Do not use them to figure your tax. Instead, see the instructions for line 44 that begin on page 36.

Schedule X—If your filing status is **Single**

If your taxable income is: Over—	But not over—	The tax is:	of the amount over—
$0	$7,550	--------- **10%**	**$0**
7,550	30,650	**$755.00 + 15%**	**7,550**
30,650	74,200	**4,220.00 + 25%**	**30,650**
74,200	154,800	**15,107.50 + 28%**	**74,200**
154,800	336,550	**37,675.50 + 33%**	**154,800**
336,550	--------	**97,653.00 + 35%**	**336,550**

Schedule Y-1—If your filing status is **Married filing jointly** or **Qualifying widow(er)**

If your taxable income is: Over—	But not over—	The tax is:	of the amount over—
$0	$15,100	--------- **10%**	**$0**
15,100	61,300	**$1,510.00 + 15%**	**15,100**
61,300	123,700	**8,440.00 + 25%**	**61,300**
123,700	188,450	**24,040.00 + 28%**	**123,700**
188,450	336,550	**42,170.00 + 33%**	**188,450**
336,550	---------	**91,043.00 + 35%**	**336,550**

Schedule Y-2—If your filing status is **Married filing separately**

If your taxable income is: Over—	But not over—	The tax is:	of the amount over—
$0	$7,550	--------- **10%**	**$0**
7,550	30,650	**$755.00 + 15%**	**7,550**
30,650	61,850	**4,220.00 + 25%**	**30,650**
61,850	94,225	**12,020.00 + 28%**	**61,850**
94,225	168,275	**21,085.00 + 33%**	**94,225**
168,275	---------	**45,521.50 + 35%**	**168,275**

Schedule Z—If your filing status is **Head of household**

If your taxable income is: Over—	But not over—	The tax is:	of the amount over—
$0	$10,750	--------- **10%**	**$0**
10,750	41,050	**$1,075.00 + 15%**	**10,750**
41,050	106,000	**5,620.00 + 25%**	**41,050**
106,000	171,650	**21,857.50 + 28%**	**106,000**
171,650	336,550	**40,239.50 + 33%**	**171,650**
336,550	---------	**94,656.50 + 35%**	**336,550**

Index

D

E

F

P

Q

R

S

T

U

V

W

X

Z

. . . Formulating and Writing an Effective Business Plan?

Business Plans That Work for Your Small Business—now in an all-new Second Edition—clearly translates complicated marketing and financial concepts into down-to-earth practical advice, explains all the essential elements and formulas, and offers concrete examples throughout. Five sample plans from real small businesses provide readers with the blueprints for their own plans, as well as a wealth of detailed information about how a successful small business should operate

This book will appeal not only to budding entrepreneurs who are planning a new venture on paper to see whether it will fly, but also to new or existing business owners who need a business plan document as part of a business loan application, and to established owners who want to create a plan for internal use.

304 pages / Book No. 0-5246-200 **$19.95***

. . . Protecting Your Assets and Limiting Your Liability?

Safe Harbors: An Asset Protection Guide for Small Business Owners is a one-of-a-kind book offering the latest techniques for preserving family wealth and legally avoiding personal liability when structuring, funding and operating a small business. Unfortunately, many small business owners retain a lawyer only after a financial crisis strikes, and usually by then it's too late, often resulting in the loss of the business and possibly a home, investments, savings, and other assets, and maybe those of your spouse as well. Almost all of these problems are preventable with solid advance planning.

Taken together, all of the strategies in this guide form a multi-layered approach to asset protection, often presenting an insurmountable barrier to personal or business creditors, even in the worst of financial circumstances. The emphasis is on easy-to-understand techniques that business owners can undertake on their own, with little or no legal assistance. Sample forms with instructions make it easy to carry out the author's advice, and extensive appendices provide detailed information on state and federal laws.

$19.95* *500 pages / Book No. 0-5436-200*

. . . Securing the Necessary Financing for Your Business?

Small Business Financing: How and Where To Get It, now in its newly revised second edition, thoroughly but simply discusses each source of debt and equity capital, whether public or private—from bookstrapping and IPOs to commercial loans and SBA-guaranteed programs, and everything in between. This book covers methods for determining the amount of capital needed, choosing an appropriate source and type of financing, selecting a business form, and planning successful applications or presentations.

Sample forms are integrated into the text to facilitate learning the details and the data-gathering skills needed for the financing process. A handy glossary is included to take the mystery out of dealing with bankers and other financial professionals.

224 pages / Book No. 0-5142-200 **$17.95***

*Plus shipping, handling and applicable sales tax

CCH® BUSINES

OOLKIT™

Do You Need Help . . .

. . . Turning Your Small Business Dreams into Reality?

Launching Your First Small Business, Second Edition, provides readers with the information they need to successfully make the transition to self-employment, concisely detailing what factors to consider when assessing personal strengths and weaknesses, deciding on the type of business to open, considering the costs involved, choosing the form of business organization, and locating and staffing the operation.

By effectively organizing the dozens of activities that go into launching a new business, this book will help first-time entrepreneurs save time and money. More importantly, it increases the chance of success by informing new business owners of the various issues needing attention when starting a business from scratch.

$14.95* *208 pages / Book No. 0-5428-300*

. . . Making the Government Your Best Customer?

All government contracts under $100,000 are targeted to small businesses. ***Win Government Contracts for Your Small Business***—now fully updated in its third edition—will show you how to get in on the action in just 10 easy-to-understand steps. By following our practical advice, you'll be accurately listed in the federal procurement system, allowing you to start receiving bids right away.

In this book you'll learn the simple most important step to take before you start bidding, where to find government buyers, the best source of bid leads for you and your company, how to write a winning proposal, listings of essential web sites, and how to use the Internet to your advantage. All together, this is the only book that covers, step-by-step and in detail, how to successfully compete for government contracts—and make more money for your small business.

*Plus shipping, handling and applicable sales tax

506 pages / Book No. 0-4494-300 **$24.95***

CCH BUSINESS OWNER'S TOOLKIT™ — Total Know-How for Small Business

On the Internet at www.toolkit.cch.com

To Order Call 1-800-248-3248

---

7 a.m. - 6 p.m. CST Select Option #3

CCH

Total Kn ure

On th